School Health Practice

School HEALTH Practice

William H. Creswell, Jr., AB MS EdD

Professor Emeritus
Department of Health and Safety Education
University of Illinois, Champaign, Illinois

Ian M. Newman, MS PhD

Professor of Health Education
University of Nebraska, Lincoln, Nebraska

TENTH EDITION

*with **117** illustrations*

 Mosby

St. Louis Baltimore Boston Chicago London Philadelphia Sydney Toronto

Mosby

Dedicated to Publishing Excellence

Editor-in-Chief: James M. Smith
Editor: Vicki Malinee
Developmental Editor: Cheryl Gelfand-Grant
Project Manager: Gayle May Morris
Production Editor: Mary Cusick Drone
Book Designer: Susan Lane

TENTH EDITION

Printed in the United States of America

Mosby-Year Book, Inc.
11830 Westline Industrial Drive
St. Louis, Missouri 63146

Library of Congress Cataloging in Publication Data

Creswell, William H., 1920-
     School health practice / William H. Creswell, Jr., Ian M. Newman.
   — 10th ed.
        p.   cm.
     Includes bibliographies and index.
     ISBN 0-8016-6746-1
     1. School hygiene—United States.   2. School health services—
United States.   I. Newman, Ian M.   II. Title.
     LB3409.U5C69   1992   92-36995
     371.7′12′0973—dc20   CIP

92   93   94   95   96   97   UG/DC   9   8   7   6   5   4   3   2   1

Preface

Since the ninth edition of *School Health Practice,* the Secretary of the United States Department of Health and Human Services, Louis W. Sullivan, has released the report *Healthy People 2000.* Like its predecessor, *Healthy People 1990,* this report has set quantifiable targets for improving the nation's health. However, in this instance, a greater emphasis has been placed on health outcomes and the importance of disease prevention. This means that health education offers an even greater potential for achieving the nation's health goals.

McGinnes and DeGraw (1991) have pointed out that more than one third of the 300 specific objectives in this report can be directly or indirectly achieved by the schools. In addition, they have added what may be the signal objective for school health education in the report:

> Increase to at least 75 percent the proportion of the nation's elementary and secondary schools that provide planned sequential kindergarten through 12th grade quality school health education

As a consequence, the report *Healthy People 2000* has been extensively referenced in this edition, and the implications of the report have been incorporated wherever appropriate. The idea of comprehensive approaches for school health continues to receive increasing support. In addition to comprehensive services, a new emphasis calls for the integration of services to avoid the fragmentation that occurs all too often for poor children and their families. Also, by integrating the health and social services with the child's educational experiences, learning becomes more meaningful, and services more effective.

Audience

Like its predecessors, the tenth edition is based on the assumption that an effectively functioning school health program calls for a clear vision of the total school health program.

Because the program is described as school-based, the primary audience for whom the book is written includes elementary and secondary level schoolteachers, specialists in health education, school social workers, school psychologists, school health service personnel, and school administrators.

New in this edition

As in the ninth edition, this tenth edition of *School Health Practice* has given continued attention to new developments and issues that directly bear upon the school health program. Never in the history of this country has so much been written in both the professional and the popular press about the health, educational, and social needs of children and youth. To help keep abreast of these developments, new material has been added to each chapter in the form of an "Emerging Issue." The purpose of these problem-solving exercises is to give the preprofessional student an awareness of and an opportunity to engage in a type of constructive controversy that deals with a "real world" problem affecting today's school health and health education. Each of the 17 issues is correlated with the Instructor's Manual and accompanying reference material. Other changes are as follows:

- Get Involved boxes are included in each chapter that provide information about related professional organizations and career opportunities.
- Updated information has been included on school-linked and school-based clinics. Professionals from medicine, public health, social work, and education are calling for a better integration of education, health, and social services to meet the needs of students and the "social morbidities" such as child abuse, school-related violence, teenage pregnancies, and AIDS.
- New material has been added on low-birth-weight infants and mothers who use drugs such as alcohol and cocaine and the implications of these problems for the school.
- New information has been added on bystander care and the importance of preparing students so they may be able to respond with lifesaving skills in emergencies.
- A new section has been added to Chapter 11 to show how learning theory may be applied to classroom management and teaching strategies.
- Nine of the eleven priority areas identified in the nation's health objectives for the year 2000 have been considered as source material for the secondary school health education curriculum.
- A new teaching unit on "Preventing Violence Through Non-Conflict Resolution" is included.
- Finally, a new addition has been made to the Appendixes: a self-appraisal check list entitled "How Healthy Is Your School?"

Acknowledgments

As was true of previous editions, many persons have made important contributions to this edition of *School Health Practice*. To each of these persons who has made sacrifices and accommodations that have allowed us to complete the tasks and to meet deadlines, we express our gratitude.

There are persons who have made special contributions to this revision whom we wish to recognize. Dr. Alan Braslow, a specialist in health education and emergency health care services, has contributed new material to Chapter 9 relating to bystander care. Dr. O. E. Byrd, Professor of Health Education, Emeritus, Stanford University, was the inspiration for the "Issue Insights," which evolved from his problem-solving teaching methods.

Special acknowledgments are due Jean Creswell, Katherine Farrell, and Michelle Wiese for their writing, editorial, and word processing skills; Tammy Reis, who made important contributions in the early stages of the project through her detailed and comprehensive literature searches; to Bill Weigand whose photographic skills are an important addition to the attractiveness of the tenth edition; and to Leslie Lewis and Kristine Jankowitz, who assisted in the development of the new teachers' manual.

We express our thanks and appreciation to the Mosby staff, including Vicki Malinee, Cathy Waller, Cheryl Gelfand-Grant, Mary Drone, and Susan Lane for their skill and efficiency in bringing the book to publication and, most of all, for their patience and good humor in shepherding the project to its conclusion.

We are grateful to the following reviewers whose insightful comments helped to shape the tenth edition:

Cindy Christie
Washington State University

Paul Finnicum
Arkansas State University

Laura Kann
Division of Adolescent and School Health
National Center for Chronic Disease Prevention and Health Promotion

Mary Paonessa
Wayne State University

Christina Perry-Hunnicutt
University of Nebraska–Lincoln

Myrna Yeakle
Eastern Michigan University

Finally, we wish to acknowledge the contributions of our wives, Jean Creswell and Enid Newman, over and beyond technical and professional support, for their patience and encouragement, despite the disruption and postponement of family schedules.

William H. Creswell, Jr.
Ian M. Newman

Contents

Part ONE

Organization of the School Health Program

1

School health

The challenge and the source of inspiration

OVERVIEW

From the beginning of time human beings have sought to protect their health by controlling disease, improving the environment, caring for the sick, and protecting food and water supplies. Passing accumulated knowledge from one generation to another through formal and informal education has led to significant advances in the ability of humankind to protect and maintain health.

This chapter highlights the principal issues that challenge all those involved and interested in improving the health of children and youth through work in the school. These challenges are set against the history of dealing with illness and protecting health, the changing nature of the population, and the changing attitudes toward health care and health promotion. The challenge is clear. To improve the health of the nation, we must influence the health knowledge and health practices of young people. To begin to capture the full effects of the educational system and the productivity inherent in the work force, we must improve the health of students and workers.

OBJECTIVES   After reading this chapter the student should be able to:

1. Describe the challenges facing teachers interested in promoting the health of children and youth
2. Identify the principal health problems facing children and adolescents
3. Discuss the nature and importance of the nation's health goals for the year 2000
4. Explain the relationship between the nation's educational goals and its health goals
5. Identify and describe the basic elements of a comprehensive school health education program
6. Describe an historical view of the development of public health and of today's school health program
7. Explain how a successful school health program balances the need to help students manage health risks with local mores and practices

THE CHALLENGE

The challenge to all persons involved in school health programs is to improve the health of children and youth. Responding to this challenge is not as simple as it sounds, but the challenge is exciting; and, when it is achieved, it represents a significant contribution to individual students and to society.

The epidemiologic challenge

Epidemiology is the study of the causes and distribution of disease and the starting point for anyone interested in improving health. Over the years the U.S. and state governments have gathered volumes of data on the distribution of death and disability and on many other aspects of the nation's health. On the basis of these data, and with consultation of a wide range of professionals, the U.S. Public Health Service has produced a set of health-related national goals to be reached by the year 2000. These goals include all age groups and cover a wide range of health concerns. They are significant because they reflect the nation's hopes for health. By default they also identify problems important to the nation's health, which may require more effort to overcome.

The school's contribution to the achievement of the nation's health goals for the year 2000 is both direct and indirect. Directly the school affects knowledge and skills, which can be translated into healthier student life-styles. Indirectly the health of the next generation will be affected by the health knowledge and practices taught to present-day students because students in today's schools are the next generation of parents.

Children. Today communicable diseases among children have been replaced to a large degree by injuries as the principal cause of death. The significance of injuries unfortunately has been downplayed by their association with the term "accidents." Accident suggests a random event over which one has little control. This implies that injuries from accidents represent a health problem that is unavoidable. The reality is that most injuries result from events directly related to conscious decisions and behavior. There are indeed few "accidents" that could not have been avoided had people been better informed or acted differently.

Although motor vehicle crashes are the greatest source of injuries, the rate of child deaths from automobile crashes has fallen 41% for children ages 1 to 4 since 1970 and 31% for children ages 5 to 14. This decline is largely the result of successful education programs to encourage the use of child safety seats and safety belts in automobiles. This trend illustrates how education and conscious decisions can change the rate of injuries and that injuries are not necessarily the result of "accidental" occurrences.

Other sources of injury-related deaths are drowning, falls, poisonings, and fires. Each of these has also declined over the past few years.

Drownings and fires rank second to motor vehicles among causes of deaths of children. Drownings are most frequent among children under 5 years of age. Household fires are most dangerous for younger children because they are less able to escape. Children living in substandard housing are at special risk.

Violence toward children involves approximately 2% of all children. Although this percentage sounds small, it represents approximately 1,000,000 children. The number of reported cases of child abuse has increased in the recent past. It has also become increasingly clear that many cases of child abuse go unreported. The most common type of child abuse is physical, followed by sexual and emotional abuse. Related to child abuse are child homicides, some of which are committed by other children. The rate of child homicides has not declined in recent years.

Children from low-income families are particularly vulnerable to developmental problems such as emotional and learning disorders and the long-term consequences of neglected physical conditions such as hearing, vision, and speech problems.

Lead poisoning is one of the nation's most preventable childhood problems. In the severe stage, lead poisoning can lead to mental retardation and death. Low levels of lead poisoning can lead to delayed cognitive and physical growth and development.

Adolescents. Like the health problems faced by children, the health problems of adolescents are diverse and in many instances not recognized when the health status of the nation is discussed.

An easy way to recognize the range of health problems faced by adolescents is to examine the nation's health goals for adolescents. Over the past few years the U.S. Public Health Service has developed and refined a list of 298 health goals to be achieved by the year 2000; approximately 15% of these goals relate directly to adolescents. Three important overriding changes should occur as the year 2000 goals are achieved:

1. Health status should be improved. The proportion of the population with a specific condition should decline.
2. Risky behavior should be reduced. The proportion of the population who participate in a particular behavior that increases their risk of a health problem should decline.
3. Services and protection should be more accessible and more widely used. The proportion of the population participating in or having access to services that would correct health problems and reduce risk should increase, and ultimately the likelihood of future health problems should decline.

These changes should result in:

1. An increase in the span of healthy life for all.
2. A reduction in health disparities among different groups of people.
3. The achievement of access to preventive services for all people.

Box 1-1 shows selected health goals related specifically to adolescents. The American Medical Association has excerpted them from the 298 national health goals for the year 2000. The adolescent health goals are specific for the age range 10 to 24 years. They identify the nature and diversity of the challenge to improve the health of young people.

Just as the nation has set its goals for health, it has also done so for education (Box 1-2). In 1989 the Secretary of Education endorsed a set of educational goals for the nation that focus educational effort over the next few years. The reciprocal nature of these two sets of goals, health and education, illustrates the complexity of the task of achieving each of them. To meet the challenge presented by the educational goals, it is clear that the health of students will need to be improved. Educational losses resulting from absenteeism, early dropout, and the inability to study and learn because of health problems and needs illustrate this point. Conversely, improving teaching and increasing what is learned will ultimately encourage appropriate

BOX
1-1

Selected health goals that apply to adolescents

These goals illustrate the aspirations for adolescent health and at the same time identify areas in which present standards are considered unacceptable. Unfortunately, current baseline data are not always available. Where available, the baseline rate in percentage is included in parentheses, along with the year the baseline data represents.

1. Increase to at least 75% the proportion of children and adolescents ages 6 through 17 who engage in vigorous physical activity that promotes the development and maintenance of cardio-respiratory fitness 3 or more days per week for 20 or more minutes per occasion (66%, 1984)
2. Increase to at least 50% the proportion of children and adolescents in first through twelfth grade who participate in daily school physical education (36%, 1987-1986)
3. Increase to at least 50% the proportion of school physical education class time that students spend being physically active, preferably engaged in lifetime physical activities (27%, 1984)
4. Reduce overweight to a prevalence of no less than 15% among adolescents ages 12 through 19 (15%, 1976-1980)
5. Increase calcium intake so at least 50% of youth ages 12 through 24...consume three or more servings daily of foods rich in calcium (7% of females and 14% of males ages 19 through 24, 1985-1986)
6. Reduce the initiation of cigarette smoking by children and youth so that no more than 15% have become regular cigarette smokers by age 20 (30%, 1987)
7. Reduce smokeless tobacco use by males ages 12 through 24 to a prevalence of no more than 4%. (6.6%, 1988)
8. Reduce deaths among people ages 15 though 24 caused by alcohol-related motor vehicle crashes to no more than 18 per 100,000 (21.5/100,000, 1987)
9. Increase by at least 1 year the average age of first use of cigarettes, alcohol, and marijuana by adolescents ages 12 through 17 (age 11.6 for cigarettes, age 13.1 for alcohol, and age 13.4 for marijuana, 1988)
10. Reduce the proportion of young people who have used alcohol, marijuana, and cocaine in the past month, as follows:

Substance/age	2000 Target (%)	Baseline (%, year)
Alcohol/12-17	12.6	25.2, 1988
Marijuana/12-17	3.2	6.4, 1988
Cocaine 12-17	0.6	1.1, 1988

11. Reduce the proportion of high school seniors and college students engaging in recent occasions of heavy drinking of alcoholic beverages to no more than 28% of high school seniors (33%, 1989)
12. Reduce alcohol consumption by people ages 14 and older to an annual average of no more than 2 gallons of ethanol per person (2.54 gallons, 1987)
13. Increase the proportion of high school seniors who perceive SOCIAL DISAPPROVAL associated with the heavy use of alcohol, occasional use of marijuana, and experimentation with cocaine, as follows:

Behavior	2000 Target (%)	Baseline (%, year)
Heavy use of alcohol	70	56.4, 1989
Occasional use of marijuana	85	71.1, 1989
Trying cocaine once or twice	95	88.9, 1989

Continued

Selected health goals that apply to adolescents—cont'd

14. Increase the proportion of high school seniors who associate risk of physical or psychological harm with the heavy use of alcohol, regular use of marijuana, and experimentation with cocaine, as follows:

Behavior	2000 Target (%)	Baseline (%, year)
Heavy use of alcohol	70	44, 1989
Regular use of marijuana	90	77.5, 1989
Trying cocaine once or twice	80	64.9, 1989

15. Reduce to no more than 3% the proportion of male high school seniors who use anabolic steroids (4.7%, 1989)
16. Reduce pregnancies among girls ages 17 and younger to no more than 50 per 1000 (71.1/1000 for girls ages 15 to 17, 1985)
17. Reduce the proportion of adolescents who have engaged in sexual intercourse to no more than 15% by age 15 and no more than 40% by age 17 (27% of girls and 33% of boys by age 15; 50% of girls and 66% of boys by age 17; 1988).
18. Increase to at least 40% the proportion of adolescents ages 17 and younger who have ever been sexually active and who have abstained from sexual activity for the previous 3 months (26% of sexually active girls ages 15 through 17, 1988).
19. Increase to at least 90% the proportion of sexually active, unmarried people ages 19 and younger who use contraception (78% at most recent intercourse, 63% at first intercourse, for females ages 15 through 19, 1988)
20. Increase to at least 85% the proportion of people ages 10 through 18 who have discussed human sexuality, including values surrounding sexuality, with their parents and/or have received information through another parentally endorsed source, such as youth, school, or religious programs (66% ages 13 through 18, 1986)
21. Increase to at least 67% the proportion of primary care providers who provide age-appropriate preconception care and counseling (no baseline data available)
22. Reduce suicides among youth ages 15 through 19 to no more than 8.2 per 100,000 people (10.3 per 100,000, 1987)
23. Reduce by 15% the incidence of injurious suicide attempts among adolescents ages 14 through 17 (no baseline data available)
24. Reduce to less than 10% the prevalence of mental disorders among children and adolescents (estimated 12% in 1989)
25. Reduce homicides to no more than 7.2 per 100,000 people (8.5 per 100,000 in 1987)
26. Reverse to less than 25.2 per 1000 children the rising incidence of maltreatment of children younger than age 18 (25.2 per 1000, 1986)
27. Reduce rape and attempted rape of women ages 12 through 34 to no more than 225 per 100,000 (250 per 100,000 in 1986)
28. Reduce by 20% the incidence of physical fighting among adolescents ages 14 through 17 (no baseline data available)
29. Reduce by 20% the incidence of weapon carrying by adolescents ages 14 through 17 (no baseline data available)
30. Increase the high school graduation rate to at least 90%, thereby reducing risks for multiple problem behaviors and poor mental and physical health (79% of people ages 20 through 21 had graduated from high school, 1989)
31. Reduce deaths among youth ages 15 through 24 caused by motor vehicle crashes to no more than 33 per 100,000 people (36.9 per 100,000 in 1987)

Selected health goals that apply to adolescents—cont'd

32. Reduce drowning deaths to no more than 1.3 per 100,000 people (2.1 per 100,000 in 1987)
33. Reduce dental caries (cavities) so that the proportion of children with one or more caries...is no more than 60% among adolescents age 15 (78% of adolescents ages 15, 1986-1987)
34. Reduce untreated dental caries so that the proportion of children with untreated caries is no more than...15% among adolescents age 15 (23% of adolescents age 15, 1986-1987)
35. Increase to at least 50% the proportion of children who have received protective sealants on the occlusal (chewing) surfaces of permanent molar teeth (11% of children ages 8, 8% of adolescents age 14, 1986-87)
36. Increase to at least 60% the proportion of sexually active, unmarried young women ages 15 through 19 whose partner used a condom at last sexual intercourse (26%, 1988)
37. Increase to at least 75% the proportion of sexually active, unmarried young men ages 15 through 19 who used a condom at last intercourse (57%, 1988)
38. Reduce gonorrhea among adolescents ages 15 to 19 to no more than 750 cases per 100,000 (1123 per 100,000 in 1989)
39. Increase to at least 50% the proportion of adolescents ages 13 through 18 who have received, as a minimum within the appropriate interval, all of the screening and immunization services, and at least one of the counseling services appropriate for their age and gender as recommended by the U.S. Preventive Services Task Forces (no baseline data available)

---

health-related behaviors. As education improves, so does health; as health improves, education is enhanced (Fig. 1-1).

The demographic challenge

By the year 2000 the population of the United States will grow 7% to nearly 270 million. This is a relatively slow rate of growth. But the nature of the population will change significantly. The average household size will have declined from 2.7 persons in 1985 to 2.5 persons by the year 2000. Two-parent households will have decreased from 58% to 53%. The median age will have moved from 29 years in 1975 to 36 years by the year 2000. The proportion of the oldest segment of the population, those over 85, will have increased by about 30% to a total 4.6 million.

The racial and ethnic composition of the population is also changing. The proportion of whites will decline from 76% to 72%. The Hispanic population will increase overall from 8% to 11.3%, with more than 31 million Hispanic citizens by the year 2000. In some cities the majority of the population will be Spanish speaking. The proportion of the population that is black will increase from 12.3% to 13.1%. Other groups such as American Indians, Alaskan Natives, Asians, and Pacific Islanders will also increase.

These changes challenge the notion of minority and majority. Worldwide, 75% of the population is of color. In the United States, the Hispanic population is the fastest growing segment of the population. Approximately two thirds of the Hispanic population is located in three states (California, Texas, and New York). In California 23 of the 25 largest school systems are "majority minority."

Demographic realities are reflected in the health problems of young people in many ways. For example, age affects death rate as illustrated in Fig. 1-2. High school dropout rates may

BOX
1-2   **National education goals for the year 2000**

Like the health goals, these education goals represent aspirations and areas of needed improvement. These goals are more general than the health goals, but the added objectives provide some specificity for measuring success. The education goals lack the extent of baseline data available to support the health goals because education is a local/state issue, whereas health is considered more of a national issue.

Goal 1

By the year 2000, all children in America will start school ready to learn.

Objectives

- All disadvantaged and disabled children will have access to high quality and developmentally appropriate preschool programs that help prepare children for school.
- Every parent in America will be a child's first teacher and devote time each day to helping his or her preschool child learn; parents will have access to the training and support they need.
- Children will receive the nutrition and health care needed to arrive at school with healthy minds and bodies, and the number of low-birthweight babies will be significantly reduced through enhanced prenatal health systems.

Goal 2

By the year 2000, the high school graduation rate will increase to at least 90 percent.

Objectives

- The nation will dramatically reduce its dropout rate and 75% of students who do drop out will successfully complete a high school degree or its equivalent.
- The gap in high school graduation rates between American students from minority backgrounds and their non-minority counterparts will be eliminated.

Goal 3

By the year 2000, American students will leave grades 4, 8, and 12 having demonstrated competency over challenging subject matter, including English, mathematics, science, history, and geography; and every school in America will ensure that all students learn to use their minds well, so they may be prepared for responsible citizenship, further learning, and productive employment in our modern economy.

Objectives

- The academic performance of elementary and secondary students will increase significantly in every quartile, and the distribution of minority students in each level will more closely reflect the student population as a whole.
- The percentage of students who demonstrate the ability to reason, solve problems, apply knowledge, and write and communicate effectively will increase substantially.
- All students will be involved in activities that promote and demonstrate good citizenship, community service, and personal responsibility.
- The percentage of students who are competent in more than one language will substantially increase.
- All students will be knowledgeable about the diverse cultural heritage of this nation and about the world community.

National education goals for the year 2000—cont'd

Goal 4

By the year 2000, U.S. students will be first in the world in mathematics and science achievement.

Objectives

- Mathematics and science education will be strengthened throughout the system, especially in the early grades.
- The number of teachers with a substantive background in mathematics and science will increase by 50%.
- The number of U.S. undergraduate and graduate students, especially women and minorities, who complete degrees in mathematics, science, and engineering will increase significantly.

Goal 5

By the year 2000, every adult American will be literate and will possess the knowledge and skills necessary to compete in a global economy and exercise the rights and responsibilities of citizenship.

Objectives

- Every major American business will be involved in strengthening the connection between education and work.
- All workers will have the opportunity to acquire the knowledge and skills, from basic to highly technical, needed to adapt to emerging new technologies, work methods, and markets through public and private education, vocational, technical, workplace, or other programs.
- The number of quality programs, including those at libraries, that are designed to serve more effectively the needs of the growing number of part-time and mid-career students will increase substantially.
- The proportion of qualified students, especially minorities, who enter college, who complete at least 2 years, and who complete their degree programs will increase substantially.
- The proportion of college graduates who demonstrate an advanced ability to think critically, communicate effectively, and solve problems will increase substantially.

Goal 6

By the year 2000, every school in America will be free of drugs and violence and will offer a disciplined environment conducive to learning.

Objectives

- Every school will implement a firm policy on use, possession, and distribution of drugs and alcohol.
- Parents, businesses, and community organizations will work together to ensure that schools are a safe haven for all children.
- Every school district will develop a comprehensive K-12 drug and alcohol prevention education program. Drug and alcohol curriculum should be taught as an integral part of health education. In addition, community-based teams should be organized to provide students and teachers with needed support.

NATIONAL
EDUCATION
GOALS

↓

**Improved
education
outcomes**

**Improved
health
status**

↑

NATIONAL
HEALTH
GOALS

FIG. 1-1. The interplay of national priorities acknowledges how improvement in school health programs will assist in meeting the educational goals for the nation. In turn, improvements in education will enhance the likelihood of meeting the nation's health goals.

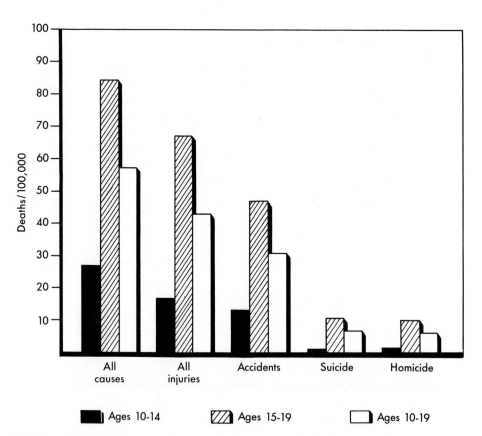

FIG. 1-2. Death rates among U.S. adolescents ages 10 through 19 by external causes of death, 1987.

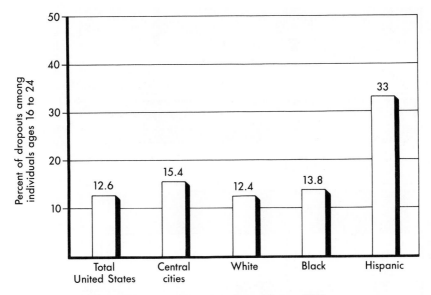

FIG. 1-3.   High school dropout rates in the United States, 1989.

reflect items other than health, but without all the benefits of education, the likelihood of good health is decreased. Ethnicity and place of living, such as the inner city, affects school dropout and indirectly affects the hope of a full measure of health (Fig. 1-3).

The importance of the national goal to reduce the disparity in the levels of health among different groups of people is clearly evident in the data presented in Fig. 1-4, which describes the leading causes of death among black and white adolescents.

The educational technology challenge

Technology has become an integral part of the education scene. The slide projector, computer, tape recorder, and interactive videodisc player all add to the effectiveness of the teaching-learning process. Many teachers and administrators have had to develop new skills to evaluate and use these resources. Of course, many of these people have also had to develop fundraising skills as they search for ways to purchase these teaching aids.

Coupled with the availability of technology is the question of who produced the resource and whether that affects the decision to use it. Attractive teaching materials have a natural appeal. But what happens when the resource is provided by a trade organization that promotes a particular product—for example, a pharmaceutical company, the Dairy Council, or the Tobacco Institute? Can use of a product in education be considered a subtle endorsement of the organization and should this influence the decision to use it?

It is important to remember that the best technology and the best teaching aids do not replace a dedicated and skilled teacher but, rather, they support the teaching/learning process. Despite the availability of so much technology, the effective health teacher will still need to determine the basic elements of the teaching learning process:

1. What are the critical health problems?
2. What knowledge and appropriate skills are needed by students to reduce the risk of a particular health problem?

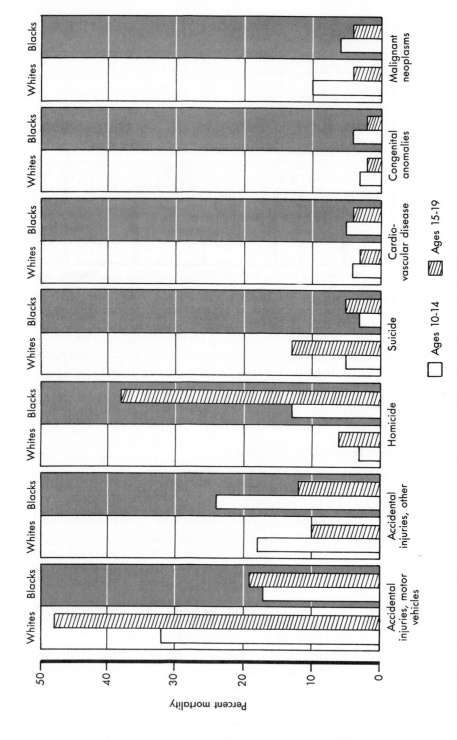

FIG. 1-4. Percent mortality caused by seven leading causes of death for black and white U.S. adolescents ages 10 through 14 and 15 through 19, 1987.

3. What educational programs and strategies will most likely encourage the desired knowledge and health promoting/protecting behavior?

The data-data challenge

Adolescence is a time of relatively low death rates. It is also a time when behavioral patterns are established. Knowing about these behavior patterns is important for all those planning and carrying out school health programs.

Twenty years ago data about the health of young people were scarce. Now, in addition to data on causes of death, there is a much improved recording system for the distribution of diseases. More important to the educator, considerable information on the health knowledge and behaviors of young people is now available.

The Centers for Disease Control (CDC) has pioneered the collection of data on health knowledge and practices of young people. These data provide an especially useful foundation for planning comprehensive school health programs.

Like many recent health-related actions, the collection of new data on adolescent health behaviors was stimulated by the human immunodeficiency virus/acquired immune deficiency syndrome (HIV/AIDS) epidemic. In 1987 the staff of the Division of Adolescent and School Health of the Center for Chronic Disease Prevention and Health Promotion at CDC began to refine a set of questions to be used to learn what young people thought and did about HIV/AIDS. In subsequent years this survey has been revised to ask students about injury prevention; nutrition; alcohol and other drug use; suicide and violence; sexual behavior and protection from sexually transmitted diseases, including HIV; and exercise and physical activity. These same questions have been used in surveys of students in Grades 9 to 12 in many states and local educational authorities. In addition, CDC has asked these same questions of a national sample of students for several years. These surveys have provided local data for planning and national data for comparison. Never before have so much data on adolescent health knowledge and practices been available. Unfortunately they have no value unless they are used. Interpreting these data for planning is one more challenge for the school worker interested in helping improve the health of young people.

The community relations challenge

The educational process has two distinct and sometimes conflicting objectives. The first is sharing the community's knowledge with the next generation, ensuring an element of continuity and stability. The second task is encouraging the application of new knowledge and the development of new behaviors to meet new challenges. When responses to new challenges appear to contradict the values of the community that ensure stability, controversy and conflict may result. Because many health-related items change as science produces new data, health is often an area of conflict and controversy. Similarly, some health-related behaviors appear to reflect moral or religious principles; thus changes to these behaviors sometimes generate controversy.

Even widely accepted practices and health programs can create controversy. For example, childhood immunization programs have generated community controversy when immunization standards are strictly enforced, resulting in the banning from school of children who are not immunized. Most schools allow exceptions to immunization for religious reasons, but not others. Despite wide public concern and the "war on drugs," drug education programs sometimes generate controversy. Some citizens are concerned about education that goes beyond knowledge and deals with values and skills. Although syphilis and gonorrhea have been at epidemic proportions among young people for a number of years, some communities are reluctant to allow open discussion of sex and the use of condoms as a health-protecting behavior. The recognition of the widespread nature of HIV/AIDS has compounded the condom/sex education dilemma in many communities.

Schools and, quite often, teachers are caught in the middle of these controversies.

The health service challenge

The scope of the school health program has been traditionally described as including *health instruction*, providing basic *health services* such as screening for vision and hearing, and providing emergency care and ensuring that the *school environment* is a safe and healthful place to learn. Recently, however, an expanded role for school health services has been proposed and adopted by some schools. This issue will receive a lot of attention in the next few years.

An increasing number of young people do not have access to traditional health care in their community; thus a number of private foundations and state governments have encouraged schools to initiate their own health clinics. These clinics may be located on the school campus as part of the school's administrative structure. Such clinics are called *school-based clinics*. Other clinics are located off the school property but usually are near the school and affiliated with it. These are referred to as *school-linked clinics.* School-linked clinics may have already existed within a community and, through the establishment of a close working relationship with the schools, thus may develop strategies to provide more effective health services for students.

In this way a wide range of primary health services is provided at low cost or no cost to students through the support of state agencies or private foundations. The close working relationship between these clinics and schools means that students often get speedier and more appropriate care than is readily available through the mainstream health care system. In 1991 the Center for Population Options reported that there were 327 school clinics serving junior and senior high schools in 1989 and 1990. Of these clinics, 306 were school based, and 21 were school linked.

This concept has caused concern among some members of the public—a concern that often focuses on the provision of services and counseling related to pregnancy, the prevention of unwanted pregnancy, and sexually transmitted diseases. Despite this area of controversy, the clinics have been shown to provide a wide range of other important care services directly related to helping students stay in school or gain greater benefit from their school experience (Fig. 1-5).

The curriculum squeeze challenge

The school day has a finite number of hours. Although the school year in the United States is shorter than in most countries, efforts to lengthen it have met with resistance. More time must be available for learning, but there will likely never be enough! The challenge to those interested in improving the health of young people is to determine how to use the available time to advance the school's health objectives. In addition to direct teaching, school health workers need to explore all the ways that health-related issues can be taught. The possibility of infusing health-related topics into the curriculum's major subjects—for example, mathematics,

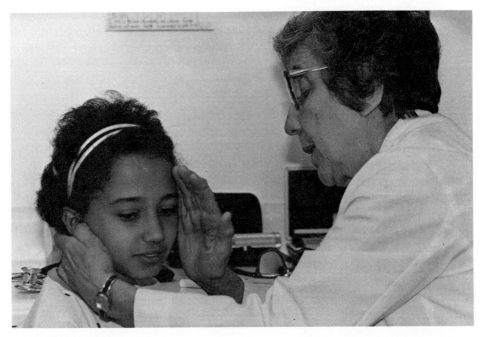

FIG. 1-5. The modern physician, like the Greek physician, accepts disease as an understandable and therefore potentially treatable condition. Health is the result of appropriate life-style, an adequate environment, and prudent care. The title "doctor," from the Latin *doctŏr*, means 'teacher'—a concept well understood by medical practitioners throughout time.

English, or social studies—would greatly increase the opportunity to raise levels of health knowledge and skills without detracting from the ongoing education in these subjects.

To encourage teachers to infuse health-related issues into their classes requires inservice education to increase their sensitivity to the health needs of youngsters and to show how health issues can be integrated into their subject matter areas. This requires careful planning and considerable cooperation and insight on the part of the school's faculty and administration.

Other opportunities for teaching health exist through the school's food service programs, physical education classes, and counseling services; through joint activities with the community; and even through the school board by the development of policies and administrative priorities.

The challenge of change

Alert health workers always expect the unexpected. Epidemics can be expected, but their nature and extent cannot be predicted. New knowledge concerning diseases and patterns of prevention present another type of challenge. Earlier this century, some thought the rapid growth of scientific knowledge would lead to the control and even elimination of disease. Rene Dubos, in his 1961 book, *The Mirage of Health*, was more insightful. He noted that solutions to problems often created new problems. Decreasing death rates, for example, contributed to a population expansion that created other problems. Dubos predicted that we will always be faced with health problems of one type or another.

For example, improving life-styles has so upset the environment that the environment itself has presented new threats to health. Early in 1992 the National Aeronautics and Space Administration reported an unusually high concentration of chlorine monoxide (ClO) in the atmosphere over the northern hemisphere. ClO is a by-product of the chlorafluorocarbons that are used as refrigerants and in a variety of industrial processes throughout the world. The increase of the use of fluorocarbons and their release into the atmosphere has seriously depleted the earth's ozone layer. The areas of greatest depletion tend to be above the Arctic and Antarctic, but now in the northern hemisphere ClO has been detected as far south as the Caribbean Sea. With ozone depleted, the sun's potentially harmful ultraviolet radiation can reach the earth's surface with increasing intensity. These ultraviolet rays are associated with increased incidence of skin cancer; interference with photosynthesis in crops, thus reducing yield; interference with the body's immune system; and a potential nutritional imbalance in the oceans.

Already faced with a 50% reduction in ozone over the Antarctic, southern hemisphere nations have taken action. Australian schools have had to teach a new set of practices for exposure to sunlight. Schools are now teaching knowledge and practices that contradict the traditional social value of people who prized suntans. School children have been instructed to wear hats and shirts and use sunscreens, not to play outdoors between 10:00 AM and 3:00 PM, and to limit their exposure to direct sunlight at all times. Ozone depletion represents just one possible challenge.

Obviously the schools cannot be the sole respondent to all changes, but this example does serve to illustrate the necessity for the school to respond to changing health problems and to produce, on relatively short notice, new curricula and services to encourage new competencies and skills among students and teachers.

The challenge to be comprehensive

How many components are there to a well-planned comprehensive school health program? Traditionally the school health program included three parts: health education, health services, and the school environment. Allensworth and Kolbe have described the school health program as including eight elements, each with a unique role to play in promoting the health of students. The challenge is to ensure that each of these elements is actually serving the school's health objectives. The eight elements are:

1. Health services
2. Health education
3. Healthy environment
4. Physical education
5. Food services
6. Counseling
7. School-site health promotion programs for faculty and staff
8. Integration of school and community activities to promote student and staff health

These eight components add to the meaning of the traditional three and serve to identify areas of student and staff health promotion that are often overlooked: for example, school counseling and food services. These eight components suggest a degree of comprehensiveness not evident when only health education, health services, and health environment are considered.

HIV/AIDS prevention

EMERGING ISSUE   Assume that you are a member of a school health council for a large urban school district. The charge of the council is to make recommendations to the school board in relation to school health issues. In a recent address before the city health department, a physican representative of the U.S. Public Health Service has called attention to the growing threat of the HIV/AIDS infections. In addition to a comprehensive health education program in schools, this official recommends that the health department undertake a joint effort with the schools to include the identification of students who are at high risk of HIV infection. Such students should be given individual counseling and referred for appropriate medical care, if needed.

An emergency meeting of the council has been called to consider this proposal. In an effort to determine the thinking of the council, the chair has asked each member to respond to the following statements. Please indicate whether you generally agree or disagree by placing a plus (+) or a minus (−) sign before each statement.

_____ 1. Since I believe that the school's primary role is education, I would have serious reservations about this proposal.

_____ 2. I would be opposed to the school becoming involved in such a program since I believe that it would compromise the confidential relationship with students.

_____ 3. I would favor placing greater emphasis on the school's role through preventive health education.

_____ 4. Important as education is, I believe that threat of this disease is so great that schools are going to have to do more to help control this disease.

_____ 5. I am opposed on moral grounds to the idea of schools teaching "safe sex" rather than emphasizing abstinence.

_____ 6. I would favor this proposal as it relates to male students since I believe that they present a greater HIV risk.

_____   If limited to a single choice, I would choose this number.

REFERENCES
Kerr DL: Condom availablity in New York City schools, *J Sch Health* 61(6):279, 1991.
Naughton SS, et al: AIDS/HIV risk assessment and risk reduction counseling in a school-based clinic, *J Sch Health* 61(10):443, 1991.

Another question related to comprehensiveness is what subjects should be taught, at what grade levels, and what should be the content of the health lessons?

Phil Nader, a physician vitally interested in the school's role in promoting the health of children, suggests that the eight components listed above need to be viewed in their relationship with the family, the community, and the media if we are to have a truly comprehensive model of the school health program (Fig. 1-6).

Nader notes that children's health status is related to education and that their ultimate education is related to their health status. He also notes that the activities in the school directed at health concerns are directly related to and reflect the school's community. He adds a factor not often suggested as integral to the school health program: the media. Not only do the media serve to link the community with great amounts of information and sometimes misinformation, but they also constitute a powerful force in shaping behaviors. Even when they impart

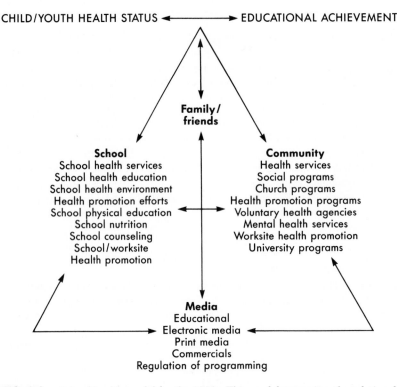

CHILD/YOUTH HEALTH STATUS ◄──────► EDUCATIONAL ACHIEVEMENT

**Family/
friends**

School
School health services
School health education
School health environment
Health promotion efforts
School physical education
School nutrition
School counseling
School/worksite
Health promotion

Community
Health services
Social programs
Church programs
Health promotion programs
Voluntary health agencies
Mental health services
Worksite health promotion
University programs

Media
Educational
Electronic media
Print media
Commercials
Regulation of programming

FIG. 1-6.   School health model for the 1990s. This model recognizes the relationship between student health and education and the interplay between school, family, friends, and the community and the media. Each affects health in a different way and therefore must be considered in planning school health programs.

health messages not necessarily positive or directly health enhancing, the media are an important part of the community.

The interplay of all these factors represents a truly comprehensive model of the forces shaping a young person's health. Given the limited resources of the school system, the ultimate challenge is to decide which of all these factors are most important, and what shall be done about them?

Our response to these challenges is based on a history of successes and failures in dealing with health problems. The remainder of this chapter highlights the history that gives inspiration to school health workers facing the challenges of school health today.

THE INSPIRATION—THE QUEST FOR HEALTH

Controlling communicable disease, improving the physical environment, providing care and medical assistance to the sick, and maintaining safe and adequate supplies of food and water are never-ending tasks. Our knowledge today represents the accumulated experiences of all human history. Our recollection of this history usually begins with the Greeks; but, as we point out, the earliest knowledge actually preceded the Greeks by thousands of years.

Early contributions

Although the Greeks are credited as a source of much of our public health knowledge, it is important to note that other civilizations preceded them for thousands of years and no doubt contributed significantly to the Greek concepts of health and disease.

Evidence of earliest humans left us few details of how health was protected. But archaeologic evidence from as early as 5000 BC suggested that people were well aware of ways to protect health and avoid disease. Beyond pictures of hunting for food, there is evidence that health protection practices were institutionalized.

In the area now known as Iraq and Syria, Mesopotamia flourished in the Tigris-Euphrates valley between 5000 and 1600 BC, long before the ascendancy of Greek culture. Evidence suggests the use of medicines and the management of water supplies to control infection. In China, in the fertile valley of the Yellow River, signs of early cities and sophisticated civilizations suggest a people sensitive to their environment and coping well with health and disease.

In the Indian subcontinent, in what is Pakistan today, there is clear evidence that the cities of the Indus River valley were built in accordance with laws that allowed the easy drainage of waste water and provided for the distribution of fresh water for human use.

In Egypt the civilizations of the Nile valley flourished from 4000 BC. Egypt's natural lifeline is the Nile River, which flows out of eastern central Africa. This raises interesting and challenging questions about how much of the sophisticated practices of the Egyptian culture, which preceded that of the Greeks, can be traced to earlier civilizations further south on the Nile in central Africa.

Western public health is often described as based on Greek ideals. One of their ideals was balance: balance between the individual and the environment, balance between mind and body, balance between nutrition and excretion, and balance between exercise and rest. Greek learning was concerned with cleansing and exercising not only the mind but also the body. Hygiene and physical fitness at the height of Greek culture were implemented to a degree unparalleled in later history.

The Greeks considered disease a natural, not a supernatural, process; therefore disease was understandable and potentially manageable and had little to do with a person's spiritual condition. Epidemiology, the study of disease, was developed by the Greeks. The first clear accounts of clinical characteristics of communicable diseases such as mumps, pneumonia, malarial fevers, and diphtheria are present in their literature.

The idea of the balance between humans and nature was best expressed by Hippocrates in his *On Airs, Waters, and Places* (1939). Noting that human well-being depended on climate, soil, water, mode of life, and nutrition, Hippocrates drew the distinction between endemic and epidemic diseases. The Hippocratic writings remained the underpinnings of public health practice until the nineteenth century when microbiology and bacteriology developed.

The Greeks are responsible for the following concepts:

1. The application of scientific thinking to matters of health
2. The recognition of the relationship between environment and health
3. The development of personal hygiene based on the concept of a balanced life
4. The provision of basic health services by the state

Despite the great idealism and concern for the health of the average citizen exhibited by Greek culture, the benefits derived from Greek medicine and hygiene remained the domain of the wealthy, the privileged, and the powerful and were not shared universally with the masses. Idealism and democratic intent aside, matters related to health were a privilege, not a right, in Greek society.

Roman contributions

Rome conquered the Mediterranean world and, with the destruction of Corinth in 146 BC, took over the legacy of Greece. The Romans accepted almost completely the Greek ideas of health and medicine but did little to advance them in the ensuing years. The Romans' outstanding contributions to public health were in the areas of engineering and administration. Their administrative skills provided the basis for their system of water supply, sewage disposal, refinements in the delivery of health services, and improved patterns of health administration.

With the migration of Greek physicians to Rome, the practice of medicine in Rome shifted from a spiritual to a secular base, from the priests to the physicians. By 200 AD Rome had established a public medical service patterned after that of Greece. Public physicians were appointed by town councils. Salaried physicians were expected to provide free care for all who could not afford to pay. Private practicing physicians were available to people of means. These aspects of Roman medical service followed the Greek precedents. Rome, however, set an important new precedent by establishing an elaborate system of public hospitals. In fact, Rome established two parallel systems of hospitals, one for the general public and one for the military.

With the fall of Rome many aspects of its public health organization and practice were lost. The health teachings of the Greek physicians were essentially discarded, except in the Christian monasteries, where some persisted. Also, these teachings were kept alive by the Islamic nations of the eastern edges of the Roman Empire, who absorbed and translated vast amounts of Greek and Roman writings, adding their own contributions to the development of public health over the next few centuries. One of the great Moslem teachers and physicians was Rhazes (Abu-Bakr Mohammed Ibn Zakaryyaar Razi), who lived between 865 and 923 and taught and practiced in Persia in modern-day Bagdad. His writing and teachings contributed to the long flow of health knowledge from which we still benefit today (Fig. 1-7).

Later this health knowledge, which had been protected by the Islamic practitioners and teachers and by monks in the Christian monasteries, would be "rediscovered" and reintroduced to Europe as part of the Renaissance.

The Middle Ages (476 to 1453)

The evolution of medieval towns with congestion on the inner sides of city walls and squatters' slums on the outside directly contributed to the decline in community hygiene standards. The walled cities were ideal environments for the spread of contagious diseases. Many who moved to the towns brought with them not only their country ways but also their livestock. Barns were as common in Paris as were houses, and it was not until 1641 that the citizens of Berlin, for example, introduced a law to forbid the building of pigpens adjacent to streets.

Against the background of early urbanization developed the first of the three great eras of pestilence or plague that swept the world in the Middle Ages: leprosy. Black death was the second, and syphilis was the third.

Leprosy marked the onset of the Middle Ages, and black death marked their waning. During this period, Europe and the Mediterranean countries were also ravaged by a variety of

FIG. 1-7. Physician and philosopher Abu-Bakr Mohammed Ibn Zakariyya ar Razi (865-932 AD), referred to today as Rhazes, represented the contribution to modern health practice provided by the Arabic world. The Arab scholars protected and added to the knowledge of Greeks passed on by the Romans after the downfall of Rome and the onset of the Middle Ages.

communicable diseases; smallpox, diphtheria, measles, influenza, tuberculosis, scabies, anthrax, and trachoma were but a few. None of these diseases, however, caused as much suffering and death as leprosy and black death.

Leprosy. During medieval times, no disease aroused more fear than leprosy, based on the facts that it (1) spread rapidly, (2) caused physical disfigurement, and (3) was regarded as a sign of spiritual impurity.

Long before the principles of contagion were validated, the practice of isolation was introduced in an attempt to control the spread of the disease. In fact, the ceremonial instructions of the Book of Leviticus (13:1-59 and 14:1-57), as well as other early writings, contain explicit references to quarantine and other means of combating leprosy. The biblical references indicate that the principle of isolation and quarantine was at first as much a religious as a medical concept.

The treatment of leprosy was the first clear example of what is now called a *prophylaxis,* that is, the control of a disease by systematic treatment: isolating or quarantining the carrier of a disease and thereby preventing the contagion from spreading. Despite these efforts, however, leprosy was not eradicated. Even today it persists in many parts of the world.

Black plague. From the wild rodents of the steppes of Asia, a plague swept westward and reached the Black Sea around 1346. The plague was referred to as the ''black death'' because of the hemorrhaging of its victims. From the Black Sea the plague was carried on shipboard to the ports of Europe. By 1348 the first of many successive waves of black plague blanketed Europe. Individuals afflicted with leprosy were especially susceptible to the plague, and the majority of lepers died, which precipitated a decline in the prevalence and severity of leprosy.

Panic, flight, prayer, and penance were initial reactions to this plague. More rational thinking soon followed. Stringent standards of quarantine were established, much like those set down for leprosy control. The gates of cities were closed to outsiders, houses of the sick were marked, and food and water supplies were carried in only by authorized people who themselves were then quarantined to ensure no contagion. Venice, for example, in 1348 held ships and their crews at an isolated island in the harbor for 40 days before entry to the dock to unload, a practice that was then widely adopted. The term *quarantine* means 'pertaining to 40.'

Approximately 20 to 35 million people, one third to one half of the European population, died from the plague. The effects were devastating. In England, for example, the labor supply became so short and the economy so restricted that Parliament in 1350 had to freeze prices and forbid laborers to migrate to other towns.

Syphilis. The last of the great plagues of the Middle Ages was syphilis. Although there is some debate as to where it originated, there is no disagreement with the fact that syphilis reached epidemic proportions in Europe in the late 1400s. By 1497 the spread of syphilis was well documented and was reported to have spread as far as remote areas of Scotland. At that time syphilis was an acute and often fatal disease. This acute version seems to have attenuated into the less virulent chronic condition present today. The decreasing virulence of the disease no doubt reduced its threat and the chance of widespread prophylaxis. Unlike leprosy and the plague, syphilis is still present in epidemic proportions.

Many people still respond to plagues in much the same way they did in the Middle Ages: with fear, suspicion, panic, and isolation and by appealing to or blaming the supernatural. Epidemics and plagues are essentially the same. HIV/AIDS represents an epidemic—a disease that occurs at higher rates than normal. Despite all the advances in health attributed to science, many people's reactions to HIV/AIDS have been much the same as reactions to leprosy or the black plague in the Middle Ages.

The Renaissance

In the period extending roughly from the fourteenth through the sixteenth centuries, a rebirth of interest in the learning, literature, and artistic achievements of classical Greece and Rome, called the *Renaissance,* began in Italy and then spread throughout western Europe.

Among the forces that led to the Renaissance were the invention of the printing press, which allowed for the widespread distribution of ideas, and the introduction of gunpowder, which led city planners to cease building walls around cities, opening them to free passage of people. This rebirth of learning extended into areas related to public health and medicine. Many people contributed new ideas that now went beyond those of the Greeks, Romans, and the Islamic world; and the increasing movement of people and ideas meant that again knowledge was being shared widely. Scholars at centers of learning in Paris, Oxford, and Cambridge began to reorder knowledge into the classical disciplines of law, medicine, theology, and philosophy. Humanists, with their emphasis on the natural, began to accept sickness and disease as phenomena to be investigated and understood.

Mercantilism

With the humanism of the Renaissance, the seventeenth, and the eighteenth centuries also came the rise of commerce and industry and the development of the new economic theory of mercantilism. Increased economic activity and trade resulted in increased wealth and led to the clear identification of the nation state. As a nation's wealth became important, the value of the nation's workers increased. This fact, along with the spirit of humanism, led to a concerted interest in solving the health problems of the day, especially as they affected the workers. A sick and ailing work force meant less production and therefore less wealth. The positive results for the work force, however, were lost temporarily in the Industrial Revolution as it developed later in the 1800s.

Beginning of the modern era

In seventeenth century London, bills of mortality were published weekly. These were basically an account of the causes of death, an early example of biostatistics. John Graunt (1620-1674) made the first systematic study of these bills of mortality and in 1662 published *Natural and Political Observation upon the Bills of Mortality*, a text that indicated some of the real meaning of mortality in his society. He observed that more boys than girls were born but that the ratio of the sexes was soon equalized because the rate of death during childhood was higher for boys than for girls. Graunt also noted that death rates were higher in urban areas than in rural areas and that death rates varied by season.

William Petty (1623-1687) went beyond Graunt in the analysis of numeric data on population, education, disease, revenue, and economic structure. Petty established the statistical basis for health planning, which involved the identification of existing needs, medical work force, medical care, and ancillary medical services designed to satisfy those needs. Petty's efforts to relate statistics to the real needs of the day became known as "political arithmetic" (Petty, 1699).

Humanism, mercantilism, and the pioneering work of Graunt and Petty led to a gradual increase in community involvement in matters related to their own health; however, the quality of medical practice available to the average citizen changed little.

The eighteenth century marked an early triumph of preventive medicine. The practice of inoculation had been known in India and China for hundreds of years. This practice was first introduced into Europe around 1713 and made famous by Mary Wortley Montague, wife of the English Ambassador to Turkey, who had her 3-year-old son inoculated against smallpox in Constantinople in 1718.

The lag between the development of a medical or preventive technique and its eventual success in the eradication of a worldwide health problem is a lesson of history worth noting. Edward Jenner (1749-1823), a British physician, made inoculation with smallpox obsolete by discovering that the application of cowpox virus to scratched human skin produced an immunity to smallpox. According to the World Health Organization, smallpox was eliminated in 1979.

The era of modern bacteriology ushered in by the work of Louis Pasteur and Robert Koch marked the first major redirection of medicine since the time of the Greeks. The discovery that a specific organism causes a specific disease transferred attention from the general environment to specific elements in the environment. The recognition that the spread of disease could be prevented by blocking routes over which the disease traveled resulted in emphasis on the sanitation of water, milk, and other foods; the elimination of insects; and the disposal of sewage. Sanitary engineers, sanitary inspectors, bacteriologists, and laboratory technicians became essential to the health program. This era reestablished many of the important principles first recorded by the early Greek physicians. These developments, from earliest times until today, are summarized in Fig. 1-8.

Control of the ill person, who was the source of the disease, became an established practice. Isolation and quarantine measures were enforced. Progress in the prevention and control of infectious diseases included immunization, antiseptic procedures, and chemical treatment. Immunization was a natural outcome of the interest in bacteriology. In 1883 Pasteur developed the inoculation against rabies. Von Behring's development of diphtheria antitoxin was first used in 1894. Wright developed typhoid inoculations in 1904. Lord Lister's development

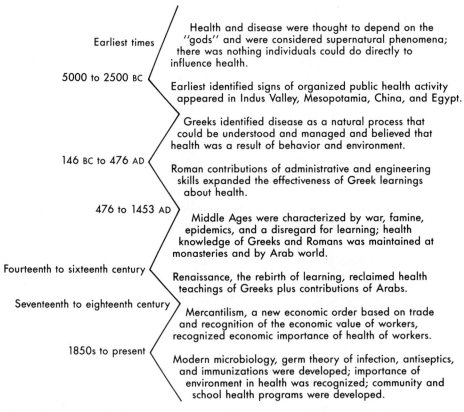

FIG. 1-8.   Major periods in public health history. Moving from an era of complete acceptance of disease as supernatural, humankind has come to view disease as a natural and therefore understandable phenomenon. The Greeks thought that if disease could be understood, it could be limited. Many of the Greeks' notions of balance, moderation, and recognition of the importance of environment were lost during the Dark Ages, only to reemerge during the Renaissance as important principles in modern public health thinking.

of carbolic acid (phenol) and Ehrlich's discovery of the value of arsenic compounds in the treatment of syphilis lowered the death rate from communicable diseases.

The dramatic progress of this era made it seem as though with time all disease could be conquered. By environmental management, improved care, and the widespread use of the dramatically successful inoculations, anything seemed possible. Public health focused its efforts on doing things to and for people. Only gradually did it become clear that people must be involved in their own health. Basic education about hygiene and nutrition developed. To become more responsible, people needed more knowledge and stronger encouragement to exercise that knowledge.

As communicable diseases were controlled and the environment improved, new patterns of disease emerged that emphasized the need for new knowledge and higher levels of personal responsibility for improved health. Today the principal causes of death are in varying degrees the result of the way persons act and what they do to and for themselves. To control the spread of modern diseases and thus lower the death rate, the public needs not only knowledge, but also help to behave in a responsible way. Changing and improving behavior is the objective of education (Fig. 1-9).

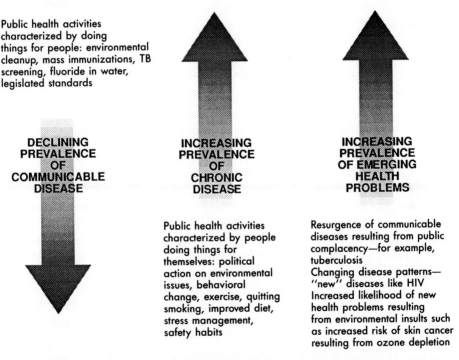

Public health activities characterized by doing things for people: environmental cleanup, mass immunizations, TB screening, fluoride in water, legislated standards

DECLINING PREVALENCE OF COMMUNICABLE DISEASE

INCREASING PREVALENCE OF CHRONIC DISEASE

INCREASING PREVALENCE OF EMERGING HEALTH PROBLEMS

Public health activities characterized by people doing things for themselves: political action on environmental issues, behavioral change, exercise, quitting smoking, improved diet, stress management, safety habits

Resurgence of communicable diseases resulting from public complacency—for example, tuberculosis
Changing disease patterns—"new" diseases like HIV
Increased likelihood of new health problems resulting from environmental insults such as increased risk of skin cancer resulting from ozone depletion

FIG. 1-9.   The changing nature of public health problems involves changes in strategies to improve health. In the past, control of chronic diseases was achieved largely by doing things *to* the environment and *to* people. To reduce the number of deaths from degenerative diseases and accidents and to prolong life, public health workers will have to work with people to bring about changes in individual health practices. With the resurgence of some communicable diseases, the continuing prevalence of chronic diseases, and emergence of environmentally caused conditions, both personal behavior and environmental conditions will need to be changed to protect health.

Beginning of school health movement

As early as 1790 Bavaria provided free school lunches for the underprivileged. In 1832 Edwin Chadwick, an assistant commissioner, studied the operation of the poor laws of England. From his studies of the conditions of child employment came reforms recognizing the health needs of children.

Physicians were placed on public school staffs in Sweden in 1868, Germany in 1869, Russia in 1871, and Austria in 1873. In Brussels, Belgium, the first organized, regular medical inspection system was instituted in 1874. In 1892 nurses began looking after the health of children in a school in London's Chancery Lane.

It is significant that all these early school health activities were directed toward doing something *for* the child. The concept of preparing children to do something for themselves had not yet evolved.

Modern school health programs are built on the developing philosophies of education and the rapidly evolving knowledge of health and disease (Fig. 1-10).

Before 1850 the schools in the United States were dominated by the church. The type of imposed pedagogy that prevailed before 1850 did not lend itself to health education. However, by 1850 tax-supported public schools became a reality in most of the United States, particularly in the north.

The publication of the *Report of the Sanitary Commission of Massachusetts* (Shattuck, 1850) expressed an awakening concern for matters affecting public health. The report, which dealt with a large number of health topics, included a plan for school health instruction. Shattuck wrote:

> Every child should be taught, early in life, that to preserve his own life and his own health and the lives and health of others, is one of his most important and constantly abiding duties.

Shattuck's report attracted much attention. It recognized the school as an agency for health promotion. For the next 20 years this seed of recognition was nourished by influential leaders in education such as Rousseau, Pestalozzi, and Froebel. This influence, which stressed education as growth from within, not imposed from without, stimulated an interest in understanding children, their needs, and the best means to meet these needs.

In the late 1800s physical education and health were considered identical. Since many of the early physical education leaders were physicians, this point of view is not surprising. Not until 1910 did it change. In that year the seventeenth meeting of the American Physical Education Association used "School Hygiene and Physical Education" as its theme. Not until 1937 did the American Physical Education Association become the American Association for Health and Physical Education and thus recognize the distinction between health and physical education.

The end of the first decade of the 1900s marked two important developments in the school health movement. The first White House Conference on Child Health and Protection was held in 1910, and in 1911 the Joint Committee of the National Education Association and the American Medical Association was appointed. This committee, representing the official position of the two parent bodies on health programs affecting schools, became an authoritative source of recommended policies and practice for health programs.

In 1918 the Commission on the Reorganization of Secondary Education named health as the first of the seven cardinal objectives of education.

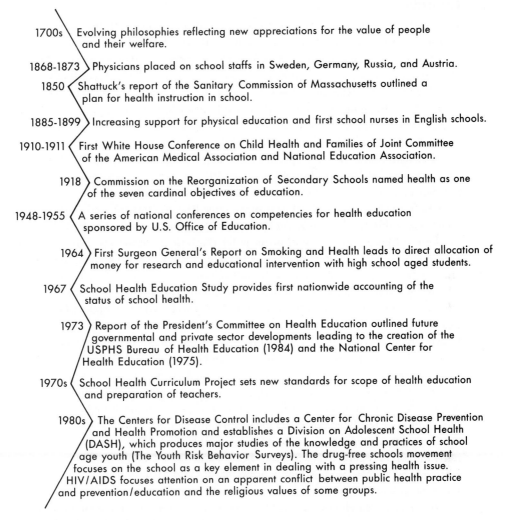

| 1700s | Evolving philosophies reflecting new appreciations for the value of people and their welfare. |

1868-1873 — Physicians placed on school staffs in Sweden, Germany, Russia, and Austria.

1850 — Shattuck's report of the Sanitary Commission of Massachusetts outlined a plan for health instruction in school.

1885-1899 — Increasing support for physical education and first school nurses in English schools.

1910-1911 — First White House Conference on Child Health and Families of Joint Committee of the American Medical Association and National Education Association.

1918 — Commission on the Reorganization of Secondary Schools named health as one of the seven cardinal objectives of education.

1948-1955 — A series of national conferences on competencies for health education sponsored by U.S. Office of Education.

1964 — First Surgeon General's Report on Smoking and Health leads to direct allocation of money for research and educational intervention with high school aged students.

1967 — School Health Education Study provides first nationwide accounting of the status of school health.

1973 — Report of the President's Committee on Health Education outlined future governmental and private sector developments leading to the creation of the USPHS Bureau of Health Education (1984) and the National Center for Health Education (1975).

1970s — School Health Curriculum Project sets new standards for scope of health education and preparation of teachers.

1980s — The Centers for Disease Control includes a Center for Chronic Disease Prevention and Health Promotion and establishes a Division on Adolescent School Health (DASH), which produces major studies of the knowledge and practices of school age youth (The Youth Risk Behavior Surveys). The drug-free schools movement focuses on the school as a key element in dealing with a pressing health issue. HIV/AIDS focuses attention on an apparent conflict between public health practice and prevention/education and the religious values of some groups.

FIG. 1-10. In the modern period it became increasingly clear that human behaviors were major contributors to disease and death. The federal government and the schools became more interested in teaching people to value and protect their health.

In 1930 the Second White House Conference on Child Health and Protection grappled with the task of synthesizing various aspects of child health and its concomitant problems. The conference report served as a guide for two decades.

An interest in the professional preparation of those who teach about health emerged during the 1960s when the American Association for Health, Physical Education, and Recreation sponsored a series of national conferences to develop standards for accrediting colleges and universities offering training in health education (Means, 1975). Schaller (1978), summarizing several of these reports, identified the common areas of professional preparation in health education as: (1) the physical and biologic sciences, (2) the behavioral sciences, (3) a core of health content courses, and (4) the skills of professional practice.

Government support

In 1971 President Nixon appointed the National Committee on Health Education. Earlier that year, in his health message to Congress, the President had stated that there was no national instrument, no central force to stimulate and coordinate a comprehensive health program (Report of the President's Committee on Health Education, 1973). Accordingly, the committee was charged with doing the following:

1. Describing the state of the art in health education
2. Defining the nation's need for health education
3. Establishing goals, priorities, and objectives for health education
4. Determining the most appropriate structure, organization, and function for a national health education foundation

The President's report led directly to the establishment of the Bureau of Health Education in 1974 as a part of the U.S. Public Health Service. The bureau provided a focal point for health education within the federal government and encouraged industry to build health education into existing programs. Another purpose for the bureau was to fund the training of health education specialists. A further outgrowth of the President's report was the establishment in 1975 of the National Center for Health Education.

Besides the creation of the Bureau of Health Education, the *Report of the President's Committee on Health Education* triggered other federal activities. For example, Congress has written new charters for the National Cancer Institute and the National Heart, Lung, and Blood Institute. In addition to their traditional biomedical research missions, it is now mandated that more attention be given to prevention, education, and control measures.

The creation of the Alcohol, Drug, and Mental Health Administration (ADAMHA) that included the National Institute on Drug Abuse and the National Institute on Alcoholism and Alcohol Abuse focused additional government resources on health education. More recently the creation of the Office of Substance Abuse Prevention within ADAMHA has supported significant health education initiatives through its Drug-free Schools programs and many other initiatives related to confronting alcohol and other drug abuse. The government is now reorganizing the National Institute on Alcoholism and Alcohol Abuse and the National Institution on Drug Abuse to become a part of the National Institutes of Health.

In 1978 the Bureau of Health Manpower of the U.S. Public Health Service sponsored a workshop on the preparation and practice of professional health educators. Conclusions from the conference suggested developing national standards to establish health educators' credentials. This work, the Role Delineation Project, was continued by the National Center for Health Education and resulted in a precise listing of skills and competencies basic to entry-level health education practice (Focal Points, 1980) and a system for establishing credentials. Through this system, health education graduates can pass an examination and become Certified Health Education Specialists.

For the first time, health education became a prominent part of a federal policy statement when the National Forward Plan for Health, FY 1978-1982, issued in 1976 offered several recommendations directly related to school health education. The Public Health Service was charged to give priority attention to the following:

1. Fostering research and pilot programs aimed at improving health education principles and techniques

2. Conducting specific health education activities in accident prevention
3. Conducting research to determine the best methods of teaching children about the harmful effects of smoking, alcohol, drug abuse, and careless driving
4. Developing lifelong attitudes toward health and the improvement of health in later years as a major goal of child health; health activities cited in this report were immunizations, nutrition, dental health, and mental health

Today the result of this work is evident in the prominence of health education–related goals in the nation's health goals for the year 2000. These goals suggest a wide recognition for and appreciation of the contributions of the school in promoting the health of young people.

The Centers for Disease Control

With the reorganization of the Center for Disease Control into the Centers for Disease Control, health education initiatives were grouped in the Center for Health Promotion and Education. With subsequent reorganization, school health activities were administered by the Center for Chronic Disease Prevention and Health Promotion. Later, the Division of Adolescent and School Health (DASH) was formed. DASH has become a visible and effective force in promoting comprehensive school health programs nationwide.

Two other government reorganizations have led to the development of initiatives to support school health. Within the Alcohol, Drug Abuse, and Mental Health Administration the creation of the Office of Substance Abuse Prevention has been instrumental in promoting school programs related to alcohol and other drugs. Similarly, within the Office of the Secretary of Education, the initiatives of the drug-free schools movement has greatly supported school health activities.

At the same time the private sector has supported initiatives for improving the health of young people. A number of groups have published significant documents to spread word about the need to improve the health of children and youth. Three such documents are:

Turning Points: Preparing American Youth for the 21st Century, published in 1989 by the Carnegie Council on Adolescent Development.

Code Blue: A Call to Action for Healthier Youth, published in 1991 by the National Commission on the Role of the School and the Community in Improving Adolescent Health of the National Association of the State Boards of Education.

Adolescent Health, Volume 1, Summary and Policy Options, published in 1991 by the Office of Technology Assessment of the U.S. Congress.

Summary

Although much of the health-related knowledge of the Greeks, Romans, and earlier civilizations was disregarded during the Middle Ages, many of their principles are now important again. Supplementing the rediscovery of old knowledge has been an enormous quantity of new scientific health-related findings within the last 100 years. Despite these advances in knowledge, one fact continues to be clear: What individuals do to and for themselves in terms of personal behavior has the greatest influence on health. Education, especially education in schools, therefore becomes critical. The elements of the school health program (i.e., education, environment, and services) are, in fact, microcosms of all that is critical to the health of our community, our country, and our world.

The school health worker faces a range of complex issues that will both frustrate and excite. The changing nature of the population and of disease will affect the nature of both the educational and the health problems to be confronted. New challenges crowd the school day, and new knowledge means new ways of doing things—often not to the liking of all people. New initiatives in the government and the private sector have clearly highlighted the potential contributions to be made by schools and their faculty and staffs. How successful we are in meeting all the challenges will determine the levels of health to be enjoyed by the young people of the 21st century.

GET INVOLVED!

As you approach the completion of your undergraduate studies, it is time to begin planning for your career as a professional. Among the organizations you may wish to consider joining, one of the largest and most influential is the American Public Health Association (APHA).

APHA has a membership of approximately 32,000 health care providers, scientists, administrators, educators, students, and others. A special strength of APHA is its multidisciplinary character. In effect, it is an organization of organizations, addressing the many special interests within the broad field of health. There are approximately 30 different sections and primary interest groups in public health, ranging from alcohol, tobacco, and drugs to veterinary medicine. For students majoring in school or community health education, there are the sections on School Health Education and Services and the Public Health Education section.

Membership in APHA offers a number of benefits important to your career advancement. As a participant in the Association, you will become part of an organized structure that will help you develop relationships with other health professionals, not only within your own specialty but in many others in the field of public health. You will develop long-lasting contacts and friendships within the Association while increasing your visibility and recognition among peers. APHA offers a job placement service for its members. You will receive two publications, the *American Journal of Public Health* and *Nation's Health,* which will help you to keep informed about current developments in the field. Each state has a state public health association that addresses local health issues and maintains a close working relationship with the national organization, APHA.

For membership information, write to:
The American Public Health Association
1015 15th St. S.W.
Washington, D.C. 20005

STUDY QUESTIONS

1. Explain how the nation's educational goals and health goals actually complement each other.
2. Select any four challenges outlined in this chapter and suggest three actions that will confront these challenges with positive health outcomes.
3. Why are the nations with the highest level of health also the nations with the greatest political, economic, and social advances? What political, economic, and social advances have these nations achieved?
4. Which developments in the past decade do you consider to be of major importance to health education?
5. What are the major health risks facing today's children and adolescents?
6. The Roman contributions to public health differ from those of the Greeks in which important dimensions?

7. Why was the development of mercantilism so important to the development of public health practice?
8. Select any three goals for the year 2000 that pertain to adolescents and suggest three specific actions that could be taken by school personnel to meet these three goals.
9. If the nation's goals are not met, what will be the impact on the nation's health?

REFERENCES

Agency for Toxic Substances and Disease Registry: The nature and extent of lead poisoning in children in the United States: a report to Congress, Washington, DC, 1988, US Department of Health and Human Services.

Allensworth DD, Kolbe LJ: The comprehensive school health program: exploring an expanded concept, *J Sch Health* 57:409, 1987.

American School Health Association, Association for the Advancement of Health Education and the Society for Public Health Education, Inc: The national adolescent student health survey: a report on the health of America's youth, Oakland, Calif, 1989, Third Party Publishing.

Bagnall P: One hundred years old and fitter than ever: school nursing in Britain, *J Sch Health* 61(9):402-404, 1991.

Breslow L: A health promotion primer for the 1990s, *Health Affairs* 9:6-21, 1990.

Carnegie Council on Adolescent Development, Carnegie Corporation of New York: Turning points: preparing American youth for the 21st century, Washington, DC, 1989, The Carnegie Council on Adolescent Development.

Chadwick E: *Report on an inquiry into the sanitary condition of the laboring population of Great Britain (poor law commissioners)*, London, 1842, W. Clowes for Her Majesty's Stationery Office.

Compas BE: Promoting positive mental health during adolescence. In Millstein SG, Petersen AC, and Nightingale EO (editors): Adolescent health promotion (in preparation for the Carnegie Council on Adolescent Development, Carnegie Corp. of New York), 1990, Washington, DC.

Congress of the United States, Office of Technology Assessment: Adolescent health, vol. 1, Summary and policy options (OTA-H-468), Washington, DC, 1991, US Government Printing Office.

Dryfoos J: *Adolescents at risk*, New York, 1990, Oxford University Press.

Dubos R: *Mirage of health*, Garden City, NY, 1961, Anchor Books.

EdnaEpp J: Achieving health for all: a framework for health promotion, *Health Promotion* 1(4):419-428, 1987.

Focal points, Atlanta, July 1980, Bureau of Health Education, US Department of Health and Human Services, Public Health Service.

Hippocrates: On airs, waters, and places. In *The genuine works of Hippocrates*, Baltimore, 1939, Williams & Wilkins. (Translated by Francis Adams.)

Kann L, et al: Establishing a system of complementary school-based surveys to annually assess HIV-related knowledge, beliefs and behaviors among adolescents, *J Sch Health* 59(2):55-65, 1989.

Males J: Youth behavior: subcultural effect or mirror of adult behavior? *J Sch Health* 60(10)505-508, 1990.

Means RK: *A history of health education in the United States*, Philadelphia, 1975, Lea & Febiger.

Nader PR: The concept of "comprehensiveness" in the design and implementation of school health programs, *J Sch Health* 60(4):133-138, 1990.

National Center for Health Statistics: Health, United States, 1989 and prevention profile, DHHS Pub. No. (PHS) 90-1232, Hyattsville, Md, 1990, US Department of Health and Human Services.

National Commission on the Role of the School and the Community in Improving Adolescent Health: *Code blue: uniting for healthier youth*, Alexandria, Virginia, 1990, National Association of State Boards of Education.

National Highway Traffic Safety Administration: *Fatal accident reporting system*, 1987, Washington, DC, 1988, US Department of Transportation.

National Highway Traffic Safety Administration: NHTSA's 19-city survey, Washington, D.C., (no date), U.S. Department of Transportation.

Petty W: *Political arithmetic or a discourse concerning the extent and value of lands, people, buildings, etc.*, ed. 3, London, 1699, Robert Clavel.

President's Committee on Mental Retardation: Preventing the new morbidity: a guide for state planning for the prevention of mental retardation and related disabilities associated with socioeconomic conditions, Washington, DC, 1988, Department of Health and Human Services.

Report of the President's Committee on Health Education, Washington, DC, 1973, US Government Printing Office.

Schaller WE: Professional preparation and curriculum planning, *J Sch Health* 48(4):236, 1978.

Shattuck L: *The report of the sanitary commission on Massachusetts*, Cambridge, Mass, 1948, Harvard University Press. (Originally published in 1850.)

Sobal J, et al: Health concerns of high school students and teachers' beliefs about student health concerns, *Pediatrics* 81(2):218-223, 1988.

Society for Public Health Education Ad Hoc Task Force on Professional Preparation and Practice: Guidelines for the preparation and practice of professional health educators, *SOPHE Health Educ Monogr* 5(1):75, 1977.

Tolsma DD: Activities of the Centers for Disease Control in AIDS education, *J Sch Health* 58(4):133-136, 1988.

US Department of Health and Human Services: The 1990 health objectives for the nation: a mid-course review, Washington, DC, 1986, US Government Printing Office.

US Department of Health and Human Services: Healthy people 2000: National Health Promotion and Disease Prevention Objectives, DHHS Pub. No. (PHS) 91-50212, Washington, DC, 1991, US Government Printing Office.

US Preventive Services Task Force: Guide to clinical preventive services: an assessment of the effectiveness of 169 interventions, Baltimore, Md, 1989, Williams & Wilkins.

Vincent ML: With high tech are we loosing touch: the time to re-emphasize affective health education, *J Health Educ* 22(5):272-281, 1991.

Waszak C, Neidell S: School-based and school-linked clinics: update 1991, Washington, DC, 1991, The Center for Population Options.

CHAPTER

2

Basic plan of the health program

OVERVIEW

Strongly organized and effectively coordinated programs are essential to the goal of furthering school health education. The two facets of a school health plan, services and education, must be integrated to serve adequately the changing needs of a modern society. On the basis of these precepts, this chapter outlines the organization of health services and the organization of health instruction within the schools. The importance of integrating health services and health education is stressed while recognizing that the programs offered by the school have important ties to health agencies in the community.

The first three sections of this chapter deal with the organization of health programs. Organizational studies of public health for all levels of government are presented, including international, federal, state, and local health agencies. This larger perspective of health services provides a context within which the school health program operates and reveals some of the origins of its health activities. A discussion of the three basic divisions of the school health program follows.

The final section of the chapter deals with the importance of integrating not only school and community programs but also health services and health education programs if society is to meet the health and educational needs of today's school age population.

OBJECTIVES After reading this chapter, the student should be able to:

1. Describe the organization of health services at an international, federal, state, and local level
2. Identify the five major services of the World Health Organization (WHO)
3. Describe the major functions and organization of the U.S. Public Health Service
4. Explain the state's role in public health
5. Trace the process of authorizing school health programs
6. Distinguish between permissive and mandatory state legislation
7. Explain the roles of state education departments and local boards of education in the authorization process
8. Outline the benefits of programs that combine health services and education
9. Discuss the arguments for and against school-based clinics
10. Describe Newman's six principles for integrating programs

33

A basic plan or blueprint is essential to any important undertaking, particularly one such as the school health program, which is expected to deal with the diversity of factors and situations related to human well-being. Although the plan for school health must have a basic pattern or framework, it should be sufficiently flexible to adapt to any situation or need. To be functional it must be practical. It should be adjusted to the needs of the students and must be in harmony with the background of both the school and the community.

There is no such thing as a single school health program. Many plans have their merits. However, it is important to recognize that school health programs in the United States are legal responsibilities of both public education and public health. School health laws in the state of Illinois reveal the shared legal relationship of the two community governmental agencies of education and health. The school code pertaining to the physical examination states in part that "physical examinations," as prescribed by the Department of Public Health, including vision screening tests, "shall be required." The Critical Health Problems and Comprehensive Health Education Act for Illinois Schools states that the office of the Superintendent of Public Instruction (Illinois Office of Education) "shall establish the minimum amount of instruction time to be devoted to comprehensive health education at all elementary and secondary grade levels."

Because of this mutual concern, several different administrative patterns of school health programs are often used. The school health service aspect of the program may be placed under the jurisdiction of the local health department. Some schools operate under a joint administration of school health shared by the board of education and the health department. The most common pattern places the school health services under an associate superintendent for special services or associate superintendent for pupil personnel services.

How the program is administered is not of great importance as long as there is agreement on program objectives and a very real and cooperative working relationship exists between the school personnel and the health professionals. Serious difficulties have arisen in schools that have not had the benefit of leadership from professionally trained school health nurses and school health educators. Without such leadership, misunderstandings may arise over program priorities, based on a failure to understand the difference between the educators' objective to teach and the health professionals' goal to treat or to correct. Although the objectives of school personnel and health professionals are different, they are not mutually exclusive but instead serve to complement and strengthen each other. The student's full effectiveness in the teaching and learning situation cannot be achieved if he or she is not at optimal health, and optimal health cannot be achieved or maintained without benefit of education.

THE CONTEXT OF HEALTH PROGRAMS

The school health program must be understood in the total context of health programs and services. To be effective, the goals and functions of school health must be integrally related to all levels of health service, including the international, federal, state, and local levels.

Government health services have been concerned primarily with those functions that require organized community action, rather than services that can be easily provided on an individual basis. Government health agencies have undergone and continue to undergo considerable change. Earlier activities were concerned primarily with the prevention and control of communicable diseases on the local, national, or international level. This emphasis is changing to meet new health problems and the evolving needs of people.

Modern public health organizations have a variety of responsibilities that go far beyond efforts to control communicable diseases. Such diverse activities as mental health, crippled children's services, health hazards of the environment, medical care of the indigent, home health services, and the ever-increasing problems of chronic disease are now included. With the growing number of older citizens in U.S. society comes a need to devote more services to those with chronic illness.

International health services

The World Health Organization (WHO) is the major international health agency; its headquarters is in Geneva, Switzerland. Several regional WHO offices are located around the globe. The Western Regional Office, known as the Pan-American Health Organization, is located in Washington, D.C. and has responsibilities for the western hemisphere. The major health service functions of WHO are as follows:

1. Supplying technical assistance to countries throughout the world to improve their own health services. For example, WHO may send a team of public health specialists to help a country control a malaria problem.
2. Coordinating a worldwide health program by encouraging nations to assist each other in raising their health standards.
3. Providing a variety of special services to member nations, such as epidemiologic reporting, collection and dissemination of statistical data on prevention of diseases, standardization of public health and drug usage data, and dissemination of health information procedures.
4. Operating an extensive program of education and training in public health. For example, WHO may assign a public health specialist to a country to serve as a university instructor in order to help strengthen that country's program of professional education in the public health field. WHO has assisted the University of Ibadan in Nigeria in establishing a school of public health where public health education specialists are trained for service in Africa.
5. Carrying out a variety of research programs to acquire new knowledge of communicable diseases, nutritional methods, and public health administration.

Federal health services

In recent years, government health organizations and public health agencies have undergone many changes because of the federal government's growing involvement in programs such as Medicare and the delivery of health services.

As shown in Fig. 2-1, the U.S. Public Health Service has six major operating agencies, which carry out the principal activities of public health. Each of these agencies is under the administrative authority of the Assistant Secretary of Health, who in turn is responsible to the Secretary for Health and Human Services (HHS). The U.S. Public Health Service is administratively divided into 10 regional offices. Each of the regions has an administrator and staff that are representatives of the Assistant Secretary for Health. According to Grant (1981), "Public Health Services is the federal agency charged by law to promote and to assure the

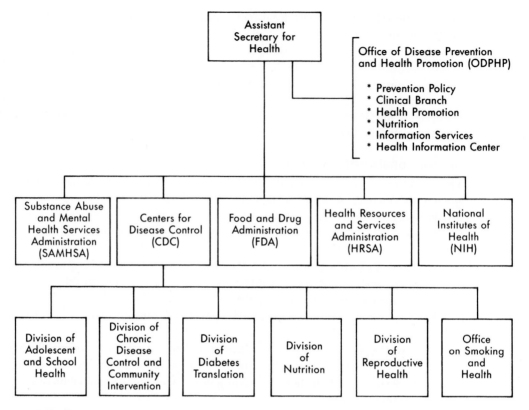

FIG. 2-1.   U.S. Public Health Service: organizational structure.

highest level of health attainable for every person in the United States and develop cooperation in health programs with other nations."

The major functions of the U.S. Public Health Service are as follows:

1. To stimulate and assist states and communities with the development of local health
   resources and to further the development of education for the health professions
2. To help improve the delivery of health services for all Americans
3. To conduct and support research in medical and related health sciences and to dissem-
   inate this scientific information
4. To protect the health of the nation against unsafe drugs and other potential community
   hazards
5. To provide leadership in the prevention and control of communicable diseases

State health services

Each state is responsible for the protection of the health of its citizens. The state, in fact, is the
sovereign power. According to the U.S. Constitution, the federal government possesses only
those powers in the field of health that have been delegated to it by the state. Local govern-

ments also derive their power and authority from the state. Public health laws vary considerably from state to state. Typically states will have a board of health or some similar authority such as a department of public health that has specific public health responsibilities. These responsibilities may be advisory in nature, but they also may be policy making. The health authority may have the power to enact regulations that are to be implemented throughout the state.

State organizations, like federal agencies, have undergone many changes in the organization of health services. The nature of problems confronting public health agencies is also changing. Some states have created large, umbrella types of organizations, analogous to the U.S. Department of Health and Human Services structure at the national level. Such an organization may encompass all agencies having to do with human services, such as the department of welfare, department of mental health, and department of public health.

Because the state health department is the agency vested by law with responsibility for protecting and promoting the health of its citizens, much of the burden for providing services falls on the states. However, the federal government often provides special grants either for conducting or for assisting the state in providing needed health services. Although state programs may vary considerably, state health departments usually are responsible for recording vital statistics and providing programs of environmental health and maternal and child health, public health laboratory services, communicable disease control, public health nursing, and health education.

With the emergence of new health problems in society, new structures and programs in state health departments have developed. Some of the more recent programs include special programs for mental health and retardation, chronic disease control, accident prevention, and medical care for the indigent, as well as special functions, such as the licensing of nursing homes for the aged.

Local health services

As at the other levels of public health, recent developments have had a profound effect on the local health department. Populations have shifted, with the more affluent citizens moving out of the cities and rural dwellers moving into the cities. Many people are moving to the southern and southwestern regions of the country. The resultant changes in racial, ethnic, and age distribution in the population present new problems for public health. Many city health departments now have to provide a disproportionate share of services for the elderly, the very young, and the poor. At the same time, local tax resources are being reduced because the more productive members of the cities' population have moved away.

AUTHORIZATION OF SCHOOL HEALTH PROGRAMS

Inherent in the American system of schools is the principle that the local board of education is responsible for the schools of its district. This principle acknowledges that the closer a government agency is to the people, the more likely it is to be in tune with the situation in which it functions. Accordingly, extensive authority and responsibility have been delegated to the local school board. However, as illustrated in Illinois, state laws often require that the school districts enact certain policies. In addition, state departments of education, through regulation, have set standards that local school districts must meet. Such legislative and regulative requirements have applied to school health programs.

State legislation

States pass two forms of legislation that affect the school health program: permissive laws and mandatory laws. In practical terms, permissive legislation simply recommends or encourages the local board of education to institute certain procedures that are beneficial to the health and well-being of schoolchildren. Permissive laws are couched in such language as "school districts should provide" or "are encouraged to provide." The conditions or procedures outlined in the law are recommended but not required. Therefore the school board has the option to accept or not accept the recommendation set forth in the law.

However, in the case of mandatory legislation, laws are authoritatively ordered. The state requires the local districts to carry out the provisions of the law; no exceptions are permitted. Ideally, such legislation is drafted in broad outlines so that the state department of education can interpret the legislation and write guidelines to schools for implementing the requirements. Such guidelines are usually developed by persons who have had extensive school experience and who are recognized for sound administrative judgment and knowledge of successful school practices. The terminology of mandatory legislation contains such phrases as "The school district shall provide" or "must include." Statutes may further indicate the areas of health instruction and charge the state superintendent of instruction with responsibility for providing materials and advisory services for the schools throughout the state. The state department of education, in cooperation with the state department of health, may also prescribe a program of health examinations of students in the elementary and secondary schools. The state superintendent of public instruction is charged with the implementation and enforcement of these statutes. Enforcement is exercised through school standardization requirements.

Among other requirements, in order to qualify as standard, the school district must meet the state standards for health services, health instruction, and school sanitation. Failure to meet these requirements may place the district in a probationary status for a specified period of time. Failure to meet requirements within this time period may disqualify the district from participation in certain state school aid funds.

Advocates of legislation to ensure health protection and promotion for *every* schoolchild in the state assert that many school boards have very little understanding of school health work. The thinking of board members and administrators is conditioned by the old classical education they received. The practical value of health in the school may not be fully appreciated. State recognition of its importance will ensure *every* schoolchild of at least a minimum of health promotion and health education.

State education department initiative

Some states seek to achieve the same goal through prescription by the state board of education. The state board sets up standards for school health services, health instruction, and a healthful school environment. Again, those districts failing to meet requirements may be declared substandard and ineligible for certain state financial aid.

In practice, these provisions are not carried out ruthlessly and dictatorially. Great leniency is granted by giving ample time for the development of health programs. Only in those districts in which the school board or administration actually resists the development of an adequate school health program will the ultimate enforcement be exercised. The important thing is the health of the students, not the state aid or the prerogative of school boards and administrators.

Responsibilities of the local board of education

Sovereignty, or ultimate authority, rests with the people. Except for such authority as the states have granted to the federal government through the federal constitution, the people have vested their authority in the 50 states to be exercised within their own borders. Local government units have only such authority as has been granted to them by the state legislature through specific legislation and accepted practice. Unless otherwise specified or prohibited, local school boards have broad authority to make such provisions for their schools as they deem necessary to discharge their responsibilities to the school-aged children of their district. From common practice, certain authority and responsibility of the school for health promotion have become generally accepted.

1. School health promotion is vested in the board of education. Although in practice the superintendent and his or her professional staff propose the program, such a proposal is merely a recommendation to the board. Only as the board approves the plan can the program have official status. The board can make the program as extensive as it sees fit. It can appropriate such funds as it deems necessary for the health program.
2. All phases of the school health program must comply with state laws and their implementing regulations. In practice, the state provisions serve as minimal standards. A board of education properly may set standards or requirements higher than the state provisions, but not lower. If a state statute provides that all students participating in interscholastic athletics must have a health examination before the season in which they are to compete, the local board on its own initiative may go further and require such an examination of all who participate in intramural sports.
3. A board of education has the authority to require every child to have a health examination before entering school and at such other times as it deems reasonable. Some boards have made provisions for exceptions on religious grounds. Other boards have made no exceptions, contending that a health examination does not constitute medication. The Washington State Supreme Court has upheld this point of view.
4. A school board can require immunization against a particular disease as a condition for admission to school. Here religious rights definitely do enter in, and provisions for exceptions should be made. In the event of an epidemic or threatened epidemic, the board may exclude those children from school whose parents refuse permission for immunization on religious grounds.
5. The school can pass rules governing school attendance. It can extend this authority to include provisions for exclusion and readmission in control of communicable diseases. Although legal isolation and quarantine are functions of the health department, the school can assert control of communicable diseases insofar as this control is part of the school program.
6. A board may require daily inspections for indications of communicable disease.

7. A child may be excused from sex education if the parents of that child object to the instruction on the basis of religious belief.

8. School boards may specify the areas of health instruction, going beyond state requirements but including them in the program.

BASIC DIVISIONS OF THE HEALTH PROGRAM

In a world that gets progressively more complicated, it is refreshing to find a group, especially an education group, that is striving to simplify its program. Two decades ago the school health program in general use consisted of seven phases or divisions. Repeated reassessment and realignment have sifted down to the following three basic divisions: (1) school health services, (2) health instruction, and (3) healthful school living (Fig. 2-2).

In a well-integrated school health program no pronounced demarcation of the divisions exists. They are interdependent and support and supplement each other. In actual operation the divisions do not exist; they are essentially creations for organizational and administrative convenience. There is *one* school health program with three different aspects. Whether a particular activity belongs under one aspect or division is primarily academic. How effectively it functions is the significant consideration.

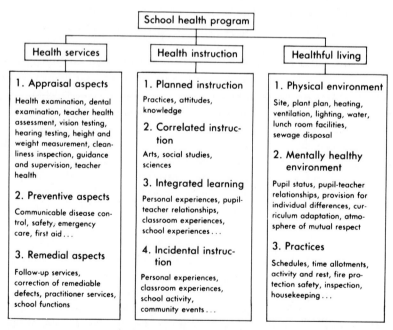

FIG. 2-2.   Organization of the school health program. For purposes of planning and administration, three distinct phases of the program are recognized, but in actual function the three phases constitute a cohesive, integrated contribution to the total school program.

School health services

Nader (1990), a nationally known pediatrician and authority on school health, observes that historically school health has been an underemphasized and neglected area of the nation's health care system. Typically, this has meant that school health services have been relegated to routine, mandated health service activities such as immunizations, the screening of vision and hearing, and the treatment of minor traumas. However, under present-day conditions, the school is becoming an increasingly important arena for dealing with some of society's most pressing health issues. These health problems are now called the "new morbidities": preventing and reporting cases of child abuse, preventing AIDS, and providing AIDS education. For those who would argue against the role of school health, Surgeon General Antonia C. Novello (1991) reminds the public that: "Of the many rights extended to American children two are paramount—the right to be educated and the right to be healthy."

For children to be ready to learn and to move toward their optimum development educationally and socially, society must address the fundamental relationships between health and education.

School health services constitute those school activities directly concerned with the present health status of the schoolchild. It is only natural that the school should concern itself with the health condition of children because the health of the students and the type of education program in which they participate are interdependent. The children can do their best work only if their health will permit them to participate to the extent that the school program requires. A child with low vitality will have little interest in any school program. A school program in turn not only must be adapted to the physiological and emotional health levels, as well as the intellectual level, of the child, but it must be designed to develop the child's highest possible level of physical and emotional health.

School health services can reinforce the efforts of the parents and the family physician in promoting the health and well-being of children. The school setting provides an unusually good vantage point from which to observe and assess the health of children. Teachers and nurses, because of their experience of observing many children, have a ready-made standard against which to compare and evaluate a child's health status and behavior. Those children who deviate from the expected normal range of health status or behavior are readily apparent to teachers and nurses. As Eisner and Callan (1974) have stated:

> The classroom teacher should become the focus of case finding and the child's behavior and functioning should become the primary indicators of his or her health. If this were done, school physicians could devote their time and attention to those children who have been identified as having problems.

School health services of this type can have a profound effect on children's health and their eventual development as healthy and mature adults. The healthy adult whose preadult years were marked by proper supervision of health, growth, and development enjoys a high level of well-being built on a solid foundation of two decades of planned health promotion. An accumulation of 12 years of organized school health services will have a beneficial effect on a person's health for the remaining years of life. The healthy, well-educated student in school becomes the effective and happy adult citizen of the community, freely giving of his or her services and influence to neighbors and the nation.

Scope. Recent reviews (Nader, 1990) of school health services reveal that there is no one organizational pattern or stance for school health services. In some communities these services may be viewed as the central program for delivering preventive health care to the school-age population, whereas in others they are limited to a much lesser role. The responsibility for school health services varies from state to state. Whether the program is administered under the health department or the board of education, certain advantages and disadvantages accrue. Michael Usdan (1990), President of the Institute for Educational Leadership, states:

> There is a growing concensus among educators, health service professionals, and other providers of human services that there is a compelling need to more effectively coordinate the myriad of fragmented services currently available to poor children and their families.

Effective programs cut across education, health, and human services. They have similar goals, and characteristics include programs designed to provide comprehensive and intensive services for prenatal care and for children as part of families and neighborhoods. Programs must transcend bureaucratic and professional boundaries to give staff the time, space, and opportunity to establish relationships and perceived trust with their clients. Beyond this, it is absolutely essential that these collaborative linkages not only better serve the clients, but also broaden the base of support that is so desperately needed in the political and business communities.

There are clear advantages of school health services that must be acknowledged. Most important among these is the fact that schools have contact with almost every school-age child. Therefore, there is the potential for establishing a direct linkage with the source of community primary care—whether it is for a crisis, for episodic care, or to provide comprehensive and continuous care. The operating principle is to establish through formal and informal channels a connection between school health services and the sources of community primary care. This includes all children, whether they have their own personal physician or whether the school or a community agency provides the complemental or supplemental services needed by the child. Schools provide an opportunity for integrating health services into the health education curriculum (Fig. 2-3). If teachers are adequately trained, they have a unique opportunity to identify children with problems (Klein and Sadowski, 1990).

What all school and community officials must come to appreciate is the ominous threat posed by the worldwide AIDS epidemic. For example, public health officials (USDHHS, 1990) estimate that the total number of persons now infected with HIV ranges from 800,000 to 1.3 million. Further, it is expected that the number of new cases that will occur during the coming decade will rise to approximately 100,000 per year. Even though medical science has provided the public with the information to prevent this disease, the great proportion of AIDS cases occurring among adolescents results from intravenous drug use and unprotected sexual contact. Solving this public health problem will require a well-designed health education program carefully integrated with health services. Such an approach need not overburden or detract from the school's educational mission. Rather, it can mean that the school becomes a focal point where a variety of community health and human services are delivered. Such a community-wide approach will require a new vision of how the school is to function.

> Demographic imperatives and dramatic changes in family structure, together with the growing emphasis on delivering education and related services at the grass roots or school building level will

Health education curriculum

Health service activities	ELEMENTARY SCHOOL					MIDDLE SCHOOL							HIGH SCHOOL							
	Grow. & devel.	Cleanliness	Dent. health	Eat. practic.	Exer. & rest	Care of senses	Safety	Body changes	Sexuality	Disease	Diet-wt. cont.	Phys. act.	Family life educ.	Disease prevention	Std. aids.	Chronic dis. prev.	Subs. abuse prev.	Diet-exercise	Health care	Accident prev.
Health Appraisal																				
Health Exam	X	X				X				X	X		X	X	X				X	
Dental Exam	X	X	X	X												X		X		
Blood Pres.								X		X	X	X	X			X		X	X	
Health Screening	X					X	X	X		X			X						X	
Vision	X					X		X					X						X	
Hearing		X				X				X			X						X	
Dental	X	X	X							X	X		X					X	X	
Ht. & wt.	X		X					X				X						X		
Scoliosis	X							X		X		X	X						X	
Comm. Dis. Cont.		X					X	X					X	X	X				X	
Skin Infects.		X						X					X						X	
Infestations		X						X												
Sex. Trans. Dis.							X	X					X	X	X		X		X	
Immunizations								X					X	X					X	
Emergency Care						X					X	X	X				X		X	X
First Aid						X	X				X	X	X				X			X
Health Care					X	X		X					X					X	X	X
Minor Illness			X			X				X			X	X						
Injury						X	X			X	X	X	X	X		X		X	X	X
Counseling	X	X		X	X	X		X	X	X	X	X	X	X	X	X	X	X	X	X
Referral Follow-up	X	X			X	X				X			X	X	X	X	X	X	X	

FIG. 2-3. Example of integration of health services into health education curriculum.

provide new opportunities for health professionals and others to provide comprehensive human resources to disadvantaged children (Usdan, 1990).

Nader (1990) has proposed that school health services provide for every school child the following:

1. Access to primary health care
2. Health screening and health maintenance activities

Teaching to prevent HIV infection

EMERGING ISSUES Recently the state legislature passed mandatory legislation requiring teaching about AIDS in the public schools. In response to this development, the Board of Education created a special ad hoc committee composed of some Board members and some members of the city Public Health Department to study the problem and to develop recommendations to guide the district's teachers.

After holding a series of hearings and discussions, the committee found itself at an impass, unable to reach an agreement on the instructional objectives. The committee's difficulties seem to revolve around the question of (1) whether to advocate the use of condoms and, if so, whether to make them available to high school students, or (2) whether to advocate a position of abstinence as the best way to prevent AIDS.

As a member of the health education faculty in the district and as one who will be responsible for implementing the program, you have been asked to respond to the following statements.

Please indicate whether you generally agree or disagree by placing a plus (+) or a minus (−) sign before each statement.

_____ 1. I believe that the best way to combat the AIDS virus is to teach the scientific truth about this virus and its transmission.

_____ 2. Evidence shows that high school students are going to be sexually active. Therefore we must teach safe sex.

_____ 3. Believing that the prevailing moral value in America is sexual abstinence until marriage, I would not favor teaching "safe sex" to teenagers.

_____ 4. I believe that we should make an appeal to the students higher moral and intellectual values. "They must either master the biology of their own bodies or the biology of their bodies will master them."

_____ 5. I believe that we should emphasize abstinence, but students should also be taught that condoms are effective in preventing the disease.

_____ 6. As a health educator, my responsibility first and foremost is to stop the spread of this disease.

_____ 7. As a professional, I must set aside my own moral values and teach whatever is necessary to prevent this disease.

_____ If limited to a single choice, I would choose this number.

REFERENCES

Brown LK, et al: AIDS education: the Rhode Island experience, *Health Educ Q* 18(2):195, 1991.
Holtzman D, et al: HIV instruction, HIV knowledge, and drug injection among high school students, *Am J Public Health* 81(12):1596, 1991.

   3. Identification of health problems with appropriate referral and follow-up
   4. The development of additional optional health maintenance and health promotion activities

The school has a fundamental concern for all aspects of the child's health and well-being. No child should suffer the burdens of illness or defects resulting from conditions that are preventable or correctable. Although the parents have primary responsibility for the health care and supervision of their children, the school cannot ignore the needs of children who are neglected or abused. In fact, when parents fail in these responsibilities, the school must be the child's advocate, as well as defender.

Traditionally, school health services have been considered a part of preventive medicine. Emphasis is given to health appraisal activities that identify those conditions or problems interfering with the child's educational progress, and the results of that appraisal are used to inform the parents about their children's health needs. Such programs have operated on the assumption that any treatment needed by the child should be provided by the family physician. Unfortunately, large numbers of children today come from families and homes that do not have or cannot afford the cost of private medical care. Nevertheless, the emphasis on prevention is still the proper role for school health programs in the total health care scheme.

School officials have had a tendency to view their child health responsibilities too narrowly. As a consequence, school health services have, in too many instances, become isolated and unrelated to the community health program. Even though the focus of such services is on preventive activities, it is essential that they be related to and coordinated with other agencies in the community so that comprehensive and continuous health care may be available for children and families.

New patterns of health care have been developing. Title XIX of the Social Security Act is intended to make comprehensive medical services available for those families who are unable to pay for them. This program is popularly known as Medicaid. For services to be effectively used, the interrelationship of school and community health programs must be fully understood so that the necessary cooperation and coordination can be achieved (see Fig. 1-6).

Appraisal. Complete evaluation of each child's health includes health examinations by a physician, dental examinations, health assessments and observations by the teachers and nurses, screening of vision and hearing by the teachers, weighing and measuring, and inspections of cleanliness.

Health guidance and supervision. In a well-conducted school health program, provision is made for aiding students in maintaining their own health. This includes all processes necessary to acquaint students with their health status and the sources and channels for developing their health assets. It aims to help the students in their health self-care. The school supervises the children in caring for their own health. An important part of the health education program includes individual and small group counseling of both students and parents. Such supervision must be planned and well organized and have recognized spheres of responsibility.

Recommendations of the education commission of the states. One of the most important and authoritative policy statements supporting school health education was issued by an educational task force representing the education commissions of the 50 states. The task force was appointed as a mechanism to study educational policy and to offer recommendations on behalf of the 50 state school offices. The health education task force was charged with conducting a review of current school health practices to identify the issues and problems hampering the implementation of effective school health education programs. After these deliberations, a series of recommendations that the task force deemed essential to establish these recommendations called for each state education agency to:

1. Take the lead in encouraging local school boards and administrators to include health education as an integral part of the elementary and secondary school curriculum.
2. Promote health education as a responsibility shared by the family, school, and community.
3. Support the development and improvement of school health education with whatever resources are available.
4. Provide technical assistance to local districts to facilitate the planning necessary for the implementation of school health education programs and to "promote the development of comprehensive school health education programs."
5. Take the lead in establishing standards of preparation that would ensure the availability of qualified teachers in health education.

To make clear the commission's intent, the following definitive statements concerning health education and its reference to comprehensive programs were offered. In addition, Fig. 2-3 is presented as a conceptionalized model of the comprehensive school health program illustrating all elements of a total program and its integrated relationships to the school and to the community. It is in this theoretic construct that the comprehensive health education program can make its maximum contribution to the health and educational development of the schoolchild.

School health education. The Commission (1981) offered several important principles to ensure that local schools provide for an effective health education component within the concept of the comprehensive school health program. Accordingly, the program should:

Be planned by both school and community.
Demonstrate scope, sequence, progression, and continuity.
Be planned for grades kindergarten through 12.
Be taught by teachers trained and prepared in health education.
Be designed to develop critical thinking and individual responsibility for one's health.
Be structured to incorporate current and emerging health problems.
Be focused on the dynamic relationship between physical, mental, emotional, and social well-being.
Be strengthened by integrating available community resources into classroom teaching (Northern California paper, 1980).

Preventive services. Strategies for health promotion or disease prevention include counseling, screening, control of communicable diseases, immunizations, safety promotion, first aid, and emergency care. For schools this is the acceptance of responsibility for doing everything reasonable to prevent unnecessary illness or injury (OTA, 1991).

Control of communicable diseases, safety promotion, first aid, and emergency care not only are opportunities for school service but also are responsibilities for doing everything reasonable to prevent unnecessary illness or injury.

Remedial measures. Although the school is not expected to treat or to correct defects, it does have a responsibility to assist the child and family in securing necessary health care. Whether such services are provided by the private physician or through some community agency will depend on the circumstances of individual students and their families. Effective follow-up depends on school personnel. Health education can play a fundamental role in developing an understanding as to why health care is needed and where the needed service may be located.

Health instruction

Formal planned classroom health teaching is designed to prepare students to make the proper decisions throughout their lives on matters affecting their health. The very nature of health allows for a great variety of approaches in instruction. Diverse methods, techniques, and combinations have been effective in health instruction. In the final analysis any program of health instruction must be appraised in terms of the extent to which it modifies persons in their understanding and practice of health principles. Instruction that promotes the development of favorable attitudes and understanding and that results in a pattern of living enabling the individual to attain the highest possible level of health meets the true goal of all health teaching.

Elementary school. During the early years of school life, health instruction is directed primarily toward the establishment of recognized health practices and the inculcation of desirable health attitudes. Health knowledge may be used as a vehicle for promoting health practices and health attitudes. Elementary schoolchildren will acquire valuable health knowledge that may be associated with pleasant experiences, but health knowledge should always be considered a means to an end—better health. As such, health knowledge should be regarded as secondary to health attitudes and practices in promoting an effective elementary school health instruction program.

Middle school or junior high school. The idealism and group tendencies of middle school students make an ideal setting for the promotion of community health interests and ideals. Interwoven with the concept of respect for the welfare of one's neighbors are the interrelationships that exist between personal and community health. Practices and attitudes are fortified with further knowledge.

Senior high school. Health attitudes and practices developed in previous years are fortified by knowledge gained in the high school from a sound scientific basis. Since for many students this will be their last opportunity for formal health instruction, high school health teaching should prepare young people to accept their responsibilities as adults to care for and promote both their own health and well-being and that of their future families and communities. Ideally, the health education experience should serve to sustain the individual's interest through self-directed study of health problems. Developing students' ability to select appropriate sources of health information, health services, and health products is of particular importance in high school health instruction.

HEALTHFUL SCHOOL LIVING

From the beginning of public school education in the United States, communities have shown a special pride in new, up-to-date school buildings. The school building denoted a monument to the culture of the community and the people's concern for their children. This concept implied that the school environment consisted of the physical plant and that a costly building constituted an ideal environment for learning. However, physical structures per se are static concepts.

The present-day dynamic concept of the environmental factors in the school is well expressed in the designation *healthful school living.* It denotes a social situation in which children develop their potential in effective and enjoyable living. Children's educational, emotional, and physical development will have the stimulation and motivation essential to their fullest attainment. It is expressed in the atmosphere of the classroom, the corridors, the gymnasium, the playground, and every other place about the school. It incorporates factors that affect the physical, mental, and social health of the child. In so doing, it includes the physical plant, its equipment, the personnel, and the practices within the school.

If an atmosphere of wholesome living is to be created, all plans and activities must be focused on the child's need for wholesome development. All aspects of the experiences and needs of the child must be met by the school, including the physical, esthetic, cultural, moral, emotional, and social aspects. The school should create in every child a pride in being a part of the school.

The physical plant, with its site, proper living conditions, ideal sanitary equipment, and general attractiveness, is basic to healthful school living. How the teaching staff uses and incorporates these assets into the life of the student will determine whether the school is truly a place of healthful living. To have a lunchroom with adequate space and sanitary equipment is not enough. The practices in the lunchroom and the general atmosphere are equally important. Children need guidance in learning to appreciate and live fully in even the most ideal physical environment. Out of this appreciation should evolve the social values so important to the present and future citizen.

When the condition of the physical plant is not acceptable, the intrepid teacher can instill in the children a desire to better the conditions under which they are learning. Even to appreciate what is and what is not commendable in the school is an achievement in personal growth. Out of these experiences can come improvements in school, home, and community.

After all, people are the most important elements in the school environment. The quality of these people can be noted in their values, attitudes, activities, and attainment. Healthful school living is an important aspect of the quality of life.

Responsibility for environmental health

Parents, school board members, architects, administrators, teachers, custodians, lunchroom personnel, and students are responsible for the environment of the school. United responsibility combined with collective effort produces the environmental conditions conducive to the atmosphere necessary for healthful school living.

Factors influencing environmental health

The attitude of the school community constitutes the all-important background for environmental health. First, those concepts that the parents hold as standards and put into effect by their own contribution and interest establish the pattern or mold for a healthful school environment. Through the board of education, this attitude will project itself into attractive, functional school buildings that are safe, efficient, sanitary, and commodious. It will lay the groundwork for an effective school program that will ensure that the children have an opportunity to develop their potential. This community support makes it possible for the school staff to create an atmosphere in which children can live effectively and enjoyably.

A second factor is a well-planned, well-constructed sanitary school plant. This implies a suitable site; functional architecture; adequate heating, ventilation, and lighting; safe water supply; approved disposal facilities; and essential accessory school equipment.

A third factor incorporates the practices of the school. From custodial housekeeping to lunchroom decorum, to group courtesy, to opportunities for self-status, many practices contribute vitally to healthful school living. Capable teachers can use fully the available facilities and opportunities to create a mentally and physically healthy environment.

Healthful school living can be reduced to a rather simple equation:

$$\frac{\text{Functional}}{\text{school plant}} + \frac{\text{Wholesome}}{\text{practices}} = \frac{\text{Healthful}}{\text{school living}}$$

Public health's relationship to school health

The titles of the six operating agencies of the U.S. Public Health Service (see Fig. 2-1) illustrate the types of program activities that relate directly to the school health program. For example, the Alcohol, Drug Abuse, and Mental Health Administration provides scientific information, as well as support and expert guidance, to schools on alcohol and drug education and ways of handling problems stemming from the misuse of these substances. Also, the knowledge gained from the scientific study of disease prevention is ultimately translated into policies and program practices at the local health department level, including the school health program.

The Health Services Administration has a great impact on schools through a variety of health care programs. The most visible programs are the Maternal and Child Health Act and Early Periodic Screening, Diagnosis, and Treatment (EPSDT). Both of these programs provide health care services to children and youth of low-income families. They work in close coordination with the Education for all Handicapped Children Act, PL 94-142. This law recognizes the rights of all handicapped children and their need for special services. All these children, 3 to 21 years of age, are to receive "a free and appropriate education." Examples of the kinds of health services activities provided through these programs include comprehensive health assessments, immunizations, physical examinations, vision and hearing screening, laboratory tests such as those to detect the presence of lead in children's blood, diagnostic evaluation, and treatment and rehabilitation services for children who suffer from handicapping or chronic conditions. Other examples of services include physical, speech, and occupational therapy and the provision of dental care. New areas of service that are now receiving special attention are programs of adolescent health, child abuse, and mental health services, including outpatient therapy.

Two units within the U.S. Public Health Service that are especially important to state and local school health programs are the Office of Disease Prevention and Health Promotion (ODPHP) and the Division of Adolescent and School Health. The organizational structures of these two agencies are shown in Fig. 2-1. As its title implies, ODPHP's special mission is preventing disease and promoting health, with special emphasis on health education. The Division of Adolescent and School Health is the only public health service unit solely devoted to the health of the school-age population and services to school health programs.

Despite the problems faced by these programs, including a lack of resources and the difficulties of achieving effective coordination among various programs, a report (Better Health for Our Children, 1981) to Congress has cited significant accomplishment. A panel of experts has pointed to important progress in the effort to reduce disabilities of handicapped children. Medicaid and EPSDT programs have made health care available to more children. There has been a substantial increase in the availability of mental health services.

Because the need for health care is great and the ability to provide it where most needed is difficult at best, the weaknesses or shortcomings of these programs are often overemphasized. Nevertheless, these programs demonstrate effective participation in the provision of health services at all levels of government: federal, state, and local. Because schoolchildren and youth are the intended beneficiaries of many of these services, school officials should become informed about them to ensure that children receive needed services. The health of children is integrally linked to their success in school. Enhancing the health of children makes it possible for them to gain the fullest measure of benefit from their educational experience.

INTEGRATING HEALTH SERVICES AND HEALTH INSTRUCTION

Although it has been shown that both the education and the health of the public are legal responsibilities of the state, as specifically defined by the federal constitution, this does not guarantee adequate or equal development of both program areas. In fact, quite the opposite may be the case. Some communities may have a well-developed educational program with little in the way of school health services, whereas other school systems may have a strong health service program and an almost nonexistent health instruction program. Some schools may have strong programs in both health services and health instruction, but these programs may operate independently and in isolation from each other.

Newman (1982) has spoken out forcefully against this separation of health services and education. He has reminded school officials that the justification for health services in schools rests on the assumption that such services contribute to the school's educational goal. Therefore, if health activities in the school are to be an educational experience, it is essential that health services and health education be integrated.

Such integration benefits the school in several distinct ways. Those in the health services can aid the educator by creating the best atmosphere for learning for both the student and the school as a whole. By identifying health problems or conditions that handicap the child's ability to learn, such as visual or auditory deficiencies, the health services staff promotes the health and learning potential of the child. By maintaining immunization levels that prevent or reduce school absenteeism, the health services program assists the goals of the educator.

The assistance of the health services staff may increase the effectiveness of teachers. The support and consultation of the health services staff can often help to identify the causes of student behaviors that disrupt the teaching-learning process. For instance, many student behavior problems stem from emotional difficulties that may require the assistance of a health professional to identify and treat.

Furthermore, the coordination of health services with health instruction makes a direct contribution to the students' health knowledge, as well as health practices. When the health educator and the school nurse work with the school dietitian to improve student eating habits, the school lunch program becomes more than a food service; it becomes a laboratory for learning.

To help school officials achieve this objective, Newman has offered the following six guiding principles in the planning for integration of health services and health education.

1. *The means for integrating health services and health education should be clearly identified and stated as a set of program objectives.* There is also the need to inform the public or the community about these objectives. The reasons for health services in the school, the objectives, and program activities should be thoroughly understood. Moreover, if the program is to be effective, many different people should be involved.

2. *The program objectives should reflect the various interests of the community.* If these two programs are to be integrated, school administrators, teachers, students, parents, health and social service professionals should be involved.

   By reducing absenteeism, by decreasing discipline problems, improving teacher morale, and improving the school's relationships with parents and the community at large, integrated health programs, when properly coordinated, can improve the school. If administrators are to be convinced of the importance of an integrated program, they need the opportunity to observe the benefits that result from the coordinated efforts of health and education personnel.

   All too often teachers have only a superficial understanding of the health program and its impact on the school. How many teachers consider the state of the student's health as a possible contributing cause of classroom disruptive behavior or as a cause of learning problems? There is a failure, also, to appreciate the important relationship between the health of the teacher and that person's role as an educator. The problem of teacher burnout illustrates this point. Teachers who do not appreciate the importance of their own health can hardly be expected to be sensitive to the health of their students.

   Parents and students both need to understand the role of school health in order to complement the efforts of the school in promoting the student's health. The role of parents and students is central to any follow-up efforts to ensure the students' optimal growth and development.

   Medical and health professionals must understand the services and educational aspects of the school health program. A mutual support and trust between the school's and the health professionals' programs will strengthen the entire effort. To achieve this integration, all of the constituent groups must understand (1) the need for health education, (2) the importance of health services, and (3) how these programs can be mutually supportive.

3. *Knowing how young people use the school health services provides yet another basis for the integration of health services and health education.* Typically, more data are available at the national level concerning the health problems of children than the health problems of students in the schools. In this regard, Newman has reported on the recent study of schoolchildren's use of school health services in which he was able to document the rate at which students use the nurse's office. One interesting observation reveals that there is a seasonal pattern to the use of health services, with headaches and gastrointestinal complaints most often occurring during the cold months and wounds, trauma, and skin problems occurring most frequently during the warm months. Conclusions drawn from these observations indicate, too, that many of the health service visits were unnecessary, at least from a medical perspective. Even at this early age, it appears that children have learned to play the "sick role" and use illness as a reason for visiting the nurse's office to avoid some other school activity. In this case the solution to an apparent health problem was found in the way classroom activities were being conducted. With the high cost of health care, misuse of health services is an important problem. Even at the elementary school level, students can be taught the appropriate use of health care services.

   Knowing that headaches and stomach problems occur more often in winter months and wounds and trauma occur more often in the spring and fall provides an opportunity to structure the health education curriculum to address these trends so that students can anticipate and better manage these health problems. The important conclusion from this discussion is that school health service records, if carefully maintained and regularly analyzed, can serve as a useful basis for the development of a program of instruction.

4. *The integration of services in education will depend to a great degree on the quality of persons employed.* Unfortunately, not all schools hire school nurse practitioners nor do they hire fully qualified health education teachers. In the best situation the school would have a staff of trained health teachers and trained school nurse practitioners. Anything less might compromise the quality of the program. However, despite limitations in the training of various personnel, nurses and teachers with appropriate administrative support can be encouraged and assisted to work together to develop good programs. If resources are lacking, obviously the scope of the program must also be reduced. It is still fundamentally important, however, to capitalize on the available staff resources and, in the most vital subjects, to maintain standards commensurate with those in better-staffed schools.

5. *The basis for integrating health personnel and education personnel is the clear delineation of responsibilities.* The integration of education and health personnel does not mean that each must learn the other's job. It should be evident that health professionals can best conduct health service programs and education professionals can best conduct the instructional program. The understanding and acceptance of this point are important to avoid confusing roles and unhappiness with responsibilities that may develop among staff members. Experience has shown that interdisciplinary programs do work when people are well trained and confident in their roles and committed to the objectives of the program.

6. *To strike the best balance between services and education, clear data on program outcomes should be developed.* A search of the literature reveals a lack of scientific research on school health services and health education. In other words, there is a lack of scientific basis for school health services and little objective information available on the practice of school health services and the behavior of students who are using school-based services. Even less information is available on the problems and the benefits involved in the coordination of the education and health service programs. If this information on the coordinated program and its outcomes is not made available to administrators, school boards, and the public, it will be all the more difficult to solicit their support for program development (see Fig. 2-3).

School-based clinic

The first school-based clinic was opened in Dallas, Texas approximately 20 years ago. Since that time there has been steady growth in the number of clinics, with recent reports placing the total at 190 now established across the country. The clinic is seen not only as a means of providing basic health care to medically underserved teenagers, but as a promising way of addressing some of the nation's most intractable and complex health and social problems such as unintended pregnancies and substance abuse. Some of the major problems affecting the adolescent's access to health care and related services are poverty, lack of insurance, limitations in health insurance, lack of information and availability of services, lack of parent availability, and lack of appropriate care for adolescents. Although there are some questions about the value of school-based clinics, there have been enough positive benefits reported to create a widespread interest in the potential of school-based clinics. Consequently, leaders in the Federal Congress have requested the Office of Technology Assessment (OTA) to conduct a special study of the physical, emotional, and behavioral health status of American adolescents and to consider the potential of the school-based clinic as a means of improving health care of the adolescent.

Among the conditions that are making it more difficult to provide adequate care for adolescents is the fact that there are relatively few practitioners trained in adolescent health care. Moreover, many of these providers who are currently serving the adolescent population agree that their training is deficient. This has led the OTA to conclude that "even if adolescents do gain access to treatment services, the services may not be appropriate to their development and experiential level" (OTA, 1991).

Adolescence is marked by a period of profound biological, emotional, intellectual, and social transformation unmatched by any other period of life save infancy (Turning Points, 1989, p. 21). In some respects adolescents are still children, whereas at the same time their physical development places them at or near the level of adult status. This appearance of maturity in their growth and development often leads to unrealistic expectations on the part of parents, teachers, and other adults, leaving the adolescents confused and unsure about their independence, conformity, and responsibility.

It is true that adolescents, as a group, are among the healthiest in American society. Their death rate is among the lowest of any age group in the United States. At the same time, however, the leading causes of death among adolescents differ from those of other age groups.

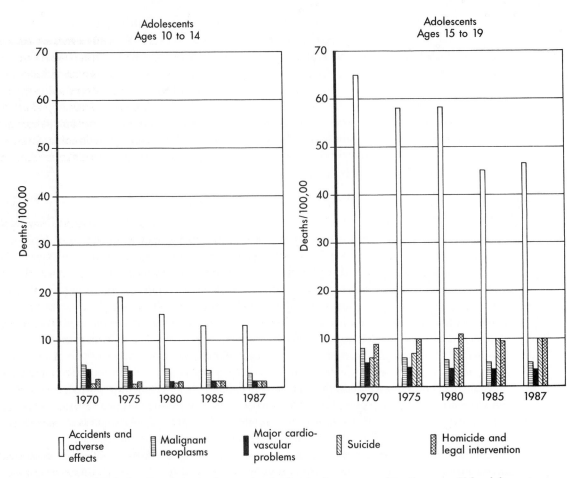

FIG. 2-4.   Trends in death rates for the five leading causes of death among U.S. adolescents ages 10 through 14 and 15 through 19, 1970-1987.

They are much more likely to die of injuries than those who are younger and older than the adolescent (Fig. 2-4).

Another difficulty in dealing with the adolescent is that data are often deficient because of the way in which vital statistics are recorded. Instead of using adolescent age groupings such as ages 10 to 14 and 15 to 19, data have traditionally been reported in age groupings of 1 to 14 and 15 to 24 years. Such groupings mask over important differences within these age categories.

Recent studies (OTA, 1991) reveal that adolescents have some unique problems stemming from family difficulties. For example, they may suffer from neglect or physical, sexual, and emotional abuse, resulting in depression and other psychological difficulties. Today's adolescents have an unacceptably high dropout rate, which may in part stem from the school's failure to meet their educational and social growth needs. Many adolescents appear to be affected by

TABLE 2-1. Percentages of school-based clinics offering medical services

Medical service	%
Assessment	
Referral to community for care	90
Referral to private physician	85
Chronic illness management	87
Dental services	
Diagnosis/treatment of minor injuries	98
Diagnosis/treatment of sexually transmitted diseases	90
Dispense medication	74
EPSDT screening	48
General physicals	96
Gynecologic examinations	88
Immunizations	87
Laboratory tests	97
Pediatric care (inflants of adolescents)	38
Physical examinations (sports/work)	97
Pregnancy tests	93
Prenatal care (on-site)	36
Prescribe medication	92
Referral for prenatal care	91

Adapted from Hyche-Williams H, and Waszak, Co.: School-based clinic update 1990, Washington, DC, 1990, Center for Population Options. Data based on senior, junior/middle school, n = 95.

a complex of interrelated problems, including academic failure, mental-emotional problems, substance abuse, unintended pregnancies, and family financial difficulty.

It is against this background that the school-based clinic is viewed as having potential for early positive health and educational intervention for today's troubled teenager.

The Center for Population Options recently conducted a survey of 153 school-based clinics for the purpose of providing a profile of these clinics as they currently exist. (Hyche-Williams HJ, Waszak C, 1990). Tables 2-1 through 2-4, adapted from this report, present information about school-based clinics, including the medical, counseling/educational services that they are providing, sources of funding, operating budgets, and community sponsoring agencies.

With the increasing attention being given to the health care of children and adolescents, the school-based clinic as an innovation is receiving careful analysis and evaluation. The following arguments both for and against the concept are being examined.

Proponents of the school-based clinic offer the following points:

1. These clinics have had success in getting adolescents to disclose their behavioral and life-style problems, enabling caregivers to provide more effective care for the adolescent.
2. Some clinics have been able to show reductions in school absenteeism, alcohol consumption, cigarette smoking, sexual activity, and rates of pregnancy.
3. Often the school-based clinic is the only health service available to the teenager.
4. Students say that they like the school-based clinic because they feel secure and confident that personal information is kept in strictest confidence.

TABLE 2-2. Percentage of school-based clinics offering counseling/educational services

Service	%
Drug and substance abuse	66
Family counseling (students and parents)	82
Health education	100
Job counseling	30
Mental health/psychosocial counseling	91
Nutrition education	99
Parenting education	62
Pregnancy counselling	91
Sex education In the classroom	85
Sexuality counseling	96
Weight reduction programs	90

Data based on senior and junior high/middle school reporting, n = 95.

TABLE 2-3. Sources of funding for school-based clinics

Funding source	% Total budget
Federal government (MCH, EPSDT, Medicaid, Title XX)	17
School district	2
Community health center	4
State health department	28
City	19
Private foundation	26
Private insurance	2
Student fees	<1
Other	1
TOTAL	100

Note: Average operating budget for school-based clinics (1989–1990) $143,827, n = 79.

TABLE 2-4. School-based clinic sponsoring agencies

Agency	% Total budget
Public health departments	33
School systems	19
Community clinics	18
Hospitals	18
Other	9
TOTAL	100

Mean number of sponsoring agencies equal 1.7, n = 94 schools responding.

5. School-based clinics provide more comprehensive service and preventive services such as health counseling, laboratory tests, reproductive health care, and examinations for athletics.
6. Some clinics are moving beyond health care and are providing legal services, vocational counseling, and in general serving as an advocate for the adolescents.

Those opposing school-based clinics argue as follows:

1. Schools should not take on yet another responsiblity that simply adds to the already overburdened educational infrastructure.
2. School-based clinics provide contraceptive services, abortion counseling, and organized medical care, which many communities oppose.
3. There is a lack of adequately trained, professional staff to provide services.
4. Convincing data are lacking to support the claims of effectiveness in reducing the socially visible adolescent problems being made by these programs.
5. There is a lack of adequate financing to support such clinics.

Summary

The school health program is presented as a formal entity and as the responsibility of two primary governmental agencies of the state—public health and public education. The context of the school health program is examined in relation to the larger picture of public health. School health is an aspect of the health and educational functions revealed in health organizations at all levels of government, ranging from the local health department to the state, national, and international health organization.

Public health, as an arm of government concerned with school health, gained much of its momentum in the early days after passage of state and federal laws requiring compulsory attendance in the public or common schools. This influx of children into the public schools was soon followed by a series of communicable disease outbreaks, which called for a major public health effort to control epidemics such as smallpox. Large cities like New York, Boston, Philadelphia, and Chicago employed physicians and nurses to serve as medical visitors to examine children who were believed to be ill. Although the communicable disease threat has lessened, except for the problem of AIDS and sexually transmitted diseases, the control and prevention of the major chronic diseases are now receiving much attention. Because each of these agencies, health and education, has a legal responsiblilty for school health, the program often is administered under a variety of organizational patterns, with some programs being jointly administered by education and health officials. Under such a divided authority pattern, the school health services are administered by the local health department, and the school health instruction part of the program is administered by the school administration in charge of curriculum. In still other instances, the total program is under the direction of school district employees, some of whom may be physicians and nurses hired by the school district. However, despite the fact that they may be fully qualified health specialists, they are technically and legally under the authority of the health department for all school health services relating to public health laws.

Regardless of the type of administrative organization, both of these official educational and health agencies have responsibilities that must be recognized. Carrying out these functions and the day-to-day activities calls for special administrative skills and knowledge of the interrelationships that exist. An inherent difficulty is the tendency to conduct the health instruction program as though it were separate and unrelated to the health services, or, on the other hand, to conduct a health service activity like screening for visual defects without considering its implications for health education.

Nader, a national authority on school health, has called attention to the fact that, unfortunately, school health programs have been too long neglected. However, under present-day conditions, the school is becoming an arena for dealing with some of society's most pressing health problems. The "new morbidities" such as child abuse and education for prevention of AIDS are but two examples. The Surgeon General has reminded the American public that all children have two basic rights: (1) to be educated, and (2) to be healthy.

There is a new awareness of the role that schools must play if these rights of children are to be fulfilled. This calls for access to health and social services. Children cannot progress educationally without provision for their basic health and social needs.

The latest developments in school-based and school-linked clinics are discussed. Increasingly, school-based clinics are being accepted as a way of providing health and social services for the underserved teenagers. The strengths and weaknesses of such clinics are now being considered as a possible model for the integration of health and social services for all school children.

GET INVOLVED!   It's time to be thinking about your career as a professional and to join a professional organization. By becoming a member of the American School Health Association, you will join with many other professionals working in schools who are committed to safeguarding the health of school-age children. The Association is a multidisciplinary organization composed of administrators, counselors, dentists, health educators, physical educators, school nurses, and physicians. These professionals are advocates for high quality school health instruction, health services, and a healthful school environment.

The ASHA has more than 3500 members in 56 countries. Most of the members work in elementary and secondary schools, advising or overseeing health education or health service programs in schools or state agencies charged with managing school health programs.

As a member of the ASHA, you join with other professionals in doing the work of the Association. You will be invited to join one of the three existing sections: (1) health educator, (2) school nurse, or (3) physician. You may elect to join with others in developing a new section such as counselors, food service personnel, physical educators, school psychologists, or social workers.

All members are urged to identify their interests from a list of 11 different councils, including early childhood health education, health behavior, international health, nutrition education, physical education and physical activities program administrators, research, school health instruction, sexuality education, or young professionals. Through the councils and committees you will help to develop new publications relating policies and standards that will help to promote better health of children and youth.

For membership information, write to:
The American School Health Association
7263 State Route 43
P.O. Box 708
Kent, Ohio 44240

STUDY QUESTIONS

1. What are the merits and demerits in the American system that places responsibility for public school education in a local board of education?
2. Courts have held that, when a school requires that a child be immunized, the child's parents can object on religious grounds, but requiring a health examination is not an infringement on the child's religious rights. How do you explain the possible paradox?
3. Compare the relative merits of having a public health nurse serve the school and having a school nurse hired by the school district.
4. From an administrative and organizational perspective, explain why it is highly desirable for school officials to create a school health advisory council. Which groups or agencies should be represented on the council?
5. From a legal perspective, where does the ultimate authority rest for protecting and promoting the health of school children?
6. Identify the three major areas of the school health program and explain the principal program activities in each of these areas.
7. Explain the apparent inconsistency of legislation that mandates certain health services and health instruction standards, despite the fact that extensive authority and responsibilty have been delegated to the local school board.
8. What are school-based clinics and what purposes do they serve?
9. Give an example of health programs or needs at the global, national, and state levels affecting school health programs.
10. How are the "new morbidities" affecting school health programs?
11. Which steps can be taken to bring about a more effective integration of school health instruction with health services?

REFERENCES

American Academy of Pediatrics: School health: a guide for health professionals, Elk Grove Village, Ill, 1987, the Academy.

American Academy of Pediatrics, Association for the Advancement of Health Education, American College Health Association, American Public Health Association—Public Health Education and School Health Education and Services Section, American School Health Association, and Society for Public Health Education: Report of the 1990 Joint Committee on Health Education Terminology, *J Health Educ* 22(3):173-184, 1991.

Carnegie Council on Adolescent Development of New York: Turning points: preparing youth for the twenty-first century: the report of the task force on education of young adolescents, New York, 1989, The Carnegie Council on Adolescent Development.

Children's Defense Fund: EPSDT: does it spell health care for poor children? A report by the Children's Defense Fund of the Washington Research Project, Washington, DC, 1977, Children's Defense Fund.

Education commission of the states: Recommendation for school health education: a handbook for state policymakers, Report No. 130, Denver, 1981, The Commission.

Eisner V, Callan LB: *Dimensions of school health,* Springfield, Ill, 1974, Charles C Thomas, Publisher.

Grant M: *Handbook of community health,* ed 3, Philadelphia, 1981, Lea & Febiger.

Hyche-Williams HJ, Waszak C: *School-based clinic: update 1990,* Washington, DC, 1990, Center for Population Options.

Illinois Prevention Resource Center, Prevention Forum, vol 11(3) Springfield, Ill, Spring, 1991, Illinois Department of Alcoholism and Substance Abuse.

Kirby D, et al: Six school-based clinics: their reproductive health services and impact on sexual behavior, *Fam Plan Perspect* 23(1):6-16, 1991.

Klein JD, Sadowski LS: Personal health services as a component of comprehensive health programs, *J Sch Health* 60(4):164-169, 1990.

Miller DF: *School health programs: their basis in law,* New York, 1972, AS Barnes.

Nader PR: The concept of "comprehensiveness" in the design and implementation of school health programs, *J Sch Health* 60(4):133-138, 1990.

Newman IM: Integrating health services and health education: seeking a balance, *J Sch Health* 52(8):498, 1982.

Northern California Chapter of the Academy of Pediatrics paper cited in Physician's Guide to the School Health Curriculum Process, 1980, Amercian Medical Association.

Novello Antonia C: Healthy children ready to learn: the Surgeon General's initiative for children, *J Sch Health* 61(8):133-138, 1991.

Usdan M: Restructuring American educational systems and programs to accommodate a new health agenda for youth, *J Sch Health* 60(4):139-141, 1990.

US Congress, Office of Technology Assessment: Adolescent health, vol I: summary and policy options, OTA-H468, Washington, DC, April, 1991, US Government Printing Office.

US Department of Health and Human Services: Better health for our children: a national strategy. The report of the Select Panel for the Promotion of Child Health to the US Congress and the Secretary of Human Services, DHHS (PHS) Pub No. 79-55071, Washington, DC, l981, US Government Printing Office.

US Department of Health and Human Services, Public Health Service, Centers for Disease Control, National Center for Health Statistics: Health, United States, 1990, Washington, DC, 1990, US Government Printing Office.

Wallace HM, et al: Maternal and child health practices, ed 3, Oakland, 1988, Third Party Publishing.

Part TWO

The School-Age Student

Health and the normal student

OVERVIEW

Health no longer means only the absence of disease. Today's concept of health implies adaptability and incorporates the notion of reaching an optimal level of health that differs for each person. Teachers and school personnel need to understand that health implies normality but that all deviations from normal do not necessarily mean an absence of health or the presence of disease.

Health results from the interaction of a person and the environment, which means that those interested in health must be sensitive to both personal and environmental concerns. History clearly shows that the greatest gains in health improvement result as much from changes in the environment and changes in the way we do things as from changes in the quality of health care.

OBJECTIVES   After reading this chapter, the student should be able to:

1. Describe and illustrate how a full understanding of the concept of normal will affect a teacher's approach to teaching and a school administrator's approach to facilitating the educational process
2. Describe health as a process of adaptation
3. Illustrate the differences between primary, secondary, and tertiary prevention and explain why these concepts are useful to school health personnel
4. Explain how health practices can vary among different groups of people and how they all can represent normal
5. Describe the basic characteristics of a healthy child in terms of physical and psychosocial health

For teachers who dedicate their lives to student welfare and improvement, understanding the concept of health and translating its meaning into terms relevant to students is important for several reasons. First, increasing students' educational levels, more than any other social variable, including wealth, will increase the likelihood of better health and longevity. Second, teachers must be informed about their students' health and understand their students' growth and development in order to assist them with the rigors of growing up. Third, teachers present to their students a model in their own behavior and appearance; teachers must appreciate and maintain their own health at an optimal level. And fourth, because we lose our entire effort and investment in education if a person dies prematurely or greatly decrease the investment if a person is disabled or frequently ill, it is important to help students protect their own health. Health, indeed, has not only personal value but also economic value to the entire society.

Although it is not necessary that all teachers have a high level of health expertise, all teachers should know something about health, and some teachers in key positions must have considerable health knowledge. In addition, a comprehensive health planning group is recommended for each school district. Such a group could involve health teachers, nurses, parents, school administrators, counselors, and students. The school physician or a local physician would also be a valuable member of such a group. These people should be expected to identify health problems and recommend solutions.

To be a competent health educator, the teacher does not need to be an expert. Experience indicates that certain basic knowledge is adequate for the position the teacher rightfully holds on the health team. Primarily, that knowledge includes an understanding of normal growth and development, normal health status, and common deviations from the normal. A study of deviations does not imply that the educator is to be a diagnostician, but rather a "suspectitian." The teacher may be in the best position to recognize first that a child does not appear to be normal in some respect.

Professional preparation should develop in the teacher an attitude toward health that focuses attention on the child and proceeds to identify existing health problems. Just as the lawyer must develop a certain frame of mind and approach to problems of law, the health educator must develop an approach to problems of health founded on an understanding and appreciation of the individual child's health.

THE CONCEPT OF NORMAL

Health is not a single static state. Neither is the concept of normal a single point on a scale. Teachers see a wide range of students and therefore are expected to judge individuals' health from many perspectives.

"Normal" is that which we accept as the usual. It must be understood as encompassing a range of variables rather than a single entity. "Normal" includes the average but extends considerably on both sides of average. No two persons are exactly alike; each is unique. A person may be clearly normal on a series of measures and abnormal by one measure, but the total outcome may still be healthy. A very short person, for example, may not be anything but healthy when viewed in total.

The range of normal can be illustrated by a statistically normal curve. In any group of persons, measures of health will tend to cluster around the average. The farther persons or

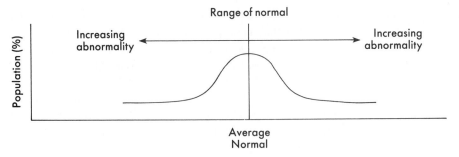

FIG. 3-1. The range of normal is a function of the tendency to cluster around the average. Average dictates normal, but deviation from the average (abnormality) does not necessarily imply anything in terms of health.

measures of health move from the average, the more they will be outside the range of normal. However, as Fig. 3-1 shows, the number of people who deviate greatly from normal declines as deviation increases. By definition, deviations are uncommon and therefore abnormal.

What constitutes the normal, or usual, is easy to determine in some instances but extremely difficult to ascertain in others. To say with assurance that the normal range of glucose in human blood is between 0.08 and 0.14 mg/100 ml is easy because in more than 96% of analyzed blood samples the glucose content falls in this range. Many physiologic norms are well established; yet the normal range for certain physical measurements is not so easily set down. For example, what is the normal range of height for American women? Should one arbitrarily say it is between 5 feet, 2 inches and 5 feet, 7 inches? What of the woman who is 6 feet, 1 inch in height? Should she be considered abnormal? According to Fig. 3-1 and its accompanying discussion, she should. Deviations such as 6 feet, 1 inch are uncommon and therefore abnormal. Whether that woman is healthy is another matter.

If normal for physical factors is a precise quantity, consider how variable it can be when applied to social and psychologic phenomena. What is the normal range of emotional responses for junior high school boys frustrated by losing election to an office or to a group? Standards of normal social acceptance vary from community to community, from school to school, and from family to family. Yet determining what is normal usually does not pose too difficult a problem for the sensitive teacher.

Different cultural groups in a school may also challenge the concept of normal. For example, nutrition education may stress the importance of eating three meals a day. To eat three meals a day is a normal expectation, although teenagers as a group frequently skip breakfast and the three-meals-a-day pattern is broken by frequent snacking. Different cultures can add to the variety of nutrition behaviors considered normal. Some people, Hindus and some Seventh Day Adventists, for example, do not eat meat. Children and adults of the Moslem faith abstain from all food during daylight hours for the holy period of Ramadan. Such behavior may be atypical by nutrition standards, but in the context of that culture it is not abnormal.

Beyond physical characteristics and sometimes buried under the heading of culture is an array of variables that influences our understanding of normal. Fig. 3-2 illustrates some of these variables and suggests how they tend to overlap one another, often going unnoticed.

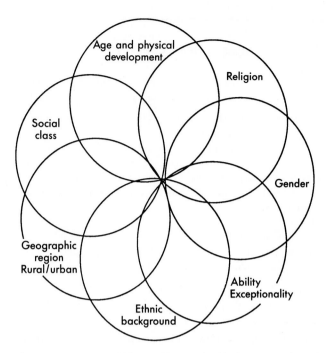

FIG. 3-2. Any group of students includes a variety of traditions and types. Although these differences tend to merge, as in the center of this figure, they are also separate and distinct, as on the edges of the figure. At one time the teachers deal with a group of individuals with few differences; at other times the teacher has to recognize many variations as normal.

There was a time when teachers tended to see their classes as a relatively homogeneous group. Not so today. Teachers now recognize the significance of the diversity of students found in many classes. Different ethnic groups and religions are common. Young people with different intellectual and physical abilities can share a common desire to learn and the same classroom. Dealing with cultural differences, described as multicultural education, is not always easy. Identifying differences, including our own, and establishing realistic notions of normal are important for the health worker. These differences are often evident in health practices and values. The box on p. 66 outlines a series of questions designed as a simple checklist to help teachers maintain a realistic view of normal when working with a multicultural class of students.

In other words, normal is determined by many conditions. For the practicing health teacher or health worker, developing a sensitivity to accept a wide range of "normal" is important. However, normal does have limits. The child who fasts for Ramadan, for example, but eats regularly during the rest of the year, is more normal in a nutritional sense than a young person who never eats breakfast. Nutrition education needs to recognize these different dimensions of normal and accommodate them in instructional practices.

In actual school practice most cases—physical, psychologic, or social—fall in the normal range. In the relatively few borderline instances the decision of an expert or the collective judg-

BOX
3-1   **A "multicultural as normal" checklist**

To establish an orientation for normal in a multicultural setting, a teacher or students can ask themselves the following questions about the cultural groups represented in their classes.

1. How am I different? (*not* how are *they* different?)
2. Do I understand nonverbal cues and communication styles of others?
3. Am I really interested in different cultures?
4. Am I sensitive in recognizing myths and stereotypes of other cultures?
5. Am I concerned about the welfare of other cultural groups?
6. Can I accept social practices different from my own as still being normal?
7. Can I accept different health practices as not necessarily bad and possibly good, even though they *are* different?
8. Do I know the reasons for different health-related practices?
9. Can I describe a situation in another cultural group to a person from that group in a way that will reflect the values and perceptions of that group?

ment of several competent teachers can usually serve the needs of the particular case. Even more important, many deviations from normal are of little significance in terms of effective and enjoyable living. Every human being has imperfections, most of which go unnoticed or are accepted by this imperfect world of imperfect people. To be abnormal in some respects, perhaps, is normal.

THE CONCEPT OF HEALTH

"Health" is a word that is used frequently but is difficult to define. The World Health Organization states that health is the "state of complete physical, mental, and social well-being and not merely the absence of disease." Health, in other words, represents a completeness that goes beyond the simple absence of illness. The word *health* implies physical, mental, and social well-being, yet society tends to measure health in disease-oriented terms. If a physician cannot find anything wrong with the patient, the patient is likely to be declared "healthy." If a country has fewer deaths, a longer life span, and a lower incidence of disease, that country is considered to have a healthier population than one with a higher death rate, a higher incidence of disease, and a shorter life span. In other words, health is frequently measured against the quality and quantity of disease and not the quality or quantity of life.

The simplest way to think of health is as the absence of disease, but a person can experience many levels of health without exhibiting clinical signs of illness. Look at the structure of the word *disease:* dis-ease. Disease implies that for one reason or another a person is not "at ease." Disease, in this sense, may not necessarily represent a clinical illness such as what a physician would diagnose, but it may represent a departure from ideal, or optimal, health. On any given day a person experiences varying degrees of "dis-ease" without actually being ill.

A person's optimal level of performance is limited only by genetic inheritance. Optimal health therefore does not mean that a person is simply stronger or taller or faster than others

Requiring the use of bicycle helmets

EMERGING ISSUE Assume that you are the Middle School Curriculum Coordinator for Health and Safety in a large, metropolitan school district. In this position, you also serve as a school representative on the city Safety Council. A reporter from the evening paper has been invited to speak to the council concerning a series of articles she has written on the topic of child safety. Several council members are concerned about bicycle safety and the number of serious head injuries that children have suffered. Data presented by the reporter show that head injuries account for 70% to 80% of the deaths and serious morbidity of bicycle-related injuries; physicians at Children's Hospital have treated over 100 children for such injuries. These physicians have recommended that the Safety Council support the passage of a city ordinance requiring cyclists to use helmets. As a member of the school representatives, you have been asked to respond to the following statements:

Please indicate whether you generally agree or disagree by placing a plus (+) or a minus (−) sign before each statement.

_____ 1. As an educator, I have some concerns about mandatory behavioral intervention.

_____ 2. I would favor an educational approach but doubt that it would receive enough community support to be effective.

_____ 3. I believe that a campaign led by the physicians and supported by others would be successful.

_____ 4. I am opposed to such a law because it encroaches on one's personal freedom.

_____ 5. I would favor a middle ground approach that would include a strong safety education program coupled with a school requirement that all school-age cyclists wear helmets.

_____ 6. Although I favor the use of helmets, I believe that it would be too difficult to implement such a requirement.

_____ If restricted to a single choice, I would choose this number.

REFERENCES
Cushman R, et al: Physicians promoting bicycle helmets for children: a randomized trial, *Am J Public Health* 81(8):1044, 1991.
Runyan C, Runyan D: How can physicians get kids to wear bicycle helmets: a prototypic challenge in injury prevention, *Am J Public Health*, 81(8):972-973, 1991.

but that the person operates at a level close to his or her personal potential. All persons have a potential to achieve their optimum even after serious illness or injury greatly changes the dimensions of that goal. For example, an athlete may be seen as a "picture of health." An automobile accident may injure that same athlete so that she cannot walk. To the extent that the athlete adjusts to an injury, accepts a new level of optimal health, and works to improve herself within the new limitations, she can be described as healthy. The trauma of the accident greatly reduced certain potentials and caused enormous "dis-ease," but the potential to reestablish health exists. At some point, recovery will be complete, and physicians will no longer be able to find actual clinical illness—only a reduction in certain functions.

Remember also that health encompasses more than just physical dimensions. For example, it is possible for an athlete to allow training to so affect her life and her behavior as to cause significant "dis-ease" and actual illness. In this case a person appearing physically healthy may actually be experiencing mental illness.

Health as ability to adapt

Health is a particularly delicate condition affected by tangible forces such as trauma, bacteria, and viruses and by less tangible forces such as stress and grief. Students are well aware that they can feel "dis-eased" before examinations and especially well (at ease) on receiving an "A" grade. Sudden fright can change the body temperature and the body metabolism in such a way as to represent disease. How well a person responds to changes, how well he or she adjusts, represents the state of health. Health, in other words, depends on an ability to adapt: to adapt to trauma, to pathogens of various types, to social stresses, to emotional crises, to varied foods, to different temperatures, and to all the forces in the world. To the extent that persons cannot adapt to these changes, they are not "at ease"; they are "diseased." These varied levels of health and disease are shown in Fig. 3-3.

Fig. 3-3 illustrates a continuum of health that ranges from optimal health to death. At the highest level of health on this continuum is optimal health. Although optimal varies among people, it is absolute for each individual. This condition is often referred to as a state of wellness. Wellness is achieved when everything is optimal: a condition that can be imagined but not actually measured, since we tend only to measure states of disease. When measures do not identify even the slightest degree of disease, we assume a state of health. The concept of wellness suggests that even when no disease is present, a range of wellness exists. In traditional terms, optimal health marks the highest degree of wellness.

Just below optimal on this continuum is a range we commonly accept as a state of health, even though it might include mild discomforts, minor traumas, muscle soreness from over-

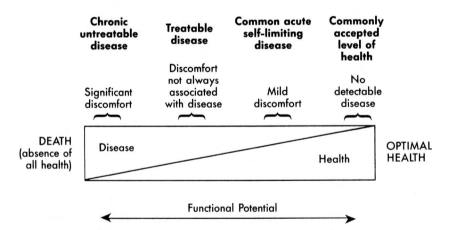

FIG. 3-3. A person's state of health is constantly varying in degree, ranging from optimal health through varying degrees of disease to death—the total absence of health. At any given time a person's health represents his or her ability to adapt to varying degrees of stress and pathology.

exertion, and common, mild, self-limiting diseases such as the common cold. In a general sense these conditions are accepted as normal; and persons do not think of themselves as diseased when they experience them. When a condition becomes serious enough to require medication, some type of remedial action, or diagnostic assistance from a medical practitioner, persons might recognize that they are not well but might not yet acknowledge that they are diseased. There is a clear indication, however, that functional potential has been reduced and that whatever is done to overcome these conditions will move a person back up the continuum of health toward the optimal level. Diseases that are chronic can seriously jeopardize function and are represented on the lower levels on this continuum. When these conditions continue and functional potential decreases, death results. It is important to note that a position on this continuum is not necessarily dictated by age. As persons get older, they tend to have more diseases, and their ability to adapt declines, but increasing proportions of older people maintain high levels of health. Age alone does not imply disease. Age does affect the nature of one's optimal potential, but it is still possible to maintain optimal health. Similarly, discomfort does not always relate to illness. At certain times, for example, chronic untreatable diseases may be asymptomatic. People do not know they have the disease.

The teacher's challenge is to help young people develop skills to facilitate their adaptation to a variety of stresses and to provide them with sufficient knowledge and skills to deal with specific health-threatening situations. This should include knowledge to seek appropriate diagnosis and treatment to gain complete recovery from illness when it does strike. It also means helping young people avoid situations that will threaten health and make knowledgeable decisions that facilitate adaptation. One significant part of health education is to help young people accept their potentials and their limitations: their own range of normal. Recognizing strengths and weaknesses, playing to strengths, working to strengthen weaknesses, and developing a feeling of self-confidence are basic to both physical and mental health. In other words, the well-adjusted student with a wide range of basic skills has the greatest potential for good health.

Most persons are born healthy and lose their health to disease through actions they or others take. Heart disease, for example, is caused by five major risk factors: diet, exercise patterns, heredity, cigarette smoking, and stress. Only heredity is beyond a person's behavioral control. Cancer presents a similar picture, as do accidents, stroke, and suicide. Cancer also represents a striking example of how the conscious or accidental behavior of others affects health. The release of a carcinogen into the environment, either intentionally or accidentally, contributes to cancer.

There was a time when disease (i.e., infectious disease) could reach almost anyone. Today, however, infectious diseases are largely controlled in North America and most of Europe— through improvements in the environment, often by eliminating the reservoir of infections— but some still persist. Because we are able to treat many common infectious diseases relatively simply, we often overlook their significance. Infectious diseases depend on human behavior to encourage their spread. Failure to wash hands regularly, for example, contributes to the spread of gastrointestinal and upper respiratory infections. Sexual intercourse spreads sexually transmitted diseases (STDs). Using condoms reduces but does not eliminate the risk of STDs. Behaviors, in other words, contributes to both chronic and acute diseases.

Because most persons are born healthy, the challenge is to protect that health and to prevent the onset of disease. Public health workers over the years have conceptualized several ways of thinking about prevention and how persons can increase their chances of preventing disease. Teachers generally deal with healthy populations; thus an understanding of prevention is useful to envisage how education can contribute to the maintenance of health.

THE CONCEPT OF PREVENTION

Public health workers describe prevention as having three levels: *primary, secondary,* and *tertiary.* Primary prevention focuses on the environment and how the environment facilitates or prevents the spread of disease; secondary prevention focuses on individuals and how they react to the onset of disease; tertiary prevention relates to the complete process of rehabilitation so that the chances of reinfection or recurrence are minimized. Fig. 3-4 describes these levels.

Primary prevention

Primary prevention relates to those actions that change the environment, physical and social, to reduce the likelihood that disease will occur or will be transmitted to another person.

The environment around us. Primary prevention is best illustrated by considering diseases that were once common and are now relatively rare. For example, as recently as 100 years ago conditions such as malaria, scarlet fever, tuberculosis, and diphtheria were common in North America. These diseases are no longer prevalent, but simply identifying and treating people with these diseases could not account for their almost total elimination. Mortality from tuber-

Primary prevention	Precedes the earliest signs of a disease and involves changes in the physical or social environment to reduce the likelihood that the disease can or will occur
Secondary prevention	Identifies diseases at their earliest stages and initiates appropriate treatment to limit the course and consequences of the disease
Tertiary prevention	Maintains appropriate treatment through its full course to complete rehabilitation and returns a person to optimal health, thereby minimizing the likelihood of recurrence

FIG. 3-4.   Three levels of prevention. Primary prevention attempts to prevent conditions from occurring. Secondary prevention and tertiary prevention attempt to prevent unnecessary development of health problems once they have been detected.

culosis infections in England and Wales declined from almost 4000 cases per million population in 1838 to 2000 cases per million population in 1880. This decline was in advance of any
modern treatment techniques and actually predated the identification of the tubercle bacillus
in 1882. After the identification of the tubercle bacillus the incidence of the disease continued
to decline. By 1944, when an effective chemotherapy was developed (para-aminosalicylic
acid), the rate was down to about 500 cases per million population. Shortly thereafter, an even
more effective treatment, isoniazid, was perfected.

Why did the incidence of tuberculosis decline so greatly before the introduction of effective treatment? Noticeable improvements in housing, management of water and sewage, production and marketing of milk, quality and availability of food, and the work environment
took place mid-century. From today's perspective it is hard to judge the years of the Industrial
Revolution as a time of great improvement in living conditions, but in relative terms they were.
In short, the decline in tuberculosis can be attributed mainly to improvements in the environment and not to increased capabilities for treating disease.

This same lesson is true for most of the other infectious diseases that are no longer present.
Even something as common as dental caries is prevented only by changes in the environment.
Careful attention to the care of teeth helps reduce dental caries, and frequent visits to a dentist
lead to the early detection and treatment of caries and other dental problems. However, the
introduction of fluoridated water contributed more to the decline of dental caries than any
other measure. Primary prevention, in other words, means changes in the environment that
reduce the likelihood of the condition's initial occurrence.

The examples just cited are mostly examples of infectious diseases. Today, however, many
diseases are not infectious and can be attributed to life-style. Cancer, heart disease, strokes,
accidents, suicide, homicide, and drug abuse are all problems of the modern age. These result
to a large degree from decisions relating to behavior. The question arises: How can primary
prevention apply? The answer is simple. Whereas tuberculosis and similar infectious diseases
were related to the physical environment, the conditions of today, such as heart disease, are
largely attributed to the social environment. Changing social attitudes toward behaviors such
as eating, exercise, overindulgence in alcohol, and tobacco use will ultimately change the incidence of diseases to which these behaviors contribute.

The environment within. How does immunization contribute to the control of infectious diseases? Immunizations, particularly effective in reducing several infectious diseases, are an
aspect of primary prevention. The immunizing agent changes the environment in which the
disease occurs, namely, the body. The injected substance in the immunization process triggers
a response that changes the body's environment so that the disease cannot occur. Even if the
causative agent enters the body, the body's environment will not sustain it. Immunization is
an excellent example of primary prevention, that is, a change in the environment.

Secondary prevention

Secondary prevention is the common practice of the majority of people. Secondary prevention
indicates early detection and treatment. Most persons are more conscious of secondary prevention than primary prevention. When a person aches or feels ill or believes he or she has the
early signs of disease, that person either initiates some type of treatment or seeks an expert

opinion from a health professional to identify the disease and set a course of treatment. Early detection and treatment are effective ways to reduce the course and the cost of a disease. However, early detection, or secondary prevention, differs from primary prevention. Secondary prevention means the condition has occurred, has been detected, and will now likely be limited by effective treatment. The modern world has focused the majority of its health care efforts on early detection and treatment rather than on primary prevention.

Tertiary prevention

Assuming that early detection is carried out and treatment initiated, tertiary prevention implies the complete course of treatment through rehabilitation. A person who breaks off treatment before full recovery increases the chance of a relapse. Rehabilitation then is prevention, in this case the third level—tertiary prevention.

Prevention and the school health program

Health is a dynamic state, and these three levels of prevention offer three levels of opportunities to deal with the maintenance of health or the management of disease.

The school health program is most effective at the first two levels. The school's responsibility is to provide an environment conducive to health and to reduce the risks of disease, including accidents. The school's educational program is responsible for teaching knowledge and skills so that individuals can relate responsibly to their environment and, along with others, work to establish an environment that is conducive to health. This may involve knowledge about such things as air pollution; it may also involve knowledge to take political action to get air pollution levels changed. This may mean helping students gain the social skills to be able to say no in a social environment that encourages the abuse of substances or behaviors that increase the risk of disease. Schools should also help students develop sensitivity to provide a supportive environment to others who are potentially at risk or who are recovering from an illness.

Also, the school health program should provide opportunities, through screening, health appraisal, and teacher observation, for the early identification of persons who have initial signs of disability or disease so that specific diagnostic services can be sought and treatment initiated. Early intervention in certain health conditions means that treatment can be initiated so that the person can return to school. Left undetected, some conditions limit the potential to learn or severely handicap a person's ability to put that learning to productive use in later life.

Schools can also serve as a site for tertiary prevention. Schools that accommodate and facilitate rehabilitation contribute to tertiary prevention. The student with physical limitations who can use the expertise of the physical education teacher and the facilities of the gymnasium to continue treatment to full recovery is a common example of the practice. A less common but equally important example is found when school teachers and counselors establish ways to enable a student returning from drug treatment to continue rehabilitation.

THE HEALTHY STUDENT

When health is regarded as the quality of well-being that enables people to live effectively and enjoyably, it must be considered a means to an end (Fig. 3-5). To a person who is ill, health

FIG. 3-5. Optimum physical growth and development is fundamental to the child's social, emotional, and intellectual development.

may be an end to be gained, but to the person who possesses health, it is a vehicle for effective and enjoyable living.

It is to the best interests of young people in a schoolroom that the teacher be conscious of the health status of every student, whether the student has normal health or is ill. The teacher must have a positive attitude and think in terms of the attributes or qualities of health each student possesses. This requires an evaluation of the natural qualities of each student. One student may have great vitality and almost unlimited energy, endurance, and ability to recover, although neither the student nor the parents may follow any of the accepted practices of good health. Another student may possess a constitution that is adequate for typical living but so near to inadequacy that every principle of health promotion must be practiced to maintain a normal level of health. Gradients between these two types require thoughtful discrimination by teachers who strive to understand the health capacity, just as they seek to understand the intellectual capacity, of each student.

In appraising students' health, one must give consideration to the personality dynamics of individuals. A student who is not extremely active physically nevertheless may possess a high level of health, both physical and mental. The less-active student may possess a level of health as optimal as that of the athletic student whose activity is obvious.

A young person's capacity to measure up to life's demands should be the cardinal criterion used by a teacher who attempts to appraise the health of a child. Health is one overall condition of well-being encompassing the physical, mental, emotional, and social aspects of well-being.

A clinical examination by a physician, supplemented by laboratory tests, is necessary for a thorough inventory of a person's precise status of physical health, but for practical purposes a teacher can observe certain outward indices as a general gauge. These landmarks of health are of special significance in the school situation where the teacher observes the same young

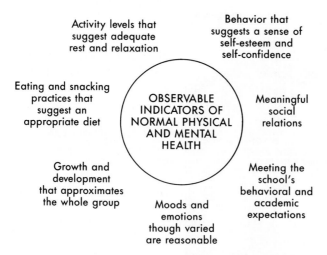

FIG. 3-6.   Observable signs of normal, healthy functioning provide a reference point for teachers to compare students with other students and with themselves over a period of time.

people daily. This day-to-day observation builds an inventory of each student's general pattern of health. Being familiar with the student's normal condition, the teacher can readily observe any deviation from normal. Fig. 3-6 illustrates a variety of important characteristics of normal mental and physical health that can be used as a guide for the observant teacher at the beginning of the year to establish a baseline for each student. Clear deviations and rapid changes are easily noticed. Some examples that relate to Fig. 3-6 illustrate the utility of this model.

It is not often that teachers observe students at rest; however, signs of fatigue or nervousness can be observed. Similarly, students' abilities to sit and relax for a few moments are observable. Inability to relax and lack of rest—demonstrated by excessive fatigue and limited physical activity—are important indicators of possible health-related problems.

Although growth and development patterns differ greatly, students who deviate significantly from the norm, while not necessarily being unhealthy, may deserve some extra attention and assistance. Often the needed help can come in health classes that explain why students differ in their rates of development.

Teachers have significant opportunity to observe the eating patterns of students. Food selection and eating patterns in the school cafeteria and snacking patterns that occur throughout the day may indicate poor nutrition and suggest possible remedial action; so might self-reported actions like regularly skipping meals.

Physical health and mental health are clearly intertwined. Just as teachers can observe variations in the physical health of their students, so they can observe indicators of mental health.

Self-esteem and self-confidence suggest a degree of coping that should be reflected in reasonable levels of achievement. Serious discrepancies between self-esteem and self-confidence and actual performance levels represent difficulties in acknowledging reality and may suggest special needs.

Normally, students maintain meaningful social contacts throughout their school years. This does not mean that all students need to be part of large social groups; but they should relate to other students, even if it is just a few, in a meaningful manner. A student without friends or a student who identifies with a group of people but is ignored by them may need assistance with social interaction.

Changes in mood are natural. All students experience feelings of happiness and sadness. This range of moods usually is realistic and reasonable. Rapid mood swings and extreme moods suggest underlying problems worthy of attention.

Perhaps the most observable indicator of appropriate mental health is the students' ability to meet the school's expectations, both academic and behavioral. This acknowledges that students get into trouble at certain times and that most students have difficulty with some of the school's academic expectations. However, a pattern of failure to achieve either academic or behavioral expectations should suggest a need for special help.

GET INVOLVED!

As a student studying for an undergraduate or graduate degree in health education, you should consider joining the Association for the Advancement of Health Education (AAHE). As the leaders of this professional organization correctly claim, AAHE is the only national association devoted solely to programs of health education at all levels of education (early childhood, elementary, secondary, college, and university), as well as nonschool adult health education.

AAHE has a membership of approximately 10,000. As a member, you may choose the particular areas that meet your professional needs or interests. There are 11 different interest areas that relate to program development in health education at all levels of schooling, professional preparation, continuing education, and research. It also includes health care providers, hospitals, and governmental and voluntary health agencies.

AAHE is one of six national organizations affiliated with the Alliance (The American Alliance for Health, Physical Education, Recreation, and Dance). One of the unique features of joining the Alliance is that you can become a member of two professional associations relating to your specialization or interest at no extra cost.

As an affiliated association with the Alliance, AAHE holds annual state, regional, and national meetings. Other services important to the professional member include a choice of four different professional journals. Health education members have the opportunity to acquire health education hours, contact hours, or continuing education units that enable members to maintain professional competence and health education credential status.

For membership information, write to:
Association for the Advancement of Health Education
1900 Association Dr.
Reston, VA 22091

SUMMARY

Falling outside normal is not necessarily a deviant condition. As this chapter has suggested, it is sometimes difficult to establish a normal range. However, a teacher is in a unique position to watch students over a period of time and to be able to compare one student with another. Teachers today are also fortunate in that there are many more referral options for special assistance for students than there were in the past. Most schools have clearly established referral procedures that teachers can use. Many schools also have clear working relationships with helping agencies in the community to support the school's special services and programs. However, none of these services is of much value unless the classroom teacher first notices the students who are exhibiting special needs and enters them into the referral process so that their special needs can be met as early as possible. It is equally important to be able to detect deviations from the normal and to be familiar with the full range of services available to students for possible referral.

STUDY QUESTIONS

1. What is normal in one situation may not be normal in another. Interpret this statement with examples.
2. How will the physical health of a pupil affect his or her mental health?
3. "The most difficult task in health education is to develop an appreciation of health in a child who already has good health." How does a teacher deal with this situation?
4. What is the responsibility of the school in understanding the present health of the child?
5. How is it that a child can be outside the bounds of normal as described in this chapter but still be healthy?
6. In terms of health, what does "normal" mean?
7. If health is a dynamic state, how is it most commonly measured?
8. Differentiate among primary, secondary, and tertiary prevention and describe an example to illustrate these differences.
9. Why are most screening programs not classified as primary prevention?
10. What would you regard as the best single index of normal health?

REFERENCES

American Medical Association: Youth speak out, Washington, DC, May 11, 1990, American Medical Association Adolescent Health Conference.

Better health for our children: a national strategy, vol 1, Major findings and recommendations—report of the Select Panel for the Promotion of Child Health to the United States Congress and the Secretary of Health and Human Services, Washington, DC, 1981, US Department of Health and human Services, Public Health Service.

Brindis CD, Lee PR: Public policy issues affecting the health care delivery system of adolescents, *J Adoles Health Care* 11:387-397, 1990.

Center for the Study of Social Policy: Kids count: state profiles of child well-being, Washington, DC, January 1990.

Dagg NV: Primary prevention: health promotion and specific protection. In Wold SJ, editor: School nursing: a framework for practice, St. Louis, 1981, Mosby–Year Book.

David R: The fate of the soul and the fate of the social order: the waning spirit of American youth, *J Sch Health* 60(5):205-207, 1990.

Dryfoos JG: Preventing high risk behavior, *Am J Public Health* 81(2):157-158, 1992.

Gollnick DM, Chinn PC: *Multicultural education in a pluralistic society,* New York, 1990, Macmillan.

McBride LG: Teaching about body image: a technique for improving body satisfaction, *J Sch Health* 56:76, 1986.

Novello AC: Healthy children ready to learn: the Surgeon General's initiative for children, *J Sch Health* 61(8):359-360, 1991.

Sobol J, et al: Health concerns of high school students and teachers' beliefs about student health concerns, *Pediatrics* 81(2):218-223, 1988.

Steinberg L: Autonomy, conflict and harmony in the family relationship. In Feldman SS, Elliott GR, editors: *At the threshold: the developing adolescent,* Cambridge, Mass, 1990, Harvard University Press.

Physical growth and development

OVERVIEW

This chapter provides a general understanding of growth and development from the intrauterine period through the adolescent stage. Some effects of heredity, environment, and nutrition on growth and development are discussed, together with the importance of health care during these various stages. A distinction between growth and development is made in order to emphasize the wide variation that occurs in normal, healthy growth. Characteristics of various stages of healthy growth and development are discussed. Characteristics of the growth and development of girls and boys are examined in regard to the issue of whether girls should compete with boys in sports and athletics. Recently developed national standards for height, weight, and skinfold-thickness measure of body fat for age, sex, and race are presented. Such measures help to characterize healthy growth and development, enabling the school to carry out its role of disease prevention and health promotion.

OBJECTIVES   After reading this chapter, the student should be able to:

1. Make a distinction between the terms *growth, development,* and *maturation*
2. Differentiate between *prematurity* and *low birth weight*
3. Explain why today's youths *are* or *are not* nearing their maximal growth potential
4. Identify possible educational, physical, and social impacts of "cocaine babies?"
5. Identify growth and development characteristics of children that have important implications for their health and education
6. Explain why age, height, and weight measures *may not* be a good method of classifying children for sports competition.
7. Describe how differing maturation levels of children can be of major importance in the planning of school programs
8. Explain what is meant by the expression "adolescent growth spurt" and how this phenomenon is related to adolescent development
9. Explain on the basis of growth and developmental characteristics why athletic competition between the sexes is an acceptable or unacceptable activity
10. Identify the abuse substance that, in your opinion, has the potential for the most harmful effect on American society and explain your position

The school deals in futures. How the child develops into the mature adult is a concern of the school. Physical growth and development are no less important than other phases of the evolving youngster. Physical growth and development represent a special phase in the maturing process but are entwined in the total pattern of maturation. Understanding physiologic change and the rate of change enables the teacher to understand each youngster in terms of his or her own particular development and relationship to the normal pattern. It is fascinating to watch the development of a child. It is most fascinating when one has an understanding of the developmental process.

Growth and development are individual matters, and each child is distinctive. However, there are typical or recognized ranges of growth into which most children fall. A conscientious teacher is eager to understand each child in terms of individual patterns of growth and development. Perhaps the teacher should think of the child as a "human becoming." After all, human beings require one third of their life span to reach maturity, and the school deals in that future.

GROWTH—CELLULAR AND INTERCELLULAR

Growth occurs at the cellular level in three ways: (1) increase in the size of the cells, (2) increase in the number of cells by cell division or multiplication, and (3) increase of the substance between the cells (intercellular).

This cellular growth consists in the addition of proteins, carbohydrates, fat, water, and minerals to the cell substance. Although vitamins are not directly involved, their regulatory function is also necessary. At least 45 nutrients are needed for healthy growth. However, recent research has led to the conclusion that the most important elements required are proteins and calories. Growth is work, and calories are the units providing the fuel for the energy needed to grow.

Calories are needed for cell multiplication, whereas protein is related primarily to increase in the size of cells. Elements of the major food groups, including carbohydrates, fats, and proteins, can be oxidized and used for energy. However, food must also provide the necessary raw materials for the growth and replacement of cells and cell products. All the molecules of the body must either be obtained directly from the food that is eaten or be synthesized from other compounds in the diet.

Some molecules are needed in great numbers because they form the structural material making up the tissues of muscle, bone, and cell membranes. Other molecules, such as vitamins, are required in lesser amounts because they are involved in the activities of the enzymes of the body. Although enzymes control chemical reactions, they are not used up in the reaction but can be used repeatedly.

Intercellular growth consists in the addition of organic and inorganic materials between cells. Fat, calcium, phosphate, or other substances retained between cells, although having a relation to the cells, must be considered a part of body growth if they are added to the total mass. Intercellular calcium is the principal constituent of bone growth. The noncellular part of tissue undergoes considerable increase in mass during the stage of physical growth of life.

DEVELOPMENT

Development, or maturation, is an increase in the complexity and effectiveness of bodily functions, whereas growth usually refers to an increase in size. For example, there is relatively little difference in the physical size of the head of a 3-month-old infant and that of a 16-year-old adolescent. But, obviously, the changes that have occurred over this period in the nature and complexity of the brain and its capacity to function are enormous.

In a comparison of the maturational differences between infancy and childhood, a comparatively shorter period of time, the 3-month-old infant is still a bundle of reflexes dominated by the need for food, warmth, and rest; whereas the child of 5 years, about to enter school, has already developed a wide range of abilities and skills.

As Krogman (1972) expresses it, "The postnatal growth period of twenty years is like a race: we all run it, but some run it fast and some run it slow." Thus at any point in time during this period some are biologically ahead, and some are behind.

An individual's pattern of growth and development is unique. Because of this uniqueness, the concept of biologic age has come into use. Standards have now been established for determining an individual's maturity by using x-ray examinations of the wrist or knee joints. Experimental investigations using standards of skeletal age are able to establish quite accurately the degree of maturity. Skeletal age is determined by the number of ossification centers and the amount of cartilage material separating those centers from the main body of bony structure in the extremity. Separation means that the epiphysis is open and that the limb or bone is still growing. Gradually these bony centers grow together, converting the cartilaginous material into bone and concluding growth in adult maturity.

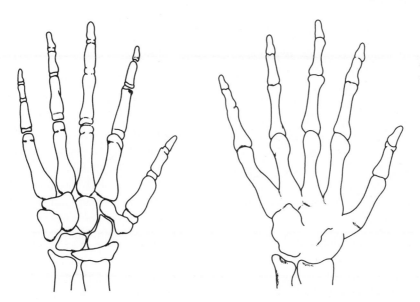

FIG. 4-1.   Variations in skeletal age.

Fig. 4-1, which is based on x-ray films taken by J. Roswell Gallagher, M.D., former Chief of Adolescent Medicine of Children's Hospital in Boston, illustrates the growth maturity of skeletal-age differences between two adolescent boys who are of the same chronologic age, 14 years and 11 months. The illustration on the left reveals a skeletal-age rating of 13 years, 6 months, whereas the bone development pictured on the right is considered to be 16 years, 10 months. This represents a maturational difference of nearly 3½ years, thus demonstrating the necessity for school officials to consider more than chronologic age when classifying students for athletic competition or evaluating age-group performances. Tables portraying averages in growth and development are useful, but so-called normal development encompasses a very wide range of differences.

In addition to these differences in growth patterns of normal children, there are variations caused by calorie and protein deprivation. Such malnourished children may never attain their normal complement of cells. Lack of protein in the diet will cause their cell growth to be limited, resulting in smaller stature throughout their growth period and into adulthood.

Since the various systems of the body develop at differing rates, it is desirable that a teacher understand the patterns of maturation of the various systems. Their separate, as well as composite, developmental patterns can be the avenue through which the teacher may better understand each child and thus better serve his or her interests.

BIOLOGIC DETERMINATION

Potential biologic growth and development are determined at fertilization. The genetic combinations at that moment set the biologic potential and limit for both.

Inheritance

Growth and development are governed or regulated primarily by the hormones of the body, and a child's genetic endocrine endowment is the principal asset for both growth and development. General body size depends on the output of *somatotropin,* the principal growth hormone, which is produced by the anterior pituitary gland. Carbohydrate, fat, and water balance are affected by other secretions from this gland. Thyroxin from the thyroid gland governs the growth of long bones, the rate at which energy is used, and the rate at which the body matures. Sex hormones affect maturation and determine secondary sex characteristics. *Cortin,* the principal secretion of the adrenal cortex, which is located at the tip of the kidneys, greatly affects the rate of maturation. An overactive adrenal cortex produces precocious children.

Considering hormones alone, geneticists calculate at least 40 million possible patterns of genetic endocrine endowment. The particular combination of factors that a child inherits appears to be a matter of mere chance. Once fertilization takes place, nothing can be done to change the inherited characteristics. Therefore a teacher who understands that there are many possible genetic combinations will be more likely to better understand and appreciate each child in the class.

ENVIRONMENTAL FACTORS

No one attains the absolute genetic maximum in growth and development because environmental factors retard or obstruct normal processes. If it were possible to provide the perfect environment for all life processes, the individual would develop more rapidly than he or she presently does and would attain greater growth. This would entail a better internal bodily environment through scientifically perfected nutrition and respiration, as well as freedom from infection, and an external environment of temperature, humidity, and other factors that best permit processes to function.

A study of growth trends over the past century provides information on the effects of improved health care, improved nutrition, and a more healthful environment on the growth and development of the young. Data collected throughout this period have shown an increasingly earlier age of maturation and an increasing size with each succeeding generation. According to health officials, this universal trend among the young of the Western world has served as a good biologic index of the effects of the environment. Although it is not likely that the perfect environment will ever be created to enable the individual to reach maximum genetic growth potential, there are indications that humankind may be nearing this growth ceiling. For example, after observing several generations of Harvard youth, Damon (1968) concluded that the growth trend had stabilized. The average heights of Harvard students were no longer increasing and, in fact, had leveled off and were remaining at a consistent average height.

Damon's findings were confirmed by an analysis of growth trends conducted by the National Center for Health Statistics (NCHS) (1976). A comparative analysis of the growth measurements taken from representative samples of children and youth from 2 to 18 years of age in the early 1960s shows that the average heights are essentially the same as those taken in the 1970s. It would seem that the average heights of children and youth have stabilized over the past 20 years. However, children in the lower end of the distribution of heights provide an exception. Those of the fifth and tenth percentile levels have continued to show slight increases in height, whereas the height of children at the twenty-fifth percentile level and above has stabilized. A possible explanation of this fact is that more children from lower socioeconomic backgrounds constitute the fifth and tenth percentile levels. Therefore it follows that these children have not had the full benefits of good nutrition and health care and have a greater potential for improvement in health. An increase in their height would be more likely than would an increase in that of children from the upper socioeconomic levels.

Children from disadvantaged backgrounds become a special concern to the school. Although the school represents only a part of their total environmental influences, it can play a vital role in their healthy development. The school health services can protect and supervise healthy growth by promoting effective nutrition and providing health education. As expressed in the NCHS report, "When the stragglers will finally achieve their genetic potential to full stature can probably be better predicted by economic and social factors than by biological ones."

FULL-TERM INFANT

If the normal gestation period is estimated at 280 days after the beginning of the last menstruation, it is interesting to note that 35% of all births occur within 1 week on either side of this estimate and 65% of births occur within 2 weeks of it. A child who is born at 37 weeks of gestation (within 3 weeks of the 280 days) is considered a full-term infant.

Medical research has revealed that the early stages of pregnancy, between the second and tenth weeks, constitute the most important growth period of life. During this time cell differentiation takes place, and the special tissues of the limbs, eyes, ears, and vital organs are formed. Special emphasis should be given to protecting the mother's health during this period because an illness or adverse condition may affect the intrauterine environment and damage the developing tissues of the fetus. For example, many childhood defects of hearing, vision, and vital function have been traced to an incident of German measles contracted by the mother during this first trimester.

Antibodies passing from the mother through the placenta to the developing fetus give the child an infantile immunity until about 6 months of age. The immunity may be against diphtheria, smallpox, tetanus, measles, and poliomyelitis. This does not give the child the ability to produce antibodies. Thus, when the antibodies received from the mother disintegrate, the immunity ceases unless the child has been immunized by other means.

Although usually smaller at birth, girls are about 1 month in advance of boys according to bone development or skeletal-age measures. Girls entering school continue to be more mature than boys in terms of skeletal age. (This advantage increases progressively to 12 years of age.)

LOW BIRTH WEIGHT AND GROWTH RETARDATION

Until recently, all infants weighing less than 5½ lb (2.5 kg) were classified as premature. However, results from medical research have shown that low birth weight (LBW) may be caused by two distinct conditions: (1) prematurity or (2) growth retardation. *Prematurity* means that such infants are born before completing the normal period of intrauterine life (37 weeks) (Fig. 4-2). Therefore premature infants weigh less because they have not had enough time to grow and develop fully. On the other hand, *growth-retarded infants* may have been born after a full-term pregnancy of 40 weeks but still be far below average weight at birth. As many as one third to one half of the incidents of LBW are believed to be caused by conditions that retard normal growth. Among the factors believed to be responsible are inadequate placental development, insufficient blood supply to the uterus, genetic defects, the mother's health, and other environmental conditions.

Several techniques are used to distinguish between the premature and the growth-retarded infant. The ultrasonic sound device is used to measure fetal size, and a precise measure of the duration of pregnancy can be obtained by amniocentesis. Standards describing the various neuromuscular reflexes typical of the neurologic behavior of the different stages of development are used. For example, the growth-retarded infant would be expected to demonstrate behavior patterns similar to those of the full-term infant with normal swallowing and sucking reflexes, whereas the premature infant would not display fully developed reflexes. In general, the premature infant would be expected to be behind the full-term infant in development.

Because of the difficulty in obtaining accurate and objective data concerning the exact length of the gestation period, a birth weight of less than 2500 g (5 lb, 8 oz) has been accepted internationally as the clinical criterion of prematurity. Further, the World Health Organization Expert Committee has recommended that the concept of prematurity be replaced by that of

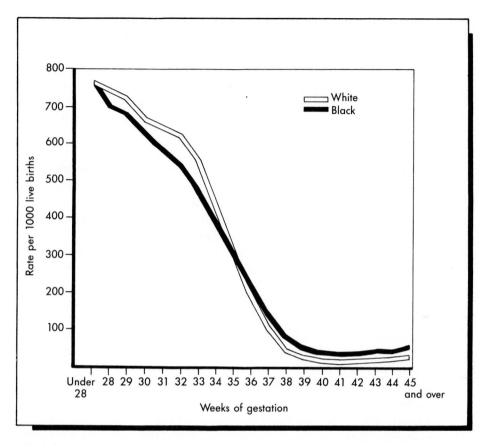

FIG. 4-2.   Weeks of gestation per 1000.

LBW as a more accurate definition of prematurity. However, the committee has also recommended that the term prematurity be reserved for those neonates (first 6 weeks following birth) who are within the LBW group when there is clear evidence of incomplete development (Thomas, 1985).

Medical science has devoted increasing attention to the LBW problem. To be more exact in the study of this morbidity, further distinctions within this condition have been adopted. Officials at the National Center for Health Statistics (NCHS) in their periodic health examination surveys have used at least three different categories of LBW: (1) the international classification for LBW—less than 2500 g, (2) moderately low birth weight (MLBW)—1500 to 2499 g, and (3) very low birth weight (VLBW)—less than 1500 g or 3 lb, 4 oz. With the advancement of science, it is now possible for physicians to save more of these LBW babies who were once thought to be beyond the reach of medicine. Collins et al. (1991) conducted a follow-up study of extremely LBW infants (less than 1000 g, 2.2 lb). The survival rates of such infants were once as low as 4%. With scientific advancements, survival rates have now risen to 50% to 60%. This has led to a shift in medicine from an emphasis on survival toward intensive study of the morbidity in order to increase the infants' chances of leading a normal and productive life.

Although LBW is not a good predictor of a future handicapping condition, research has demonstrated that these infants are at high risk. Their development should be carefully monitored well into their preschool years. It is important that children with handicapping conditions be identified at the earliest possible time to increase the prospects of ameliorating, if not eliminating, their handicapping condition. In addition to the regular testing at infancy, Collins et al. have recommended that such children be reexamined between 36 and 56 months of age to assess their verbal and perceptual performance, their quantification, memory, and motor abilities to evaluate their continuing development.

Impact of maternal substance abuse. The association of substance abuse with detrimental effects on the fetus has been extensively documented in the literature. Substances such as alcohol, cocaine, tobacco, marijuana, and other drugs are widely used. Unfortunately, the trend is toward increasing usage for some of these substances. Further, it has been shown that persons abusing substances are often users of multiple drugs.

Data from the National Longitudinal Study of Youth reveal that 45% of young, pregnant women in this group use at least one of these substances (alcohol, cigarettes, or marijuana) (Abma and Mott, 1991). The significance of this statistic is underscored by the fact that alcohol abuse is now considered to be the major cause of mental retardation in the world (NIAAA, 1991).

A study of 1776 pregnant women conducted over a 2-year period recorded an alarming increase in use of cocaine. With the exception of alcohol, these data suggest that women who have had less education are more likely to use tobacco, cocaine, and other substances. These same women are more likely to have poor nutritional habits and to receive less prenatal care, which places them and their infants at greater health risk. According to pediatric nurses (Bresnahan et al., 1991), among the most negative outcomes of the mother's abuse of cocaine and her inability to stop are the subsequent guilt feelings and self-hatred that accompany usage. To cope with these feelings, the mother continues to use cocaine as a form of self-medication, thus sinking ever deeper into dependence.

Why has cocaine abuse become such a threat to mother and child? Contributing factors are cocaine's wide availability and the ease with which it can be used, that is, by sniffing or smoking without resorting to injections. Unlike alcohol or other opiates, cocaine dependence does not lead to the typical physical withdrawal characteristics of other dependencies. Rather, its effect on the neurotransmitter systems of the central nervous system and the characteristic withdrawal and crash that follow the cocaine binge include a state of agitation, depression, craving for more cocaine, and increasing fatigue. Addiction to cocaine can develop in a matter of weeks or months following first use. Once into the mother's system, it diffuses quickly across the placenta into the blood system of the fetus. Also, cocaine readily crosses the blood-brain barrier, where it has a special affinity for concentrating in the brain.

This intense craving for cocaine is believed to be related to its effects on the central nervous system, including the dopaminergic and the norepinephrine systems. Cocaine blocks the reuptake of these neurotransmitters at the postsynaptic juncture. This blocking causes a neurochemical magnification of the pleasure response (Spitz and Rosecan, 1987). These aftereffects on the mother leave her with little energy or desire to care for herself. The depression and feeling of low self-esteem, together with a loss of appetite, further undermine the health of the mother and her unborn child.

Cocaine effects on the fetus and newborn. Obstetric data were compared for two groups of pregnant women, an experimental group who had tested positive for cocaine use and a control group who were nonusers of cocaine. The results of this study showed that the cocaine-using mothers had a significantly higher incidence of the following situations than did the control group of nonusers:

1. Pre-term deliveries
2. Premature ruptures of membranes
3. Birth of small-for–gestational age infants
4. Abruptio placentae (tearing away of the placenta)

With regard to the perinatal morbidity associated with the mother's cocaine abuse during pregnancy, the data revealed that these infants had many more complications, including withdrawal symptoms such as tremulousness, irritability, poor feeding, diarrhea, abnormal pneumograms (measure of respiratory function), ventricular septal defects, and alarmingly higher infant mortality rates. Of special concern to the child's future potential for development are the brain malformations that cause dysfunction of the higher cognitive abilities (Neerhof et al, 1991).

CHARACTERISTICS OF THE PRESCHOOL CHILD

The period from infancy to the school years is a critical one for the child's growth and development. Recently worldwide attention has been focused on the health and nutrition of very young children and the dramatic effects brought about by extreme malnutrition. Pictures of children from underdeveloped countries of the world suffering from marasmus or kwashiorkor stir a sense of concern and compassion in the viewer. But malnutrition is not restricted to distant lands. Actually the breast-fed infant from an underdeveloped country may be better nourished than an infant from the United States who is not breast-fed and fails to get an adequate diet from bottle feedings. It is after weaning that the infant from an underdeveloped nation suffers from malnutrition and diarrheal infection from unhygienically prepared food. As a result, these children suffer the severe effects of kwashiorkor, which retards their growth and leaves them dull and listless with the possibility of permanent brain damage. Research has shown that nutritionally deprived children may have brain cell counts 20% lower than those of normal children.

Surveys of child nutrition in the United States show that malnutrition exists in this country to a far greater extent than had been realized, and it is not restricted to poor children who do not get enough food or suffer from dietary deficiencies. Malnutrition also refers to the state of "overnutrition" that can be found in many children from financially stable families. They may suffer from a form of malnutrition that involves taking in too many calories. Overfed children may develop into obese children and adults. Some researchers believe that the consumption of too many calories causes the body to develop an excess of fat cells, thus predisposing the individual to a lifelong tendency to obesity and perhaps to the chronic diseases associated with that condition.

The preschool period marks a transition from the very rapid growth of infancy to the slower but steady, continuous growth of childhood. By the time children reach 5 months of age they will have doubled their birth weight. Moreover, their bodies will have changed from the rounded, plump appearance of infancy to the longer-limbed body type characteristic of childhood.

During this preschool period certain normal growth characteristics predispose children to upper respiratory tract illnesses. Tonsils and adenoidal tissue grow very rapidly, reaching full adult size by the time the child is 5 years old. This large growth of tissue in the relatively small nose and throat area of the child often encourages an infection in the middle ear. Since the child of this age has a shorter eustachian tube leading from the throat to the middle ear, bacterial infections often invade the middle ear. Such infections should receive prompt treatment to avoid a possible hearing loss. Teachers and parents should be alert to identify those children with hearing difficulty and a pattern of mouth breathing. Such a condition may indicate the presence of infection.

During the first 2½ years of the child's life, the cerebellum portion of the brain influences to a large extent the child's posture, coordination, and ability to perform certain movements. Efforts to teach neuromotor skills such as those that are involved in walking or in toilet training will be of no avail until the child is "ready" developmentally, that is, until the neural pathways have been established. After a child has attained sufficient physical maturity, it has been dem-

FIG. 4-3. Children of the same chronological age and grade level often reveal wide variations in their patterns and rates of growth and development.

onstrated that preschool programs have a significant and positive effect on the child's development.

Among so-called normal children, there is a variation in physical, social, and intellectual maturity. Some lag behind, some are on schedule, and some race ahead. In a group of preschoolers a variation in maturation of 6 months is not unusual (Fig. 4-3). However, this seemingly short period of time can represent the equivalent of nearly one fourth of a young child's life span. Children whose birthdays occur in late summer or early fall may be as much as 10 to 11 months behind developmentally. Such children may not be ready for school simply because of this lack of maturation. Pushing them ahead can lead to difficulty.

THE ELEMENTARY SCHOOL-AGE CHILD

Technically the elementary school growth period includes the time span from kindergarten up to and including the preadolescent growth spurt of puberty. However, since the timing of the growth spurt varies widely and often extends well into the middle or junior high school years, pubertal growth is discussed with adolescence.

The growth stage of the early elementary school years has often been described as undramatic, compared to the rapid growth changes that characterize both the earlier and later growth periods. The gradual and steady rate of growth that began in preschool continues well into the elementary school years. Children tend to become heavier in relation to their height. The tendency toward lower back curvature, or lordosis, ends, creating a more erect posture. During this period children lose all their primary teeth, except for the second and third molars, and acquire their permanent teeth. These children may continue to have problems because of the abundance of lymphatic tissue that makes up the tonsils and adenoids.

The preschool child usually is farsighted, which he or she does not outgrow until about the sixth year of age. At this time both the involuntary and voluntary muscles of accommodation mature to give the child the visual apparatus necessary for reading. At the 6-year level of visual maturity, a child can read large type (12 point) but not without sustained effort.

If a child is nearsighted, the condition usually appears early (Fig. 4-4). Eyestrain in school is not necessarily a deficiency in visual acuity but may be a tendency of the relatively immature muscles of accommodation to fatigue very easily. The normal eye reaches its maximum growth and acuity at 12 years of age. It is the first organ to mature. At 7 years of age children tend to become daring, adventuresome, boisterous, and vigorous in their play. Running, chasing, skating, jumping rope, bicycle riding, and swimming appeal to them. Joy, as an expression of self, motivates the child to master a skill that actually becomes a means to an end.

Manipulative skills begin to improve greatly at 8 years of age. The child normally becomes progressively stronger and sturdier. Legs lengthen rather rapidly, but the rate of general body growth is slower. Considerable variation in muscular development and coordination occurs. The child fatigues quite easily but recovers just as readily. At 8 years of age, the smaller muscles begin to be used, though not too skillfully. Rapid improvement in manipulative skill and eye-hand coordination results in a surprisingly high level of dexterity.

By 11 years of age rapid muscular growth has begun, particularly in the girl. At 12 years of age a child attains a near-adult level of perfection in control of the shoulder, arm, and wrist

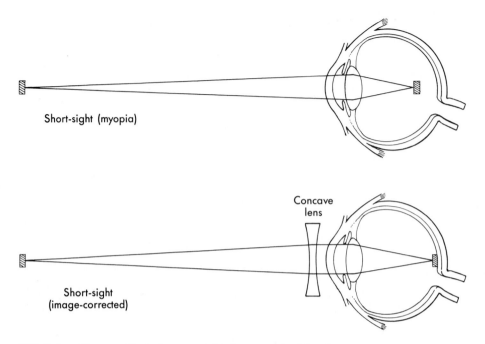

Short-sight (myopia)

Concave
lens

Short-sight
(image-corrected)

FIG. 4-4.   Diagrams illustrating nearsightedness and farsightedness.

muscles. Finger control is slower. Development of large muscle skills first and then small muscle skills is a sound practice.

Handedness becomes noticeable by the time a child enters school. Neurologically most persons are right-handed or left-handed. This preference is inherited; right-handedness is a dominant trait, and left-handedness is a simple recessive trait. About 7% of all males and 6% of all females are strongly left-handed. About 20% of the members of both sexes are mixed handed and can use either hand about equally well. The hand that is used more depends on training. These persons can be truly ambidextrous.

These early years of the schoolchild's life, coming between two periods of rapid change, are often termed the healthiest period of the entire human growth span. Children at this age have the lowest death rates and the lowest rates of serious illness of the entire society.

But children of this age group do have health problems. Their leading cause of death is accidents. A common example is the tendency to dash suddenly across the street. Certain forms of cancer, principally leukemia, constitute a major cause of death. The most common illnesses are episodes of infection causing respiratory illness and digestive upsets. Vaccines have been developed for many of the so-called childhood diseases, such as measles, mumps, and German measles, and have brought them under control.

In recent years health authorities have become concerned over the increasing use of cigarettes and marijuana by elementary school children. Community and social pressures to smoke have persisted, despite major efforts to inform children about the hazards of smoking. The tendency of children to experiment with drugs and alcoholic beverages has caused many school systems to strengthen and extend health education in the schools.

Preschool vision screening

EMERGING ISSUE The public health nurse/Health Department representative on the School-Community Health Council has spoken to the council about the department's dissatisfaction with its "lazy eye" (amblyopia) screening program. As she explained, the department's clinics are reaching only 10% of the children. Therefore the Health Department wishes to make a change. However, before instituting a new program, it is important to have the approval and support of the council.

Under the new plan proposed by the Health Department the parents would do the screening. After they had been given an orientation about the problem of ambylopia, each family would be provided with a "do-it-yourself" screening kit. A group of volunteers are also being organized—the "Lazy Eye, Ltd." This group will assist the parents as needed and will raise funds to help pay for the cost of materials and the follow-up care.

As a member of the Council you are asked to share your views on the proposal and to indicate your position relating to each of the statements listed below.

Please indicate whether you generally agree or disagree by placing a plus (+) or a minus (−) sign before each statement.

_____ 1. This is an important problem and I agree that we must take steps to ensure that all preschool children are screened.

_____ 2. If parents failed to cooperate in the department's clinic screening program, I'm not very optimistic about the prospects for success of a plan that puts even more responsibility on parents.

_____ 3. In my opinion, a plan that involves parents and a group of volunteer citizens working together with the local health department to protect the health of children should at least be given a trial period.

_____ 4. Since all children must have a physical examination before entering school, I would favor delaying the vision screening until the child enters kindergarten when the screening can be done by a health care professional.

_____ 5. I would be concerned about the validity and accuracy of screening done by lay persons and would be opposed to the plan.

_____ 6. I think we should first discuss this proposal with the county medical society before proceeding with the plan.

_____ If limited to a single choice, I would choose this number.

Although the emphasis of this chapter is on the child's physical growth and development, many emotional health problems have a direct and important effect on physical development and well-being. The child's adjustment to school; his or her fear of separation from parents; the effect of broken homes or incomplete families; and the tendency to become too involved in and stimulated by academic, athletic, and social activities are often sources of difficulties that affect both health and school progress.

PUBERTY AND ADOLESCENCE

With the exception of the growth period of infancy, the pubertal growth spurt, which precedes adolescence, is perhaps the most dramatic stage of human development. It is widely discussed, but a great deal of misunderstanding still continues about this phase of growth. *Puberty* marks the time in life when a person is first capable of sexual reproduction, whereas *adolescence* is designated as that period of transition between puberty and maturity. Researchers designate *pubescence* as the period extending from the first evidence of sexual maturation (breast development in girls and changes in the genitals of boys) to the onset of menstruation in girls and the production of spermatozoa in boys. Adolescence is defined as the period in a person's life extending from menstruation or spermatogenesis to the time of physical growth maturity. *Maturity* in this sense means the culmination of linear growth when the epiphyses have closed and the person has reached maximum height.

To appreciate the magnitude of the growth change that takes place during puberty, one should compare the amount of growth during this time with that of other periods. Fig. 4-5 depicts the velocity curves (amount of gain in height at various age levels) from infancy to

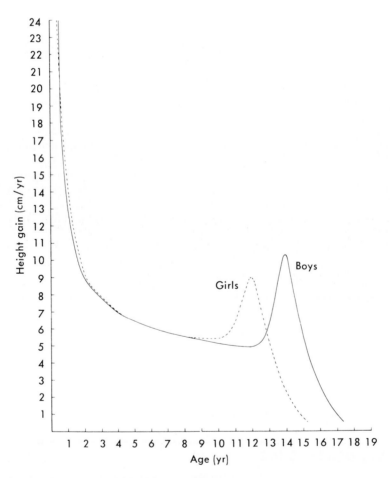

FIG. 4-5.   Typical individual velocity curves for supine length or height in boys and girls. These curves represent the velocity of the typical boy and girl at any given instant.

puberty. The amount of gain, though steady, gradually declines until the sharp upsurge takes place at puberty. This spurt of growth occurs at approximately 12 years of age for girls and 14 years for boys. Extensive study and research of the pubertal growth phenomena have revealed that more is involved than simply an abrupt change in linear growth. Instead, puberty consists in a complex sequence of interrelated events. The mechanisms, which are not fully understood, involve an orchestration of interrelationships between the endocrine gland system and the various other body systems.

The research by Dr. Li at the University of California (NIH, 1972) has helped to explain the role of the endocrine glands in growth. His studies have provided more information about the pituitary gland and its production of the human growth hormone (HGH), which causes an increase in size. In addition to the growth-promoting qualities of HGH, it also serves an important regulatory function in many metabolic processes. For example, the pituitary gland is believed to initiate the secretion of *gonadotropins,* after which the gonads or sex glands begin to secrete sex hormones. These sex hormones, in turn, promote such effects as protein synthesis, muscle development, bone growth, and the development of secondary sex characteristics (Fig. 4-6).

The female sex hormones *estrogen* and *progesterone* are responsible for inducing the menarche. According to Tanner (1973), the male sex hormone, testosterone, which is also stimulated by a hormone from the anterior pituitary gland, is responsible for much of the adolescent

FIG. 4-6.   The influence of the endocrine glands can be seen in the adolescent girl's development of secondary sex characteristics.

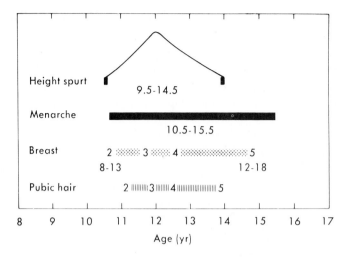

FIG. 4-7. Sequence of events of puberty in girls at various ages is diagrammed for the average child. The curve in the bar labeled "height spurt" represents the peak velocity of the spurt. The bars represent the beginning and completion of the events of puberty. Although the adolescent growth spurt for girls typically begins at 10.5 years of age and ends at 14 years, it can start as early as 9.5 years of age and end as late as 15 years. Similarly, menarche (the onset of menstruation) can come at any time between 10 and 16.5 years of age and tends to be a late event of puberty. Some girls begin to show breast development as early as 8 years of age and have completed it by 13 years; others may not begin it until 13 years and complete it at 18 years. First pubic hair appears after the beginning of breast development in two thirds of all girls.

growth spurt in boys. The presence of testosterone leads to the development of the male reproduction cell spermatozoa in the testes. This event of sexual maturation or spermatogenesis in the male usually occurs some 2 to 3 years after the onset of puberty.

Charts developed by Tanner (1966) (Figs. 4-7 and 4-8) from the Institute of Child Health in London illustrate the sequence of major events occurring at puberty for boys and girls. The symbols on the charts represent the typical ages at which these changes occur. For example, the G rating in Fig. 4-8 refers to maturational staging, with 5 representing adult level maturity. The timing and coordination of these various events, which include height gain, breast development, and menarche in girls and changes in the sex organs along with height gain in boys, demonstrate the interrelationship of growth and glandular functions discussed in Li's research.

On the basis of several longitudinal studies, researchers at the Harvard School of Public Health describe the variations in physical growth patterns as characteristic of "early" and "late" maturers. In Fig. 4-7 the concept of velocity curves (yearly increments in growth) is again used to illustrate the differences in the timing of the growth spurt among girls and boys. Although this dramatic increase usually occurs at 12 and 14 years of age, respectively, individual growth patterns may vary greatly from these norms. Tanner speaks of these variations as the individual's "tempo of growth." Variations are present at all ages; however, these differences are more dramatic during adolescence. For example, the range of chronologic ages within which menarche may normally fall is approximately 10 to 16½ years of age. For boys,

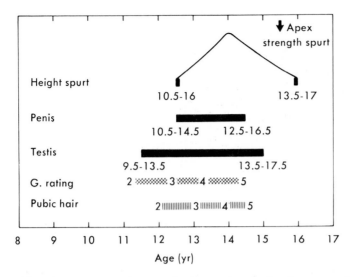

FIG. 4-8.   Sequence of events of puberty in boys is also shown at various ages for the average child. The adolescent growth spurt of boys can begin as early as 10.5 years of age or as late as 16 years and can end anywhere from 13.5 years of age to 17.5 years. Elongation of the penis can begin from 10.5 to 14.5 years of age and can end from 12.5 to 16.5 years. Growth of the testes can begin as early as 9.5 years of age or as late as 13.5 years and end at any time between 13.5 and 17 years of age.

the chronologic age when the growth of the penis begins may also vary widely, from 10½ to 14½ years of age. This means that some boys and girls have finished their pubescent growth before others of their same chronologic age have started (Fig. 4-9).

Because of these variations, growth authorities recommend the use of other measures in addition to chronologic age to make a more accurate assessment of maturity. Bone growth or skeletal age correlates much more closely with growth changes. In this regard, Tanner has developed a technique for the assessment of bone age or maturity (Fig. 4-10) that uses x-ray pictures of the bones of the hand and wrist. Successive changes in the shape and density of the margins of each of the ossification centers are illustrated. In Fig. 4-10, *b* to *h* illustrate the various stages of maturation of the first metatarsal bone of the foot. Bone development is traced from a tiny speck of calcium at stage *b* to the adult state of development or maturity at stage *h*.

Standard percentile curves have been developed so that a boy's or girl's bone age or degree of maturity can be determined by comparison of bone age with chronologic age (Marshall, 1977).

BONE-GROWTH PROBLEMS

Promoting healthy growth and development of children and youth calls for a special awareness of the bone-growth characteristics of this age group. As illustrated in Fig. 4-10, bone growth proceeds from the centers of ossification forming the shafts of the long bones and ulti-

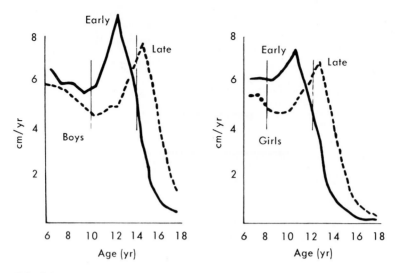

FIG. 4-9.   Annual increments in height of early and late maturing boys and girls (means of 20 in each group).

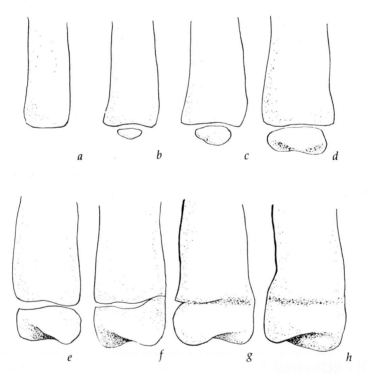

FIG. 4-10.   X-ray technique showing successive stages in the maturation of the first metatarsal bone. At stage *a* the calcium is not yet discernible. Beginning at stage *b* the successive stages show a gradual development of the bone to full maturity at stage *h*. Standards of bone development have been established showing stage of bone maturity or development.

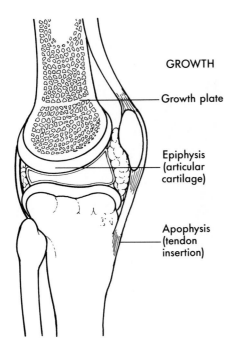

GROWTH

— Growth plate

Epiphysis
(articular
cartilage)

Apophysis
(tendon
insertion)

FIG. 4-11. Growth cartilage at three sites, side view diagram of knee (apophysis).

mately fusing with the secondary centers of ossification at the ends of the long bones. However, this area between the two centers of ossification where new bone growth is occurring presents the greatest potential for injury. The epiphyseal, or growth plate, area is composed of growing cartilage cells that are nourished by a network of blood vessels. Injury to the blood vessels and growth plate can interfere with nourishment of these cells, resulting in a disturbance of the normal growth process.

During this period of rapid growth the potential for handicapping injuries caused by stresses arising from vigorous physical activity or sports participation is a special concern of medical authorities. Without the aid of x-ray films it is very difficult to determine an individual's state of skeletal development and to know when a youngster may be at special risk of injury.

Medical authorities have distinguished between two types of trauma that can occur to the epiphyses, or growth plate area: (1) a traction type of injury, or (2) a pressure type of injury. An example of the traction type of injury is Osgood-Schlatter disease, which affects the tibial tuberosity, or apophysis, a bony projection just below the kneecap (patella). This is the location where the large thigh muscles (quadriceps) attach through the patellar tendon to the lower limb (Fig. 4-11). This injury causes the tibial tuberosity to become very tender and irritated. This condition usually occurs between 9 and 14 years of age. Although the danger of permanent growth injury may not be great, the person can suffer considerable pain and discomfort. Proper care may require special protective padding and restriction from all vigorous activity. Under conditions of excessive strain to the leg, a traumatic separation of the tibial tuberosity may occur.

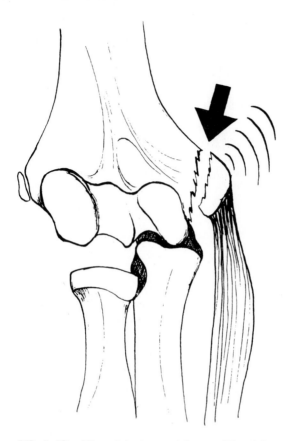

FIG. 4-12.   Elbow joint in an adolescent. The violent contraction of the flexor-pronator group of muscles to the forearm in the act of throwing causes a strain in the growth plate of the medial epicondylar epiphysis of the humerus, arrow. This is a traction epiphysis.

Scheuermann's disease is an example of the pressure or weight-bearing type of injury to the growth plate. This condition also occurs during the adolescent growth spurt between 12 and 17 years of age. In this instance pressure may cause a wedgelike deformity to one or more vertebrae of the spine, resulting in a rounding of the upper back, or kyphosis of the spine.

Two other conditions that are of special interest to school officials include Legg-Calvé-Perthes disease, a deformity of the hip joint area, and an injury that has become known as "Little Leaguer's elbow." Fig. 4-12 illustrates an epiphyseal separation occurring on the inner side of the elbow, or the medial epicondyle. The muscles to the lower arm are attached here. The separation is caused by a violent contraction of this muscle group during the act of throwing. Efforts to protect children from such injuries have led to modifications in the rules governing little league baseball such as restricting the amount of pitching and the throwing of curve balls by these young players (Larson, 1973).

Evidently the physiologic processes controlling the ossification and growth of bones are also rather closely related to the other events that occur during this spurt of growth. Early-maturing girls start the growth spurt at 9 years of age, whereas late-maturing girls start at 11 years. Early-maturing boys start at 11 years of age, and late-maturing boys at 13 years. In addition to the difference between early and late maturers of both sexes, there is also a difference in the amount of incremental gain or height increases. In each instance those entering the growth spurt earliest also achieve the greatest amount of gain. This would seem to indicate that those who enter this growth cycle first not only have an early advantage but also maintain their height advantage in later life. However, this is not always the case. Some late-maturing boys may have a longer growing period and eventually catch up with and in some instances achieve greater height than their age mates.

Because individual growth characteristics loom so important to the adolescent and his or her self-image, the condition of early or late maturity can have lasting personality effects. Since girls begin their growth spurt first, they may suddenly find themselves taller than boys in the same classroom and become very concerned about being "too tall." Boys, on the other hand, especially those who mature late, are greatly concerned about their lack of height and size. Boys are said to be at greater risk for personality problems than girls, since their changes in strength and size are correspondingly greater. Teachers need to understand the effects of these changes on students. Patterns of growth should be explained, as should the differences between male and female growth rates. Physicians and counselors can help to allay what, in most instances, is an unnecessary concern about growth. For those relatively few adolescents who have medically diagnosed growth problems, medical science has made great strides in treating growth abnormalities, so that even these boys and girls may be able to grow to heights similar to those of their peers.

Girls begin to taper off in motor performance at 15 years of age. Boys taper off at about 18 years of age. Although both will develop further skills after these ages, the rate of improvement will be much slower, and the maximum skill attained will not be appreciably higher. Biologic maturity is a stage at which motor skill approaches the maximum potential. The girl's maximum potential will be attained at about 20 years of age, and the boy's will be attained at about 23 years of age. Girls generally fall far below their potential skill, largely because of inadequate educational programs.

A question that is often posed is whether or not children today are bigger and taller than their ancestors? A frequently made observation, though not based on scientific data, is that today's college football and basketball players are much larger and taller than their predecessors. In this respect, the age-height-weight tables of some 25 years ago are now outdated. The scientifically based data that provide an answer to this question are drawn from what are called "secular-trend studies." Tanner (1978) cites such trend studies of English boys in which he compared the heights of boys in the mid-nineteenth century with those of English boys in 1965. These data indicate that the differences may result from the effects of environment and nutrition. Although today's youth tend to be taller and heavier than their predecessors, this may result from the differences in their rates of development and maturation rather than from true differences in height. For example, records based on nineteenth-century English working boys revealed that they continued their growth in height until well into their middle twenties.

By comparison, such boys would be shorter in height during their teens, but, because of their continued growth, they might eventually be as tall as the earlier maturing boys of the twentieth century. At the same time, there is little doubt that the advantages of superior medical care, nutrition, and environmental conditions have contributed to greater average heights and weights among the youth of today.

Researchers in the fields of growth and development and in early childhood education point to some of the skills and abilities that can be expected of the nursery school child. For example, most of these children are able to feed and dress themselves, with certain qualifications, of course, as teachers and parents of children of this age can attest. Tying shoelaces and donning heavy winter clothing present special problems. Most children have established bowel control by 3 years of age, but bladder control comes later. These behavior patterns respond to emotional pressures, and teachers working with preschool children must be alert to the fact that stresses may cause temporary loss of these controls and regression to previous levels of behavior. The adult's ability to handle these situations with sensitivity and understanding is of paramount importance to the child's satisfactory adjustment and continuing development.

MALE-FEMALE DIFFERENCES

One of the major outcomes of the civil rights movement of the 1960s was legal enforcement of the constitutional right of every person, regardless of race, age, sex, or religious preference, to receive fair and equal treatment, as well as the opportunity to participate fully in all aspects of American life. This has led to major changes in society and in the public school programs. In the past, girls were rarely given the same opportunity as boys to enter certain fields of study, to practice the professions, or to participate in certain activities included in interschool athletics. Many of these restrictions were based on misconceptions and stereotyped attitudes about female interests, mental and physical capacities, and athletic capabilities in particular. Now that these barriers are being removed, many high schools are giving girls an opportunity to participate in school athletics. However, the fact that few secondary schools have the budget, staff, or facilities to provide such an expanded program has, in numerous instances, forced girls to compete with boys "to make the team." Although this effort to give girls opportunities in athletics is commendable, a single, combined sports program for boys and girls cannot be justified. On the basis of their physical growth characteristics, such programs place girls at a distinct disadvantage.

Because girls have a 1- to 2-year maturational advantage over boys that lasts from infancy through childhood, many observers have reached the false conclusion that girls can compete favorably with boys in athletics. However, with puberty comes the emergence of the male-female sex differences in height, weight, strength, and speed. Several of these developing characteristics are highly correlated with success in sports activities. For example, boys have the advantage of greater size, both in height and in weight, and an inherited capacity for speed and endurance. Although the female's maturational advantages during childhood are well known, the fact that boys have a muscle cell advantage over girls is not generally appreciated. Studies have revealed that, as early as 3 weeks of age, boys already have a larger complement of muscle cells than girls have. This advantage continues throughout childhood, and adolescent growth increases the difference. By the time a girl has reached 10 years of age, she has undergone a fivefold increase in the number of muscle cells. However, at this stage, the girl's muscle growth has just about reached its maximum. For boys, however, the adolescent growth spurt means an increase in the number of muscle cells, possibly by as much as 14 times by 18 to 20 years of age.

Other well-known findings have established the fact that females have a greater proportion of fatty tissue to muscle cells than males have. Moreover, adolescent growth causes girls to develop an even greater proportion of fatty tissue.

Until 8 years of age, there is a slight difference between the basal metabolic rate (BMR) of boys and girls. From that age until 20 years, the BMR of both sexes is equal. From 20 years of age onward, a man's basal requirement is 10% greater than a woman's of the same height, weight, and age.

At about 9 years of age a radical change occurs in the rate of growth of boys and girls. This pronounced sex difference in growth is believed to be caused by the male's greater responsiveness to the effects of growth hormone at the tissue level. Boys evidence a more rapid cell multiplication in muscle tissue and in the epiphyseal plates relating to bone growth (Figs. 4-13 and 4-14). This change in the male is characterized by a remarkable increase in lean body mass and a correspondingly greater intake of calories and protein. Although the amount of fat tissue also increases in males during this period, it occurs at a lesser rate than it does for the female. It is believed that the hormone estrogen restricts the stimulating effect of the growth hormone in girls. Also, it is believed that the female responds differently to the effects of insulin, resulting in a greater increase in fat tissue (Fig. 4-15) (Grumbach, Grave, and Mayer, 1974).

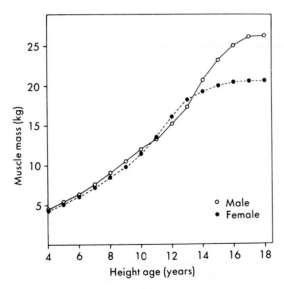

FIG. 4-13. Muscle mass is plotted against height age for boys and girls. Notice that muscle mass doubles in boys from 10 to 17 years of age.

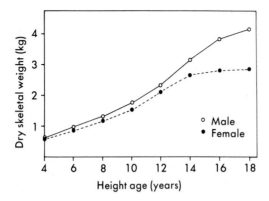

FIG. 4-14.   Garn's data (1970) show the growth of skeleton versus height age. Clearly the greater gain in body and muscle of the boy is associated with the greater gain in skeletal mass.

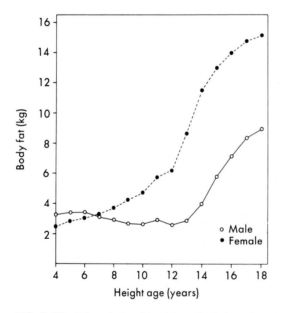

FIG. 4-15.   The relationship of fat to body length and the increasing fatness of boys and girls during the adolescent period are shown. The greater increase in fat tissue among girls is also demonstrated.

Boys not only possess greater amounts of muscle cells (which determine the development of strength and power), but they also develop larger hearts and lungs in relation to their size. This means that they develop higher systolic blood pressure and lower resting pulse rate, with a greater capacity for carrying oxygen in the blood. As a result, they have a greater capacity for neutralizing the waste products or lactic acid accumulating from physical exertion. As a consequence, boys recover from fatigue more quickly. The comparatively greater oxygen-carrying capacity of the blood of the male is a result of the greater number of red cells and hemoglobin present in the blood, caused by the presence of the male sex hormone *testosterone*.

Another difference reported by Tanner (1971) shows that boys develop larger forearms than girls do. This difference is undoubtedly reflected in the greater arm strength of boys.

As a direct result of the anatomic and physiologic differences that develop in the adolescent period, athletic ability increases greatly in boys during this period. The unusually gifted girl may be able to compete successfully with boys of her peer group, especially during childhood, but the male-female differences that develop during adolescence necessitate that public schools provide a separate program for average girls to allow them to develop athletic skills to their individual level of excellence.

However, with the recent developments in girls' athletics, new records and higher levels of performance from the older, more mature girls and adult women can be expected in the future. In fact, there are several examples of women athletes in their mid- to-late twenties competing successfully at world class competition levels in track and skating events.

Recent world-record performances in running the marathon suggest that the female may eventually equal or exceed the performance of the male in this event. These performances have led to speculation that sex differences such as weight and endurance may favor the female (Fig. 4-16).

FIG. 4-16.   World-class female athlete.

NATIONAL STANDARDS FOR GROWTH

The two factors of height and weight in the National Center for Health Statistics (NCHS) charts can be used as a practical growth profile for students. The charts show percentile distribution of boys and girls for height (in centimeters) by age and for weight (in kilograms) by age. These height and weight curves make it possible to compare the height and weight of an individual youth or group with that of all others in the United States who have the same characteristics. Children should be weighed without shoes and with sweater or jacket removed. Height is also measured with the shoes removed. As a minimum procedure, each child should be measured in September, January, and May. At each measuring period, the point, or child's location on the chart, is determined by the intersection of two lines formed by a vertical line extended from the base or age line and a horizontal line from the weight or height (stature) portions of the chart. After successive measurements over a period of 2 or 3 years have been recorded, curves of progress can be traced (Fig. 4-17).

The graphs outline six percentile levels: very tall, moderately tall, average, moderately short, short, and very short. The particular zone in which a child's height point falls indicates his or her position with reference to the heights of other children of the same age and sex. The same principle applies to the location of weight points. The height and weight points of most children fall in corresponding zones; for example, if the weight falls in the average zone (at the 50th percentile level), the height also falls in the average zone for height (at the 50th percentile level). The child is of average size in terms of both height and weight.

When a youngster's weight and height points do not fall in corresponding zones, two possible interpretations may explain the dissimilarity: (1) it may indicate natural slenderness or stockiness, or (2) it may reflect a poor quality of growth. A child with dissimilar height and weight percentile zones may need medical evaluation. Once the child is established in a particular growth zone, a generally consistent pattern of growth can be expected. Some variation from the pattern may occur, but such events should be carefully evaluated. It thus is apparent that the physical growth record can indicate possible health deficiencies, as well as portray normal growth progress.

The most common method used to measure overweight has been to compare the height and weight of a person with a table of standard weights. Ideal body weight has been defined as the 50th percentile level for age and sex. The formula for calculating ideal body weight (IBW) and then making a comparison between the actual weight and the standard is as follows:

(actual weight) divided by (ideal weight) $\times$ 100

For example, assume that John Smith, a 12-year-old sixth grader, weighs 99 pounds. To compare his weight with the 50th percentile or IBW standard, divide John's weight of 99 pounds by the IBW of 89 pounds. This equals 1.11 $\times$ 100, which equals 111%. Thus John is 11% overweight but still within the normal weight range.

The several percentile level standards included in the two figures (Fig. 4-18 and Fig. 4-19) provide a visual pattern for comparing an individual child's growth with his/her age and sex group peers. An individual child's growth pattern is likely to follow the more central or intermediate percentiles (25-50-75) typical of normal growth. However, a change in growth before pubescence that depicts a marked downward or upward trend should be carefully evaluated (Hamill et al., 1979).

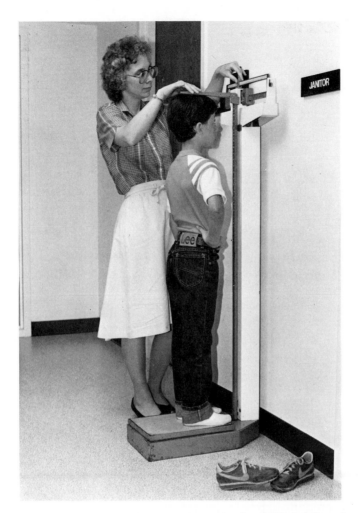

FIG. 4-17. Maintaining accurate records of a child's height and weight during the elementary school years serves as a general index of a child's general growth and development.

The widely used age-height-weight tables developed by the Metropolitan Life Insurance Co. have provided the standard for determining overweight. These standards are based on the morbidity and mortality data drawn from the company's life insurance experience. However, use of these tables in addition to age, height, and weight measures also requires that a judgment be made about the individual's type of body frame.

In an effort to develop a less complicated and a more convenient method of determing the unhealthy condition of overweight (obesity), a special consensus panel of experts was convened in 1985. An outgrowth of this conference was the recommendation to use a ponderosity index, now more commonly termed a body mass index (BMI). The formula for determining the index is as follows: weight in kilograms divided by height in meters squared. The National Center for Health Statistics for their National Health and Nutrition Examination Survey II

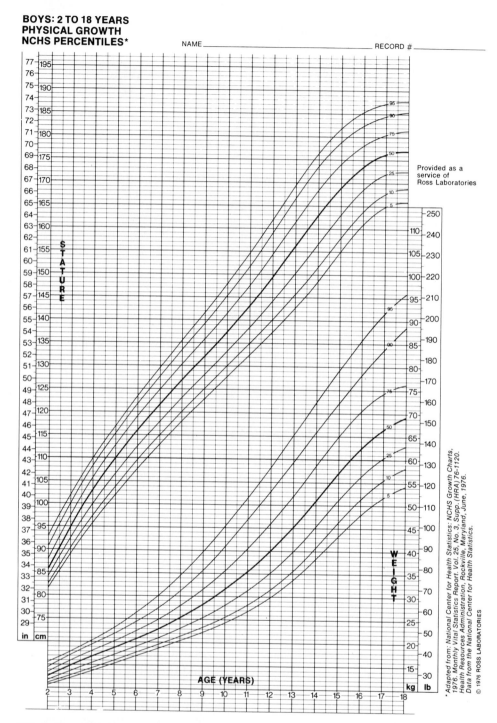

FIG. 4-18.   NCHS growth chart for boys.

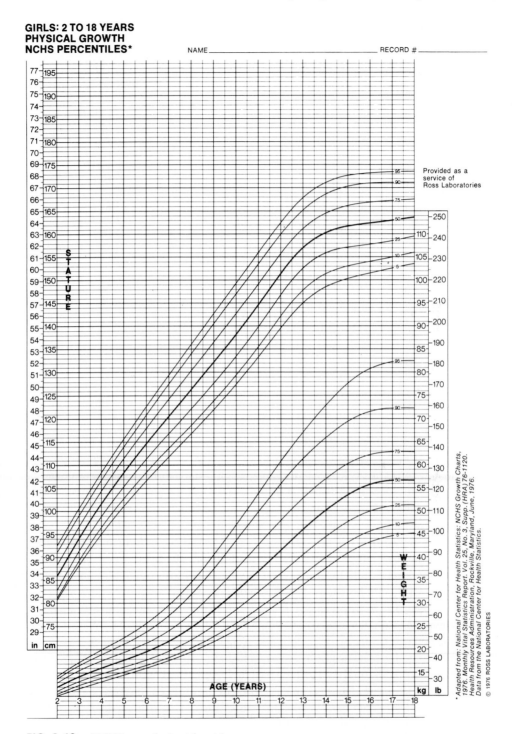

GIRLS: 2 TO 18 YEARS
PHYSICAL GROWTH
NCHS PERCENTILES*

FIG. 4-19.   NCHS growth chart for girls.

TABLE 4-1. School-age height, weight, BMIs, and percentile rankings for boys

Age	BMI (15th %tile)	Height (inches)	Weight (pounds) (50th %tile)	BMI (85th %tile)
5	14.3	43.3	41.1	16.8
6	14.5	45.7	45.5	17.5
7	14.5	47.9	50.3	17.3
8	14.7	50.0	55.7	18.7
9	14.9	52.0	61.9	18.6
10	15.6	54.1	69.2	20.4
11	15.6	56.4	78.1	22.5
12	16.3	58.9	87.5	21.6
13	16.7	61.6	98.9	22.2
14	17.7	66.2	111.7	23.1
15	18.3	66.5	124.8	23.0
16	19.0	68.3	136.6	25.4
17	18.7	69.4	145.9	25.6
18	19.4	69.3	151.5	26.0

$$BMI = \frac{\text{Weight in kilograms}}{(\text{Height in meters})^2} = \frac{45 \text{ kg}}{(1.50 \text{ m})^2} = \frac{45 \text{ kg}}{2.25} = 20$$

EXAMPLE : 12-yr-old boy—wt. 99 lb, ht. 59 in

Convert pounds to kilograms $\frac{99 \text{ lb}}{2.2} = 45 \text{ kg}$

Convert inches to meters $\frac{59 \text{ in}}{39.37} = 1.50 \text{ m}$

(1983) defined the criterion points for determining "overweight" as a BMI at the 85th percentile equal to or greater than 27.8 for men and 27.3 for women. These values correspond approximately with the 20% above desirable weight established by the Metropolian Life Insurance Co. In this regard, the National Institutes for Health Consensus Conference 1985 stated that an increase of 20% or more above desirable weight constitutes a health hazard (AMA, 1985).

The BMI has become widely accepted for use with adults. Combining height and weight into a single index has made it possible to measure height in relation to weight. Through use of the index, a judgment may also be made about whether a person has too much or too little weight in relation to height. Several investigators have shown that the index correlates positively with other health risks such as blood pressure.

Using the BMI, Tables 4-1 and 4-2 provide the additional data that are needed for a more complete evaluation of the school-age child's growth and development. These tables include the percentile rankings of height and weight for boys and girls ages 2 to 18 years. The 50th percentile for both height in centimeters and inches and weight in kilograms and pounds is provided. Additional data include BMI rankings at the 15th and 85th percentile levels for each age and sex group. These rankings represent the outer parameters or extremes for identifying the "underweight" or "overweight" student who is at risk, as determined by United States Public Health Service (NCHS, 1989).

TABLE 4-2.   School-age height, weight, BMIs, and percentile rankings for girls

Age	BMI (15th %tile)	Height (inches) (50th %tile)	Weight (pounds)	BMI (85th %tile)
5	14.0	42.7	38.8	17.2
6	14.1	45.1	42.9	17.3
7	14.1	47.5	48.5	17.8
8	14.4	49.8	54.6	18.1
9	15.0	52.0	62.6	19.6
10	15.1	54.5	71.6	20.9
11	15.7	57.0	81.3	21.6
12	16.3	59.6	91.4	22.7
13	16.5	62.9	101.4	23.2
14	17.8	63.2	110.6	24.5
15	17.9	63.5	118.1	22.6
16	18.6	63.9	123.0	25.4
17	18.9	64.2	124.7	25.5
18	19.1	64.5	124.6	25.5

$$BMI = \frac{\text{Weight in kilograms}}{(\text{Height in meters})^2} = \frac{44.5 \text{ kg}}{(1.57 \text{ m})^2} = \frac{44.5 \text{ kg}}{2.46} = 18$$

EXAMPLE: 14-yr-old girl—wt. 98 lb, ht. 62 in

Convert pounds to kilograms $\dfrac{98 \text{ lb}}{2.2} = 44.5 \text{ kg}$

Convert inches to meters $\dfrac{62 \text{ in}}{39.37} = 1.57 \text{ m}$

Data from recent national surveys show a marked increase in the prevalence of pediatric obesity in the United States. Reports issued by the Department of Health and Human Services and the President's Council on Physical Fitness show a 40% to 64% increase in the prevalence of obesity among school-age children in the last decade. Sports medicine specialists express a further concern about the nutritional status of school children. Practices associated with some of the youth sports in regard to weight loss can lead to growth retardation. Weight loss in such sports as wrestling, crew, gymnastics, and dance are problem areas. According to these physicians, eating disorders such as anorexia nervosa and bulimia are relatively common among young athletes participating in gymnastics and dance. Finally, problems associated with the use of anabolic steroids can cause a premature closing of the epiphisis (the growing ossification center of bones) (McKeag, 1991).

Benefits of figures and tables

When teachers and other school personnel have an adequate understanding of growth indices such as the NCHS growth charts, they become valuable tools of teaching and health screening. The growth of all children should be evaluated periodically, including at the time of their general health examination. A chart of the child's growth record becomes a valuable adjunct to the physican's examination. By keeping a record of the child's growth over a period of years, a much more accurate assessment of the child's ultimate development can be made.

SUMMARY

The growth and development process covering the period from prenatal period through adolescence is discussed. At its most fundamental level, cellular and intercellular, the quality of growth depends on a variety of factors, genetics, environment, and good nutrition. As many as 45 nutrients are involved in healthy growth. A diet composed of the essential proteins is needed for cell multiplication and growth, whereas carbohydrates and fats supply the calories or energy demands of growth. The concepts of growth and development are differentiated. Growth is a quantitative dimension meaning an increase in size, whereas development refers to complexity or maturity. Between infancy and adolescence the child's height, weight, and body grows and increases greatly in size. However, there is relatively little change in respect to the child's cranium or brain size but a great change in development or complexity of the brain and central nervous system. These concepts are also illustrated with reference to bone growth. During the pubertal growth spurt there is rapid bone growth. However, there may be great variance in the maturation of bones or skeletal age. Skeletal age is determined by the number of ossification centers and the amount of cartilage material between the bony structures. Children of the same age and weight may vary greatly in their skeletal-age maturity. All humans follow a predictable sequence of events in their growth and development. In some respects they are *like all* other human beings, yet in certain aspects they are unique or *unlike* all others.

The pubertal growth spurt, which ushers in the transition from childhood to adolescence and eventual adulthood, is the most dramatic period of growth and development in the life of the school-age child. Puberty marks the point in life when the human is capable of sexual reproduction. Pubescence, the period leading up to puberty, marks the interval between the first signs of sexual development, which is evident in girls as breast development and in boys as genital development and puberty itself. Typically girls begin this spurt of growth apparently 2 years earlier than boys, at 12 and 14 years of age, respectively.

This period of growth and the varying rates of adolescent development have been the subject of much study. With the advent of interscholastic athletics, competition for girls has raised the question of male and female differences. Although adolescent girls are now establishing physical achievement records far superior to those of the recent past, studies have shown that there are biologic differences in body structure, which means that adolescent boys typically have greater skeletal and muscle mass than girls, a finding that supports the principle of maintaining separate athletic programs for boys and girls. Charts depicting national standards for height and weight growth for boys and girls covering ages 2 to 18 are presented. Height and weights are graphically portrayed at six different levels for the very tall, moderately tall, average, moderately short, short, and very short. The concept of BMI is included, and its value in identifying the underweight and overweight child are presented.

Once a healthy child's pattern of growth is established, he or she should follow a relatively consistent pattern of growth. Variations from this pattern should be clinically evaluated.

GET INVOLVED!   Undergraduate students enrolled in health and health-related curriculums have a number of career options available to them. One such field is that of physical therapy, an important and growing profession. The American Physical Therapy Association guides the profession through its various levels of local, state, and national associations. As a member, one participates in chapter and section meetings, annual conferences, and workshops. These sessions are devoted to keeping members informed about the latest developments in education, practice, research, and legislation. The Physical Therapy Association has made a commitment to the recruiting and training of minority students. To this end, the national association has created an Office of Minority Affairs to assist students in locating schools, sources of financial aid, and the names of members who can assist students with further information.

Physical therapists work closely with physicians and other health care personnel in carrying out treatment plans for patients. This includes exercise programs and the application of treatment programs to aid the patients' rehabilitation.

The American Physical Therapy Association now encourages students to enter the profession at the postbaccalaureate level. With the growing status of the field, physical therapists are now given more freedom and regarded with greater esteem in the health care community. Twenty-four states now permit physical therapists to evaluate and treat patients without a physician's referral. The national association reports that there is 100% employment for graduates of accredited physical therapy programs.

For more information about this profession and its career opportunities, write to:

The American Physical Therapy Association
P.O. Box 37257
Washington, DC 20013

STUDY QUESTIONS

1. Define the terms *growth* and *development* and give an example of each to show how they differ.
2. Recent growth surveys indicate that certain groups may be nearing their growth potential, whereas others apparently have not yet reached their potential. What is the basis for these observations?
3. Explain how the concept of skeletal age is important to the planning of school programs.
4. What is the meaning of the terms *prematurity* and *growth retardation?* How does the physician distinguish between these conditions in the newborn infant?
5. Give an example of a health problem that is related to growth and developmental characteristics among the preschool age group, elementary school youngsters, and the adolescent age group.
6. Explain the sequence of events that takes place during the adolescent growth spurt for both girls and boys.
7. On the basis of growth and developmental characteristics, why should separate athletic programs be provided for boys and girls?
8. Assume that height and weight records kept on John,

a 12-year-old boy, during his first 6 years of school show that his growth curves for both height and weight have consistently followed the 50th percentile growth level for his age group. On this basis, project his height and weight at age 18.
9. Select a classmate to work with and take the following measurements: (a) height, (b) weight, (c) skinfold thickness, and (d) blood pressure. Also calculate the BMI for both. After recording the data, compare the measures with national standards.
10. State some of the principal health implications to be gained from monitoring the growth and development of children and youth: (a) potential for immediate health benefit, and (b) potential for long-range health benefit.

REFERENCES

Abma JC, Mott FL; Substance use and prenatal care during pregnancy among young women, *Fam Plann Perspect* 23(3):117, 1991.

Abel EL, Sokol RJ: Fetal alcohol syndrome is now leading cause of mental retardation, *Lancet* 2:1222, l986.

American Medical Association: Consensus panel addresses obesity question, *JAMA* 254:254, 1985.

Breckenridge ME, Murphy MN: *Growth and development of the young child,* ed 8, Philadelphia, 1969, WB Saunders.

Bresnahan K, et al: Prenatal cocaine use: impact on infants and mothers, *Pediatr Nurs* 17(2):123-129, 1991.

Collins MF, et al: Emerging development sequelae in the "normal" extremely low birth weight infant, *Pediatrics* 88(1):115, 1991.

Creswell WH, et al: A longitudinal study of adolescent health characteristics and behavioral risk indicators. In the 12th World Conference on Health Education, Dublin, Ireland, Shannon, September 1985, Irish Elsevier Printers.

Damon A: Secular trend in height and weight within old American families at Harvard, 1870-1965, *Am J Phys Anthropol* 29(1):45, 1968.

Gallagher JR: *Medical care of the adolescent,* New York, 1960, Appleton-Century-Crofts.

Gesell A, Ilg FL, Ames LB: *Youth—the years from ten to sixteen,* New York, 1956, Harper & Row.

Grumbach MM, Grave GD, Mayer FE, editors: *Control of the onset of puberty,* New York, 1974, John Wiley & Sons.

Hamill V, et al: Physical growth: National Center for Health Statistics Percentiles, *J Clin Nutr* 32:607-629, 1979.

Illingworth RS: *Development of the infant and young child,* ed 4, Baltimore, 1970, Williams & Wilkins.

Johnson F, Roche EAF, and Suranne C, editors: *Human physical growth and maturation: methodologies and factors,* New York 1980, Plenum Press. (Published in cooperation with NATO Scientific Affairs Bureau.)

Krogman WM: *Child growth,* Ann Arbor, Mich, 1972, The University of Michigan Press.

Larson RL: Physical activity and the growth and development of bones and joint structures. In Rarick G, editor: *Physical activity: human growth and development,* New York, 1973, Academic Press.

Marshall WA: *Human growth and its disorders,* New York, 1977, Academic Press.

McKeag DB: The role of exercise in children and adolescents, *Clin Sports Med* 10(1):117-130, 1991.

National Center for Health Statistics: Dietary intake and cardiovascular risk factors. Part I, Blood pressure correlate, United States 1971-75. Data from the national survey series 11, no. 226, Hyattsville, Md, 1983, US Department of Health, Education, and Welfare, Public Health Service, National Center for Health Statistics.

National Center for Health Statistics growth charts: 1976 monthly vital statistics report, US Department of Health, Education and Welfare (HRA) 76-1120, vol 25, no. 3 (suppl.), June 22, 1976.

National Institutes of Health: How children grow, Pub. No. (NIH)72-166, Bethesda, Md, 1972, US Department of Health, Education and Welfare, General Clinical Research Centers Branch, Division of Research Resources,

Neerhof MG, et al: Cocaine abuse during pregnancy: peripartum prevalence and perinatal outcome, *Am J Obstet Gynecol* 161:633-638, 1989.

NIAAA, Alcohol Alert Supplement, 1991, US Public Health Service, no. 13, PH. 297, four pages.

O'Neill DB, Micheli L J: Overuse injuries in the young athlete, *Clin Sports Med* 7(3):591-610, 1988.

Rarick GL, editor: *Physical activity: human growth and development,* New York, 1973, Academic Press.

Sinclair D: *Human growth after birth,* ed 3, London, 1978, Oxford University Press.

Smith DW, Bierman EL, Adkinson NW, editors: *The biologic ages of man: from conception through old age,* Philadelphia, 1978, WB Saunders.

Spitz HI, Rosecan JS: *Cocaine abuse: new directions in treatment and research,* New York, 1987, Bruner/Mazel.

Stuart HC, Prugh DG, editors: *The healthy child: his physical, psychological and social development,* Cambridge, Mass, 1960, Harvard University Press.

Tanner JM: Sequence, tempo, and individual variation in the growth and development of boys and girls aged twelve to sixteen, *Proc Am Acad Arts Sci* 100(4):904, 1971.

Tanner JM: Growing up, *Sci Am* 229:35, 1973.

Tanner JM: *Foetus into man: physical growth from conception to maturity,* London, 1978, Open Books Publishing.

Tanner JM, et al: *Textbook of pediatrics,* Edinburg, 1962, Churchill Livingston.

Thomas CL, editor: *Taber's cyclopedic medical dictionary,* Philadelphia, 1985, FA Davis.

Valadian I: The adolescent—his growth and development. In Proceedings of National Education Conference, November 2-4, 1971, US Department of Agriculture, Miscellaneous Pub. No. 1254, Washington, DC, 1973, US Government Printing Office.

Watson EH, Lowrey GH: *Growth and development of children,* ed 5, Chicago, 1967, Year Book Medical Publishers.

Psychosocial development

OVERVIEW

Just as the physical person grows and develops in sequential fashion, so does the psychosocial person. For today's teacher *psychosocial development* replaces the more simple notion of emotional development. This change acknowledges that the nonphysical development aspects are the products of a person's psychologic makeup and the continuing interaction of that person with society.

In this chapter the nonphysical aspects of normal growth are discussed from the perspective of a widely accepted theory of personality development and from a perspective of students' evolving sense of right and wrong: their moral development. The interaction of physical and psychosocial aspects of development is acknowledged.

Knowledge about intellectual and physical development, as well as psychosocial development, is vital to the teacher. Many physiologically mature young people have difficulty adjusting to their social environment. What commonly has been spoken of as mental health is the balance between emotional development, physical development, and the ability to interact with all aspects of the environment—now referred to as psychosocial development.

OBJECTIVES   After reading this chapter, the student should be able to:

1. Recognize various stages of psychosocial development
2. Outline the physiologic basis of emotions and illustrate how the physical and psychologic characteristics of a person interact
3. Describe a set of developmental tasks that represent psychosocial development among preschool children, school-age children, and adolescents
4. Identify the role of the autonomic nervous system and the endocrine system in psychosocial development
5. Using Erikson's "stages of man" theory, illustrate the conflicting pressures that young people express
6. Explain how young people develop a sense of right and wrong
7. Explain how peer pressure is an important element in psychosocial development but not necessarily a negative pressure
8. Recognize the value of the concept of in loco parentis in developing a school environment to support psychosocial development

Understanding various levels of psychosocial development enables a teacher to understand each child more fully. The informed teacher not only knows what to expect in emotional responses from children but is also able to interpret unusual social behavior in terms of psychosocial maturity.

PHYSICAL BASIS OF PSYCHOSOCIAL DEVELOPMENT

All overt human conduct arises from a physical source: the protoplasm of the body's cells. Each person possesses a particular constitutional endowment from which emotions arise. When stimuli from the external environment produce an emotional response, virtually all the body is involved, but two systems—the neural and the endocrine—play major roles. These systems function in all coordination and adjustment and are particularly involved in emotional responsiveness. The responses of the neural system are immediate and quick acting, whereas endocrine functions are slower.

A person is conscious of emotional states, which involve the cortex of the brain, where consciousness is located. Original external stimuli reach the cortex of the brain and are relayed to the thalamus, where autonomic impulses originate.

Autonomic nervous system

The autonomic system is particularly important in emotional responses. It is sometimes referred to as the vegetative system, since it maintains functions necessary to sustain life. This involuntary system has two divisions: the *sympathetic nervous system,* which speeds up action, and the *parasympathetic nervous system,* which has the opposite effect. All organs of the thoracic and abdominal cavities have a dual supply of autonomic nerves—sympathetics and parasympathetics—to maintain the balance of function. During emotional states these nerves are stimulated; at times the sympathetics arouse the organs, and at other times the parasympathetics reduce organ activity.

The brain's emotional center is in the thalamus, a large mass of gray matter located toward the center and base of the brain. It also is the area of the pain and temperature-regulating centers. That some people are emotionally highly responsive and others much less so is understandable in biologic terms. Sensitivity may be inherent in the nerve structure and may be further enhanced by particular endocrine influences. However, neither social conditioning nor conscious training should be discounted.

Endocrine nature of temperament

Generally temperament is regarded as the emotional mold distinguishing a person. Each person's endocrine endowment greatly affects his or her temperament. Most endocrine influences are rather subtle, but some manifestations are more definite. Irritability, fatigability, apathy, enthusiasm, depression, indifference, and aggressiveness are all understandable in terms of the endocrine system.

The term *endocrine type* presumes a great deal. Persons whose basic makeup is entirely the result of extreme endocrine malfunction are rare, but examples do exist. Persons with an overproduction of thyroxin (hyperthyroidism), in addition to a tendency to lose weight and be thin, are restless, energetic, active, impatient, easily upset, impulsive, and alert. At the other pole are persons with an underproduction of thyroxin (hypothyroidism). For these individuals it is an effort, almost, to live. They maintain a low level of functioning, react slowly, fatigue easily, are usually behind in everything, rarely are enthusiastic about anything, are not easily disturbed or upset, and are usually easygoing and easily pleased.

Most persons represent various intergrades of endocrine balances. A teacher must recognize that students react as they do, partly because of each student's particular biologic makeup. A wise teacher tries to understand students' conduct in terms of their basic constitutional makeup and the environment in which they live.

What motivates human conduct? What gives force and direction to what one does? Why does a person become angry or elated? Through what channels are emotions mediated? These are significant questions to all persons. They are of special importance to teachers, who, to be of the greatest value in guiding children in self-development, must understand why children act as they do (Fig. 5-1).

Human beings are biologically self-centered, self-interested, and selfish. Knowingly and unknowingly they seek self-gratification. These characteristics are principally biologic. Individuals respond physiologically to external threats in terms of survival, meaning to flee or to fight. As social creatures, however, human beings learn to ignore these biologic response patterns. Social learning and biologic urges are to varying degrees at odds, creating a tension often manifest as stress. When persons handle this tension well, it is seen by others as a mark of

FIG. 5-1.   Each student is unique, but each student also shares much in common with peers. The competent teacher recognizes differences and similarities, understands something of the reasons for these differences, and plans classroom activities accordingly.

maturity, but even handling tension "well" can affect physical health as manifested in stress-related diseases.

Children are born with certain physiologic needs, such as hunger, thirst, and pain. The infant's self is gratified by satisfying physiologic needs as hunger and thirst, by relieving pain, by being active, and by eliminating discomfort. If the infant is in pain, hungry, or restrained, he or she responds emotionally by exhibiting emotions of dissatisfaction or fear.

All through life, gratification of these physiologic patterns is a factor in a person's emotional responsiveness. However, as one matures emotionally, emotional control rises accordingly. Although teenaged children may not cry or show an infant's intense emotional responses, their responses differ when they are hungry from when they are not, or when they are active from when they are inactive.

The basic principles of psychosocial development are less well documented than those of physical development for two reasons. Historically, less attention has been paid to documenting the stages and phases of psychosocial growth than the stages of physical growth. Also, psychosocial development is exhibited in behaviors rather than in the structure of physical growth; therefore it has been more difficult to document and understand.

UNIVERSAL SOCIALLY CONDITIONED MOTIVES

Children become social beings and learn to obtain self-gratification through certain socially conditioned and universally accepted motives. All normal people want attention, affection, approval, praise, and security. They seek mastery, superiority, and achievement.

The exhibition of success and failure varies from person to person. Although all persons have much in common, each is unique, and therefore reactions to similar situations differ. Just as physical health was described earlier in terms of what is normal, so too can behavior based on psychosocial development be compared to a range of normal. Unlike the physical characteristics of health wherein the range of normal is essentially the same for all people, the range of normal behaviors varies greatly. Behaviors considered normal among the people who live in the Kalahari Desert of Africa, for example, may be considered abnormal if carried out in New York City. Similarly, some acceptable behaviors in New York City would likely be considered abnormal in an Eskimo village in Alaska.

Although psychosocial development has unique characteristics and is hard to judge in terms of normality, all people share similar experiences. Some groups, however, differ in certain experiences because they belong to different cultures and societies. The French, for example, share much in common with people from Greece, but each national group has certain special experiences because of their cultural heritage. Families in any culture share some experiences of their heritage, but within this cultural grouping all families remain unique. Of course, individuals within a family share certain experiences, but every individual in the family experiences events differently. This overlaying of similarities binds people together in cohesive groups, but the experiences make each person unique. The range of normal for psychosocial behavior is broad and is determined largely by the dominant cultural group in any given area (Fig. 5-2).

Although the character of every person is unique, there is basic agreement about important stages of psychosocial development in our society. It is acknowledged that growth of this

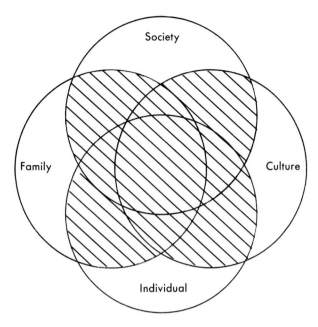

FIG. 5-2. Psychosocial development is influenced by the shared and unique characteristics of the individual, family, society, and cultural grouping.

type is an epigeneric process, that is, a process that builds one stage on another. These stages are often viewed as developmental tasks. Completion of these tasks not only represents health progress, but also is essential to complete subsequent tasks. These developmental tasks are described here in terms of the preschool child, the school-age child, and the adolescent. The family, the school, friends, and the community all contribute to the achievement of these tasks. Box 5-1 suggests the characteristics of a school that fosters psychosocial growth and the achievement of developmental tasks for young people.

Preschool child

Developmental tasks of the preschool child include:

1. Settling into a healthful daily routine of rest, activity, and elimination
2. Mastering good eating habits
3. Developing large- and small-muscle coordination and movement skills
4. Becoming a participating member of the family
5. Beginning to master impulses and conform to parental expectations
6. Developing healthy emotional responses for a wide variety of experiences
7. Communicating effectively with others
8. Developing the ability to respond correctly to potentially hazardous situations
9. Using initiative tempered by own conscience
10. Laying the foundation to understand one's place in relation to the physical and spiritual world

---

BOX
5-1
Characteristics of a school sensitive to the psychosocial needs of students

1. Regular inservices for teachers that (a) provide practical suggestions on assisting student psychosocial development, (b) develop teacher's sensitivity and skills in developing multicultural programs and opportunities, and (c) review crisis management techniques such as how to handle reports of suggested suicide and assisting students who have experienced a personal or family crisis
2. Close working relationship between teachers and the school's counseling staff
3. Close working relationship between school counseling staff and community agencies that provide support services for students and families
4. Crisis management plan in place for such events as the death of a student or teacher
5. A system that is known and trusted by students for reporting such events as discrimination, assault, physical abuse, rape, and alcohol or other drug use
6. A valued student assistance program
7. A range of student support groups with opportunities for others to develop; a school administration that allows the allocation of teacher time to assist student support group activities
8. A plan for assisting students who have been absent from school for special needs such as injury rehabilitation, pregnancy, alcohol and other drug treatment, and study abroad to be reintegrated into all school activities
9. Widespread knowledge of and easy access to crisis hotlines and special emergency services
10. A policy responsive to faculty needs: faculty sick leave and leave for personal needs and crises; the encouragement at faculty support groups; the encouragement of special interest groups among the faculty; support for study leave and special events

---

Teachers generally expect children to have achieved these tasks before first grade. Preschool and kindergarten can contribute greatly to their mastery. Because psychosocial development involves interaction with others, the increased social contact in school can help children achieve these tasks. Social contact alone, however, does not necessarily contribute to the developmental achievement of these tasks. The role of the skilled and understanding teacher is important and, outside the family, represents the most constructive monitor to ensure adequate psychosocial development.

School-age child

Developmental tasks of the school-age child include:

1. Mastering basic fundamental skills and a rational approach for problem solving
2. Developing concepts and reasoning abilities for everyday adult living
3. Mastering age-appropriate physical and self-care skills
4. Developing a socially accepted understanding of money: how to get it, how to spend it, and how to save it
5. Assuming an active, responsible, cooperative role within the family
6. Relating effectively to peers and other adults outside the family by making and keeping friends
7. Handling feelings, emotions, and impulses appropriately
8. Learning age-appropriate sex behaviors and adjusting to prepubertal body changes
9. Developing self-respect for one's own behavior and individuality

FIG. 5-3.   The accomplishment of each of a series of developmental tasks is greatly facilitated by the opportunity to interact with others, to learn how they do things, and to experiment personally with a variety of ways of doing things.

10. Developing loyalties to religion, culture, morale values, and social institutions
11. Accepting the eternal realties of birth, death, and infinity

Developing skills to master each of these increasingly complex tasks, students grow in emotional, psychosocial maturity. Many of the skills have clear health implications beyond those related to simple psychosocial development. These school-age tasks compare with many things taught in health classes today. As students gain the ability to respond to others and build a feeling of self-worth, it becomes less difficult to teach young people to value their own bodies. It is then possible to teach students to avoid risky health-related situations such as illicit drug usage, unnecessary risk taking, and promiscuous sex (Fig. 5-3).

Adolescent

Developmental tasks of the adolescent include:
1. Accepting one's changing body and learning to use it effectively
2. Achieving a satisfying role as a woman or a man
3. Finding oneself as a member of one's own generation and establishing mature relations with peers
4. Achieving emotional independence from parents and other adults
5. Selecting and preparing for an occupation and economic independence
6. Developing intellectual skills and social sensitivities necessary for civic competence
7. Developing a workable philosophy of life that makes sense in today's world

Adolescence is not a stage bounded by specific age limits. It takes some longer than others, and unless preceded by adequate achievement of earlier developmental tasks, it may be an especially difficult period. Health-related activities for adolescents relate to these tasks in several ways. Education can address the principal public health problems of adolescence, that is, accidents and associated factors of substance abuse and risk-taking behavior; but unless this learning occurs concomitantly with appropriate psychosocial development, students will not be able to act on the basis of their knowledge. It is very difficult, for example, for a student who lacks an adequate self-concept to deal with social or peer pressures to participate in certain high-risk behaviors.

STAGES OF DEVELOPMENT

A different way to view the psychosocial development of the school-age child is through the eight stages described by Erikson (1963). These stages are as follows:

1. Trust vs. mistrust
2. Autonomy vs. shame and doubt
3. Initiative vs. guilt
4. Industry vs. inferiority
5. Identity vs. identity confusion
6. Intimacy vs. isolation
7. Generativity vs. stagnation
8. Integrity vs. despair

Erikson identifies these stages as characteristic of a person's life span. Clearly stages 3 to 5 pertain to school-age children and youth.

The *initiative* vs. *guilt* stage is characterized by the tremendous energy, opportunity, and action of childhood contrasted to defeatism, anger, and the feeling of responsibility for things he or she can't control. Encouragement, a chance to experiment, and opportunity foster initiative, whereas excessive restrictions or excessive expectations may encourage guilt. In the early stages of childhood, young people experience both of these pressures. For preschool and early-school children the mastery of this stage occurs at the same time they are moving away from solitary patterns of play toward parallel and cooperative patterns of play. Children are also beginning to realize that there are others, besides the family, who provide models to learn from and imitate. Also occurring at this time is the rapid development of language with all its accompanying advantages. Vocabulary increases from about 90 words at age 3 to 2000 words at age 5, thus providing greatly increased communication power.

Industry vs. *inferiority* represents the focus of energy to solve a particular problem versus a feeling of inferiority, a sense of not doing things well enough or not finishing tasks. Neither of these feelings may bear any resemblance to actual competency. Feelings of inferiority may override actual achievement.

Involvement in constructive activities that can be completed and acknowledged provides clear rewards for the sense of industry and combats feelings of inferiority. This stage occurs as the school becomes an increasingly important part of a young person's life, and there is a distinct change in the nature of family relationships. Establishing friends and friendship groups is a way to deal with inferiority and an important step in establishing independence from the family. Friends can assist one another with the difficulties of development. The loner and the social isolate may find this time especially difficult. However, such persons may be known to the teacher, who with skill and patience can help such students cope with any inferiority feelings and capitalize on their energy for creative industry.

Identity vs. *identity confusion* is usually a characteristic of adolescence. The onset of adolescence is associated with the physiologic changes that accompany the beginning of sexual maturity. For girls this is initiated by *menarche,* or the onset of menstruation, beginning at about 10 to 11 years of age with development continuing for about 3 years. For boys development toward sexual maturity begins at about 12 years of age and usually continues for a 4-year period. The beginning of adolescence is marked by physiologic signs, but its ending is less clear.

The rapid growth of adolescents frequently provokes feelings of awkwardness, and new roles often create a sense of identity confusion. Young people respond by trying to emulate different roles, seeking a zone of comfort. Even apparently mature young people may revert to childlike behavior just as they may assume clear adult roles. They may also emulate one adult role and then another. The subsequent reactions of others to these roles and their own desires to be "grown up" leads to a degree of role confusion. Who am I? Why am I different? What do I want to be like? Can I be like I want to be? These are all questions to be dealt with in establishing personal identity.

Conflict with parents is frequent. Parents have a range of expectations, and the role experimentation of adolescents frequently exceeds the range of tolerance established consciously or unconsciously by parents. Young persons seek support and reinforcement in the various roles they try. The degree of reinforcement received encourages the acceptance of one role over another and therefore is an important force in shaping adolescent behavior. Reinforcement comes from many sources—parents, teachers, and peers; and in fact the most appropriate behaviors may not always be reinforced.

Responding to young people in various stages of development is a challenge. Teachers need to understand reasons for individual differences and be skilled at responding to the needs of different students. The organization and administrative structure of the school encourages teachers with this difficult task. Box 5-1 lists a series of school characteristics that illustrate how schools can be responsive to the changing needs of students. Aspects of this list are discussed in detail in subsequent chapters.

MORAL DEVELOPMENT

While physiologic and psychosocial changes are taking place, so too is a developing sense of what is right and what is wrong. Kohlberg (1964) has described moral development as related in part to cognitive development. In the early years, from ages 4 to 10, Kohlberg suggests that morality is based on recognition of an action's physical consequences. Right or wrong is defined by punishment. The presence of the threat of punishment indicates a wrong. This is a premoral or preconventional stage of development in Kohlberg's typology.

From about 10 years of age there develops what Kohlberg calls conventional morality. In this stage individuals are pressured to "obey the rules" by the expectations of others and desire to conform out of a sense of duty and respect. This is the level at which the majority of the population operates most of their lives. However, in late adolescence some develop what has been called "postconventional morality."

Postconventional morality operates apart from the pressures to conform to the will of others and represents the development of autonomous moral principles based on an individual's unique experiences. This postconventional morality is linked with the development of cognitive knowledge, past experience, and reasoning ability. Only a small proportion of the popu-

BOX
5-2

Promotion of sound psychosocial development

Teachers and school administration working together provide an environment that supports healthy psychosocial development. Note that the box on page 000 highlights actions that result mostly from administrative decisions and actions; this box shows actions that resulted from teachers' actions that could occur without administrative or policy actions.

A school promotes sound psychosocial development when:

1. Its buildings and facilities reflect pride and concern for the welfare of students and staff.
2. Faculty recognize and promote the contribution that all cultures can make.
3. Teachers use praise rather than punishment.
4. Teachers clearly communicate their expectations of success for all students.
5. Good communication is a priority for students, teachers, and administrators.
6. Teachers emphasize the need to learn to cooperate.
7. Faculty and staff share and accept responsibility for planning and discipline.
8. The life of the school and the life of the community are closely integrated through classroom activities.
9. Subjects, materials, and activities are selected on the basis of interest and aptitude rather than gender.

lation operates at the postconventional level of moral development. They are free of the preconceived constraints of others' expectations and therefore often make significant contributions to society. They dare to break barriers and to lead and experiment, and as a result society often benefits.

In the school years young people break free from the family, develop physiologically, develop a sense of identity, and become moral beings at the same time that they attempt to master the cognitive and affective challenges of schooling. From a psychosocial perspective this is a turbulent period. Many changes take place within each individual, and the individual also lives in a changing environment. The family is changing; social conflict within the community is unsettling; and such things as global tensions cannot be forgotten, for each indirectly affects the developing student. Teachers, individually and collectively, have an opportunity to help students through this period. Box 5-2 lists characteristics that support sound psychosocial development and result from teachers' actions.

PEER PRESSURE

Peer pressure and how students react to it indicate something about psychosocial development. Similarly, how well a teacher understands peer pressure determines how well he or she can capture some of its energy and use it to positive ends.

Conventional wisdom too frequently suggests that peer pressure is the base of most teenaged problems and there is little that can be done about it. The concept of peer pressure makes an excellent generic whipping boy to blame for so many failures to "improve" adolescents' behavior.

Peer pressure is not limited to adolescents: it is a phenomenon all people experience. However, for adolescents who are seeking an identity of their own and developing an adequate self-concept, peer pressure is a difficult force to deal with. Young people respond variously to the pressures of others; sometimes they seek to belong and to be like others, but at other times they contradict pressures, seeking to stand alone, testing possible identity roles. Understanding how adolescents interpret and respond to pressures applied by others is critical for teachers who work with young people. The term *peer pressure* oversimplifies a complex process.

Peer pressure is often considered a single force where one youngster is encouraged to do something by others. Careful analysis, however, indicates that this is not the case. Although peer pressure is discussed as a single force, it is in reality a combination of forces. These forces may appear singular in effect, but to consider them as a single entity in planning health education and school health programs overlooks several options. It is well accepted today that peers, media, and parents are the major pressures seen by young people. Parental and media messages present an environmental backdrop against which young people interpret their peers' expectations.

The tendency to see peer pressure as overt acts to coerce one individual to comply with the will of others is only one perspective of this phenomenon. Another perspective is more subtle. It involves pressures presented as others' expectations to which young people respond. All persons, for example, seek recognition; therefore they interpret the expectations of others and act so that they will receive recognition. Adolescents in particular seek to appear "grown up" and to be like adults, and so they emulate adult images and models. Young people also report that there is significant pressure to have fun, but frequently the role of fun overlaps the role of risk-taking behavior, sometimes with unfortunate consequences.

It is important to recognize therefore that peer pressure is in reality a perceptual issue. Peer pressure results from perceptions that others want a person to act in a particular way. Perceptions result from messages received, and like other messages, their meaning is determined by the receiver, not the sender. Adolescents, however, do not have much experience in interpreting these messages. Many adults also inappropriately determine the perception of pressures and have difficulty in dealing with them. In the health area, a critical way to help young people deal with the perceptions of others is to ensure that they have adequate factual knowledge to use in interpreting perceptions. There is good evidence that young people can be significantly helped in this area. For example, Martin and Duryea (1981) report that junior and senior high school students consistently overestimate the proportion of their peers, older adolescents, and teachers who smoke cigarettes. Because adolescents seek to identify a role for themselves and want to be like the majority of people, this misinterpretation encourages them to smoke. The reality is that less than half of the population smokes, and to be like the majority, one need not smoke.

The environment also provides a large number of perceptual cues important to young people passing through adolescence and to which health personnel must be sensitive. For example, the media present messages that imply ways to have fun, establish individuality, establish sex roles, and appear mature, successful, and grown up. The media also present a wide variety of messages that are not health enhancing. Helping young people cope with so many conflicting messages present in their environment is an important contribution to their psychosocial development.

Reducing cigarette sales to minors

EMERGING ISSUE As an employee of the local health department, you have been appointed by the health officer to serve on the Community Adolescent Health Council. A member of the Council has expressed concern about the extent of teenage smoking. She makes a forceful case, citing research that shows that most smokers begin the habit during their teenage years. In addition, she points out that well over $1 billion worth of cigarettes are sold illegally each year. There is general recognition on the part of the Council that high school students can easily obtain cigarettes, despite local laws prohibiting the sale of cigarettes to minors.

After extended discussions and several meetings, a subcommittee of the Council proposes that a public relations/information campaign be undertaken. According to this plan, each store manager in the community would be personally contacted to enlist his or her cooperation in banning tobacco sales to teenagers. A second phase of the plan would involve both teenagers and the police. In this follow-up, the teenagers in effect would test the system to see whether the ban on tobacco sales is working. The police would be informed of the plan to enable the teenagers to carry out the follow-up.

Please indicate whether you generally agree or disagree by placing a plus (+) or a minus (−) sign before each statement.

_____ 1. I like the idea of personally contacting the merchants and I believe they would be willing to cooperate.

_____ 2. I like this approach because I believe the merchants need more support in enforcing what I consider to be a difficult law.

_____ 3. I have doubts about the plan because it puts the merchant in the difficult position of limiting his own profits.

_____ 4. I would like the plan better if it involved a stronger cooperative approach between police and merchants.

_____ 5. As presented, I think the plan is incomplete and needs more emphasis on preventive education.

_____ 6. I have serious reservations about the ethics of this approach.

_____ 7. I am concerned that in the long term the council's relationship with the business community will be jeopardized.

_____ If limited to a single choice, I would choose this number.

REFERENCE
Altman D G, et al: Sustained effects of an educational program to reduce sales of cigarettes to minors, *Am J Public Health* 8(7):891, 1991.

Role models in person and in discussion are also critically important. If adulthood is not realistically described and presented in the educational process, the idealized images of the mass media may create unrealistic expectations in adolescents.

Because peer pressure is essentially a conforming force, psychosocial development must involve the establishment of an adequate self-concept and the achievement of developmental tasks so that a balance can be struck between the conformity of society and individuals' needs and responsibilities. Later, this text describes educational programs that provide ways for the teacher to help young people in a critical stage of psychosocial development deal with peer pressure in the interest of their personal health.

ADAPTATION

Just as adaptation is a critical component of health, so too is it a critical element in psychosocial well-being. The environment includes physical dimensions, as well as other people, to which individuals need to adapt. At the same time, individuals adapt to the idiosyncratic changes occurring within themselves as developing individuals. The school nurse and health teacher must help students to recognize that, although they are unique persons, they are also like most others. However, this should not imply that each student is able to survive these times alone just by knowing others are going through a similar experience. The process of healthy psychosocial development can be facilitated by conscious efforts to adapt the environment, both physical and social. In the school environment, for example, teaching stress-coping skills as a part of physical education or health classes can provide an invaluable skill. Teachers can coordinate weekly tests so that all are not always given on Fridays. Pleasant work and study environments and judicious use of colors and textures can improve the "spirit" of the school.

The establishment of clear and consistent codes of behavior and discipline clearly delineates expectations and removes one more uncertainty. Within clear discipline guidelines "space" for social experimentation will facilitate adolescents' need to try different roles in establishing self-identity. This means teachers should expect change in their students. Unfortunately, schools and school personnel sometimes have a tendency to "type" students and may not reinforce positive changes.

Physical health is clearly visible, and any deviations are usually visible to the teacher. Teachers are accustomed to dealing with physical health problems and in the main do an adequate job of handling them. Mental health problems and difficulties in psychosocial development, on the other hand, are less noticeable unless they are extreme.

The fact that suicide and homicide rank third and fourth as causes of adolescent death illustrates the significance of psychosocial issues (see Fig. 1-2). Abuse of alcohol and drugs, fatal automobile accidents, and unwanted teenage pregnancy all are manifestations of difficulty with psychosocial development.

Most schools have counseling services, but too often the organization of health services within a school may not recognize student health as a total concept. One way to assess how well the school has accepted health as a central issue in education is to check the organizational pattern of academic services, health services, and counseling services. Is there provision for a regular review of students who experience educational difficulty by a team of academic personnel, the school nurse, and the school counselor, or are students referred from one to another of these specialists?

The necessity of interaction between physical health, psychosocial development, and academic performance is clear. A school organization should develop some formal opportunity for records of students with problems to be reviewed by an interdisciplinary team (i.e., teachers, physicians or nurses, and counselors) representing the three initial aspects of education, physical growth, and psychosocial development. The student must be reviewed as a whole to identify how the school can be most effective.

The school in loco parentis

Establishing an ideal environment to nurture psychosocial development is not easy. Schools traditionally struggle with issues of class size, discipline, behavioral and academic expectations, and student-teacher relations as they seek an ideal mix to promote student well-being. One approach in clarifying the school's policy in support of psychosocial development is to recall the in loco parentis role and take a lesson from the principle of the value of clear "parental" guidelines.

In determining what these guidelines should be, it is useful to review what young people feel about parents and schools. Although much has been written about this topic, we will only cite data from a Minnesota study of 37,000 seventh- to twelfth-grade students. Of these students in 86 different school districts, only 41% thought that "school people" cared about them. Of this same group of young people, 90% thought "adults" cared about them. Only 65% reported their parents cared about their feelings, however, and only 50% said their parents paid attention to them. Less than half (45%) of this sample of students believed that their parents understood them and only 45% reported having fun with their parents.

If school and parents are not seen as caring, then schools in their "in loco parentis" role and parents in their traditional role may want to assess the reasons for this perception. This reassessment can be guided by considerable literature on parenting. This literature suggests a complex of factors that can be characterized as including warmth, democracy, and specific and reasonably high expectations.

Baumrind (1987) describes these homes as authoritative: not to be confused with "authoritarian." Authoritative parents embrace traditional values but are not punitive or authoritarian. Parents tend to be more demanding than lenient and more responsive to their children. Authoritative parents state their expectations and values clearly and expect respect and a good degree of conformity. At the same time, they are supportive, loving, and provide a stimulating and challenging environment for their families (Fig. 5-4).

Adolescents who grow up in homes that are described as authoritative score higher on tests of psychologic development that include such measures as self-image, ability to relate socially with others, and ablity to make independent decisions.

Authoritative parents focus on issues and not personalities and promote opportunities for their young people to express their disagreement, encouraging them to take an active role in

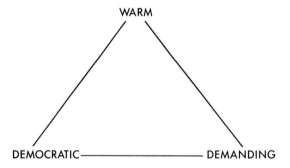

FIG. 5-4.   Authoritative model for psychosocial development. Parenting literature suggests that families that exhibit warmth toward their children have realistically high expectations, allow a degree of participation in decision making, and foster psychosocial development. Schools, as well as in loco parentis agencies, can use this model to create environments that foster psychosocial development.

important family debate and decision making. These parents differ from authoritarian parents who emphasize rigid social controls and absolute authority and show little or no tolerance for dissent.

If these are the conclusions of the literature on parenting styles, then the question is how can a school in its "in loco parentis" role be "warm," "democratic," and "demanding?"

Warmth can be both a physical and a psychologic state. In a physical sense, warmth is portrayed by the physical environment in a number of ways. Perhaps the simplest way for a school to show warmth in its physical environment is to emphasize the role of the students. Posters, exhibits, displays of class work, awards, and plaques are useful indicators of a student-centered school environment. Students showing respect for teachers and teachers deserving that respect suggest warmth. Teachers knowing students by name, speaking to students outside of class, and participating in activities with students add a sense of warmth. Schools that value their multicultural nature are warm schools.

Democracy does not mean that students have an equal vote. Teachers are in charge. Democracy does imply an informed citizenry, however. Students deserve to know why things are the way they are or why certain decisions were made. Understanding and accepting decisions can be facilitated by discussion and debate. Occasionally decisions may be revised as a result of this discussion. Involvement, however, is the critical element in establishing warmth and respect.

Demands affect performance. Within reason, higher demands generate higher quality in performance. Demands may be academic and should be rewarded. Demands may also be behavioral and discipline related and may involve negative rewards (punishment). In either case, the demands, better called expectations, will only be effective if they are clearly understood. What a student needs to know to pass a course or get an A should be clear. Behavioral expectations should also be clear, as should the consequences of not meeting these expectations. The consequences of good behavior or bad should be swift in appearing. Just as an exam should be graded quickly and the grade made known to the student, so should the penalty for inappropriate behavior be swift and exactly as expected.

A school with an environment that reflects warmth, democratic values, and clear and demanding expectations provides a positive environment for psychosocial development. Schools, as in loco parentis agencies, can use this model to create environments that also foster psychosocial development.

SUMMARY

Physical growth and development are easily observed. Psychosocial development can be determined only by observation of behaviors or the consequences of behavior. The challenge to school personnel is to interpret an ever-changing scene filled with rapidly growing young people and still be able to identify students who may need special assistance.

A good school health program exhibits sensitivity to the physical well-being of students. An excellent school health program shows the same sensitivity to the psychosocial needs of its students. This includes knowing the psychosocial skills that are normal for preschool, elementary, intermediate, and adolescent youngsters. All school activities should be geared to helping students develop these psychosocial skills. The challenge is to keep the student's total development in perspective. A math teacher who sees students as junior computers and a coach who emphasizes sports as total commitment are examples of failures to recognize the principles presented in this chapter.

It is important to remember that all development occurs in a social environment, a community. Therefore the psychosocial environment within a school community is important. Developing a supportive environment and helping students understand their place in this environment so that they can develop a sense of self-worth and skills to interact with others facilitates psychosocial development and is a vital part of the school's total health program.

GET INVOLVED!

With the increasing importance of health and safety protection for high school and college athletes, the field of athletic training provides an opportunity for an exciting and rewarding professional career. An important requirement for becoming an athletic trainer is a sincere interest in athletics and the well-being of the athlete. Undergraduate preparation for athletic training includes course work in prevention and evaluation of athletic injuries and illnesses, first aid and emergency care, therapeutic modalities, and many of the courses similar to related fields such as health education and physical education or kinesiology.

The certified athletic trainer should give serious thought to becoming a member of his or her state and national athletic trainers' association. The National Athletic Trainers' Association, Inc. (NATA) is dedicated to the advancement, encouragement, and improvement of the athletic training profession.

Both the national organization and its state affiliates offer certification and continuing education programs to ensure that members maintain high standards of professional practice. In addition to the state and national athletic training associations, the national organization is composed of 10 districts or regional directors and secretaries who carry out much of the association's business.

Important professional service provided by NATA and the district offices include career information, certification, grants and scholarships, membership, placement, and professional and continuing education.

For membership information, write to:
Membership Committee
National Athletic Trainers' Association, Inc.
2952 Stemmons St., Suite 200
Dallas, TX 75247

STUDY QUESTIONS

1. Why is psychosocial development a more appropriate title than mental development?
2. If all behavior has a physiologic basis, what is the difference between the sympathetic and parasympathetic nervous systems and how do they offset behavior?
3. What role does the endocrine system play in behavior?
4. If all behavior is biologically based, what distinguishes the human species from other species?
5. How is it that a person can be said to be part of a social unit yet at the same time be a unique being?
6. Outline the principal developmental tasks that should be achieved by (a) preschool children, (b) school-age children, and (c) adolescents.
7. Which factor makes it more difficult to define "normal" psychosocial development compared with normal physical development?
8. In which ways are Erikson's stages of development useful in helping school health personnel deal with students?

9. The idea of teaching morals or moral education is an especially controversial topic, but why is it important for teachers to understand how the ability to make moral decisions is related to cognitive development?
10. In which ways can peer pressure be seen as a positive force for school health personnel?
11. Identify some important health problems that may result from poor psychosocial development.
12. How can a health teacher assist students in psychosocial development?

REFERENCES

Berkovitz IH: *The role of schools in child, adolescent, and youth suicide prevention,* New York, 1985, Springer Publishing.

Capuzzi C: Herschi's bond theory, juvenile delinquency and the school nurse, *J Sch Health* 52:280, 1982.

Chavez E, Edwards R, Oetting E: Mexican American and white American school dropouts; drug use, health status, and involvement in violence, *Public Health Rep* 104(6):594, 1989.

Crabbs M: School mental health services following an environmental disaster, *J Sch Health* 51:165, 1981.

Donovan JE, Jessor R: Structure of probelm behavior in adolescence and young adulthood, *J Consult Clin Psychol* 53:890, 1985.

Erikson E: *Childhood and society,* New York, 1963, WW Norton.

Harter S: *Adolescent self and identity development; at the threshold: the developing adolescent,* Cambridge, Mass, 1990, Harvard University Press.

Hughes C, Aluli N: A culturally sensitive approach to health education for native Hawaiians, *J Health Ed* 22:6 1991.

Jessor R, Jessor SL: *Problem behavior of psychosocial development: a longitudinal study of youth,* New York, 1977, Academic Press.

Kohlberg L: Development of moral character and moral ideology. In Hoffman M, Hoffman L: *Review of child development research,* vol 1, New York, 1964, Russell Sage Foundation.

Martin G, Duryea E: The distortion effect in student perception of smoking prevalence, *J Sch Health* 51:115, 1981.

Moore RS, Moore D: When education becomes abuse: a different look at the mental health of children, *J Sch Health* 56:73, 1986.

Page R: Loneliness and adolescent health behavior, *Health Educ* 21:5, 1990.

Paulk M, Kirk RH: Toward a better understanding of self-help groups in self-health care, *Health Educ* 21:4, 1990.

Richardson G, et al: The resiliency model, *Health Educ* 21:6, 1990.

Shaffer D: *Prevention of psychiatric disorders in children and adolescents: a summary of findings and recommendations from project prevention,* Rockville, Md, 1989, US Department of Health and Human Services.

University of Minnesota and Minnesota Dept. of Health: School survey results: the Minnesota adolescent health survey adolescent health database project 1986-1987, Minneapolis, 1988, Minnesota Dept. of Health.

Departures from normal health, growth, and development

OVERVIEW

Knowledge of departures from normal health is important to teachers so that they can interpret routine information in student files and be sensitive to the daily referral needs of students. Today's philosophies of education and health care mean that teachers are almost assured of having students in their classrooms who would previously have been precluded from regular school because of health conditions. Usually major changes are unnecessary to accommodate these young people, but the professional teacher will want to know about these conditions to make knowledgeable decisions about classroom activities and individual learning activities.

In addition, teachers will frequently be the first to notice deviations from normal health or growth and development that are often visible through changes in student performance or student appearance. Teachers are not responsible for diagnosis or treatment, but knowledge of the most common health problems experienced by their students improves their ability to plan and carry out effective learning activities.

OBJECTIVES   After reading this chapter, the student should be able to:

1. Identify and describe the most common medical conditions likely to be found among the student population
2. Recognize and use opportunities to help students understand and accept health conditions among their fellow students
3. Assist students who may need additional care or referral and initiate appropriate referrals with confidence
4. Recognize a teacher's professional role in working with students whose growth, development, or health deviates from normal

Every school can expect to have children who deviate from the normal. Some minor deviations affect the youngster little or not at all. In other instances the deviation may greatly limit the student so that special provisions must be made. Whatever the deviation, there are correct and incorrect ways to deal with the situation. Young people with significant disabilities can still reach their optimal levels of health. Handled incorrectly, students with disabilities can be made to feel that they are outsiders, with resulting harm to mental and physical health.

Perhaps nothing in a teacher's experience could be more rewarding than to make a normal or near-normal school life possible for the student who has some departure from the normal. Sometimes the demand on the teacher may be great; at other times it may be small. Whatever the situation, the teacher's present contribution may well benefit the person throughout life.

Teachers are eager to do everything reasonable for children who have a disability or deviation in growth and development but are sometimes hesitant to act because they lack confidence in their knowledge of such conditions. No teacher, whether an elementary classroom teacher or a secondary school health educator, should be considered an expert on any of these conditions, but the teacher should understand their essentials.

Schools do not have a recognized legal responsibility for the correction or improvement of health defects in any child, but they do have a responsibility to ensure that all students receive an adequate education to function well in society. When health problems interfere with learning, the school is obligated to concern itself with these problems. Obviously the sick student cannot learn as well as the healthy student; therefore both the student and society are shortchanged in their investment in education if health problems are overlooked.

Health problems among students interfere with learning in several ways. An illness or health condition that affects the rate of learning may attract a disproportionate amount of the teacher's time and energy to that student at the expense of other students. Health problems are often manifest as disciplinary problems, and the resulting class disruption interferes with the learning of the entire class. Students with untreated infectious conditions run the risk of infecting others and causing undue absenteeism; they also increase the risks of illness for the teacher.

The responsibility to do everything reasonable for the health and well-being of the student is the basic obligation of the school. This commitment to deal with health issues can be fulfilled in various ways, such as the following:

1. Bringing the student's condition to the parents' attention
2. Following up such a referral
3. Counseling the parents regarding means of obtaining necessary professional services
4. Seeking outside financial assistance to obtain the correct services
5. Carrying out at school certain instructions from the student's physician or other practitioner
6. Adapting the school program to the needs of the specific student
7. Helping the student to help himself or herself in solving health problems that are not directly under the supervision of any practitioner
8. Most important, understanding fully the student's condition and problems and making adjustments in school life to provide a more enjoyable and effective school environment

The role of the teacher is neither that of diagnostician nor therapist. The teacher needs to know which health conditions can affect the student both favorably and unfavorably to plan in the best interests of the student (Fig. 6-1).

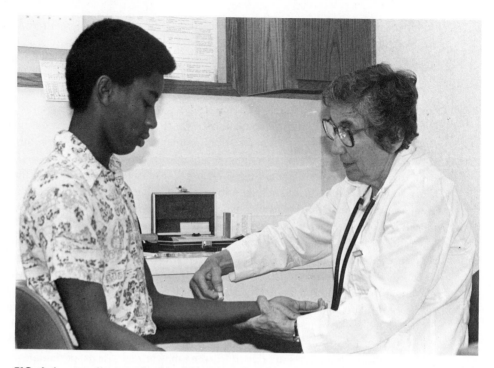

FIG. 6-1. An effective school health program has the potential to aid in the early referral of students with possible health problems. Effective communication between school administrators, local physicians, and health department personnel often facilitates the obtaining of health services for students.

UNDERACHIEVEMENT AND LOW VITALITY

The one condition that is most noticeable to teachers and may not have identifiable health-related causes is underachievement, or low levels of vitality. Underachievement may result from many causes, ranging from diagnosed medical conditions to social, psychologic, or other environmental concerns. Heredity, prematurity, lead poisoning, and malnutrition are a few of the conditions that can cause low vitality and underachievement. More common, however, are conditions related to parental support, peer pressure, and family and community problems.

A useful way to consider causes of underachievement is to divide possible contributing factors into two categories: external and internal. Most causes are external, associated in one way or another with the student's environment rather than actual clinical health. Thus it is not unusual to find children with clear records on both health examinations and health screenings who still exhibit chronic underachievement. However, it is important that children exhibiting low achievement and low vitality be referred for medical examination to ensure that no correctable internal conditions are contributing to the problem.

Students who have a record of underachievement with no clear internal causes for this problem should be examined in terms of inappropriate class placement, family problems, and poor relationships with others. Each of these factors represents an important contribution to understanding and dealing with underachievers.

Inappropriate class placement, for example, can result in a student's boredom with or inability to understand the class content because of failure to master earlier concepts. Personality clashes with teachers are also possible causes, as are many other class-related issues. Families suffering economic hardships, serious illness, marital tension, or recent bereavement may partly explain underachievement. Unrealistic parental expectations and overprotective parents may contribute to this condition. Lack of motivation may result from social messages that do not place a high value on educational achievement and from parents who present models of low achievement and low motivation. Family or community members may be economic and social successes but may not show respect or value for formal education.

Low vitality also results from functional conditions in the environment. Homes that lack any semblance of a regular schedule, in which children get little sleep or sleep irregular hours, are a principal contributing cause. Involvement of children in outside work may also figure prominently in low vitality in school.

The nature and extent of underachievement from internal causes have not been clearly described. A host of terms has been used to describe conditions related to underachievement and low motivation. These terms include minimal brain dysfunction, learning disability syndrome, and the hyperactive child syndrome. In general, these conditions can be classified as attentional deficiencies and have been grouped in the third edition of the *Diagnostic and Statistical Manual of Mental Disorders* (American Psychiatric Association, 1987) as attentional deficit disorders.

Each of the conditions now grouped under attentional deficit disorders has been described in the past as having some element of attentional dysfunction. The term *minimal brain dysfunction,* for example, implied organic causes or abnormalities, which may not have always been the case. Minimal brain dysfunction correctly covers a group of wide-ranging conditions, and the implication of organic abnormality is unwarranted. *Hyperactivity* is a term that has been used rather loosely and is manifest in schools most prominently as an attentional problem. *Learning disabilities* referred to cognitive deficits, often but not necessarily associated with hyperactivity.

The vagueness of these terms and the likelihood that these conditions are interrelated have led to the more general term of *attentional deficit disorders.* Attentional deficit disorders are separate and distinct from the conditions of mental retardation, sensory disorders, and emotional disorders and can be more objectively identified.

Attentional deficit disorders are more common among boys than among girls. Estimates of prevalence range from 1 per 1000 to 5 or 6 per 100. This discrepancy results from different diagnostic criteria and variation in rates from one population to another.

The *Diagnostic and Statistical Manual of Mental Disorders*, sometimes referred to as DSM III, describes the diagnostic criteria for attentional deficit disorders as follows:

1. There is excessive general hyperactivity or motor restlessness for the child's age. In preschool and early school years there may be excessive, haphazard, impulsive running, climbing, or crawling. During middle childhood or adolescence, up-and-down activity, an inability to sit still, and fidgeting are characteristic. Activity differs from the norm for the age in both quality and quantity.

2. The child exhibits difficulty in sustaining attention, an inability to complete tasks, or a disorganized approach to tasks. The child frequently "forgets" demands made or tasks assigned and shows poor attention in structured situations or when independent unsupervised performance is required.
3. Impulsive behavior is manifest by at least two of the following:
   a. Sloppy work despite reasonable efforts to perform adequately
   b. Frequent speaking out of turn or making inappropriate sounds in class
   c. Frequent interruption of or intrusion into other children's activities or conversations
   d. Difficulty waiting for one's turn in games or group situations
   e. Poor frustration tolerance
   f. Fighting with children in a fashion indicating low frustration tolerance rather than sadistic or mean intentions
4. The condition lasts at least 1 year.

It is not the teacher's task to diagnose students with any condition, but a review of these conditions should help the teacher who needs to make a referral. Most children with attentional deficit disorders are usually referred for assessment in the first two or three grades of elementary school.

MALNUTRITION

Severe or pronounced malnutrition is relatively uncommon among young people in the United States today, but moderate and mild malnutrition are far more prevalent than is commonly known. A teacher easily recognizes pronounced obesity and underweight, but children who lack sufficient protective foods to meet the *recommended dietary allowances* (RDAs) are not readily detectable. Although the general school health program should promote the nutrition of every school student, certain students merit special attention because of recognized or suspected nutritional needs. Teachers should also be aware of nutritional influences of their own school administration's policies and practices. Too often school administrators respond to student and parental pressure to install vending machines that dispense nonnutritional, high-calorie, salt- and additive-laden items. Alert teachers can encourage school administrators to provide nutritious snacks in school vending machines.

The U.S. Centers for Disease Control reports that adolescents between 10 and 16 years old are most likely to have the poorest nutritional status of any age group. Nutritional needs vary with sex and age, with the greatest nutritional need associated with greatest physical growth. The most accelerated growth periods tend to be between 12 and 17 years of age. Among girls, the height and growth spurt begins between 10 and 11 years of age and lasts 2½ to 3 years. Among boys this period starts around 12 years and may last to 15 years of age. Malnutrition represented by underweight may have both physiologic and social causes (e.g., parental neglect).

OBESITY

Young people more than 10% overweight for their age are considered obese. In some children overweight by more than 10% may not affect health adversely during childhood, but the long-term effect may lower the level of health. The American Academy of Pediatrics (1987) notes that 15% of adolescent girls and about 7% of adolescent boys are obese. About 80% of obese children become obese adults. Although no physical effect may be discernible, obesity reduces both the effectiveness and enjoyment of living. A child who carries around excess weight is likely to fatigue easily. Although the added burden may not tax a normal heart, a slightly defective heart may be strained seriously. Obesity handicaps play and muscular reactions. Obese children are frequently taunted and ridiculed and may be considered different by their peers. Being classed out of the normal category is not conducive to the best mental health for a developing student.

Obesity results from eating more calories than one uses. Even when a glandular disorder exists in which organic substances readily turn to fat, the organic compounds come from what a person eats. The remedy for obesity is to eat less or expend more calories or both. Any child who is obese has been eating too much. Long-established family dietary customs may well produce obese children who become conditioned to excessive eating. Once this psychophysiologic pattern is established, obese children find it progressively more difficult to reduce their food intake. Their problem is both physiologic and psychologic.

Hunger is basically physiologic, governed by the glucose (sugar) level of the blood. When the blood glucose level is low, a person experiences sensations of hunger. Immediately after a meal, the blood glucose level is high. This high level affects the output of insulin from the pancreas. Over time insulin converts excess blood glucose to stable glycogen, which is stored in the liver and muscles. This results in a low blood glucose level and hunger. Only limited amounts of glycogen can be stored in the liver and muscles, and the excess is converted to body fat. To meet energy needs and reduce the buildup of fat is the challenge of good nutrition.

About 12% of daily calories in United States diets comes from protein, about 42% from fat, and 46% from carbohydrates. Experts suggest that fats be reduced to 30% and the proportion of carbohydrates increased.

Carbohydrates, especially complex carbohydrates (fruits, vegetables, dried peas, beans, cereals, breads, rice, pasta), are the recommended energy source compared to sugars, syrups, and candies, which contribute almost nothing to the diet but calories.

Obese students who can reduce their caloric intake by 600 calories per day should lose 1 pound (454 g) per week. This is a wholesome weight-reduction rate. Cutting down on portions and increasing the proportion of complex carbohydrates in the diet to allay between-meal hunger are the two points that must be emphasized. If at all possible, dieting should be done under medical supervision. Encouragement from the teacher and cooperation from the family increase the likelihood of controlling the diet.

When there is a combination of underweight and illness, it is the province of the medical profession to find the underlying causes. The observant teacher initiates the chain reaction to bring the child and physician together.

The school correlates its efforts with the home and the family physician. At minimum, the teacher should confer with the parents when concerned about a child's weight. Often parents, too, are concerned and express the wish that something could be done. Proposing a health examination is in order. From the examination may come a recommended program or the identification of the child as healthy and normal in all respects, including weight for his or her particular constitutional type (Fig. 6-2).

FIG. 6-2.   Observations by teachers provide an opportunity for a continuing assessment of student health. Teachers are often the first to notice signs of illness. An effective school health service involves teachers, nurses, parents, physicians, and counselors to ensure students a maximal opportunity to learn.

EATING DISORDERS

Anorexia nervosa

Anorexia nervosa occurs most frequently among females (10:1). It is seen often among persons 11 to 35 years of age and peaks in prevalence in the late teens. Clinically the dramatic weight loss is associated with (1) refusal to eat and maintain normal weight, (2) a loss of 15% or more of expected body weight, (3) intense fear of becoming obese, and (4) amenorrhea for 3 consecutive months when menstruation has previously been regular. These conditions appear in the absence of organic disease that would otherwise account for weight loss.

In effect, the anorectic student loses control over eating and out of an extreme fear of being "fat" ceases to eat. The resulting condition interferes with development and produces fatigue, depression, and ultimately a total loss of appetite. Anorexia nervosa is not a loss of appetite attributable to nerves, as the name may suggest. Persons with this condition do not actually lose their appetites until a very late stage of their illness.

Bulimia

Bulimia is an eating disorder characterized by periodic binge eating followed by purging. During binges there is a fear of not being able to stop eating. Purging usually includes self-induced vomiting and the use of laxatives and may also include patterns of extreme dieting or exercise to overcome the excessive eating. The clinical definition (DSM-III) indicates that for confirmed diagnosis of bulimia a person binge eats at least twice a week for at least 3 months.

For the teacher, any evidence of binge eating or discussion of this possibility by a student should be addressed with information about the condition and its consequences. The current trend of "dieting" and the often unrealistic images of the ideal body encourage behavior that can lead to the development of nutritional problems along the continuum of eating disorders. A person may begin to reduce food intake, may begin to believe he or she can control the process, and, when he or she feels excessively hungry, may overeat. Guilt follows, and purging is seen as a way to reduce guilt and "get back on the diet." The pattern is established and becomes habitual.

Anorexia nervosa and bulimia are two distinct conditions that result from similar underlying causes: poor self-esteem, insecurity, and the need to be perfect or to control. It is possible for students to exhibit signs of both conditions. To understand the way these two conditions may occur together, it is useful to think of them as two ends of a continuum, with the area in the middle reflecting some combination of the two.

For the developing adolescent this critical problem needs expert attention. In a well-established form, anorexia nervosa and bulimia are not easy to treat; thus referral in the early stages is important. Classes in nutrition, health, and physical education help adolescents understand normal growth and development, and the school staff should facilitate the development of strong and adequate self-concepts and the acceptance of individual differences. Such efforts help prevent anorexia nervosa and bulimia, facilitate early identification and referral, and help others understand and be supportive of those with eating disorders.

Digestive system disturbances

Most digestive disturbances in school-age children are accompanied by symptoms and signs that warn that something is wrong. The symptoms might include a mild upset from which the child recovers in a relatively short period of time, or they may be chronic in nature, ultimately involving the need for medical service, hospitalization, home care, or special school programs.

Symptoms describe the sensations that the patient experiences. These may include nausea, pain, elevated temperature, irritability, or headache.

Signs describe what can be seen by observation of the patient. These include flushed skin, restlessness, red, watery eyes, or facial grimaces. Mild symptoms and signs do not necessarily denote a mild illness.

Iron deficiency anemia

Anemia literally means "without blood" (Gr. *an-*, without; *haima*, blood), but in its practical sense anemia is a condition in which the red corpuscle count or the hemoglobin content of the blood is low or both deficiencies are present.

Iron deficiency anemia is more common in girls than in boys. Approximately 5% of adolescent boys have confirmed iron deficiency anemia. Among adolescent girls from affluent homes the prevalence is 12%, and among those from low-income homes the rate is as high as 20%. The reason for the difference in the male and female rates is related to the female body's poorer ability to shepherd iron, the low level of testosterone (a principally male sex hormone), which stimulates the production of red blood cells, and the loss of blood associated with menstruation.

The presence of iron deficiency anemia is indicated by low hemoglobin and hematocrit levels. Hemoglobin is the red pigment of erythrocytes that has the ability to carry oxygen. Hematocrit levels represent the proportion of whole blood volume occupied by cells after centrifuge. Symptoms of iron deficiency are irritability, fatigue, difficulty concentrating, headache, and in females heavy menstrual flow.

Iron deficiency anemia can be corrected relatively easily with an improved diet, including iron-rich foods such as liver, red meats, green vegetables, whole grains, and the prescription of ferrous sulfate. Required diet changes are significant, however, because females need four times more iron than males do.

ENDOCRINE DISTURBANCES

Diabetes mellitus

Although it is generally considered a disease of later life, *diabetes mellitus* does occur among school-age children and occasionally among preschool children. One child in 1000 is affected by diabetes mellitus, and although this prevalence may seem low, it is the most common chronic endocrine disease among young people between 10 and 19 years of age. Medical authorities point out that for every four known cases, three unrecognized cases of diabetes exist.

Most people who have diabetes can stay well and lead healthful and useful lives. Careful attention to the physician's instructions safeguard the student's health. In this respect the school can be of appreciable service to the diabetic student.

Diabetes mellitus usually results from a deficiency in the insulin output of the islands of Langerhans in the pancreas. It also may be caused by a deficiency of the glycogenic hormone of the anterior pituitary gland. A deficiency of these hormones results in a high level of blood glucose (*hyperglycemia*) and glucose in the urine (*glycosuria*). Lassitude and weariness result, as well as pronounced thirst after meals and, with the subsequent consumption of water, frequent urination. Increased hunger, a drawn expression, and a loss of weight may occur. The mouth is dry, and the tongue is red and sore. Dry skin, itching, eczema, and boils may occur. The eyes are affected, and neuritis, numbness, and tingling of the hands and feet occur. Pronounced weakness results from the inability of the muscles to use available fuel.

Some diabetic students may be on a restricted diet, often sufficient to control the condition.

The physician or parents should inform the school of the prescribed diet and routine for physical activity. The teacher guides the child in adherence to the prescription.

Exercise lowers insulin requirements so that blood glucose levels and insulin dosage levels are also lowered. The American Academy of Pediatrics recommends the following guidelines (1987):

1. During physical activity needed insulin may be 20% to 30% less than other times. Insulin should be injected in muscles not heavily used in the sport or activity.
2. Insulin dosage may need to be adjusted so that peaks do not coincide with high-activity periods.
3. High-carbohydrate foods should be eaten an hour before strenuous exercise. Food with readily available glucose should be available during periods of exercise, and additional food may be needed the day after strenuous exercise to replenish glycogen stores.
4. Coaches and teammates should be taught to recognize and treat insulin reactions.
5. Rapid weight-loss regimes, such as those sometimes unwisely practiced by wrestlers or others, are especially dangerous to diabetics and should be avoided.
6. Medical advice should always be sought and followed.

Students being treated with insulin will probably receive their injection at least 1 hour before coming to school; some may take injections during the day. Occasionally fluctuations of the effect occur, and a low blood glucose level (*hypoglycemia*) may result. In extreme forms the condition is commonly spoken of as *insulin shock*, the early signs of which are trembling, faintness, palpitation, unsteadiness, excessive perspiration, and hunger. Crackers, bread, or juice produces recovery in a few minutes. Some children carry a small supply of crackers or bread and eat them immediately on appearance of symptoms.

Hypoglycemia

Abnormal behavior in children can arise from an unusual body metabolism and, as a consequence, mask the true cause and nature of the illness. *Hypoglycemia* is one of these conditions. The dominant factor is a low level of glucose in the blood, responsible for periods of irritability, confusion, depression, lethargy, complaints of weakness in the extremities, and inability to concentrate. When a physician puts the patient on a selective diet, the patient's behavior improves.

Teachers need to be aware that the signs of hypoglycemia may be mistaken for other behavioral problems. Children who are irritable, confused, or lethargic may be mistaken for being drunk, drugged, or acting out. To overlook the possibility of hypoglycemia or to treat it as a discipline issue can have unfortunate consequences. Teachers who observe these signs should check the student's health records for indications of hypoglycemia or refer the student to the school nurse.

CARDIOVASCULAR DISORDERS

Approximately 1% of schoolchildren in the United States have a diagnosed cardiac disorder. Together, rheumatic fever and its accessory, rheumatic heart disorder, cause more disability than any other disease of childhood. A second important cardiac disorder of childhood is congenital heart defect. In both, the everyday management or supervision of the child is all important. A teacher who knows what should and can be done makes an invaluable contribution to the child's well-being.

Rheumatic fever

Rheumatic fever, an insidious disease, overtakes a child stealthily. Although it undoubtedly is infectious, the causative agent is unknown. However, physicians generally agree that a certain type of infection is the forerunner of rheumatic fever. Group A *beta-hemolytic streptococcus,* which produces a sore throat, is the recognized source of rheumatic fever. From this primary infection two additional phases delineate the evolution of rheumatic fever:

1. The middle (dormant) phase lasts 2 to 3 weeks after the sore throat, during which no visible symptoms appear; child seems completely recovered.
2. The final phase (acute rheumatic fever) lasts from 2 to 3 weeks to several months.

Although most afflicted children have a physician's services, some children appear in the classroom without the benefit of medical advice. The teacher who recognizes certain danger signals contributes immeasurably to the child's welfare by bringing the matter to the parents' attention. Early detection may prevent the most serious complication—rheumatic heart disease.

Specific symptoms do not exist in every case of rheumatic fever, but common symptoms include irritability; undue fatigue; nosebleeds; pallor; pain in the joints, arms, and legs; jerky and twitching motions; poor appetite; loss of weight; and a lack of interest in school activities. The teacher must contact the parents of a child with several of these symptoms because there obviously is something wrong.

Rheumatic fever is not communicable; therefore prevention is directed toward the conditions that precede it. Preventing the spread of throat infections in the school should indirectly reduce the incidence of rheumatic fever. Prompt medical treatment for any throat infection prevents it from becoming the forerunner of rheumatic fever.

Because rheumatic fever tends to run in families, members of the patient's family should be informed of the need for a well-balanced diet, adequate rest, early treatment of respiratory infections, and regular medical supervision. A child with rheumatic fever will receive long-term medication from the physician to prevent repeated attacks.

Rheumatic heart disease

Two out of three patients with rheumatic fever suffer damaged hearts. A single attack may cause minor damage, but recurrence of the disease will likely cause further damage. With regular medical supervision, recurrent attacks can be prevented.

During the acute stage of the infection the heart muscle may be affected. This muscle inflammation *(myocarditis)* may weaken and enlarge the heart. At times the outer heart covering is inflamed *(pericarditis).* As the infection declines, the heart tends to return to normal size. Permanent injury usually results from inflammation of the valves on the left half of the heart. During the healing process scar tissue forms, which prevents the valves from opening or closing properly.

About a third of children with rheumatic fever show no evidence of heart damage; about one third more show signs of cardiac injury but lead practically normal lives.

No limitations should be placed on the child except those advised by the physician. These could include between-meal snacks and rest periods. As much as possible youngsters should be made to feel that they are not abnormal but can, with few exceptions, participate in the regular classroom work.

Congenital heart defects

A child may be born with a defective heart. Some congenital heart conditions benefit from surgery; others cannot be helped by methods now known. Some congenital heart disorders are so minor that they can essentially be ignored. Others are not serious enough to prevent a child from attending school, yet the child needs supervision and management. From this range, it is apparent that knowledge of these defects enables the teacher to cooperate effectively with the child's physician.

Many cardiac patients can participate in regular classroom activities. Restriction or limitation should not be imposed, except on instruction from the child's physician. Many of these children limit their own activity when necessary because of the distress of fatigue. A physician may rule out competitive sports for some children. It is essential that young people develop a wholesome, positive attitude toward their capacities and abilities. The teacher should emphasize what they can do and give less emphasis to what they cannot do if they are on a restrictive regimen.

Hypertension

High blood pressure is not frequent among children of school age but does occasionally occur. Evidence indicates that young people with elevated blood pressure at two successive annual or biannual examinations are likely to have high blood pressure as adults (National Heart, Lung and Blood Institute, 1982).

Even in a normal person systolic blood pressure may vary considerably, but in *hypertension* the blood pressure consistently will be above 140 mm Hg systolic and 90 mm Hg diastolic. Sometimes the condition is functional, the result of mental and emotional tensions. If tensions are relieved, these persons improve considerably. Sometimes the condition is organic. Certain renal, endocrine, vascular, and cerebral disorders may cause hypertension.

MENSTRUAL DISORDERS

Menstrual irregularities are common in adolescence and concern the school when they cause absence or prevent full involvement in school activities. The pain of *dysmenorrhea* is usually short and recurring and occurs just above the pelvic bone and in the midabdomen region. Medications can reduce the discomfort; thus referral to a physician is recommended. Normal course content should prepare students for the onset of menstruation, and the nurse or counselors should be seen as an accessible source of advice and explanation.

DISORDERS OF POSTURE

In the typical school situation, posture is not regarded as an important factor in student health. Although a deviation in posture usually does not produce a serious threat to health, postural defects should be a concern.

A child does not stand in a straight line but in four counterbalancing curves: cervical, thoracic, lumbar, and sacral. These vertebral curves are not in perfect compensating alignment but must be supported by the skeletal muscles. Whether a child is standing, walking, or sitting, four criteria can be applied as the index of good posture: (1) head erect, neck back, and chin level; (2) no exaggeration of vertebral curvatures; (3) chest lifted slightly; and (4) shoulders held broadly, without tension.

In walking, a rhythmic gait with a free and easy leg swing should be supplemented by a free and easy arm swing. The feet should be nearly parallel. In sitting, the hips, knees, and ankles should point ahead and be flat on the floor.

Most poor posture is functional, that is, resulting from careless habits; and a considerable amount results from poor muscle tone. Deformities of the skeleton and joints account for a very small percentage of poor posture.

Scoliosis is a condition in which there is a lateral curvature of the vertebral column. To identify a curvature the student is viewed from behind while standing erect and then as he or she bends forward. Pronounced lateral curvature can be seen easily. The condition often occurs first among junior high students and appears more frequently in girls. Screening procedures for scoliosis are described in Chapter 7. In time scoliosis can interfere with cardiopulmonary function and cause chronic back pain and psychologic problems related to self-image.

Other posture concerns include *round shoulders*, *lordosis* (swayback), and *visceroptosis* (abdominal paunch). Students with these conditions can often be helped with exercise programs that develop improved muscle tone.

DEVIATIONS OF THE RESPIRATORY SYSTEM

Some noninfectious chronic conditions of the respiratory system are of minor consequence. Others are significant in terms of reducing the effectiveness and enjoyment of life. Occasionally life itself may be threatened.

Nasal congestion

All persons experience some congestion of the nasal passages, but usually it is temporary, resulting from an excessive production of mucus associated with respiratory infection. Although temporarily distressing, the accumulation of mucus is not serious, being a natural response to irritation of the mucous tissue. A chronic or permanent congestion may be caused by mucus or a mechanical obstruction such as a stemmed growth (polyp) of mucous tissue and need medical care or surgical correction.

Sinusitis

The sinuses of the skull are air cavities lined with the same type of mucous tissue that lines the nasal passages. Two frontal sinuses, one above each eye, and two maxillary sinuses, one in each upper jawbone beneath the eyes, have narrow passageways, or ducts, that empty into the nasal passages. Exhaled and inhaled air passes into the ducts and sinuses. These structures are properly considered part of the respiratory tract. Normally the mucous tissue lining the sinuses secretes a small-to-moderate amount of mucus. Mechanical or bacterial irritation produces an excessive amount of mucus with resulting congestion. Until the irritation is removed, the overproduction of mucus is likely to continue. Persons with constricted ducts may have painful sinus congestion.

The school should identify children with chronic sinusitis and suggest to parents the need for medical attention.

Deviated septum

At least half the adults in the United States have some degree of deviation of the partition separating the nares, but most deviations are of no particular significance. Deviation can occur without a nasal fracture.

In children, when the deviation is so pronounced that one of the nasal passages is closed, surgery will be advised by the physician. When the condition is obvious, the teacher will observe that, although the youngster has no difficulty in breathing under ordinary conditions, slight exertion requires mouth breathing. Closing the open naris by pressure with the finger and asking the child to exhale forcibly indicates the degree of obstruction in the other passage. Mouth breathing is not necessarily objectionable, but the chronic condition that produces it usually requires correction.

Allergies

Studies have shown that 10% to 28% of the population suffer from major allergic problems. In the United States an estimated 2.5 million young people have asthma. Asthma is one of the leading causes for missing school.

Hypersensitivity can affect the respiratory tract in a variety of ways. Hay fever, bronchial asthma, bronchitis, and croup are end products of allergies that affect the respiratory system. Although some of these conditions exist when the child enters school, others do not become evident until the child is a teenager. Sometimes allergies do not appear until adulthood. Because of the factor of inheritance, children with a family history of allergies should be considered to have a possible respiratory allergy if they display chronic respiratory disturbances. Student health records, therefore, are a valuable asset in helping students with allergies.

Under medical supervision, children with respiratory allergies usually carry on the normal activities of school life. An asthmatic attack in school may appear dramatic but should not be alarming. Generally the students themselves know what action to take. Medication, usually administered by an inhaler, frequently controls the attack.

Teachers should be aware that, although asthma treatment is improving in efficacy, physicians report that the number of children and young people affected with asthma has increased 50% in the last ten years. The reasons for this increase include an increased sensitivity to certain allergies, greater levels of air pollution, and possibly a decreased access to health services for many poor and inner city youth.

DISORDERS OF THE ORAL CAVITY

Disorders of the oral cavity are not an urgent life-and-death matter; yet they play an important role in the quality of health, the length of the prime of life, and life expectation. Thus early detection and correction are dictated. Dental health is improving. In 1940 90% of young people had some form of dental decay; today that number is less than 50%.

Child care safety

EMERGING ISSUE   As Curriculum Coordinator for Health and Safety in a large metropolitan school system, you also serve as the school district's representative on the city Safety Council. A recent report of the city's organized child care facilities reveals a number of serious environmental health and safety deficiencies in these facilities. The report is based on an independent, statewide study conducted by the State University's Safety Center. Examples of some of the problems include the failure to restrict objects that could cause choking among children, the lack of CPR-trained staff members, the failure to provide safety education for both children and parents, and in many instances a lack of safety standards for playground equipment.

Several community groups have become concerned about these conditions. As a consequence, a group of citizens has called on the Safety Council with the request that something be done to correct the situation. Accordingly, the executive committee of the council has selected several points for consideration in an effort to assess the council's thinking and to develop a consensus for a plan of action.

Please indicate whether you generally agree or disagree by placing a plus (+) or a minus (−) sign before each statement.

_____ 1. Health and safety concerns of the community are the primary responsibility of the local health department.

_____ 2. I believe the problem should be presented to the city government to determine whether there has been a violation of city ordinances.

_____ 3. Since child care programs are such a recent development, I assume that there is a need to establish rules and regulations governing such programs.

_____ 4. I suspect that the problem is simply a matter of inadequate inspection.

_____ 5. I believe we should hire a safety specialist to advise both the council and the child care program managers.

_____ 6. I believe the role of the Safety Council must be that of child advocacy; therefore the council must take leadership in whatever plan is adopted.

_____ 7. There is so much negative feeling about government regulations that I would favor a voluntary compliance approach.

_____ 8. Since the Safety Council is a nonregulatory body, there is very little that can be done.

_____ 9. Although I would push for local policy initiatives, ultimately we must have federal standards governing these programs.

_____ 10. If limited to a single choice, I would choose this number.

Caries and cavities

The process of dental decay is called caries; the result is the cavity. The process is initiated by the *Lactobacillus acidophilus* (LA) organism and can be expressed in the equation:

LA enzyme + Carbohydrate = Acid

Disintegration of the dental enamel occurs from the acid.

Dental cavities occur more frequently than any other disorder of schoolchildren. Of itself, a simple cavity may have no effect on health. However, it may progress to a point at which the tooth is destroyed or must be extracted. Loss of several teeth, without compensating dentures, can affect a person's dietary practices; and, more seriously, the oral cavity can become an avenue of invasion for disease-producing organisms that pass, via the pulp cavity, to the apex of the tooth root and produce an abscess.

Good dental hygiene should be taught to all students, and parents made aware of untreated dental condition.

Abscess

An infection in the gum or at the apex of a tooth root may be painful or virtually painless. Toxins produced at the *abscess* can travel about the body and seriously impair vital tissues. Any gum involvement, including the gum boil, which is an abscess, demands professional attention. Prompt action may save the tooth and prevent injury to the general health.

Pyorrhea

Pyorrhea is an infectious or mechanical irritation of the periodontal membrane, which attaches the tooth to the gum and bone. A red margin of the gum around the neck of the tooth is indicative of this irritation. If permitted to continue, the irritation seriously damages the membrane. Because the periodontal membrane does not have the capacity to rejuvenate itself, the tooth becomes permanently loosened and may have to be extracted.

Gingivitis

Any inflammation of the gum may be termed *gingivitis,* but in its general usage the term designates infection by two known pathogens, *Bacillus fusiformis* and *Borrelia vincentii.* Commonly called trench mouth, or Vincent's disease, it is characterized by inflammation and even ulceration of the gums and other parts of the mouth, bleeding, excess salivation, and considerable soreness.

Gingivitis does not often occur in a healthy child. Malnutrition, poor general health, inadequate rest, and poor mouth care predispose to gingivitis. The infections can be treated successfully by a dentist.

Malocclusion

Pronounced overbite or underbite and poorly aligned teeth create mechanical problems that eventually destroy supporting tissue. For children with these conditions, the services of an orthodontist are a necessity, not a luxury.

DISORDERS OF EYES AND VISION

With a function as complex as vision and a structure as remarkable as the human eye, the wonder is that the incidence of defective vision is not greater. Standard screening tests usually detect students with pronounced vision disability. A professional practitioner's examination locates even the slightest disability. Teachers who observe their students closely can detect children whose posturing, squinting, inattention, or poor progress may be caused by their inability to see normally.

Myopia

Myopia, or nearsightedness, is a heritable tendency and is usually caused by elongated eyeballs. The image falls in front of the retina unless the object is close to the eye. Therefore close objects can be seen quite clearly, but distant objects are blurred. Concave lenses will compensate for the extra length of the eyeball. Although nearsighted children may be able to read without glasses, they will become less distressed and fatigued if they use proper eyewear.

Hyperopia

Hyperopia, or farsightedness, is caused by an eyeball so short that the image literally falls behind the retina. With a great deal of effort, a farsighted student can see near objects by over-working the delicate muscles of accommodation, although visual fatigue sets in very quickly. A tendency to become cross-eyed is possible. Convex lenses can compensate so that the student can read with a minimum of strain and fatigue.

Astigmatism

Irregularities in the curvature of the cornea and lens prevent a true focus of the eye, and a blurred image with discomfort results. Astigmatism requires carefully prescribed glasses and sometimes frequent renewal of the prescription.

Amblyopia

Vision dimness without known cause can occur in people of all ages. Amblyopia may begin with a central or peripheral spot where there is little vision. The condition may enlarge slowly and will progressively interfere with vision.

Fortunately, amblyopia in children usually clears up spontaneously, but every young person with dimness of vision should be under the supervision of an ophthalmologist for periodic checkups.

Strabismus

Cross-eye, not cross-eyes, is descriptive of strabismus, since only one eye is crossed because of a shortened extrinsic muscle that turns the eye inward. Ophthalmologists can correct many types of strabismus by treatment or surgery or a combination. Early attention is essential. The accommodation or acuity of one or both eyes may be affected in some children if the condition is untreated. Such children exhibit posturing and other signs of difficult vision. The alert teacher calls this difficulty to the attention of the child's parents.

Ptosis

A drooping of one or both upper eyelids, ptosis, is usually an inherited condition in which the nerves that stimulate the elevating muscle do not conduct impulses. Paralysis of the muscle may come on gradually during the school years. If the paralysis is bilateral, children will naturally tilt their heads back to see through the small apertures formed by the backward tilt of the head.

Conjunctivitis

Conjunctivitis, or pinkeye, is a highly communicable condition caused most often by pneumococci and staphylococci. Characterized by a mucous discharge in the eyes, a burning and itching sensation, and bright red coloration of the conjunctiva, the disease is easy to detect. Overnight the discharge may seal the eyelids closed. Because of the highly contagious nature of this condition, children with conjunctivitis should be isolated and excluded from school with a suggestion to parents to consult a physician. With medication the condition is quickly managed, but the student should not return to school until the physician's clearance is received. Even at home the child with pinkeye should be careful not to use items such as towels that could be used by others.

HEARING DISABILITIES

Most children who have some hearing loss acquire it gradually. The audiometric test determines hearing disabilities, but the alert teacher can observe indications that a child has hearing difficulties. Children who cannot hear well often posture, are inattentive, copy, and make poor progress. Faulty pronunciation and an unnatural voice are hints that the child does not hear well.

Conduction deafness

Almost all hearing loss in children is caused by disturbances of the outer and middle ear that interfere with the conduction of sound. Excessive wax (cerumen), ruptured or rigid tympanic membrane, rigidity of the ligaments of the bones (ossicles) of the middle ear, mucous congestion of the middle ear, and rigidity of the oval window of the spiral shell (cochlea) all interfere with sound conduction. Some conditions of conduction deafness can be corrected, and most are amenable to treatment.

Sensorineural deafness

Sensorineural deafness, or perception deafness, is relatively rare in school-age children. It may be caused by an injury or disease in the neuron or inner part of the ear. Infected gums or gallbladder can be the primary cause of perception deafness. It also can result from meningitis, influenza, and drugs such as quinine and salicylates. Extremely high body temperature can also cause perception deafness.

Some types of hearing loss cannot be prevented or corrected. However, hearing aids may compensate for much of the deficiency in persons with impaired hearing. Today prescriptions for hearing aids are written with the same precision as prescriptions for glasses.

NEUROLOGIC DISORDER: EPILEPSY

Epilepsy can cause the uninformed teacher considerable concern. An understanding of the condition and the proper care of afflicted children gives teachers the assurance necessary for dealing with an episode of epilepsy.

From its Greek derivation, the word *epilepsy* literally means a seizure. Being merely descriptive of clinical symptoms, the term is not satisfactory, but it usually is used to designate recurrent seizures and periods of unconsciousness.

Grand mal is the more serious type of epileptic seizure. Essentially it is a convulsive seizure with the following characteristics:

1. Aura, or sensory disturbances (e.g., light or taste), which sometimes precedes and warns of the attack
2. Sometimes a shrill and startling cry
3. Sudden loss of consciousness and falling backward
4. Pupils dilated; eyes open at beginning of seizure
5. Tonic spasm—drawing up limbs in rigid, flexed position
6. Clonic spasm—intermittent contraction and relaxation, with thrashing about of arms and legs
7. Spasm of respiratory muscles—no breathing and blueness of the face
8. Spasm of jaw muscles—biting the tongue, which results in bloody foam
9. Relaxation, prolonged stupor, and profound sleep

The active convulsion lasts less than 1 minute and terminates in exhaustion. During the seizure, attempt to protect the child from injury. It is sometimes possible to catch the person and prevent a fall. Moving the child to a clear space away from hot and sharp objects prevents injury. The seizure should not be resisted. Children who have only two or three grand mal seizures during the school year usually continue school attendance. When seizures become so frequent as to disrupt the class, alternative means of education should be considered. The cause of epilepsy is unknown, but sedatives reduce the severity of seizures and increase the length of time between seizures.

Typical minor attacks *(petit mal)* are characterized by a transitory (3- or 4-second) loss of consciousness without falling and only minor, if any, muscular twitching. These children may attend school without any particular problems. Others, however, may be classified by teachers as "spacy," "slow," or "inattentive." It is possible to experience as many as 200 *petit mal* attacks per day, and so teachers need to be aware that classroom behavior and deviation from the normal performance may have health-related origins.

With any student whose performance level changes or who repeatedly fails to meet normal expectations, one of the first questions should be, Could this situation be caused by or contributed to by a medical or health problem? In this way school personnel can more responsibly address their mandate to educate by identifying impediments to learning.

SKIN DISORDER: ACNE

Most adolescents suffer from some degree of acne, but about 5% may suffer from severe cases with associated discomfort and embarrassment. Boys are more frequently affected and likely to experience severe cases. For girls, acne problems occur between 14 and 16 years of age and for boys between 16 and 19 years of age. Professional care from a dermatologist minimizes the cosmetic consequences and limits the psychologic stress this condition causes. Teachers can be most effective in correcting some widespread misconceptions about acne. Acne is a natural consequence of the increased flow of androgens associated with puberty and changes in the skin occurring with growth. Acne is not, as often believed, the consequence of diet, and restricting the consumption of chocolate, cola, and candy is not necessary to manage the condition. Scrubbing with soap and water will not necessarily reduce the condition and may produce an irritant dermatitis. Acne is not the consequence of poor personal hygiene, but bacterial soap will limit the spread of the associated bacteria.

PREGNANCY

Pregnancy is a normal, healthy process; but, when it occurs in junior and senior high school youth, it can be a high-risk situation. Younger bodies are not fully prepared for pregnancy; thus there is physiologic risk for mother and child. Early parenthood clearly puts at risk the prospect of future education, employment, and personal growth. The United States, among countries of the developed world, has one of the highest rates of teen pregnancy. At the same time, there is no evidence that American students are more sexually active than students in other countries. The difference clearly seems to be ignorance and failure to use birth control techniques, including abstinence.

Instruction about birth control techniques, including abstinence, is difficult for many schools to carry out because of prevailing community attitudes against any discussion of this topic. However, school personnel should be open in their discussion about pregnancy and pregnancy risk and honest and complete in answering students' questions.

Prenatal care in the first 3 months of pregnancy is very important to ensure the health of the mother and the baby. Schools, therefore, should be responsive to pregnant students by providing support to continue their education and encouragement to seek medical care as early as possible.

CHILD ABUSE

It is estimated that more than a million children are abused or neglected each year. The majority of the abuse occurs in the first 6 months of the child's life. Although the incidence of abuse has declined by the time children enter school, the individual consequences are often so evident that they interfere with learning and relating to other people.

Every state now has child protection laws that mandate the reporting of child abuse to the appropriate authorities, and so school personnel can find themselves in a situation in which they are required to act as an extension of law enforcement. This creates a difficult situation for schools because it thrusts them directly into the midst of what typically are family problems, usually of long standing, and often sets school personnel in adversarial relationships with parents. Reporting evidence of child abuse also potentially involves teachers in investigative and judicial proceedings, which may result in the state assuming responsibility for the child's custody, thus splitting a family.

Despite these consequences, it would be unprofessional, unconscionable, and illegal for a teacher or any other school personnel to overlook evidence of possible chid abuse.

The U.S. Child Abuse Prevention and Treatment Act (PL 93-247) defines abuse and neglect as physical and mental injury, sexual abuse and exploitation, and negligent treatment of any child under 18 years of age by persons who are responsible for their welfare. This would include others besides the child's natural parents.

Physical abuse

Beating, burning, and kicking are the most common forms of physical abuse, but such things as exposure to weather, suffocation, strangulation, and stabbing or cutting have also been identified. Injury results from the hands of the abuser or from whatever item is available to use as a weapon: brooms, bats, electrical cords, hairbrushes, cigarette lighters, coat hangers, cigarettes, flames, hot plates, hot water, or scissors.

Abuse is evident by observation of physical signs and is also suggested by a child's behavior. Signs of physical abuse include:
1. Unusual bruising patterns or bruises in unusual places.
2. Bruises that reflect the outline of an instrument.
3. Burns.
4. Swelling around the mouth and eyes.
5. Broken nose.
6. Ears torn or injured.
7. Unusual skin rashes.
8. Lacerations.
9. Dental injury or missing teeth.
10. Dirty or inadequate clothes.

It is not only the existence of these signs but also the fact that they appear with some degree of frequency that indicates child abuse. For the teacher, the school nurse can be an invaluable assistant in identifying abuse. The nurse can examine the child more carefully and keep a record of the youngster's health. School counselors can also be of assistance by noting a child's behavior.

Often abused children also present behavioral patterns that will raise a concern among school staff. Abused children do not look to their parents for assurance; are apprehensive of other children or their parents; do not react under conditions that would normally cause children to cry; are withdrawn, preoccupied and forlorn, and aggressive in their behavior; seek assurances from others in unusual ways such as asking to stay with them; abuse drugs; run away; or are sexually promiscuous.

Abusive parents also present behavior patterns that can alert the professional teacher, nurse, or administrator. Parents may be overprotective, not allowing their children to participate with other children, give explanations for signs of abuse that are inconsistent with reality, saying, for example, "He fell off a stool," to explain a black eye. Such parents may give vague and evasive answers to direct questions. Parents may blame the child, saying, for example, "She's just a klutz, always banging into something." Parents may seek medical help for the consequences of abuse, but it may be from different emergency rooms or distant hospitals or a variety of physicians and nurses so that patterns of abuse cannot be easily detected.

Almost all child abuse occurs at the hand of parents. Child abuse is a family problem sometimes referred to as the "battered child syndrome." Families under stress, lower socio-economic families, single-parent families, parents with limited educations, and poorly housed families experience higher incidences of child abuse. However, teachers should not overlook the fact that children from sophisticated families may also suffer child abuse.

Sexual abuse

Sexual abuse is most common in the form of incest between father and daughter. It is the most difficult to identify and deal with. Signs of injury to the external genitalia and anal region with bleeding and swelling would be evident to physicians and nurses but not be detectable to others. Positive tests for sexually transmitted diseases and spermatozoa also may indicate sexual abuse.

Inability to sit still or signs of tenderness when sitting is often a sign of sexual abuse. With careful counseling children may admit to sexual abuse.

Steps to deal with child abuse

Because child abuse reporting initiates a legal action, teachers should act with care.

1. Note possible signs of abuse in some detail in writing. Record date, time, and circumstances under which the signs were noticed.
2. If a pattern develops or signs are obvious, check with the school nurse for confirmation.
3. Report information to school principal. The principal should initiate the reporting.
4. A decision may or may not be made to contact the parents, but the law in each state mandates reporting to the appropriate authorities.
5. If the primary law enforcement agency does not respond appropriately, contact may be made with other child protective social agencies.

Because child abuse involves families in highly emotional issues, there is sometimes a hesitancy on the part of all authorities to interfere. However, if these conditions exist, the law requires that they be reported.

SUICIDE

According to the Committee on Adolescence of the American Academy of Pediatrics (1987), suicide is the most frequent cause of death among young people 10 to 19 years of age, and there is evidence the prevalence is increasing. Although suicides are not likely to take place at school, gestures for help and attention are. Suicide attempts are more frequent among girls than boys, but boys are more often successful when they do attempt suicide. It is estimated that as many as 100 attempted suicides occur for every recorded suicide. The nature of attempts is so varied that there is no way to assess the extent of the problem. Automobile accidents, drug overdoses, falls, firearm accidents, and drownings may all represent suicide attempts. Gestures likely to be observed in school include depression; daredevil acts; truancy; delinquent behavior; somatic complaints such as headache, fatigue, and gastrointestinal pain; and behavioral conditions such as hyperactivity. Outright questions or statements about suicide should not be taken lightly. Because open discussion of this topic does not make it more likely to occur, questions or statements should be discussed. If teachers identify students whom they consider at high risk, they should involve other student personnel in a conference to explore their concern and develop a plan of action. Other teachers and the nurse and counselors usually constitute the primary team, which may then consult the school psychologist for advice.

ALCOHOL AND OTHER DRUG USE

Although tobacco is the drug that leads to the most drug-related deaths in the United States, alcohol is the drug that will most likely interfere with learning and be related to adolescent injuries and deaths. Other drugs are no less important; despite their public visibility, they are simply less common. They represent a problem, but one of lesser magnitude than alcohol. Teachers should recognize that alcohol and other drug abuse can occur at any age. Obvious failure to meet academic and behavioral expectations are early indicators of possible substance abuse. However, like all other health problems, the teacher is not a diagnostician and should refer students to specialists for a full assessment.

Unfortunately, parents are often not receptive to the suggestion that a youngster may be using alcohol and other drugs; thus the school should have clear policies on how parents are notified and what is expected of the parents. In many schools, teams of specially trained teachers help decide when alcohol and other drug referrals are made and how they should be made. This topic is discussed more fully in the chapter on screening.

DEVIATIONS IN MENTAL HEALTH

Numerous behavioral characteristics indicate that a student's mental health or psychosocial development may not be typical. Any of these characteristics taken individually may have little significance, but a complex of factors observed over a period of time gives rise to concern. Major deviations from mental health are relatively obvious, but small differences are difficult to interpret because the accepted range of "normal" is not clearly defined. Accordingly, the teacher's first role is to observe a student's behavior carefully and then seek advice and assistance from counselors and other specialists in the school or community.

Behavioral characteristics that may indicate deviations in psychosocial development may include the following:

1. Undue shyness
2. Tendency to be a loner
3. Restlessness and easy distraction
4. Excessive daydreaming
5. Belligerent, pugnacious and quarrelsome attitudes
6. Suspiciousness and distrust
7. Selfishness
8. Hypochondria

Although any one of these conditions may identify a student as different, it does not define a child as sick or in need of medical attention. If the conditions exist in the absence of a medical basis, they may just represent individual differences that we all will learn to live with. For the teacher the task is to ensure that small differences in individual students are not masking major problems.

As with communicable illness, people can contribute to the spread of mental illness or the promotion of mental health. Just as a teacher should be free from communicable disease, so too should a teacher be mentally healthy. Introspection may be useful at this point. Certain things can rightfully be expected of teachers in their role as educators:

1. Understanding his or her own behavior
2. Separating personal problems from the classroom and school life
3. Respecting each youngster
4. Understanding individual differences
5. Understanding the cause-and-effect relationship of deviant behavior
6. Maintaining an atmosphere neither too rigid, too severe, nor too permissive
7. Strengthening desirable behavior through recognition and praise
8. Dealing with behavior problems not serious enough for professional care
9. Substituting acceptable behavior for deviant behavior

In addition, the psychologic or mental health environment of the school should be conducive to good relations among teachers and between teachers and administrators. Teachers should be competent in dealing with students in a guidance and counseling role, although they should not usurp the role of the trained counselor. Schools should have an infrastructure of guidance and counseling services, often incorporating community resources to support teachers in their everyday classroom activities.

Skilled teachers with adequate knowledge of deviations from normal growth and development effectively help young people gain the most from their educational experience. The ability to note carefully developmental or health-related irregularities and adapt educational programs accordingly or make appropriate referrals is the mark of a truly professional teacher.

GET INVOLVED!   If you are presently majoring in or are considering majoring in community or public health education, you should become acquainted with the Society for Public Health Education; the organization is known among professionals as SOPHE. This organization was formed in 1950 to promote the health of all people by stimulating research and by working for high standards of professional practice in health education.

SOPHE membership includes health educators who work in local health agencies, the U.S. Public Health Service, colleges and universities, hospitals, health care and mental health agencies, and voluntary organizations.

SOPHE is well known for its Code of Ethics, which helps to set the standards of professional practice for health educators, its policy statements, and its outstanding publication, the *Health Education Quarterly*.

In addition to the national organization, there are state chapters that deal with both local and national issues. Annual meetings are held in conjunction with the national and state Public Health meetings. Undergraduate students enrolled in health education who are sponsored by an active member may apply for membership.

Application forms are available in the *Health Education Quarterly*, and by writing to:
Society for Public Health Education, Inc.
2001 Addison St., Suite 220
Berkeley, CA 94704

Summary

This chapter reviews a wide range of possible departures from normal. Teachers should have considerable tolerance to allow individuals to develop their own unique characters, but they should also be alert to identify differences that may indicate a larger problem. Developing teachers who are referral agents and keen observers is the desired outcome of this chapter.

STUDY QUESTIONS

1. Indicate some deviations from the normal in children that should be disregarded or even ignored in the school.
2. What is the professional responsibility of the teacher for the correction of defects in a pupil?
3. What role can a teacher play in aiding the excessively obese child to lose weight?
4. What should be the course of action of the school in dealing with a student who is listless, slow, inactive, disinterested, and chronically late?
5. After a child has had an epileptic seizure while in school, what should the teacher say to the other children in the class?
6. Why can it be said that there is as great a danger for a child with a defect or disorder to underparticipate as there is for that child to overparticipate?
7. What does it mean and what should the teacher do if a child's physician reports, "The child has a functional heart murmur, but it should be disregarded, and she should be treated like any other child"?
8. Explain the statement, "For the growing child with a malocclusion, the services of an orthodontist are not a luxury."
9. Which agencies or organizations in your community are interested in helping children with vision and hearing disorders?
10. A schoolchild needs a hearing aid, but the parents do not buy one. What should the school do?
11. What can be done by a teacher for the youngster who does not enter into group activities but always tends to be alone?
12. In terms of its influence on the mental health of the students, what is the most important factor in a classroom?
13. What are some resources a teacher can call on for consultation relating to students with health problems?

REFERENCES

Adeyanju M, Creswell WH: The relationship among attitudes, behaviors, and biomedical measures of adolescents "at risk" for cardiovascular disease, *J Sch Health* 57:326-331, 1987.

Adeyanju M, et al: A three-year study of obesity and its relationship to high blood pressure in adolescents, *J Sch Health* 57:109-113, 1987.

American Academy of Pediatrics: *School health: a guide for health professionals,* Elk Grove Village, Ill, 1987, the Academy.

American Psychiatric Association: *Diagnostic and statistical manual of mental disorders,* ed 3 (revised), Washington, DC, 1987, the Association.

Dale S: School mental health problems: a challenge to the health professional, *J Sch Health* 48:526, 1978.

Drucker M, Slade R: *Anorexia nervosa and bulimia: how to help,* Philadelphia, 1988, Open University Press.

Ensminger ME: Adolescent sexual behavior as it relates to other transition behaviors in youth, In Hofferth SL, Hayes CE, editors: *Risking the future: adolescent sexuality, pregnancy, and childbearing,* Volume II: Working papers and statistical appendixes, Washington, DC, 1987, National Academy Press.

Feldman SS, Elliott G: *At the threshold: the developing adolescent,* Cambridge, Mass, 1990, Harvard University Press.

Fennell R: AIDS/HIV articles published in selected professional health journals: 1981-1990, *J Sch Health* 61:385-387, 1991.

Forrest JD, Singh S: The sexual and reproductive behavior of American women, 1982-1988, *Fam Plann Perspect* 22:206-214, 1990.

Forrest JD, Hermalin AI, Henshaw SK: The impact of family planning clinic programs on adolescent pregnancy, *Fam Plann Perspect* 13:109-116, 1981.

Goodrich SW, McDermott RJ: Changing role and challenges for teachers of students with diabetes, *J Sch Health* 59:341-345, 1989.

Hodgson C, et al: Adolescent health needs: perspectives of health professionals, *Can J Public Health* 76:167-170, 1985.

Irwin CE Jr: *New directions for child development: adolescent social behavior and health,* No. 37, San Francisco, Fall 1987, Jossey-Bass.

Kempe RS, Kempe CH: *Child abuse,* Cambridge, Mass, 1978, Harvard University Press.

Kornguth M: Preventing school absences due to illness, *J Sch Health* 61:272-274, 1991.

Ladner JA: Black teenage pregnancy: a challenge for educators, *J Negro Educ* 56:53-63, 1987.

Lansky D, Brownell K: Comparison of school-based treatments for adolescent obesity, *J Sch Health* 52:384, 1982.

Malus M, et al: Priorities in adolescent health care: the teenager's viewpoint, *J Fam Pract* 25:159-162, 1987.

McGovern JP, DuPont RL: Student assistance programs: an important approach to drug abuse prevention, *J Sch Health* 61:260-264, 1991.

McHutchion ME: Student bereavement: a guide for school personnel, *J Sch Health* 61:363-366, 1991.

Meyer R: Accepting the challenge of child abuse and neglect: a golden opportunity for school health, *J Sch Health* 49:480, 1979.

Miller D, Lever C: Scoliosis screening: an approach used in the school, *J Sch Health* 52:98, 1982.

National Asthma Education Program: Expert panel report to provide clinical guidelines for diagnosis and treatment of asthma, *J Sch Health* 61:249-250, 1991.

National Heart, Lung and Blood Institute: Arteriosclerosis: report of the working group on arteriosclerosis, vol. 2, NIH Pub. no. 82-2025, Washington, DC, 1982.

Neinhuis M: As the health care system bypasses children, pressure mounts on schools to fill the gap, *J Sch Health* 57:144-146, 1987.

Newacheck PW, Taylor WR: Childhood chronic illness: prevalence, severity and impact, *Am J Public Health* 82:364-371, 1992.

Nishioka E: Helping children of alcoholics, *J Sch Health* 59:404-405, 1989.

Novello AC: Healthy children ready to learn: the Surgeon General's initiative for children, *J Sch Health* 61:359-360, 1991.

Ojanlatva A, Hammer AM, Mohr MG: The ultimate rejection: helping the survivors of teen suicide victims, *J Sch Health* 57:181-182, 1987.

Pigg RM: The contribution of school health programs to the broader goals of public health: the American experience, *J Sch Health* 59:25-30, 1989.

Resnicow K: The relationship between breakfast habits and plasma cholesterol levels in children, *J Sch Health* 61:81-85, 1991.

Weiss G, Hechtman L: The hyperactive child syndrome, *Science* 205:1348, 1979.

Winpisinger KA, et al: Risk factors for childhood homicides in Ohio: a birth certificate-based case-control study, *Am J Public Health* 81:1052-1054, 1991.

Part THREE

School Health Services

Health appraisal aspects of school health services

O VERVIEW

Secondary prevention activities involve early detection of possible illness and initiation of treatment. Despite the fact that illness is at its lowest levels among school-age children, sufficient deviations from normal health go unnoticed to justify regular health examinations and health screening of the school-age population. This chapter describes the relationships between student health and the school's educational mission. A distinction is made between health examinations and health screenings, and the basic screening techniques are described.

O BJECTIVES   After reading this chapter, the student should be able to:

1. Describe the relationships between health appraisal activities and the educational objectives of a school
2. Differentiate between a health examination and health screening
3. Describe the advantages and disadvantages of a health screening program
4. Identify possible errors in screening outcomes
5. List the basic methods in health screening for vision, hearing, height and weight, dental care, and scoliosis
6. Illustrate the use of various types of vision screening equipment
7. Describe the sweep test and the threshold test used to determine hearing acuity
8. Identify observable behaviors that indicate possible vision and hearing difficulties
9. Describe the ways height and weight data can be effectively used in health screening
10. State the basic reasons for measuring body fat (adiposity) and describe a means of measuring body fat
11. List basic points of an effective referral follow-up
12. Describe the basic principles governing confidentiality of student health records

Preventive activities that reduce the likelihood of a condition's occurring are preferable to treatment activities designed to overcome illness. This is the fundamental difference between primary prevention and secondary prevention described in Chapter 2. Unfortunately, it is not always possible to prevent an illness. The next best option is secondary prevention: prompt identification of the earliest discernible pathogenesis and initiation of appropriate treatment. The ultimate objective of early detection is the reduction of any illness-related disability and the avoidance of the costs and inconvenience of long-term treatment. For the school and students, the most important immediate cost is absence or distraction from the learning process.

The success of secondary prevention efforts depends on the early detection of disabling conditions. Schools are an excellent place for appraising students' health and detecting early signs of illness. Health appraisal efforts are principally of two types: (1) required physical examinations carried out by physicians at set times during the elementary and secondary school years and (2) health screening activities carried out in school under the supervision of the school nurse or a physician.

Sick and injured students do not learn as well as those who are fit and healthy. Health examination and screening programs that identify conditions interfering with learning and that aid in the early initiation of treatment improve the school's efforts on behalf of learning. When health conditions reduce a student's ability to learn, the teacher tends to focus special attention on that student, thus depriving others. The recognition that some learning problems are actually health problems can lead to the initiation of treatment, freeing the teacher to attend to the whole class.

Unrecognized health problems contribute not only to underachievement but also to inattention, class disruption, absenteeism, tardiness, and disciplinary problems. Early detection of students with communicable diseases, their subsequent removal from the school, and the initiation of treatment reduce the likelihood that other students or teachers will contract the disease and suffer unnecessary absenteeism.

Health examinations and health screening programs also have educational value. Students' participation in health examinations and screening activities allows them to learn values of personal health, monitor their own health status, and understand the need to seek further diagnosis and special care when appropriate. An effective means for young people to reduce the likelihood of early death from degenerative diseases is to learn skills and responsibilities for early detection and referral to treatment.

HEALTH EXAMINATION

The health examination is a means to an end and potentially a very effective instrument for improving health standards. In keeping with the present-day positive approach, the physician's examination of a child is designated a health examination, not a medical or physical examination as it may have been in the past (Fig. 7-1).

The frequency of school children's health examinations is usually set down by law. Where no legal directives exist, the decision must be made by local school and medical officials. The American Academy of Pediatrics (1987) suggests that the order of priority of health examinations should be (1) when children are identified as having special problems, (2) on beginning school, (3) in midschool (grade 6 or 7), and (4) before leaving school (grade 11 or 12). In addi-

FIG. 7-1. School-age children are at the healthiest time of their lives. Careful monitoring of health through regular health examinations and screening programs guarantees that any problems are treated early to ensure continued good health.

tion, special health examinations are recommendeded for students participating in athletic programs.

Students entering school for the first time

Children who are to begin school in the fall should be examined early enough to permit follow-up observation on recommendations of the examining physician. June and July are the most satisfactory months for preschool examinations. Parents are usually asked to complete a health history form for each new student. This form (Box 7-1) begins the student's health file.

Parents of students entering school for the first time are often invited to the school for a meeting with staff and general orientation before the start of classes or early in the semester. This is an ideal time to help parents understand why health is so important to learning. They should understand what the school will do to protect and enhance the health of their children. Also they should be reminded of their responsibilities in health promotion and education. Parents sometimes forget that they are important role models for their young students. Their eating patterns, use of medicine, and alcohol and tobacco habits all shape their children's behavior. The school cannot neutralize bad habits learned at home. Because the school's policy is to promote the health of its students, it must use every opportunity to recruit parents to participate in this effort.

BOX
7-1

Sample health history form*

1. Name of child _____ Birth date _____

2. **Pregnancy, birth and development**   *Circle one*
   a. Were there any difficulties during pregnancy, labor, or delivery?   Yes   No
   b. If yes, explain: _____
   c. Was this child carried for a full 9 months?   Yes   No
   d. Birth weight was _____ lb. _____ oz.

   Did this child:
   e. Have any trouble starting to breathe after birth?   Yes   No
   f. Have any problems in the hospital after birth?   Yes   No
   g. Sit alone before 7 months of age?   Yes   No
   h. Walk alone before 15 months of age?   Yes   No
   i. Say words by 1½ years of age?   Yes   No
   j. Check any of the following that have occurred with this child:
      ☐ Sleeping problem   ☐ Eating problem
      ☐ Excessive drooling   ☐ Coordination problem

3. **Illnesses and accidents**
   Has this child:
   a. Had more than one ear infection each year?   Yes   No
   b. Had more than two throat infections each year?   Yes   No
   c. Had a hearing problem?   Yes   No
   d. Had a vision problem?   Yes   No
      If yes, when last fitted for glasses? _____
   e. Had allergy problems, such as eczema, hives, wheezing, or asthma?   Yes   No
   f. Had frequent colds, sinus infections, or hay fever?   Yes   No
   g. Received any routine medications?   Yes   No
   h. Had any serious reactions to any medicine or injections?   Yes   No
   i. Had any difficulty passing urine?   Yes   No
   j. Ever had convulsions?   Yes   No
   k. Had a weight problem?   Yes   No
   l. Had any serious accidents?   Yes   No
   m. Been hospitalized for serious illness or accidents?   Yes   No
   Please explain any "yes" answers (use back of sheet if necessary).

4. **Family health**
   Do any other family members have any serious health problems?   Yes   No
   Explain a "yes" answer.

5. **Additional health concerns**
   Please let any additional health concerns or physical limitations of this child.

   _____

   _____

Filled out by _____ Date _____

*To be completed by parent or guardian.

Communication on this topic to the parents of new students should not only raise these issues, but should be very specific in encouraging parents to take action on behalf of their own health behavior and that of their children. For example, a listing of all the local health promotion agencies should be distributed. This list should include general health promotion agencies such as fitness centers; agencies and support groups providing special assistance such as smoking cessation groups and Alcoholics Anonymous; agencies such as the YMCA that provide recreation services and other services; and adult education options offered through community colleges, crisis intervention groups, and hot lines. As parents more actively accept this role and recognize the school's responsibilities, the basis for an effective working relationship between parents and school personnel begins.

Students new to the school system

If an acceptable health record is received from the student's previous school, a health examination may be unnecessary. If there is no health record or a doubtful health condition exists, health examination requirements should be part of the admission procedures, as should be the completion of a health history form.

Students entering midschool grades

For schools organized on the grade 6-3-3 basis, health examination as a requirement for admission to junior high school is both sound and an easy procedure to administer. Middle schools (5-3-4) should have the examination in the eighth grade. For schools on the 8-4 plan, the requirement should apply for admission to high school.

Entering junior high school or middle school often involves students having opportunities to select courses and become active participants in planning their education. Often schools invite parents to orientation meetings so they may have a better understanding of the school's role. This may be the first time since the parent orientation associated with students entering elementary school that most parents attend a school function. It is an ideal time to remind parents of their role and responsibilities in protecting and promoting their student's health.

Students participating in vigorous athletic programs

All students participating in interscholastic activities should be examined at the beginning of their particular sports program. Physician certification of the student's fitness to participate will indicate any limitations or restrictions and should be on file in the school before the student is admitted to practice. After an injury, illness, or other incapacity, the student should be admitted to further participation only on recommendation and supervision of a physician. Students participating in intramural sports should be examined by a physician yearly.

Graduation

Some school districts require health examinations before graduation from high school so that students graduate with an evaluation of both their academic and health status. Other school districts seek the assistance of community service groups and provide examinations as a gift to the graduating seniors. Examinations late in the student's education have little value to the school but do serve as an important reminder to the student of the importance of regular health examinations throughout life. Unfortunately, this practice is declining as the cost of health examinations is increasing.

Students referred through screening by teacher or nurse

Health screening programs frequently identify conditions requiring medical follow-up observation. When the physician evaluates the findings of the health screening, he or she typically provides a thorough health examination. Alert teachers and nurses also can frequently detect an unhealthy child. Both minor and serious deviations can be recognized by the observant teacher and referred to the school nurse, who will in turn contact the child's parents. Although the teacher may be unsure, it is prudent to err on the side of caution and speak to the nurse or the parents about the advisability of having the child examined by a physician.

Health examination procedures

Most commonly, the student's family physician conducts the health examination. In some cases health department physicians may be used, and in others, physicians may conduct examinations in the school. The student's usual health provider is the most desirable health examiner. The results and their usefulness to the school are greatly enhanced by standardized reporting forms. Information needs vary among school districts and may be dictated by state law. An example of a health examination form is given in Box 7-2. Notice that this form asks the physician only for information on any immunizations he or she may have given as part of the examination. Most states now require parents to submit a full immunization history when the student enters school (Box 7-3).

Periodic examinations of healthy schoolchildren rarely reveal major pathologic conditions. Children participating in health examinations are usually healthy, and childhood and adolescence are generally the healthiest periods of life. Nevertheless, there are several advantages to scheduling a periodic health examination.

First, an alert physician may identify an important unrecognized problem. Second, student-physician contact in the absence of a crisis (illness) enhances a healthy physician-student relationship. Third, routine conferences provide opportunities for parents to ask questions that they might not normally ask if they had to initiate a physician visit on their own. Fourth, the opportunity for physicians to tell children and adolescents that they are perfectly normal in their developmental stages is reassuring in times of rapid growth and development.

Health history

The American Academy of Pediatrics (1987) suggests that a medical history or health history may be the most important part of any health examination. In addition to a record of past health problems, both physical and emotional, the health history reviews the body systems and seeks information on any special health problems of other family members. A history identifies practices that may influence health such as smoking, exercise, diet, and sleep. Past immunizations and the current use of medication will also be reported (see Box 7-2). Information on emotional problems, parent-child relationships, leisure time activities, school performance, conflicts with authority, and use of drugs, alcohol, or tobacco are also explored.

BOX
7-2

Identification and school health data

Name _____ Sex _____ Entry date _____

Grade level K 1 2 3 4 5 6

Birth _____ Place of birth _____

Month   Day   Year   City/state

(Please bring copy of birth certificate.)

Present home address _____ Phone number _____

_____ Zip _____

Parents' names: Date of birth   Birth place   Nationality   Education   Occupation

_____   _____   _____   _____   _____   _____
(Father)

_____   _____   _____   _____   _____   _____
(Mother)

_____   _____   _____   _____   _____   _____
(Guardian)

Father deceased _____ Mother deceased _____ Parents divorced _____ Parents separated _____

| *Brothers* | *Sisters* |
Name	Birth date	Name	Birth date
_____	_____	_____	_____
_____	_____	_____	_____
_____	_____	_____	_____
_____	_____	_____	_____

Former school attended: _____

Health information: Family physician _____

State law requires all children be immunized against rubella, measles, polio, DPT, and mumps.

Please list below the date (month and year) of each dose given. To keep the health record up-to-date, please send dates of immunizations given after this form is sent to school.

1. Immunization against diphtheria, tetanus, and pertussis (combined)
   (three doses 1 month apart) Dates of doses 1. _____
   2. _____ 3. _____
2. DPT boosters: Date of doses _____
3. Sabin (oral) polio: Dose 1 _____
   Dose 2 _____ Dose 3 _____
4. Sabin polio boosters: Date of doses _____
5. Rubeola (hard measles): Date of dose _____
6. Rubella (German measles): Date of dose _____
7. Mumps: Date of dose _____
8. TB test date: _____ Results: _____

Please list below any medication the child takes on a daily or routine basis.

_____

Please write in date if the child has had any of the following:

Scarlet fever _____ Measles _____ Mumps _____

Other _____

Pneumonia _____ Three-day measles _____ Chickenpox _____

Other _____

Rheumatic fever _____ Poliomyelitis _____ Whooping cough _____

Operations (type and year): _____

Signed (parent or guardian) _____ Date _____

BOX
7-3   **Sample physical examination form**

Dear Parent:

State law requires that each child enrolled in kindergarten and seventh grade present a physical examination report from the family physician. It is extremely important that any physical limitations be discovered at these age levels to prevent more serious difficulties in your child. A physical examination within 6 months of entering kindergarten or seventh grade is acceptable.

Name _____ School _____ Grade _____

Address _____ Zip _____ Age _____ Sex _____

Physical Findings

Height _____ Weight _____   Nose and throat _____

Blood pressure _____ Pulse _____   Heart _____

Urinalysis _____   Lungs _____

Hemoglobin _____   Abdomen _____

Vision report _____   Musculoskeletal:

_____   Spine _____

Audiometric screening: Upper extremities _____

  Method _____   Lower extremities _____

  Results _____   Neurologic: ___ No ___ Yes

General appearance _____   Evidence of scoliosis: ___ No ___ Yes

_____   Evidence of hernia: ___ No ___ Yes

Immunizations given at this time: _____

Significant findings and remarks: _____

_____

Have you any further recommendations to teacher or school nurse for promoting this child's physical and mental health?

_____

Require medication on a daily or episodic routing: _____

_____

Please check classification:

_____ Regular: Student may participate in the regular program of physical education, recreation, intramurals, athletics, or related activities without undue risk or injury.

_____ Adapted: Student has a condition that might risk sustaining injury from participating in the regular program or needs a special adapted program as indicated by the consulting physician. Reexamine each year.

_____ Exempt: Student has a severe handicap that might risk sustaining injury from participating in the regular or adapted program. This student should be reexamined for possible reclassification at the end of the exemption period.

Date _____ Signed _____ (examining physician)

Because of the wide range of information gathered in a health examination, it is important for parents to be present unless the examination is being conducted on an older adolescent. Some physicians prefer to visit with parents and children separately.

For school health examinations, the physician pays special attention to any conditions requiring modification of the child's current or future school program. Thus parents must understand the importance of providing full information. Reluctance to record such information as epilepsy, mental retardation, or emotional illnesses increases the possibility that the school is unaware of these conditions as well as the likelihood that manifestations of these conditions may be misinterpreted when they occur.

In addition to the health history, a standard health examination usually includes a careful evaluation of the following:

1. General appearance
2. Height and weight
3. Head and neck, nose and throat
4. Vision and hearing
5. Thorax, heart, and lungs
6. Abdomen and genitals
7. Skin
8. Muscular and skeletal systems
9. Posture, gait, and feet
10. Neurologic system

Many schools require parents or guardians to complete a health history for the school's cumulative health record. An example of this form is shown in Box 7-2.

Dental examination

Most schools require periodic dental examinations when they require physical examinations. Routine annual or semiannual visits to the dentist are relatively common, and the prevalence of dental conditions interfering with learning has decreased significantly. The addition of fluoride to the drinking water in many communities has further reduced the prevalence of dental caries among young people.

For the school's purpose it is important to know whether the dentist has identified problems and whether appropriate care has been initiated or completed. The reporting form for dental health examinations given in Box 7-4 is relatively simple. Side 1 advises parents of the school's recommendation for regular dental examination, and side 2 provides space for the dentist's report.

Confidentiality of records

The quality of data and usefulness of records of health examinations are greatly increased if all cooperating physicians use standardized forms for reporting results. This not only standardizes procedures in data gathering but also encourages the inclusion of only pertinent information concerning the development of the child's educational program.

Passage of the Family Education Rights and Privacy Act in 1974 meant that all written records from physicians to schools receiving federal funds be open to parental inspection. According to the Family Education Rights and Privacy Act, parents may review their child's

---

BOX
7-4   **Dental referral card**

Dear Parents or Guardians:

The (name of school or health department) recommends that you see your family dentist for regular dental care.

Early and regular care will ensure better dental health throughout life. Only you, as a parent or guardian, can see that your child receives regular dental care. Poor dental health is a menace to general health.

Therefore you are urged to take _____ to your dentist for examination and, if any dental service is required, continue with treatment until all corrections are made. Please have your dentist sign as indicated on other side of card.

_____
(teacher or school nurse)

(over)

THIS SIDE FOR DENTISTS USE ONLY

I have examined _____

☐ All necessary treatment completed

☐ Patient currently under treatment

☐ No treatment necessary

Date _____ Signed _____ D.D.S.

---

educational records on request, challenge the accuracy of any part of the record, and seek deletion or correction.

Because written records are subject to misinterpretation and the potentially destructive effects of labeling are well recognized, schools must develop clear policies on the nature of information recorded and the ways health records are used.

HEALTH SCREENING

In technical terms screening is the identification of unrecognized illness or defect by the application of tests, examinations, or other procedures which can be applied rapidly. In simple terms screening identifies students who deviate from the average on one or more of a series of tests. Not all deviations indicate health problems, but the presence of a measured deviation indicates the need for a more careful examination.

Health screening can take several forms. Most health screening activities in schools are conducted by the school nurse, teachers, and trained volunteers (often parents) to assess vision, hearing, dental health, tuberculosis (TB), postural problems such as scoliosis, and growth and development. Various screening tests can be conducted separately or, more commonly, as a battery of tests administered in a single screening session, frequently referred to as *multiphasic screening.*

Another type of screening sometimes used in schools is referred to as case finding. *Case finding* is a specific screening activity carried out to identify a specific high-risk or suspicious condition such as head lice (pediculosis capitis) infestation. Still another variation is *selective screening,* carried out for portions of the school population who are for various reasons at special risk. Examples of high-risk children may be those of low socioeconomic status, those performing poorly in school, or those who are often absent or exhibit frequent disciplinary problems.

The usefulness of the school's health screening program depends on (1) the quality and care with which the program is carried out and (2) the uses made of the findings. Screening is one way of alerting people of the possible need for special care. The entire value of the screening process depends on how well the results are communicated to the participants and whether parents of students identified "at risk" follow through and seek definitive diagnosis and subsequently cooperate in any recommended treatment regimen.

The value of early detection made possible through a screening program must be constantly assessed against the time and personnel required to carry it out. Similarly, the decision on exactly which problem areas the screening program will assess must be judged against the utility of such a program. The following 10 principles of early disease detection were suggested by Wilson and Jungner in 1968 and still apply to screening program decisions:

1. The condition screened for should be an important health problem.
2. There should be an accepted treatment for persons with the recognized disease.
3. The facilities for subsequent diagnosis and treatment should be available.
4. There should be a recognizable latent or early systematic stage identifiable through screening.
5. There should be a suitable, easily administered screening test.
6. Screening procedures should be acceptable to the population.
7. The natural history of the condition, including the development from latent to declared disease, should be well understood.
8. There should be an agreed-upon policy on who treats patients.
9. The costs of the screening program should be economically balanced against the costs of other case-finding procedures and subsequent medical care.
10. Screening and case finding should be a continuing process.

If these conditions are met, screening can be a useful tool contributing to secondary prevention.

As described here, a screening is usually considered a special event when all students are screened for a particular condition, as in vision screening. It is important to remember that the teacher is invaluable in a continual process of screening. Each day that teachers see students they have an opportunity to notice deviations from the normal for each student in their class. This opportunity, when fully accepted by the skilled teacher, may mean the difference between success and failure for a student. Box 7-5 illustrates how a sensitive teacher noticed a difference in a student's performance and took action that will probably benefit that student for the rest of her life.

BOX
7-5.

School health services at work

Mrs. Jacobsen, a third grade teacher, noticed that Cindy often seemed out of touch when asked questions about the lesson. It was early in the school year, so Mrs. Jacobsen asked Cindy's teacher of the previous year about the student.

"Oh, she's just a little slow," the other teacher said.

Over the next few weeks Mrs. Jacobsen noticed that Cindy could usually answer questions about her classwork if she was working on something on her desk, but still seemed "slow" when asked about things the whole class was discussing and that were being illustrated on the blackboard. Mrs. Jacobsen first suspected that Cindy became shy when asked a question in front of the whole class. But further observation discounted shyness as a factor. Cindy had lots of friends and wasn't shy with them. She didn't seem to participate much in play activities at recess, but she did like to talk and play close to her special friends. Mrs. Jacobsen began to suspect Cindy's vision was the cause of her problems.

Mrs. Jacobsen moved Cindy's desk to the front of the room and immediately observed a difference in Cindy's ability to answer questions. This confirmed her suspicion that vision was the cause, so Mrs. Jacobsen sent Cindy to the nurse for a vision test. Sure enough, the test results indicated Cindy needed an eye examination.

How did Cindy get past the entry physical? A look at her records showed that she had transferred midway through the previous year and no health records had been sent.

The school nurse called Cindy's home and learned that her mother was unaware of Cindy's condition. She also learned that Cindy's mother was a single parent and Cindy's father was delinquent in his child support payments. Cindy's mother had moved to town to seek better employment, and the previous month her car had broken down. The repairs to the car were expensive, and she was just making it financially. The cost of a full eye examination and possibly glasses was more than she could manage. In 4 months the car repair would be paid, and glasses would be possible. That meant Cindy would spend half of the school year with poor vision.

The nurse suggested the ophthalmology clinic at the state medical college 100 miles away. Cindy's mother didn't want to ask for time off from her new job. Unemployment was high at the time, and many people were seeking jobs. The employer could afford to be tough.

Every day that went by Cindy fell further behind, even though she was sitting in the front of the classroom. Now she was self-conscious about being singled out to sit in front of the room.

The school nurse contacted the county health department's family medicine clinic. After explaining the case in detail she was referred to the local Lions Club, a civic group with a special interest in vision problems. The case was presented to the club president. He referred Cindy's case to a club member who was an ophthalmologist. He agreed to see Cindy at no cost.

The examination indicated that Cindy needed glasses. Cindy's mother was embarrassed that she didn't have money for the glasses at that time. The Lions Club agreed to meet half the cost of the glasses and Cindy's mom paid the balance to the club over six months.

Cindy could see better and was happier. Her mother's dignity was maintained since she made a substantial contribution to the cost of the glasses. Mrs. Jacobsen was able to help Cindy achieve. The nurse was proud of her role in being able to help.

Cindy's story is an example of the results that can be achieved when an observant teacher is able to detect a health-related problem underlying poor academic performance.

Quality of information gathered

Screening results should be reviewed in terms of (1) validity, (2) reliability, (3) yield, (4) cost, (5) acceptance, and (6) follow-up services.

The *validity* of a screening test is the ability to identify individuals who have the condition. Do the persons identified by the screening test actually have the condition when examined by a physician? Validity is assessed in several ways.

Persons identified at screening as being "at risk" subsequently fall into two groups: those who actually have the condition and those who do not. Persons identified who are actually diagnosed as having the condition are called *true positives*. Those identified at screening as having the condition but in whom the condition is not confirmed in subsequent diagnosis are called *false positives*.

Similarly, persons not identified in the screening process as having the condition fall into two groups: those not identified in the screening program who do have the condition *(false negatives)*, and those not identified in the screening program who actually do *not* have the condition *(true negatives)*. The ability of a screening test to identify the condition for which the screening is done is referred to as the test *sensitivity*. The ability of a test to identify correctly those who do not have the condition is referred to as the *specificity* of the test. Both sensitivity and specificity are usually expressed as percents.

$$\text{Sensitivity} = \frac{\text{Diseased persons with positive test}}{\text{All persons in population with the condition}}$$

$$\text{Specificity} = \frac{\text{Nondiseased persons with negative test}}{\text{All persons in population with the condition}}$$

Reliability of a screening test refers to the result consistency. Tests are reliable only when the same results are obtained repeatedly over time or when the test is carried out by different people and the same results are presented.

The *yield* of the screening test simply refers to the number of people identified. Screening tests should be reserved for a reasonably common condition to make them worthwhile.

Cost considerations relate both to personnel and to equipment. In the main, school screening programs are carried out with relatively inexpensive equipment that nurses, trained teachers, health aides, or volunteer parents can operate.

Today, *acceptance* of screening programs is seldom a problem. Care should always be taken to inform parents of regular screening activities and allow them to ask questions about procedures.

Follow-up activities ultimately determine the value of the screening endeavor. No matter how carefully the program is conducted, its value depends on communicating the results to parents who must get the necessary medical examinations and follow through on any suggested treatment activities.

Vision screening

Vision screening should be carried out each year of a child's elementary and secondary education and should be required of all students transferring into the school system unless the results of earlier screenings are included in the student's health record. Children with glasses should be checked annually by their health care professional. Eye characteristics change rap-

---

Nutritional and fitness status of school-age children

EMERGING ISSUE The chair of the School Health Council has called a meeting to review recent reports and to consider the implications for the school health program. For example, the Surgeon General's report *Healthy People 2000* and a report from the National Heart, Lung and Blood Institute (NHLBI) have called for reductions in dietary fat. As a consequence, the Institute has recommended that children over the age of 2 years follow the same low-fat, low-cholesterol dietary guidelines recommended for adults. The concern is that Americans, as a whole, have blood cholesterol levels that are too high, putting them at risk for coronary heart disease. Life-style factors contributing to elevated blood cholesterol are saturated fats in the diet and a sedentary life-style. In fact, recent surveys indicate that children and youth are becoming less fit because of their diets and lack of exercise.

These reports have sparked considerable interest in the community. Several parents have called to inquire about the dietary standards of the school lunch program and the amount of exercise that children receive in physical education.

The Council has been asked to make a report to the school board on any recommendations that the committee thought were needed. As a Council member, you are asked to indicate your thinking on this issue by placing a plus (+) or a minus (−) sign before each of the following statements with which you agree or disagree.

_____ 1. I believe that school lunches, as a rule, make a positive contribuiton to the diets of school children.

_____ 2. I believe that this is an example in which schools are being asked to take responsiblities that are more properly assumed by the home.

_____ 3. I believe that this is a problem that can be best addressed through parent education.

_____ 4. I find it difficult to debate over the quality of school lunches when some children depend on the school feeding program to sustain them.

_____ 5. The type of food provided by the Department of Agriculture relates to surplus commodities such as meat and dairy products, a prime source of dietary cholesterol.

_____ 6. I believe that this calls for a comprehensive approach that includes school staff, teachers, administrators, and parents to make program practices consistent with the promotion of health and well-being.

_____ 7. This, in part, is a political issue and a question of values (e.g. food available for school feeding and the degree of emphasis that can be directed to health and fitness).

_____ If limited to a single choice, I would choose this number.

---

idly in childhood and adolescence, and the frequency of vision disorders increases with age. Only 5% of first-grade students have refractive errors (*myopia,* nearsightedness; *hyperopia,* farsightedness; *astigmatism,* irregularities in the curvature of the cornea), but as many as half of the students may have similar problems by high school graduation. *Strabismus* (cross-eye, esotropia) and differences in the visual acuity of the two eyes (*anisometropia*) are found in approximately 5% of children (Fig. 7-2).

Screening for visual acuity is most frequently done with a Snellen or similar test. For some children the illiterate *E* or the STYCAR (Sheridan's test for young children and retardates) is more effective. The illiterate *E* uses the capital *E,* sometimes called the tumbling *E,* with the

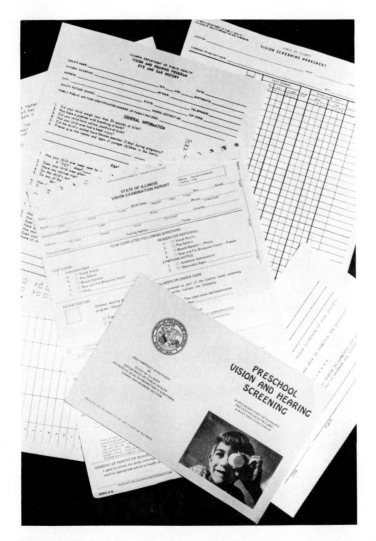

FIG. 7-2. Vision screening records provide a valuable aid for monitoring changes in students' vision and making referrals and follow-up observations. The school nurse, counselors, and teachers can refer to these records to help plan special student learning activities and possibly to help understand unusual behavior.

arms of the *E* facing at random either left, right, up, or down. Students are asked simply to point the direction of the arms of the E. The STYCAR test uses the letters *H, O, T,* and *V,* and children match letters on the screen chart with the same letters on a card they hold in their laps.

The wall chart for the Snellen test is placed at eye height 20 feet (6 m) from the person to be tested. The chart should be well lit (20 to 30 footcandles) with bright lights from sources such as windows eliminated. Both eyes are open during testing; a card covers the eye not being tested. The right eye is tested first, then the left eye, and then both. Children should be able to read at least half the letters and symbols on a given line to "pass" that line. The American Academy of Pediatrics (1987) suggests that "children at the third grade should read the 20/40 line or better with each eye; after third grade they should read the 20/30 line. A child with a difference of two or more lines between the two eyes should be referred." Children who normally wear glasses should be tested wearing their glasses.

Interpretation of the tests is not difficult in most cases. For school purposes 20/20 is normal. A child with 20/30 vision is probably nearsighted, although a definitive diagnosis must be made by the health care professional. A child with 20/10 or 20/15 vision is probably farsighted. However, a deviation from the 20/20 normal standard is simply an indication of a need for retesting and possible referral.

The test for *hyperopia*, a convex or "plus" lens test, can be carried out at the same time. This is an important test because hyperopia may eventually make reading difficult. Generally this test is given only in the early grades.

To test for hyperopia a pair of 2.25-diopter lenses on a frame are placed on the child, over his or her own glasses if necessary. A diopter (D) is a measure of refractive error. The child is asked to read the standard wall chart, described earlier. A child who can identify half or more of the letters or symbols on the 20/20 line in this case may have possible hyperopia of 2 D or more. Because of the concern and expense associated with referral, all students identified in screening as having a possible need for referral should be retested a second or third time.

Defects in *color vision* are tested for by use of the pseudoisochromatic plates in which a color figure is embedded in a background of another color. Children with normal color discrimination can identify figures; others cannot. It is estimated that 8% of boys and 4% of girls have color discrimination difficulties.

The possibility of vision problems can often be detected by observation of the student's behavior or appearance. Cross-eye; red, bloodshot eyes; and encrusted or swollen eyes are all signs suggestive of the need for referral or attention. Students' complaints about not being able to see well, dizziness, headaches, and nausea especially after close eye work, as well as reports of blurred or double vision are also signs of vision problems. Young people's behavior also can indicate the need for eye examinations: rubbing the eyes excessively, shutting or covering one eye, tilting the head, thrusting the head forward in an effort to see, difficulty in reading or other work requiring close eye contact, blinking more than usual, irritability when doing close work, stumbling over small objects, holding books close to the eyes during reading, and poor performance in games requiring distant vision can indicate the need for referral.

Children should be prepared for activities such as vision screening. They should be told in advance what will be done, why it will be done, and how it will be done. In the case of vision screening children can practice using the STYCAR or Snellen chart or illiterate *E* symbols before the actual tests. The results of screening should be carefully explained, with care being taken that the students do not see screening as a "pass" or "fail" situation and that referral for further testing is a helpful gesture made in the interest of the student's well-being. Only after careful diagnosis will students truly know the status of their eyes and their vision.

Some schools may have commercially produced binocular vision screening equipment. Testing effectiveness of this equipment can vary widely. The purchase and maintenance of vision screening equipment should be directed by a cooperating physician or a committee made up of parents and health care professionals. Good equipment, well maintained and correctly used, can enhance the efficiency of vision screening by reducing the space needed, but it does increase the time needed to screen large numbers of students. Some schools establish a policy whereby students not meeting a particular criterion using standard vision screening charts are tested a second time using the binocular vision screening equipment. This allows an increased level of specificity in the screening program.

Hearing screening

Hearing loss is frequently so gradual that it is imperceptible to the person concerned. Unconsciously a person adapts to a gradual hearing loss. People with normal hearing do a certain amount of lip reading, but a person whose hearing is declining relies more and more on lip reading. Often a teacher observes behavior symptoms of hearing difficulties, such as posturing, inattention, faulty pronunciation, unnatural voice, poor academic progress, and copying.

However, many children with hearing defects do not show behavior changes, and a hearing screening test is a more reliable device to discover hearing defects than a child's outward behavior.

Many adults with greatly defective hearing could have normal or nearly normal hearing if the defect had been discovered early. Hearing screening will identify the student with possible correctable hearing loss.

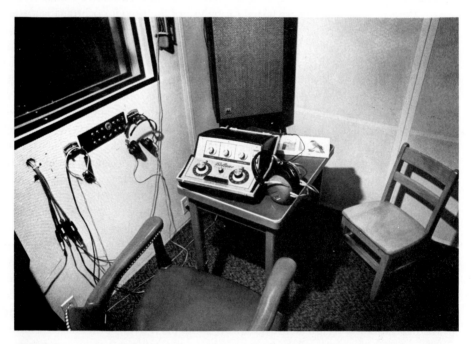

FIG. 7-3. Hearing screening involves a simple, noninvasive procedure that can be a useful learning experience for young people. How the equipment works and the procedures followed should always be explained to the person being screened.

Because of the importance of early detection and treatment, the hearing screening should be conducted on a schedule similar to that of vision screening, beginning during the preschool period. Hearing losses are often related to middle ear infections, which occur more frequently among younger children. Screening at this level should be done annually and then every 2 years in secondary school (Fig. 7-3).

The two most common types of hearing loss are *sensorineural* and *conductive.* Sensorineural loss is serious and often irreversible. Causes of sensorineural loss include damage to the auditory nerve and to the auditory center of the ear and the temporal lobe of the brain. Viral diseases such as measles and mumps, bacterial infections, prolonged exposure to loud noises from sources such as tractors, rock bands, gunfire, and trauma to the head or ears are known causes of sensorineural hearing loss.

Conductive hearing loss is a more common occurrence among children and results from problems in the external ear, the tympanic membrane, and the middle ear cavity that interfere with the transmission of sound. Causes include wax impaction, foreign objects, otitis media, congenital abnormalities, and ruptured or scarred eardrums. Fortunately, many cases of conductive hearing loss can be treated with either medical or surgical procedures. However, early attention is important to avoid the profound effects on learning that even moderate hearing loss can cause (Fig. 7-4).

An accurate and reliable hearing screening program requires a pure tone audiometer and an audiometrician or trained operator to do the testing. The conventional program involves two stages: a sweep check test and a threshold test. A sweep check test establishes frequencies that can be heard when the volume is constant. The threshold test establishes the lowest volume level at which a child hears tones of a given frequency.

Hearing screening should be carried out in a room that is as quiet as possible and free of background noises such as fluorescent lighting, toilets, music classes, shop classes, cafeterias, and typewriters.

Young people should be prepared by receiving a clear description of the testing process, an equipment demonstration, and instructions for response when they hear sounds in the headphones. Children are usually instructed to raise a hand or signal with a forefinger to acknowledge that they have heard a sound. For actual testing, students should remove glasses and earrings and should not chew gum. Care should be taken that the headphones fit properly and that hair is pulled back from around the ear.

In the sweep-check screening a tone is presented at a consistent 20-decibel (dB) level of intensity, starting with a frequency of 1000 hertz (Hz), or cycles per second, and then sweeping through several different frequencies as follows: 250, 500, 2000, and 4000 Hz. If no response is received from the students at 1000 Hz, the tester has the option of proceeding through the other frequencies or increasing the intensity to 25 dB. If a response is received at 25 dB after the sweepthrough of the frequencies at this level, the tester returns to the 20 dB.

According to the American Academy of Pediatrics, children who fail to hear 1000 or 2000 Hz at 20 dB or 4000 Hz at 25 dB in one or both ears should be retested after several weeks. Because respiratory tract infections can cause temporary hearing loss, students must be retested after a period of weeks before the final referral decision is made.

The results of a hearing test are recorded on an audiogram as shown in Fig. 7-5.

Hearing needs lifetime protection

FIG. 7-4. Often students take their ability to hear for granted. Colorful posters and informational brochures used at screening times and throughout the year are an important reinforcement for a good health education and hearing screening program.

The second step in hearing screening is the threshold test, which determines the exact decibel level at which a tone can be heard at various frequencies. Each ear is tested at 250, 500, 1000, 2000, and 4000 Hz with the intensity of tone beginning at O dB and increasing to louder levels until a response is obtained. Next the intensity is reduced in steps of 10 dB from the first obtained response level until no response is obtained. Then the tone is presented at 5-dB increments until the child can hear the tone. This procedure is repeated for each frequency. The American Academy of Pediatrics (1987) suggests that a child needs further diagnostic evaluation if the hearing threshold is 25 dB or greater at two or more frequencies in one or both ears or 35 dB or more for a single frequency in either ear.

False-positive hearing tests often occur because the audiometer has not been correctly calibrated. Before any large-scale screening effort is begun, a check should be made of the equip-

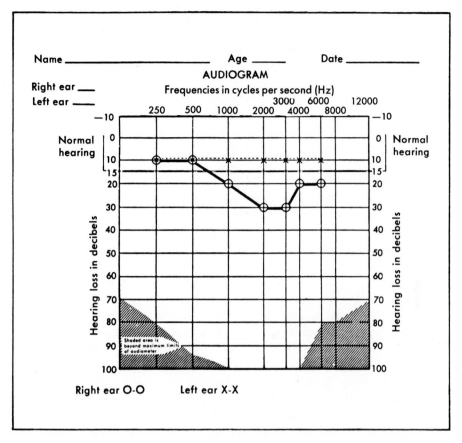

FIG. 7-5. Audiogram. The diagram indicates normal hearing in the left ear, but in the right ear a loss of 20 dB at frequencies of 1000, 4000, and 6000 hertz and a loss of 30 dB at frequencies of 2000 and 3000 hertz.

ment and the background noise of the room, and if possible an electroacoustic calibration should be carried out to ensure that the equipment is working correctly.

Tympanometry. New technology now provides some added options in hearing screening. Audiometry provides for the subjective assessment of the threshold of sound. The student provides an indication of when he or she first hears the sound. New equipment designed to check the integrity of the middle ear now also provides an objective measure of sound threshold.

Tympanometry is the measurement of the integrity and sensitivity of the middle ear and combines the resources of miniaturized circuitry, computerized capabilities, and immediate printed test results. Using sound emitted from a hand-held probe, tympanometry compares the emitted sound to sounds reflected by the eardrum. In this way the equipment calculates the ratio of absorbed sound to reflected sound. Infections such as *otitis media* reduce the ability of the ear to absorb sound; thus, if the tympanometer instrument measures a high degree of reflected sound compared to absorbed sound, further testing and diagnoses may be necessary.

At the same time this equipment is able to detect the small muscular reflexes associated with the response of the ear to sound. Muscular reflexes can be assessed against different sound thresholds, and an objective measure is provided of the ear's ability to detect sound. Auditory sensitivity is thereby measured without the subject's subjective assessment of the threshold.

The equipment necessary for tympanometry is widely available, but it will take time for it to replace the audiometric devices already in use in many school districts. In the future, audiometric screening in schools will incorporate this new technology and will become significantly more sophisticated.

Dental screening

Even though children are referred to the family dentist for thorough examination before admission to school and at other set times, there is no guarantee that additional dental care will occur.

Dentistry has been especially effective in encouraging good preventive practices and prophylactic care every 6 months, but some parents still believe that first teeth, or deciduous teeth, do not need special care because they will ultimately be replaced by permanent teeth. Dental screening programs provide an excellent opportunity to encourage students to take care of their teeth, eat correctly, and see a dentist frequently.

Absence of clear defects in teeth and the oral cavity at screening does not ensure that no problems exist. Dental caries occur more frequently than any other disorder among schoolchildren, and until caries reaches an advanced stage, it is likely to cause little pain or concern. Similarly, infected gums may occur painlessly. However, dental screening programs, along with their educational impact, can identify *pyorrhea,* usually indicated by a red margin of the gum around the neck of the tooth, and *gingivitis,* sometimes called trench mouth or Vincent's disease, characterized by inflammation or even ulceration of the gums and other parts of the mouth, bleeding, excessive salivation, and considerable soreness. Gingivitis usually does not occur in healthy children but is associated with malnutrition, poor general health, inadequate rest, and poor personal hygiene. Chronic *halitosis,* or bad breath, may also indicate a problem, especially when it occurs in the presence of an otherwise clean mouth. Changes in the color of a person's teeth also indicate possible problems (Fig. 7-6).

Pronounced overbite or underbite and poorly aligned teeth that will eventually create mechanical and cosmetic problems are also easily detectable. In many cases orthodontists will delay treatment of these conditions until the student reaches a particular growth stage, but the conditions should still be brought to the parent's attention. If orthodontic care has been initiated, a note should be made in the student's health record.

Measuring height and weight

The practice of weighing and measuring is perhaps the most firmly established aspect of the school health program. Nevertheless, little evidence supports the value of height and weight data alone as a useful tool in identifying health problems that are not otherwise suspected. However, although growth charts such as those in Chapter 4 are useful in comparing the serial measurements of an individual student's height and weight, they are far from effective in detecting possible nutritional problems such as obesity or growth disorders.

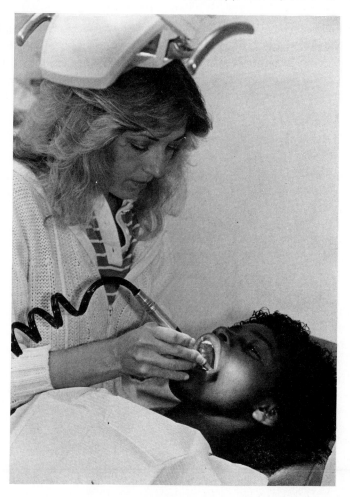

FIG. 7-6.   Dental screening that results in referral for a specific problem will usually result in the student receiving a full dental examination plus prophylactic care and instruction on the care of teeth and gums.

As a health education aid, however, height and weight measurements are invaluable. Emphasis should be placed on interesting children in their own uniqueness, not comparing themselves with the standard table or with other children. In addition to the educational use, height and weight measurements are also useful in the follow-up observation and evaluation of specific nutrition programs such as weight control classes or as useful adjuncts to nutrition surveys, provided that height and weight measures are supplemented with skinfold measures and possible laboratory tests. Eisner and Callahan (1974) also suggest that height and weight measurements may be useful in geographic areas where there are common treatable conditions, such as hookworm and other chronic infections, that retard growth.

The National Child Health Survey (1983) has shown that height and weight measures combined into a body mass index (BMI) and a skinfold measure of body fat tissue (adiposity) are related to blood pressure, both diastolic and systolic. As such, height, weight, and adiposity measures become useful screening devices.

BMI represents a simple extension of height and weight data as described in Chapter 4. The higher the index, the greater the deviation from normal.

$$BMI = \frac{Weight\ (kg)}{(Height\ [ml])^2}$$

Adiposity measures are relatively new in routine school health appraisals. Adiposity, or body fat, is estimated with specially designed calipers that measure body fat under the skin at spe-

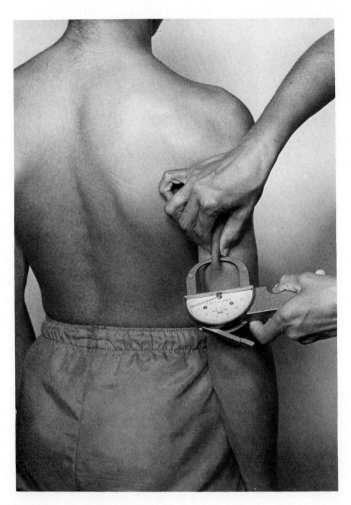

FIG. 7-7. Skinfold measurement is taken in the triceps area approximately midway between the elbow and the head of the humerus.

cific points. This is done by pinching skin between the forefinger and thumb and measuring the thickness with the calipers (Fig. 7-7). The two most commonly used landmarks for screening purposes are (1) the *triceps,* the back of the arm, midway between the elbow and tip of the shoulder, with the skinfold parallel to the axis of the arm and (2) the *subscapular* area, 1 cm below the inner angle of the end of the scapula (shoulder blade), in line with the natural cleavage of the skin (American Alliance for Health, Physical Education, Recreation and Dance, 1980) (Fig. 7-8). Usually the physical education teacher is trained in taking these measurements and can assist with adiposity screening.

Approximately 1 cm of skin is pinched, and the caliper tips are placed 1 cm above the part held by the thumb and forefinger and 1 cm in from the extended edge of the fold. The full pressure of the caliper is gradually released, and the reading is taken within a few seconds. Two or more measures at a given site should be averaged to represent the screening value. Percentile norms for the triceps area for boys and girls are presented in Table 7-1.

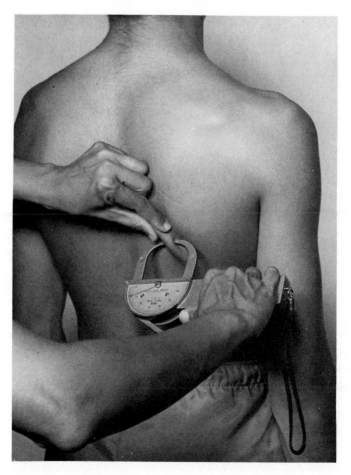

FIG. 7-8. Landmarks for taking skinfold measurements in triceps and subscapular area.

TABLE 7-1. Percentile norms for 6 to 18* years of age for triceps skinfold (mm)

Age (years)	6	7	8	9	10	11	12	13	14	15	16	17
Boys												
Percentile												
5	5	4	4	5	5	5	5	4	4	4	4	4
10	5	5	5	6	6	6	6	5	5	5	5	5
25	6	6	6	7	7	7	7	7	6	6	6	6
50	8	8	8	8	9	10	9	9	8	8	8	8
75	9	10	11	12	12	14	13	13	12	11	11	11
90	12	12	14	16	16	19	20	19	17	16	16	16
95	13	14	17	20	20	22	23	23	21	21	20	20
Girls												
5	6	6	6	6	6	6	6	6	7	7	8	8
10	6	6	6	7	7	7	7	7	8	9	9	10
25	7	8	8	9	9	9	9	9	11	12	12	12
50	9	10	10	11	12	12	12	12	14	15	16	16
75	11	12	14	14	15	15	16	17	18	20	21	20
90	14	16	18	19	20	20	22	23	23	25	26	25
95	16	17	20	22	23	23	25	26	27	29	30	29

Based on data from Johnston F, Hamill D, Lemeshow S: Skinfold thickness of children 6-11 years (Series II, No. 120, 1972) and Skinfold thickness of youth 12-17 years (Series II, No. 132, 1974), Washington, DC, US National Center for Health Statistics. US Department of Health, Education and Welfare.
*The norms for age 17 may be used for age 18.

Scoliosis screening

In the typical school situation posture is not regarded as an important factor in the promotion of student health. A deviation in posture usually does not produce a serious health threat, yet, as with other physical disorders, postural defects are a concern.

Lateral curvature and rotation of the spine, or *scoliosis,* lead to significant disability later in life and are a principal focus for postural screening. It is estimated that 2% of the population has scoliosis, a treatable condition that goes largely undetected; thus the potential for the schools to greatly reduce the prevalence of this disease is significant.

Scoliosis occurs most frequently during the years of rapid growth (10 to 15 years of age); accordingly, screening programs should be arranged to check children in grades 5 through 10 annually.

Scoliosis goes undetected in the early years because many students visit a physician only irregularly and because the condition in its early stages is asymptomatic. Girls more often than boys exhibit the condition, as do those who have close relatives with scoliosis. Linking the school health records of members of an individual family may be a useful administrative practice.

Scoliosis screening can be carried out by the school nurse, physical education teacher, visiting physical therapist, or health aide who has received special training. Ideally both boys and girls should undress to the waist for screening purposes and should not wear leotards or other physical education clothes. A brassiere will not interfere with the screening of girls. Shoes must be removed so that both feet are level on the floor.

The student stands erect, head up, eyes straight ahead, shoulders back, and arms hanging to the sides. Feet should be together. Five points of perspective of the student's back are examined: (1) shoulders should be the same height, (2) shoulder blades should appear at the same height, (3) the space between each of the free-hanging arms and the body should be equal, (4) flanks of the hips should be equal, and (5) the alignment of the spinal processes of the spinal cord should be straight (Fig. 7-9).

Standing directly behind the student, the screener asks the student to bend forward to right angles at the hips, head hanging in a relaxed position and the arms dangling relaxed from the shoulders with the palms pressed together and the knees remaining straight (Fig. 7-10). The screener observes the surface of the back at eye level to detect any unevenness. Box 7-6 identifies points of observation and presents a sample reporting form to record deviations that represent criteria for further referral. Students with noted deviations should be referred to a physician for evaluation.

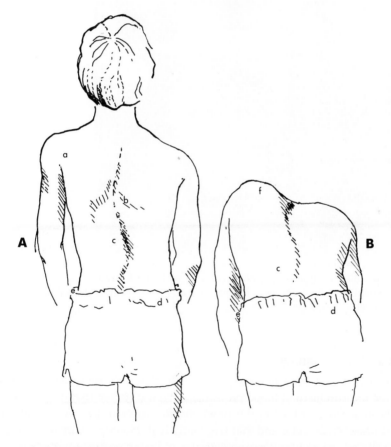

FIG. 7-9.   Screening points for scoliosis. **A,** Student standing erect, feet together, arms hanging naturally. *a,* Shoulder elevation uneven; *b,* scapula (shoulder-blades) uneven. **B,** Feet together, hands with palms together, bending forward, arms hanging perpendicular to floor. *c,* Misaligned spine; *d,* uneven hip prominence; *e,* unequal arm to body space; *f,* uneven rib prominence.

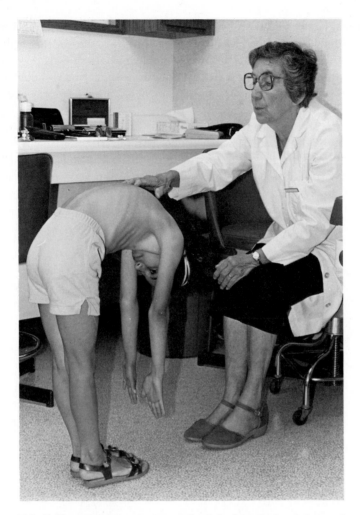

FIG. 7-10. Physician viewing student's back as she bends forward to check for indications of scoliosis. Student should also be viewed from the rear. Notice that this student's hands are not palms together as they should be.

Blood pressure screening

The inclusion of blood pressure screening in school health appraisals is relatively new. Although the measurement of blood pressure is a typical part of routine medical care, it has not often been a part of school health programs. Recognition that high blood pressure is a major heart disease risk factor and that frequently high blood pressure is asymptomatic has led to an increased concern for the early detection of high blood pressure.

Blood pressure is simply the force of the blood pulsing against the arterial wall. Blood pressure is measured with a sphygmomanometer in a simple and painless procedure. Persons deviating from established norms can easily be identified and referred.

BOX 7-6

Sample scoliosis reporting form

Name _____ Age _____ Date _____ M/F _____

Address _____ School _____ Grade _____

Examiner _____

Back toward examiner and forward bend away from examiner:

1. Head and neck base off center over sacrum?   ☐ Yes ☐ No

2. Shoulder elevation uneven?   ☐ Yes ☐ No

3. Shoulder-blades uneven?   ☐ Yes ☐ No

4. Waist creases uneven?   ☐ Yes ☐ No

5. Obvious spinal curvature?   ☐ Yes ☐ No

6. Hip prominences unequal?   ☐ Yes ☐ No

7. Arm to body space unequal?   ☐ Yes ☐ No

Forward bend toward examiner:

8. Ribs prominent on one side?   ☐ Yes ☐ No

Side bend toward examiner:

9. Increased round back?   ☐ Yes ☐ No

10. Increased swayback?   ☐ Yes ☐ No

• • •

Is the student presently under treatment for scoliosis? ☐ Yes ☐ No
Student referred to: ☐ Family physician or orthopedist
                     ☐ Services for handicapped children or other clinic

---

Blood pressure should be measured in a quiet area with the student relaxed. Support the student's arm at midchest level and wrap the blood pressure cuff around the upper arm. Blood pressure cuffs come in several sizes, and it is important that the cuff fit snugly and cover at least two thirds of the upper arm. Given the choice of a cuff that is too large or too small, choose the larger cuff. Inflate the cuff to approximately 30 mm Hg above the point at which the radial pulse can no longer be heard. Then deflate the cuff while listening to the pulse through a stethoscope placed over the brachial artery. The point at which a clear pulsing sound is heard represents the measure of systolic pressure. The point at which the pulsing sound disappears represents the diastolic pressure.

Routinely, blood pressure should be measured two or three times to overcome the possibility of a single unusually high reading. Repeated deviations of 10% from established norms indicate the need for referral.

Students and parents need to be frequently reminded that, as with all screening procedures, deviation from the norm simply warrants further investigation by a medical doctor and does not necessarily indicate the existence of any clinical condition.

Cholesterol screening

Not yet common in school health screening programs but increasingly available in public screening programs is the measurement of blood cholesterol. Generally agreed to be a major risk factor for heart disease, cholesterol can now be checked quickly and easily with relatively inexpensive new technology. However, a drop of blood is required for testing. The skin must be punctured; thus usually medical supervision is required.

The identification of elevated cholesterol levels will need medical interpretation. Frequently, however, modifying the diet; reducing food of animal origin; and increasing fruit, vegetables, and grain products will adequately reduce cholesterol levels. In special cases medication will be prescribed.

Nutrition

Students' nutrition practices may vary greatly. The advent of computer-based nutritional analysis programs has meant that students' diets can now be easily analyzed. Home economics teachers may help students quantify recent dietary recalls, which can then be entered into a computer for analysis. The resulting report can be used individually or as the basis for nutrition class.

Risk profiles

Computer-based risk profiles that assess the interaction of personal health risks based on personal behavior profiles are available for high school students but not for elementary or middle school students. These profiles incorporate measures on smoking, exercise, alcohol and other drug use, safety practices, nutrition, and exposure to sexually transmitted diseases; and they give students an assessment of their own health risk. The advantage of these types of programs is that students themselves can often complete them by entering their own data in response to computer-programmed questions. Assistance is often needed for interpretation of the results and the development of personal action plans. These activities form a part of the health curriculum for students as they learn to take responsibility for their own health.

Screening for teachers

More and more teachers are asking school nurses for health-related screening. Weight measures, blood pressure checks, and access to computer-based risk profiles are probably the most common services requested by teachers. The school that actively encourages teacher and staff health promotion will do well to develop a policy to encourage teachers to monitor their own health and will provide regular screening services to their teachers and staff.

The school exists to facilitate learning. Obviously, the early identification of health problems that interfere with learning is important. But schools are not health care institutions.

Screening programs that require technology or specialized personnel or that seek to detect relatively rare conditions may be appropriately conducted through required routine medical examinations conducted by physicians.

In the final analysis, school personnel, parents, and representatives of the medical community should be involved in determining the extent of the school's screening program and its value. More important, perhaps, than expanding traditional program screening is ensuring adequate follow-up observation of cases.

Follow-up observation

Health appraisal activities consist of four phases: (1) planning, (2) conducting the health appraisal, (3) follow-up observation, and (4) summarizing and interpreting the screening results to aid in curriculum development.

Health screening disrupts the normal educational pattern of the school day and poses a different pattern, not necessarily less educational but designed specifically for another purpose. Efficiency is important. Careful planning ensures that classroom disruption is held to a minimum. Efficiency can be improved by seeking help in the actual screening activities from local health departments and voluntary health agencies, from volunteer parents, and physical education and speech teachers. All cooperating personnel must be skilled in their tasks, and all equipment must be checked in advance.

Planning should be carried out in detail. The actual screening activities should be carried out in an organized manner with special care to gather accurate information and record it clearly.

For effective follow-up study, screening results must be properly recorded so that they can be clearly understood and interpreted at a later date. Before conferring with parents, other school records should be reviewed.

Follow-up centers around referral. A screening exercise simply identifies a person who needs further careful examination. Care should be taken to avoid unnecessary referrals because of anxiety and expense placed on parents and unnecessary burdens placed on local health care resources.

The simplest referral device is a letter sent directly to parents or guardians with a clear explanation of what was done, the results, and recommended follow-up actions. Care should be taken not to alarm parents or guardians. Include a simple letter or card the health care provider can complete, to be returned to the school with referral results. School personnel should establish a time frame for the referral and should state this clearly in the letter. Suggest telephone contact with the school nurse or aide if questions arise.

If compliance with the referral is not achieved in a set time, a conference with the parents is recommended. Ideally both parents should attend the conference because they may see the problem from different perspectives. Parent conferences may include other school staff such as the nurse or physician, teacher, administrator, or possibly staff members such as the physical education, speech, or special education teacher. Parent conferences provide a forum for explaining the possible problem and its significance, but, just as important, they should develop a plan of action, including suggestions for care sources, means of payment, and limits of the school's responsibilities. The school needs to establish a policy clearly outlining just how far a school will go to ensure parental follow-up observation and just how much of the school's resources will be devoted to such an activity.

Records

A critical element to follow-up relates to interpretation and use of records. Individual student records are confidential documents. Access to these documents is specified in the Family Education Rights and Privacy Act of 1974, Title IV, PL 93-380 (as amended).

A student's individual health record includes health examination results, screening results, and records of routine health activities within the school such as accident and illness. This is a confidential document. All members of the school staff should recognize this fact. Health records are also cumulative documents of long standing; thus statements that could damage a student's school career should not be included. Certain entries in the record may be appropriate, but the likelihood of later misinterpretation should always be considered.

Under the terms of the Family Education Rights and Privacy Act all student records must be available to parents and can be subpoenaed as court evidence. Parents, or students who have reached 18 years of age, may review their children's or their own records on request. Further, they have a right to challenge the accuracy of these records and seek corrections or deletions of offending sections. Records cannot be released to a third party without informed consent and only for specified purposes. Summary or aggregated data that do not identify individual students, however, can be compiled for planning purposes without violating the confidentiality of student health records.

The school health examination and routine health screening activities provide a significant opportunity to improve students' health. Early identification of health problems is the next best option to actual primary prevention. Even the healthy child can benefit from participation in a health examination and health screening program.

HEALTH GUIDANCE AND SUPERVISION

Health appraisal information is obviously useful to individual students and their parents. In summary form, these data are also useful to classroom teachers and curriculum planners. Classroom activities should address common health conditions among students. School nurses and counselors can also work with individual students and their parents to help overcome health problems. Individual counseling and direct supervision of a student's educational activities are important follow-up aspects of health appraisals and also form part of the school's educational responsibilities.

Traditionally, schools accept the role of supervising all aspects of a student's activities during the school day. In practice, such supervision at school corresponds to the supervision a conscientious parent exercises in the home. However, inherent in the school's role is more than just the protection and maintenance of the child's health.

Any school health program must be appraised in terms of its effect on individual students' health. No phase of the program has a more direct effect on the student than does the guidance and supervision phase. The effect will be reflected in the student's future well-being and the student's ability to accept responsibility for his or her own health.

Basic concepts

Guidance helps young people plan their own actions, in full light of all facts about themselves and the world in which they live and work.

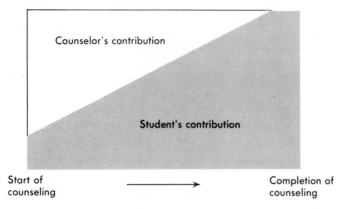

Counselor's contribution

Student's contribution

Start of counseling ———————> Completion of counseling

FIG. 7-11. Counselor and student contributions in health counseling. At the outset the counselor makes a considerable contribution but reduces his or her role as students increase their contributions. The final objective is to develop students' abilities to rely on their own resources.

Health guidance acquaints persons with various ways in which they may discover and use their natural endowments to live as well as possible. Guidance means accepting each pupil as an independent personality. Effective guidance develops the student's ability for self-guidance; if the student continues to lean heavily on the counselor, the guidance has not been effective. As revealed diagrammatically in Fig. 7-11, the counselor should play a diminishing role, and the student an increasing role in the process.

Responsibility

In the United States, the school health program and the school general guidance and counseling program experienced parallel growth, since both grew out of the transition to functional education. Both are concerned primarily with students as individuals and with their overall well-being.

Education leaders support the view that all teachers have a role in guidance. These leaders also recognize that school health personnel are in a strategic position to contribute to the school guidance program and consequently to each student's fullest development. Clearly, from a school's perspective, the only issue more important than education is the child's health.

In this context, health education should not be considered exclusively an academic subject. Health instruction is a means to an end, with a goal of the student's fullest possible development. The quality of well-being the student maintains and his or her ability to make necessary decisions relating to personal health reveal the application of health knowledge.

Counseling is a procedure of guidance and a form of mutual deliberation that involves examination of items that will aid a child in comprehending his or her problem and understanding its solution. The school counselor does not make the final decision but aids the student or parent in arriving at a solution. Counseling helps a child see his or her health needs and find the medical or other service required. It may be a matter of working out a pattern of living to attain a maximal level of health. Counseling can also help each child develop a full appreciation of the value of good health and inculcate a determination to promote and protect

TABLE 7-2. Similarities and differences between teaching and counseling

Teaching	Counseling
The teacher needs to know pupils so that educational objectives are attained and normal growth processes encouraged.	The counselor needs to know pupils in terms of specific problems, frustrations, and plans for the future.
The subject matter outcomes (or objectives) to be attained are known to the teacher and the students.	The subject matter of the interview is known to the counselor and sometimes unknown to the counselee.
The teacher is responsible for encouraging growth toward objectives partially determined by the social order (citizenship, honesty). The teacher has a responsibility for the welfare of the culture.	The counselor is responsible for helping the counselee resolve personal problems. The counselor has a responsibility for the welfare of the counselee.
Teaching starts with a group relationship, and individual contacts grow out of and return to group activities.	Counseling starts with an individual relationship and moves to group situations for greater efficiency or to supplement the individual process.
The teacher is responsible for the welfare of many children at one time.	The counselor is responsible for only one person at any one time.
The teacher carries on most work directly with children.	The counselor works with and through many people. Referral resources and techniques are of considerable importance.
The teacher uses skill in group techniques with great frequency, whereas interviewing skills are used less often.	The counselor uses interviewing skills as a basic technique.
The teacher uses tests, records, and inventories to assist the instructional (educational) process.	The counselor uses tests, records, and inventories to discover factors relating to a problem. The results are used for problem-solving (therapeutic) purposes.
The teacher has many tools (curriculum outlines, books, workbooks, and visual and auditory aids) to increase effectiveness.	The counselor has no tools that are used with all the counselees. The first task is to help the counselee discover problems and their causes, and then the individually appropriate sources of assistance.
The teacher needs to increase personal information relating to instructional activities.	The counselor needs information not frequently used by teachers: information about occupations, training institutions, colleges, apprenticeship programs, community occupational opportunities, placement, referral resources, social service agencies, and diagnostic and clinical instruments.
The relationship between teacher and student is compulsory. Children are required to be there.	The most effective counseling comes from a voluntary association. The counselee must want help and must feel that the counselor can be helpful.

TABLE 7-2.   Similarities and differences between teaching and counseling—cont'd

Teaching	Counseling
The teacher deals with children, the majority of whose adjustments are happy and satisfying.	The counselor's clients are disturbed by frustrations. They are often characterized by emotional tensions, previous disappointments, and lack of confidence.
The teacher is concerned with the day-to-day growth of pupils and with their general development.	The counselor is concerned with the counselee's immediate problems and choices but is also interested in helping the counselee develop workable long-term plans.
The skillful teacher tries to develop many abilities that increase instructional effectiveness.	The skillful counselor tries to develop many of the abilities used by a wide variety of highly technical specialists: psychiatrists, clinical psychologists, test technicians, occupational information specialists, social workers, visiting teachers, juvenile delinquency workers, and placement officers.

that asset. Counseling may be an avenue through which a student visualizes future needs and accomplishments.

Primary responsibility for a child's health must always rest with the parents, but the school is in a strategic position to complement and supplement the effort by dealing with expressed and observed health problems. After all, the best and fullest development of each child is the school's cardinal objective. Subject matter is important, but it serves as a means to an end in the development of the student. It is incongruous to teach children about health yet disregard their existing health problems.

The guidance role of the elementary school teacher and the secondary school health educator is to help students understand their problems, to see possible solutions, and to know which professionals and agencies may be of service in helping them solve their problems.

Organized health guidance focuses the students' interest on the appraisal of their own health status, making health knowledge personally identifiable and more meaningful.

Teaching and counseling

In many respects teaching and counseling are similar. Many of their objectives are the same. Teaching attempts to obtain these objectives through classroom situations. Counseling seeks to reach these objectives through counseling relationships. The principles developed by the Michigan State University illustrate the differences between counseling and teaching (Table 7-2).

SUMMARY

Health appraisals seek to identify health conditions that will detract from the general welfare of the student and interfere with learning. This responsibility is shared with the parent, who should report past and present illnesses and handicapping conditions; the physician, who checks the child's health at specific times during his or her school career; and school personnel, who routinely have the opportunity to check a few important measures of health.

The school screening programs, which identify deviation from the norm, can be dealt with only to the extent that parents and community resources join together to help identify health problems and to provide the means for treatment.

School screening programs are important but limited. They identify students with deviations from a preestablished norm but do not confirm the presence of specific health problems. Screening programs identify the need for further analysis and should clearly be recognized as such. When significant conditions are identified, follow-up observation to ensure that the proper medical opinion is obtained is critical.

Equipment and personnel costs and the yield of true positive results, considered in light of the philosophy of the local school board and community, will dictate the nature and extent of the school's health appraisal practices.

G**ET INVOLVED!**   School counselors play an important role in providing for the health and well-being of school children. Given the challenges faced by today's schoolchildren, school counselors are being asked to assume a greater role in the lives of their students and their students' families.

Counselors in today's schools are much more developmental and positive in their work with students. The long-range goals of school counselors are to help students become effective learners, responsible people, and productive workers. In terms of the school's health program goals, counselors help students develop a healthy self-concept. Counselors are often the student's main source of support and counsel in problems such as acquired immune deficiency syndrome (AIDS), child abuse, problem family life and parenting education, substance abuse counseling, and school dropouts.

The school counselors work with students with regard to these broad areas, including personal/social goals, and education and career goals. In the area of personal/social goals, students are encouraged to develop a self-awareness and develop positive attitudes, respect for others, relationship skills, and ways to resolve conflicts. In the area of education goals, counselors help the student to apply effective study skills, set goals, become an effective learner, and gain skills. With regard to career goals, counselors help the student form a career identity, develop a plan for the future, learn to use career information, and begin to set career goals.

If you wish to learn more about counseling as a career, write to:
The American School Counselor Association
5999 Stevenson Ave.
Alexandria, VA 22304

STUDY QUESTIONS

1. Explain the contention that health appraisal is a continuing process.
2. What is the primary objective of the health examination?
3. If certain parents do not arrange to have their children checked by a dentist, what can the school do?
4. Who should have access to the child's health record form?

5. Referral of a child by the school is to the parents, not to the physician. What is the significance of this procedure?
6. Why is it important to start the screening for vision and hearing in preschool?
7. Propose a program to have all elementary school children have at least one dental examination per year.
8. What measures should the school take when a child has been found to have a hearing defect?
9. Why is it unnecessary for all schoolchildren to have a threshold test of their hearing?
10. What is the purpose of a screening examination as opposed to a health examination?
11. What are some of the benefits that can come to students from effective health guidance?
12. What are some common objectives of teaching and counseling?
13. Why should the school administration concern itself with the health of all teachers in the school district?
14. Why is the health of the teacher a significant factor in the school health program?
15. What is the difference between false-positive and false-negative results in a screening test?
16. Distinguish between validity, reliability, and yield in health screening.
17. Why is a federal law needed to govern access to student records?
18. What is the difference between the sensitivity and the specificity of a screening test?
19. List and explain the significance of three common visual defects found in young children.
20. Explain the screening process for scoliosis.
21. Demonstrate the correct way to administer a vision screening test using (a) the Snellen chart, (b) the STYCAR test, (c) the illiterate E, and (d) the test for color vision defects.
22. How do sensorineural and conductive hearing losses differ?
23. How does a threshold test differ from a sweep test?
24. Why is dental screening so important, and what are the basic dental problems that can be detected in a screening program?
25. Describe the limitations of height and weight as a screening device. How do BMIs and measures of adiposity add to the value of height and weight data?

REFERENCES

American Academy of Pediatrics: *School health: a guide for health professionals,* Elk Grove Village, Ill, 1987, the Academy.

American Alliance For Health, Physical Education, Recreation and Dance: *Lifetime health related physical fitness,* Reston, Va, 1980, the Alliance.

Appelboom T: A history of vision screening, *J Sch Health* 55:138, 1985.

Bagnall P: One hundred years old and fitter than ever: school nursing in Britain, *J Sch Health* 61:402, 1991.

Blum R, Pfaffinger K, Donald W: A school-based comprehensive health clinic for adolescents, *J Sch Health* 52:486, 1982.

Bonaguro JA, McLaughlin, M, Sussman K: An exploration of health counseling and goal attainment scaling in health education programs, *J Sch Health* 54(10):403, 1984.

Bosse JD, Mallett J, Santoro J: Preliminary report of the Colorado school vision screening interdisciplinary task force, *J Sch Health* 61:407, 1991.

Brink SG, Nader PR: Comprehensive health screening in elementary schools: an outcome evaluation, *J Sch Health* 54(2):75, 1984.

Brown E: Multidisciplinary assessment of learning problems: school nurse's role, *J Sch Health* 51:595, 1981.

Bryan E: Administrative concerns and the school's relationship with private practice physicians, *J Sch Health* 49:157, 1979.

Eisner V, Callan LB: *Dimensions of school health,* Springfield, Ill, 1974, Charles C Thomas.

Eisner V, Oglesby, A: Health assessment of school children. III. Vision, *J Sch Health* 41:408, 1971.

Family Educational Rights and Privacy Act of 1974, Title IV, PL 93-380 (as amended), *Fed Reg* 40:1208, 1975.

Fox G, Harlin V: Role and responsibilities of the school physician, *J Sch Health* 44:369, 1974.

Griffith B, Whicker P: Teacher-observer of student health problems, *J Sch Health* 51:428, 1981.

Kaplan DL, et al: Transferring a clinic-based health education program for children with asthmas to a school setting, *J Sch Health* 56(7):267, 1986.

Knecht L: Consent and confidentiality: legal issues in adolescent health care for the school nurse, *J Sch Health* 51:606, 1981.

Litwack J, Litwack L: The school nurse as a health counselor, *J Sch Health* 46:590, 1976.

Mallick MJ: Anorexia nervosa and bulimia: questions and answers for school personnel, *J Sch Health* 54(8):299, 1984.

Marino L: Pre-kindergarten health visitation day in Boardman, Ohio, schools, *J Sch Health* 61:269, 1991.

Miller JSA; Implications of role expansion for school nurse managers, *J Sch Health* 60:29, 1990.

National Child Health Survey (NCHS): Dietary intake and cardiovascular risk factors. I. Blood pressure correlate, US, 1971-1975. Data from the National Survey Series 11, No. 226, Hyattsville, Md, Feb. 1983, US Department of Health and Human Services, Public Health Services.

Newman I: Integrating health services and health education: seeking a balance, *J Sch Health* 52:488, 1982.

North A: Screening in child health care: where are we now and where are we going? *Pediatrics* 54:631, 1974.

Silver G: Redefining school health services: comprehensive child health care as the framework, *J Sch Health* 51:157, 1981.

Puskar K, Lamb J, Norton M: Adolescent mental health: collaboration among psychiatric mental health nurses and school nurses, *J Sch Health* 60:69, 1990.

Roeser RJ, Adams RM, Watkins S: Cerumen management in hearing conservation: the Dallas (Texas) independent school district program, *J Sch Health* 61:47, 1991.

Spalj N, et al: The school nurse's role in managing athletic injuries, *J Sch Health* 59:271, 1989.

Walter HJ, Connelly PA: Screening for risk factors as a component of a chronic disease prevention program for youth, *J Sch Health* 55(5):183, 1985.

Weinberg AD, et al: Cholesterol screening using the school as a worksite, *J Sch Health* 62:45, 1992.

Wilson J, Jungner G: Principles and practices of screening for disease, World Health Organization, Public Health Papers No. 34, Geneva, 1986.

Zanga JR, Oda DS: School health services, *J Sch Health* 57(10):413, 1987.

CHAPTER
8

Preventive aspects of health services

Control of communicable diseases

OVERVIEW

Although most communicable diseases are no longer a principal cause of death, they are not eradicated. Only smallpox has been totally eliminated. Many other fatal communicable diseases are present and are more prevalent than the public realizes. Recent outbreaks of measles, Hepatitis B, *Giardia,* and influenza and the continued prevalence of venereal diseases, including AIDS, illustrate how communicable diseases still pose a threat to public health. The control of the spread of communicable diseases rests entirely on the ability of society to maintain high standards of personal hygiene, effective sanitary engineering practices (especially the management of sewage and water), good housing, adequate nutrition, and high levels of immunization within the entire population. Infectious diseases have always been a scourge of the young, and even today the young are more prone to infections. Because infection depends to a large degree on the close association of many people, the school presents a great potential both for spreading infection and for controlling infectious diseases. Teachers must understand the dynamics of infection, the principal infectious diseases of school-age children, and the ways to control infection.

OBJECTIVES   After reading this chapter, the student should be able to:

1. Identify and describe paths of infection and disinfection
2. Differentiate between types of resistance to communicable disease and different forms of immunity
3. Diagram and describe the course of an infectious respiratory disease
4. Describe the (a) source of infection, (b) mode of transmission, (c) incubation period, and (d) possible school control measures for common infectious conditions of childhood and adolescence
5. Outline various responsibilities for controlling infectious diseases
6. Explain legal and administrative reasons for excluding sick children from school
7. Detail the immunization schedule for school-age students and explain needs for legal mandate to enforce immunization schedules
8. Recognize the different sexually transmitted diseases and explain why they present a special challenge to school personnel

Today's school is concerned with the prevention of diseases and defects. The school's main effort focuses on the prevention of communicable disease. Communicable disease rates have declined significantly, perhaps in part because of the school's past efforts.

COMMUNICABLE DISEASE

Disease is a harmful departure from the normal state of health. A *communicable* disease is one transmitted from one person to another or from other animals to humans. It involves parasites that are pathogenic to humans. Most of the organisms are microscopic, although some worms and even mites are visible to the unaided human eye. Microscopic pathogens include bacteria, viruses, fungi, and protozoa.

INFECTION AND DISINFECTION

Infection is the successful invasion of the body by pathogenic organisms under conditions that permit them to multiply and harm it. The mere presence of organisms in the body, however, does not mean infection. At a given moment many persons harbor *Pneumococcus* bacteria in the lungs without having pneumonia, and many persons have billions of *Streptococcus albus* on the skin without having acne. Bodily harm is usually caused by an organism-produced toxin (biologic poison), although some organisms invade and damage tissues directly. To multiply and thrive, human pathogens require a temperature of about 98.6° F (37° C), moisture, alkalinity, darkness, and nutrients. The human body provides optimal conditions.

The body reacts to infection by increased production of white blood cells, elevated temperature, inflammation, and pain. These body defenses may be sufficient to overcome the infection.

Disinfection kills, removes, or arrests the activity of the pathogens of infection so that the body's defense mechanisms can overcome the invader. Chemical disinfectants are generally used for infections. Tincture of iodine, mild silver protein (Argyrol), gentian violet, mercocresols (Mercresin), nitromersol (Metaphen), thimerosal (Merthiolate), benzalkonium (Zephiran), and alcohol dilutions are examples. A disinfectant must be effective without causing damage to living tissues.

CONTAMINATION AND DECONTAMINATION

Contamination is the presence of human pathogens or nonpathogenic organisms on inanimate objects. Thus one speaks of a *contaminated* handkerchief, glass, water supply, or quart of milk; but one speaks of an *infected* finger, tonsil, or intestine. *Escherichia coli,* a contaminant from human feces, is an example of a pathogen that may contaminate a water supply. Milk and water are hospitable media for human pathogens. Inanimate objects are less hospitable because pathogens live only seconds in light, dryness, or low temperatures. Inanimate articles, other than milk, water, and solid foods, that harbor pathogenic organisms are called *fomites.*

Decontamination is killing or removing the pathogens in or on inanimate objects. Several methods can be used, such as burning, heat drying, ultraviolet rays, and highly concentrated chemicals.

CLASSIFICATION OF COMMUNICABLE DISEASES

Different systems have been devised to classify communicable diseases. A simple yet comprehensive classification accepted by many in the health field encompasses five different classes. Each class title describes the diseases in the group and suggests the mode of transmission.

The five classes and some of the more common diseases in each class

Respiratory-borne diseases
Chickenpox
Coryza (head cold)
Diphtheria
German measles (rubella)
Influenza
Measles (rubeola)
Meningococcus meningitis
Mumps (parotitis)
Poliomyelitis (infantile paralysis)
Rheumatic fever
Scarlet fever
Smallpox (variola)
Streptococcal throat infection
Tuberculosis
Whooping cough (pertussis)
Alvine (intestine) discharge diseases
Amoebic dysentery
Bacillary dysentery
Salmonellosis
Typhoid fever
Serum hepatitis
Viral hepatitis

Open-lesion diseases
Furunculosis (boils)
Impetigo (gym itch)
Scabies
Rabies
Insect-borne diseases
Malaria
Rocky Mountain spotted fever
Tularemia
Yellow fever
Sexually transmitted diseases
Chlamydia
Gonorrhea
Syphilis
Herpes
Genital warts
HIV/AIDS

In the normal school situation, respiratory diseases constitute the greatest problem in disease control. Students have more days of restricted activity and school absenteeism because of respiratory conditions than any other condition.

TRANSMISSION OF INFECTIOUS DISEASE

Humans are the greatest reservoir of disease-causing organisms. Although other reservoirs exist, the great problem in controlling communicable disease is preventing transmission of organisms from one person to another. The increase in population, travel, and general congestion of people increases the problem of control. Pathogens are transmitted by direct or indirect contact or by an intermediate host.

Direct contact is the most common means to transfer infection. Three conditions are necessary for transfer: the infectious materials must be fresh, the distance traveled must be short, and the lapse time must be brief. Material may be transferred through hand shaking, kissing, coughing, or sneezing. Normal air does not usually contain enough virile pathogens to cause infection by inhalation, but sneezes and coughs may provide a means of transfer. Respiratory diseases are transferred by direct contact, and most are acquired when the organisms are carried to the mouth via the person's own hands. Open-lesion diseases also are transmitted by direct contact.

Indirect contact involves an intermediate vehicle between the reservoir and the new host. The infectious material may be old, the time interval long, and the distance great. Alvine discharge diseases are usually transmitted indirectly via water, milk, or foods. Respiratory diseases may be spread by indirect contact via handkerchiefs, towels, and eating utensils, although the usual method is by direct contact.

An *intermediate host,* the third method of transmission, accounts for the transfer of insect-borne diseases. An insect acquires the organism from an infected person or lower animal and transfers the organism to another person. In some instances the organism spends part of its life cycle in the intermediate host, but in other cases the transmission is a mechanical transfer.

BLOCKING ROUTES OF TRANSMISSION

If one person is the original reservoir of infection and another person is a prospective new host, the organisms must travel by one of several routes between the two. If these routes are blocked, the new host will be protected from contracting the disease. First the organisms must escape from the reservoir. Their ability to travel is limited; thus they must rely on vehicles of transmission. Because conditions outside the human body are decidedly unfavorable to pathogens, the organisms must enter the new host shortly after leaving the reservoir. Several means are available for blocking the routes of transmission of disease.

Early diagnosis is essential to block routes of transmission. Because diseases vary in their mode of transmission, disease identification indicates routes over which the organisms of that disease may travel.

Control of the direct contact route is the most difficult to handle effectively. In a society where citizens enjoy personal freedom, voluntary or compulsory restriction on personal contact is difficult to establish. The control of disease spread by direct contact depends on a willingness to undergo personal inconvenience for the protection of others.

Isolation of persons with diagnosed cases can be an effective means to control direct contact. Also helpful is quarantine of exposed susceptible persons during the period in which they might transmit the disease if infected. These are legally enforceable measures, although voluntary isolation is the most desirable means of disease control.

Control of the air route is based on the three principal ways by which infection may be spread by aerial contamination: droplets, droplet nuclei, and dust. *Droplets* are the fine drops of moisture composing the spray of coughs and sneezes. Moisture sustains the bacteria for several seconds so that inhalation could carry virile organisms into the respiratory tract of a susceptible host. *Droplet nuclei* are minute particles from the evaporation of droplets, which, being small and light, may float in the air for minutes. *Dust* can become contaminated from droplets and droplet nuclei and thus can be a vehicle for the transmission of disease.

Control of the water route is highly effective through community water treatment plants, sewage treatment, and the prevention of stream pollution. The same procedures apply to private and semipublic water supplies. Chlorine added to water effectively controls most waterborne diseases.

Control of the milk route is possible through testing of herds for tuberculosis and brucellosis, milk pasteurization, dairy inspection, and examination of dairy employees.

Control of the solid food route focuses on sustained inspections and sanitary safeguards for food cultivation, production, distribution, and preparation. Foods that are consumed raw, such as fruit and vegetables, are given special attention. Supervision of sanitation in restaurants and other establishments where food is produced or prepared, such as canneries and bakeshops, is effective.

Control of the insect route depends on knowledge of the pathogen, the insect, and the disease itself. Control measures are directed toward the destruction of the intermediate host. Elimination of breeding places and insecticide and larvicide use are highly effective direct means. Theoretically, insect-borne diseases can be controlled completely.

RESISTANCE AND IMMUNITY

Resistance is the body's general ability to ward off pathogens. Several body factors act as barriers or defenses against organisms pathogenic to the human being. These mechanisms, nonspecific in their action, attack all foreign organisms with varying degrees of effectiveness.

Human skin is a *mechanical* barrier, and its moderate acidity provides an unfavorable medium for pathogens. *Mucus secretions* of the respiratory tract interfere with pathogens, which are propelled outward by the hairlike cilia of the mucous cells. The *acid* of the stomach and the high alkalinity of the intestines defend against pathogens. *Salinity* of the tears protects the eyes and eyelids against infection. *Fever* is the body's response to invading parasites. Because temperatures above 100° F (38° C) inactivate most pathogens, a fever aids the body's task of destroying organisms.

Perhaps the most important defense mechanism is *phagocytosis,* in which microorganisms are enveloped, dissolved, and absorbed. White blood cells (leukocytes) and fixed (endothelial) cells of the liver, spleen, and lymph nodes are phagocytes, capable of destroying pathogens.

Immunity, complete resistance to a disease, is specific to a particular disease. Immunity is the result of specific chemical substances (antibodies) that neutralize a particular toxin or cause bacteria to precipitate or stick together.

Active immunity exists when a person's own body produces the antibodies either through an attack of a disease or by inoculation. The time that active immunity lasts varies with different diseases. Second attacks are common in the common cold, influenza, and pneumonia and are rare in chickenpox, measles, mumps, poliomyelitis, and scarlet fever. Inoculation during infancy against diphtheria and pertussis may produce lifelong immunity. Artificial active immunization is available for diphtheria, measles, mumps, poliomyelitis, rabies, Rocky Mountain spotted fever, scarlet fever, smallpox, tetanus, typhoid fever, and whooping cough.

Passive immunity occurs when antibodies formed in animals or human beings are injected into another person. Passive immunity is of short duration; the borrowed antibodies tend to exhaust their cycle and disappear as the blood is renewed. An example of passive immunity is the *infantile immunity* of the first 3 to 6 months of life. Antibodies from the mother diffuse through the placenta into the bloodstream of the fetus.

CYCLE OF RESPIRATORY INFECTIOUS DISEASES

Respiratory infectious diseases follow a characteristic cycle of six stages or periods: incubation, prodrome, fastigium, defervescence, convalescence, and defection (Fig. 8-1).

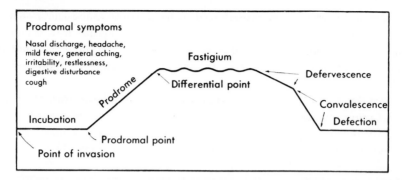

FIG. 8-1. Course of an infectious respiratory disease. All respiratory infections follow the course this graph indicates. In the school the prodrome and convalescence periods pose the greatest problems in disease control because the infected person may be well enough to be up and around, exposing others.

Incubation is initiated by the invasion of pathogens. During the incubation period organisms multiply, but the infected person displays no symptoms. The incubation period varies both from one disease to another and with the same disease. Usually the disease is not communicable during the incubation period, although measles and chickenpox can be transmitted during the last 3 days of the incubation period.

Prodrome is initiated by the first symptoms of illness. Symptoms of the prodromal period, those of the common cold, are the same for all respiratory infections: nasal discharge, watery eyes, mild fever, headache, general ache, irritability, restlessness, digestive disturbances, and perhaps a cough. This period lasts about a day, and a definite diagnosis cannot be made. Since the person often believes the symptoms are mild, he or she may continue a usual mode of life and expose many people during this highly communicable stage. Teachers should be alert to observe prodromal symptoms in children as the signal of impending danger.

Fastigium represents the height of the disease, initiated by the differential point at which characteristics of the specific disease allow diagnosis. Because the person is now home or hospitalized, not many people are exposed, although this period is highly communicable.

Defervescence is a decline in the severity of the disease. A new disease may produce a *relapse,* but usually the case proceeds to convalescence.

Convalescence, or recuperation, represents a difficult control problem because the disease may still be transmissible.

Defection is casting off organisms and may coincide with convalescence. Recovery from a disease does not imply the end of communicability. Isolation time is based on the length of defection, when the person has cast off all infectious organisms.

INFECTIOUS RESPIRATORY DISEASES

Although the list of known infectious respiratory diseases is extensive, certain ones affect the school population and are of particular interest to the teacher. An understanding of the characteristics, mode of transmission, and control measures for these diseases aids the teacher's efforts to prevent the spread of disease. Although the teacher never attempts to diagnose a particular ailment, knowledge of various diseases gives him or her the necessary confidence to take effective action.

With improved environmental sanitation and the wide acceptance of immunizations, many communicable diseases are no longer common. Teachers should never see advanced cases of these conditions among their students.

Because the early (prodromal) stages of many of these conditions appear similar, teachers should be aware of the guidelines used by nurses and others when deciding to send a student home. Standards may vary, but the presence of any rash warrants a call to parents with a request for the student's removal from school until a physician indicates the condition is not contagious. Students with temperatures of 100° F (38° C) or above are usually sent home, as are students with sore throats, swollen glands, clearly inflamed throats, badly bloodshot or irritated eyes, and obvious cold symptoms. Other less specific conditions, such as headache and nausea, must be judged more subjectively. Elevated temperature, but less than 100° F (38° C), along with sore throat, rash, headache, and nausea in some combination clearly indicates exclusion. Ideally the school nurse, aide, or teacher with special training should be responsible for the exclusion decision. Decision guidelines should be developed with the assistance of the local health department, school physician, or school health committee.

Chicken pox. Chicken pox is a fairly prevalent, although not serious, disease among schoolchildren that can become widespread.
1. *Infectious agent:* unidentified virus
2. *Source of infection:* respiratory discharges; lesions of the skin of infected persons
3. *Mode of transmission:* directly from person to person; indirectly through objects with fresh respiratory discharges from the mucous membranes and skin of infected persons
4. *Incubation period:* 14 to 16 days
5. *Description:* mild constitutional symptoms; slight fever; few eruptions and mostly on covered surfaces; eruption at various stages of development in the same area (Fig. 8-2)
6. *Control measures for the school:* exclusion for minimum of 7 days

Head cold. Typical head colds (coryza) merit more attention than they are usually given. They can be a forerunner of other diseases.
1. *Infectious agents:* unidentified viruses
2. *Source of infection:* nose and mouth secretions of infected person
3. *Mode of transmission:* directly by sneezing and coughing; indirectly from objects with fresh respiratory discharges of infected person
4. *Incubation period:* 1 to 3 days
5. *Description:* nasal discharge; watery eyes; mild fever; headache; general aches; irritability; cough
6. *Control measures for the school:* exclusion of most severe cases

German measles. Often referred to as 3-day or German measles, rubella is a distinctive disease.
1. *Infectious agent:* unidentified virus
2. *Source of infection:* nose and mouth secretions of infected persons

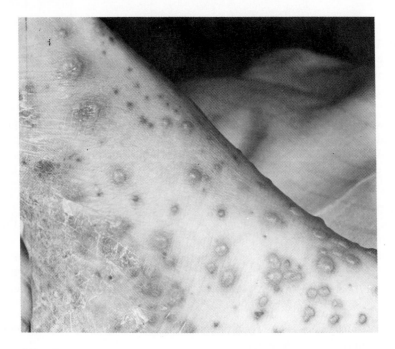

FIG. 8-2. Chickenpox. A severe case of chickenpox with lesions at various stages of development on the foot and ankle area.

3. *Mode of transmission:* directly from person to person; indirectly from objects contaminated with fresh discharges from nose and mouth of infected person
4. *Incubation period:* 16 to 18 days
5. *Description:* mild symptoms; slight fever; eruptions varied but often rose pink and small; lymph nodes on neck behind the ear swollen and sensitive
6. *Control measures for the school:* exclusion for sake of infected child
7. *Preventive measure:* immunization
8. *Special caution:* possible damage or deformity of the fetus if women in the first trimester of pregnancy contract German measles; thus immunizations are especially important

Infectious hepatitis. Infectious hepatitis is an acute involvement of the liver that occurs sporadically or epidemically. It occurs most frequently in autumn. Hepatitis can be of two types: infectious or serum. Infectious hepatitis is caused by the virus entering the body through the mouth; serum hepatitis is caused by a similar virus found in blood and tissue and enters the body by contaminated blood transfusions and contaminated needles or syringes. Poor sanitation and overcrowded living conditions appear to increase its spread. An uneventful recovery after a 7- or 8-week illness is usual. Mild symptoms and malfunction of the liver may persist for more than a year. About 12% of patients suffer a relapse, usually because of overactivity or other indiscretions.

1. *Infectious agent:* heat-resistant virus
2. *Source of infection:* usually milk or other food contaminated by fecal discharges of an infected person; feces and blood may be infectious before, during, or after the occurrence of hepatitis
3. *Mode of transmission:* both sporadic and epidemic types usually transmitted from feces of infected person by way of the hands, which come into contact with milk, food, and water; infectious hepatitis spread from direct contact or fomites, and direct fecal contamination of water is possible; serum hepatitis spread by contaminated blood transfusions, medical instruments, or drug-abuse paraphernalia
4. *Incubation period:* 15 to 35 days
5. *Description:* prodromal signs, including fever, headache, lassitude, nausea, anorexia, fatigue, and pronounced tenderness and pain in the liver; jaundice appearing about the fifth day, followed by subsiding fever (not all patients develop jaundice)
6. *Control measures for the school:* recognition of the disease; exclusion from school until readmitted by attending physician; improvement in sanitary and hygienic practices in food handling, hand washing, and disposal of sewage; checking of food handlers in school cafeteria for possible latent infectious hepatitis

Serum hepatitis

1. *Infectious agent:* virus
2. *Source of infection:* blood transfusions, plasma therapy, and inoculations
3. *Mode of transmission:* inoculation or transfusions
4. *Incubation period:* 2 to 4 months
5. *Description:* rather gradual onset with clinical manifestations and treatments similar to those for infectious hepatitis
6. *Control measures for the school:* because this disease is transmitted by inoculation or transfusion, the school is not directly involved in control; indirectly, drug education can help students understand the risk of using unsterilized needles and paraphernalia; it is apparent that serum hepatitis can be prevented by laboratory blood tests of prospective donors; a history of the donor's health problems can be helpful as a preventive measure, but an accurate assay of the blood is most reliable

Measles. Measles (rubeola) is a highly communicable disease.

1. *Infectious agent:* unidentified virus
2. *Source of infection:* secretions from nose and mouth of infected person
3. *Mode of transmission:* directly by sneezing and coughing from person to person; indirectly from objects contaminated with fresh respiratory discharges of infected person
4. *Incubation period:* 10 to 12 days
5. *Description:* nasal discharge; eyes red and sensitive to light; swollen eyelids; irritability; moderate fever; hacking cough; Koplik's spots on buccal surface of mouth; dusky red skin eruptions that tend to coalesce (Figs. 8-3 and 8-4)
6. *Control measures for the school:* exclusion for not less than 5 days after appearance of rash; exclusion of contacts only if symptoms appear; immunization recommended

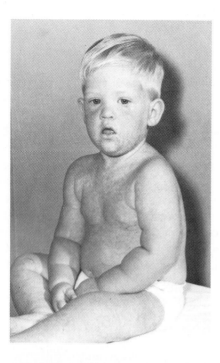

FIG. 8-3.　Measles. The characteristic rash occurs 3 to 5 days after onset of symptoms. It begins on the face and neck and spreads to trunk and extremities as it begins to fade on the face.

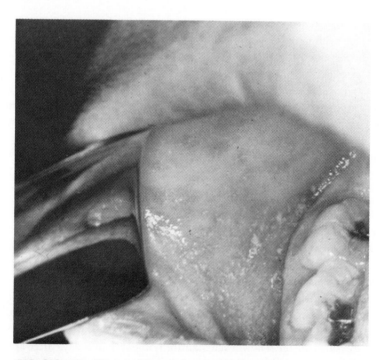

FIG. 8-4.　Koplik spots. These red and white pinpoint eruptions on the buccal mucosa are one of the most important signs of measles.

Meningococcus meningitis. One of the most feared of the respiratory diseases, meningococcus meningitis can now be treated successfully if discovered early.

1. *Infectious agent:* meningococcus (spheric bacterium)
2. *Source of infection:* nose and throat discharges of carrier or person with active case
3. *Mode of transmission:* directly from person to person; indirectly from objects contaminated with fresh discharges from nose and throat of carrier or person with active case
4. *Incubation period:* 6 to 8 days
5. *Description:* acute onset; intense headache; fever; nausea; stiff neck; irritability
6. *Control measures for the school:* exclusion until recovery, usually minimum of 14 days, or until released by health department after negative laboratory tests; exclusion of contacts in same household for 7 days from last exposure

Mononucleosis. Mononucleosis is an acute infection that may occur in epidemic form among children and youth but more often is sporadic. It usually lasts from 1 to 3 weeks, but involvement of the lymph system and general fatigue and weakness may go on for months. Recurrences are frequent but usually short lived.

1. *Infectious agent:* unidentified virus
2. *Source of infection:* probably discharges from nose and throat of infected person
3. *Mode of transmission:* probably by direct contact with infected person
4. *Incubation period:* 5 to 15 days
5. *Description:* fever; sore throat; headache; fatigue; chilliness; malaise; general involvement of lymph systems (white cell count of the blood varies between 10,000 and 20,000); excessive agglutinins present in the blood
6. *Control measures for the school:* recognition of disease; no legal isolation, but patient should not return to school until so advised by attending physician

Mumps. Mumps (parotitis) involves primarily the salivary glands, but it is classified as a respiratory disease.

1. *Infectious agent:* unidentified virus
2. *Source of infection:* saliva of infected person
3. *Mode of transmission:* droplets spread by direct contact; indirectly from objects contaminated with fresh saliva of infected person
4. *Incubation period:* 18 days
5. *Description:* light fever; tenderness and swelling over the jaw and in front of the ear, one side or both sides; possible involvement of ovaries and testes in persons with mature reproductive systems
6. *Control measures for the school:* exclusion until the disappearance of swelling and tenderness; immunization of 12- to 18-year-old boys recommended
7. *Preventive measure:* immunization

Rheumatic fever. Signs of rheumatic fever may occur 1 to 3 weeks after a sore throat. The associated fever and pain in the joints may not indicate the possible damage done to the heart muscle. Because of these characteristics, rheumatic fever is described as an insidious disease.

1. *Infectious agent:* group A beta-hemolytic streptococcus, producing sore throat
2. *Description:* primary phase identified as severe sore throat; middle (dormant) phase

with no particular symptoms or signs, may last for 4 weeks with apparent complete recovery; final phase acute rheumatic fever lasting 2 to 3 weeks; without treatment, recurrence of primary phase possible; damage to heart or other organs possible

3. *Control measures for the school:* effective prevention by use of antibiotics at early stage of recognized infection

Scarlet fever and streptococcal throat infection. Scarlet fever and streptococcal throat infection are commonly classed together.

1. *Infectious agent:* hemolytic streptococci
2. *Source of infection:* nose and throat discharges of person with active case or a carrier; articles soiled with discharges
3. *Mode of transmission:* directly by coughing and sneezing from person to person; indirectly via handkerchiefs, clothing, and other objects that reach the mouth; from contaminated milk
4. *Incubation period:* 3 to 5 days
5. *Description:* sore throat; fever; nausea; vomiting; flushing of cheeks; pallor about mouth; if rash occurs, it is on the neck and chest and is a fine scarlet goose-pimple type that blanches when pressure is applied
6. *Control measures for the school:* exclusion for at least 7 days or until all abnormal discharges have disappeared; sore throat is always a signal for exclusion

COMMON SKIN INFECTIONS AND INFESTATIONS

Communicable skin conditions are not a life or death matter but can be a trying problem to the school. Much of the nuisance effect can be reduced by an understanding of the common communicable skin diseases.

A skin *infection* occurs when the pathogen penetrates the skin and causes harm. A skin *infestation* occurs when the parasite remains *on* the skin and causes harm.

Impetigo contagiosa (gym itch). In elementary schools impetigo may spread quite widely from a single unrecognized case; thus early recognition is important.

1. *Infectious agent:* streptococci and staphylococci
2. *Source of infection:* skin lesions of infected persons
3. *Mode of transmission:* directly by contact with discharge of skin lesions; indirectly from objects contaminated with such discharges
4. *Incubation period:* 2 to 4 days
5. *Description:* systemic manifestations usually absent except in infants; lesions first appear as pink-red stains that are fluid filled and wet, then fill with pus, and finally form a crust that appears as though it were pasted on; the face (particularly the butterfly area about the mouth) and hands are commonly involved, but other parts of the body may be affected, particularly the scalp; pressure generally releases pus from beneath the oval crusts
6. *Control measures for the school:* exclusion from school until the pustules have healed
7. *Preventive measures:* encourage prompt treatment, which consists in soaking crust until

it can be removed and applying 5% ammoniated mercury ointment or sulfonamide ointment to the infected area; some schools have ointments available for the student's own use, and in some instances the parent or student requests the teacher's assistance; a physician's services should be obtained if possible; emphasis on general personal health helps to avoid any wide spread of impetigo

Pediculosis. Pediculosis (lousiness) is a classic example of infestation.

1. *Infesting agent:* head or body louse
2. *Source of infestation:* infested person or his or her personal belongings
3. *Mode of transmission:* directly from infested person; indirectly by contact with clothing of infested person
4. *Incubation period:* ova hatch in 1 week and mature in 2 weeks
5. *Description:* the louse egg (nit), larva, or adult louse on the scalp or other part of the body or in the clothing; nits attached to the hair shaft; occasionally a severe secondary infection
6. *Control measures for the school:* exclusion until adequate treatment received and proper insecticide applied to scalp, skin, and clothing; inspection of possible contacts and use of effective insecticide for infested pupils
7. *Preventive measure:* emphasis on body cleanliness

Ringworm. The term *athlete's foot* applies to ringworm (tinea) of the feet; however, ringworm can affect all parts of the body. Common dermatophytes are often present on healthy skin and cause disease only when favorable conditions prevail.

1. *Infectious agent:* several types of fungi
2. *Source of infection:* lesions on body of infected persons; objects contaminated by the fungi or their spores
3. *Mode of transmission:* directly by person-to-person contact with lesions; indirectly from objects contaminated by the fungi or their spores
4. *Incubation period:* unknown
5. *Description:* lesions often circular, clear in the center, with vesicular (fluid) borders; not widely distributed; crusting not present, itching common; foot ringworm (athlete's foot) more common in adults; body, face, and head forms more common among children, especially in warm weather
6. *Control measures for the school:* exclusion until treatment initiated and lesions dry or covered; in foot ringworm, exclusion from privileges of swimming pool and gymnasium
7. *Preventive measures:* personal cleanliness; thorough drying of feet after bathing; gymnasium and shower room cleanliness; regular inspections and treatment; keeping feet dry to deny moisture to fungi

Scabies. The common term *7-year-itch* is often used to designate scabies. Both male and female mites live on human skin, but the female burrows into the superficial layer of the skin to deposit eggs. The female can be seen with the unaided eye, but the male, being half her size, is not readily detected. The parasites are short lived, the male dying after mating and the female after she has laid her eggs. Larvae are hatched in 4 to 8 days.

1. *Infectious agent: Sarcoptes scabiei* (itch mite)
2. *Source of infection:* person infected with the mite
3. *Mode of transmission:* directly by contact with infected persons; indirectly from underclothing, bedding, towels, and other objects of the infected person
4. *Incubation period:* 1 to 2 days
5. *Description:* itching of the skin often unbearable; frequent locations: the waist, armpit, and crotch; at times, lesions on the face, scalp, and arms; when infection is mild, systemic symptoms are negligible, but severe infections may result in fever, headache, and discomfort
6. *Control measures for the school:* exclusion from school until successfully treated with an effective miticide
7. *Preventive measure:* personal cleanliness

SEXUALLY TRANSMITTED DISEASES

Among infectious diseases, sexually transmitted diseases (STDs) have always been problematic for school health personnel. The incidence of the most common sexually transmitted diseases is higher than most people realize and is epidemic. In 1991 in the civilian U.S. population, there were 602,677 reported cases of gonorrhea and 41,006 reported cases of syphilis. *Chlamydia* is probably the most widespread reportable sexually transmitted disease. Unfortunately reporting is not as complete as it is with the other sexually transmitted diseases. With 11 states not reporting and some states providing only partial reports, the Centers for Disease Control reported 362,016 cases of *Chlamydia* in 1991. Of these cases, 265,427 were in females. Until testing procedures are more established, it is likely that *Chlamydia* will continue to be underreported.

Because the spread of these conditions involves sexual activity, school personnel have been reluctant to discuss them. In fact, whole communities are reluctant to support discussion of sexuality issues in schools. Because morality is involved, denial often exists. Many parents believe that discussion related to sexuality should be reserved for the home and openly discourage school personnel from discussing such matters. Teachers are reluctant to deal with sexuality because they feel ill prepared. Today, however, public awareness of the prevalence of sexually transmitted diseases, high rates of adolescent pregnancy, and the advent of HIV/AIDS have led to a more receptive environment for educators to teach about and provide services related to sexually transmitted diseases. All school personnel should be concerned about the spread of sexually transmitted diseases and, although they are sometimes reluctant to address this health topic, there are several things they can do. Abstinence from sexual contact can be taught as the most effective way to reduce the risk of contracting a sexually transmitted disease. Recognizing that not everybody follows abstinence, consistent correct use of condoms can be taught. Some schools have chosen to make condoms available at school. Condom use is a useful public health option, but not as safe as abstinence because condoms do fail. Important aspects of any STD education program are: where to get condoms if they are not provided at school; and where to get STD screenings and early intervention, treatment, and counseling.

Sexually transmitted diseases are transmitted during sexual intercourse, during homosexual and heterosexual relations, and through other sexual contacts. Among the STDs, of most concern to the school are *Chlamydia*, gonorrhea, syphilis, herpes simplex type 2, and HIV/ AIDS.

Chlamydial diseases. Trachoma, caused by *Chlamydia*, is sometimes classified as a nonspecific sexually transmitted infection (NSI). The prevalence of nonspecific sexually transmitted infections is unknown because they are not reportable. However, data now indicate that NSIs are more prevalent than gonorrhea. About 80% of NSIs are reported to be caused by *Chlamydia trachomatis*. The second species, *Chlamydia psittaci*, is responsible for the remainder of the chlamydial diseases.

1. *Infectious agent: Chlamydia trachomatis*, a bacteria that, like a virus, grows only within cells
2. *Source of infection:* direct contact with the infected person
3. *Mode of transmission:* sexual contact
4. *Incubation period:* 7 to 28 days
5. *Description:* Many females experience no symptoms. If symptoms exist, they will include vaginal pain and itching, and in males, pain and itching in the genital area and a urethral discharge. In an advanced stage, the disease can cause pain throughout the pelvic area for women (pelvic inflammatory disease). Because *Chlamydia* often is accompanied by no symptoms, its detection often follows the testing for other sexually transmitted diseases.
6. *Control measures for the school:* effective education, encouragment of family to communicate behavioral expectations to children, conscious abstinence from sexual activity

Gonorrhea. Gonorrhea is a widespread sexually transmitted disease.

1. *Infectious agent: Neisseria gonorrhoeae*
2. *Source of infection:* sexual activity
3. *Mode of transmission:* contact with infected person
4. *Incubation period:* males, 2 to 4 days; females, 7 to 21 days
5. *Description:* For males the lining of the urethra is usually infected, causing a burning sensation on urination and a puslike discharge from the urethra. For females, the first indications include a mild burning sensation in the genital region and possible vaginal discharge. Later the disease may spread to the vagina, uterus, fallopian tubes, and ovaries, causing pain and fever. However, women may have no indication that they are infected. Symptoms may disappear with time.
6. *Control measures for the school:* effective education, encouragment of family to communicate behavioral expectations to children, conscious abstinence from sexual activity

Syphilis

1. *Infectious agent: Treponema pallidum* (spirochete)
2. *Source of infection:* skin lesion of infected person
3. *Mode of transmission:* transmitted through mucous membrane or skin abrasions
4. *Incubation period:* 10 to 28 days
5. *Description:* Syphilis enters the body through small skin breaks, usually in the mucous

membranes of the genital tract, rectum, or mouth. After incubation, a chancre, or small, moist lump appears at the site of the infection. The chancre is often not visible or is in a location not observable. Without treatment, spirochetes travel in the bloodstream throughout the body. In the second stage, symptoms may appear any time from a few weeks to a year after the disappearance of the chancre. Symptoms include skin rash, small flat sores in moist areas of the skin, whitish patches in the mouth and throat, fever, headaches, and swollen glands. A person with syphilis in this stage is highly infectious. After this secondary stage, all signs and symptoms of the disease disappear. During this latent stage spirochetes invade various body organs, including the heart and brain, but it may be as long as 20 years before the patient suffers serious incapacitating conditions. Pregnant women may transmit the disease to their unborn children. The infection may kill the fetus or produce various malformations.

6. *Control measures for the school:* effective education, encouragement of family to communicate behavioral expectations to children, conscious abstinence from sexual activity

Herpes simplex. Herpes simplex was once a relatively rare condition, but it is estimated that between 300,000 and 1 million cases may now occur each year. There is no cure for herpes at this time.

1. *Infectious agent:* herpes virus hominis type 2 (HSV-2)
2. *Source of infection:* direct contact with blisterlike sores of an infected person
3. *Mode of transmission:* sexual contact
4. *Incubation period:* 4 to 7 days
5. *Description:* Blisterlike sores in the genital area that may spread to buttocks and thighs. Sometimes swelling of the legs, difficult urination, watery eyes, and fatigue will result. HSV-2 is cyclic in nature, with the virus retreating to the base of the spine from time to time, leaving the patient symptom-free and at low risk to spread the disease. Symptoms recur periodically, often in association with sexual activity or stressful life events.
6. *Control measures for the school:* avoid sexual contact with an infected person

Human immunodeficiency virus/acquired immune deficiency syndrome (HIV/AIDS). Although the incidence of AIDS is relatively low, it is increasing, and the fact that no known cure exists means that this increase will continue. In 1991 there were 43,389 cases of HIV/AIDS reported in the United States. The cumulative total number of cases of HIV/AIDS through March 1992 was 218,301. At that same time, 141,223 deaths from AIDS had been reported.

For schools the problems caused by HIV/AIDS are related to public hysteria and fear of catching HIV/AIDS from an infected person. Children infected through blood transfusions have been shunned by the public and have been excluded from normal educational activities. The school's challenge is one of community and student education and the development of policies to protect both the public and the infected student, while at the same time providing quality education.

1. *Infectious agent:* virus HTLV-3
2. *Source of infection:* infected person or contaminated blood products or contaminated syringes

3. *Mode of transmission:* sexual contact, primarily male homosexual contact, intravenous drug use, and sexual contact with intravenous drug users, transfusion of infected blood or blood products
4. *Incubation period:* a few months to several years
5. *Description:* No obvious signs during incubation period. Later the victim will develop night sweats, unexpected weight loss, diarrhea, loss of appetite, swollen glands, and fatigue. Still later when the body's defense system is weakened (specifically the helper T-cells), other ordinary diseases develop unchecked. Often the victim suffers from *Pneumocystis carinii* pneumonia and Kaposi's sarcoma, a rare form of skin cancer. Many carriers of the virus have not yet developed symptoms, whereas others develop mild versions of the symptoms referred to as AIDS-related complex (ARC).
6. *Control measures for the school:* effective education of the risks of sexual contact and sharing intravenous drug equipment. There is no clear evidence that casual contact with an infected person actually transmits the disease. Children with HIV/AIDS can safely attend school without endangering other students. Some special precautions may, however, be required.

In the control of infectious disease, the teacher need not be limited to specific detailed symptoms. Any time a student has a sore throat, fever, or watery eyes, the teacher should prudently assume that he or she has the beginning of an infectious respiratory disease. Skin eruptions exhibiting inflammation are likely to be infectious, as contrasted with noninflamed skin areas such as those occurring in eczema.

A teacher who watches for typical prodromal symptoms quickly identifies the student in the early stages of any usual infectious respiratory diseases. Skin disorders will also be recognized early in their development.

RESPONSIBILITY FOR CONTROL OF COMMUNICABLE DISEASES

Both legal and professional responsibilities must be considered in the control of communicable diseases. Responsibilities written into law or health codes represent the minimal desirable control, usually in terms of restrictions. Beyond these legal responsibilities are the moral or professional responsibilities of individuals and groups.

Public health personnel

Health authority is vested in the police power of the state. *Police power* is the authority of the people vested in government to protect society's health and general welfare. Health departments have police power and promote public welfare by regulating and restraining the use of property and liberty. Police power is based on the concept of the greatest good for the greatest number and may inconvenience some people in the interest of the common good.

State legislatures delegate authority to a state board of health to set rules and regulations governing health. Accordingly, the health board passes regulations to control communicable diseases. This includes the imposition of isolation and quarantine, milk control, water treatment, and all other measures necessary to disease control. The state code specifies the time and terms of isolation, quarantine, and other control measures. States may also promulgate these standards in law.

Multicultural education and health education

EMERGING ISSUE

The chairperson of the health education curriculum committee has called a meeting of all health education teachers, including school counselors, to discuss multicultural education and its implications for health education.

Although the chairperson readily admits little knowledge of "multicultural education," she is concerned about the growing number of incidents marked by antagonistic and hostile actions that are occurring between white and black students. Moreover, recent reports from large city schools indicate serious social relationship problems between racial and ethnic groups. A high proportion of African-American male students are being suspended and are dropping out of school.

The chairperson challenges the group with the statement, "If we really believe in the concept of 'holistic' health, including social well-being, I think we need to consider carefully the goals of the health education program."

You are asked to reflect on this situation and to share your thoughts by marking a plus (+) or a minus (−) sign before each of the following statements with which you agree or disagree.

_____ 1. This suggests to me that our educational programs as conducted are failing to give adequate consideration to the needs of the African-American males.

_____ 2. I think that the inner city community influence is having its most disruptive effect on the African-American male.

_____ 3. I believe that the economic situation, especially the lack of job opportunities, has make schooling appear irrelevant to African-American males.

_____ 4. I believe that the health education curriculum should include the study of conflicts and conflict resolution in an effort to reduce the incidence of violent acts.

_____ 5. I believe that the teachers' perceptions and low expectations for the African-American males are having a negative effect on their motivation and school achievement.

_____ 6. I believe that more emphasis should be given to cultural and ethnic factors in the study of health and health behavior.

_____ 7. I believe that the emphasis of American education must be shifted from primarily Eurocentric to include more information about various cultures, including African-Amercian.

_____ If limited to a single choice, this is the number I would select.

REFERENCE

Rist MC: "Ethnocentric education: is a rainbow curriculum right for American schools?" *Am School Board J*, 178:26, 1991.

The state may delegate many of its powers to subdivisions of local governments. The state grants charters to cities giving them absolute self-rule (home rule) to exercise within their own borders and within specific limits or fields. Police power thus delegated to the municipalities enables them to control communicable diseases within their own geographic borders.

In terms of direct effect on individual citizens the county or city health department is charged with legal responsibility for communicable disease control. Standards may not be lower than those of the state code, but they may be higher. Thus, if the state code sets the isolation period for a particular disease as 7 days, the local code may require 9 days but not 6 days. Generally the local code coincides with the state code.

Local health personnel enforce isolation and quarantine, immunization, and other provisions as they pertain to disease control. To fulfill their respective duties concerning children's health, school and health department personnel usually establish some means of liaison.

Private physician

Practicing physicians have always been key figures in communicable disease control. Because they diagnose and supervise each case, they are in the best position to advise the patient.

Practicing physicians advise and perform immunizations as a routine part of family medical care.

Parents

An obvious responsibility of parents is the protection of their children's health. Parents observe their children for symptoms of disease, keep them out of school when symptoms of communicable disease are present, and follow the practices recommended by the school and the physician. Parents have legal responsibilities when isolation has been imposed officially.

School personnel

Promotion of immunization, early recognition of disease symptoms, and effective control of exclusions and readmissions allow the school staff to carry out its communicable disease control responsibilities.

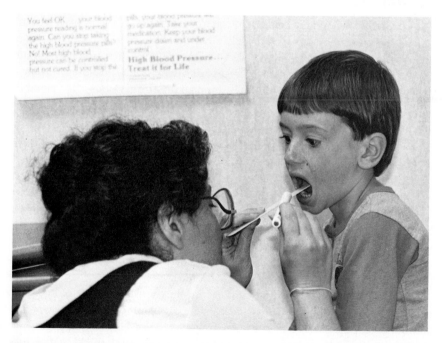

FIG. 8-5. Qualified school health personnel can detect communicable diseases early and develop effective programs to control their spread. In this way school health services help keep as many students in school as many school days as possible so that school personnel can provide a complete education for their students.

Teachers who recognize early symptoms of communicable disease aid in their control. Early disease detection and early exclusion benefits both the affected student and the student's classmates. It is relatively simple and highly effective to exclude students and to refuse readmission until all communicability has passed (Fig. 8-5).

Teachers, as well as the school nurse, can advise students and parents on matters relating to disease control and suggest a desirable course of action.

ISOLATION OF A STUDENT AT SCHOOL

A student with the symptoms of a communicable disease should be segregated from other students. The nurse's office is ideal for a student who appears only slightly ill and may recover in a short time, or who may not have a communicable disease. This student should lie comfortably on a cot in a moderately darkened room and be kept warm with blankets. Someone should be in attendance or visit the student at regular intervals.

If the isolated student does not improve in a reasonable time, the parents should be contacted, and arrangements made to take the student home. If the student becomes seriously ill and no contact with the parents can be made, the family physician should be called, and his or her advice followed.

EXCLUSIONS

A question of considerable concern to classroom teachers is their responsibility for the exclusion of students who appear to have a communicable disease. Ideally a school nurse makes the decision, but if the teacher must decide, a set of established guidelines should be followed. Teachers readily recognize their professional responsibility to do everything reasonable on behalf of the student's health, but the administrative dimensions often cloud the issue.

Legal aspects

Do teachers have the right to exclude a student they suspect of having a communicable disease? If it develops that the student's condition was not communicable, can teachers be held legally liable for their action? These two vital questions have been answered by the courts. The classic decision was laid down by the court in the case of *Stone v. Probst*, in which parents instituted a civil suit against a public school educator for excluding their child from school because of suspected communicable disease. The key sentence of that decision is this: "Pupils who are suffering, or appear to be suffering, from a communicable disease may menace the well-being of all pupils and therefore should be denied the privilege of school attendance" (Supreme Court of the State of Minnesota, 1925).

It is significant that the court emphasized the mere *appearance* of symptoms of communicable disease as sufficient basis for exclusion. The court did not require proof that the well-being of other pupils was menaced but merely that their well-being *may* be menaced. The court did not assert that the school may exclude the student but that it *should* exclude the student. This decision means that, if a teacher has reason to believe a student has a communicable disease, the student should be excluded. If it is subsequently found that the student did not have a communicable disease, no jury would ever hold the teacher liable for such reasonable actions.

Administrative procedures

Various situations require different methods, and typical examples illustrate standard procedures:

1. If the student is not well, but doubt exists as to whether the condition is communicable, he or she may be isolated in the nurse's suite or similar area.
2. If no doubt exists that the student is quite ill and very likely has a communicable disease, the student should be sent home. First, the parents should be called, and one of the student's parents should come after him or her. Under no circumstances should the ill student walk home alone. All decisions to exclude a student should be channeled through the principal's office.
3. In a doubtful case when a school nurse or physician is unavailable, two or three teachers may share their collective judgment. Ultimately the decision rests with the principal.
4. When the ill student must ride home in a school bus, the bus driver should be informed, the student seated near the driver, and the parents notified.

READMISSIONS

The problem of readmission of students does not occur as frequently as the exclusion of students with questionable symptoms. However, school personnel may face this problem. When a medically confirmed communicable disease is no longer communicable, it should be so certified in a physician's note sent with the student when he or she returns to school.

Generally, courts hold that it is the parents' responsibility to demonstrate that the student is not in a communicable state and thus should be readmitted to school. This interpretation is expressed in the case of *Martin v. Craig:* "It is the responsibility of the parents to prove otherwise if the child is not to be denied the privilege of school attendance" (Supreme Court of North Dakota, 1919).

When doubt exists as to communicability, the parents must resolve the doubt by obtaining a written clearance from the health department or a practicing physician.

In practice, when a student has been absent for a day or two, the nurse or teacher should attempt to judge whether symptoms such as nasal discharge or rash have abated and indicate that the student can return to school. Review of Table 8-1 shows a set of possible indicators for exclusion or readmission.

Repeated controversy on readmission indicates an inadequate program for educating parents on policies and procedures of disease control. Where parents are well informed and cooperative, students will be kept out of school until there is no doubt that the student should be readmitted.

The other side of this issue is the parent who excludes a child from school for even the slightest deviation in health. Although doing no harm to other children, such a parent unduly interferes with the educational process. Here again the school has a professional responsibility to discuss this matter with the parents and explain the school's health care responsibilities, the

TABLE 8-1. Communicable disease inspection points for teachers to use in observing students

Inspection	Directions to child	Signs
For respiratory disease		
General condition	"How do you feel?"	Facial expression, listlessness, irritability, sneezing
Eyes	"Move your eyes about."	Watery eyes, inflammation, puffiness, redness
Nose	"Tilt your head back."	Discharge, inflammation, odor
Skin	"Do you feel hot?"	Flushing; hot, cold, or clammy feeling
Forehead	"Raise the hair from your forehead."	Eruptions along hairline
For skin infection		
Chest	"Open your shirt (or dress)."	Eruptions, redness, irritation
Hands and wrists	"Pull up your sleeves and spread your fingers."	Eruptions, redness, irritation

resources, and the effect of such behavior on a child's education. A school nurse, physician, or counselor may be able to assist in this situation.

Special cases

Today readmissions are likely to follow many health-related conditions other than communicable diseases: alcohol and other drug treatment and pregnancy and childbirth are two common examples. The readmission of students with special health problems who have undergone treatment or are continuing treatment represents an increasingly frequent readmission issue. These readmissions deserve different attention than those involving contagion.

Associated with these cases are clear educational opportunities for both the students being readmitted and for their classmates. Understanding, acceptance, and support should be a focal point. Because we can expect to see more of these situations in schools and in work places, the educational opportunities associated with these readmissions are becoming especially important.

Although not related to contagion, these cases are health and/or illness related and should be viewed as health education opportunities. Understanding the underlying health issues should be a regular part of the curriculum for students involved with these readmissions. The insight that comes from knowing and understanding should be the basis for social behaviors that are supportive of readmission. The students themselves could become a part of the readmission process if they feel comfortable doing so: talking about their condition and their personal experiences.

For such readmissions to be a positive experience, teachers may need to do some special study so they can be a useful resource. Teachers may have to review carefully their own attitudes toward the students involved.

EPIDEMICS AND SCHOOL POLICIES

Experience demonstrates that during an epidemic it is better to keep schools in session unless the epidemic is extreme and all public gatherings are prohibited. This is a decision for the health department. When students remain in school, their contact with others is limited to their peers, and careful observations are possible.

If the health department recommends school closings, prohibiting groups of children in theaters, recreation centers, churches, and other places is also in order. School personnel can assist by appealing to parents and students to follow health department regulations and remain away from public places.

Occasionally a widespread outbreak of influenza or other respiratory disease in a school population may prompt school officials to close the school. If more than half the student body is absent because of influenza, it may be sensible academically and economically to close the school temporarily. Most of the schoolwork for that week would have to be repeated for those who were absent.

IMMUNIZATION PROGRAM

Even in a well-educated democracy such as the United States, it has not been possible to maintain voluntary immunizations at a level high enough to stop the spread of preventable diseases. Today most states have legislated mandatory immunizations, linking immunization with permission for children to enter school.

This situation illustrates a dilemma of public health. When a disease can be prevented or quickly, if not cheaply, controlled and cured, the public quickly forgets the threat and ceases to participate in the measures that reduced the incidence of the disease in the first place. Short-term success in the public health may, in other words, increase the risk of long-term failure. The most effective educational means of increasing immunization levels would be an epidemic, although the public effect would likely "wear off" as the threat diminished.

Among the preventable diseases, immunization levels must be kept around 90% to 95% in the vulnerable population to prevent the spread of these conditions.

Schedule for immunizations

Various immunization schedules have been recommended. The recommendations of the Committee on Infectious Diseases of the American Academy of Pediatrics present perhaps the most widely followed standards; these are shown in Table 8-2. Immunization status is checked on admission to kindergarten or first grade. Parents are usually asked to complete an entry health history that includes questions similar to those shown in Box 8-1. State law usually allows for exemptions under certain conditions; for example, religious objections. If immunization status is not complete, the school will notify parents to have their children immunized by a specific date. Exemption requests must be reviewed and filed in the student's permanent health record. Box 8-2 gives a simple form for parents to notify the school of refusal to have a student immunized.

TABLE 8-2. Recommended schedule for active immunization of normal infants and children

Recommended age	Immunization(s)*	Comments
2 mo	DTP, OPV	Can be initiated as early as age 2 wk in areas of high endemicity or during epidemics
4 mo	DTP, OPV	2-mo interval desired for OPV to avoid interference from previous dose
6 mo	DTP	A third dose of OPV is not indicated in the U.S. but is desirable in geographic areas where polio is endemic
15 mo	Measles, mumps, rubella (MMR)	MMR preferred to individual vaccines; tuberculin testing may be done at the same visit
18 mo	DTP,†‡ OPV,§ PRP-D	
4-6 yr	DTP,‖ OPV	At or before school entry
14-16 yr	Td	Repeat every 10 yr throughout life

Adapted from Report of the Committee on Infectious Diseases, Elk Grove Village, Ill, 1988, American Academy of Pediatrics. A second dose of MMR recommended at entrance to middle or junior high school (American Academy of Pediatrics, Committee on Infectious Diseases current immunization policy, *Pediatrics* 84(6):1110-1113, 1989).

*DTP, diphtheria and tetanus toxoids with pertussis vaccine; OPV, oral poliovirus vaccine containing attenuated poliovirus types 1, 2, and 3; MMR, live measles, mumps, and rubella viruses in a combined vaccine; PRP-D, Haemophilus b diphtheria toxoid conjugate vaccine; Td, adult tetanus toxoid (full dose) and diphtheria toxoid (reduced dose) for adult use.
†Should be given 6 to 12 months after the third dose.
‡May be given simultaneously with MMR at age 15 months.
§May be given simultaneously with MMR at 15 months of age or at any time between 12 and 24 months of age.
‖Up to the seventh birthday.

Special immunization practices

In practice, immunization against certain diseases is not advocated except under certain circumstances. When a disease is peculiar to a special area (endemic), health authorities may recommend immunization of all persons in that area, particularly those who risk exposure.

For mumps, prepuberty immunization protects the body through the critical transition years to adulthood. As a preventive measure for exposed men who lack prior immunity, a special gamma globulin is used to give temporary immunity and thus prevent possible sterility. High school boys exposed to mumps and lacking prior immunity should consult a physician on the advisability of gamma globulin administration.

Because German measles in a mother during the first 3 months of pregnancy can cause the birth of defective infants, it is urgent for all girls to be immunized before 12 years of age.

National immunization objectives

Immunizations represent one of the most effective means of primary prevention. However, without public understanding and cooperation, immunizations will remain an underused resource. Immunization effectiveness is especially clear when differences in morbidity and mortality are compared between the years of their initial development and recent records:

- Whooping cough: approximately 200,000 cases and approximately 5000 deaths annually in the early 1930s; 2575 cases in 1991

BOX
8-1

Sample section of school-entry health history form

State law requires all children be immunized against rubella, measles, poliomyelitis, DPT, and mumps.

Please list below the date (month, day, and year) of each dose given. To keep the health record up to date, please send dates of immunizations given after this form is sent to school.

1. Immunization against diphtheria, tetanus, and pertussis (combined):
   3 doses 1 month apart. Dates of doses: 1. _____
   2. _____ 3. _____
2. DPT boosters. Dates of doses: _____
3. Sabin (oral) polio. First dose: _____
   Second dose: _____ Third dose: _____
4. Sabin polio boosters. Dates of doses: _____
5. Rubeola (hard measles). Date of dose: _____
6. Rubella (German measles). Date of dose: _____
7. Mumps. Date of dose: _____
8. TB test. Date: _____ Results: _____

Please write in date if the child has had any of the following:

Scarlet fever: _____ Measles: _____ Mumps: _____
Other: _____ Pneumonia: _____
3-day measles: _____ Chickenpox: _____ Other: _____
Rheumatic fever: _____ Poliomyelitis: _____
Whooping cough: _____

Date signed _____ Parent or guardian _____

TABLE 8-3. Reduce indigenous cases of vaccine-preventable diseases as follows:

Disease	1988 Baseline	2000 Target
Diphtheria among people ages 25 and younger	1	0
Tetanus among people ages 25 and younger	3	0
Polio (wild-type virus)	0	0
Measles	3058	0
Rubella	225	0
Congenital rubella syndrome	6	0
Mumps	4866	500
Pertussis	3450	1000

From US Department of Health and Human Services: Healthy people 2000: national health promotion and disease prevention objectives (Full Report, With Commentary), Washington, DC, 1991, US Government Printing Office, DHHS Publication No. (PHS) 91-50212, p. 513.
Baseline data source: Center for Prevention Services, CDC.

BOX 8-2

Refusal of immunization

As the parent/guardian of _____

         Name   Age   Birth date

                         _____

         School   Grade

I do not wish to have my child receive the following immunizations:

(check disease)
- ☐ Rubeola (measles)
- ☐ Rubella (German measles)
- ☐ Mumps
- ☐ Poliomyelitis
- ☐ Diphtheria
- ☐ Tetanus (lockjaw)
- ☐ Pertussis (whooping cough)

Comments _____

_____

                                     _____

                                     Signature of parent/guardian   Date

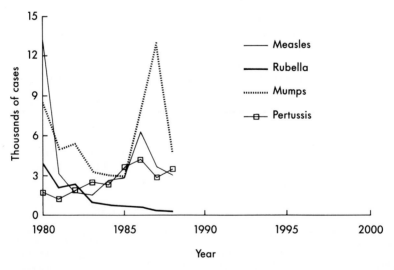

FIG. 8-6.   Vaccine-preventable diseases. Even with available immunization, the control of these vaccine-preventable diseases is not guaranteed.

- Mumps: 152,000 cases in 1968; 4031 cases in 1991
- Rubella: 60,000 cases in 1969; 1372 cases in 1991
- Measles (rubeola): 480,000 cases in 1962; 9276 cases in 1991

So strategic are immunizations that specific national goals, the *National Immunization Objectives for 2000,* have been set. If the goals are achieved, these infectious diseases will be almost eliminated. Table 8-3 lists the national goals for the year 2000 and compares them with baseline rates for 1988. Fig. 8-6 illustrates the patterns of several preventable diseases, showing that, even when immunization technologies are available, a consistent decline in incidence is not guaranteed. National goals will be achieved only if individuals use available technology. The technical knowledge for widespread immunization exists, and cost no longer is a barrier for the majority of families. Technology to reduce health risks in the environment also exists, and when communities share the costs, they are not exorbitant. Human behavior at personal, family, and community levels is the critical element of prevention. Education provides the knowledge and skills to affect behavior. Education, especially health education in elementary, middle, and secondary schools, is critical in how individuals accept prevention options, how society devotes resources for prevention, and ultimately how much society benefits in terms of health.

G ET INVOLVED!   Therapeutic Recreation is a relatively new field of human and health service concerned with the the delivery of leisure services to persons with mental, physical, emotional, or social disabilities. Therapeutic recreation provides three types of services in a variety of different settings.

1. *Treatment/rehabilitation programs* are designed to improve the functional ability of patients. These programs are usually offered in hospitals or in treatment centers.
2. *Leisure education programs* focus on the acquisition of skills and attitudes of individuals, enabling them to develop a meaningful leisure and a healthy life-style. These programs are offered in both treatment centers and in community agencies.
3. *Recreation and leisure participation programs* are guided by the philosophy that all individuals have the right to personal enjoyment through recreation, regardless of their disability, place of residence, or special needs.

The programs of preparation for therapeutic recreation are offered by colleges and universities. Approximately one half of the students' course work is general education, including communication, social science, humanities, anatomy, and physiology. In addition to a core of professional courses in recreation and leisure studies, preparation is required in the clinical aspects of therapeutic recreation; in problems of aging; and concerns of the physically disabled, mentally ill, and developmentally disabled. On completing degree requirements, graduates are eligible for certification in the National Council for Therapeutic Recreation.

If you would like to learn more about this field, write to:
National Recreation and Park Association
3101 Park Center Dr.
Alexandria, VA 22302

STUDY QUESTIONS

1. Explain the possible paradox that all cases of communicable disease are infectious diseases but not all cases of infectious diseases are communicable.
2. What is each citizen's responsibility for the health of his or her neighbor?
3. "Infectious disease is but the reaction of the host to a parasite." Explain this statement.
4. What are the sources of disease that threaten a schoolchild?
5. What class of communicable diseases poses the greatest problem for the school, and why are these diseases so difficult to control?
6. What forms of isolation can a school use to prevent communicable disease spread?
7. What are the responsibilities of the county health department in controlling communicable diseases in the schools of a community?
8. Why do health officials contend that teachers are the first line of defense against the spread of communicable disease?
9. Why do epidemiologists maintain that at least 90% of children entering school be immunized against diptheria, smallpox, and poliomyelitis to prevent a major epidemic?
10. Explain why, in communicable disease control in the school, problems of readmission can be more difficult than those of exclusion.
11. How would parents establish that their child is no longer in a communicable state and should be readmitted to school?
12. Under what circumstances should a school be closed because of an epidemic?
13. List the communicable diseases that a teacher may have and that he or she may transmit to students.

REFERENCES

American Academy of Pediatrics, Committee on Infectious Diseases: Measles: reassessment of the current immunization policy, *Pediatrics* 84(6):1110-1113, 1989.

American Academy of Pediatrics: *School health: a guide for health professionals,* Elk Grove Village, Ill, 1987, the Academy.

American Medical Association: *Healthy youth 2000: national health promotion and disease prevention objectives for adolescents,* Chicago, 1990, AMA.

Beilenson P, Santalli J: An urban school-based voluntary MMR booster immunization program, *J Sch Health* 62(2):71, 1992.

Burnet F, White D: *Natural history of infectious disease,* ed 4, London, 1972, Cambridge University Press.

Carvey A, Kittell SB, Hadeka MA: A method for documentation in school health services, *J Sch Health* 57(9):390, 1987.

Ewert DP, et al: Measles vaccination coverage among Latino children aged 12 to 59 months in Lost Angeles County: a household survey, *Am J Public Health* 81(8):1052, 1991.

Facts About AIDS, a special guide for NEA members from the health information network; insert in September 1987 issue of NEA Today.

Kann L, et al: HIV-related knowledge, beliefs, and behaviors among high sachool students in the United States: results from a national survey, *J Sch Health* 61(9):397, 1991.

Kendig EJ, Chernich V, editors: *Disorders of the respiratory tract in children,* ed 3, Philadelphia, 1977, W.B. Saunders.

Krugman S, Ward R, Katz S: *Infectious diseases of children,* ed. 7, St. Louis, 1981, Mosby-n-Year Book.

Lehr KW, Shrock MM: A school program for children of alcoholics, *J Sch Health* 57(8):344, 1987.

Lenaway DD, et ak: An outbreak of pertussis-like syndrome in Boulder County Colorado, *J Sch Health* 60(1):31, 1990.

National Center for Health Statistics: *Vital statistics of the United States 1985,* vol 2, Mortality, Part A, Atlanta, 1985, US Department of Health and Human Services, Public Health Service, Centers for Disease Control, NCHS.

National Education Association: Recommended guidelines for dealing with AIDS in the schools from the National Education Association, *J Sch Health* 56(4):129, 1986.

Newton J: *School health handbook,* Englewood Cliffs, NJ, 1984, Prentis-Hall.

Nishioka E: Helping children of alcoholics, *J Sch Health* 59(9):404, 1989.

Pacheco M, et al.: Innovation, peer teaching, and multidisciplinary collaboration: outreach from a school-based clinic, *J Sch Health* 61(8):367, 1991.

Price JM: AIDS, the schools, and policy issues, *J Sch Health* 56(4):137, 1986.

Shanley DA, Gagliardi BA: The nurse's role in identifying children with communication disorders, *J Sch Health* 58(2):1988, 75.

Supreme Court of North Dakota, April 22, 1919, 42ND213, 173, NW 787, Mand. 81 Schools 157.

Supreme Court of the State of Minnesota, 165 Minn., 1925, 361, 206 NW 642; appeal from the District Court, Hennepin County.

Thompson J: School health services in the United States: a view from the United Kingdom, *J Sch Health* 59(6):243, 1989.

Update: serologic testing for antibody to human immunodeficiency virus, *MMWR* 36(52):833, January 1988.

US Dept of Health and Human Services: *Healthy People 2000: national health promotion and disease prevention objectives,* Washington, DC, 1990, Government Printing Office.

Preventive aspects of health services

Safety, emergency care, and first aid

O VERVIEW

Accidents are the leading cause of death for school-age children and youth, and motor vehicle accidents are the most frequent cause. However, most accidents do not happen "by accident" as the word incorrectly implies. Most accidents repeat previous accidents and have quantifiable contributing factors that can be prevented. Although the school itself is relatively safe, the school environment presents its own hazards and safety concerns. The Healthy People 2000 national health objectives pertaining to the prevention and control of accidents provide a useful guide for school safety. The number and rate of accidents in the schools are relatively low when compared with other youth activities, but children and youth do get injured and die while engaged in school activities. The school requires a system for preventing accidents, as well as dealing with them immediately and effectively when they do occur. Because the school is an ideal peer-referenced environment, important opportunities exist for teaching health and safety education. The possibililty of encountering an emergency requires that everyone should be prepared to administer lifesaving care. This chapter prepares the responsible teacher and administrator to deal with these events.

O BJECTIVES   After reading this chapter, the student should be able to:

1. Explain the concept of "injury control" and the factors that contribute to an accident
2. Explain the terms "external controls" and "internal controls" and how they contribute to the prevention of accidents
3. Explain why school officials are often surprised when an accident occurs
4. Interpret the expression, "There hasn't been a new type of accident in 50 years"
5. Identify areas of the school environment that pose a potential threat for accidental injury to students
6. Explain the concept of negligence and the conditions under which teacher liability may be determined in cases of student injury
7. Describe the community Emergency Medical Services and the role of the school in the handling of a school emergency
8. Explain the components of a basic training program for school personnel that will enable them to handle a school emergency appropriately
9. Explain the "Bystander" program and what has led to its development   **221**

ACCIDENTAL DEATH AND INJURY AND THE ROLE OF THE SCHOOL

The leading causes of death for *all* ages (child to adult) are heart disease, stroke, and cancer, followed by accidents. But accidents are the leading cause of death for school-age children and youth. For the period from 1 to 44 years of age, *accidents* claim the most lives (Table 9-1).

Although children and youth between 5 and 18 years of age spend roughly one third of their lives, or most of their waking hours, engaged in school activities, most injuries and deaths do not occur there. The school is a controlled environment, and accidents are generally the result of an uncontrolled behavior occurring in an uncontrolled environment. Most school activities are planned and take place within prescribed boundaries. Therefore, if an accident is going to happen to a student, it is going to occur within a certain room, building, or in an outside area and be part of an organized activity (i.e., a health education class, a physical education class, lunch, or recess). Most activities within the school are planned and therefore can be controlled. Knowing when, where, and how a student is to be involved in an activity makes it possible to recognize patterns over time that can lead to accident behaviors. With enough experience, these behaviors can be controlled. Therefore, when accidental injury and death do occur in the school, the administration and teachers are called to question not only because of their legal responsibility for the health and welfare of the students, but also because the accident occurred in a controlled environment during a controlled activity. The actions that led to the injurious behavior should have been predicted and controlled (Table 9-2).

SCHOOL SAFETY PROGRAM

The release of the report *Healthy People 2000: National Health Promotion and Disease Prevention Objectives* challenges the nation's schools (46 million children and youth) to help the nation reach a new level of health for the twenty-first century. The report contains a set of 300 national health objectives.

Dr. J. M. McGinnis, Director of the Office of Disease Prevention and Health Promotion (McGinnis and Degraw, 1991, p. 305) has stated that the schools can play a major role in

TABLE 9-1. Percentages of death from injury and other causes in the United States by age

Age	Injuries (%)	Congenital anomalies (%)	Cancer (%)	Pneumonia/ influenza (%)	Heart disease (%)	Liver disease (%)	Stroke (%)	Other (%)
1-4	46	13	7	3	4	—	—	27
5-14	55	5	14	—	3	—	—	23
15-24	79	—	5	—	3	—	—	13
25-34	62	—	10	—	6	3	—	19
35-44	31	—	21	—	20	6	4	18
45-64	7	—	32	—	36	4	5	16
65+	2	—	19	3	48	—	10	18

Adapted from Committee on Trauma Research, Commission on Life Sciences, National Research Council, and the Institute of Medicine: Injury in America, a continuing public health problem, Washington, DC, 1985, National Academy Press.

TABLE 9-2. Student accident rates by school grade

The table below summarizes more than 7,500 school jurisdiction accidents[a] reported to the National Safety Council for the 1984-85 and 1985-86 school years. The rates are accidents per 100,000, student days. In the "total" column only, a rate of 0.10 is equivalent to about 8000 accidents among the nation's enrollment.

The rates indicate principal accident types and locations within grade groups. Since reporting is voluntary, the experience may not be representative of the national accident picture. These rates are not comparable to rates of previous years because of a decrease in the number of schools included. See footnotes.

Location and type	Total[b]	Kgn.[c]	1-3 Gr.	4-6 Gr.	7-9 Gr.	10-12 Gr.	Days lost per injury
Enrollment reported (000)	*720*	*46*	*167*	*153*	*176*	*153*	
Total school jurisdiction	**5.86**	**4.81**	**4.01**	**6.89**	**8.27**	**6.11**	**1.19**
Shops and labs	**0.24**	**0.00**	**0.00**	**0.01**	**0.63**	**0.40**	**0.87**
Homemaking	0.02	0.00	0.00	0.01	0.07	0.02	0.63
Science	(d)	0.00	0.00	0.00	0.05	0.02	0.82
Vocational ind arts	0.12	0.00	0.00	(d)	0.28	0.25	0.97
Other labs	0.01	0.00	0.00	0.00	0.03	0.04	1.35
Other shops	0.01	0.00	0.00	(d)	0.02	0.03	0.92
Building—general	**1.26**	**1.35**	**0.85**	**1.33**	**2.00**	**1.17**	**1.14**
Auditoriums and classrooms	0.47	0.92	0.45	0.60	0.55	0.37	1.04
Lunchrooms	0.08	0.05	0.07	0.07	0.14	0.07	1.00
Corridors	0.31	0.15	0.19	0.25	0.58	0.30	1.15
Lockers (room and corridor)	0.05	0.00	(d)	0.03	0.12	0.08	0.87
Stairs and stairways (inside)	0.18	0.02	0.04	0.16	0.36	0.21	1.24
Toilets and washrooms	0.06	0.12	0.08	0.09	0.06	0.02	1.11
Grounds—unorganized activities	**1.16**	**1.93**	**1.99**	**2.40**	**0.32**	**0.22**	**1.17**
Apparatus	0.36	1.18	0.75	0.68	0.01	(d)	1.44
Ball playing	0.22	0.24	0.23	0.59	0.12	0.03	1.01
Running	0.20	0.15	0.37	0.39	0.04	0.08	1.14
Grounds—miscellanenous	**0.32**	**0.36**	**0.29**	**0.57**	**0.28**	**0.22**	**1.23**
Fences and walls	0.02	0.02	0.02	0.02	0.02	0.02	1.07
Steps and walks (outside)	0.11	0.15	0.10	0.16	0.17	0.12	1.08
Physical education	**2.14**	**0.82**	**0.66**	**2.28**	**4.02**	**2.36**	**1.12**
Apparatus	0.17	0.51	0.15	0.23	0.22	0.09	1.04
Class games	0.14	0.19	0.09	0.30	0.13	0.10	1.05
Baseball—hardball	0.01	0.00	(d)	(d)	0.01	(d)	1.25
Baseball—softball	0.11	0.00	0.02	0.13	0.19	0.16	1.15
Football—tackle	0.05	0.00	0.00	0.05	0.12	0.05	1.07
Football—touch	0.12	0.00	0.00	0.04	0.21	0.26	0.88
Basketball	0.32	0.00	0.01	0.17	0.67	0.53	0.95
Hockey	0.02	0.00	0.00	0.01	0.04	0.06	1.10
Soccer	0.15	0.00	0.08	0.16	0.26	0.15	1.24
Track and field events	0.12	0.00	0.02	0.17	0.27	0.04	1.07
Volleyball and similar games	0.19	0.00	0.01	0.16	0.38	0.29	0.89
Other organized games	0.17	0.05	0.09	0.21	0.29	0.18	0.95

Source: Reporters to the National Safety Council: Accidents Facts 1987, Chicago, 1987, p. 100.
[a]Accidents are those causing the loss of one-half day or more of (1) school time or (2) activity during nonschool time, or any property damage as a result of a school jurisdictional accident.
[b]All totals include data not shown separately.
[c]Adjusted for half day.
[d]Less than 0.005.

Continued

TABLE 9-2.   Student accident rates by school grade—cont'd

Location and type	Total[b]	Kgn.[c]	1-3 Gr.	4-6 Gr.	7-9 Gr.	10-12 Gr.	Days lost per injury
Physical education—cont'd							
Swimming..........................	0.05	0.00	0.00	0.01	0.12	0.08	0.98
Showers and dressing rooms...........	0.06	0.00	0.00	0.01	0.17	0.06	0.72
Intramural sports......................	**0.07**	**0.00**	**0.00**	**0.01**	**0.20**	**0.10**	**1.12**
Football—tackle	0.01	0.00	0.00	0.00	0.02	0.01	0.75
Basketball	0.02	0.00	0.00	(d)	0.04	0.04	1.28
Interscholastic sports...............	**0.42**	**0.00**	**0.00**	**0.01**	**0.53**	**1.38**	**1.65**
Football—tackle	0.18	0.00	0.00	0.00	0.19	0.64	2.39
Basketball	0.07	0.00	0.00	0.01	0.09	0.22	1.02
Track and field events	0.02	0.00	0.00	(d)	0.03	0.08	1.47
Special activities........................	**0.06**	**0.05**	**0.03**	**0.06**	**0.08**	**0.08**	**1.23**
Trips or excursions	0.03	0.05	0.02	0.04	0.04	0.02	1.32
Going to and from school (MV)	**0.11**	**0.24**	**0.10**	**0.08**	**0.13**	**0.16**	**2.60**
School bus..	0.08	0.10	0.08	0.06	0.08	0.10	2.99
Other motor veh.—pedestrian	0.02	0.10	0.01	0.01	0.02	0.02	2.19
Other motor veh.—other type.........	0.01	0.00	0.00	(d)	0.01	0.04	3.00
Going to, from school (not MV)	**0.07**	**0.05**	**0.07**	**0.12**	**0.09**	**0.01**	**1.10**
Bicycle—not motor veh.	0.01	0.00	(d)	0.01	0.01	(d)	0.81
Other street and sidewalk...............	0.04	0.02	0.04	0.06	0.05	0.01	0.93

Source: Reporters to the National Safety Council: Accidents Facts 1987, Chicago, 1987, p. 100.
[a]Accidents are those causing the loss of one-half day or more of (1) school time or (2) activity during nonschool time, or any property damage as a result of a school jurisdictional accident.
[b]All totals include data not shown separately.
[c]Adjusted for half day.
[d]Less than 0.005.

attaining one third of these objectives by the year 2000. Examples of the objectives contained in the report that directly concern the safety, emergency care, and first aid programs of the schools are as follows:

> **Objective 9.18** Provide academic instruction on injury prevention and control, preferably as part of quality school health education, in at least 50% of public school systems (grade K through 12).

Injuries cause more deaths among children and young adults than all of the other major diseases. The most recent survey shows that 37% of the deaths were related to motor vehicles. This also includes bicycle and pedestrian deaths involving motor vehicles. For ages 0 to 14 years, the five leading causes of death from injuries were occupancy of a motor vehicle, drowning, pedestrian accidents, house fires, and homicide.

Bicyclist deaths accounted for 12% of the motor vehicle-related deaths in the 5- to 9-year age group and 16% of the pre-adolescent group 10 to 14 years of age (Waller et al, 1989).

Data from the National Health Interview Survey indicate that injuries were responsible for 8.5% of all school-loss days (U.S. Congress, 1991, p. 119)

> **Objective 9.19** Extend requirement of the use of effective head, face, eye, and mouth protection to all organizations, agencies, and institutions sponsoring sporting and recreation events that pose risk of injury.

Supporting information documenting the importance of this objective shows that trauma to the head, face, eyes, and mouth accounts for a large proportion of athletic injuries. Experience with the use of mouth protectors and face guards in football has greatly reduced the incidence of mouth and face injuries in this sport. "In contrast, 10 percent of baseball and 13 percent of ice hockey injuries are to the mouth and face. Mouth protectors and face guards are not currently required in these sports" (McGinnis and Degraw, 1991, p. 311).

For the adolescent ages 13 to 19, sports participation accounts for the greatest number of injuries requiring medical treatment. A special report to the U.S. Congress (1991) shows that 1 in 14 adolescents required hospital treatment for sports injury and 20% of those injuries were from football. The data presented in Table 9-3 show that football has the highest injury rate per 100,000 participants, followed closely by baseball, ice hockey, and basketball (National Safety Council, 1991).

> **Objective 9.12** Increase use of occupant protection systems such as safety belts, inflatable safety restraints, and child safety seats to at least 85% of motor vehicle occupants.
>
> **Objective 9.13** Increase the use of helmets to at least 80% of motorcyclists and at least 50% of bicyclists.

These two objectives can and should be an important part of the school's health and safety education program. The results of the National Adolescent Student Health Survey (1989) revealed that many adolescents are engaging in behaviors that place them at risk. For example,

TABLE 9-3. Sports injuries per 100,000 participants

Sport	Rates per 100,000
Archery	66
Baseball	2089
Basketball	1858
Bicycle Riding	905
Football	2171
Golf	104
Horseback Riding	465
Ice Hockey	2089
Ice Skating	335
Racquetball	168
Roller Skating	349
Skate Boarding	878
Soccer	910
Swimming	93
Table Tennis	13
Tennis	118
Volleyball	370
Water Skiing	199

Adapted from National Safety Council: *Accident facts,* 1991 edition, Chicago, 1991, the Council. Rates rounded to nearest whole number.

92% of all bicycle riders *do not wear a helmet*. Of the adolescents surveyed, 62% believed that their friends would think that wearing a helmet would be "a silly thing to do." However, results of the survey show that most adolescents have correct information about safe practices (Fig. 9-1). For example, 81% of these teens agree that wearing a seat belt is a very important procedure to protect one in a motor vehicle crash. However, only 41% of those same adolescents wore a seat belt the last time they were in a vehicle. The educational implication of these findings emphasizes the importance of peer influence and the inconsistencies between knowledge, attitudes, and practices in safety education.

>   ***Objective 7.16*** Increase to at least 50% the proportion of elementary and secondary schools that teach nonviolent conflict resolution skills, preferably as a part of quality school health education.

The National Adolescent Student Health Survey reveals that students are aware of certain dangerous behaviors such as hitchhiking, which they avoid. On the other hand, adolescents frequently go into places that are known to be dangerous, placing them at high risk of becoming victims of violence. At the same time, positive factors operate to increase the potential for preventing violence among school-age youth. These include parental attitudes, school rules, the influence of friends, and the likelihood of injury.

Observational research shows that some families are more prone to violence than others.

FIG. 9-1.   Helmet use reduces the risk of injury for bicyclists.

For example, abusive families are unable to resolve conflicts, whereas nonabusive families are able to resolve negative family interactions quickly. This has led researchers to conclude that the skills that prevent conflict from escalating to the point of violence can be taught.

The U.S. Surgeon General's Report identified violence as a major cause of death of young people (Fig. 9-2). Accordingly, the report has called for increased efforts on the part of health professionals to teach skills to prevent conflict in order to reduce the morbidity and mortality resulting from violence. For the schools, the goals of such a curriculum seek to "change knowledge about and attitudes toward violence and to develop interpersonal skills for resolving conflicts nonviolently" (McGinnis and DeGraw, 1991).

The school deals with accidental injury and death in three ways: by teaching students to avoid or deal with risky situations, by reducing hazards in the school environment, and by teaching skills to cope with accidents and care for accident victims when accidents do occur.

It is apparent that safety in the school does not imply that the physical environment be converted into an accident-proof situation or that children's actions be completely restrained so that an accident cannot possibly happen. Rather, it means pursuit of the normal demands of life in an environment in which hazards are reduced to a practical minimum and the behavior of the pupils is adapted to safe and effective living (Fig. 9-3).

Student rates for accidents occurring in school-related activities give some indication of the relative risks associated with school activities. In terms of days lost per injury, travel to and from school in a motor vehicle is the most dangerous school-related activity. Activities apart from organized athletics and class work but carried out on the school property are the next most costly. Among formal school activities, interscholastic activities rank third for girls, and physical education class accounts for the third most frequent loss of school days for boys. The accident death rates are beginning to rise during the ages 10 to 14 years and then increase dramatically during the teenage years of 15 to 19 (Table 9-4).

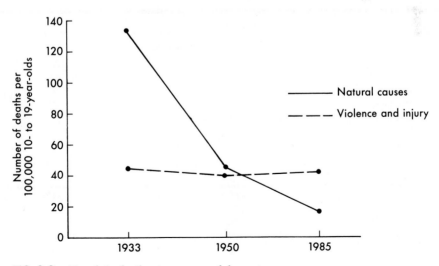

FIG. 9-2.   Trends in death rates among adolescents.

FIG. 9-3. Posted directions and emergency drills reduce the potential risk when real emergencies do occur.

TABLE 9-4. Average annual accidental injury deaths and death rates among U.S. adolescents ages 10 to 14 and ages 15 to 19, 1984-86

	Ages 10 to 14		Ages 15 to 19	
	Deaths	Rate (per 100,000)	Deaths	Rate (per 100,000)
Vehicle-related				
Motor vehicle occupant	458	2.69	3,770	20.18
Drivers	56	0.33	2,094	11.21
Passengers	402	2.36	1,676	8.97
Motorcycles	87	0.51	639	3.42
Pedestrians	294	1.72	515	2.76
Bicycles	219	1.28	142	0.76
Other & vehicle unspecified	203	1.19	1,526	8.17
Other				
Drowning	280	1.64	566	3.03
Firearms	169	0.99	248	1.33
Fires/burns	174	1.02	238	1.27
Falls	39	0.23	143	0.77
Other accidental	324	1.90	752	4.02
TOTAL ACCIDENTAL	2,248	13.18	8,537	45.69

Sources: U.S. Department of Commerce, Bureau of the Census, *Current Population Reports, Series P-25, No. 1000, Estimates of the Population of the United States by Age, Sex, and Race: 1980 to 1986* (Washington, DC: U.S. Government Printing Office, 1987); U.S. Department of Health and Human Services, Public Health Service, National Center for Health Statistics, *Vital Statistics of the United States, Volume II, 1984-1986 Mortality, Part A* (Washington, D.C.: U.S. Government Printing Office).

School driver education

EMERGING ISSUE You are a member of the high school health and safety education curriculum committee. The school district's coordinator for the safety and driver education program has just returned from a meeting in Washington, D.C. sponsored by the National Highway Traffic Safety Administration (NHTSA). She has requested a meeting of the committee to consider some of the major issues discussed at this conference.

The concern of governmental and legislative officials over the traffic accident problem and, in particular, the high rates of adolescent injuries and fatalities resulting from motor vehicle crashes has led to the conference. Research presented there indicated that, if proper safety procedures had been followed, a great proportion of injuries and deaths could have been prevented. Various approaches for reducing the accident rate were considered, including the introduction of new laws and regulations, development of new equipment and automatic safety devices, and educational and incentive programs that would cause people to be more safety conscious.

Of special concern to the committee is research suggesting that safety education efforts have been the least effective in reducing accidents. Driver education, as presently conducted in schools, is generally ineffective. Further, there is some indication that, by enabling a student to obtain a driver's license at a younger age than without training, driver education may actually cause an increase in motor vehicle accidents.

Given the background of information from this conference, the question that is placed before the committee is "What, if anything, should be done about the school's driver education program?"

Please indicate your thinking on this issue by marking a plus (+) or a minus (−) before each of those statements with which you generally agree or disagree.

_____ 1. I believe that the committee should critically evaluate the way the course in driver education is being taught. Is 6 hours of behind-the-wheel experience enough to qualify a student for the learner permit?

_____ 2. Judging from my observation, more emphasis should be given to developing the proper attitudes toward driving and less given to the mechanical skills of driving.

_____ 3. Considering school priorities, as well as budget constraints, I seriously question whether schools should be conducting driver education programs.

_____ 4. I believe that students should have a more extensive and realistic driving experience, including demanding traffic situations, night driving, and adverse weather conditions.

_____ 5. I believe a partial solution would be a system of incentives that would raise the standards to qualify for the course and make licensure for driving a greater reward.

_____ 6. I would favor including a unit on alcohol and drug education as a part of the driver education course.

_____ 7. Considering the magnitude of this problem, I believe that the schools have a moral obligation to society to upgrade the quality of this program and to continue driving education as an integral part of the curriculum.

_____ If limited to a single choice, I would choose this number.

ACCIDENTS AND THE INJURY CONTROL MODEL

The word "accident" is a poor and inappropriate descriptor. To the lay person, most accidents happen "by accident," but in reality most injury and deaths attributable to accidents are a repeat of other accidents or injuries. In fact, there is a saying in the field of safety education and research that "there hasn't been a new type of accident in 50 years." Motor vehicle accidents are a good example, not only because the number and type of car accidents are repeated virtually every year, but also because of the magnitude of the problem. A car can run into another car or stationary object in only one of several ways. The number and type of collisions are limited. They include hitting another object, fixed or moving; being hit in the front or rear; or, in fewer situations, being hit on the side. After the car impacts, the "second collision," occurs, where the occupants actually impact on the inside of the car. This second collision causes injury and death. This scenario plays itself out thousands of times each year, resulting in just under 50,000 deaths annually. All aspects of this type of accident have been analyzed over and over, yet the circumstances repeat, every day of every year. Other factors involved in motor vehicle death also repeat themselves. For example, alcohol consumption has a strong relationship to motor vehicle accidents (Table 9-5).

The concept of *injury control* is a useful model for school administrators and teachers to use in the prevention and control of accidental injury and death. The model quantifies the accident scenario and makes it possible to control factors that contribute to the event. An accident happens to a particular person within a particular environment in contact with a particular "object" (e.g., a car, a jungle gym, a floor, a large piece of meat in the case of a choking) during a particular activity. It then becomes possible to observe and control the environment, the activity, the person, or any combination of these to prevent the accident event from happening. It is possible to quantify all factors related to environment, object, and person engaged in the activity and then effectively control these factors. The injury-control model uses the fact that contributing factors of a particular accident type can be found within three categories: the person, the object, and the environment. These categories can be factored out, and effective controls can be implemented (Fig. 9-4).

Once these factors are known, they can be removed or "controlled" to lessen the possi-

TABLE 9-5.   Teenage drivers—fatalities and accidents by age and licensed drivers

Age group	No. of fatalities	No. of accidents	Driver fatalities per 100,000 licensed drivers	Drivers in all accidents per 100 licensed drivers
Under 16	500	90,000	1316*	237*
16	1200	560,000	81	38
17	1700	680,000	73	29
18	2200	770,000	77	27
19	2200	750,000	71	24

Adapted from data presented in National Safety Council: *Accident facts, 1991 edition,* Chicago, 1991, the Council.
*Rates for drivers under age 16 are substantially overstated because of the high proportion of unlicensed drivers involved.

FIG. 9-4. It is not the school's responsibility to remove all potential hazards from a student's environment, but school personnel do have a responsibility to teach students how to use equipment safely and to be prepared in case accidents do occur.

bility of accident. Controls that relate to the environment or object are called *external controls.* Controls relating to the person involved in the performance of the activity are called *internal controls.* External controls involve changing the environment or creating rules or regulations for the behavior. Speed limits and warning lights are examples of external controls. Internal controls involve modifying the behavior of the individual involved in the unsafe behavior. A person who recognizes the hazards involved in driving around a curve at a high speed and slows down illustrates internal control. Educational programs are designed to promote internal control, or control of the person. Many individual behaviors that contribute to accidental death are played out among students in the school setting, and the health educator and school administrator can capitalize on these real-world teaching moments. Internal control of risky behavior can be promoted through effective health and safety education programs that capitalize on peer-referenced learning.

As logical as the injury approach may seem, the assumption that accidents occur accidentally and cannot be controlled pervades society. Therefore the accident rates in certain categories are still high. The school administrator and health education instructor can use the injury control model to quantify the factors in the school setting that have demonstrated a history of contributing to accidents.

Prevention of accidents in school

Not all accidents can be anticipated, and not all situations that cause accidents can be foreseen. Yet most hazardous conditions and unsafe practices can be recognized through the use of a well-organized school safety program. Safety programs, financially speaking, are not costly. They do demand vision, organization, leadership, and cooperation. They should be enacted, not just exist on paper.

A well-planned program begins with an evaluation of the school conditions and practices that relate to the school's safety and accident prevention program.

A survey should be conducted to detect all potentially hazardous conditions. The survey form provided in Appendix C has proved to be an effective instrument for this purpose and one that can be easily adapted to the needs of most schools.

Legal aspects

Although the number of injury-producing accidents that happen in and around schools is low compared to other childhood hazards, children and youth *do* die or get injured at school, and the potential for accidental death and injury is always present. Because the school is a controlled environment (i.e., most activities are well defined and take place within a defined space), it is possible to quantify and control specific behaviors that could lead to injury. From a legal point of view, since the environment is controlled and most accidents can only repeat previous ones, it would be reasonable to assume that the school should have an effective injury control program.

Emergency health needs always involve trauma. Trauma is experienced by the victim and to a lesser degree by the teacher or other school personnel who tends to the victim. To lessen this trauma, teachers should be skilled in emergency health care procedures and be aware of their legal responsibilities.

Teachers and other school personnel are required to provide basic emergency care. In more technical terms, school personnel can apply nonmedical and nonsurgical procedures of an immediate and temporary nature until a physician or medical emergency person is available. This means that efforts can be made to stem excessive bleeding but no medication such as aspirin may be administered, nor should a procedure such as removing a sliver from a finger be undertaken.

Teachers and other school employees run the risk of being sued by injured students because of alleged negligence unless careful emergency procedures are followed. In general, *negligence* is any conduct below the legally established standard for the protection of others against unreasonable risk of harm. Two basic types of negligence are as follows:

1. Performance of an act that a person of ordinary prudence or judgment would realize involves unreasonable risk to others
2. Failure to act for the protection of another person

Thus negligence can be an act of commission or omission. The specific details of each case determine whether or not behavior has been negligent.

The following set of guidelines (Harper, 1938) illustrates a variety of possible negligent actions:

1. Failure to use or properly carry out appropriate care
2. Creating undue risk through the circumstances under which care is provided

3. Unreasonably risking direct and immediate harm to others
4. Creating a situation that is unreasonably dangerous to others because of the action of a third person
5. Entrusting dangerous devices or instruments to persons incompetent to use or care for them properly
6. Failing to use due care to give adequate warning
7. Failing to exercise the proper care in looking out for persons whom one has reason to believe may be in the danger zone
8. Failing to use appropriate skill in performing the acts undertaken
9. Failing to make adequate preparation to avoid harm to others
10. Failing to inspect and repair devices to be used in emergencies
11. Preventing a third person from assisting in an emergency

Liability for negligent conduct is affected by the nature of both the act and its results. Carelessness is a relative term. In general, a person is considered to be careless or negligent when the actions taken are not those of an ordinarily prudent individual. If a pupil is injured because a teacher's actions were not prudent or the teacher failed to act, a lawsuit may be instituted by the parents, and the teacher may be held liable. Each teacher is responsible for negligence that results in physical harm to others. A teacher's administrative superior is held liable when he or she directs the teacher to perform a dangerous act resulting in injury to a pupil or fails to correct a hazardous situation that has been reported by a teacher. The teacher must have tangible evidence that the administrator was notified of the hazard.

School boards are not usually held liable for negligence, but several state supreme courts have removed this immunity by making it possible to sue the school board, as well as the teacher.

Teachers are not often defendants in lawsuits that allege negligence resulting in an injury to a pupil. Teachers tend to be conservative, and their conduct usually is prudent. Courts recognize the problem of close supervision of 35 to 40 children at a given moment, and only when the teacher has displayed deplorably poor judgment does the court tend to hold him or her liable. The relatively low cost of premiums for liability insurance for teachers attests to the limited likelihood that a teacher will be a defendant in a lawsuit resulting from injury to a pupil.

The best safeguard against such a lawsuit is a well-planned, functioning program for the prevention of accidents to pupils. Such a program also assures the parents that the school has taken definite steps to reduce student injuries to a minimum. The safety of the students is the primary consideration, and student and faculty interests are as one.

EMERGENCY CARE

In any situation in which relatively large numbers of young people are assembled, emergencies occur despite the best precautions. Wisdom dictates preparation for such emergencies. Experience indicates that such preparation need not be elaborate but must be well organized.

Although students visit the nurse or aide for routine matters such as health screening, the most likely reason for a student visit to the school nurse's office is an emergency. The emergency may be relatively minor, but to the student or the referring teacher, the condition is important enough to warrant interruption of classroom activity. A review of the patterns of use of the nurse's office indicates the variety of health problems of young people and also indicates the types of services that school health personnel should be prepared to render.

In one small (240 students) midwestern elementary school (K through 6), all visits were carefully documented. Reasons for visiting the nurse's office ranged from attempts to avoid an unpopular class to major illness and injury. Occasionally parents know about the health problem and send the sick child to school to get "free" medical advice from the school nurse or aide. The data gathered in this school survey indicate that young people, even elementary school students, use health services (in this case the nurse's office) in very much the same manner that adults use their health services (clinics and private physicians). More girls than boys come to the nurse's office in the course of a day. Occasionally the condition requiring care could have been attended to earlier and simply represents parental neglect. Accidents are the most common cause of a visit. And young people, like adults, frequently use sickness or at least sick role behavior to avoid doing things they do not enjoy. (Note: Students with wounds [trauma] should not visit the nurse. Rather, the nurse or first responder should visit the injured student at the scene of the accident. In many cases, an injured child should not be moved.)

The percentage distribution of complaints that students presented when they reported to the nurse's office is shown in Table 9-6. It is interesting to note that the incidence of headache was most frequent during the winter months when children had little opportunity to play and exercise outside during the school day. In the second year the school administrators made a conscious effort to provide activities, exercise, and recreation during the school day, including out-of-doors recreation unless the weather was especially bad. The rate of headaches declined. This implies that student health, at least as reflected by visits to the nurse's office, is affected by such things as physical hazards and accidents but also by administrative organizational patterns.

In this school it was also noticed that those students who used the nurse's office frequently were not the same students who were absent most often. Respiratory complaints accounted for the largest number of health/illness–related absences (20.4%), followed by gastrointestinal problems (11.1%), fever (10.2%), and skin problems (10.2%). Interestingly, respiratory complaints were not prominent among the causes of sick room use nor was fever. The skin

TABLE 9-6.   Elementary students' reasons for visiting school nurse's office*

Boys			Girls		
	Year 1	Year 2		Year 1	Year 2
Wounds (trauma)	39.5	51.5	Wounds (trauma)	30.5	43
Headache	19.5	8.5	Headache	19	11
Gastrointestinal	14.5	12.5	Gastrointestinal	17	12
Skin	8	9.5	Skin	10	14
Mouth	5.5	2.5	Mouth	9.5	6
Eye	5	4	General malaise	6	3.5
General malaise	3.5	3.5	Respiratory	4	5.5
Respiratory	3	4.5	Ear	2.5	2.5
Ear	2.5	3.5	Eye	2	2.5

*All figures are given as percentages.

problems seen by the nurse or health aide (sunburn and exposure to cold) were very different from those causing absence. Gastrointestinal complaints were the only category of complaints where visits to the nurse's office and absenteeism appeared to be related. This relationship is probably a direct result of the nature of the illness, with early symptoms occurring at school and convalescence taking place at home.

A total of 7.3% of all school absences were attributed to visits to the physician or dentist. Only 5% of the reported absences were on a physician's recommendation. Causes for another 25% of the absences ranged from helping with harvest to baby-sitting and accompanying parents on vacation.

Facilities and procedures for emergency care

Effective emergency care begins with adequate facilities and well-established procedures. These include:

1. Nurse's office or health room with at least two cots, adequate blankets, pillows, washbasin, soap, towels, and chair; (a contingency plan should exist that identifies space and supplies for more than two children in case of a major emergency)
2. Established procedures in case of an emergency and the clear posting of emergency phone numbers for police, fire department, physicians, ambulance, and hospital
3. Student files listing location and phone numbers (home and work) for all children's parents
4. Established protocols concerning the role of the principal, nurse, aide, secretaries, and teachers in case of emergencies
5. Adequate first aid supplies

With an organized plan of action the school is well prepared to meet its responsibility during emergencies. If the school emergency program is part of the community emergency response program, the school should rehearse its procedures as part of the community rehearsal. Otherwise, on its own initiative the school should go through simulated emergencies.

PLAN OF ACTION WHEN ACCIDENTS OCCUR

Most people do not recognize that accidents are an expected part of daily living. Therefore an accident takes people by surprise. This surprise may cause the victim of an accident to lose the critical benefit of immediate, necessary, and appropriate care. Fortunately, most school systems have been required to develop written guidelines for handling emergencies. Unfortunately, that often constitutes the extent of the response to accidents. Whether these plans are realistic and up-to-date regarding current practices in emergency medical care is always in question. Because society still views the saving of lives as an activity reserved for physicians and hospitals, the important actions that need to take place when an emergency occurs in the school often go undone.

Emergency medical services (EMS) is a relatively new area of health care, and the critical role that lay bystanders (e.g., general public, teachers) play in saving lives has not been totally realized. A victim can die or suffer permanent disability when care is not rendered during the first critical moments following an accident. On the other hand, untrained bystanders relying on "common sense" can often cause real harm and must be controlled. The critical role of the

FIG. 9-5.   Emergency phone.

trained bystander is: (1) to recognize that an emergency situation exists, (2) to summon help effectively, and (3) to maintain life function until EMS arrives (Fig. 9-5). Without this effort, lives can't be saved.

Unfortunately, an uninformed public often assumes that accidental death is an inevitable consequence of an accident. In many cases accidental death is caused by lack of or inappropriate emergency care in the first few minutes following the accident.

BYSTANDER CARE

The importance of "bystander care" is illustrated by the experience of Dr. Henry Bock and his colleagues at Memorial Hospital of Indiana. Indianapolis Speedway race car drivers who have suffered head injuries often recover quickly, whereas persons suffering similar head injuries on rural highways never regain consciousness. Analysis of these injuries has led medical experts to conclude that the reason so many of the race car drivers survive is the fact that rescuers are on the scene within seconds after the crash to make certain the injured driver has a clear airway. It is now believed that many of the fatalities attributed to brain injuries may be caused by a lack of oxygen.

This research has led the National Highway Traffic Safety Administration to conclude that the implementation of a national bystander care program has the potential to reduce the annual highway traffic death toll by more than 22,000. Dr. P. Safar (1985), an authority on emergency care, has suggested that school systems should teach emergency care as a part of the health education curriculum.

Analyses of rural highway traffic accidents reveal that many fatalities could have been prevented if the following steps had been taken:

1. Recognizing the emergency
2. Deciding to help
3. Contacting the Emergency Medical System
4. Preventing further injuries
5. Assessing the victim
6. Providing life-sustaining care if needed (ABCs)

THE MODEL FOR SAVING LIVES: THE COMMUNITY EMERGENCY MEDICAL SERVICES SYSTEM

An EMS system is a coordinated means of providing care to victims of injury and sudden illness. It involves many of the community's human and physical resources linked together and trained to provide specialized emergency care. It involves police, fire, ambulance, and hospital personnel cooperating through well thought-out planning to provide specialized care within precise times related to the physiologic life-death function of the victim. EMS systems have had tremendous "save" rates when victims are readily accessible and appropriate care can be rendered quickly. For example, when a victim is located on the street or in a home, access to care can be virtually unimpeded.

But lives are often lost when care is delayed. When an accident occurs in a facility such as a school, shopping mall, or stadium, access to care and adequately trained personnel often are not present. Or, as in some cases in the schools, unrealistic procedures such as delaying necessary care during a life-threatening emergency to contact parents can cost lives. Relying on untrained personnel or on school staff assumed to be trained in first aid can lead to negative consequences.

The school system should be an integrated submodel of the community's EMS system. When an emergency situation occurs, everyone inside the school environment should know what to do. This includes teachers, bystander students, and all other school personnel. In certain emergencies, the care that is provided immediately and continued to the hospital can determine whether the child will live or suffer disability. Personnel must not only be trained, but also practiced in what to do.

TRAINING OF SCHOOL PERSONNEL

It may be advantageous but cost prohibitive to have all school personnel trained in advanced techniques of emergency care. But advanced training for all personnel may not be necessary. To have effective management of most medical emergencies, at least two levels of trained personnel must be present.

1. All personnel on the school staff should have basic training in the management of emergency situations and the basic ABCs of first aid: (*A*irway, *B*reathing, *C*irculation—heartbeat and bleeding; Fig. 9-6). This training does not necessarily contain extensive

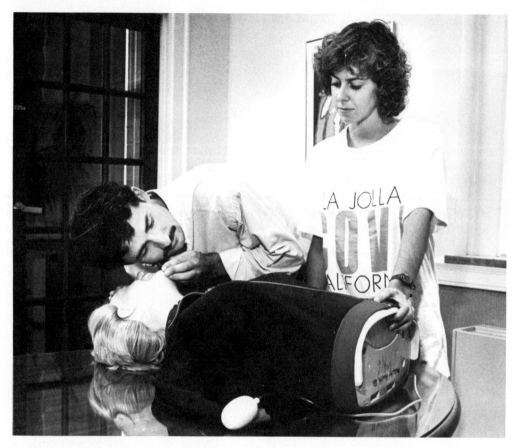

FIG. 9-6.   Teachers practicing the ABCs of emergency care: *A*irway, *B*reathing, *C*irculation—heartbeat and bleeding.

first aid procedures but teaches the teacher how to recognize an emergency situation, make sure that conditions are safe for the injured and bystanders, efficiently and correctly notify the school and community's EMS system, protect the victim from other inappropriate acts, and provide basic care until the school's first responder and community's EMS system arrives.

This basic care includes managing problems that could lead to death during the first few minutes while the next level of care is responding. This care would include keeping the victim's airway open to breath, rescue breathing, cardiopulmonary resuscitation (CPR), and control of severe bleeding.

Training that goes beyond the ABCs and calling for help is not necessary if the school has the next critical provider immediately available. Basic first-level training is sometimes difficult to find. Many training programs teach unnecessary skills for this level of training, such as splinting. This type of training can confuse the lay person and does not foster helpful behavior when the emergency occurs.

2. Each school building and grounds should employ one person trained to the first

responder level. A *First responder* is a person who has had basic professional training to provide basic care until the ambulance and other components of the EMS system arrive. This person has sufficient training in scene management and basic life support to sustain life until the EMS system arrives. This trained first responder should be located within each building or wherever he or she can react to the emergency scene within 3 to 5 minutes. A lay person can be taught these skills. The school nurse may or may not be the best candidate for this training depending on such factors as availability to the school. Such first aid training, especially the recommended first responder training, can be made available to school staff by contacting the community's local EMS office.

Adequately trained personnel, together with well-conceived and practiced EMS planning, will prepare the school to deal effectively with typical emergency situations and offer a good defense in the event of litigation.

FIRST AID SUPPLIES

Every school building should have at least one fully stocked, conveniently located first aid cabinet. The cabinet should be placed in the nurse's office if there is one. Otherwise the emergency rest room or principal's office is an acceptable place to store these items. (Table 9-7).

DRUG ABUSE: A SCHOOL EMERGENCY

Drugs either depress or stimulate the central nervous system. The individual's behavior under the influence of a drug may range from extreme sluggishness to hyperactivity. Needle marks may be apparent, especially on the arms or legs. In addition to the effects from taking drugs there are also the after effects from drug withdrawal. For example, frequent eye blinking and jerky eye movements may indicate drug withdrawal.

First aid

1. First, if drug use is suspected, assess the emergency. Can the situation be handled by one person? If not, summon help.
2. If the victim is conscious, the first responder should ask what drug has been taken and when.
3. Drug users may become violent. If it is known that the individual took a drug and is able to cooperate, vomiting should be induced by tickling the back of the throat with a finger or tongue depresser. Make sure that the victim does not choke on the vomit.

Alcohol abuse

Alcohol intoxication slows or depresses the actions of the central nervous system. Alcohol impairs psychomotor skills, slows reaction time, and reduces coordination. It also affects areas of the brain that control speech, hearing, and eye movements. Perhaps more important, alcohol impairs reasoning power by lowering inhibitions and conscious self-control. Because alcohol can give a false sense of euphoria, the person may appear stimulated, but in reality alcohol depresses.

TABLE 9-7. Inventory for first aid cabinet

Suggested supplies	Purposes
Glass jars (2)	For applicators and blades
Blades, wood (500)	Splints, depressors
Wooden applicators (1000)	Swabs, remove particles
Toothpicks (750)	Remove particles
Tincture of green soap	Wash injured parts
Absorbent cotton roll	Large pads or dressings
Sterile gauze, 4" roll	Dressings
Sterile gauze, 3 x 3" (7.5 x 7.5 cm) squares (100)	Protect injuries
Sterile gauze, 2 x 2" (5 x 5 cm) squares (100)	Protect injuries
Compress on adhesive band, 1" (2.5 cm) (111)	Protect injuries
Roller bandage, 1" (2.5 cm) (12 rolls)	Dressings
Roller bandage, 4" (10 cm) (12 rolls)	Dressings
Triangular bandage (4)	Sling, area coverings
Safety pins (23)	For triangular bandage
Adhesive tape, roll (widths ½-2") (1.25-5 cm)	Fasten splints, dressings
Scissors (blunt or bandage)	Cut dressings
Forceps (3") (7.5 cm) pincer or tweezer type	Grasp small objects
Tourniquet (3' ¼" rubber tube)	Check excessive bleeding
Splints (metal or yucca) (10)	Support
Quick cold packs	Relief of swelling
Hot-water bottle (with cover) (2)	Local relief of pain
Mineral oil or petroleum jelly (nonmedicated)	Relieve irritation
Paper cups (100)	Receptacle
Thermometer	Temperature checking
Elastic bandage	Sprains and strains
Inflatable splints	Fractures
Ample supply of ice	Bone and joint injuries
Pocket resuscitation mask	For protection of first responder from disease

Signs of alcohol overdose. A lack of coordination, slurred speech, or even unconsciousness, when accompanied by a strong odor of alcohol, characterize alcohol overdosage.

First aid in responding to alcohol overdose

1. If the victim appears to be sleepy, with normal respiration and pulse, and if he/she can be roused by shaking or shouting, no immediate treatment is required. The victim should be placed in a position so that he/she will not harm himself/herself. The victim should be checked periodically to see that he/she is breathing normally.
2. If the victim is breathing abnormally or is unconscious or in a coma and cannot be aroused, immediate action must be taken to establish an *airway* and restore *breathing* and *circulation* (ABCs). The EMS should be called immediately.

Withdrawal from drugs

Drug withdrawal signs and symptoms include trembling hands and head, vomiting, frightened response to sounds, objects, and lights. He/she may be hallucinating (hearing and seeing objects not present). The individual may have a high fever or he/she may display other unusual behavior.

First aid for a drug withdrawal

1. Open airway, restore breathing and circulation if necessary.
2. If vomiting, check to see that he/she does not choke.
3. Calm and reassure the person.
4. Call for medical attention.

Stimulant overdose

Stimulant drugs include inhalants, antidepressants, tranquilizers, cocaine (coke, crack, rock, snow), amphetamines (speed, uppers, black beauties), and pep pills . Other stimulants include glue, paints, lacquers, thinners, gasoline, kerosene, lighter fluid, and nail polish remover.

Signs and symptoms. Stimulant overdose is characterized by overly active or aggressive behavior, mental confusion and disorganization, repetition of particular acts, irritability, fear, suspiciousness, and exaggerated perception of abilities.

First aid

1. Approach the victim carefully.
2. (A-B-C) estabish *A*irway, restore *B*reathing and *C*irculation, if necessary.
3. Call for medical attention.

SUMMARY

Accidental injury is the leading cause of death for age groups 1 to 44 years. Accidents result from uncontrolled behavior or uncontrolled environmental factors. However, the school environment is a relatively controlled environment and the activities in which the student participates are usually prescribed and controlled. Consequently, teachers and school officials have a greater responsibility for anticipating situations that could cause injury to students.

An injury control model should include the student, the hazardous object or equipment, and the environment. The external factors of the model include the object and the environment. Examples of external control include rules, regulations, and laws such as speed limits. Internal controls are designed to modify the individual's behavior so safe practices on the part of the student are promoted. Safety education emphasizes internal controls.

Legal concepts of prudent behavior on the part of the teacher or school administration are the basis for determining negligence. If the individual's acts of commission or omission fail to meet a legal standard of acceptability, then he or she may be held liable for injuries suffered by the student. All schools should have a written plan of the procedures together with facilities needed in the event of an emergency. This should enable the school to respond appropriately in the first critical moments of an emergency. This plan covers maintaining life if necessary until the community's EMS arrives. It is especially important that the school's emergency care program be planned as an integral part of the community's EMS. This means that the school has appropriately trained personnel who would be able to maintain life until medical help arrives. Such a first responder should be on the scene in 3 to 5 minutes and should be able to manage the emergency scene and administer the ABCs of first aid, which are *Airway, Breathing,* and *Circulation*—heartbeat and bleeding.

G**ET INVOLVED!** Paramedics or emergency medical technicians (EMTs) have a career that is often highly dramatic, calling for immediate, lifesaving actions and often performed under stressful and dangerous conditons. The EMT must recognize, assess, and manage emergencies of acutely ill or injured persons outside the hospital setting.

Typical emergencies encountered in the line of work are treating victims of automobile crashes, heart attacks, near drownings, unexpected childbirths, poisonings, and gunshot wounds. All of these demand urgent medical attention.

Each condition, whether resuscitating a heart attack victim, immobilizing fractures, handling an emotionally disturbed person, or handling a fatal accident, requires appropriate action. The EMT is a key member of the health care team.

The student enrolled in health career fields has often taken courses related to EMT training. A national training program of 110 hours has been designed by the U.S. National Highway Traffic Safety Administration. This field training is offered by specified police, fire, and health departments, by hospitals, and by colleges and universities.

**For more information about the training and qualifications
for becoming a certified Emergency Medical Technician, write to:**
National Association of Emergency Medical Technicians
9140 Ward Parkway
Kansas City, MO 64114

STUDY QUESTIONS

1. Should a school board and the faculty of a school district be held legally responsible for preventing risks of injury to students?
2. What are the elements of an "injury control" model?
3. In reference to the model of "injury control" above, where should the emphasis be placed to reduce the threat of injury to children and youth?
4. What is the minimum level of training required of all school staff to be able to respond to serious injury?
5. What constitutes a community emergency medical service (EMS) and how does a school relate to such services?
6. What is meant by the expression "teachers may be held legally liable for acts of commission and omission in situations of accidental injury to students?"
7. What do we mean by the ABCs of first aid?
8. Two levels of training are required to enable schools to respond effectively and efficiently to a medical emergency. What are they?
9. What teaching implications do you draw from the national survey of adolescent risk behaviors?
10. With reference to your school safety survey, what were your findings and recommendations for improving the school safety?
11. Ask three male and three female classmates why people tend to ignore a highway emergency? What educational implications did you draw from these responses?
12. How do you distinguish between the effects of a drug overdose from alcohol and from crack cocaine?

REFERENCES

American Red Cross, Adult CPR, Washington, DC, 1992.
American Red Cross, Infant and child CPR, Washington, DC, 1992.
American Red Cross, Standard first aid, Washington, DC, 1991.
ASHA, AAHE, and SOPHE, Inc.: *The national adolescent*

student health survey: a report on the health of America's youth, Oakland, Calif, 1989, Third Party Publishing.

Bergeron D: *First responder,* ed 2, Bowie, Md, 1986, Robert J. Brady.

Braslow A, et al: National standard curriculum for bystander care, Metropolitan Dade County Office of Trauma Services, Technical Report, Contract No. DTN 422-88-Z-05215 prepared for the U.S. Department of Transportation, National Highway Traffic Safety Administration, Office of Enforcement and Emergency Services, Emergency Medical Services Division, 1991.

Committee on Trauma Research, Commission on Life Sciences, National Research Council, and the Institute of Medicine: *Injury in America, a continuing public health problem,* Washington, DC, 1985, National Academy Press.

Hafen B: *First aid for health emergencies,* St. Paul, Minn, 1985, West Publishing.

Kozlowsky JC: "Illinois wrestler alleges coach reckless in post-injury treatment," Halper v. Vayo, Recreation and Parks Law Reporter, vol. VIII (2), March 5, 1991.

McGinnis JM, Degraw C: Special issue on healthy people 2000: national health promotion and disease prevention objectives and healthy schools, *J Sch Health* 61(7):292-328, 1991.

National Safety Council: *Accident facts, 1990 edition,* Chicago, 1990, the Council.

National Safety Council, *Accident facts, 1991 edition,* Chicago, 1991, the Council.

Reinberg S, Pendagast E: *The first minutes, what to do until the ambulance arrives,* Westport, Conn, 1984, Emergency Training.

Safar P: Disaster resuscitology: report on the second world congress on emergency and disaster medicine, *J World Assn Emerg Disas Med* I:(suppl 1)159-167, 1985.

US Congress, Office of Technology Assessment: *Adolescent health.* Volume 2: Background and the effectiveness of selected prevention and treatment services OTA-H-466, Washington, DC, 1991, US Government Printing Office.

Waller AE, et al: Childhood injury deaths: national analysis and geographic variations, *Am J Public Health* 79(3):310-315, 1989.

Waller J: *Injury control, a guide to the causes and prevention of trauma,* Lexington, Mass, 1985, Lexington Books.

Zydlow SM, Hill JA, editors: The American Medical Association handbook of first aid and emergency care, revised edition, New York, 1990, Random House.

Tertiary prevention and special populations

OVERVIEW

Primary prevention involves efforts to prevent a health problem before it occurs. Secondary prevention involves the early detection and treatment of a health problem to limit its effects. Tertiary prevention addresses the need to carry treatment forward into full rehabilitation and ensure complete recovery or adaptation to any long-term disabilities. Ensuring that treatment continues through full rehabilitation decreases the chances of recurrence or the development of a secondary condition. This chapter describes the school's involvement in tertiary prevention.

Although schools teach about cigarette smoking and its accompanying risks, it is not their primary responsibility to "treat" students who smoke by providing clinics to help them quit smoking. On the other hand, schools do have a responsibility to help students with specific health-related conditions and handicaps so that they receive the best education possible. This may mean providing services to deal directly with health-related conditions and with handicapping conditions to facilitate the education process for these students.

Because education is in part a social process, schools have a responsibility to educate all students, including students with special handicapping conditions, in a similar environment and in the company of others. So important is this principle that the U.S. Congress in 1977 passed PL 94-142, the Education for All Handicapped Children Act, and in 1990 PL101-336, the Americans with Disabilities Act, to ensure that all students, regardless of their special needs, receive the best possible education in the least restrictive environment, carried out as often as possible in the normal school setting.

This chapter outlines the responsibilities of the school and especially school health personnel in meeting the needs of special students. In this chapter special students include those with physically handicapping conditions, chronic health problems, handicaps brought on by family financial situations, and unusual learning abilities.

More than in past years, educators are recognizing many health conditions that are not truly handicapping but do interfere with the process of education as it is traditionally conducted. Young people who are not close to their optimal level of health are certainly not able to learn at optimal levels. The interference with education by health conditions is now more prevalent than before because health care is increasingly difficult to get for a large segment of society, because behavior patterns have encouraged the spread of certain health conditions, and because society in general has expanded its definition of who is educable in the public schools. School-based clinics and school-linked clinics represent the beginning of a new trend toward a future in which schools will be more involved in providing health care for many conditions to fulfill their educational responsibilities. These conditions and the school's increasing involvement in providing health services have been discussed in other chapters. This chapter deals specifically with tertiary care and special populations. Even here the school now provides services to a much wider range of students than in years past.

OBJECTIVES   After reading this chapter, the student should be able to:

1. Describe how the goals of tertiary prevention complement the goals of education
2. Identify the major clauses specified in PL 94-142 and PL101-336, and explain the implications of each for the school health worker
3. State the meaning and significance of the terms *mainstreaming* and *least restrictive environment*
4. Explain the principal handicapping conditions found among the school-age population and briefly discuss implications of each condition for school personnel
5. Outline the major steps in the medical and psychosocial assessments of handicapped students
6. Describe various specific actions school personnel can take to ensure the least restrictive environment for all students
7. Illustrate the role and functions of related services in the education of a handicapped student
8. Identify the elements of an individualized educational program (IEP)
9. Justify the need for and nature of a school policy addressing the giving of medication to students during school hours
10. Outline how the Early Periodic Screening Diagnosis and Treatment Program of the Social Security Act can contribute to a school's health service program

At any given time a significant number of students will be experiencing handicapping conditions. However, for a large number of these students the conditions will be transitory in nature, including such things as common colds, asthma, allergies, mild emotional disturbances, gastrointestinal upsets, and minor injuries. In most cases these minor handicapping conditions will have little effect on the educational process. However, there are many students who experience handicapping conditions in the more traditional sense.

The term *handicap* usually refers to severe musculoskeletal disorders, neural disorders, cardiac disorders, disorders of vision and hearing, and intellectual and emotional disorders.

For the school's purposes handicapping conditions identify students with special needs who require changes in one or more elements of the regular school program. Changes may be required in classroom facilities, classroom activities, teaching equipment, transportation, or the nature of auxiliary school personnel.

EDUCATION FOR ALL HANDICAPPED CHILDREN

For these students Congress passed PL 94-142, the Education for All Handicapped Children Act, in November 1975 and implemented nationwide in 1977. The principal intent of this legislation includes the following:

1. Guarantee free, appropriate public education at no cost to the parents of all handicapped children 3 to 21 years of age
2. Identify, locate, and evaluate all handicapped children regardless of the severity of their disabilities
3. Evaluate yearly each handicapped student and develop an individualized education plan
4. Provide educational services in the *least restrictive environment,* a process that often has been referred to as *mainstreaming*
5. Ensure for parents a clear role as a participant in the identification, evaluation, and placement of students
6. Ensure that students who are placed in private schools or special schools receive special educational services at no cost to parents; also that these students receive the same rights and programs as children enrolled in public education institutions
7. Provide in-service training for all teachers and support staff
8. Develop and implement public awareness programs to ensure greater sensitivity to and understanding of handicapped students

This legislation describes supportive services, including but not limited to speech therapy, audiology, psychologic services, physical and occupational therapy, recreation, counseling services, and medical diagnosis and evaluation. The intent of the legislation is to guarantee for handicapped children the removal of all obstacles to education (Fig. 10-1).

The Americans With Disabilities Act (PL 101-336) states that its purposes are to:
- Provide a clear and comprehensive national mandate for the elimination of discrimination against individuals with disabilities.
- Provide clear, strong, consistent and enforceable standards addressing discrimination.
- Ensure that the federal government plays a central enforcement role, backed by "the sweep of congressional authority."

Therefore, PL 100-336 strengthens the procession of earlier legislation and expands the scope of the earlier legislation to include the fields of employment, public service, and public accommodation. Schools are covered in the public service/public accommodation sections.

FIG. 10-1. Programs in special education enable children to achieve their optimum growth and development potential.

PRINCIPAL HANDICAPPING CONDITIONS

Mental retardation

Mental retardation is a major category of developmental disabilities, which includes learning disabilities, cerebral palsy, and several other conditions such as autism, epilepsy, congenital rubella, fetal alcohol syndrome (FAS), and fetal alcohol effect (FAE). Mental retardation is the third most prevalent handicapping condition of school-age children after speech impairments and learning disabilities. Mental retardation identifies a state of impairment recognized in the person's behavior. Severe retardation is frequently the result of overt brain damage; approximately 11% of children described as mentally retarded fall into this category. Mild retardation frequently results from cultural or familial conditions, and children who are mildly retarded can benefit significantly from special education programs and early efforts at developmental stimulation.

Generally two types of programs address varying degrees of mental retardation. The first type is directed at infants and children with clearly recognized early developmental delays usually diagnosed by physicians. Carefully structured educational programs, designed to maximize the developmental potential of these children, can prevent secondary contributions to retardation that develop from within the student's social environment as a result of the handicapping condition. The other type of educational program focuses principally on students whose retardation has a cultural or familial base. Project Head Start is a program aimed at the developmentally deprived young person. One of the goals of this program is to prevent borderline mental retardation from resulting in school failures and subsequent social, emotional, and cognitive difficulties. This type of program aims to give children maximal stimulation and reward frequently missing in their own social environments and to provide a structure in which they can function at maximal potential. Frequently these programs involve parents in an attempt to overcome the lack of stimulation or support that may exist in the family or social community.

Learning disabilities

Students with attentional deficit disorders, described on p. 131, are categorized as learning disabled. So are students with multiple forms of dysfunction that may be initially quite severe but are potentially responsive to special education. Special education techniques are designed to strengthen the student's existing abilities and to discourage inappropriate behavior in the school or social setting.

The development of educational programs for mentally retarded and learning disabled students is frequently produced by interdisciplinary effort. Individualized educational programs (IEPs) for these students may involve close collaboration of the child's family physician, teachers, therapists in the areas of various deficits, and school counselors. Developing IEPs is not easy, but when children's difficulties are clearly identified, objectives aimed at overcoming these difficulties and educational programs and activities designed to achieve these objectives can be developed. In this way PL 94-142 strives as much as possible in the regular classroom to provide for handicapped students educational programs designed specifically for their individual needs.

Hearing difficulties and deafness

Approximately 2% of handicapped students have significant hearing deficits. Because speech patterns clearly depend on hearing ability, it is critical that hearing loss be identified before school age.

Many students with hearing difficulties can be accommodated in the traditional classroom, if teachers are sensitive to such things as seating arrangements, supplemental speech and lip-reading instruction, the acceptance of hearing aids by fellow students, and occasionally the seeking of support services through community organizations. It is not the school's responsibility to treat these conditions, but one of the school's objectives is to facilitate education, and thus it is often in the interest of education for school personnel to stimulate family, community, or agency action to ensure that students have appropriate assistance. Frequently school personnel have been effective in getting necessary services for students with hearing and vision difficulties simply by making contact with appropriate community agencies and initiating action that ultimately leads to the improvement of the student's education.

Vision difficulties

Less than 1% of the handicapped population have severe vision difficulties, and unless the impairment to vision is severe (beyond 20/70 on the Snellen chart), students can usually be accommodated in the traditional classroom. Students who are partially sighted (20/70 to 20/200) cannot function in traditional classrooms without special aids, and although these children are not specifically defined as blind, special provision must be made to facilitate their education.

Because of difficulty in determining the exact status of vision in very young children, quite frequently children in kindergarten and the early grades manifest vision difficulties that have not been recognized by parents. Screening and observation of children therefore become especially important. There are several relatively simple steps the school can take to accommodate children with impaired vision. These range from making available large-type books printed on low-glare paper to using special dark pencils or felt pens, large-faced typewriters, and special seating arrangements in the classroom.

Orthopedic handicaps

Problems for orthopedically handicapped children are not so much problems of learning as those of ambulation and transportation. Accordingly the schools are faced with the problems of removing architectural barriers and providing special transportation. In addition, special facilities may be necessary (1) for orthopedically handicapped students to participate in adaptive physical education programs and to receive physical and occupational therapy and (2) to provide special assistance for students who may be catheterized.

Emotional disturbances

As many as 5 million, or 10%, of schoolchildren in the United States are described as having emotional problems, but as few as 14% of these receive specific care. Although some of these students need therapeutic treatment outside the school's competency, significant numbers can benefit from school-based services. The addition of special classroom activities, specially trained teachers, and counselors and psychologists can present a low-cost alternative to the possible intensive care that may be required later in life if these conditions are over-looked.

Gifted students

Students with special talents and with ability for especially high performance should also be the subject of special attention from the school. As many as 5% of the school-age population fall into this category and have been generally ignored, especially at the elementary school level. Consequently a large number of gifted students become frustrated and bored with the educational process. Although gifted students do not present any special health problems for the school to deal with, meeting their needs with special programs will help to further the educational progress of students whose abilities may enable them to become important contributors to society.

MEDICAL ASSESSMENT

The medical examination of the student with a handicap differs only in terms of detail and focus from the medical examination of an apparently healthy child. Because of the detailed nature of the examination, it will likely be carried out by a team of specialists who will confer after the results of all tests are received to plan a specific course of action. The intent of the examination, any resulting prescriptions, and the development of a prognosis will clearly identify the student's strengths and establish objectives to develop these strengths. Limitations and specific pathologic conditions will, of course, be explored, but from the school's view guidance concerning positive developments is just as, if not more, important than statements of specific limitations and problems.

The health examination begins with a specific and detailed history that explores family history to identify possible hereditary trends and seeks data on the mother's health during the pregnancy. Detailed information from prenatal records often helps in understanding handicapping conditions. A detailed neurologic examination is completed; growth and development records are examined; and vision and hearing are carefully tested. In addition, a careful examination of the skin is carried out. Often the skin provides useful information concerning neurologic disorders. Anatomic defects are assessed to identify the extent of limitations and activity restrictions, and ways to maximize movement potentials are identified.

Like most examinations, medical examinations provide an opportunity to gain new knowledge and increase understanding. In the course of the examination, physicians seek to understand the parents' knowledge of the handicapping conditions and identify any misconceptions that may exist. They show parents how they can assist their child's growth and development.

PSYCHOSOCIAL ASSESSMENT

The most critical point in the psychosocial assessment of students is the final designation of handicapped. PL 94-142 calls for the identification of all handicapped students; it also clearly specifies that assessment must be nondiscriminatory. Because of the tendency for many tests to exhibit a degree of bias and also for factors of ethnicity, poverty, and culture to affect test outcomes, considerable caution is needed to avoid the unfortunate outcomes of labeling. To reduce the risks associated with assessments, several points are important (Johnson, 1980).

1. Because so many handicapping conditions are health related, a comprehensive medical assessment should be completed before any psychosocial assessment.

2. Parents should be involved in all phases of the screening and assessment program to ensure that they understand what is being done and why. Fully informed parents will give greater cooperation and support when and if special programs need to be established.

3. Assessment should focus on the present level of educational functioning and what can realistically be achieved, rather than identify what cannot be achieved. Such information should include but is not limited to the following:

   a. Academic level in the essential subjects
   b. Communication and language skills
   c. Motor and perceptual skills
   d. Social and emotional skills
   e. Prevocational and vocational skills

A comprehensive assessment of a student cannot be carried out without careful attention to the environment in which the student learns: the school. In the past, students have frequently been assessed in isolation from their environment. Handicapping conditions and their resulting psychosocial behaviors are influenced by the environment, and therefore the environment must be assessed. Among other things that affect the psychosocial development of the student and should be examined are the following:

1. Organizational climate of the classroom
2. Management style of the principal
3. Behavior of the teachers

Deviant social behavior indicative of emotional or physical problems can be the result of real handicapping conditions or reactions to specific environmental cues. Psychosocial assessment is therefore carried out with a recognition that the person being assessed is not a lone individual but is actually part of a social system, and the system must also be examined to understand the individual. Recognition of the social system's interconnecting nature decreases the likelihood of incorrect assessment results and the potentially damaging effect of inappropriate labeling.

Assessment is a team process and therein lies a significant safeguard. However, for a team approach to work, all members must have complementary ways of viewing the task. Recognizing the interaction of person and environment makes the assessment more difficult but increases the likelihood of a quality process and results leading to an effective individual education program.

IMPLICATIONS FOR SCHOOL HEALTH PERSONNEL

Most handicapping conditions are related to health problems; therefore school health personnel, nurses, health teachers, physicians, and aides are likely to be the first to notice such conditions. Once a handicap is noticed, and even when treatment is initiated, an advocate within the school may be needed to ensure that specific needs are met. Again, health service and

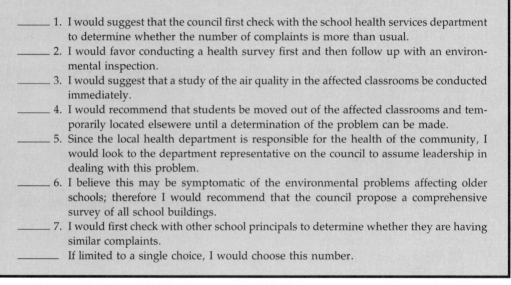

E MERGING ISSUE   As a school health specialist, you are the chair of a school health council for the elementary schools in a large city school system. The purpose of the council, as the title implies, is to serve as a communication and coordinating mechanism for school health–related matters such as health instruction, health services, and environmental health. The council meets on a regular basis to carry out its function and to respond to issues or special problems as they arise. The council is composed of representatives from the school administration, school nurse association, curriculum supervisors, medical society, PTAs, and the local health department. One of the elementary schools has reported a problem of odors in its second and third grade classrooms. Teachers and students from this school have complained about headaches, dizziness, and nausea.

As the chair, you have presented this problem to the council for their review and recommendations for advice that may be appropriate. Please indicate whether you generally agree or disagree with the following statements by placing a plus (+) or a minus (−) sign before each of them.

_____ 1. I would suggest that the council first check with the school health services department to determine whether the number of complaints is more than usual.

_____ 2. I would favor conducting a health survey first and then follow up with an environmental inspection.

_____ 3. I would suggest that a study of the air quality in the affected classrooms be conducted immediately.

_____ 4. I would recommend that students be moved out of the affected classrooms and temporarily located elsewere until a determination of the problem can be made.

_____ 5. Since the local health department is responsible for the health of the community, I would look to the department representative on the council to assume leadership in dealing with this problem.

_____ 6. I believe this may be symptomatic of the environmental problems affecting older schools; therefore I would recommend that the council propose a comprehensive survey of all school buildings.

_____ 7. I would first check with other school principals to determine whether they are having similar complaints.

_____ If limited to a single choice, I would choose this number.

health education personnel may be the most likely advocates to ensure that architectural barriers are modified, special classes or learning opportunities are provided, special services are available, and arrangements for medication, special meals, and transportation are made.

Physical environment

The school's commitment to equal access to all people has created a new set of standards for buildings and grounds. Access is not limited to the buildings but to all facilities in the building, including physical education and recreation facilities, labs, buses and other transportation, and special purpose classrooms. Inclusion means full participation on field trips, assemblies, graduation exercises, concerts, and sports events.

Expanded role of school nurse

Mainstreaming and the school's increased involvement in tertiary care have greatly expanded the role of the school nurse. Today, school nurses may use a wide range of their professional skills.

With students presenting a wide array of care needs, the school nurse may be involved in supervising the provision of technical care, including intravenous feeding, gastrostomy feeding, nasogastric tube feedings, provision of both oral and intravenous medications, medications given via gastrostomy or nasogastric tubes, administration of respiratory treatments, giving oxygen via mask or canula, nebulizer treatments, oral suctioning and tracheostomy care. In addition, nurses may be involved in catheter care, stoma care, diapering, changing dressings, treating decubitus (pressure sores), monitoring casts, collecting urine and stool or sputum samples, or maintaining special equipment.

Adaptive physical education

The law assumes that handicapped students are essentially healthy and therefore should be provided access to a full curriculum. Physical education is the only area actually mentioned in the law's description of special education. Regulations call for motor development, body mechanics, and physical and motor fitness, all central to the objectives of any physical education program but especially to adaptive physical education. Adaptive physical education is defined as "the science of analyzing movement, identifying deficiencies within the psychomotor domain and developing instructional strategies to remediate identified deficiencies" (Sherrill, 1976).

Adaptive physical education, like regular physical education, contributes to the goals of education through physical activity. As such, the teachers' concern goes beyond the qualitative and quantitative issues of biomechanics to include such concerns as posture, weight control, diet, stress management skills, relaxation, and mental health.

Depending on the extent of the handicapping conditions, the skill of the teacher, and the planned activities of the curriculum, handicapped students can be integrated into regular classes, or they can participate in an exclusive class designed to meet their needs. Exclusive classes are not prohibited by the law but must be justified as the most appropriate for the particular student.

As with all curricular areas, individual educational plans need to be developed, with the identification of the current level of psychomotor functioning, specific goals for psychomotor achievement, specific instructional objectives, suggestions for placement in classes, and evaluation plans and a specific time line.

Related services

Two essential services are outlined in the standards of PL 94-142. These are the provision of special education and related services. Special education is described as "specifically designed instruction at no cost to the parent to meet the unique needs of a handicapped child inclusive of home or hospital or classroom instruction as well as physical education" (*Education of Handicapped Children,* 1977). Related services include "professional services provided with the major goal to assist the handicapped child to benefit from special education" (*Education of Handicapped Children,* 1977). Steenson and Sullivan (1980) in identifying the relationship of related services to education suggest that "related services" could be called "student support services" and further suggest the following:

- Art therapy
- Audiologic services
- Corrective therapy
- Social work services
- School health services
- Occupational therapy
- Counseling services
- Drama therapy
- Physical therapy
- Psychologic services
- Speech therapy
- Transportation
- Orientation and mobility instruction
- Visual training therapy
- Recreation therapy
- Music therapy

The law did not intend for every student to receive every service but meant that services like these should be considered in the development of individualized educational plans.

Steenson and Sullivan (1980) further clarify the instructional goals for handicapped youth by collapsing various educational elements into eight areas: ambulation, self-care, emotion and behavior, vision, communications, hearing, health problems, and academic achievement. These areas of concern illustrate the role of school health service personnel, teachers, nurses, physicians, and aides in the planning of individualized educational programs.

Ensuring education for all in the least restrictive environment also breaks down the traditional separation of care providers (nurses and physicians) and educators (teachers). Now there is a need for partnership between health and medical personnel and educators to ensure the best possible program for all students. However, the goal of the program is not the medical goal of curing but is closer to the nursing-teaching goal of providing support services and immediate care while developing skills to enhance the ability to cope and survive.

In this way the objectives of prevention are served by enhancing a person's ability to achieve his or her full potential and reducing the chances of additional complications. Tertiary prevention, exhibited through full rehabilitation, essentially recycles a person back to the domain of primary prevention where the task is to reduce the likelihood that further regression occurs or that other health problems develop.

MEDICATIONS

In the majority of states, school nurses are responsible for administering medications during school hours. Medications may include those prescribed by physicians as part of ongoing treatment or maintenance therapy, as is frequently the case with handicapped students, but they can also include over-the-counter medications (OTCs) purchased without prescriptions by parents. Regular medication administration can become problematic for school personnel because of the need to assign persons to the task and also because of the added responsibility for treatment and maintenance services rather than preventive and educational services, the school's traditional responsibilities. Schools with full-time nurses or aides can usually perform the task of providing medications, but schools that must rely on office personnel to carry out this function have greater difficulty.

Education of parents and communication with physicians are important in establishing a school medication policy.

For example, most medications that are prescribed three times a day do not need to be given during school hours. Administration before school, immediately after school, and before going to bed in the evening meets the instructions. Medications taken with meals, however, will need to be taken at school. Parents need to understand the difference so that they do not ask school personnel to carry out an unnecessary chore. Physicians sometimes overlook this option to avoid school-time administration when explaining a prescription to parents, and so it is frequently necessary for the nurse or principal to have parents question their physician about this option. Time-release medication may also be a possibility, reducing the needed number of daily doses. Again, a simple inquiry from parents to physicians may simplify the regimen and avoid an extra task for the school.

Dorsett (1982) has noted a series of points that should be included in a school's medication policy and has suggested that such a policy should have two major concerns: (1) safety—the assurance that the correct medication is given correctly to the right person, and (2) efficiency—minimizing the time needed for administration and minimizing the time taken from the teaching-learning process.

The following are points to be considered for school medication administration:

1. The principal of each school should ensure that a medication policy exists and is followed.
2. The principal must designate certain persons to administer medications according to specific guidelines.
3. The policy should clearly state that, whenever possible, medications should be given outside school hours and that only essential medications will be given by school personnel.
4. A form should be filled out by the prescribing physician for all medications to be administered during school hours, specifying the name of the medication, how often it should be given, the expected duration of the treatment, and whether a reaction is likely and if so, what type of reaction. The medication form should be signed by the parent or guardian authorizing the school personnel to administer the medication.
5. The school personnel should not be responsible for administering the first dose of any medication in case of an allergic reaction.
6. Medications properly labeled and accompanied by an authorization form should be hand-carried to the school by the parent. Medications in containers other than the original one provided by the pharmacy should not be accepted.
7. Medication should be kept in a separate, locked facility or refrigerator accessible only to authorized persons.
8. A record should be completed for all medications administered. If for some reason a dosage of medication is not administered, a specific reason should be stated, and parents notified.
9. A copy of the daily medication schedule should be kept by the principal or the school nurse.

EARLY PERIODIC SCREENING, DIAGNOSIS, AND TREATMENT

A growing concern of educators and physicians alike is children who come to school from homes in which the parents either cannot afford or do not accept responsibility for the needed health and medical care of their children. Another complication is the lack of medical services available to the disadvantaged and to children in lower socioeconomic levels. This problem is particularly acute in many of the major cities in the United States today. Special federal legislation has been enacted, such as the amendments to the Social Security Act and Titles V and XIX (popularly known as Medicaid), which are designed to provide comprehensive health services for children and youth. This legislation intends to provide medical care for all those who are unable to pay for it. Although providing direct health care for children is not the school's responsibility, school personnel should not overlook students' health care needs. School officials should know state and federal legislative provisions for child health services. Indeed, school administrators, teachers, and school nurses, as advocates for the health of school-age children and youth, must communicate health needs to families and to appropriate community health officials.

Although not focusing on a tertiary prevention issue, the Early Periodic Screening, Diagnosis, and Treatment Program does address an important need for children of low-income families who meet the standard to receive Medicaid or Aid to Dependent Children as authorized by Title XIX of the Social Security Act. This extension to Title XIX of the Medicaid program is commonly known as Early Periodic Screening, Diagnosis, and Treatment (EPSDT). The details of the way this program is administered may differ slightly from state to state. In Illinois, for example, children who receive Aid to Dependent Children or medical assistance are eligible for services under this program for the period from birth to 20 years of age. In Illinois the program is administered jointly by the Department of Public Aid and the Department of Public Health. In Nebraska it is administered by the Department of Social Services.

The extended services provided under the Medicaid (Title XIX) program include:

1. Periodic health appraisals, including health history and physical examination, with emphasis on growth, development, and nutritional status; the schedule includes four medical checkups during the first year, annual checkups to age 6 years, and then at ages 10, 14, 17, and 20 years
2. A comprehensive immunization program and updating of previous immunization, including measles, poliomyelitis, diphtheria, pertussis, and tetanus
3. Periodic screening for urine sugar and protein, hemoglobin, or hematocrit determinations and tuberculosis testing; vision and hearing screenings are provided annually from ages 3 to 8 years and thereafter at ages 10, 12, 14, and 16 years
4. Screening when indicated to detect specific conditions including lead poisoning, sickle-cell abnormality, and venereal disease
5. Dental examinations as provided on an annual basis from ages 3 through 20 years

Emphasis is given to follow-up care and treatment of the health problems discovered through screening activities.

School officials and health educators should be informed about these federal and state services available to the children of their respective communities. With the development of new programs of health services, school health education should accept the responsibility for informing children and parents about these important community services and resources.

SUMMARY

Children with disabilities are no different from children without disabilities in their need for basic health care and educational services. The concept of mainstreaming emphasizes this principle.

Public Law 94-142, The Education for All Handicapped Children Act of 1975, defines handicapped children as those mentally retarded, hard of hearing, deaf, speech impaired, visually handicapped, seriously emotionally disturbed, orthopedically impaired, or suffering from other forms of health impairment such as limited strength or vitality, rheumatic fever, asthma, epilepsy, sickle-cell anemia, blood poisoning, diabetes, and other conditions that would affect educational performance.

For school personnel the challenge is to incorporate these children fully into the life of the school. School staff have the responsibility for planning and managing individual educational plans that involve a full range of human service professionals and helping other children learn from participating in activities with handicapped students.

All people in the school learn about human health, adaptability, the meaning of normal, and the difference between primary, secondary, and tertiary prevention when they work and learn together with handicapped students and modify the educational environment and activities to accommodate their special needs.

GET INVOLVED!

As a health student taking courses in education, health science, and health education, you should be aware of the number of health-related and education-related career opportunities that are available to you. A field you may wish to consider is that of teaching the visually handicapped.

With the implementation of Public Law 94-142, the educational rights of children with disabilities were recognized. Educational programs for the visually impaired are but one example of this development.

The typical pattern in public school districts today is to provide a central location where the visually impaired students from several school districts are enrolled for their specialized instruction. In addition to being able to develop special skills in using Braille and recording devices to compensate for the child's visual impairment, the ideal teacher for these programs should be much more child oriented. In addition to being impaired, these children have all the other health, social, and emotional needs of other children. Because of these special needs, teachers in this field are expected to work closely with parents in monitoring the child's progress. They also work closely with other school personnel, such as the school psychologist, social worker, and school nurse.

According to authorities in the field, employment opportunities are good. Programs in special education are a relatively recent development, and there is a growing demand for more teachers trained in this field.

All teachers must, as a minimum, have a bachelor's degree from an accredited program and a master's degree is ususally preferred. You may inquire at a local school superintendent's office or at any State Department of Education regarding teacher certification requirements.

For additional information, write to:
Association for Education and Rehabilitation
Office of the Blind and Visually Impaired
206 N. Washington St.
Alexandria, VA 22314

STUDY QUESTIONS

1. How can a physical defect adversely affect mental health?
2. What relationships can exist between a physical defect and academic performance?
3. Lack of family financial means should increase the determination of the school to obtain the necessary medical services for the child needing correction of a defect. Explain the implications of this statement.
4. What can be done for children with noncorrective orthopedic defects to help them be normal members of their class and to give them the type of self-gratification from accomplishment that all normal youngsters want and need?
5. In any rehabilitation, why is it important that one person have primary responsibility, even though the services of many persons may be used?
6. When a teacher recognizes that a child has a physical disorder, why should the teacher relate this to the school nurse and then to the school principal before anything is done on behalf of the child?
7. In a program to help a student adjust to a physical defect, why is it important to have the student develop a strong insight in terms of his or her status, needs, and progress?
8. How would you get a child to wear prescribed glasses when he or she does not want to wear them?
9. What can a small school system do to provide a modified program for the handicapped pupil?
10. How does the medical assessment for a healthy student differ from that for a handicapped student?
11. What does the term *handicapped* mean?
12. Why should a medical assessment always precede a psychosocial assessment?
13. Define tertiary prevention, and explain how it is different from primary and secondary prevention.
14. How does the concept of mainstreaming differ from the concept of education in a minimally restrictive environment?
15. Differentiate between acute and chronic handicapping conditions.
16. Explain the significance of PL 94-142 to (a) the health teacher, (b) the school nurse, and (c) the school principal.
17. List the major handicapping conditions found in the school-age population.
18. Describe the major aspects of a school's environment and program that should be reviewed to ensure the school is best serving its handicapped students.
19. Should school personnel be expected to give medications to students during school hours? If so, why and under what conditions?
20. What is Title XIX of the Social Security Act, and why is it important to educators?

REFERENCES

American Academy of Pediatrics: *School health: a guide for health professionals,* Elk Grove Village, Ill, 1987, the Academy.

Accardo P, Capute A: *The pediatrician and the developmentally delayed child,* Baltimore, 1979, University Park Press.

Bleck E: Integrating the physically handicapped child, *J Sch Health* 49:141, 1979.

Bryan E: Administrative concerns and schools' relationship with private practicing physicians, *J Sch Health* 49:157, 1979.

Cora-Bramble D, Bradshaw ME, Sklarew B: The sex education practicum: medical students in elementary school classroom, *J Sch Health* 62(1):32, 1992.

Dorsett T: Administration of medications during school hours, *J Sch Health* 52:444, 1982.

Education of handicapped children: implementation of part B of the education of the handicapped act, Fed Reg, Aug. 23, 1977.

Gleidman J, Roth W: *The unexpected minority: handicapped children in America,* New York, 1980, Harcourt Brace Jovanovich.

Hertel V: *Health care of special needs students in the school setting,* Denver, 1988, Colorado Department of Health School Health Nursing Division.

Joachim G: The school nurse as case manager for chronically ill children, *J Sch Health* 59(9):406, 1989.

Johnson J: Psychosocial assessment of the handicapped, *J Sch Health* 50:252, 1980.

Jones E: PL 94-142 and the role of the school nurse in caring for handicapped children, *J Sch Health* 49:147, 1979.

Levenson PM, Cooper MA: School health education for the chronically impaired individual, *J Sch Health* 54:446, 1984.

Lovick SR: School-based clinics: meeting teens' health care needs, *J Sch Health* 58(9):379, 1988.

McCubbin J, et al: Personal health training and the severely handicapped: a curriculum-based research investigation, *Health Educ Q* 15(2):217-223, 1988.

National Asthma Education Program: Expert panel report to provide clinical guidelines for diagnosis and treatment of asthma, *J Sch Health* 61(6):249, 1991.

Naughton SS, Edwards LE, Reed N: AIDS/HIV risk assessment and risk reduction counseling in a school-based clinic, *J Sch Health* 61(10):443, 1991.

Pacheco M, et al: School-based clinics: the politics of change, *J Sch Health* 61(2):92, 1991.

Pearl L, Welsch M, Brown W: Training competencies for school health professionals working with young handicapped children, *J Sch Health* 58(7):298, 1988.

Rose T: The education of all handicapped children act (PL 94-142): new responsibilities or opportunities for the school nurse, *J Sch Health* 50:30, 1980.

Sherrill C: Adapted physical education and recreation, Dubuque, Iowa, 1976, Wm C Brown Group.

Steenson C, Sullivan A: Support services in the school setting: the nursing model, *J Sch Health* 50:246, 1980.

Swisher J: Developmental restaging: meeting the mental health needs of handicapped students in the schools, *J Sch Health* 48:548, 1978.

Trupin EW, Forsyth-Stephens A, Low BP: Service needs of severely disturbed children, *Am J Public Health* 81(8):975, 1991.

Vitello SJ: The Detsel case: limitation of school health ser-
ivces for special education students, *J Sch Health*
59(1):37, 1989.

Vlasak J: Mainstreaming handicapped children: the underlying legal concept, *J Sch Health* 50:5, 1980.

Waszak C, Neidell S: School-based and school-linked
clinics: update 1991, Washington, DC, 1991, The Center for Population Options.

Zeitlin S: Assessing coping behavior, *Am J Orthopsychiatry*
50:139, 1980.

Part FOUR

Health
Instruction

A theoretical foundation for health instruction

OVERVIEW

This chapter begins with an examination of several widely published statements on health education, including definitions and purposes. These statements are discussed in the light of changing needs and conditions to determine the most appropriate role for health education. The differing perspectives of education and public health are noted: the field of education emphasizes cognitive outcomes, and public health places greater emphasis on the health behavior outcomes. A code of ethics for health education is presented, with the reminder that health educators have a special responsibility to serve the public in accordance with the highest standards of professional and ethical conduct. Since much of today's illness and disability is attributed to life-style factors and poor health habits, health education has taken on additional importance as a means of improving health. With this new recognition has come increased criticism of health education. The field is often criticized because it lacks a sound theoretical basis to provide direction for program activities and research. In an effort to establish a theoretical basis, two major theories of learning are discussed: (1) the connectionist, or behaviorist, position and (2) the cognitive position. Several of the theories and models now being applied to the field of health education are analyzed in terms of these two major theories of learning to gain a better understanding of both the theory and the methods being advocated. Among the health education applications discussed are (1) the health belief model, (2) social learning theory, (3) Fishbein's theory of reasoned action model, and (4) persuasive communication theory. The chapter concludes with a section on the application of learning theory for more effective health instruction programs.

OBJECTIVES   After reading this chapter, the student should be able to:

1. Relate various statements of definition, purposes, and goals of health education
2. Demonstrate familiarity with major purposes and goals of health education that have been adopted by professional and government agencies
3. Explain why a code of ethics is of special importance to health educators
4. Explain why theories are important to the profession of health education
5. Identify the connectionist and cognitive theories of learning and explain some of the characteristic differences between these two major orientations
6. Identify several determinants of health behavior

7. Identify several models of behavior change that have been offered to the field of health education
8. Determine how the persuasive communication matrix model could be used in developing a health teaching plan
9. Explain the appropriate uses and benefits of direct instruction, mastery learning, and cooperative learning
10. List several guidelines for developing a health instruction program

---

Health educators and other health professionals have long called for a national commitment to good health as a way of life. Health education should be one of the most dynamic components of the entire school curriculum, a program to achieve the goals of both education and public health.

Research has demonstrated that certain aspects of individual behavior are related to major causes of death in American society. In particular, long-term patterns of behavior or life-style factors have been determined to be risk factors for such major health problems as accidents, cardiovascular diseases, and cancer. Public health officials have long contended that a strong scientific basis exists for the belief that habits and patterns of living and their associated diseases have their origins early in life. This challenges the school health education program to intervene early in the life of a student to prevent disease. Health education can make its greatest impact during the formative years of the school child to develop positive, health-promoting behavior relating to habits of diet, exercise, use of health products and services, and avoidance of negative behavior such as cigarette smoking, excessive consumption of alcoholic beverages, and reckless driving.

It has become increasingly evident to both medical researchers and the general public that many of today's health problems are caused by factors that are not responsive to medical solutions. For example, at this time there is no vaccine to prevent heart disease and no cure for the problem of alcoholism. Short of a dramatic breakthrough, such as the development of a cure for cancer, it is becoming apparent that further expansion in the nation's health care system will produce only marginal improvements in the health status of Americans. Although it is obvious that providing the best health care for all citizens is of great importance, it is also apparent that, in the long run, the greatest benefits to the health of the public are most likely to come from efforts to improve the life-style and the environment in which they live and work (U.S. Department of Health, Education and Welfare, 1975).

As a result of this thinking, a new emphasis is being placed on the behavioral aspects of health. Richmond (Nightingale et al., 1978), on taking the oath of office as the nation's highest ranking health officer, stated that the importance of behavioral research must be recognized so that the public can discover how to enlist people into preventing disease and in promoting their own health. This means that health education encompasses not only the transmission of knowledge but also the full range of activities designed to provide the skills, the interest, and the motivation to help make people's lives more fulfilling and free from disease and disability.

HEALTH EDUCATION: A BRIEF REVIEW OF THE CONCEPT

Over the years, members of the field of health education have attempted to develop a philosophy or point of view and have articulated a set of goals or a statement of purpose. These definitions not only reveal the intent of a particular time but also illustrate the growth and change in purpose that have occurred.

In 1934, the Joint Committee (NEA-AMA) on Health Problems in Education proposed the following definition: "Health education is the sum of all experiences which favorably influence habits, attitudes, and knowledge relating to individual, community, and racial health." This statement recognized that all of life's experiences, both in and out of school, contribute to the individual's attitudes toward health and patterns of living. Any formal health education planned by the school must recognize those forces outside the school that shape the health behaviors of children and youth.

The 1948 Joint Committee (NEA-AMA) statement emphasized that "health education is the process of providing learning experiences for the purpose of influencing knowledge, attitudes, or conduct relating to individual, community, and world health." This definition stresses the role of the school in providing learning experiences through a formal and planned program of health instruction. The statement also provides guidance as to the purpose of the curriculum. Classroom learning must deal with contemporary problems of society to have a positive effect on what students think, feel, and do about health in the community and the world at large.

The inclusion of world health in this definition reflects awareness of the World Health Organization (WHO), which had been created during this period. WHO issued its widely quoted definition of health as a state of complete physical, mental, and social well-being and not merely the absence of disease and disability. In 1954, WHO (Expert Committee on Health Education of the Public, 1954) addressed the subject of health education as follows:

> The aim of health education is to help people achieve health by their own actions and efforts. Health education begins, therefore, with the interests of people in improving their condition of living. . . in developing a sense of responsibility for their own health betterment and for. . . the health of their families and governments.

This statement has proved especially useful to health educators working in countries other than the United States, enabling them to relate more effectively to people of different cultures and ethnic groups. It has served as a reminder to public health and school officials that health education is not something to be done for or to be given to people. Rather, this process, if it is to be truly educational, must cause change within the person through changes in knowledge and attitudes. In turn, health education is reflected in what a person does for himself or herself and for others to promote well-being and prevent illness and injury.

With the upsurge of public interest in health education in the 1970s, more statements were issued. Like the earlier efforts, these served to clarify the evolving and emerging role of health education. The statement of the President's Committee on Health Education (1973), issued in 1972, is illustrative:

> Health education is a process that bridges the gap between health information and health practices. Health education motivates the person to take information and do something with it, to keep himself/herself healthier by avoiding actions that are harmful and by forming habits that are beneficial.

Here again, the emphasis on process is apparent, speaking to the relationship between health information and health education. Only after health information is translated into health knowledge, understanding, and action does it become health education. In the schools the process of health instruction translates health information into health outcomes.

After the President's Committee statement, the Joint Committee on Health Education Terminology (1972/1973) issued a revised definition of health education as:

> . . . a process with intellectual, psychological, and social dimensions relating to activities which increase the abilities of people to make informed decisions affecting their personal, family, and community well-being. This process, based on scientific principles, facilitates learning and behavioral change in both health personnel and consumers, including children and youth.

This statement also emphasizes the idea of process, but it recognizes that education is more than an intellectual experience. Emotional and social factors also shape health understandings and behaviors. But perhaps the part of the definition most important in the development of a philosophy of health education is the expression, "the abilities of people to make informed decisions." This suggests that enabling the individual to make an informed decision about health is the central purpose of health education. Moreover, it implies that decision making is the prerogative of the individual. Although it is the teacher's responsibility to create the opportunities for decision making through the health instruction program, students must be given freedom to make decisions. If children and youth are to grow to full maturity and are to become health-educated citizens of tomorrow, they must be allowed to make decisions, choices, and even mistakes in the realm of health. The challenge of the health teacher and of parents in matters affecting health is to know when to lead, when to guide or control, and when to let the young person make the choice.

Sullivan (U.S. Department of Health, Education, and Welfare, 1977), in writing for health planning agencies, has suggested that a program of health education should meet the following criteria:

1. It should be consistent with current knowledge about how people learn.
2. It should be consistent with the rights of individuals to make their own decisions about health practices as long as these practices do not infringe on the rights of others.
3. The definition should be readily understood not only by the health educator specialist but also by the public at large.

The fact that these criteria apply primarily to programs geared to the health needs of the adult population indicates the need for an additional criterion. Health education should emphasize the fact that adults must accept responsibility for the health and safety of the young and immature. For example, it is one thing for college students to make decisions and choices about their diets or about their physical exercise program, but it is quite another matter for primary grade children to make a choice about crossing the street. Health-related decisions and actions are highly specific to the individual and to the social and environmental setting. It must also be emphasized that in any program in health education, the information presented must be consistent with the scientifically established knowledge.

The report of the 1990 Joint Committee on Health Education Terminology represents the latest step in the evolving process of the health education concept. Like its predecessor committee of 1972-1973, this committee emphasized that health education is a learning process, but also acknowledged that the term is used to define a field of professional practice. Thus instead of a single definition the committee offered the following:

1. Health education as a process . . . "is that continuum of learning which enables people, as individuals and as members of social structures, to voluntarily make decisions, modify behaviors, and change social conditions in ways which are health enchancing."
2. Health education as a field of . . . . "multidisciplinary practice, which is concerned with designing, implementing, and evaluating educational programs that enable individuals, families, groups, organizations, and communities to play active roles in achieving, protecting, and sustaining health."

CODE OF ETHICS

To guide professional behaviors of its members toward highest standards, the Society for Public Health Education, Inc. (SOPHE) adopted a Code of Ethics in 1976 and acknowledged the need for periodic review and improvement of the code. The Code of Ethics states*:

- I will accurately represent my capability, education, training, and experience and will act within the boundaries of my professional competence.
- I will maintain my competence at the highest level through continuing study, training, and research.
- I will report research findings and practice activities honestly and without distortion.
- I will not discriminate because of race, color, national origin, religion, age, sex, or socioeconomic status in rendering service, employing, training, or promoting others.
- I value the privacy, dignity, and worth of the indiviual and will use skills consistent with these values.
- I will observe the principle of informed consent with respect to individuals and groups served,
- I will support change by choice and not by coercion.
- I will foster an educational environment that nurtures individual growth and development.
- If I become aware of unethical practices, I am accountable for taking appropriate action concerning these practices.

CONTRIBUTION OF HEALTH EDUCATION TO HEALTH

The American Public Health Association, at its annual meeting in 1977, formally acknowledged the essential relationship of health education to the achievement of the association's goal of optimal health for the nation's population. Today, more than ever, methods of improving the public's health status focus on health education. The conviction is growing among health professionals that major advances in health status will come from changes in the lifestyles of individuals and from the control of health hazards in the environment. It is through the process of education that citizens in a democratic society are alerted to the personal and

---

*Courtesy Society for Public Health Education: Code of Ethics, San Francisco, Oct. 15, 1976, the Society.

societal obstacles to good health. Health education offers a channel for achieving the needed changes.

Because of the complexity of factors that interact to affect health, including the environment, social conditions, and institutional and economic politics (Fig. 11-1), the solving of health problems often requires coordinated action on the part of informed citizens.

From the public health perspective, then, the goal of health education is the health-educated consumer-citizen who adopts a health-promoting life-style and wisely selects and uses health care resources, products, and services. Ideally, this citizen will actively participate in the formulation of public policy and planning on health care issues and in the larger environmental matters that affect health (American Public Health Association, 1977).

One of the most useful statements issued thus far on the goals of consumer health is that of the Task Force Report on Consumer Health Education (Preventive Medicine USA, 1976). This report, one of eight provided by the American College of Preventive Medicine and the Fogarty International Center for Advanced Study in the Health Sciences, has served as the basis for the Department of Health, Education and Welfare *Forward Plan for Health,* FY1977-1981. According to the task force, the term *consumer health education* subsumes a set of activities that serve the following purposes:

1. Inform people about health, illness, disability, and ways in which they can improve and protect their own health, including more efficient use of the delivery system
2. Motivate people to want to change to more healthful practices
3. Help them to learn the necessary skills to adopt and maintain healthful practices and life-styles

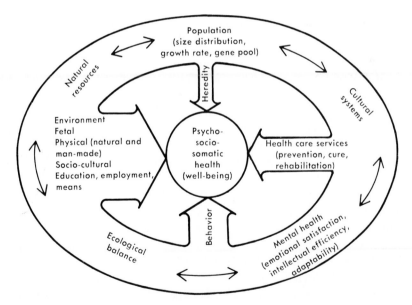

FIG. 11-1. Blum's inputs to health. The relative widths of the arrows indicate the relative importance attached to the various inputs. By inference, health education (behavior) is seen to make a major contribution to health.

4. Foster teaching and communications skills in all those engaged in educating consumers about health
5. Advocate changes in the environment that facilitate healthful conditions and healthful behavior
6. Add to knowledge via research and evaluation concerning the most effective ways of achieving the above objectives

The task force continues as follows:

> In brief, consumer health education is a process that informs, motivates, and helps people to adopt and maintain healthy practices and life-styles, advocates environmental changes as needed to facilitate this goal, and conducts professional training and research to the same end.

If the American Public Health Association statement provides the broad general goal for health education, the task force statement spells out the details and activities that characterize an effective action program. The specificity of these activities makes it clear that health education includes informing, motivating, and helping people to acquire the skills needed to protect and promote health and to recover from illness. The program pertains to people of all ages and levels of health—-the young, the aged, the handicapped, and the healthy. It covers more than academic, scientifically derived knowledge, including actions and practical skills ranging from the principles of diet selection to the lifesaving skills of cardiopulmonary resuscitation (CPR) (Fig. 11-2). For the professional health educator, this statement carries a special message: teaching and communication skills are essential. Moreover, like any other successful program activity, health education must rest on a scientific basis of ongoing research and evaluation.

A THEORETICAL BASIS FOR HEALTH EDUCATION

A theoretical statement involves terms that cannot be observed directly but that are inferred from a great deal of data. According to Snow (Travers, 1978), what first may be considered a theoretical term later may be found to refer to real objects or events. An abstract idea or theory may become fact. This relationship between theoretical statements and factual reality is well illustrated by Darwin's early ideas about evolution. Two theoretical statements, the theory of "natural selection" and the "survival of the fittest," served to guide his observations and collection of data. Darwin observed that many more individual organisms were born than could survive. Among those that survived, Darwin noted that some were born stronger, swifter, with more protective coating, or with less conspicuous marking, blending more readily into their natural surroundings. Those born stronger, swifter, and more suited to their environments were more likely to survive, thus perpetuating those organisms having the more favorable variations (Moore and Editors of Life, 1964). Hence, through evolution the surviving species or organism becomes ever more attuned to the environment.

A *theory* is a set of interacting, interlocking, or independent principles designed to account for a wide range of observations or facts (Bugelski, 1971). Travers (1978) contends that the behavioral sciences have been much less successful than the physical sciences in developing theories that eventually can be proved in the real world. In fact, many of the behavioral science theories have remained just that—-theoretical abstractions, with little or no progress toward

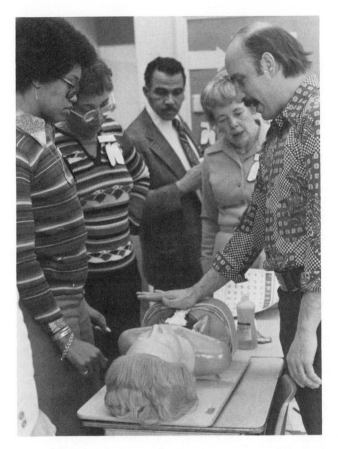

FIG. 11-2.   Health educator explaining an anatomic feature using a visual aid.

predicting real events. This discouraging fact does not diminish the importance of theories in science, for no science of any consequence has yet been built without using theoretical terms. Therefore it becomes necessary to develop a productive theory of health behavior change on which to base health education programs.

What purpose does theory serve, and how does it serve the field of health education? In the broadest sense, a theory is a way of interpreting knowledge. The interest in theories reflects a desire for unity and simplicity (Hill, 1963). Theories provide the individual with useful ways of conceptualizing his or her world. For the health educator, theories can provide an orientation, a systematic interpretation of the field, as well as a rational approach to the practice of health education.

Researchers are rarely content merely to collect more and more facts about learning. To satisfy the individual's desire for understanding, knowledge must be organized. Broad, general laws or principles from which specific principles may be deduced help to organize facts and knowledge. Unlike research in physical science, which uses general acceptance and understanding of concepts such as mass, space, and time, research in education offers no comparable agreements or general understandings on which to base a theory of learning. It is necessary to examine terms such as health and education to establish a common ground.

Theories of learning

A theory of learning is concerned with describing how learning takes place. As defined by Hilgard, Atkinson, and Atkinson (1971), learning is a relatively permanent change in behavior that occurs as the result of practice. Establishing the desired changes and bringing them about constitute the role of schools and education. It follows then that schools are interested in both theories of learning and theories of teaching or instruction. A theory of learning describes what happens when learning occurs, whereas a theory of instruction is concerned with the teaching methods and the instructional material required for something to be learned.

According to Hill (1963), most of the different theories of learning, no matter how diverse, derive from two general sources, the connectionist and the cognitive theorists. The connectionists, or associationists, as they are sometimes called, view learning as a matter of making connections between stimuli and responses. This theory assumes that all responses are caused by stimuli. Other terms used to describe these connections are habits, stimulus-response bonds, and conditional response. Research is conducted on the responses that occur, on the stimuli that elicit the response, and on the ways in which experience affects these relationships.

Those using a cognitive theory of learning are concerned with the perceptions or attitudes and beliefs that a person has about his or her environment and the ways these cognitions affect behavior. Attention is directed to these cognitions to define and describe them and to determine how they are modified by experience.

Of course, there is no "either-or" approach to learning. Both kinds of interpretations are used. The connectionist's interpretation of learning can often be identified by comments such as "I have developed a bad habit" or "Her long hours of practice produced a flawless performance." Statements such as "He has a very positive attitude about school" reveal a cognitive interpretation of learning.

Connectionist theory. Preference for one theory over another may relate, in part, to the nature of the learning task. For example, the connectionist theories lend themselves to greater precision and are used when there is need to define learning in objective and quantifiable terms that can be measured. The applied psychologists or the educational psychologists are more likely to use the cognitive interpretation. Learning, in this sense, refers to the concepts of beliefs and purpose. This interpretation holds that behavior change results from a change in what one knows or from a change in cognition. Such learning is more likely to deal with complex problems and behavior.

Whereas learning theorists may be strongly biased toward one or the other of the major learning theories, it is apparent that no one approach is followed when theories are applied in the field. A review of educational research shows how the different learning theories are reflected in educational developments. In the early 1930s, when the progressive education movement had identified "critical thinking" as an outcome of major importance for schools, Tyler (Travers, 1978) led the way in writing behavioral objectives that were detailed, objective, and explicit. His purpose was to clarify the goals of education that had been, until then, so vague that it was virtually impossible to determine whether schools were accomplishing their intended purpose. Tyler's objectives were written in behaviors that could be observed, measured, and evaluated. On this basis Skinner developed operant psychology and insisted on definitions of behavior that met the standards of objectivity and accuracy necessary for laboratory research. This trend characterized the period of the 1960s and 1970s, when great emphasis was placed on the precision of objectives as illustrated in Mager's behavioral objectives (1961).

Concepts such as readiness, motivation, and stimulus are central features of the connectionist approach, as is the importance of practice (Fig. 11-3). Thorndike, in his "laws of exercise" (Hill, 1963) stated that one learns by practicing the correct response or skill. Through repetition and practice the behavior to be learned is strengthened or is "stamped in" to the individual's neurologic processes. A key concept in the learning theory is recognition of the importance of rewarding the learner's correct or desired responses. This principle is expressed in such terms as reinforcement, operant conditioning, and feedback, which are derived from cybernetics and from the study of control mechanisms, as in engineering. Reinforcement, or positive feedback, used in today's classrooms, rewards the students for giving the correct response to a classroom learning activity, such as answering a question, solving a problem, or demonstrating the appropriate behavior, as in performing a skill in using the computer. Providing students with immediate and positive feedback has proved very effective in influencing student learning (Fig. 11-4). Examples of positive feedback would include the teacher's written comments on students' papers, class work assignments, and comments on examinations. The

FIG. 11-3.   Following directions. Gaining valuable experience in learning how to perform the skill by observing and then practicing the skill.

FIG. 11-4.   Girl practicing use of the computer illustrates the importance of repetition and feedback in learning a skill.

value or benefits of negative reinforcement, where the stimulus to an undesired response is removed, are less clear. However, negative feedback, as displayed in the learning of a skill when the individual observes his or her error of performance and is able to make the necessary adjustments to achieve correct performance, is also widely accepted in educational practice.

Much in the connectionist theories, as revealed in the works of Thorndike, Watson, and Skinner (Zais, 1976) has influenced present-day curriculum planning. For example, principles derived from these theories advocate the subdividing of curriculum content and learning activities into their most elemental components. Once separated into the basic parts, content and activities then can be restructured or arranged into an optimal sequence for learning. According to this approach, the student learns by being taught first the simplest learning task and then the more difficult. By building on prior learning, complex learning is attained.

In addition, the process of bringing the curriculum together with the learner illustrates the classic stimulus-response principle of the connectionist theory.

Although this development helped to overcome the vagueness of earlier educational thinking and goals, it did not produce the hoped-for advances in education. A chief criticism of the connectionist approach to learning is that it is too mechanistic and simplistic. According to Travers (1978), the problem with this approach is the fact that it never succeeded in providing an adequate description of human intellectual performance. Although it is useful in rote learning tasks, it does not contribute to the higher levels of intellectual learning and to general understanding.

Cognitive theory. The cognitive learning approach, as represented by those who accept the gestalt and field theories, holds that learning is determined by individual perceptions. One perceives in terms of a pattern or in dynamic, structured wholes. For example, according to this theory, the listener is not aware of all the separate tones when listening to a musical performance but rather perceives the whole, or the melody. Nor does one perceive each separate skill of all the many related skills in an athletic performance. Instead, one perceives the total configuration of integrated skills in a gymnastic stunt.

Lewin (Hill, 1963), a leader among the field theorists, argues that a clear picture of learning cannot be attained unless the entire complex, psychological world that he calls the "life space" of an individual is considered. According to Lewin, the life space includes all the forces within which the individual operates. These include both internal forces, such as the basic psychological drives for food, water, and sex, and external forces such as the interaction with people met, objects encountered and used, and geographic places within which the individual moves. It must be stressed that life space means those forces recognized by the individual's psychological perceptions. If an individual does not perceive an object in the environment, then it simply does not exist insofar as that individual's life space is concerned.

Lewin contends that there are four different kinds of changes that compose the process of learning. These include changes in (1) cognitive structure, (2) motivation, (3) group membership, and (4) voluntary muscle control, as in skills and motor performances (Fig. 11-5).

FIG. 11-5. Communication and mental health. Without talking, students are trying to put a puzzle together to illustrate nonverbal communication and interaction.

FIG. 11-6. Cognitive theory of learning emphasizes motivation and the importance of interpersonal relationships.

Of central importance to Lewin's field theory are perception and motivation. He argues that the connectionist theory of learning is inadequate to explain the different types of learning. For example, he contends that the learning of a skill is not the same as learning to like a person or learning to live without alcohol.

Applying Lewin's principles to teaching and curriculum planning involves giving increased attention to the relationships of the individual and studying the individual's motivation and behavior in the school. Small classes are important for the individuals to know each other, and the instructor should emphasize interpersonal classroom activities. This approach recognizes the importance of motivation in learning and distinguishes between the goals of the curriculum and the individual's psychological goals (Fig. 11-6). Lewin's emphasis on interpersonal learning is not only evident but relevant to cooperative learning and to programming for cultural diversity in today's schools.

HEALTH EDUCATION APPLICATION: THEORIES AND MODELS

Every health education program has as its major, long-range objective the development of a life-style that will lead to good health. Traditionally these objectives have been defined in terms of health knowledge, health attitudes, and health practices. However, health educators have long been aware of the troublesome gap that often exists between health knowledge, health attitudes, and health practices or between what the individual knows about health and what he or she does about it. The physician who fails to care for his or her own health is an often-cited example, as is the obese nutritionist, the physical educator who fails to exercise, and the health educator who smokes.

Despite this evidence, the pressure of the public's growing interest in health education as a method for preventing disease, eliminating social problems, and achieving better health often causes schools to adopt unrealistic and unattainable objectives for its health education program. As Kreuter and Green (1978) have warned, it is naive to expect health education to produce health behavior changes that result in significant improvements in health. Instead, school health education can make its most important contribution in the development of specific knowledge and skills. The school's health instruction program, since it is directed to healthy children and youth, is designed to intervene in or to prevent illness and disease before signs or symptoms are apparent.

Health behavior change is not a favorable goal or objective for schools because of its very complex nature. Even in a situation offering optimal control, as in an experimental study, it is very difficult to determine which influences of many affecting children are causally related to health behavior. Although children do spend a considerable portion of their lives in school, its influence is relatively weak compared to pressure exerted by their homes, their neighborhoods and communities, and particularly their peer group. Even under optimal conditions, such as an ideal school health instruction program, the time available for formal health instruction is relatively limited.

Therefore it becomes apparent that the major role of health instruction is to develop health knowledge and positive health attitudes. In addition, certain health behavior skills are taught, such as those related to hygienic measures, personal and interpersonal skills, selecting nutritious diets, selecting health care, participating in fitness and exercise activities, and acquiring the skills necessary to apply first aid and emergency care procedures. It is assumed that this approach will provide the developing students with the basis for making wise decisions and appropriate choices about healthful life-styles and behavior patterns that will contribute to their health and well-being.

Clarification of health behavior goals

With the development of health education and its expansion into a variety of settings outside the schools, such as public health, health care, rehabilitation, and occupational centers, it becomes important to recognize that objectives and approaches will differ. Professionals in health care settings have called attention to the need for making distinctions in the health behavior outcome in order to clarify the program objectives and related activity. This behavior can be classified as (1) health behavior—that which is related to the prevention of illness and disease, (2) sick role behavior—that which occurs after the appearance of symptoms of illness, and (3) illness behavior—that which occurs after the diagnosis of disease (Society for Public Health Education, 1976).

In light of these distinctions, the school's health instruction program will, to a large extent, focus on health behavior. Schools must also give some attention to sick role behavior, helping persons to understand their own feelings and to know how to care for themselves when symptoms appear. Learning how to use health services and how to relate to health service personnel is an important aspect of health instruction. Illness behavior, though it may be beyond the scope of the school, is within the realm of health education. It has long been recognized that a sick person is much easier to motivate to adopt a recommended health practice or to accept medical advice than is a well person. A task force of the American College of Preventive Medicine (Preventive Medicine USA, 1976) concluded that the most effective health education programs have involved persons who already had strong motivation, such as chronic illness or disability, an acute crisis such as surgery, or a job-threatening condition such as alcoholism. The logic of health education seems most appealing to those who are not well. If the person understands his or her disease, recognizes how to control it, and understands why the medication should be taken or why the treatment should be followed, then he or she is more likely to comply with the physician's recommendations (Podell, 1976).

Although health education is involved with the total spectrum of the population, the three general arenas where it takes place may include only a portion of the whole. School health education deals with young people in a generally healthy state. Therefore the instructional emphasis is on primary prevention, and the curriculum covers a wide range of topics. The objectives of school health education emphasize specific knowledge and attitudes, with health behavior change receiving much less emphasis. This is not because the health outcome is less important, but because, practically speaking, the opportunity to practice the health outcome is not always present.

Community health education covers the widest range of subjects, since it includes the total community: old, young, sick, and well. The instructional objectives for community health, however, are quite specific, focusing on programs such as glaucoma screening or measles immunization campaigns. There is greater emphasis on health behavior change, with specific actions being required to carry out the program.

Health care education deals with a narrow spectrum of subjects—sick people. The instructional objectives are very specific, concerning patient education about a particular disease, diet, or medical therapy. There is great emphasis on health behavior change, involving actions required by specific treatment, diet, or follow-up procedure.

Health belief model

How have the connectionist and cognitive theories affected the field of health education? The health belief model represents the most extensive work done thus far in an effort to develop a theory and a science of health behavior change. This model was influenced by the theories of Lewin and his phenomenologic orientation, which holds that it is the individual's perception or psychological environment that determines what his or her action will be (Rosenstock, 1974). This complex of psychological forces, which Lewin calls the "life space of the individual," explains how learning takes place. The life space includes regions of positive and negative valence that exert forces causing the individual to move away from negative and toward positive forces. Lewin considers motivation to be very important to learning, explaining that learning involves changes in both cognition (knowledge) structure and motivation (Zais, 1976).

Fig. 11-7 illustrates the health belief model and the three distinct phases—individual perception, modifying factors, and likelihood of action, which lead to a health action.

Individual perceptions. Individual perceptions include the individual's subjective risk of contracting the disease. For example, consider the issue of teenage smoking. The disease in

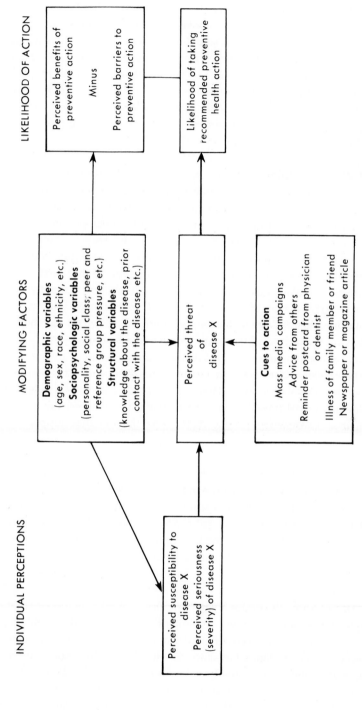

FIG. 11-7. The health belief model as predictor of preventive health behavior.

question is a smoking-related disease such as lung cancer, emphysema, or heart disease. According to the principle of this model, the teenager's smoking behavior will be influenced away from smoking to a reduced or nonsmoking state or will continue in a nonsmoking state if the teenager perceives the effects of smoking as presenting a serious threat to health and perceives conditions such as lung cancer, emphysema, and heart disease as very serious diseases. In addition, cigarette smoking must be perceived as behavior that greatly increases the likelihood of developing one of these diseases. Thus the two perceptions, personal susceptibility to the disease and the severity or seriousness of disease as a personal threat, are interacting perceptions that are the necessary conditions for modifying the smoking behavior or maintaining the nonsmoking behavior.

Modifying factors. Assuming that the foregoing perceptions or conditions are present, the ultimate decision of the individual to change or maintain his or her smoking behavior depends, to a great extent, on the modifying factors present in the teenager's situation. For example, if the individual comes from a home where smoking has not been part of the family culture and if his or her peers are nonsmokers, the prospects of changing smoking behavior to nonsmoking or for continuing as a nonsmoker are greatly enhanced. If, also, this young person has just gained knowledge from the high school health science course that further demonstrates the hazardous effects of smoking on health, the change in the student's cognitive structure (knowledge) adds an important factor to behavior change. The combined influence of the home, peer group pressure, and health knowledge gained at school acts either to modify the teenager's smoking behavior or to reinforce the continuation of nonsmoking.

The calls to action issued by the mass media and other sources are interpreted in the context of these perceptions. If the cues encourage smoking, the individual is more likely to reject them because they are inconsistent with the major predisposing forces identified in this situation. Nonsmoking media presentations and similar advice from friends and respected adults are interpreted as consistent with the many other factors that support the nonsmoking position.

Likelihood of action. According to the health belief model, individual action is determined by the balance or imbalance between the individual's perceived positive and negative forces affecting his or her health behavior. In the foregoing example, the action of stopping smoking or continuing nonsmoking wins approval for the individual from family and friends. This action also ensures consistency with the knowledge (cognitive structure) that the individual has acquired in the school health education course.

•   •   •

Admittedly, this example illustrates a situation in which all of what Lewin describes as the complex of psychological forces favor nonsmoking. In terms of the health belief model, the modifying factors and the perceived benefits favor nonsmoking. Another example might show the major forces in the student's life space as encouraging the continuation of smoking or encouraging its initiation. A more true-to-life example would show both negative and positive valences (values), some favoring and some opposing smoking, that combine to pose a genuine dilemma for the teenager. In this situation the student's health education experiences can play a major role in decision making. Obviously, the quality of this instruction, the preparation of the teacher, and the teacher's sensitivities to the student's dilemma are of critical importance.

Social learning theory

According to social learning theory a continuous, reciprocal interaction exists among the individual's behavior, other personal factors (thoughts, emotional reactions, and expectations), and the environmental consequences of behavior. Bandura calls this reciprocal determinism, a process in which all factors are interlocking determinants of each other.

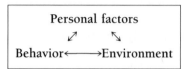

The distinction between social learning theory and the extreme behaviorist (connectionist) position is the importance attached to inner causes of behavior. The behaviorists deny that cognitive functions have any effect on behavior. In fact, behaviorists reject the concept of cognitive functions on the grounds that cognitions are unassessable or fictitious constructs that do not exist in reality. After extensive analysis of stimulus conditions, many behavioral psychologists have reached the conclusion that environmental forces control behavior.

Although proponents of social learning theory recognize the importance of environment, they believe that interaction among the three components (i.e., behavior, personal factors, and the environmental consequences) ultimately determines human behavior.

According to social learning theory, the most important factor affecting behavior is the continuous, reciprocal interaction or feedback that occurs. The relative influence exerted by this factor may vary in accordance with the changing environment, with the particular behavior, and with the variations of personal factors. For instance, there may be situations in which the environment is the all-powerful constraining force on behavior; correspondingly, there may be instances when personal factors such as emotional reactions may become the overriding control of behavior.

The feedback from behavior and the consequent effect on future behavior might be illustrated by the example of the person who attempts to engage a fellow worker in conversation by extending a friendly greeting. However, when such efforts are repeatedly rebuffed, it is highly probable that this person will cease efforts to initiate conversations. On the other hand, if the greetings are met with a friendly response, future conversations between the two persons are more likely to develop.

The social learning theory proponents also differ with the stimulus-response psychologists, who have assumed that the individual learns by directly *performing* responses and from directly *experiencing* their effects. However, according to the social learning view, nearly all learning occurs vicariously, by observing other people's behavior and its consequences. This capacity to learn through observation enables a person to acquire more rapidly large, integrated patterns of behavior without having to learn everything through the long and tedious process of trial and error. This capacity to learn through observation enables a person to accelerate the process of learning. In fact, history offers many instances wherein individual survival has been determined by the ability to learn from the experience of others.

Bandura (1977) and others argue that there is much research that demonstrates that cognitions can be activated by instruction and that cognitive effects can be assessed indirectly. Bandura points to studies that have demonstrated that people learn and retain behavior much better by using instructional techniques and other cognitive aids than by repeated practice.

In addition to learning from the experience of others, Bandura points out that a person learns from observation, from reading, from listening, and through the capacity to use symbols. Perhaps one of the most useful concepts of social learning theory is that a person has the capacity to determine many of the consequences of his or her actions (i.e., to establish a standard of behavior). Having adopted a standard of behavior or a level of expectation, the individual is now able to provide his or her own rewards and punishments, depending on whether the personal standard of behavior has been achieved.

The social learning theory (i.e., that personal standards of behavior can be acquired in many different ways) is of great practical significance to the health educator. Some of the ways in which a new behavior is learned are as follows:

1. *Learning by direct experience.* A person learns from the consequences of his or her own behavior. A student seeking advice from a teacher about a personal problem such as drug abuse will respond in terms of behavior, in accordance with the way he or she is treated by the teacher. If the student is treated with respectful attentiveness, he or she is more likely to continue to seek the counsel of the teacher (Fig. 11-9). If the consequences of the session with the teacher are perceived as threatening and unsympathetic, the student will behave negatively. In each instance, the behavior is modified, but it is the direction of change that is of critical importance from the health education perspective.

2. *Learning by observing.* Other students may learn quickly from observing the behavior of their classmates and the consequences of their actions. If students observe that their teacher is open, friendly, and supportive and that other students react favorably to interaction with the teacher, the future behavior of the observing student concerning contacting the teacher for advice will be positively reinforced.

3. *Learning by listening and reading.* Here again, the student learns about how a specific behavior (seeking advice from the teacher) and the consequences of such action are related. The "acceptance of the student by the teacher" and the "giving of valued counsel" are likely to be determining factors in the student's future behavior.

4. *Learning discriminating and generalizing.* The student develops a more sophisticated level of both understanding and consequences by analyzing human behavior. As Zimbardo, Ebbesen, and Maslath (1977) have explained, people learn "if-this" relationships. They learn by adopting tentative hypotheses about the relationships between observed events, phenomena, or variables. They also learn under which conditions these relationships are true (Fig. 11-8).

Behavior modification

The behavior modification approach is a direct application of the connectionist theory of learning and emphasizes relating observable activity or responses to antecedents and subsequent

FIG. 11-8. Positive interpersonal relationships between students and school counselors are important resources for enabling students to develop health-promoting behaviors.

events or stimuli. The stimulus-response association and the reinforcement of the desired activity or behavior compose essential elements.

One concept that has emerged from the behavior modification approach is *contingency management,* which is based on the experimental observations that the consequences of behavior, the reinforcing stimuli, determine the pattern of behavior. The reinforcer is a consequence that has the effect of making the behavior that preceded it more likely to be repeated. For example, if praise (reinforcement) is given to a boy for washing his hands before eating, he is more likely to repeat this act in the future.

The second important concept of behavior modification is *stimulus control.* This involves an analysis of how a stimulus provides the context for ongoing behavior. Stimulus control analysis is used in many behavior applications to determine exactly how the environment controls a particular problem behavior. Such an analysis usually begins with the keeping of a detailed record of the times when the behavior occurs, the physical location, the current mood, and the social context of the behavior. For example, the characteristics of each occurrence of an unwanted behavior such as overeating or cigarette smoking would be carefully defined.

Bandura (1977) has developed a five-part process for applying a behavior modification approach that includes the following:

1. Analyzing existing relevant behavior and developing behavioral objectives
2. Modeling of the new behavior by the instructor

3. Providing guided practice of the new behavior by the learners

4. Providing for reinforcement of the new behavior

5. Being able to maintain the new behavior without further assistance from the instructor

Of these five parts, reinforcement devices for new behavior are particularly important. Changes in diet, smoking, and exercise, for example, might develop such reinforcements as encouragement from the instructor, support from family members, and approval from friends and peers.

A recent development that has made behavior modification easier for the health educator is the use of self-control behavioral strategems. As expressed in the code of ethics statement for health education, self-control is in keeping with the principle of fostering an educational environment that nurtures individual growth and development. It is also consistent with the idea of helping people to make behavior changes by conscious choices rather than by coercion.

In behavior modification, changes are often brought about by environmental manipulations that force the person with the problem to modify or change behavior. Examples of such manipulation include putting a substance in the cigarette to create an unpleasant taste to the smoker, thus causing the smoker to consider stopping smoking; or, in an effort to encourage the automobile driver to wear a safety belt, installing a device that creates a loud, unpleasant noise when the key is inserted into the starter switch and the seat belt is not fastened. Such environmental manipulation is designed to force compliance rather than to help the person make a conscious choice of health actions.

Under a self-managed approach, the person with the problem behavior becomes an active participant in changing or modifying his or her own behavior.

Although educators find the self-control strategem a more acceptable method than environmental manipulation, it often proves unsuccessful because of vague or poorly defined instructions. Also, as Bandura (1977) contends, such instructions may have no immediate implications. In addition, persons using this approach have often failed to provide the necessary support that comes from reinforcement. To ensure the success of self-managed behavioral change, research has demonstrated the importance of the following steps:

1. Both immediate and long-range goals require carefully defined objectives. In keeping with the self-control approach, the person involved should choose the objectives or goals.

2. Adopting contractual agreements is an important means of increasing a person's commitment to goal achievement. For example, an agreement recommended for smoking behavior change would call for gradually restricting cigarette smoking by reducing the number of times and places where smoking is permitted. To succeed, persons must personally set the objectives and then voluntarily commit themselves to attaining these immediate objectives on a day-to-day basis.

3. Negative self-evaluations that result from deviation from a person's contractual agreement are an important element in helping counteract the undesired behavior.

4. The satisfaction resulting from an agreement and receiving a favorable social reaction from family and friends for adopting the new health behavior represents an important source of reinforcement.

5. Keeping a detailed record of behavior changes is an additional source of reinforcement, since it provides a tangible and objective measure of the progress. Experience has shown that those who record their daily activities continue to work toward achieving

objectives until they have exceeded preceding performances, thus ensuring continued improvement.

The altering of stimulus conditions under which the maladaptive or undesired behavior occurs is an effective technique in changing or modifying behavior. For example, research has shown that the problem of overeating often arises in situations in which appetizing foods are prominently displayed. To counteract this influence, altering the stimulus condition by storing foods out of sight and in less accessible places is effective. Another way of helping control the overeating problem involves limiting the circumstances under which a person eats. Special efforts are made to avoid eating in nondining settings (e.g., while watching television, reading, or listening to the radio).

It must be recognized that many of the undesired behaviors, such as smoking, overeating, and drinking, provide immediate gratification or reinforcement to a person. Because these behaviors occur in many and diverse situations and times, it is necessary for a person to narrow this stimulus control over his or her behavior.

The need for developing self-reinforcing techniques must also be recognized in self-control behavior modification. To do this, persons are taught to arrange for personally rewarding contingencies that serve as reinforcements. For example, after refraining from smoking for a certain period of time, the smokers then reward themselves by engaging in an enjoyable activity, such as taking a recreational break or watching a favorite television program.

Fishbein's theory of reasoned action

Although it is helpful to simplify the analysis of learning theories by grouping them into one of two broad categories—cognitive and connectionist, or associationist, learning theory—further attempts have been made to combine the advantages of these two theories. Many researchers have been attracted by the connectionist's objectivity in identifying behavior and precision in measuring behavior, but others have been dissatisfied with a stimulus-response analysis of behavior. These researchers have argued that, in addition to this effect, the person's behavior is also a result of his or her beliefs, attitudes, and desires to achieve a goal. The Fishbein conceptual framework is one example of the attempt to combine cognitive and connectionist approaches to learning.

According to Fishbein's theory (Fishbein and Ajzen, 1975), beliefs are the fundamental building blocks. The individual, through direct observation or by receiving information from an outside source, as in health instruction, learns or forms some beliefs about a particular object. The individual also develops beliefs about the various attributes of the object. Through this process, beliefs about health, illness, cigarettes, food, physicians, hospitals, health behavior, and many other things in life are acquired. The totality of a person's beliefs serves as the information or knowledge base that ultimately determines the person's attitudes, intentions, and behavior. This approach views the individual as an entirely rational being, one who uses the information available to make judgments, form evaluations, and arrive at decisions. An adapted and simplified illustration of the behavioral intentions model is presented in Fig. 11-9.

Formally stated, the theory holds that an individual has many beliefs about a given object. Moreover, the object is seen as having various attributes or characteristics. For example, the object *cigarette* may be seen as having various attributes; for example, cigarette smoke may represent odor, the cause of disease, and an offense to friends. If these beliefs about the attri-

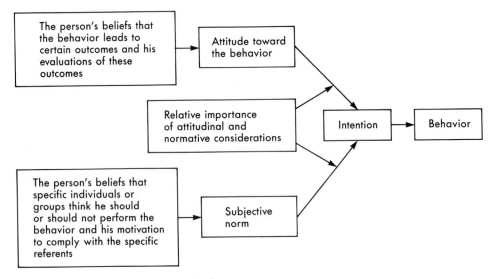

NOTE: Arrows indicate the direction of influence

FIG. 11-9. Ajzen and Fishbein's model factors determining a person's behavior.

butes of cigarettes are associated with unfavorable attitudes, then, through the process of conditioning, the attitude of the individual toward cigarettes and smoking is likely to be negative. According to this theory, attitudes toward an object are conditioned by beliefs about the attributes of the object and by evaluation of those attributes. Also, according to this theory, a person's attitude toward an object is related to his or her intention to perform a variety of behaviors relating to the object, in this case, cigarettes. If a person's overall attitude toward cigarettes is negative, his or her intention to perform certain behaviors with respect to cigarettes may be something like the following:

1. To decide against smoking a cigarette
2. To continue not smoking
3. To avoid areas where cigarettes are smoked

Fishbein points out that there may not be a direct and consistent relationship between beliefs, attitudes, and behavioral interactions. He contends that a person's intention to perform a particular behavior is a function of two basic determinants, one attitudinal and the other normative (Fig. 11-10). The attitudinal component refers to the person's attitude toward performing the behavior in question. The normative component (subject norm) is related to the individual's beliefs about people who are very important to him or her and what such people's expectations of him or her are. For example, if the individual sees all the attributes of cigarettes as being bad or negative (attitude) and believes parents and friends (subjective norm) do not want him or her to smoke, it is more likely that he or she will *intend not* to smoke.

In summary, a person's intentions (to smoke or not to smoke) are a function of two variables intervening between the stimulus conditions and the intention. These variables are (1) attitude toward the behavior and (2) the subjective norm. The individual's attitude is determined by the stimulus conditions, by beliefs about what others think he or she should do, and by his or her own desire to comply with their standards of behavior. Fishbein's general framework for behavior change with its stimulus conditions, intervening variables, and behavioral intentions response is clearly in the connectionist tradition of learning and its well-known model of stimulus-response. However, many of the precepts from the cognitive theory of learning have also been included in Fishbein's model. For example, the intervening variables of knowledge, beliefs, attitudes, and the influence of others on the individual's decisions are closely related to cognitive theories and Lewin's concept of life space.

Persuasive communication theory

The effort to influence other people by arguing, presenting facts, drawing conclusions, and predicting the future consequences of a proposed behavior has become one of the most widely used influence techniques. The adult's attempt to influence the child, the father's efforts to mold the son, and the teacher's approach to educating the pupil represent varying degrees of sophistication in applying what has become known as *persuasive communication.*

The premise of persuasive communication theory holds that an individual's attitudes (the affective component) are influenced or changed by alteration of that individual's opinions or beliefs (the cognitive or knowledge component) (Zimbardo, Esseben, and Maslath, 1977). For example, it should be possible for the health educator to change people's attitudes toward proposed legislation to raise the qualifying age for a driver's license by changing their beliefs about the advantages, the disadvantages, and the potential impact on traffic accidents of such a law. Persuasive communication theory holds that previously unknown information will affect beliefs.

An examination of school health education curriculums and teaching plans provides evidence that this assumption, though rarely made explicit, is the premise for most of today's health teaching. As Wallack (1980) has observed, common sense tells us that a change of attitude will ultimately lead to a change in behavior. Attractive as this theory may be, it is not the reality of behavioral science research. Although a positive relationship between knowledge and attitude often exists, it is painfully small; studies of the relationship between attitude and behavior have found the connection to be disappointingly small or insignificant (McGuire, 1981).

However, these apparent inconsistencies in the studies of attitude and behavior change have stimulated the interest of several behavioral scientists. Their efforts to clarify the relationship between feelings and actions has led to a delineation of the persuasive communication theory. This research has identified four processes that determine the extent to which a person will be persuaded by a communication. As applied to health education, the processes are as follows:

1. *Attention.* Obviously, the attention of students must be gained before the communication can have the effect. Regardless of how appealing, logical, or well organized the argument may be, it will not change anyone's attitude until the message has been received.
2. *Comprehension.* Even if the student is attentive to the message, it must be understood. People must first understand the argument if they are to change their attitudes or comprehend which behavior is being advocated.
3. *Acceptance.* Once the message has been comprehended, the important question is the extent to which the student agrees with or accepts the argument. Ultimately this will be determined by what the student perceives the rewards of the message to be.

4. *Retention.* How effective has the communication been? This will be determined by its retention and application at some future time.

Although these processes are all important to successful communication, they constitute only half of the communication equation. The outcome depends on the effectiveness of the inputs or the message and its transmission. Whether a message is accepted and effects a behavior change depends on several factors. Often "who said what to whom" is the critical factor in determining whether a communication is persuasive. Accordingly, researchers have identified several factors that affect the acceptance of a communication. Some of the most important factors include the following:

1. *The source.* The source of the communication often has an important effect on the attitude of the recipient. For example, if the person communicating the message is seen as one who is credible and trustworthy, that person's ability to persuade others is greatly

TABLE 11-1. Adaptation of McGuire's persuasive communication matrix for antismoking education

Output variables	Input variables	
	Source of the message	Characteristics of the message
	Viewed as credible, likable, trustworthy; attractiveness; teaching style; knowledgeable, authoritative, powerful	Effectively organized; salient information organized appeals to student's autonomy to make own decisions
Exposure to the communication: health education program designed to provide maximal exposure to message presenting arguments against smoking	Teacher designed 5-day module on hazards of smoking	
Attention: teaching methods are interesting; hold students' attention to hear message advocating nonsmoking	Introduces unit with color film on teenaged smoking	Reviews trends depicting teenaged smoking
Comprehension: communication well organized; numerous examples and illustrations enable student to understand message	Teacher conducts frequent reviews to assess students' understanding	Formal testing of students' knowledge on smoking
Acceptance: arguments and conclusions of message abstaining from smoking are accepted; appeal to student to use information in decision making; possible models for nonsmoking	Teacher discusses epidemiologic evidence linking smoking to disease	Students conduct discussions on more effective labeling of cigarettes
Retention and application: reinforcement is provided; recalls information for future use; applies information to decision making; learns; wants to resist pressure to smoke; maintains nonsmoking status	Appeals made to student to use information on smoking in decision making	Analyzes data on health benefits realized from quitting

enhanced. Other important perceived characteristics of the speaker include intelligence, experience, sincerity, likability, and attractiveness of the manner of speaking. Another favorable characteristic of the communicator as perceived by the listener is the appearance of familiarity—someone with whom the audience can identify.

2. *Communication.* The characteristics of the message can enhance or reduce its effectiveness. Such things as good organization and clear order of presentation (one-sided or two-sided) improve the presentation. The use of logic and emotions, fear techniques, the extent of the analysis, and documentation are all part of the effectiveness of the message.

3. *Audience.* The characteristics of the audience, their predispositions and attitudes, their knowledge of the subject, their previous experience, their level of intelligence, and their self-esteem all enter into the final acceptance or rejection of the communication.

Input variables		
Characteristics of the students	**Channel or method of delivery**	**Target objective of the communication**
Age; grade level; background experience; intelligence; attitude of acceptance; committed willingness to listen	Appropriate uses of visual and auditory stimuli; example of model behavior; effective use of teaching-learning activities Bulletin board advertising appeals to smoking	Specific attitude or behavior change objective (e.g., favorable attitude toward nonsmoking; avoids experimental smoking)
Conducts class experiment on composition of tar acid smoke (i.e., tar)	Collects and analyzes (e.g., smoking ads in popular magazines)	Students display attentiveness to class activities
Students practice assertive methods to resist pressure to smoke	Class discussion of nonsmokers' rights	
Students do volunteer, peer-led counseling with younger students on antismoking theme		

4. *Audience reaction.* Reaction to communication influences its acceptance. If the message presents an opportunity for a response or counterargument, it may be more effective than a "hard sell" approach, which may put people on the defensive, causing them to become suspicious and fearful of being manipulated. Overemphasis of a fear approach can cause people to reject, avoid, or fail to hear the argument.

Finally, McGuire has developed the social-influences communications matrix. It is a process by which a person (the source) communicates with another person (the receiver) about some object for the purpose of changing the person's (receiver's) attitude or behavior about the object. The *input* component of the social influence process is the communication, and the *output* is the persuasive communication effect. Table 11-1 gives an adaptation of McGuire's communications matrix applied to school health education.

FROM THEORY TO CLASSROOM APPLICATION

The guiding purpose of the scientist engaged in basic research is to reveal the truths of relationships. Scientific objectivity is of paramount importance, and in this sense the researcher divorces himself/herself from real world-problems or social issues. With respect to the development of learning theory, the role of the behavioral scientists is closer to that of their colleagues in basic research. Before learning theory, concepts, and principles are ready for real-world applications, a great deal more testing and verification in the laboratory is necessary. The combined efforts of biomedical scientists and health behavior researchers have resulted in more healthful life-styles for millions of Americans and a dramatic reduction in deaths from cardiovascular disease.

Whereas the health psychologist and the health behaviorist are primarily interested in learning theory, the school health educator is interested in both the theory of learning and the practice of teaching. Those health behaviorists engaged in learning theory research have come to accept the contributions of approaches that combine the traditional techniques of behaviorists (connectionists) and the cognitive interventionists. For example, key concepts drawn from the two theories include stimuli response and reinforcement together with intervening variables such as perceptions, emotions, beliefs and environmental factors. Both theories are now used in the improvement of classroom instruction.

Research in schools has led to the following conclusions about student learning and teaching strategies.

Student characteristics and learning

Students learn more efficiently and effectively when their basic emotional and physical needs are met. This includes their physiological needs for food and rest, their emotional and psychological needs for safety and emotional security, and their needs for a sense of confidence and self-worth (Maslow, 1954; Palardy, 1990). The benefits of school breakfasts and nutritious school lunches are well established. A Carnegie Task Force (1989) has called upon schools to create an atmosphere that meets the emotional, intellectual, and health needs of students. Although schools are not responsible for meeting every need of students, the school has no other choice but to meet the Carnegie Task Force challenge.

Success in teaching implies that one has both an expectancy of and a recognition that students have the capacity to learn. Research on mastery learning has demonstrated that when students are given sufficient time, practice, and teacher support, they can learn. Such a conclusion does not deny the fact that students do differ in their capacity for learning. This research has demonstrated the importance of one-on-one instruction, careful monitoring, and reinforcement of student learning. Research in the memorization of material has reaffirmed findings that students have different learning styles that need to be accommodated. Most students can benefit from reading, reciting, and writing of material (Bloom, 1976; Hill, 1982).

Students learn more readily when they are given positive reinforcement or rewarded for their behaviors. As Brophy, 1982, has pointed out, the appropriate use of reward can have a most powerful effect on learning. The concept of reinforcement works well in complex learning situations in which learning progresses slowly and in small steps, such as in learning a difficult skill. Here again, the opportunity for practice is important. Also, it is important to note that learning accrues from observing "important others." The opportunity to observe and to practice important social skills demonstrates the effects of modeling on vicarious learning. Teachers should provide prompt and positive feedback to students through formal and informal means. These reinforcements can take the form of spoken and written responses and acknowledgement of student success through gestures and nonverbal responses.

Motivated students learn more readily. All people have a drive (motive) for food, a drive (motive) for success and prestige, a drive (motive) for friendships and for love and sex. Hill (1982) regards learning and motivation as almost inseparable. Certainly they are closely related. Through learning, motives come into existence. For example, learning a desirable new skill is accompanied by recognition and prestige. This, in turn, becomes an incentive or motive to learn more to gain more rewards of recognition. Relatively speaking, school-age children and youth are among society's healthiest members. Thus they are likely to feel less threatened by or to be less motivated to protect themselves against a potential health threat. However, children and youth do have special needs for protection against disease and disability. Like all human beings, when children and youth suffer illness and injury, their attention is drawn to the pain and discomfort, and they are motivated to seek relief.

Classroom management and teaching strategies

The application of teaching theories to the classroom is discussed in relation to three general types of classroom organization and teaching strategies: (1) direct teaching, (2) mastery learning, and (3) cooperative learning. Each of these general approaches is characterized by a particular teaching and learning style. Direct teaching is teacher directed, mastery learning is individualized instruction–based, and cooperative learning is a noncompetitive student-centered approach. Each approach subsumes a variety of teaching methods. Their distinguishing characteristics have emerged from the teaching research conducted over the past two decades. What has become evident from this research is that no single teaching strategy is superior to all others.

Direct teaching is an academically focused, teacher-directed classroom using required structured materials (Fig. 11-10). In this approach, the goals of instruction are made clear to the student. As Cohen and Manion (1989) have stated, the interaction pattern is one in which the teacher speaks and the pupils listen. The most effective teachers are those who maintain a

FIG. 11-10. Direct teaching requires a careful structuring of the lesson, with key points of the lesson identified and arranged in a step-by-step progression.

strong academic focus and take special care to avoid spending an undue amount of time on nonacademic activities. Teachers who express strong leadership roles are most effective in teaching content and skill subjects. Although direct teaching places the teacher in an authoritarian role, research has shown that teachers who are most successful are warm, concerned, and flexible and permit freedom of movement within the classroom (Rosenshine [1979], see Kindsvatter [1988]). Because students are less actively involved in the direct teaching process, it is essential that the teacher allow time for feedback, for monitoring student progress, and to work with individual students as needed. Direct teaching is part of all teaching methods. In its most complete form, the lecture is composed of the following elements:

Phase I—Entry: preparation for learning
- Sets objectives and rationale
- Provides a context for new material
- Focuses attention on a key concept, generalization, or principle

Phase II—Presentation
- Sequences content form simple to complex
- Enhances presentation with visual aids
- Stimulates attention with verbal and nonverbal behaviors

School breakfasts

EMERGING ISSUE
The school lunch program has a long history and is well accepted as an integral part of the school program. A story in the local paper describing the school breakfast program and its positive effect on student learning has attracted much interest and discussion in the school health council. These discussions have revolved around the question, "Is breakfast feeding an appropriate function of schools?" If so, should this be considered as part of a comprehensive school health program?

Several members of the council are aware of breakfast programs operating in some of the large inner city schools. According to reports, these programs have been made available to children of low-income families who may come to school without breakfast. Under such circumstances school breakfasts seem justified. However, the issue before the council is whether school breakfasts should be considered in the same light as school lunches and be made available to all students?

Unable to reach a consensus on this question, the council has decided to open the discussion to a broader representation of school and community opinion. As the health education representative, you are asked to indicate your position on this question by placing a plus (+) or a minus (−) sign before each of the following statements with which you generally agree or disagree.

_____ 1. I would be opposed to making the breakfast program available only to poor children because of the negative sterotype effect on them and their families.

_____ 2. I think a parent education program on the importance of a good breakast for their children would be a more appropriate use of district money.

_____ 3. In view of tight education budgets, I would be concerned about the added costs to the district such as additional personnel, cost of food, and disruption of the teaching schedule.

_____ 4. Important as child nutrition is, I have difficulty justifying an action in which schools take on a social function that may detract from their primary mission of education.

_____ 5. I would favor a breakfast program for all children in the belief that it would make a positive contribution to both their health and educational development.

_____ 6. I think we should make a careful study of the costs and benefits of school breakfast programs before offering any recommendations to the district.

_____ If limited to a single choice, I would choose this number.

Phase III—Closure and review of learning

- Integrates with students' knowledge and experience
- Provides transition to next lesson or activity (Kindsvatter and Ishler, 1988)

Mastery learning is an individualized teaching approach using a structured curriculum subdivided into small units or learning steps directed toward achieving knowledge or skills objectives (Fig. 11-11). These small units are arranged by the teacher according to the scope and sequence of the curriculum.

"The purpose of mastery learning is the accomplishment of a designated learning task at a designated performance level by all students" (Kindsvatter and Ishler, 1988)

The guiding thesis of mastery learning holds that most students can achieve the instructional objectives within a flexible time period. Instruction is individualized and diagnostic. The

FIG. 11-11. Mastery learning is an individualized learning approach designed for the student to accomplish a specific objective or learning task.

teacher designs the formative test to assess the students' progress for each instructional objective. If a student fails to achieve a satisfactory level of performance, the teacher is in a position to diagnose the problem and to begin an immediate remediation program. The individualized approach is particularly well suited to accommodating the variations in student learning rates, as well as the cultural and ethnic differences that exist among America's schoolchildren.

A possible criticism of mastery learning is the fact that the mastery learning method places a heavy reliance on the teacher. Also, success with this approach requires a high degree of student motivation.

Studies have shown that students taught by mastery learning compare very favorably with regard to their performance levels in standardized achievement tests. This is a highly individualized approach, using a variety of teaching methods, including teacher-to-student relationship, peer instruction, and small group activity, in addition to the more typical tutorial approaches of one-on-one, programmed instruction, workbooks, games, and computer-based instruction.

Bloom (1980) has devised a five-phase process for mastery learning:

1. Subdivide the content into small units for student learning that are to be evaluated at incremental steps.
2. Decide on the teaching-learning activities that will enable the student to achieve the objective.
3. Develop and administer a formative test self-administered by the students at the completion of the unit.

4. For those students who have not yet achieved mastery, provide additonal instruction and materials needed to achieve mastery; for students who achieved mastery, provide enrichment materials until the class is ready to move to the next unit.

5. As the final step, give all students a summary test to determine mastery. Students receive an incomplete grade until they have reached the mastery level. Individual schools define mastery level.

Cooperative learning uses peer tutuoring and team cooperation to encourage student learning (Fig. 11-12). The importance of maturation is stressed by the development of cooperative learning. Objectives of the cooperative learning strategy are: (1) to increase achievement through group collaboration, (2) to provide an alternative to the usual competitive situation in classrooms, and (3) to improve human relations through cooperative activities by providing interdependence among class members. Proponents of cooperative learning contend that this approach not only improves student learning but also has contributed toward improving racial and ethnic harmony among students.

The teacher's role in contrast to the other approaches (direct teaching and mastery learning) is that of a facilitator to help students establish a sharing and cooperative learning relationship. Strother (1990) identifies several points that are important to consider in preparation for a cooperative learning approach: (1) provide comprehensive student orientation to the cooperative learning procedure, (2) establish expectations for effective group behavior, (3) once the class is organized into groups, keep the groups together long enough to develop cohesion and reward students for contributing to group success. Because of the importance of student incentives in cooperative learning, teachers should:

FIG. 11-12   Cooperative learning strategy is designed to increase student learning through group collaboration and to improve human relations among students

- Involve students in developing learning objectives and reward students for their efforts
- Show interest and enthusiasm for cooperative learning
- Arrange group activities that give members of the group an opportunity to contribute
- Establish group rapport and acceptance of others' opinions
- Help students to develop necessary skills for effective cooperative work
- Help students develop a sense of responsiblity for group success

SUMMARY

The purpose or goals of health education are to help people prevent disease and promote health through their own efforts. From the perspective of the practicing health educator, persuading people to change their health behavior involves an important moral and ethical problem. Changing one's health behavior implies that such decisions are made freely without coercion.

With respect to the contribution of health education to the health of the nation, health and medical authorities now recognize that major advances in health improvement will come from changes in people's life-style and from the control of environmental hazards. At the same time, a national task force has called for a broader health education responsibility—to serve as an advocate for changes in the environment to facilitate healthful conditions and behaviors.

To develop effective strategies for health education and behavior changes requires an understanding of the theories of learning. Most theories derive from two sources: (1) the connectionist and the (2) cognitive learning theory. Learning according to the connectionist is recognition of the importance of rewards or reinforcing the learner's correct or desired responses as expressed in Skinner's operant conditioning and feedback. Cognitive learning, on the other hand, refers to concepts of belief. Learning is determined by one's perceptions. Advocates of the cognitive theory argue that connectionist theory is too limited and fails to explain the different types of learning. Learning a skill is not the same as learning to like someone.

Several models of behavior change are illustrated to show different applications of learning theory. The health belief model holds that a person's perception of psychological environment determines the action a person will take.

Social learning theory proponents recognize the importance of the environmental forces on behavior. They believe that the interaction among behavior, personal factors, and the environment determine human behavior. Behavior modification, which is widely used in the health field, is a direct application of connectionist theory. The essential elements in this process include stimulus-response and reinforcement of the desired action.

In Fishbein's model the totality of a person's beliefs or knowledge base determines that person's attitude. However, the connectionist theory is reflected in the model that shows how one's beliefs become a process of conditioning the attitude one holds toward an object.

McGuire's persuasive communication theory provides a final example of the processes of changing behavior. The premise of this theory holds that one's attitudes are influenced or changed when his or her opinions and beliefs are changed. A change in attitude will ultimately lead to a behavior change. The apparent inconsistencies of this model have led to the identification of four processes: (1) attention, (2) comprehension, (3) acceptance, and (4) retention. In addition, a second set of factors that determine whether a message is accepted were identified. This includes the source of the message, the way a message is communicated, the characterics of the audience, and the reaction of the audience to the message.

The chapter concludes by tracing the relationship of theories of learning and research to that of classroom applications and instructional strategies. Results from a great deal of research have been summarized and distilled in the form of conclusions and principles designed to improve the teaching-learning proccesses. Guidelines for the improvement of instruction relate to (1) student learning and (2) classroom organization, including: enhancement of student learning, the importance of teacher expectations to student learning, providing appropriate rewards or reinforcements, and the role of motivation in student learning. Finally the discussion on teaching methods makes the point that successful teachers use a variety of teaching methods. Three principal methods of teaching are discussed: (1) direct instruction—information giving, (2) mastery learning—student-directed learning, and (3) cooperative learning—the role of student-to-student interaction and shared learning. These three general methods may be presented in a variety of permutations.

G ET INVOLVED! After selecting a health science or health education major and taking course work toward your degree, you will very probably be invited to join a professional honorary fraternity. An example of such an honorary in the field of health education and health science is Eta Sigma Gamma. It is one of the youngest and fastest growing of the honoraries.

The twenth-fifth anniversary of Eta Sigma Gamma was celebrated in April 1992. Since its founding in 1967 at Ball State University, Muncie, Ind., the honorary has grown to a membership of over 12,000, with chapters in approximately 90 colleges and universities.

The objectives of Eta Sigma Gamma are to: (1) further the professional competence and dedication of its individual members in health education; and (2) promote the discipline of health science by stimulating scientific research; by facilitating communication and discussion among individuals, agencies, and governmental jurisdictions; by recognizing service and academic achievement; and by raising professional and ethical standards.

Membership is composed of men and women (undergraduate and graduate students and faculty) who meet the national and local chapter standards. The college and university chapters are very active through the leadership of their undergraduate student members and their faculty sponsors.

Publications include the official journal of the honorary, *The Eta Sigma Gamman,* and a monograph series. The journal is published twice a year and often features articles written by student members.

Members may participate in the regular schedule of local chapter meetings and are entitled to attend the two national meetings held annually. One meeting is held in conjunction with the annual meeting of the Association for the Advancement of Health Education (AAHE) in April, and one meets with the American School Health Association in October.

For more information about the honorary, contact a local chapter or write to:

Eta Sigma Gamma
National Health Science/Health Education Honorary
2000 University Ave.
Muncie, IN 47306

STUDY QUESTIONS

1. Discuss the program implications of the following definitions of health education: (a) a process that enables the individual to make an informal decision and (b) a process whose aim is to help people achieve health by their own actions.
2. With respect to a code of ethics, what does the following statement imply for the health educator: "Health education supports change by choice, not by coercion."
3. In his model of health, Blum illustrates several inputs to health, including the gene pool, health services, and health behavior. What would you consider to be the *outputs*, or the effects, of these inputs?
4. Assume that a connectionist or behaviorist is conducting an intervention program designed to improve students' nutritional status. Which measures would he or she use? How might a cognitive theorist approach this measurement problem differently?
5. How would a health education program based on social learning theory differ from an approach based on behavior modification?
6. Explain the key elements of the health belief model.
7. Discuss the problem of unrealistic expectations for school health education.
8. What do you consider to be the major determinants of health behavior?
9. Of the theories and models discussed in this chapter, which of these do you think will be of most value to your health education efforts? Explain.
10. Assume that you are teaching a class that has a wide range of abilities. What would you choose as your principal method of instruction? Please explain.

REFERENCES

Ajzen I, Fishbein M: *Understanding attitudes and predicting social behavior,* Englewood Cliffs, NJ 1980, Prentice-Hall. American Public Health Association: Toward a policy on health education and public health. Position paper adopted by the governing council of the American Public Health Association, Washington, DC, Nov. 2, 1977.

Bandura A: *Social learning theory,* Englewood Cliffs, NJ, 1977, Prentice-Hall.

Bloom B: Human characteristics and school learning, New York, 1976, McGraw Hill.

Bloom B: Learning for mastery. In Ryan K, Cooper J, editors: *Kaleidoscope readings in education,* Boston, 1980, Houghton Mifflin.

Bugelski BR: *The psychology of learning applied to teaching,* Indianapolis, 1971, Bobbs-Merrill.

Brophy J: Successful teaching strategies for the Inner-city child, *Phi Delta Kappan* 63(8):527-530.

Carnegie Council on Adolescent Development: *Turning points: preparing American youth for the 21st century,* New York, 1989, Carnegie Corp.

Cohen L, Manion L: *A guide to teaching practice,* ed 3, London, 1989, Routledge.

Expert Committee on Health Education of the Public: First report. World Health Organization Technical Report Series no. 89, Geneva, 1954, World Health Organization.

Fishbein M, Ajzen I: *Belief, attitude, intention, and behavior: an introduction to theory and research,* Menlo Park, Calif, 1975, Addison-Wesley.

Glanz K, Lewis FM, Rimer BK, editors: *Health behavior and health education: theory and research practice,* San Francisco, 1990, Jossey Bass.

Hilgard ER, Atkinson RC, Atkinson RL: *Introduction to psychology,* ed 5, New York, 1971, Harcourt, Brace, Jovanovich.

Hill WF: *Learning: a survey of psychological interpretations,* Scranton Pa, 1963, Chandler Publishing.

Hill WF: *Principles of learning: a handbook of applications,* Palo Alto, 1982, Mayfield Publishing.

Hubbard B, Smith B, editors: *Strengthening health education for the 1990s: summary and suggestions for project replication,* Reston, 1990, Association for Advancement of Health Education supported by Metropolitan Life Foundation.

Kindsvatter RW, Ishler M: *Dynamics of effective teaching,* White Plains, 1988, Longman.

Kreuter MW, Green LW: Evaluation of school health education: identifying purposes, keeping perspective, *J Sch Health* 48(4):228, 1978.

Leventhal H, Glynn K, Flemming, R.: Is the smoking decision an "informed choice?" *JAMA* 257(24):3373, 1987.

Mager RF: Preparing objectives for programmed instruction, Belmont, Calif, 1961, Fearon Publishers.

McGuire WJ: Attitude theory and management. In *Food and nutrition research: proceedings of a symposium,* University Park, Pa, 1980, The Pennsylvania State University Press.

McGuire WJ: Behavioral medicine, public health and communication theories, *J Health Educ* 12(3):8-13, 1981.

Moore R, the Editors of Life: *Evolution,* New York, 1964, Life Nature Library, Time.

Muth K, Alverman D: *Teaching and learning in the middle grades,* Needham Heights, 1992, Allyn and Bacon.

Nightingale EO, et al: *Perspective on health promotion and disease prevention in the United States,* Washington, DC, 1978, Institute of Medicine, National Academy of Sciences.

Palardy M: Some basics about students' learning, NASSP Bulletin April 1990 pp 86-91.

Podell RN: Appendix V: physican's guide to compliance in hypertension: In *Preventive Medicine USA: health promotion and consumer health education,* New York, 1976, Prodist, Division of Neale Watson Academic Publications.

Preventive medicine USA: Theory, practice and application of prevention in personal health services: quality control and evaluation of preventive health services. Task force reports sponsored by the John E. Fogarty International Center for Advanced Study in the Health Sciences, National Institutes of Health, and the American College of Preventive Medicine, New York, 1975, Prodist, Division of Neale Watson Academic Publications.

Report of the 1972-1973 Joint Committee on Health Education Terminology, prepared by representatives of the American Academy of Pediatrics, American Association for Health, Physical Education and Recreation, American School Health Association, American Public Health Association, and Society for Public Health Education, Washington, D.C.

Report of the 1990 Joint Committee on health education terminolgy, *J Health Educ* 29(3):173-184, 1991.

Report of the President's Committee on Health Education, New York, 1973, the Committee.

Rosenstock IM: Historical origins of the health belief model. In Becker MH, editor: *The health belief model and personal health educator*, Thorofare, NJ, 1974, Charles B Slack.

Rosenstock IM, Strecher VJ, Becker MH: Social learning theory and the health belief model, *Health Educ Q* 15(2):175, 1988.

Society for Public Health Education: Code of ethics, San Francisco, Oct. 15, 1976, the Society.

Strother DB: Another look at time on task, June 1984, *Phi Delta Kappan*, 65(10):714-717, 1984.

Strother DB: Cooperative learning: fad or foundation for learning, *Phi Delta Kappan*, 72(2):158-162, 1990.

Taylor SE: *Health psychology*, New York, 1986, Random House.

Travers RMW: *An introduction to educational research*, ed 4, New York, 1978, Macmillan.

US Department of Health, Education and Welfare: Forward plan for health, FY 1977-1981, Washington, DC, June 1975, US Government Printing Office.

US Department of Health, Education and Welfare: Educating the public about health: a planning guide, Washington DC, 1977, Public Health Service, Health Resources Administration.

Wallack LM: Assessing effects of mass media campaigns: an alternative perspective, *Alcohol Health Res World* 5:18, Fall 1980.

Zais RS: *Curriculum principles and foundations*, New York, 1976, Thomas Y Crowell.

Zimbardo PG, Ebbesen EB, Maslath C: Influencing attitudes and changing behavior, Menlo Park Calif, 1977, Addison-Wesley.

Planning the health education curriculum

OVERVIEW

It is generally accepted that health education as an academic discipline originated with the 1918 report on the cardinal principles of secondary education. Health was identified as one of the seven major goals of education. The school's curriculum and the curriculum development processes are presented as background for the planning of the health education curriculum. Differing views over the goals of health education are examined from the perspectives of education and public health. Educators have stressed knowledge as a major goal, whereas public health officials have emphasized the goal of changing health behavior to promote health and to prevent disease.

The issue of what to teach is discussed in the context of the controversy over the comparative effectiveness of the comprehensive or the categorical health problems curriculum.

Forces affecting the school health curriculum are identified, beginning with the early temperance movement and continuing to the present influences of the Surgeon General's reports on health goals for the nation for 1990 and *Healthy People 2000,* which stressed the importance of health promotion and disease prevention. The influence of these developments on schools is most evident in the program leadership provided by the Division of Adolescent and School—Centers for Disease Control and the U.S. Public Health Service. The personal health risk of sexual behaviors causing disease and unplanned pregnancies, of smoking, inadequate diets, alcohol and drug use, lack of exercise, and intentional and unintentional injuries are receiving increasing attention.

Examples of health education curriculum organized according to comprehensive and categorical problems approaches are discussed. The strengths and weaknesses of these curriculums are reviewed. The chapter outlines a series of steps to guide school officials in planning an effective health instruction unit. Finally, the format and organization of lesson planning are discussed to ensure effective teaching.

OBJECTIVES   After reading this chapter, the student should be able to:

1. Identify historical events that help explain why health education has become part of the public school curriculum
2. List several steps in the curriculum development process

3. Explain why public health authorities have stressed the importance of life-style factors and health behavior in preventing disease

4. Identify and explain three different levels of decision making that determine the nature of the health curriculum

5. Identify past developments that have helped to determine the health topics or content of health education

6. Discuss the arguments favoring either a categorical health problem or a comprehensive health education approach to curriculum planning

7. Give two examples of the positive influences that the report *Healthy People 2000* has had on school health programs.

8. Explain how Goodlad's conceptual framework would help in planning a comprehensive health education curriculum

9. Identify the elements of the teaching unit

10. Develop an outline for a lesson plan and give an example for each to the three major parts of a lesson

HEALTH EDUCATION IN SCHOOLS

Although the adult's concern for the schooling of the young has existed throughout civilized history, the origin of health education in today's schools in America is most frequently identified as 1918, an important starting point for curriculum studies in the United States. On this date one of the most influential statements affecting the curriculum of American schools was issued, the report of the Commission on the Reorganization of Secondary Education, entitled "The Cardinal Principles of Education."

These principles were intended to serve as the general goals of all secondary schools and are frequently cited as the basis for the establishment of health education in the school. The following areas were included:

1. Health
2. Command of fundamental processes
3. Worthy home membership
4. Vocation
5. Citizenship
6. Worthy use of leisure
7. Ethical character

This statement has been of singular importance to education because of its widespread influence on and recognition by educational leaders. Recognizing its historical significance, the National Education Association appointed a special commission to reexamine the seven cardinal principles. The results were issued as a part of the nation's bicentennial celebration in

1976. The commission members were among the nation's most prominent leaders, representing such fields as business, industry, and labor, as well as professional and scientific fields. The commission reaffirmed the validity of the cardinal principles and their value as goals for all secondary schools. However, the principles were restated and reinterpreted to make them more relevant in terms of the needs of today's society. For example, the commission's interpretation of the goal of health was as follows, "The scope and importance of health as an educational objective has become even more important than it was in 1918." Accordingly, greater emphasis should be placed on "the need for healthy interpersonal and intellectual attitudes. . . ." The importance of a world view of health and the worldwide challenge that that entails were emphasized. Support was given to a broad concept of health, including total mental, physical, and emotional health for each person. Support of the efforts to improve drug education and support for frank discussions of family living were included. This aspect of education, the commission stated, is necessary if the youth of today are to be guided toward acceptance of responsible citizenship as tomorrow's leaders.

As previously stated, the events and concerns of the day often have a pronounced effect on the schools. Because the institution of education is close to the average citizen, the curriculum is frequently determined by the immediate concerns of the people. For example, Kleibard (1982) has identified four different interest groups that at the turn of the century also exerted a major influence on what the schools taught. These groups were the (1) humanists, (2) social efficiency reformers, (3) child study movement, and (4) social meliorists. The child study group and the social meliorists were instrumental in obtaining the inclusion of health among the seven cardinal principles.

The rise and fall of public interest create a continuous change in the school's curriculum. Because health has been identified as a priority of education at one time does not ensure that it will always continue to be so.

The growing influence of political action groups in shaping public programs means that the position of health education in the schools could change very quickly. Unless the health education curriculum is reviewed and evaluated on an on-going basis, it could become irrelevant to the needs of both the individual and society.

THE SCHOOL CURRICULUM

Any discussion of the health education curriculum requires the establishment of a common definition for the term *curriculum*. It is most often identified as the plan for schooling, which is the content that curriculum planners expect the teachers to teach and that the students are expected to learn. Curriculum development entails the selection and organization of a set of intended learning outcomes (Posner and Rudnitsky, 1978).

The term *curriculum*, in addition to its use as a definition of an education plan for the learner, also refers to a field of study. When the curriculum for health education is being considered, it is helpful to consider some general principles that have derived from work done in the field of curriculum study and the application of such knowledge to a plan for action, or a plan that guides instruction (Zais, 1976).

Curriculum foundations

Most curriculum specialists agree that the determinants of a curriculum should reflect some, if not all, of the following considerations:

1. *Philosophy and the nature of knowledge.* Basic assumptions about the nature of knowledge and the philosophy that guides beliefs about knowledge have particular relevance to the formulation of the curriculum.
2. *Society and culture.* The school is the institution invented by society to transmit the cultural heritage and to ensure its survival. Societal values, assumptions, and concepts of good and bad are translated into curriculum objectives and learning activities.
3. *The individual.* The nature of humankind and its biological and psychological characteristics, needs, and capacities to learn have placed certain limits on the curriculum, such as the content included, the organization of the curriculum, and the types of learning activities to be selected.
4. *Theory of learning.* Some elements of learning theory enjoy wide acceptance (e.g., the social learning theory), whereas other theories (e.g., behavior modification) are more controversial. The particular theory of learning embraced by the curriculum developer will exert a pronounced influence on the design. For example, Dewey's theory that the school curriculum should serve as a preparation for living has been applied directly to certain types of learning activity, including use of the project method. The theory of learning and the importance that environment places on learning have significant implications for the contemporary curriculum developer.

Curriculum development

Tyler (1975) stresses the importance of conducting a careful preliminary analysis of a society to determine clearly the needs that the curriculum should serve. Such an analysis may call for extensive work with the local community, parents, peer groups, teachers, and school officials. If the curriculum to be developed is to be accepted and used by the teachers, special efforts must be made to seek their active involvement and to give careful consideration to their needs as well (Fig. 12-1).

The process. In this extensive work in curriculum development, Tyler (1975) has developed a series of steps to be followed:

1. *Selecting and defining the objectives.* Curriculum developers must resist the temptation to write their own objectives and must, instead, involve many different groups in the selection process, seeking group deliberation and judgment. Involvement of teachers is essential to their ultimate commitment to the curriculum. Subject matter specialists, curriculum specialists, psychologists, sociologists, and specialists in human development all offer judgments in this area. The level of generality for objectives must be considered; objectives that are too general are nonfunctional, and overly specific objectives are burdensome.
2. *Developing a philosophy.* The theory of learning that is adopted influences the philosophy or point of view of the curriculum developer.
3. *Selecting and creating learning experiences.* The purpose of the learning experience is to

FIG. 12-1. Teachers planning curriculum development.

meet the curriculum objectives (i.e., to perform and to practice the behavior called for in the objective). Appropriate learning activities should invite the attention and interest of the learner and provide satisfaction. Activities should be balanced between those that can be carried out alone and those involving peer group cooperation.

4. *Organizing learning experiences.* The learning activities should provide maximal impact on the learner. They should be sequenced to build relationships, so that the student's learning builds from one activity to the next.

5. *Curriculum evaluation.* Evaluation of the curriculum involves determining (a) the effectiveness of the curriculum approach in its developmental stage; (b) the usability of the curriculum at the point of implementation; (c) the effectiveness of the curriculum in its operational stage; and (d) the extent to which students have achieved the objectives selected for the curriculum.

Posner and Rudnitsky (1978) have provided a model of the curriculum development process, including the various activities and sequence of steps or events that characterize the curriculum development enterprise (Fig. 12-2).

Making decisions about the curriculum

Goodlad et al. (1979) have identified three levels of decision making that are involved in the curriculum development process. These include (1) the *societal level,* which includes the community and the local board of education; (2) the *institutional level,* which involves the superintendent and the central office or district staff; and (3) the *instructional level,* which involves schools and teachers. According to this scheme, the societal decisions are performed by the board of education through powers delegated to it by the state board of education or state

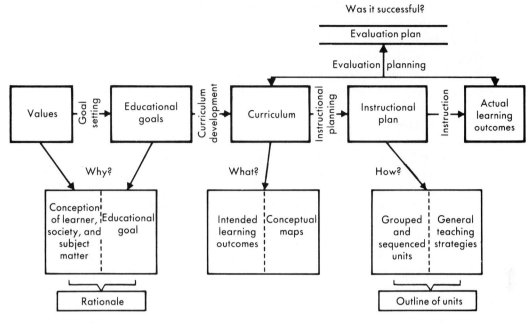

FIG. 12-2.   A model of the components and processes of curriculum development sources.

legislating authority. For instance, the Illinois State Board of Education (1983) has redefined schooling or the goals for public school students in Illinois to include the following areas: (1) mathematics, (2) language arts, (3) science, (4) social science, (5) fine arts, and (6) physical development and health. Moreover, the board has requested that schools must specify for each goal what students are to know and what they will be able to do as a consequence of having received this instruction (see Fig. 12-2).

The health instruction framework for California public schools is another example of decision making at the societal level. This document, which was issued by the California State Department of Education (Curriculum Framework Criteria Committee on Health, 1978), was developed by a committee composed of health educators and curriculum specialists for the state department of education. The framework defines the scope and sequence of the health education curriculum for California schools. As such, it is a very useful tool in helping local school district personnel decide on specific objectives and specific classroom teaching plans and student learning experiences. The health instruction framework encompasses 10 topic areas:

1. Personal health
2. Family health
3. Nutrition
4. Mental-emotional health
5. Use and abuse of substances
6. Diseases and disorders
7. Consumer health

8. Accident prevention and emergency health services
9. Community health
10. Environment

The board's responsibilities are critical to the whole curriculum development process. Typically, such decisions are made at the beginning of the process and involve actions concerning matters of board policy and questions with budgetary implications. Also, the board must adopt or establish the central goals and functions that are to be served by the schools.

Decisions at the *institutional level,* made by the superintendent and his or her administrative staff, are more likely to be concerned with curricular questions pertaining to the whole school system. These decisions include questions about the subjects to be taught and the curricular framework to which each subject area of the district curriculum is to be related. Decisions at the institutional level are concerned with the coordination and articulation of the district's instructional program to ensure that the various elements of the program are related to the educational goals adopted by the board of education.

At the *instructional level,* decisions are made about the working elements of the curriculum. Ideally this should be a teamwork process among principals, teachers, students, and parents. More typically, the classroom teacher makes the decision about the specific teaching-learning activities that will ultimately be used in the classroom. Here the general societal goals of the curriculum are translated into instructional objectives and learning outcomes.

The California state curriculum provides a good illustration of how the different levels of decision making can function effectively in providing a quality program of instruction at the classroom level. The state department uses its resources to enlist the assistance of experts in determining the state's general goals and curriculum framework. However, because it is a framework, or an outline, the school district administration may benefit from the guidance of the framework in planning its district-wide program of instruction, while at the same time one local school is given a maximal degree of flexibility in selecting specific teaching materials and learning experiences to be used in the classroom. Such flexibility enables the teacher to make the decisions necessary to meet the specific health education needs of the children in the local schools.

THE HEALTH EDUCATION CURRICULUM: DECIDING WHAT TO TEACH

The term *health* connotes a wholeness of mind and body, a condition free from disease and disability. The term *hygiene* is the forerunner of the term *health education.* Although hygiene has become archaic in today's usage, except in its limited application to industrial hygiene, the meaning (i.e., the science of preserving the health of both the individual and the community), is entirely appropriate. The teaching of hygiene was often narrowly focused because of the implied limited knowledge base of health and disease. Tracing the development of health education over the last century reveals a gradual expansion of knowledge concerning health and disease.

During the early nineteenth century the teaching of physiology and hygiene moved away from the teaching of facts about the structure or anatomy of the body to presenting information on the function or dynamic qualities of living.

Understanding the timing and events of history gives the student a greater appreciation for the growth of human knowledge and the effect of these events on the understanding of health. For example, the first law requiring the teaching of physiology and hygiene was passed in 1850, predating Pasteur's work and the development of the germ theory. With the enactment of laws requiring compulsory school attendance, there also came outbreaks of epidemic diseases in the schools. These developments and the new knowledge about infectious diseases led to the teaching of information about communicable diseases and to a further expansion of the concept of health and disease. As a consequence, awareness of preventive measures, including the importance of environmental sanitation in controlling disease, increased.

Other developments during the first decades of the 1900s that influenced the teaching of health and the health education curriculum included the scientific temperance movement, the child study movement, and World War I. These events initiated teaching in such areas as alcohol, tobacco, narcotics, physical growth, exercise, and fresh air and ventilation. Unfortunately, not all developments had a completely positive impact on health teaching in the schools. The first breakthrough of new scientific knowledge was often incomplete, and partial truths often led to errors and the spreading of both misconceptions and new facts. For example, early programs that were designed to prevent and control the spread of tuberculosis may not always have had a positive effect on the health of children. The emphasis on fresh air and ventilation may have led to an overexposure of children to the elements, thereby lowering their resistance to upper respiratory tract infections.

The scientific temperance movement provides yet another example of how a group in its zeal to stamp out the use of alcohol and tobacco can have a negative effect on education. Although the program advocated teaching scientifically verified facts (i.e., the effects of these substances on human health), often the teaching and instructional materials contained a mixture of misconceptions, myths, and facts. Moreover, the laws requiring the teaching of these subjects were often poorly conceived and educationally unworkable.

In the early decades of this century, acute infectious diseases represented one of the most serious health problems. As scientific knowledge progressed, these diseases were controlled, and chronic diseases became the focus of research.

Determining the goals and objectives of health education

The 1973 report of the President's Committee on Health Education revealed a general confusion and lack of agreement over the goals of health education. The public hearings conducted by the committee revealed the fact that two different approaches were being advocated for health education. One approach held that the goal of health education was to facilitate the achievement of the highest optimal level of health by the individual—a concept of health similar to that embraced by the World Health Organization. The other approach maintained that the goal of health education was disease prevention, emphasizing the prevention or management of specific conditions. The legislation that created the Office of Disease Prevention and Health Promotion, as well as recent publications of the Public Health Service issued under a similar title, indicate that the federal government is attempting to circumvent this controversy by including both the concept of positive health and that of disease prevention in its statement of the goal of health education.

The fact that health education originated in two fields, health and education, may explain this difference in orientation. The field of health has long been dominated by the influence of medicine, with its focus on the treatment and control of disease. Education's major influence on the field focuses on the nurturing of the individual's growth and development, or health promotion.

How are the goals of health education to be selected or defined? School programs, responsible for many different curriculums and program specialties, should maintain an on-going process of selecting or defining goals. To ensure that the goals of a particular school program are consistent with those of the larger mission or purpose of the educational enterprise, a careful survey of the educational literature pertaining to the fundamental purpose of schooling should be conducted (Fig. 12-3). Sources that may be consulted when writing or selecting program goals include the following:

1. State and federal legislation (especially that which is mandatory)
2. Literature pertaining to local and national concerns
3. Goals of other programs, especially those considered to be exemplary
4. Parental concerns and requests and special study reports on program needs

In general terms, the purposes or goals of education focus on the development of cognitive abilities and positive habits of the individual. In American society, schools play a major role in helping to establish an ideal democratic society in which respect, justice, and fair play should provide firsthand experiences with ethical values. Thus a general goal of education is to provide students with an opportunity to learn the responsibilities of adulthood and citizenship (Tyler, 1975). Although these general goals of education may not be specifically identified

FIG. 12-3.   Special references and reports used in curriculum planning.

as health goals, nevertheless it is evident that health education can play a key role in the achievement of such aims.

Other goals of education stress personal, intellectual, creative, social, moral, emotional, and physical development. The relationship of these goals to health education is more obvious. Such general concepts as personal development, including a social consciousness, hold important implications for health education (Taylor, 1975).

Traditionally health education has been characterized by its threefold objectives of health: knowledge, attitudes, and behavior. However, the degree to which these objectives are emphasized is determined largely by the point of view held regarding the purpose of health education and the theory of learning or theory of behavior change.

In this modern era the U.S. Public Health Service and the Office of the Surgeon General have exerted a major influence on all Americans and their health behavior. The release in 1979 of the report *Healthy People* and in 1990 of the report *Healthy People 2000* placed great emphasis on the role of education in developing health-promoting and disease-preventing behaviors. School health education is expected to play a key role in helping to achieve the nation's health objectives for the year 2000.

The implementation of comprehensive school health programs is essential if the effort to prevent the needless loss of life among the young is to succeed. Nearly 70% of the deaths for ages 1 to 24 years are caused by: (1) motor vehicle crashes, (2) other accidents, (3) homicides, and (4) suicides (Koble, 1990)

Personal habits play critical roles in the development of many serious diseases, as well as in injuries from violence and automobile accidents.

Analysis of the health problems affecting different age groups in American society (infants, children, adolescents, and adults) calls for changes in behavior or life-style. It is clear that health education programs committed to reducing many of these problems are attracting widespread support. The landmark Carnegie Commission report *Turning Points* (1989) stresses this point:

> Young adolescents are far more at risk for self-destructive behaviors—educational failures, drug and alcohol abuse, school age pregnancy, contracton of sexually transmitted diseases, and violence— than their age group ever was before . . .

Many of these problems, it is argued, are the result of environmental and social factors; as such, they are not amenable to medical care or to methods of medical intervention. This same point of view was expressed years earlier in former New York Governor Rockefeller's report on Social Problems and Health and Hospital Services and Costs (Governor's Steering Committee on Social Problems, 1971), "Prevention and sound maintenance are as much an individual responsibility as they are a medical responsibility."

In the field of health, education has established new concepts of disease prevention and health promotion, accepting a model of health (see Fig. 11-1) that recognizes the roles of (1) heredity, (2) environment (including physical, social, and psychological factors), (3) health services, and (4) life-style factors and behavior in an expanding concept of health.

Deciding what to teach not only calls for an examination of the structure of knowledge about health but also a determination of the most effective approach to use from the standpoint of the teaching-learning process or curriculum design.

What should be the parameters of the health education curriculum? Can a comprehensive view of health be taught, as implied in Bruner's thesis (1960) that children can be taught to understand the essential intellectual concepts of *any* subject? Or is a child-centered approach that focuses on the particular developmental stages of growth more appropriate? Regardless of the approach to be taken, Goodlad et al. (1979) have called for the establishment of a comprehensive and coherent framework for curriculum design.

A FRAMEWORK FOR CURRICULUM DESIGN

According to Goodlad et al.'s conceptual scheme (1979), content and behavior are the organized elements of a curriculum design. Such a design may be depicted graphically in the form of a chart with the behavioral elements written along a *vertical* axis and the substantive elements (subject matter) presented along the *horizontal* axis. This illustration provides an adaptation such as might be used for the development of a health education curriculum. The specific learning objectives for students are determined by the points at which the columns of subject matter elements intersect the rows of the behavioral elements. Table 12-1 depicts three elements of the teaching-learning plan for each of four health topics that might be part of a larger comprehensive curriculum. There is a progression in both the level of behavioral outcomes and for each of the subject matter topics. The squares represent segments in the total design of a comprehensive curriculum.

In terms of the levels of decision making, the squares where the learning objectives are identified constitute the points at which the decision making of superintendent and school district staffs (institutional level) separates from the decisions that are now to be made at the instructional level. The responsibility for determining student learning outcomes, teaching

TABLE 12-1. Conceptual framework for health education curriculum

Behavior elements	Smoking, alcohol, and drugs	Diet and nutrition	Safety and first aid	Family life and sex education	Organizing elements (content + objectives)
Level III behavioral objectives	Differentiate between use and misuse of alcohol	Explain relationship between nutritional status and health	Analyze the relationship between accidents and emotions	Compare and contrast male and female reproductive systems	
Level II behavioral objectives	Explain the effect of alcohol on the body	Illustrate variety of food in a good diet	Illustrate relationships between accidents and human behavior	Explain body changes occurring in puberty	Learning Objectives
Level I behavioral objectives	Identify uses of alcohol	Identify	Describe an accident and how to prevent it	List similarities and differences between boys and girls	

Adapted from Goodlad JI, et al: *Curriculum inquiry: the study of curriculum practice,* New York, 1979, McGraw-Hill.

methods, study materials, and the evaluation of student learning are decisions made at the school and classroom level. Again, according to Goodlad, the activities emanating from the learning objectives constitute the organizing centers. Traditionally these elements of the curriculum have been identified as teaching units or, in more contemporary terms, as teaching modules.

COMPREHENSIVE CURRICULUM VERSUS CATEGORICAL HEALTH PROBLEMS CURRICULUM

The scope of teaching about health and disease prevention has gradually evolved and expanded. This expansion results from the new knowledge gained from technological advances, from society's accumulated experiences in learning to apply principles of disease prevention, and from the development of ways to promote health.

With this expanding knowledge, curriculum planners and learning theorists have generally advocated the adoption of a comprehensive approach to health education. Health education specialists and school policy-making groups also support this approach. For example, in a recent statement the Education Commission of the States (1981) recommends that "state education agencies should promote the development of *comprehensive* school health education programs."

In discussing the nature of such a curriculum, the term *comprehensive* may be characterized in at least two ways. First, a comprehensive curriculum includes all grade levels from kindergarten to grade 12, and instruction should be provided for all students. Second, a comprehensive curriculum presents an all-inclusive treatment of health topics.

Essentially health educators do not differ as to whether a health education curriculum plan should be comprehensive and coherent. There are differences of opinion about *what* should be taught and *when* it should be taught to students. Some of these arguments stem from ideologic differences, whereas others are based on practical considerations and realistic expectations.

From the curriculum reform movement of the 1960s and 1970s, which supported a comprehensive treatment of subject matter, emerged the theory that the study of health can be organized into a conceptual structure, which in turn can be presented as a curriculum plan. This material can be taught in an articulated sequence of learning experiences, beginning in the elementary school and continuing through high school. The goal of this approach is the development of a health-educated citizenry.

As expressed in PL 95-561, the Health Education Act of 1978, the comprehensive school health program provides learning experiences based on the best available scientific information in an effort to promote the understanding, attitudes, behavioral skills, and practices of students (1) to prevent illness, disease, and injury and (2) to enhance the physical and mental health of the individual, family, and community.

The act identifies 21 different health topics, which are to be organized into a progressive sequence of learning activities taught through the elementary and secondary school years. Forty- two states require health education to be offered in schools . . . 28 of the 42 states requiring health education specify that they require "comprehensive school health education" (Corry, 1992). Table 12-2 contains an example of a comprehensive health education curriculum plan.

TABLE 12-2. A scope and sequence for a comprehensive health education curriculum

Suggested topics	Grade emphasis			
	K-3	4-6	Junior high	Senior high
Personal cleanliness and appearance	X	X	Omit	Omit
Physical activity, sleep, rest, and relaxation	X	X	X	Omit
Nutrition and growth	X	X	X	Omit
Dental health	X	X	X	Omit
Body structure and operation (including the senses and skin)	X	X	X	Omit
Prevention and control of disease	X	X	X	Omit*
Safety and first aid	X	X	X	Omit
Mental health	X	X	X	X
Sex and family living education	X	X	X	X
Environmental and community health	X	X	X	X
Alcohol, drugs, and tobacco	Omit	X	X	X
Consumer health	Omit	X	X	X
World health	Omit	Omit	Omit	X
Health careers	Omit	Omit	X	X

From Willgoose CG: *J Sch Health* 43:189, 1973.

*Decisions regarding which topics will receive emphasis at a particular grade level are determined at the state and local school level. However, in view of the current AIDS epidemic, no doubt the topic of infectious disease would be emphasized at all educational levels.

Despite the less than satisfactory progress to date in implementing comprehensive programs, several positive steps have been taken. In the 1988 Hawkins-Stafford Elementary Education Improvement Act, Congress reauthorized an Office of Comprehensive School Health Education within the U.S. Department of Education. The U.S. Public Health Service also established the Division of Adolescent and School Health. This governmental unit has undertaken a major effort in addressing health risks that are causing most mortality and morbidity among adolescents including (1) sexual behaviors resulting in diseases such as AIDS and unintended pregnancies, (2) drug and alcohol use, (3) tobacco use, (4) dietary patterns contributing to disease, (5) insufficient physical activity, and (6) unintentional and intentional injuries.

In a further statement of support, the report *Healthy People 2000* (1990) has included among its objectives for the nation "Increase to at least 75 percent of the nation's elementary and secondary schools provision for a planned and sequential (K-12) school health education."

Seffrin (1990) in his article on closing the gap between what is and what ought to be offers a number of specific steps to enable states to achieve commprehensive programs. He has offered recommendations that are appropriate to several levels of action, including steps to be taken at the state management level, sources of support available at the federal level, the professional preparation necessary for elementary and secondary teachers, and recommendations to state education agencies for developing up-to-date curriculum guidelines.

Proponents of the comprehensive approach contend that health-promoting principles and theories of disease causation can be generalized and that such principles may be transferred and applied by the learner to all conditions to satisfy health needs. According to this view, health is a quality of life involving a dynamic interaction and interdependence among the different aspects of health. These include the physical, mental-emotional, social, and spiritual dimensions of health. Thus it is argued that, if a person is to be truly healthy, health must be understood in its totality (Sliepcevich, 1968).

The advocates of a comprehensive health education curriculum criticize the categorical problem approach on the grounds that it often becomes the teaching of health education by crisis. Examples of a categorized problem approach would include teaching about a specific problem such as alcohol, drugs, smoking, sex education, or sexually transmitted disease. Such programs are usually launched with little planning and often without adequate resources or support. Typically, the program veers from one new development to another topical issue, moving from one crisis to the next, with health education forced to draw its support from whatever problem has temporarily captured the public's interest. For example, in the 1960s, the problem was the issue of cigarette smoking, followed by the drug crisis of the 1970s. Current problems include unintended pregnancies, sexually transmitted diseases, unintentional and intentional injuries, use and misuse of alcohol and other drugs. This approach means a constant shifting of priorities as well as program activity. Programs lack the stability essential to long-range planning, as well as the systematic progress necessary for achievement of long-term goals.

It is argued that approaching health education from a categorical disease perspective is both limiting and artificial. Teaching about health by focusing on health problems is a negative orientation that falls far short of the goal of health education. The disease, or health problems approach, is inefficient, emphasizing the disease manifestation rather than the more positive and productive approaches of disease prevention and health promotion. There is not enough time in the curriculum for health education if every health problem is to be taught. Finally, a categorical disease approach is poor pedagogy. Teaching about specific diseases, apart from the general study of health and disease, is like teaching the concepts of multiplication apart from the context of mathematics.

On the other side of the argument, however, critics of the comprehensive program contend that it is too general and too vague to be meaningful or to be communicated effectively. Instead, they argue for a specific problem approach. This approach can be communicated to people, taking advantage of their natural interest and motivation to solve problems. In support of this approach, proponents point to the many voluntary and governmental organizations that have successfully conducted programs to deal with categorical problems. Further, it is argued that organizing health education around a problem approach need not fall into the trap of overemphasis on the disease entity to the exclusion of health concerns. Instead, this approach can also develop the students' understanding of general principles of disease prevention and health promotion that are applicable to all aspects of life. In addition, directing the health education effort to the most important health problems for a particular age group offers the advantage of concentrating limited resources where the need is greatest and the greatest benefits may be achieved.

Critics of the comprehensive approach have argued that the failure of states to implement effective comprehensive school health education programs, even when such programs have carried the force of mandatory legislation, points out the weaknesses and impracticality of this approach. Such programs represent a major undertaking and commitment on the part of the school. In an era of limited budgets, state and local school systems lack the resources to implement a program of such magnitude.

Finally, in support of a categorical health problems curriculum, several voluntary, commercial, and governmental agencies have developed excellent curriculum modules around specific or categorical problems. Because there are high-quality materials already available, the school can implement specific health topic programs at relatively low cost. The fact that such programs are targeted for a specific problem often means that they are more likely to be undertaken by the school. Visibility of a categorical problem approach also may attract support from a community agency whose goals are closely related to those of the school. Instead of languishing on the shelf of the curriculum writer, these categorical programs have shown steady and consistent growth. In particular, the health education curriculums relating to cardiovascular disease, cancer, and personal risk behaviors such as smoking, diet, and alcohol are being implemented in a growing number of schools.

A major force that moved schools toward a categorical health problems approach during the 1980s was the availability of a small grants program entitled Health Education Risk Reduction Projects, which was made available to schools through state health departments. The purpose of this activity was to develop and test school health education risk-reduction curriculums. Typically these programs include the health topics identified under the health promotion category of the report, *Promoting Health and Preventing Disease: Objectives for the Nation* (U.S. Department of Health and Human Services, 1980). These health topics are included in the 15 priority areas identified in the U.S. Surgeon General's report *Healthy People* (1979) listed in Box 12-1. Schools were strongly encouraged by the U.S. Public Health Service to develop health education programs around the five areas of health promotion.

The Drug-Free Schools and Communities Act of 1986 has been an important source of funding for developing and implementing drug education in the schools. Unfortunately officials in the U.S. Department of Education apparently do not believe that drug education should be treated as part of the health education curriculum. Although on one hand comprehensive health education is advocated, on the other the use of Drug Free Schools and Communities funds for comprehensive health education is discouraged (Corry, 1992).

School Health Education Study: comprehensive approach

Health Education: A Conceptual Design for Curriculum Development is an example of a comprehensive treatment of health or a conceptual structure of health as a subject. It also represents an effort to apply learning theory to curriculum planning in health education. Often such projects are eclectic, using several different principles of learning rather than following a particular approach. In some respects, The School Health Education Study (SHES) is an example of this, drawing on principles derived from both the cognitive and the connectionist traditions. Whereas school practitioners have sometimes been criticized for failing to adopt a consistent overall theory to guide the instructional program, common sense may dictate the use of both kinds of interpretations in certain instances. As Hill (1963) has observed, some principles of

BOX
12-1
Promoting health and preventing disease: objectives for the nation

Preventive health services

1. High blood pressure control
2. Family planning
3. Pregnancy and infant health
4. Immunization
5. Sexually transmitted diseases

Health promotion

1. Smoking and health
2. Misuse of alcohol and drugs
3. Nutrition
4. Physical fitness and exercise
5. Control of stress and violent behavior

Health protection

1. Toxic agent control
2. Occupational safety and health
3. Accident prevention and injury control
4. Fluoridation and dental health
5. Surveillance and control of infectious diseases

learning appear to apply in all situations, whereas others are germane only in particular circumstances.

However, examination of the SHES conceptual model for curriculum design reveals that it is more characteristic of the field, or cognitive, theory of learning. The SHES model is based on the concept of health that serves as the focal point in formulating a structure of health and from which the framework for health education is derived (see Table 12-2).

The term *health* implies a wholeness or, as modern-day philosophers and scholars have contended, a dynamic process in which the individual is functioning in harmony both with his or her total self and with the total environment. The next step is to determine the principal ideas to be elaborated on if a structure is to be devised that is at once logical for curriculum development, meaningful to the learner, and a valid representation of ideas held to be true by the scientist and the philosopher.

Health is the comprehensive, unified concept at the apex of the hierarchy developed for the conceptual model for health and health education. It has three dimensions—physical, mental, and social. More specifically, physical health pertains to the structure and function of the biologic organism; mental health pertains to behavior and personality patterns; and social health includes the complex of interpersonal and societal forces. Health is a quality of life involving dynamic interaction and interdependence among the individual's physical well-being, his or her mental and emotional reactions, and the social complex in which he or she exists. Any one dimension may play a greater or lesser role than the other two at a given time, but the interdependence and interaction of the three dimensions still hold true (Sliepcevich, 1968).

This view of the individual and his or her health closely parallels Lewin's (Zais, 1976) contention that learning refers to a multitude of different phenomena. He argues that we cannot have a clear understanding of learning unless we take into account the entire complex psychologic world that he calls the life space of the individual.

The hierarchy of concepts portrays the unified concept of health at the apex or highest order in the model. Following immediately are the three key concepts of growing and developing, interacting, and decision making, which are considered to be the unifying threads of the curriculum (Fig. 12-4). These three features are peculiar to all human beings, and from the standpoint of health education they are essential to the understanding of the individual's health problems and the forces affecting health behavior. Thus they are considered to be the processes that underlie health.

These three concepts are consistent with the cognitive theory of motivation that may be regarded as a theory of preferential choice or of decision making. The decision to become involved is made on the basis of cognitive considerations (Hill, 1963). For example, consider the importance of the key concept of growth and development to the curriculum planner and health education teacher in the case of a 14-year-old boy whose pubescence is late in developing. Frequently such a boy suffers severe emotional disturbances because his associates of the same age are not only sexually more mature but are also bigger and stronger than he is. Consider the impact of his state of growth and development on his social interaction with boys and girls of his same age. What kind of effect will his physical development have on his choices and decisions about participating in sports and physical activity? Will it affect his decision about diet?

Next come the 10 concepts and subconcepts that represent the scope of the subject matter treated in health education. The 10 concepts and subconcept, together with the behavioral objectives, according to Goodlad's curriculum nomenclature (1963), are the "organizing elements" of the curriculum. According to this scheme, the concepts and subconcepts include 31 different health topics.

These broad content areas have been phrased in conceptual statements to give more meaning and direction to the teaching-learning process. For example, instead of using the term *accident prevention,* the following conceptual statement is given: "The potential for hazards and accidents exists, whatever the environment." This is considered to be more descriptive, as well as prescriptive, insofar as health education is concerned.

The long-range goals and behavioral objectives are derived from the conceptual structure representing that which is to be learned (see Table 12-1). The goals and behavioral objectives represent the educational outcomes that are sought (i.e., various health behaviors, including the way students think, feel, and act with regard to health). The goals are long-term, general outcomes, whereas the behavioral objectives are specific outcomes. Similarly, goals are the result of the total health education experience, whereas behavioral objectives are those designed for a particular educational level. Also in keeping with the instructional level of decision making, classroom teachers worked with the curriculum designers in developing the behavioral objectives for student instruction.

These characteristics of the SHES curriculum point to other similarities of the field, or cognitive theories, approach. For learning to occur, it is essential that the student pursue goals that the individual student considers to be his or her own. Adopting both affective and cognitive goals with constant attention to the three unifying key concepts serves as a constant reminder to the curriculum planner to be ever aware of the individual student's needs.

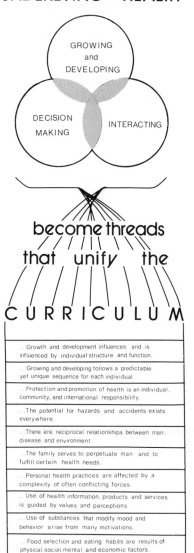

FIG. 12-4.   SHES—three key concepts.

To apply the SHES conceptual model to teaching, each concept is analyzed and translated into priority behavioral objectives at four different educational levels (as opposed to the three levels illustrated in Goodlad's framework) beginning with level I and progressing through level IV. Here the SHES model draws on the connectionist theory of learning, which calls for the writing of objectives in precise, observable, and measurable behaviors. Behaviors considered appropriate to the desired outcomes must be identified and carefully arranged in a progression of increasingly complex behaviors. This is similar to the approach used by the advocates of behavior modification, based on the principles developed by Thorndike, Guthrie, Watson, and Skinner. According to the behaviorist, establishing complex social behavior and modifying existing response patterns can be achieved most consistently through a gradual process in which the person participates in an orderly learning sequence that guides him or her stepwise toward more intricate or demanding performances (Bandura, 1969).

To illustrate how this progression is developed in the SHES model, behavioral objectives were developed from the concept: *food selection and eating patterns are determined by physical, social, mental, economic, and cultural factors* (Box 12-2). Behavioral objectives from each of the four educational levels are illustrated to show the sequences and progressions of these behaviors. The similarity to Goodlad's conceptual scheme is readily apparent.

Behavior modification: categorical health problems approach

Golaszewski (1979) developed an innovative composite behavior modification model for use in school health education programs. His proposal, similar to previous efforts to apply learning theory in schools, draws to some extent on both the connectionist and cognitive traditions of learning. This composite model provides a good example of behavior modification as the application of connectionist theory to school health education. As Golaszewski points out, in any attempt to develop an ideal program, the following points should be considered: (1) a multitude of environmental influences shape the child's behaviors; therefore the tendency to take an overly simplistic view of learning and behavior must be avoided; (2) many individual variations exist, resulting from ethnic and cultural differences; and (3) the constraints of school finances, school policies, and biases of the health educator affect curriculum decisions.

The three steps of the composite model include the following:

1. Providing for student participation through appropriate laboratory experiences. For example, in teaching a unit on heart disease, activities such as an exercise stress test, serum lipid evaluations, blood pressure measurements, and growth measurements might be included. Such measures can be related to results taken from actual student

---

BOX 12-2   **Progression of behavioral objectives by education level**

Concept 10: Food selection and eating patterns are determined by physical, social, mental, economic, and cultural factors

Level I   *Identifies* —many different kinds of foods
                   ↓

Level II   *Illustrates*—that a variety of foods are necessary in maintaining a balanced diet
                   ↓

Level III   *Describes* —the relationship between nutritional status and disease
                   ↓

Level IV   *Applies*   —criteria for selecting foods and planning meals that provide for a balanced diet

surveys of behavior, such as eating, exercise, and smoking habits. Data from this step can be used as the basis for developing goals for behavior change.

2. Providing students with the information necessary for them to build a knowledge base required for rational decision making. This procedure draws on the cognitive theory of learning for behavior change. Since the objectives of this unit are to reduce the risk of heart disease, information to be included should relate to the need to eat a nutritious diet low in fats, to avoid cigarette smoking, to exercise regularly, to control blood pressure, and to make appropriate use of health care services. A variety of teaching aids, including multimedia tapes, film reports, and guest appearances of experts, is needed to ensure the validity of the content material and to stimulate student interest.

3. Providing value clarification activities that delineate actual and ideal behavior patterns aimed at preventing disease and promoting health. A major purpose of this step is the use of student participation in the setting of personal goals. Each student is expected to formulate a written plan of action to meet this goal. The goal selected should be measurable, related to a specific time period, and realistic for the student. In keeping with the self-management or self-care approach, the student should provide a plan for monitoring progress and a system of rewarding or reinforcing the desired behavior.

To help ensure the success of a behavior modification approach in school health education, the following procedure for the teacher is recommended:

1. Review all student plans to determine their appropriateness and feasibility
2. Follow a contract-grading procedure, in which each step of progress is appropriately rewarded
3. Organize the class into small groups of students having similar goals; encourage students to make a group commitment and share both their progress and their problems
4. Include the technique of mental imagery in student learning activities; this encourages the student to visualize goal achievement, such as losing 20 pounds (9 kg) of weight or being able to jog 3 miles or stop smoking; the student then imagines being rewarded for achieving the goal and receiving compliments on the results
5. Provide opportunities for the students to give a public demonstration after goal achievement; for example, a diet group might give a "health meal" demonstration, an exercise group might sponsor a special road race, and an antismoking group might give a special class presentation to younger students in the school
6. Arrange special booster sessions or programs that will provide reinforcement for student progress toward goal achievement (e.g., giving awards to students for adopting a new behavior or recognizing students who lose weight)

Growing Healthy

Originally the Growing Healthy curriculum was known as the School Health Curriculum Project (SHCP). In its earlier form it represented a categorical health problems approach for health instruction at the elementary and middle or junior high school levels. However, since its inception, Growing Healthy has been greatly expanded. It now includes a curriculum plan that progresses from the primary grades to middle school and continues through high school. As such it can perhaps best be described as a middle-ground approach between that of a narrowly focused categorical health problems approach and that of a comprehensive curriculum. The

Health care for the adolescent

EMERGING ISSUE The U.S. Congress, Office of Technology Assessment (OTA), completed a 3-year study of adolescent health care in 1991. The conventional wisdom that the American adolescents as a group are so healthy that they don't need health-related services is not justified. In fact, adolescents face serious difficulty in obtaining needed services. Among these barriers to their health care are the following: (1) health insurance coverage may be lacking or health services may be unavailable for those in poverty; (2) the type of preventive services needed by adolescents such as dental, psychologic, eye examinations and refraction, and speech therapy may not be available; (3) laws requiring parental consent may apply; (4) in cases in which parental consent is not required, the adolescent may have concerns about the confidentiality of the services; (5) adolescents may lack information about health services and how to access them; (6) and cultural and ethnic barriers may exist.

OTA concluded that a different orientation to health services for adolescents is needed. In addition to health promotion and problem prevention, adolescents may need a specialized type of service such as suicide prevention, drug abuse information, pregnancy prevention, mental health services, and care for sexually transmitted diseases.

One strategy recommended by OTA for improving adolescents' access to health care would be the development of school-based or school-linked comprehensive health services specifically for adolescents.

As a member of the school health council you are asked to indicate whether you generally agree or disagree with this proposal by placing a plus (+) or a minus (−) sign before each of the following statements.

_____ 1. I don't believe it is realistic to think that school-based clinics can be established in the schools.

_____ 2. Although a school-based clinic approach would be ideal, I believe a community-based clinic is more feasible.

_____ 3. I like the idea of a school-based clinic, except for the areas of family counseling and pregnancy prevention services.

_____ 4. I oppose school-based clinics on the belief that this is not an appropriate function of public schools.

_____ 5. I favor the school-based clinic plan because it provides comprehensive and confidential services for the adolescent.

_____ 6. The school-based plan appeals to me because it makes needed services readily accessible to the adolescent.

_____ 7. I like the school-based clinic approach but would favor a plan that includes all students (K through 12).

_____ If limited to a single choice, I would choose this number.

curriculum began as an experimental project in California during the early 1960s and was first taught to intermediate grade school children as an in-depth study of the heart and circulatory system. It was first known as the "Berkeley Project" but was later given the title of the School Health Curriculum Project when it came under the sponsorship of the U.S. Public Health Service. Its general purpose is to help children learn how their bodies function in a normal, healthy state and the changes that occur when disease strikes. The effects of the environment and living habits on the body are stressed.

The goal of the curriculum is to help the child realize that the body is each person's greatest natural resource in life, is uniquely one's own, is exquisitely beautiful and complex in its structure and function, and is affected by the choices one makes throughout life (U.S. Department of Health, Education and Welfare, 1977). From a health perspective, children are taught about the importance of controlling events in their lives that might create a serious health problem, such as heart disease or cancer. In brief, the Growing Healthy program is (1) a curriculum, (2) a method of teaching, and (3) a training program for classroom teachers in health education. The curriculum focuses on the healthy body and ways of maintaining it. Acitivities are designed to involve and motivate a wide range of persons associated with the school, including students, teachers, school administrators, school health staff, community resource people, staffs of volunteer agencies, and parents.

The curriculum plan is designed for the elementary school, kindergarten through grade 7. The primary grades (K-3) unit studies the senses, whereas successive grade levels from four through seven represents a study of a different organ system at each level, including units on the digestive system, the lungs and respiratory system, the heart and circulatory system, and the brain and nervous system.

The curriculum uses a common organization (Fig. 12-5; Box 12-3).
- Introduction: curiosity arousal and motivation of students
- Phase one: overview of the body's system
- Phase two: appreciation of one of the body's systems and its unique function
- Phase three: structure and function of the body system
- Phase four: diseases and problems of the body system
- Phase five: care of the body and prevention of disease
- Culmination: synthesis, through group presentations of the previous phases

Developers of the curriculum contend that using the same teaching approach serves to reinforce the children's understanding of the concept that all body systems are related and that any single event affecting a part of the body affects the whole body and the total health of the person.

Audiovisual materials, including films, filmstrips, slides, tape recorders, and records, are used extensively to stimulate the children's interest. Models and dissection and analysis of animal organs make the study of health more realistic. Such concrete experiences help the student to personalize the relationship between living habits and their effect on the body.

This curriculum involves the use of a learning center of five or six stations, enabling children to participate in several different learning activities simultaneously. Children study in small groups, rotating through each of the stations in the learning center, actively involved in the learning process (see Fig. 12-5). For example, a series of activities are developed around the study of circulation, including tracing the locations of arteries and veins, examining red blood cells under the microscope, and learning to take blood pressure. Groups rotate every 30 minutes or at the end of each period, depending on the complexity of the task.

Schools wishing to initiate the curriculum are required to send a team of four or five members to a special training center. The team is composed of at least two classroom teachers who

CHART OF THE PHASES (EXAMPLE 1)

Teacher Reference
Day 3

(Diagram to make chart for use at the end of Introduction Phase)

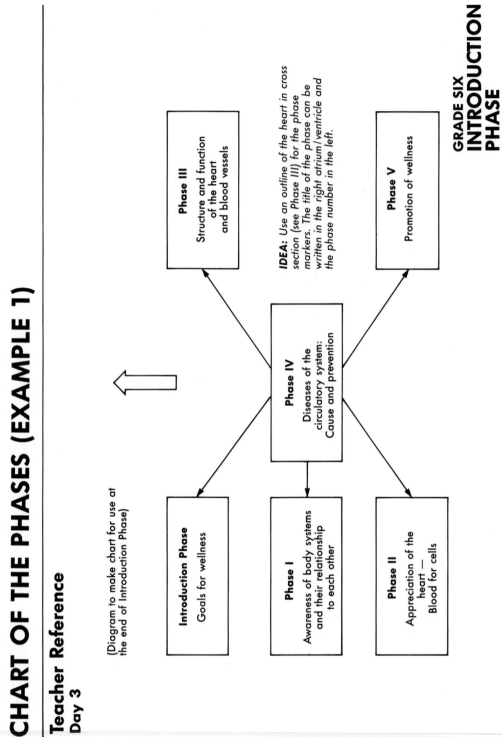

Phase III
Structure and function of the heart and blood vessels

IDEA: Use an outline of the heart in cross section (see Phase III) for the phase markers. The title of the phase can be written in the right atrium/ventricle and the phase number in the left.

Phase V
Promotion of wellness

Phase IV
Diseases of the circulatory system: Cause and prevention

Introduction Phase
Goals for wellness

Phase I
Awareness of body systems and their relationship to each other

Phase II
Appreciation of the heart —
Blood for cells

**GRADE SIX
INTRODUCTION
PHASE**

CHART OF THE PHASES (EXAMPLE 2)

Teacher Reference

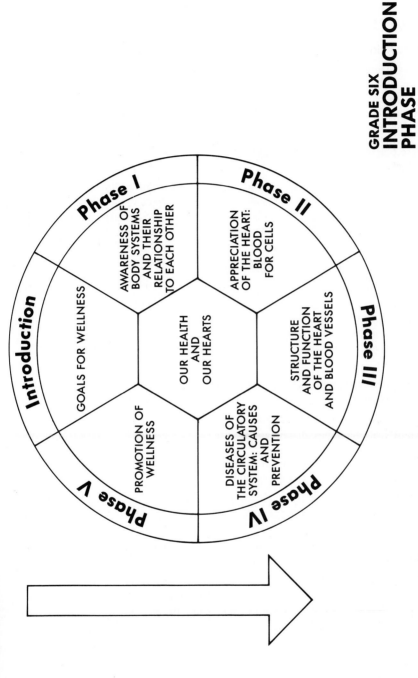

GRADE SIX
**INTRODUCTION
PHASE**

Introduction

Phase I

AWARENESS OF
BODY SYSTEMS
AND THEIR
RELATIONSHIP
TO EACH OTHER

GOALS FOR WELLNESS

OUR HEALTH
AND
OUR HEARTS

Phase II

APPRECIATION
OF THE HEART:
BLOOD
FOR CELLS

STRUCTURE
AND FUNCTION
OF THE HEART
AND BLOOD VESSELS

Phase III

PROMOTION OF
WELLNESS

DISEASES OF
THE CIRCULATORY
SYSTEM: CAUSES
AND
PREVENTION

Phase IV

Phase V

FIG. 12-5.   Five phases of *Growing Healthy: Our Health and Our Hearts.*

Unit 5—About our lungs

Introduction: Curiosity arousal about air

The existence of air
The body's need for air
Life needs air
Artificial resuscitation demonstration
Your breath can save somebody's life

Phase one: Overview of the body's systems

Skeletal system   Excretory system
Muscular system   Endocrine system
Respiratory system   Reproductive system
Circulatory system   Nervous system
Digestive system

Phase two: Appreciation of air and lungs

Essence of air
Properties of air
Functions of air
How the human body uses air
Pollution and its effects on the respiratory system

Phase three: Structure and function of the respiratory system

Nasal passages, trachea, bronchial tubes, bronchioles, alveoli, lungs, diaphragm, rib cage, cells
Inhalation, exhalation, oxygen-carbon dioxide exchange with blood, cleansing system

Phase four: Diseases and problems of the respiratory system

Communicable diseases: colds, flu, pneumonia, bronchitis, etc.
Noncommunicable diseases: allergy, asthma, emphysema, lung cancer, heart disease

Phase five: Care of body and prevention of respiratory diseases

Clean air/pollution
   Effects of tobacco smoke
   Good and harmful effects of drugs
   Nutrition
   Rest
   Exercise

Culmination: The respiratory system

Activities planned and executed by children, including skits, games, poster presentation, etc., presented to class or to the total school community, including parents

From The School Health Curriculum Project, Washington, D.C., DHEW Pub. No. (CDC) 78-8359, U.S. Department of Health, Education and Welfare, Public Health Service, Centers for Disease Control, Bureau of Health Education, Atlanta, 1977, HEW Publications.

will teach the unit at a particular grade level. Other members of the team include the principal and two other persons such as a nurse, a health educator, or a curriculum specialist. These teams participate in a training session of 60 hours for each unit. During this intensive training workshop, teachers are introduced to each step of the unit exactly as it will be taught to their classes. After the teacher has successfully taught the program, he or she then must conduct a training session for other teachers in the school district to ensure the dissemination of the model throughout the school system.

Strengths of the Growing Healthy approach include a clear definition of each unit, which facilitates the understanding and preparation of the classroom teacher. The variety of audio-visual aids, teaching materials, and learning activities makes the curriculum interesting to both students and teachers. The active participation of the student in his or her learning, the involvement of community health agencies in providing resources for the curriculum, and the interest of parents in the health problem being studied not only facilitate learning but also provide a broad base of support and reinforcement to the student (Fig. 12-6).

This curriculum has not been identified with a particular learning theory but is based on principles that have evolved from a distillation of empirically tested school practices. Widely accepted principles of instruction evident in the project include the following: (1) the active involvement of the learner, (2) the extensive use of concrete learning activities, (3) the use of cooperative group learning activities, and (4) the structured yet flexible program that allows for variation in student abilities. Several of the principles derived from the cognitive learning theory are employed in the emphasis on motivation and the recognition of structure and its interrelationship in the study of body systems. Perhaps the characteristic that would most closely relate this curriculum to connectionist theory is its recognition of individual differences and its use of a variety of individual learning activities.

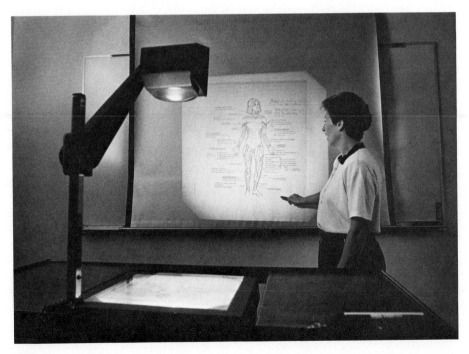

FIG. 12-6. Teachers use a variety of classroom activities to stimulate student interest and motivation to learn.

THE HEALTH TEACHING UNIT

Once the goals and the general framework of the health education curriculum have been established, the planning, organization, and instruction of the teaching unit can then proceed. Whether the unit is to be developed from its very inception or is to be adopted from a general teaching guide provided by the state or school district administration, the classroom teachers and personnel of the local school must play the central role in this final stage of curriculum construction. It is they, the teachers, who will make the decisions about the teaching strategies and learning activities that students will ultimately experience in the classroom.

The term *unit* implies a wholeness or unity of several elements. It has been defined as "an instructional sequence having distinct objectives and separate assessment" (Tyler, 1975). The unit is a manifestation of what Goodlad (1979) has called the "organizing centers of curriculum design" (see Table 12-1). Typically the unit includes (1) a title and an introduction or overview statement about the unit; (2) the goals, or long-range objectives; (3) the subject matter or health content to be learned by the student; (4) the methods or teaching strategies for presenting information or engaging the student in learning activities; (5) teaching aids to implement the effectiveness of classroom methods and learning activities; (6) the techniques for assessing the effects of the unit, in terms of the effectiveness of the teaching process and the degree to which students have achieved the intended learning outcomes; and (7) a compilation of resources for both the student and the teacher.

The unit of instruction is the basic building block of the total curriculum structure. It is the smallest complete teaching-learning segment of the curriculum (Fig. 12-7). How long should the unit be? Although no single time period meets all needs, there is general agreement that short units offer certain educational advantages. For example, a unit covering a shorter time frame provides early assessment and feedback to the student. This enables the teacher to assess the student's progress at an early point, when modification of the unit and student learning problems can be easily achieved. The demonstrated effectiveness of mastery teaching, with its relatively short teaching sequences and feedback to the student, has led to the recommendation that teaching units be planned for approximately 5 to 10 hours of instruction or 1 to 2 weeks in length.

Constructing the health unit

Title and overview. *The title and overview* of the unit often evolve from discussion and questions that are raised about a particular problem or health topic of interest. Discussions among teachers, students, school officials, parents, health officials, and other experts can be highly productive in identifying issues, concerns, and problems. Several sessions may be required to clarify questions and to determine the key ideas, focal points, or themes around which the unit can be developed. As Tyler (1975) has cautioned, teachers should resist the temptation to close this phase of planning too soon. There is much evidence to support the benefits to be derived from the appropriate involvement of such groups in planning for health instruction. Not the least of these benefits is the support for the health education program that is often engendered from such planning.

Depending on what the planning group and teaching faculty decide, the title selected for the unit may convey a particular theme. A catchy, provocative title or one that communicates

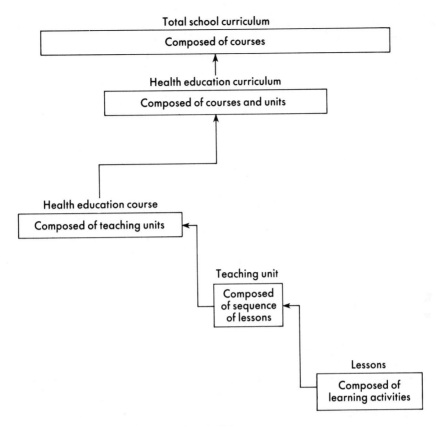

FIG. 12-7. A context for curriculum building.

simply and directly the health topic for the unit works best. For example, a title such as "The Psychology of Accidents" is intended to call attention to the importance of our emotions, attitudes, feelings, values, and interpersonal relationships as factors to be understood in the dynamics of accidents. Another example, "The Potential for Accidents Exists Whatever the Environment," serves both as a unit title and as one of the major ideas or conceptual statements making up the School Health Education Study Curriculum design. It is the organizing element for planning the teaching and learning activities that are designed to promote safety and prevent accidents.

The overview, or introduction to the unit, ideally provides a statement summarizing the characteristics, needs, and interests of the student group for whom the unit is designed. In addition, the overview contains a statement about the subject (i.e., the health problem) and its importance to the student and to the larger community or societal concerns. For example, an overview statement for a senior high school teaching unit on safety and accident prevention might include reference to the motor vehicle accident death rate for teenagers. The fact that these accidents are often related to drinking and that the rates for this age group have recently shown an increase gives added meaning to the curriculum planning.

Curriculum goals. Traditionally in health education such goals have been expressed as knowledge (cognitions), attitudes (affective domain), and health practices or applications. School curriculum goals have often been selected at the societal level (e.g., national or state goals). Examples of such goal statements are as follows:

Knowledge (cognitive domain): students will develop an understanding that accidents are related to human behavior, the physical environment, and the interaction of these factors.

Attitude (affective domain): students will become sensitive to the dangerous aspects of a changing environment.

Practice (action or application): students will attempt to make the environment safe, and they will assist or cooperate with others in such efforts (Fig. 12-8).

Instructional or behavioral objectives. Instructional and behavioral objectives are derived from the goals as long-range objectives that have been adopted by the district for the health education curriculum. Although there may be differences of opinion as to the exact nature or degree of precision required of instructional objectives, there is agreement on the purposes they are to serve. They direct the teaching process and determine the learning outcomes that are intended for the student. Accomplishing such a purpose requires special care and skill on the part of the teacher. Moreover, the writing of these objectives becomes the primary responsibility of the teachers who will teach the unit. A well-stated objective must specify the

FIG. 12-8.   Students practicing water rescue procedures.

observed behavior that a student will exhibit on achievement of the objective (Posner and Rudnitsky, 1978).

Specific behavior objectives shall also be written for the affective and practice or application domains.

Content outline. This section of the teaching unit probably should take precedence over all other aspects. The importance of the content and its relevance to the instructional objectives are fundamental to the success of the whole teaching effort. There are several steps to be taken that will help the curriculum committee develop the content section (Fig. 12-9). First, they should include or arrange to have the advice of a subject matter specialist. Because the health education curriculum includes such a wide array of health topics and technical subject matter, it becomes especially important to have the content reviewed and checked for both its timeliness and its accuracy. Although having the advice of a subject matter specialist or a discipline scholar does not ensure a correct decision on matters of pedagogy, it does protect against error and misconceptions in subject matter.

In this regard, Pratt (1980) has offered a series of questions that are useful to the curriculum writer.

1. Is the content relevant?
2. Is the material comprehensive?
3. Is the material interesting and challenging?
4. Is the quality of the material consistent?
5. Is the content logically organized?
6. Is the material current or easily updated?

FIG. 12-9. Curriculum planning calls for the special knowledge and perspectives of teachers, counselors, parents, and community personnel.

Second, a preliminary content outline should be prepared. Drawing on the ideas discussed earlier in relation to the goals, objectives, and overview statement will help to define and clarify the particular emphasis of the unit. Conducting a literature search, including the review of textbooks, periodic references, and other courses of study, is beneficial to the committee in helping them to become familiar with the subject matter. It is particularly important, at this juncture, that a well-developed and logically organized content outline be developed. Although the outline should have sufficient detail to reveal its structure, too much detail can be confusing.

Once a preliminary outline has been developed, it should be reviewed by a technical expert or subject matter specialist. This represents an important check on the curriculum committee's work—a content validation step to avoid the possibility of introducing errors into the curriculum. This step should be repeated periodically to ensure that the content is kept current and checked for scientific accuracy. The rapid growth of science and technology and its accompanying accelerated increase of information have caused psychologists and curriculum writers to seek new and more efficient ways to organize information to facilitate the teaching and learning process. The teacher and learner are confronted with a difficult problem in attempting to keep abreast of these new developments. This is the background that has given rise to a concept approach. This approach seeks out the basic principles, fundamental concepts, and methods that make up a large body of knowledge. Much of the interest in concepts learning stems from the belief that knowledge can be greatly simplified for teaching. Knowledge is not merely an accumulation of isolated bits of information, but instead is composed of a network of ideas.

One of the curriculum writers for the School Health Education Study, Means (1968) provides an example of how a conceptual approach can be used as the point of departure for the development of the major subtopics or generalizations relating to the conceptual statement: "The potential for accidents exists regardless of the environment."

The content outline for this teaching unit on high school safety is presented in its supporting detail as follows:

Subtopic—interpretation of accident data reveals a variety of implications (e.g., physical, mental, social, and economic)
1. Individual factors relating to accidents
   a. Physical defects
   b. Risk factors vary with age and occupation
   c. Mental and emotional states
2. Social and environmental factors
   a. Group pressures
   b. Laws
   c. Weather conditions
   d. Defective equipment
3. Consequences of accidents
   a. Temporary and permanent disability
   b. Mental anguish and human suffering
   c. Family and group disruption
   d. Economic costs
4. Using accident data to prevent accidents
   a. Planning safer cities

b. Improved laws and regulations
c. Safe location of public facilities (e.g., parks, schools, airports)
d. Educational programs

As each subtopic is written, it can be readily transformed into a student behavioral objective such as, "Students will be able to interpret accident data in terms of their various implications."

Posner and Rudnitsky (1978) described a method of "concept mapping" as a way of revealing the structure of a subject or discipline. Such a map provides a graphic representation of a conceptual structure and the various relationships completing the structure. Fig. 12-10 illustrates a conceptual map of the content or conceptual structure of a unit on basic rescue and water safety procedures (American Red Cross, 1983) for junior or middle school students.

The knowledge or cognitive objective: "Students will be able to explain the correct water assists to be used in attempting to rescue a potential drowning victim" (see Fig. 12-8).

Teaching strategies. Although there are no absolutes regarding the best method of teaching, there are several generalizations that can be made about teaching and that have been supported by experience and research. Certain teaching characteristics are known to have a positive effect on student achievement. For example, teachers who are effective tend to be warm, friendly, and outgoing; are enthusiastic about their teaching; are well organized in their presentations; are able to express themselves clearly; make effective use of gestures; and have a good sense of humor.

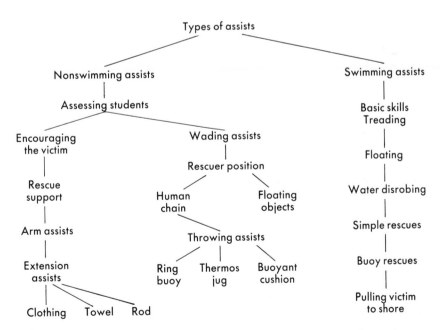

WATER SAFETY RESCUE ASSISTS

FIG. 12-10.   Conceptual mapping to develop an instructional outline for teaching a unit on water safety.

Pratt (1980) has offered a model composed of four key steps to guide the teacher and curriculum writer in selecting teaching strategies (Fig. 12-11).

Reviewing the instructional objectives should give a clear vision of what is intended as the learning outcomes for the student. This will also help the teacher decide on an effective teaching strategy. For example, the following instructional objective from the unit on water safety rescue indicates quite specifically the kind of teaching strategy to be used. "The student will be able to demonstrate how to rescue a victim using *nonswimming assists.*"

Being able to maintain student interest is of such importance that the teacher may be justified in selecting some classroom activities primarily for their interest value. Once having caught the students' interest, the thoughtful teacher should be able to focus their attention on the desired learning objective (see Fig. 12-6).

Research on teaching reveals that most teachers tend to rely too much on a limited number of teaching activities, such as teacher talk or "telling the student", teacher questioning, and student recitation. Increasing the variety of teaching methods increases student interest and teacher effectiveness. Consequently, teachers are encouraged to make a concerted effort to expand their teaching repertoire by drawing on the vast resources that are available to them. Understandably, teachers will have their preferences as to teaching style. However, using different teaching methods also recognizes that students learn in different ways.

Student motivation is also greatly enhanced by student interest. Being able to match the instructional objective with the interests and needs of the student is one of the keys to motivation. A long-accepted axiom in education holds that "success breeds success, and failure breeds failure," which is further validation of the concept of positive reinforcement. In this regard the reward system is widely used in education. Although both external and internal rewards are used, students tend to lose interest in external rewards once the goal has been achieved.

An interrelationship appears to exist between the desire for success, as a motivator, and the fear of failure. If success is perceived as too easily achieved, the lesson or learning risk may lose its value as an incentive. Correspondingly, if the learning task is sufficiently difficult that the probability of failure is about equal to that of success, the incentive value increases. Students tend to work hardest at tasks of intermediate difficulty. However, if the task is perceived as very difficult, with a high risk of failure, it is more likely to discourage the student from trying. Moreover, if the student tends to be too anxious, even a task of intermediate difficulty may lose its incentive value to the student (Atkinson, 1978).

Sequencing instruction has long been recognized as an important consideration in developing a teaching strategy. Furthermore, there is a consensus that learning should proceed from the simple to the complex, or from that which is familiar to that which is difficult and unknown. However, good reasons exist for varying the sequence of lessons. An unfamiliar,

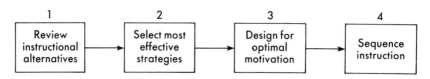

FIG. 12-11.   Main steps in selecting teaching strategies.

yet novel, learning activity may be effective in stimulating student interest. Introducing a unit by providing students with an overview or a general perspective of the problem before proceeding to the specifics may also increase student *interest* and *motivation* for learning.

Unit evaluation. In unit evaluation the emphasis is on formative rather than summative evaluation. Because the unit typically represents only 5 to 10 hours of instruction, the teacher's concern at this point is to learn how much progress students have made (formative evaluation) toward achieving the objectives. Summative evaluation comes after instruction has been completed. It is designed to answer the question, "How much did students achieve?"

The emphasis on formative evaluation provides another effective teaching method. As such, this form of evaluation must provide immediate feedback to the students. It can be done with the usual classroom tests that check student work and by informal observation of the student in class. It is important that the test results be fed back immediately, so that students may learn of and correct any errors that they may have made. When tests are used as a learning activity, they should not be used for grading purposes. Again, the emphasis of formative evaluation is on assessing, feeding back, and reinforcing by providing further encouragement, in order for the student to reach the maximal level of achievement.

Materials. There is an important distinction between the materials section of teaching and resource units. Teaching units include only those materials that have been selected by the teacher to serve a specific purpose, that is, to be used with a specific learning activity. The resource units, as the term implies, are a compilation of many materials from which the teacher may draw. Typically, the resource units are collected and kept in the curriculum library of the school district. Curriculum writing committees and classroom teachers use this resource in planning the teaching unit.

A major problem facing today's health education teacher is the challenge to keep up with all the new materials and teaching aids that are available. Fortunately, information systems such as bibliographies, indexes, abstracts, and periodicals are becoming available through computer-based information systems. Several of the computer-based indexes, including the American Psychological Association to psychological and social science literature, the readers guide to periodical literature, Index Medicus to medical and health literature, Education Resource Information Centers (ERICs), the Current Index to Journals in Education (CIJE), and related publications such as Resources in Education (RIE) information dissemination publications are available. In addition, there are several special subject indexes of topics such as smoking, drugs, and nutrition.

With the increasing availability of materials, more attention must be given to their evaluation. Teachers will need to develop their skills, using such criteria as appropriateness, coverage, and accuracy of the content. They will have to consider such questions as readability levels, suitability of the material for the school and the community, and cost of the material.

Lesson plans. Lessons are divided into three sections: (1) an introduction, (2) a presentation or development of the lesson, and (3) the closing. In addition, there are four elements of a lesson: the objectives, procedures or methods, materials, and evaluation (Fig. 12-12).

The introduction is designed to achieve two purposes: (1) to gain the attention of and to

SAMPLE FORMATS AND LESSON PLAN

Topic: Preventing Injuries
Day:
Class: Sophomore Health Education

Objectives	Procedures	Materials	Evaluation
Students 1. Understand that most injuries are not due to chance but are preventable 2. Learn about teenagers leading causes of death	Injuries just happen or do they? Examine and analyze injury data Mini-lecture based on data "Epidemiology-Etiology" 1. Typical public response: Accidents, Act of Fate, Bad Luck 2. People fascinated and repulsed 3. Becoming more sophisticated about injury prevention 4. Reading and small group work: Analyze reports, determine factors involved: knowledge, attitudes and behaviors	Class handout materials: DATA SHEETS 1. Leading causes of death in U.S. 2. Injuries versus other causes of death 3. Factors contributing to motor vehicle deaths News stories about accidents Use accident analysis sheet for nonfatal accidents, including: Type of accident Possible contributing factors: Knowledge Attitude Behavior Environment	 Write a paragraph about one of the reports explaining how the accident could have been prevented.

FIG. 12-12.   Lesson plan.

stimulate the interest and curiosity of the student in the lesson to be presented, and (2) to develop the relationship between this lesson and the previous one. This is done by establishing a framework or context for this lesson so that students can understand its relation to the larger unit. The teacher should provide a brief summary of the previous lesson and then present the objectives for the present instruction. Student motivation is enhanced when the teacher makes clear the objectives and the outcomes for the student. Approximately 5 minutes is suggested for this phase.

Characteristics of effective presentations include maintaining student interest, conducting the lesson at a brisk pace, giving students opportunities to learn new information and time to practice new skills, monitoring student progress, providing students with appropriate feedback, and maintaining a pleasant, relaxed but task-oriented class atmosphere.

Closing the lesson often presents a problem for the teacher who has failed to develop a carefully organized and time-paced lesson. Like the introduction, 5 minutes are suggested for the closing. Depending on the nature of class activities, two types of closings are required. A *content closing* calls for a brief summary of the key points developed in the current lesson and an announcement of plans for the next, including homework assignments. A *procedural closing* means providing students with adequate time to record information about class assignments, to hand in papers, and to gather their class materials in preparation for moving to the next class.

SUMMARY

This chapter provides a brief historical review of the school health education curriculum developments leading up to the present. Several events are examined, including the Commission on Reorganizing Secondary Education and their Cardinal Principles of Education, which have had a major influence on the development of health education since World War I. With respect to curriculum development, the contributions of two leaders in the field role are discussed in some detail. Ralph Tyler, a national authority on theory and practice of curriculum development, and John Goodlad, with his conceptual approach to curriculum, have had a major influence on the teaching of health education. Events that have had an influence on contemporary health education curriculums are reviewed, including the curriculum reform movement after Sputnik (1957), the President's Committee on Health Education in the 1970s, the Surgeon General's report of 1979 on *Healthy People* and the nation's health goals for the decade of the 80s, and the report of 1990, which contains the nation's health objectives for the year 2000. Examples of comprehensive and categorical health curriculums are also discussed. The rationale for these different approaches and the events that have influenced their development are also presented. The chapter concludes with a detailed analysis of the curriculum, including the teaching unit, the foundation on which all curriculums are based, and finally, a suggested format and organization for the lesson plan.

STUDY QUESTIONS

1. Why is the 1918 report of the Commission on Reorganization of Secondary Education of importance to health education?
2. What are the foundations of today's school curriculum?
3. How might the curriculum planner's theory of learning affect the organization of the health education curriculum?
4. How might the report *Health Promotion and Disease Prevention: Objectives for the Nation* influence the decision making for the health education curriculum? What level of decision making is most likely to be affected?
5. Although many leaders in health education have advocated a comprehensive health education curriculum, why does the categorical health problems approach enjoy increased interest and emphasis?

GET INVOLVED! According to the Surgeon General's report, *Healthy People 2000*, many students appear to understand the relationship between good nutrition and good health. However, when students shop for snacks, 65% say that they buy candy. Thus it becomes clear that many students do not understand the effect of sweet foods on their dental health. The dental profession has been very successful in preventing dental disease. Programs such as fluoridation of public water supplies, educating the public on effective oral hygienic practices, and seeking early preventive care of the mouth and gums are part of dental health education.

Dental hygienists play a key role in preventing dental disease. They may work in conjunction with the dentist in performing dental prophylaxis (cleaning of the teeth and gums) by removing calcareosis (limelike deposits) and stains from the teeth and by removing the accumulation of tartar from the teeth and beneath the gums. Dental hygienists are also trained to perform a number of other services under the direction of the dentist, such as applying medication and developing x-rays to assess the progress of dental decay. In addition to working in dental offices, dental hygienists work in schools and community health programs. Their work in these programs and with dentists are the primary areas for dental health education. Children from low-income families are likely to have less access to dental care. For such children the health education and prophylactic services provided by the dental hygienist in schools and community programs become crucial to their dental health and well-being.

For more information about preparing for a career in dental hygiene, write to:

American Dental Hygienist Association
211 East Chicago Ave.
Chicago, IL 60201

---

6. What is the rationale for a conceptual approach to curriculum development?
7. What are the foundations of curriculum development?
8. In what ways has the report *Healthy People 2000* contributed to the advancement of health education?
9. What is the difference between a goal of the health education curriculum and a health instruction objective?
10. What are the major elements of the lesson plan?

REFERENCES

American National Red Cross: *Lifesaving: rescue and water safety*, Washington, DC, 1982.

Atkinson JW: *An introduction to motivation*, ed 2, Princeton, NJ, 1978, Van Nostrand Reinhold.

Bandura A: *Principles of behavior modification*, New York, 1969, Holt, Rinehart & Winston.

Bruner JS: *The process of education*, Cambridge, Mass, 1960, Harvard University Press.

Carnegie Council on Adolescent Development: *Turning points: preparing American youth for the 21st century*, New York, 1989, Carnegie Corp.

Commission on the Reorganization of Secondary Education: *Cardinal principles of secondary education*, Washington, DC, 1918, US Government Printing Office.

Corry M: The role of the federal government in promoting health through schools: report from the National School Health Education Coalition, *J Sch Health* 62(4):143-145, 1992.

Curriculum Framework Criteria Committee on Health: *Health instruction framework for California Public Schools*, Sacramento, 1978, California State Department of Education.

Downey AM, et al: "Heart Smart"—a staff development model for a school-based cardiovascular health intervention, *Health Educ* 19:12, 1988.

Education Commission of the States: Recommendations for school health education: a handbook for state policymakers, report No. 130, Denver, 1981, Education Commission of the States.

Education Commission of the States: State policy support for school health education: a review and analysis, report No. 182, Denver, 1982, Education Commission of the States.

Education Development Center: *Teenage health teaching modules: preventing injuries*, Newton, 1982, EDC.

Eisner E, Valloner E, editors: *Conflicting conceptions of curriculum*, Berkeley, Calif, 1974, McCutchan Publishing.

Fodor JT, Dalis GT: *Health instruction: theory and application*, ed. 3, Philadelphia, 1981, Lea & Febiger.

Golaszewski TJ: *Influencing behavior through instruction: methodology in health education*, Washington, DC, 1979, ERIC Clearinghouse on Teacher Education.

Goodlad JI: *Planning and organizing for teaching: project on instruction*, Washington, DC, 1963, National Education Association.

Goodlad JI: *A study of schooling: some findings and hypothesis*, March 1983, Phi Delta Kappan, p. 465.

Goodlad JI, et al: *Curriculum inquiry: the study of curriculum practice*, New York, 1979, McGraw-Hill.

Governor's Steering Committee on Social Problems: Report from the Governor's Steering Committee on Social Problems in Health and Hospital Costs, New York, 1971, State of New York.

Gow DT, Casey TW: Selected learning activities. In Finwich WE, editor: *Yearbook fundamental curriculum decisions*, Alexandria, Va., 1983, Association for Supervision and Curriculum Development.

Hill WF: *Learning: a survey of psychological interpretations*, Scranton, Pa, 1963, Chandler Publishing.

Illinois State Board of Education: *Phase I mandate studies final staff recommendations*, Springfield, Ill, 1983, Illinois State Board of Education.

Killip DE, et al: Integrated school and community programs, *J Sch Health* 57:437, 1987.

Kleibard H: Education at the turn of the century: a crucible for curriculum change, *Educ Res* 11(1):16, 1982.

Koble LJ: The role of the federal government in promoting health through the schools: report of the division of adolescent and school health, Center for Disease Control, *J Sch Health* 62(4):135-137, 1992.

Lohmann DK, DeJoy DM: Utilizing the competency-based curriculum framework for curriculum revision: a case study, *Health Educ* 18:36, 1988.

McGinnis JM, DeGraw C: Healthy People 2000: Creating partnerships for the decade *J Sch Health* 67(7):292-328, 1991.

Means RK: The potential for accidents exists regardless of the environment. In Sliepcevich EM: *Health education: a conceptual approach to curriculum development*, School Health Education Study, St. Paul, 1968, 3M Education Press.

Means RK: *Historical perspective on school health*, Thorofare, NJ, 1975, Charles B Slack.

Muth KD, Alvermann DE: *Teaching and learning in the middle grades*, Boston, 1992, Allyn and Bacon.

National Center for Health Education: *Growing Healthy, Grade 6*, New York, 1987, National Center for Health Education.

Office of the Assistant Secretary for Health and the Surgeon General: Healthy people: the Surgeon General's report on health promotion and disease prevention, DHEW Pub. No. (PHS) 79-55071, Washington, DC, 1979, US Government Printing Office.

Posner GJ, Rudnitsky AN: *Course design: a guide to curriculum development for teachers*, New York, 1978, Longman.

Pratt D: *Curriculum design and development*, New York, 1980, Harcourt Bruce Jovanovich.

President's Committee on Health Education: *The report of the President's Committee on Health Education*, New York, 1973, the Committee.

Public Health Service: *Promoting health, preventing diseases—objectives for the nation*, Washington, DC, 1980, US Government Printing Office.

Redican KJ, Olsen LK, Stone DB: Health education: a positive force in increasing the reading skills of low socioeconomic elementary students, *Urban Rev* 2(4):215, 1979.

Rist MC: Antismoking policies can work in schools, *Educ Dig* 52:53, 1987.

Seffrin JR: The comprehensive school health education: closing the gap between the state-of-the-art and state-of-the-practice, *J Sch Health* 60(4):151-156, 1990.

Sliepcevich EM: *Health education: a conceptual approach to curriculum design*, St. Paul, 1968, 3M Education Press.

Tyler RW: In Schaffarzich J, Hampton DH, editors: *Strategies for curriculum development*, Berkeley, Calif, 1975, McCutchan Publishing, pp 17-33.

Tyler RW: *A place called school*, March 1983, Phi Delta Kappan, p. 462.

US Department of Health, Education and Welfare: The School Health Curriculum Project, Public Health Service, Center for Disease Control, Bureau of Health Education, Atlanta, 1977, US Government Printing Office.

US Department of Health, Education and Welfare, Office of Education, Health Education Program: Proposed regulations governing award of grants to state and local educational leagues, II, *Fed Reg* 44(115):34024, 1979.

US Department of Health and Human Services, Public Health Service: *Promoting health and preventing disease: objectives for the nation*, Washington, DC, 1980, US Government Printing Office.

Willgoose CE: *Health teaching in secondary schools*, ed 3, Philadelphia, 1982, WB Saunders.

Willgoose CE: Saving the curriculum for health education, *J Sch Health* 43:189, 1973.

Zais R: *Curriculum principles and foundations*, New York, 1976, Thomas Y Crowell.

Elementary school health instruction

OVERVIEW

Several curriculum and scheduling patterns for health instruction in elementary schools are discussed; these include integration, correlation, and direct teaching. Successful programs use each of these approaches. The alert teacher has many opportunities to integrate and correlate health-related activities and opportunities for health education in all areas of the curriculum, as well as the regular school activities. However, for a program to be fully successful, the direct formal teaching of health is basic. Such a program has a planned set of learning activities, teaching materials, and a formally designated schedule for health instruction. The program is directed toward the accomplishment of clearly defined health education objectives. The role of the school health coordinator is discussed both at the school district and school building level. Emphasis is placed on the coordination in contrast to the administration or direction. Coordination calls for cooperating with and facilitating and in general providing support for the classroom teacher who is the central figure in the elementary school health instruction program. The health interests of primary and intermediate level students are identified, together with ways of motivating students. Providing opportunities for students to achieve and to gain recognition for their improved health status is emphasized. Showing the individual how he or she can accept responsibility for self-care and take pride in self is part of effective teaching.

Criteria are offered for evaluating textbooks and other health education materials so that materials of high quality may be selected. Several examples of available health education curriculums are presented to aid the teacher in his or her own curriculum planning. Health teaching units and sample teaching plans for several health topics such as sex education, human relationships, environmental health, smoking, and dental health are included. Also included is an example of the material from the Growing Healthy Curriculum, which is now available through the National Center for Health Education in New York. A section on critical thinking and decision making encourages teachers to create more opportunities for students to participate in decision making and to develop more complex thinking skills.

OBJECTIVES   After reading this chapter, the student should be able to:

1. Explain several patterns for offering health instruction at the elementary school level
2. Name several health topics to be included in the health curriculum for an elementary school

3. Explain the role of a school health coordinator in the health instruction programs
4. Suggest criteria for evaluating textbooks and other forms of health education literature
5. Identify several topics that would be included in sex education at the primary and intermediate grade levels
6. Explain some of the typical concerns parents are likely to have about a sex education program
7. Explain the several different unit formats that are represented by the various curriculums now available
8. Explain the general organization of the *Growing Healthy* curriculum, as well as some of its potential strengths and weaknesses

---

The school is not the sole agency that contributes to the health education of a child. However, the core of health instruction must come from the school. Other health instruction should be considered an intensification and extension rather than an embellishment of the school program (Fig. 13-1). The school must proceed on the principle that it will provide the best possible

FIG. 13-1. The study of health can help elementary school children develop their basic skills of reading, writing, and locating information.

health instruction for the pupils and that other sources of health instruction will add to it. This is altogether sound because some children have limited opportunities for health instruction outside of school.

In the elementary school, health instruction, like all other instructional areas, should be a meaningful experience of permanent value. In an effort to make health interesting and enjoyable, the means should not become so important that it obscures the real purpose of the activity. Poster construction, puppet shows, and plays can be effective vehicles for health instruction, but when the poster, the puppets, or the play becomes the purpose of the experience, little is derived in the way of health education. Health instruction must be an effective experience, not a delightful diversion. An elementary school teacher should resolve to affect the health of each child favorably.

ORGANIZING FOR EFFECTIVE HEALTH INSTRUCTION

Once the health curriculum or course of study has been established, the next logical step is the organization of the implementation of the curriculum. Health instruction must be fitted into the total school schedule. More than time is involved. Effective instruction requires that all possible teaching opportunities be included in the class organization. The schedule for health instruction should allow for planned teaching, incidental learning, correlation, and integration. Although flexible, the schedule must be sufficiently definite to ensure effective health instruction. Certain current practices in education indicate the principles that will guide scheduling for health instruction:

1. A weekly schedule provides for extended time periods and allows for necessary flexibility.
2. A daily health period is not required for health instruction.
3. Two fairly extended periods per week may be sufficient for health instruction in the primary grades, and three periods per week can serve the intermediate grades.
4. A flexible schedule allows for continuation of an activity that is particularly challenging.
5. Opportunities should be provided for the varieties of activities that health instruction entails.
6. When special health needs or interests require, the schedule should be rearranged. Extra time invested in health instruction during one week can be followed by incidental instruction in the following week or weeks.
7. Opportunities for incidental and integrated health instruction should not be sacrificed to maintain a rigid schedule.
8. To be effective, correlation of health with other areas must be given a definite place in the organization for health instruction.

District health coordinator's role

The health director should be thought of primarily as a supervisor. Recent studies reveal that competent supervision more than justifies its cost in the added effectiveness that it gives to the school program. A supervisor who can help each teacher improve his or her services by 5% has made a considerable contribution.

The help of a supervisor enables teachers to do a more effective job. In helping teachers to organize their health instruction program, the coordinator may give them the benefit of his or her professional preparation and experience, as well as knowledge of the total school health program. The health coordinator becomes the key to the grade-to-grade integration of health instruction and is also familiar with state requirements and resources. He or she does not hand classroom teachers a schedule or plan for organization but instead works with them in developing or reviewing proposals for improving the program. An experienced health coordinator recognizes individual differences in teachers and accordingly recognizes that each teacher organizes his or her teaching plan in a pattern that best fits his or her particular abilities. Variation from grade to grade in the organization of health instruction is an indication of a vital program.

During the course of the year the coordinator or supervisor may serve as a consultant with the teacher in working out problems or in developing approaches that might be introduced. The coordinator appraises the program both during the year and at the conclusion of the year.

Administrator's responsibility

If there is a health coordinator, the principal should serve as a resource person for organizing health instruction. Some elementary school principals have an excellent health background and can provide valuable health supervision. However, even principals with a very limited health background can help the classroom teacher resolve specific problems that may be particularly vexing.

School building health coordinator

Some elementary schools have regular staff members who serve as resource people in music, art, geography, health, and other areas. An elementary school teacher with a minor in health may well serve in these roles. This health resource person may serve as a consultant to other teachers in the building.

Classroom teacher's function

Minimal health preparation of the elementary school teacher should be course work in general health, school health services, and the school health curriculum. Further health preparation would be highly desirable. However, in-service preparation could include such course work as the health of the school-age child, physical growth and development, and mental health, as well as other courses.

Classroom teachers are the key persons in the implementation of elementary school health instruction. Others may advise teachers and assist in various ways, but, because of their strategic location, only teachers are in a position to appreciate the total situation and the health implications inherent in it. Because they will direct children in learning, it is essential that they have a good grasp of the health instruction plan and organization. If an inflexible plan and organization are handed to them, they are not likely to do an effective job of health teaching. On the other hand, if they have been prime figures in the development of a health instruction plan and organization, their familiarity with the *what, how,* and *why* of the program should make their contribution a more meaningful and effective one.

When teachers are left to their own resources, they are justified in using plans and programs that have been developed by others, then modifying and adapting them to their own classroom situations. Such curriculums should be treated as guides, and teachers should feel free and be encouraged to make adaptations to suit the needs of their students. The use of several sources may provide teachers with the substance from which to organize their own health instruction. Whatever the approach or source of reference, the health needs and interests of the children in a particular classroom should be the focal center from which the program emerges. The health concerns and outcomes in terms of the students are the vehicle that propels the program. The guiding motive in the organization of health instruction is to provide students with opportunities to explore health concerns and to solve vital health problems.

Certain universal health needs and interests of pupils make it possible for teachers to use available materials and to apply them effectively to the immediate situation. Yet each group of children has need for special health emphasis or the consideration of a different type of health program. For this reason, in a new situation an elementary school teacher might consider the organization of health instruction for a half year. A reappraisal at that time will indicate the strengths and weaknesses of the program and the modifications that are in order.

CLASSROOM INSTRUCTION

Motivating pupils sufficiently so that they want to establish desirable health practices is the basis for all health instruction. Motivation is the catalyst of all teaching, but it is particularly important in health teaching.

Fundamental to motivation in elementary school health instruction is giving each pupil status in the classroom. A *team* concept—*us, we, all of us*—must permeate the atmosphere. This relationship within the groups should be supported by a strong teacher-pupil relationship. Active participation in health projects is needed for all pupils. Neither passive nor vicarious participation will establish health practices. Above all, an organic relationship of pupil to group and group to pupil must be maintained for effective health instruction.

Pride in oneself, in one's own accomplishments, and in one's own progress is basic to everyone. Developing this pride constitutes a most effective means for initiating a health practice and for continuing the practice until it becomes ingrained in a pupil's mode of life. Appeal to pride in personal appearance can be as effective at the elementary school level as at adolescence, if attention and praise are properly distributed.

Self-progress reinforced by an understanding of that progress motivates pupils in their quest for advancement. Competition with themselves can be wholesome motivation for pupils when realistic standards are the guide and when counseling in appraisal of their advances, plateaus, and failures is offered. Achievements that are visible to children can stimulate them to further achievement. It may be necessary to help them see their achievements.

Unless children themselves internalize health instruction, the whole opportunity for education has been missed. They must be the center of action—the vital element of greatest consideration. Moreover, they should believe this and be stimulated by it. This, of course, is the necessary ingredient for any teaching situation to be effective.

At all times the elementary school teacher should direct health instruction toward the establishment of certain desirable health practices. Knowledge and attitudes can grow out of the establishment of health practices, contributing to their formation and permanence. These practices should be related to recognized factors in health such as play and rest, vision promotion, hearing protection, care of the teeth, cleanliness, general appearance, use of the toilet, avoiding infection, work practices, sleep, safety at school, safety at home, going to and from school, bicycle safety, fire safety, water safety, courtesy, self-reliance, self-discipline, and social adjustment. Specific practices will be listed in the units and other sources that follow, but the teacher with some degree of ingenuity can develop a list of practices suited to the particular group of youngsters in the room.

In a well-organized, system-wide health program, certain specific health practices should be common to all elementary schools as a guide in health education. This common core of practices provides continuity and intensification. It ensures some measure of performance in health practices. In an elementary school in which teachers agree on health practices to be established, the health program is ensured of reasonably effective long-term results. In addition to the reinforcing effect of such an established program, the likelihood of omissions is reduced, if not eliminated.

Various approaches to health instruction are in general use. Each has merit and can be used to advantage when adapted to particular needs and situations. Four approaches are of special interest:

1. Integrated living as health instruction
2. Planned direct formal and informal instruction
3. Incidental instruction
4. Correlated health instruction

Because all four approaches have special attributes and merits, the prudent elementary teacher uses all of them in conducting an effective health instruction program. Together the four approaches tend to ensure the maximum in effective health instruction.

INTEGRATED LIVING AS HEALTH INSTRUCTION

Life is not cast in a mold of isolated islands or separate compartments. Interwoven in each child's daily activities are health implications, values, and factors. All adaptations that pupils make have implications for either mental or physical health. In some activities health occupies a prominent role, and in others it assumes a lesser role. Yet whether it occupies a major or minor role, if the opportunity for health instruction is fully developed, the resulting health education can be both effective and lasting. If learning is a meaningful and functional experience, it becomes an established, integral part of the mode of living of a child—the true goal of the school.

Pupil-teacher relationships

No one has objectively measured the specific influence of a particular teacher on a given pupil. Yet there is ample evidence that the teacher can modify the child's behavior in a beneficial way. Perhaps no phase of the school health instruction program can have a more beneficial, lasting effect than the teacher's interest in and encouragement of each child's health. The approval of the teacher can develop the self-interest in health that is necessary to the promotion of personal health. From such experiences will develop worthy health goals, which, because of self-esteem, each person will strive to maintain. Teachers make a lasting wholesome impression when they recognize and commend the child's cleanliness, appearance, dental care, posture, safety measures, dietary practices, courtesy, thoughtfulness, social adjustment, vitality, buoyancy, and general development. To the child, health truly becomes a matter of personal concern and gratification. It is the seed from which will develop a lifelong interest in personal health promotion.

Most teachers are interested in the well-being of schoolchildren. However, this interest should be expressed by interest in the child's health and his or her efforts in its behalf. Could there be a more worthy outcome of the total program of the school than students with a wholesome concern for their own health and with the necessary preparation to make the decisions that relate to their health and to that of their families? Pupil-teacher relationships provide the most effective means for motivating children to accept responsibility for the promotion of their own health.

School experiences

Many school activities with health aspects provide opportunities for effective education. At times the instructional opportunities are missed completely. Perhaps more frequently, the experience is given cursory treatment. An alert teacher not only uses the unusual event for instructional purposes but also recognizes opportunities for health instruction in the regular program.

There are many opportunities to apply health knowledge in daily school experiences. The acts of coming to school and going home involve problems in safety for pedestrians, for bicycle riders, for general traffic, and for bus riders. Within the school, safety is an ever-present problem. Lighting, ventilation, cleanliness, dental health, posture, activity, rest, lunchroom practices, and social problems provide a diversity of opportunities for learning and its application.

Unusual experiences can have health implications of instructional value. The illness of a child can have learning value for classmates if the teacher directs the learning into constructive channels. An appendectomy can be discussed in terms of early indications, the desirability of avoiding self-diagnosis and self-medication, the need for immediate medical care, the effectiveness of modern medicine, and the importance of relying on the physician to restore health. Thus the fact that it is the individual who promotes health and the physician who restores health can be reemphasized.

If a child in the class wears glasses because of a physician's advice, the wisdom of wearing glasses can be emphasized by a class study of the problem. If the situation is dealt with openly, the supposed onus that youngsters may associate with glasses is removed. The children can learn that wearing glasses is not a stigma, but the badge of a person who is wise enough to use the fruits of modern science, just as a wise person uses other modern inventions.

Occasionally, sensitive circumstances that relate to health arise in the school. Discretion indicates that the teacher consider the situation carefully. After extended deliberation, a means of using the event for instructional purposes may be devised. Perhaps the solution will be to consider related problems rather than the specific event. If a child has been hospitalized with influenza, a discussion of the measures for control of communicable disease rather than of influenza alone may be less disturbing but educationally just as valuable (see Fig. 2-3).

Many school experiences merit repeated consideration. A single discussion may create an interest but may not result in effective learning. Correlation of the factors in two or more experiences adds interest to the discussion and provokes thinking.

Is mandating sex education the answer?

EMERGING ISSUE   As a health educator in a large school district, you have been elected to the Executive Committee of the State Association for Disease Prevention and Health Promotion. Recently, the state Association has requested that the Executive Committee seek passage of a law mandating the teaching of sex education in the public schools. The Executive Committee and the officers of the Association have conducted a series of hearings around the state for the purpose of shaping the legislation and refining the language of the proposed bill. A number of questions and suggestions have been made regarding the details of the proposed legislation. You are asked to share your thinking by responding to the following statements.

Please indicate whether you generally agree or disagree by placing a plus (+) or a minus (−) sign before each statement.

_____ 1. Because of the extent of self-destructive behaviors among adolescents such as pregnancies, and sexually transmitted diseases, including AIDS, I agree that legislation is needed.

_____ 2. I believe the legislation for sex education should be explicit about the topics to be taught such as human sexuality, human reproduction, birth control, sexually transmitted diseases, and pregnancy.

_____ 3. I believe conservative politicians would oppose legislation containing explicit language about sex that would lead to the defeat of the bill.

_____ 4. Instead of labeling the bill "sex education," I would prefer the title "family life education."

_____ 5. I believe that the language of the legislation needs to be clear so that teachers have an accurate direction as to what they will be expected to teach.

_____ 6. I am somewhat pessimistic about the prospects for improving the teaching of sex education because I believe that it is usually poorly integrated into the school curriculum; that it is often taught by inadequately trained persons; and that it rarely has enough resources to support the program adequately.

_____ 7. I strongly favor this legislation on the belief that a quality sex education program would help reduce the problem of unwanted pregnancies and sexually transmitted diseases.

_____ 8. Although I favor the teaching of sex education, I doubt that legislating it is the answer.

_____   If limited to a single choice, I would choose this number.

Community experiences

Events in the community may be a concern of schoolchildren. In the primary grades pupils have only slight community interest, which tends to develop as they reach the intermediate grades. Expansion of the municipal water facilities, construction of a sewage disposal plant, restaurant inspection, control measures for communicable disease, medical services, air pollution, safety programs, industrial health, recreation, and special health drives should be of interest to the future adults of the nation. Community health personnel can serve as a resource for stimulating the interest of children in community health.

Interest in local health can be projected to the state and nation. Children can acquire health understanding from epidemics, disasters involving health problems, new health experiments and discoveries, reports on the conquest of disease, extension of life expectation, and population growth. Indeed, international health can become interesting.

PLANNED DIRECT INSTRUCTION

With the elementary school program fragmented, as it tends to be, a scheduled time for health instruction is helpful. Doubtless a few teachers, highly skilled in incidental, correlated, and integrated health instruction, may do an effective job of health teaching without a scheduled period for health, but most teachers will need definite scheduled time to provide the necessary core instruction. A daily period is not necessary, but a period of 30 minutes twice a week for primary pupils and three periods a week for intermediate children should serve as a minimum for core health instruction if supplementary health teaching makes a reasonably strong contribution. Such scheduling does not make an inordinate demand on school time.

Direct teaching is the core of the instructional program. Other procedures can supplement it advantageously, but the base of the instruction pyramid should be direct teaching. It serves many purposes and has definite advantages, such as the following:

1. Gives status to health as a subject area
2. Ensures at least a minimum of emphasis on teaching
3. Provides an organized approach
4. Deals with realistic specific needs
5. Makes effective results possible for a teacher of average ability
6. Tends to emphasize the positive aspects of health
7. Can be applied even with incidental teaching
8. Can emerge from correlated teaching
9. Can be channeled into integrated and other approaches
10. Provides for outcomes in terms of interpretations, values, and other worthwhile attributes

The imaginative teacher can use direct teaching as an adventure in health education, as effective as it is interesting.

Allocation and gradation

Emphasis for areas of special teaching should be allocated in the overall plans for health instruction. The key must be the interests and needs of the children at each age level. Health instruction is effective when it begins with children and their concerns or problems. If they can identify with a health problem and associate themselves with it, it takes on a personal meaning. The most effective health education is achieved when it seems to emanate from children rather than to be imposed on them from above. Complexity of treatment is adjusted to the psychological level of the pupils. Interests of the students indicate levels of maturity.

Areas of emphasis

Teachers can obtain an overview of the health needs, interests, and problems from observing the children; from their questions; from observing school, home, and community life; from statements of parents; from suggestions of health personnel; and from school records. Teachers will notice that children in their early years tend to be individualists, which is reflected in their health interests. Starting in about the fifth grade, the tendency toward gangs begins to be expressed in an interest in group and community health.

Several studies have revealed the almost universal health interests and needs of children at various levels. An elementary teacher can be guided by these studies if no other data are available. When allocations of areas have been made on a school basis, results of these studies have frequently been used as a guide. Usually kindergarten and grades 1, 2, and 3 are grouped; and in grades 4, 5, and 6 individual assignments of areas are given. It will be noticed that the health of the individual is emphasized in the early years and community health is emphasized beginning with the fifth grade. Repetition and duplication are not necessarily objectionable. Certain duplications are inevitable, even desirable, but specific emphasis changes with the maturity of the pupil. Nutrition in the primary grades deals with a few simple dietary practices. In the intermediate grades an understanding of the *how* and *why* of certain nutritional needs is of interest to the pupils (Tables 13-1 and 13-2).

TABLE 13-1. Areas of emphasis in kindergarten and primary grades and grade 4

Kindergarten and primary grades	Grade 4
Physical health	
Personal cleanliness	Vision and hearing
School cleanliness	Illumination
Rest and sleep	Ventilation
Eating practices	Clothing
Posture	Cleanliness
Play practices	Activity
Dental health	Dental problems
Lighting	Nutrition
Common cold	Preventing infection
Safety to and from school	Illness
Schoolroom safety	Avoiding poisons
Playground safety	Fire prevention
Home safety	Traffic safety
Body growth	
Mental health	
Sharing	Sportsmanship
Working together	Self-direction
Kindness	Confidence
Being friendly	Our friends
Orderliness	Being grown up
Depending on ourselves	Courtesy
Attaining goals	Accepting disappointments
Community health	
Home life	Family health
Sources of water and milk	Helping the neighborhood
Sunshine and health	Improving the neighborhood

TABLE 13-2. Areas of emphasis in grades 5 and 6

Grade 5	Grade 6
Physical health	
Appraisal of personal health	Bicycle safety
Personal health promotion	Safety patrol
Balanced diets	Health examination
Food preparation and care	Body function
Communicable diseases	Growth and development
Recreation needs	Grooming
Developing skills	Posture
Body development	Rest and sleep
Relaxation	Communicable diseases
Types of school accidents	Home and farm safety
Playground accidents	Emergency care
Fire prevention	First-aid procedures
Fire drills	Safety patrol
Mental health	
Family relationships	Interesting people
Peer groups	Personality
Loyalties	Emotional adjustment
Social status	Life goals
Emotional maturation	Self-improvement
Community health	
Home sanitation	Community disease control
Health advertising	Community water supply
Community safety program	Milk control measures
School sanitation	Community sanitation

Motivation

A cue to all motivation in education is the natural human desire for self-esteem through attention, achievement, advancement, improvement, superiority, praise, and recognition. Motivation in health instruction should be relatively simple because health deals directly with a pupil's own welfare, but the whole experience must begin within the child.

To promote self-identification in health areas, effort should be made to introduce each topic as a problem that is the concern of all who are present. By using a question as the vehicle, the problem should be launched with emphasis on *you, we, all of us,* or *you and I.* The question should include or imply self-improvement. How can *we* keep clean so that *we* always look nice? Out of this appeal to appearance and improvement emanate subquestions of keeping the hair clean, having clean fingernails, and other specific activities. How can *you* keep *your* teeth healthy and looking nice? The approach can apply equally to *our* school, *our* community, and *our* nation.

Questions can serve various purposes in making the instruction effective, such as the following:

1. Arouse curiosity, stimulate interest, and develop purpose (Fig. 13-2)

FIG. 13-2.   The art of questioning requires skill in framing the question and sensitivity to the student's answer.

2. Prepare pupils for learning by encouraging them to draw from their own experiences
3. Cause the student to think and evaluate
4. Understand the pupil's thinking
5. Help the student discriminate
6. Direct the pupil's attention to significant elements
7. Introduce new concepts
8. Help the pupils express their thinking
9. Help the pupils explore the various choices or alternatives

Once the project is launched, guidance and individual recognition are necessary. Children find gratification in their achievements. Self-esteem becomes a wholesome motivating force. Every child can achieve some degree of success in feeling well, in improving personal appearance, and in following recognized health practices.

Teaching methods and techniques

The versatile teacher uses a diversity of methods and adapts teaching to the needs and purposes of the situation. Certain teaching procedures are especially adaptable to the elementary school level. These include group discussion, counseling, construction, independent study, oral presentation, problem solving, project method, reports, demonstration, dramatization, exhibits, field trips, and audiovisual aids.

In kindergarten and the primary grades the health instruction program can be based effectively on the development of desirable health practices.

Personal health practices
1. Wash carefully each morning.
2. Wash hands before and after eating.
3. Wash hands before leaving the toilet area.
4. Keep fingernails clean.
5. Wash hair at least once a week.
6. Keep hair well-groomed.
7. Bathe regularly.

Daily living practices
8. Stand, sit, and walk tall.
10. Keep materials organized.
11. Hang up clothing when not in use.
12. Play out of doors regularly, if weather permits.
13. Work cooperatively with others.
14. Be friendly.
15. Finish tasks that are begun.

Healthy eating practices
16. Drink low-fat milk with each meal.
17. Eat fruit at least twice each day.
18. Eat green and yellow vegetables daily.
19. Include protein foods in daily diet.

Health care and disease prevention
20. Keep fingers and other objects out of mouth.
21. Use a clean handkerchief or tissue to cover a sneeze or cough.
22. Remain at home when ill.
23. Brush teeth after eating and floss before going to bed.
24. Visit dentist regularly.
25. Go to bed on time.

Safety practices
26. Be alert for hazards that may cause accidents.
27. Follow all safety rules.
28. Use proper lighting for all needs.

In the intermediate grades the health instruction program can be effectively incorporated into the general theme of daily living. This is functional instruction at its best.

The use of health texts or health readers and other written materials can be effective when these materials serve as a source of knowledge for pupils and do not constitute the total sum of the health instruction.

Critical thinking, decision making, and problem solving

How is critical thinking developed? Disinger (1990) observes that behaviors associated with creative thinking include fluency, metaphorical thinking, complexity, intuition, insight and imagery. Such thinking, referred to as new thought patterns, provides unique and innovative solutions to problems. A characteristic of creative people is their interest in seeking solutions and delight in the challenge to solve problems. Most people are not inherently creative. However, according to Disinger, teachers can develop their creative talents, which will enable them to teach and encourage the development of creativity in their students. Woolfolk and McCune-Nicolich offer the following guidelines for encouraging creativity in the school:

1. Accept and encourage divergent thinking
2. Tolerate dissent
3. Encourage students to trust their own judgment
4. Emphasize that everyone is capable of creativity of some sort
5. Be a stimulus for creative thinking

Practically every method and teaching strategy used by the teacher involves questioning of some form. Kindsvatter et al. (1988) have made a useful adaptation of Bloom's *Taxonomy of Educational Objectives* (1956). This analysis has divided teacher questions into four levels. Low level I consists of convergent questions that require the student to recall and recognize information actions such as identifying, listing, and yes or no responses. The purpose of such questioning is to determine the levels of the student's knowledge and develop a base on which subsequent knowledge can be built. Level II consists of high-order convergent thinking. Here the teacher's purpose is to have the student go beyond simply recalling concepts by demonstrating and organizing information. In terms of the taxonomy, at this level the student is called on to make comparisons, describe, comprehend, and apply information. The ability to apply information has been classified as a skill objective as distinguished from a knowledge objective. Level III is low-order divergent thinking requiring the student to think critically about information, to discover reasons and causes, and to be able to draw conclusions. Level IV is high-order divergent thinking. Here the student performs original thinking and evaluative thinking such as developing designs, making judgments, hypothesizing, and speculating.

This model describes thinking from a basic level to the highest order. According to Kindsvatter, students may not be able to respond at Levels III and IV. Three components in the teaching of basic thinking skills have been identified. All students should be given the opportunity to:

1. Observe someone demonstrate or perform the skill accurately
2. Practice the skill
3. Have corrective feedback on the performance of the skill

High-order or critical thinking skills can be taught directly or indirectly. When taught directly, the focus of the lesson is on the skill itself without regard to the subject matter. For example, teaching primary students to develop higher-order thinking might follow this example.

The teacher would write the following instructions for the students on the chalk board.

Class objective.

Developing skill in classifying objects. (*Classifying*—placing objects into groups and then naming the groups)

Steps in classifying:

1. Look over all objects.
2. Choose two that are alike.
3. Name or label that group.

4. Look at remainder to see whether any others belong in that group.
5. Add any other like objects to the first group.
6. See if any other objects belong together.
7. Name or label the second group.
8. Repeat process of looking at remainder and adding to the second group.
9. Repeat the process until all the objects are grouped.

The teacher placed the following objects before the students: sandwich, apple, fork, milk, salad, straw.

Another class exercise requires a higher thinking skill in classification relating to nutrition.

Class objective:

Classify foods into the four food groups necessary for a healthy diet.

Foods

1. Banana	7. Peas
2. Salad	8. Broccoli
3. Hamburger	9. Butter
4. Bran flakes (cereal)	10. Egg
5. Fish	11. Orange
6. Milk	12. Hard roll

Using the same procedure, classify the food into the appropriate groups.

Andrews and Turner (1991) have developed a classroom activity designed to give primary-level children the opportunity to discuss decision making and to help them (1) become aware of and actively involved in the methods of making decisions, (2) become aware of the basis on which decisions are made, and (3) accept responsiblity for the consequences of their decisions. The teaching strategies used by these authors included decision-making charts related to children's literature. One such selection could be Winnie the Pooh and the story "Pooh gets stuck in a tight place." After reading the story, the children make a list of (1) the decisions Pooh makes, (2) the consequences of Pooh's decision, and (3) the alternative decisions that Pooh could have made.

A second teaching strategy includes the making of a decision web. This procedure places Pooh's problem as the center of the decision web. A variety of ways of webbing (decisions that were made) may be developed: who made the decisions, what was decided, what other decisions could have been made, what were the consequences, and what were other possible consequences.

Helping students develop their talents for creativity and critical thinking is believed to offer the greatest potential for increasing student interest in learning and enhancing their capacity for complex thinking. Establishing a classroom environment that encourages student creativity and divergent thinking poses a special challenge to the teacher. The traditional disciplinary curriculum organization is more structured and compartmentalized, causing students to be more convergent or narrow in their thinking. In contrast, curriculums that encourage creativity are more open-ended and unstructured. Students are encouraged to be more open-minded, less bound by time constraints, and more tolerant of learning outcomes that are less definite and predictable. At the same time, teachers are cautioned to guard against class discussions in which students are lacking in preparation and basic understanding.

Materials

The busy elementary school classroom teacher must obtain instruction materials for a multitude of purposes. To assemble materials for health instruction poses an especially difficult task because of the diversity of topics encompassed by the term *health instruction.*

To assist the classroom teachers, several examples of health instruction units have been included in this chapter.

Two problems may be especially difficult for the elementary classroom teacher: "What text should be used?" and "Should commercially prepared materials for health instruction be used?"

A textbook should be regarded as a reference. If textbooks are to be used in health instruction, certain standards in relation to health needs should then be met, in addition to the general criteria for all textbooks:

1. Primary emphasis should be on normal well-being.
2. Health principles should be stressed.
3. Discussion should be directed to the interests and needs of the pupils.
4. The topics of personal appearance, physical health, and mental health are important in the primary grades.
5. Community health should be included in the intermediate groups.
6. Basic anatomy and physiology are of interest to elementary school students, but health is more than anatomy and physiology.
7. An overview of each section can be of special value.
8. The literary style should be lucid and interesting.
9. Stimulating examples and original approaches add to the book's value.
10. Vocabulary should be adapted to the grade level.
11. A variety of suggested activities for pupils should be included.
12. Illustrations should be meaningful to the students.
13. Pupils should be able to understand and use the graphs and charts.
14. Suggestions for evaluation should be presented.

Commercial film makers, voluntary health organizations, and governmental agencies are producing an ever-increasing quantity of health education materials. Although the motivation in some instances may be to sell a product, much of this free and inexpensive material is of excellent quality. Because most schools have limited resources, it is important for teachers and curriculum coordinators to be aware of this potentially valuable source of instructional materials. However, it is essential that the teacher conduct a careful evaluation of such materials to determine their suitability for specific class needs. To aid the teacher in this effort, an evaluation form is included in Appendix A. The form has been adapted for use in the Office of the Superintendent of Public Instruction in the state of Washington. These general criteria can be readily adapted for use in health education.

Evaluation

In the final analysis, the effectiveness of the health instruction program should be measured in terms of improved health of the pupils. To a limited degree, this can be done both objectively and subjectively. The teacher can observe and measure the effect of health instruction in terms of the child's behavior. Health attitudes, knowledge (Fig. 13-3), and practices can be appraised

FIG. 13-3.   Health knowledge is an important aspect of health education evaluation.

in a practical way. Instruments for measurement are presented in Chapter 17. In considering specific evaluation of the health instruction, the teacher should ask one cardinal question: Is each child building a body of health knowledge and understanding that will contribute to his or her ultimate well-being?

ELEMENTARY SCHOOL CURRICULUMS: EXAMPLES

Several examples of health instruction materials for the elementary school have been selected to illustrate both subject matter and curriculum organization. Materials for the primary grades include the topic of sex education, which is illustrated by grade level units on human interrelationships. *Growing Up Healthy* illustrates a horizontal curriculum plan. It is designed as a year-long health teaching program composed of nine units to be taught by integration of the material with other basic subjects taught at the kindergarten level. The environmental health section illustrates the unit organization.

Not to be confused with *Growing Up Healthy* is *Growing Healthy*, the new collective name for the Primary Grade Health Curriculum Project. It has been included because it is an integrated part of a larger curriculum, which includes the School Health Curriculum Project (see Chapter 12) for grades 4 to 7. Thus *Growing Healthy* provides an articulated health education curriculum from kindergarten to grade 7. An outline of the units for each of the primary grades is presented.

For the intermediate grades Unit 1, "Food Campaign," has been selected to illustrate the teaching of nutrition at the intermediate grade level. It is part of the National Dairy Council's comprehensive nutrition learning system. This sequentially planned curriculum includes instructional materials for preschool, the elementary grades, and the junior and senior high school levels.

The last example at the intermediate level is the level II oral health unit from the American Dental Association. The association has extensively field-tested all of its health education materials. Both the teaching format and content organization should be useful to the teacher.

Sex education in the elementary school

Too many adults assume that the absence of formal sex instruction means that no sex education is occurring. However, the important question is not whether the child will receive sex education but rather what kind of sex education he or she will receive. The reality of the home and parent relationship, how parents react to each other as sexual beings, the attitudes parents reveal toward their children's explorations of their bodies, the effect of parental efforts to establish the child's toilet habits, and family members' ability to give and to express love for each other are all factors that represent powerful forces shaping the child's sexual feelings and attitudes.

All too often sex education tends to be a narrowly based reproductive education or a kind of moralistic teaching. Children are very much interested in and curious about their bodies. Thus a study of the reproductive process can provide a good starting point from which to develop adolescents' understanding of their roles and relationships as men and women in the family context and in situations outside the family. Teaching about the anatomy and physiology of reproduction provides the teacher with a comfortable, objective, and impersonal approach to sex education. Eventually, such topics as dating relationships, sexual behavior, and moral codes must be considered. In these areas, students must be given a greater role and encouraged to enter into open discussions and exchange of ideas—especially when questions such as standards of sexual behavior and the development of moral values arise. However, such discussions hold the potential for involvement in a school-community controversy. The teacher must be aware of the anxieties that many parents have about their child's sexual development. Such anxiety may be characterized as parental hopes that their child will grow up to lead a conventional life and will avoid "getting into trouble." However, there is also a kind of parental ambivalence, with some parents fearful that, on the one hand, children may *not* be getting the kind of education they need to become responsible adults or that, on the other hand, children may get the wrong kind of information, which may lead them into trouble.

Examples of instructional objectives for the primary student are as follows:

1. Develops a concept of self-worth and sexual identity
2. Recognizes that there are sex differences between boys and girls
3. Recognizes his or her role in the family
4. Accepts reproduction as a natural process of life
5. Develops an understanding and respect for the rights of others

6. Develops respect for the body and uses correct terminology in referring to parts of the body

Some instructional objectives for the intermediate student are as follows:

1. Continues to develop an understanding of the roles of each member of the family
2. Develops the self-image as a worthy member of society
3. Continues to develop an emotional acceptance of sex as a normal aspect of life
4. Develops an understanding of puberty and associated growth changes
5. Assumes more responsibility for his or her own care and for the care of others
6. Develops an ability to discuss sex objectively and in a dignified, unembarrassed manner

Human interrelationships: primary grades

The study of interpersonal relationships can provide an important vehicle for teaching sex education in the primary grades. Interpersonal relations are at the core of all sexual expression. Until about 10 years of age, a boy's output of male sex hormones (androgens) is but slightly greater than his output of female hormones (estrogens). In a 10-year-old girl the output of estrogens is little more than the output of androgens. At this stage of life children are neutral in sexuality and have no particular interest in anything of a sexual nature. Thus certain social conditioning must occur to help the boy and girl develop their roles as male and female.

AIM OF THE UNITS ON HUMAN INTERRELATIONSHIPS

Develops in children those qualities of personal worth that will command respect from others and will have a mutual respect for others.

OBJECTIVES

Develop in children attributes of:

1. Wholesome pride in self
2. Respect for parents
3. Respect for brothers and sisters
4. Respect for classmates
5. Respect for teachers
6. Respect for other people
7. Respect for authority
8. Respect for the rights of others
9. Respect for privacy
10. Respect for property
11. Thoughtfulness
12. Kindness
13. Fair play
14. Sharing
15. Obedience
16. Cooperation
17. Honesty
18. Courtesy
19. Responsibility
20. Consideration
21. Neatness

GRADE LEVEL UNIT TITLES

Kindergarten

Unit Title—Every Boy and Girl a Friend

Grade 1

Unit Title—Social Development

Grade 2

Unit Title—Social, Emotional Growth

Grade 3

Unit Title—Growth and Maturing

SAMPLE UNIT

The grade 3 unit has been selected to illustrate the unit format and the content.

Concepts and activities

I. Life and growth
   A. Discussion
      1. All life has a beginning, grows, changes, matures, and eventually dies.
      2. In which ways are plants and animals like and different?
      3. All life reproduces itself.
      4. How do plants reproduce themselves?
      5. What do plants need to keep alive, and where do these things come from?
      6. Plants grow, change, and carry on certain activities.
      7. How important are plants to the lives of all of us?
      8. Animals have young that are hatched from eggs or are born by the mother.
      9. Care of the young is important for all animal species.
      10. Care of their babies is important to our parents too.
      11. Discuss the nature of human growth.
      12. How do we change from babyhood through each stage to adulthood?
      13. Discuss how boys and girls differ in their growth patterns.
      14. All life needs nourishment for what purposes?
      15. How does what we feed the baby differ from what children 8 or 9 years old are fed?
      16. Discuss what is meant by a well-balanced diet.
      17. How does the school lunch provide for growth?
      18. Evaluate personal diets.
   B. Construction
      1. Have an aquarium or terrarium in the room to demonstrate the "web of life."
      2. Grow plants from seeds and seedlings.
      3. Make a chart of the four basic food groups.
      4. Plan a single meal such as breakfast.
      5. Plan a menu for a day.
      6. Make a chart of stages of growth using cutouts as models.
      7. Make a bulletin board or mural titled "What helps us grow?"
      8. Make lists of how children differ: physical characteristics, manners, grooming, speaking, opinions, interests.
   C. Dramatization and other activities
      1. Get information from parents on family growth characteristics and report to the class.
      2. Report on human growth differences throughout the world.
      3. Using a veterinary resource, report on rate of animal growth over a period of several weeks.

    4. Have a nurse, physician, or other resource person talk on human life, growth, and well-being.

    5. Bring baby pictures to school and have children try to identify the person.

II. Maturing

  A. Discussion

    1. How does maturing differ from growth?

    2. What does it mean to act grown up?

    3. What feelings or emotions do we have?

    4. How do we control the emotion of anger?

    5. How do we control selfishness or meanness?

    6. Why do people dislike us if we cheat?

    7. What is meant by:

      a. Happiness

      b. Honesty

      c. Courage

      d. Respect

      e. Forgiveness

      f. Responsibility

    8. How do our thoughts about ourselves influence the way we think about others?

    9. Why does self-respect promote respect for others?

    10. Why should we always try to have more friends?

    11. How do we get more friends?

    12. What qualities do you like in others?

    13. What do we mean when we say a certain third-grader acted like a first-grader?

    14. What do we mean when we say a certain third-grader acted like a fifth-grader?

    15. Notice individual differences and qualities.

    16. How do we show others we value their friendship?

  B. Construction

    1. Place on the blackboard each week a question relating to behavior, asking if all students have exhibited a certain quality each day (e.g., "Am I courteous?" "Am I thoughtful?" "Am I dependable?").

    2. Post pictures displaying desirable mature conduct.

    3. Have children keep records of their good deeds.

    4. Have children make an appraisal of their best qualities and those in which improvement is needed.

  C. Dramatization and other activities

    1. Tell stories to the class about people with exceptional courage, thoughtfulness, dependability, or other qualities.

    2. Have children report an exceptional case of helpfulness, courtesy, industriousness, or other quality they have observed.

    3. Prepare a skit that demonstrates courtesies toward other children.

    4. Demonstrate courteous conduct toward adults in various walks of life.

    5. Have each of a panel of five give a description of a middle-grade student who is unusually mature and explain why he or she is so regarded.

Evaluation

Observe class members regarding:

    1. Interest in life about them

    2. Concern for life

    3. Interest in their own growth

    4. Interest in children in other parts of the world

5. Interest in nutrition and nutritional practices
6. Concern about growth of others
7. Desire to improve relationships with other children
8. Interest in expanding friendships
9. Respect for adults and pupils
10. Increased sense of responsibility
11. Honesty
12. Obedience
13. Ability to make amends for mistakes

Growing Up Healthy: environmental health*

The President's Committee on Health Studies issued a special background paper entitled "Health Education of Preschool Children and their Parents" (1972) that stressed the need for health education throughout the entire program of early childhood education, with emphasis placed on the preschool and primary grades. *Growing Up Healthy,* a health education curriculum guide for the kindergarten level, provides an excellent example of an innovative response to this challenge. This curriculum project was supported by the Zellerbach Family Fund and was originally developed in conjunction with the San Francisco Unified School District. It is a multidisciplinary curriculum designed to enhance and reinforce the basic subjects of language arts, reading, and mathematics. These basic areas provide the avenues for the teaching of health. Materials included have been selected to illustrate the goals and one of the nine student behavioral objectives. Unit 8, "Environmental Health," a unique topic for teaching health at this level, has been chosen to show how the unit is organized.

An inexpensive workshop leader manual that contains guidelines and procedures for conducting a short 2- to 3-hour workshop session is available. It is all that is required to prepare teachers to use the program. The curriculum is designed to cover one school year; each of the nine units covers approximately 1 month of instructional time. Another unique feature of the curriculum is its multilingual character. Parent letters are available in five languages: English, Spanish, Chinese, Tagalog, and Vietnamese. The curriculum has three major goals and one student behavioral objective for each of the nine units. To illustrate the program, the goals and the student behavioral objective for Unit 8 are presented.

GOALS

1. To encourage kindergarten children to take an active role in developing and practicing good health habits
2. To improve compliance with Assembly Bills 2068 and 4284, which require children to have a physical examination before the third month of first grade
3. To assist parents and teachers in helping children make positive health habits an integral part of their daily lives

STUDENT BEHAVIORAL OBJECTIVE

The student identifies ways to keep the environment safe and clean.

The *Growing Up Healthy* curriculum is organized into nine lesson units. The topics of these units are:

1. The physical examination

---

*The material in this section is from Hazlett SH: *Growing up healthy,* 1983, Zellerbach Family Fund.

2. Cleanliness
3. Dental health
4. Nutrition
5. Safety
6. Foot health
7. Movement and relaxation
8. Environmental health
9. Mental health

Each lesson unit is divided into three major sections: preactivity, activity, and enrichment activities. The preactivity sections offer a variety of individual learning experiences. The activity section combines several learning experiences and offers suggestions for presentation of a half-hour lesson. Examples from Unit 8 are presented here.

Growing Healthy*

The *Growing Healthy* curriculum is organized around the theme "Me, my feelings, my senses, and my body."

Kindergarten - Happiness is Being Healthy
Grade 1—Super Me
Grade 2—Sights and Sounds
Grade 3—The Body Framework and Movement
Grade 4—Our Digestion Nutrition and Health
Grade 5—About our Lungs and our Health

This curriculum, like its predecessor the Primary Grades Health Education Curriculum Project, is developed according to a common unit format for each topic and grade level. The following outline is the framework for the content material of all grade units.

Introduction	Curiosity arousal and motivation of students
Phase 1	Overview of the feelings and the five senses (grades K-2) or the body systems (grades 3-7)
Phase 2	Appreciation of specific senses (grade K-2) or body systems (grade 3-7)
Phase 3	Structure and function of the senses (grades K-2) or body systems (grades 3-7)
Phase 4	Diseases and problems of the senses (grades K-2) or body systems (grades 3-7)
Phase 5	Care of the body and prevention of disease
Culmination	Synthesis of previous phases

The pattern of development is to present the overall interrelationships among the systems of the body, then to focus in each grade unit on specific sense organs of the body, and finally to return to a concept of the interdependence of all body systems. The factors that change from unit to unit are the body senses or body systems studied in depth. This same outline is also the framework for grades 6 and 7 of the *Growing Healthy* curriculum. The first grade unit "Super Me" is selected to illustrate the five-phase organizational structure.

Food—your choice: a nutrition learning system †

The lesson selected to illustrate the intermediate level curriculum is taken from the National Dairy Council's comprehensive nutrition learning system. It is designed for the fifth- or sixth-

---

*The material in this section is from the *Growing Healthy* curriculum. Kathleen Middleton, Project Director, National Center for Health Education 30 E. 29th St., New York, NY 10016.

†From *Food—your choice*, Rosemont, Ill, 1981, The National Dairy Council. Courtesy National Dairy Council.

First Grade: "Super Me"

The first grade unit elaborates some of the concepts introduced in kindergarten and focuses on three senses: taste, touch, and smell.

Major Concept Development

Introduction: Each person is unique and important at the same time that each person shares common needs with others. The special quality of being human is to cherish and take care of one's self and one another.

Phase I: The body is a super machine of many identifiable parts which work together in wonderful ways. The children learn the names of body parts, how they function, and the motor skills that use these body parts, such as skipping, hopping, tying shoes, and riding a bike. They express what they feel about their own body features.

Phase II: Taste, touch, and smell communicate information about the human body and its environment and can contribute to safe and healthful living.

Phase III: The structure and function of the tongue, skin, and nose bring experience of the world through taste, touch, and smell. Students learn (1) the specific sense organs of taste, touch, and smell; (2) the function of the nerves and the brain in relation to these organs; (3) the major structures of the skin and the functions of each; (4) the major functions of the nose, and (5) the major structure and functions of the tongue.

Phase IV: Diseases and environmental hazards can affect the senses of taste, touch, and smell. Diseases have symptoms and causes (virus, germs), and some diseases, communicable diseases, can spread (for example, colds, flu, pneumonia, mumps, measles, chicken pox, polio). Medicines can be helpful or harmful, depending on how they are used.

Phase V: The spread of disease can be prevented by health habits such as covering a sneeze, washing hands, caring for cuts, and being immunized. Overall health of the super machine is promoted through sleep, exercise, good nutrition, safety, good decisions about substance use and abuse, and relationships with others.

Culmination: In group activities, the children express what they have learned about taking care of their bodies, especially the senses of taste, touch, and smell.

grade student. As illustrated by the learning activities, the psychological and sociological dimensions of food choices are introduced to clarify students' values and to make them aware of the factors that influence their choices. The unit for this grade level comprises 14 different learning activities, each of which is related to a specific learning outcome. An interdisciplinary content chart is provided in which each of the 14 learning activities is correlated with the traditional subject matter areas taught at this grade level.

The elementary school program of *Food—Your Choice* is divided into three levels. Each level is packaged in its own box.

Level 1, for kindergarten and first and second grades, introduces 5- to 7-year-old students to basic nutrition concepts.

Level 2 builds on and extends the concepts introduced in Level 1. Level 2 serves students in the third and fourth grades. It provides 8- and 9-year-old students with opportunities to manipulate materials as they acquire additional knowledge about nutrition.

Level 3, designed for fifth and sixth grades, introduces students to the economic and sociologic ramifications inherent in nutrition. It broadens the scope of the earlier programs and moves 10- to 12-year-old students from a personal and family food orientation to a more global one.

This material includes a list of 14 learning activities and shows how these activities are related to learner outcomes. Finally, the interdisciplinary content chart is an example showing how the content of this curriculum has been developed to correlate to all subjects of the school curriculum.

Learning About Your Oral Health, level II: 4 to 6

The following unit illustrates another way in which the subject matter (content) of health education can be organized. The unit on human interrelationships or sex education for kindergarten through third grade presents a grade-by-grade progression of the social, emotional, and physiological aspects of sex education. The oral health unit, however, presents a horizontal structure emphasizing a particular sequence of topics—integrating dental health with other school subjects such as art, drama, language arts, science, history, and social studies. The unit offers an in-depth study of dental health, focusing on preventing dental disease by controlling of plaque in the mouth through oral hygiene (flossing and brushing), use of fluorides, and proper diet. In addition to the benefits afforded by integrated learning, the unit provides some classroom activities designed to stimulate student interest and understanding of the importance of dental health to total health.

When curriculum materials such as the American Dental Association's oral health program are used, teachers must make special adaptations for the particular school system and give careful study to the materials to understand the guiding philosophy of the developers. This unit is designed as a health instruction resource for children in the intermediate grades (4 to 6). The teacher must decide which grade level is most appropriate for teaching the unit. Regardless of the grade level selected, experience indicates that the oral health program should be taught as a unit and that the topics covered should be presented in the sequence suggested by the guide.

Research experience at the University of Illinois has demonstrated that fifth-grade teachers with a minimum of preparation can use this program to achieve effective results with their fifth-grade students.

The material from the *Learning About Your Oral Health* curriculum* has been selected to illustrate certain unique features. The design of each grade-level guide in the curriculum has been developed to serve as a complete teaching package. For example, the sections "Forward

---

*Material that follows is from Learning about your oral health, Chicago, 1980, Copyright by the American Dental Association. Reprinted by permission.

to the Teacher'' and ''Dental Health Facts for Teachers'' provide the teacher with the essential background information needed to teach the unit. A section of the teaching guide has been selected to illustrate the horizontal or parallel column structure of the teaching unit. This structure shows the interrelationship of the behavioral objective content, suggested learning activities, and finally the related activities that provide for the correlation of dental health learning to other school subjects.

INCIDENTAL INSTRUCTION

Opportunities and a need for casual or incidental health instruction arise naturally in the course of a school day. Some phases of health teaching may best be handled by such incidental instruction. Problems that are of deep personal concern to a particular pupil or particular types of pupils may be dealt with most effectively by incidental treatment. However effective such instruction may be for certain purposes, if the teacher relies entirely on incidental health instruction, a decidedly limited health instruction program results, regardless of how skillful the teacher may be.

Pupil-teacher conferences and counseling frequently include incidental health instruction. When a teacher discovers the particular needs and problems of a child, the person-to-person relationship promotes a clarifying discussion of the problems. The conference may proceed beyond the original problem and explore related problems of interest and importance.

In class a pupil's question on a health matter may be an occasion for the whole class to learn. At times a discussion of a question considerably removed from health may gradually shift to its health aspects. An alert teacher uses expressed class interests and explores a whole area of health, perhaps leaving the class with several questions to ponder over, and concludes the discussion at a later date.

Simple incidents in school can have meaning in health terms, and the teacher can make effective use of such realistic teaching situations. Health terms occasionally are used in areas aside from health instruction, and opportunities are presented for the pupils to expand their vocabulary. Examinations usually offer opportunities for incidental health instruction. This is particularly true during the review of the examination after the tests have been scored and returned.

Daily newspaper, radio, and television reports frequently have health topics of interest to the pupils. A new health discovery, an epidemic, a person who has reached 100 years of age, and a physician who has practiced for 50 years are examples of news items that provide both the opportunity and necessity for consideration in the classroom.

Opportunities are plentiful for the alert teacher who uses incidental instruction to fortify and amplify planned health instruction (Fig. 13-3). Spontaneous, live instruction is usually most stimulating to the pupils.

CORRELATED HEALTH INSTRUCTION

Correlation is a reciprocal relationship, and a kindred relationship or alliance exists between health and other cognate areas, which provides opportunities for effective instruction. Health aspects can enrich other fields and make experiences more stimulating and rewarding for the child (Fig. 13-4). There are many opportunities in health for teaching basic academic skills and

FIG. 13-4. Classroom strategies that attract attention and interest of students are essential to effective learning.

life experiences. In health instruction, diction, pronunciation, spelling, coherence, and clarity are important. In a very real sense health involves history, art, and the people of other lands.

Reading

Health readers are available at various levels. They are interesting, are written to be understood by children, and can be used to encourage general supplementary reading. For the teacher who seeks to enrich the curriculum of the superior pupil, health readers and health projects offer a fertile field of exploration.

Language arts

In writing and speaking assignments, health topics are a frequent choice of pupils. Reports on special health topics, field trips, and health experiences are used. Articles on health in the school may be written for newspapers. Letters asking agencies for health materials and requests to the health department provide correlated health and writing experience.

Spelling also can be included. Of the 2000 basic words in common usage, which are the core of instruction in elementary school spelling, many are in health literature. From classroom health study an instructor can find ample material for spelling purposes.

Art

Paper cutting, crayon fill-in, and free drawing can deal with health topics. Paste-on or original posters can be health posters. Health report cards can be a health project.

Music

Implications of mental and physical health in vocal and instrumental music are of interest. Many musical compositions have references to health. Health parodies on recognized songs should be avoided.

Arithmetic

Keeping records of changes in height and weight, attendance, and illness provides problems in arithmetic. Calculation of sleeping time and the amounts of certain foods consumed in a given period of time can be interesting experiences in arithmetic. The intermediate grades may be interested in rates for various health factors.

Geography

Health customs, life span, health problems, and dietary practices of peoples of other lands can be of interest to pupils. How other people live usually interests children.

History

The influence of health and disease on history challenges the imagination of youth. Health problems of different periods in history and health problems of famous historical figures are of special interest. Celebrated men and women health heroes live in historical perspective.

Nature study

The life and habits of lower animal forms have health implications. Feeding habits are particularly germane. The interrelationships that exist between humans and the plant and animal world are concepts that children should acquire as fundamental education.

Children must be helped to see relationships in life. Especially important are the relationships of health to the many aspects of everyday living.

SUMMARY

This chapter is introduced with a general discussion on the conditions necessary for establishing an effective health instruction program in the elementary school. Although local school curriculums vary in pattern and the details of their curriculums, experience has shown that certain organization factors contribute greatly toward achieving an effective health education experience for children. To this end, a list of eight suggestions for scheduling the health motivation program is included.

In this regard the role of school district health education coordinators can be an invaluable asset to the program. Typically the coordinator is a specialist in health education with a strong preparation in the content and instruction materials of health education.

As such, the coordinator oversees and monitors the overall program, reporting directly to the associate superintendent for instruction on the status and progress of the health education program. The coordinator becomes an important support person to the busy classroom teacher by providing assistance when needed, consulting, giving demonstrations, and conducting special in-service workshops for teachers. Experience has shown that school districts with a health educator coordinator have superior programs.

The four patterns of instruction traditionally used in the elementary schools are discussed; in addition, the pupil-teacher relationships, school experiences, and community experiences are discussed as rich resources for creative classroom teaching in making health teaching both interesting and vital in the lives of children.

Because of the scope and varied nature of health interests and health needs of children, organizing a curriculum that is both flexible and organized to ensure appropriate progression of learning experiences becomes a challenging task. To assist the classroom teacher and curriculum coordinator in this task, subject matter topics of interest at the various grade levels are suggested, along with the normal school day activities that can become effective teaching methods. Goodlad's conceptual framework (1979) (see Chapter 12, p. 309) for organizing the curriculum can be readily adapted to the local school curriculum. Sex education in the elementary school is discussed, and examples of objectives for this instruction are provided.

This chapter concludes with several examples of health teaching units at both the primary and intermediate grade levels.

GET INVOLVED!

Most respiratory therapists work in hospitals, where they perform procedures crucial to maintaining the lives of seriously ill patients with breathing problems. They perform tests to determine the patient's lung capacity. In addition, they analyze the oxygen, carbon dioxide, and pH levels of the blood.

To analyze carbon dioxide and pH levels, the respiratory therapist draws arterial blood. This must be done with special care to avoid damage to the artery that could interrupt the flow of oxygen-rich blood to the tissues.

Respiratory therapists, like hospital nurses, generally work in hospitals on a 40-hour work week schedule. Because hospitals are open around the clock, respiratory therapists also may work a varied schedule, including evenings, nights, or weekends. Much of their work time is spent in attending patients and in responding to respiratory emergencies. Respiratory therapists advance in their work from attending "general care" patients to the "critically ill" patients.

Respiratory care equipment has become increasingly complex, requiring formal training to enter the field. In addition to respiratory care, these therapists are now performing ECGs and providing care as cardiopulmonary technologists.

Training includes psychology, communication skills, medical ethics, human anatomy, physiology, chemistry, physics, microbiology, and mathematics, in addition to technical courses relating to the procedures, equipment, and clinical tests.

There are two levels of training that vary in length. Qualifying as a technician takes a shorter period, equivalent to an associate degree. To be accredited as a therapist involves a 4-year training program. Respiratory therapy training is offered at the postsecondary level in hospitals, medical schools, colleges, and universities.

For more information about opportunities in this field, write to:

The American Association for Respiratory Care
1720 Regal Row, Suite 122
Dallas, TX 75235

STUDY QUESTIONS

1. How is health instruction presented under an integrated, correlated, and direct teaching plan?
2. What are the functions of a school health coordinator?
3. What criteria should be considered in evaluation of health textbooks and other health education materials?
4. In terms of curriculum planning what is meant by terms such as *scope, sequence progression,* and *articulation?*
5. What are the sensitive and controversial aspects of teaching sex education?
6. Assuming you have the responsibility for planning a primary level health instruction program, what five high-priority health units would you include?
7. How does the *Growing Healthy* curriculum differ in its curriculum organizational scheme from that of the American Dental Association's Oral Health Level II Program?
8. What classroom activities would you emphasize to develop critical thinking and problem-solving skills in students?

REFERENCES

Allendorff S, et al: Student heart health knowledge, smoking attitudes, and self-esteem, *J Sch Health* 55:5, 1985.

Allensworth D: Teaching materials on world hunger and other international health problems, *Health Educ* 18:41, 1987.

American Dental Association: *Learning about your oral health: preschool, level I: K-3, level II: 4-6,* Chicago, 1980, the Association.

Andrews S, Turner C: *Sowing seeds of democracy in the first grade classroom,* Indianapolis: National Council of Teachers of English, 1991, ERIC.

Bloom B, editor: *A taxonomy of educational objectives, Handbook 1: cognitive domain,* New York, 1956, McKay.

Bridges D: *Education, democracy and discussion,* Berks, England, 1979, NFER.

Cornacchia HJ, Olsen LK, Nickerson CJ: *Health in elementary schools,* ed 6, St. Louis, 1984, Mosby-n-Year Book.

Cvetkovich G, et al: Child and adolescent drug use: a judgement and information processing perspective to health-behavior intervention, *J Drug Educ* 17:295, 1987.

Disinger J: *Teaching creative thinking through environmental education,* no. 3, ED 331699, Washington, DC: Effect of Educational Research, 1991, ERIC.

Eggen D, Kanckak D: *Learning and teaching,* Boston, 1989, Allyn & Bacon.

Frank C, Goldman L: Growing up healthy in New York City, *Phi Delta Kappan* 69:454, 1988.

Hazlett SH: *Growing up healthy: health education curriculum guide for kindergarten,* ed 4 (developed in the San Francisco Unified School District), 1983.

Health education of preschool children and their parents: a background paper prepared for the President's Committee on Health Education, New York, 1972, Xerox Corp.

Hufford A, Lipnickey S: Promoting self-responsibility using the school nurse in a health awareness program for primary students, *J Sch Health* 57:195, 1987.

Kindsvatter R, et al: *Dynamics of effective teaching,* New York, 1988, Longman.

Mayshark C, Shaw DD, Best WH: *Administration of school health programs: its theory and practice,* St. Louis, 1977, Mosby-n-Year Book.

Nagy C, Nagy MC: Administrative perceptions of health education in the special education curriculum, *Teacher Educ Special Educ* 10:131, 1987.

National Dairy Council: Food—your choice: a nutrition learning system, Rosemont, Ill, 1981, the Council.

Oei T, Fea A: Smoking prevention program for children: a review, *J Drug Educ* 17:11, 1987.

Pollock MB, Middleton K: *Elementary school health,* St. Louis, 1984, Mosby-n-Year Book.

Raper J, Aldridge J: What every teacher should know about AIDS, *Child Educ* 64:146, 1988.

Roberts SW: Food first, educating our children, *Health Educ* 18:17, 1987.

Shupe SD, Sandoval WM: Nutrition education: from the lunchroom to the classroom, *J Sch Health* 57:122, 1987.

Steinberg V, Fry T: The writing process in the health class, *Health Educ* 19:50, 1988.

Tucker AW: Elementary school children and cigarette smoking: a review of the literature, *Health Educ* 18:18, 1987.

US Department of Health and Human Services: Better health for our children: a national strategy. The report of the Select Panel for the Promotion of Child Health, Pub. no. 79-55071, 1981, Public Health Service.

Woolfolk AE, McClure-Nicolich L, *Education psychology for teachers,* ed 2, Englewood Cliffs NJ, 1984, Prentice-Hall, p. 47.

CHAPTER

14

Health instruction in secondary schools

OVERVIEW

Although controversy over the goals of secondary education has always existed, there appears to be less disagreement among today's critics than in the past. The arguments over the school's role tend to polarize between the so-called compassionate critics, who argue that the curriculum should be focused on the needs of the student, and the "back to basics" critics, who argue that the school should confine its efforts to teaching fundamental skills and those subjects that prepare the student for entrance to a college or university.

This chapter describes the departmental structure of the secondary school and its separate course (subject matter) orientation. Although the study of subjects from a separate course perspective offers certain advantages, the pattern of separate courses tends to create an isolated and unrelated approach to teaching that may make learning more difficult for the student. Several different curriculum patterns, including correlation, integration, and a broad-fields approach, are presented in relation to this problem. Modular scheduling, which divides the curriculum into smaller units or modules, offers the promise of more flexibility in class schedule and the hope of improving student learning.

The recommended schedule and the health content for a comprehensive health education program are presented. Also given is an illustration showing how the Teenage Health Teaching Modules program organizes a comprehensive curriculum. A summary of some of the most important health problems facing the nation is provided, together with a list of suggested health education objectives.

Materials from three innovative approaches to teaching health at the secondary school level are included. The handling of controversial topics is discussed. Several different types of controversies are examined, and suggested guidelines are offered to help schools handle controversies. Recent developments in professional preparation for health education are reviewed, including the minimum competencies required of all health educators. An example of teacher certification standards and undergraduate preparation in school health education is presented.

OBJECTIVES   After reading this chapter, the student should be able to:

1. Identify the controversies over the purposes or goals of secondary education
2. Explain the organizational patterns that are typical of most secondary schools

3. Identify the health education curriculum content recommended by the education commission of the state
4. Identify the characteristics of the secondary school student that have important implications for the health instruction program
5. Identify several major adolescent health problems that have important implications for the health education curriculum
6. Explain how the school health program can make a direct contribution toward achieving at least three of the nation's health objectives for the year 2000.
7. Distinguish between a moral and moralistic perspective in teaching a topic such as human sexuality
8. Identify several techniques and interpersonal skills that can help adolescents resolve conflicts nonviolently
9. Identify some of the conditions giving rise to teenage pregnancy.
10. Discuss the code of ethics for health educators proposed by the Society of Public Health Education

GOALS OF SECONDARY EDUCATION

Secondary schools are the principal vehicle for youths' transition into adulthood. As such, there is general agreement that the major purpose of American secondary education is to define and establish education for American contemporary life. Although there is general agreement on this broad purpose, there have always been a variety of interpretations. The differing conceptions of what constitute desirable goals of secondary education persist. The broad general direction in which education is going is toward a useful education for all American youth, stressing individually and socially significant learning. The exact nature of such education continues to be a matter of controversy. However, as Van Til (1978) has observed, the areas of agreement appear to be expanding, and the swing back and forth between extreme positions of critics seems to be narrowing. The extremes of these differences are between the critics of secondary education characterized by the compassionate critics, who are calling for a youth-centered school stressing the needs and interests of the individual, and the back-to-basics critics, who are calling for emphasis on the three R's and solid content courses to ensure the graduates' successful entrance to college.

The reaffirmation of the cardinal principles of education is perhaps a good indication of this larger consensus that is developing in regard to the purposes of schooling. Because of the historical significance of this statement, the National Education Association (1976), as part of the bicentennial celebration, appointed a panel of nationally prominent leaders and asked them to reexamine the cardinal principles. The panel reaffirmed the validity of these principles and their value as goals for all secondary schools. However, the panel chose to restate and to reinterpret each of the goals in order to make them more relevant in terms of the needs of today's society. For example, the panel's interpretation of the goal of health was as follows, "The scope and importance of health as an educational objective has become even more important than it was in 1918."

ORGANIZATION OF THE SECONDARY SCHOOL CURRICULUM

Frequently, secondary schools have a departmental structure that is organized by subject matter or disciplines. A typical schedule for the secondary student would include courses such as English, mathematics, science, social studies, health, art, music, and physical education. Other characteristics that are typical of secondary education in the United States center around the school day, class schedules, and the role of teachers and students. Typically the school day begins at 8:30 AM and concludes about 3:30 PM. Students usually attend school starting after Labor Day and continuing until the first week of June. The pattern of secondary schooling has become so standardized that it is assumed that students will study certain distinct and separate subjects. Moreover, the knowledge gained from some of the subjects will not be for practical purposes or immediately useful but instead will be of value in its own right. Classes in secondary schools are usually taught by a teacher who specialized in that subject matter. Typically classes have approximately 30 students, and the class functions as a group, with the teacher playing a dominant role in the classroom. Students are usually assigned homework to be carried out between classes, which includes assigned readings in the class textbook in addition to other class activities or study materials provided by the teacher.

One of the problems of departmental organization is that, in the horizontal structure of disciplines, the subject matter tends to become isolated and compartmentalized. Moreover, when several subjects are taught simultaneously, they may not be well coordinated and are taught separately and unrelated to other subjects in the curriculum. When this occurs, it becomes difficult for the student to assimilate the information. To overcome this difficulty, secondary schools have experimented with several different patterns of course organization. Such an example is the teaching of two courses according to a correlated plan: for instance, the teaching of U.S. history and English, the teaching of mathematics and science, and, to a lesser degree, the teaching of biology and health as correlated subjects.

The broad-fields approach represents still another attempt to integrate and show the relationships between subjects. An example is social studies, which combines history, geography, economics, and political science; language arts is another example in which elements of English, speech, literature, spelling, reading, and grammar are combined. In this regard some educators have advocated a broad-fields approach for the teaching of health-related topics under a title such as health and physical fitness, which would include aspects of health, exercise, physical development, safety, and recreational activities.

Still another approach is that of the core curriculum, which is also designed to establish meaningful relationships between subjects. This interdisciplinary curriculum seeks to bridge broad fields of study by designing courses or study themes such as the study of an American city or the family or the study of problems such as community health, consumer spending, and social problems.

The quest for better organization of the secondary school program goes on. Sometimes it takes the form of core or common learning programs, team taught or community-oriented. Through such programs, students can work together on interdisciplinary problems encountered by young people in our society. Sometimes it assumes the form of individualized instruction through contracts, learning packages, learning centers, technology, and independent study (Van Til, 1978).

In an effort to overcome the disadvantages of rigid subject matter categories and school scheduling, a modular plan for class scheduling has been developed. The major objective of this approach is to provide a more flexible plan for individualizing instruction. This objective is accomplished by allowance for greater variability in the scheduling of time, space, staff, and students. The conventional seven-period day of 55-minute modules is changed to a series of 21-minute modules each day, or a total of 105 such modules in a weekly cycle. The advantages of this plan include the varying of class size to allow for small-group seminars, large lectures, or laboratory classes of predetermined size. Moreover, the time length of a class can be varied to accommodate differing instructional needs. By use of the computer a variety of scheduling configurations can be developed.

Traditionally the recommendation for health instruction in secondary schools has called for a one-year or two-semester health course to be offered at both the junior and senior high school levels with the minimum for such instruction being a one-semester course at each level. However, with the creation of more flexible scheduling patterns has come the development of health education curriculum modules. The module is a smaller version of the traditional instructional unit. It allows for greater flexibility in scheduling and in the teaching of health. The Teenage Health Teaching Modules (Education Development Center, 1982) exemplify this development. This curriculum is a health education curriculum, composed of 16 modules, each comprising 4 to 15 hours of instruction. The modules are designed so they can be taught independently or as part of a larger course of study.

During the past 15 to 20 years investigators have studied several different patterns of health instruction, including the core course concept, integrated health instruction, correlated instruction, and several patterns of scheduling health instruction. Unfortunately, the results of most of these experiments are not clear and lack careful documentation and evaluation. On the other hand, studies have sought to determine the comparative effects of different scheduling patterns such as the teaching of health on an alternate-day schedule with physical education or the teaching of health on a block-of-daily-time schedule. The latter approach, namely, direct teaching, is preferred by most health educators. Also, as McClendon and Tayeb (1982) have pointed out, when health instruction is offered as a separate semester course, students have been found to achieve higher health knowledge and application test scores.

A pattern of alternating 9-week blocks of class time between health instruction and physical education has become a fairly widespread practice in secondary schools. Although such a plan does offer the advantage of a concentrated time period for instruction and subject matter continuity, there are other disadvantages. All too often, this pattern results in a single teacher having responsibility for teaching the two courses without being adequately qualified in both areas. A further disadvantage of this arrangement stems from combining classes that are not compatible in terms of scheduling class size, use of facilities, and course evaluation.

MIDDLE SCHOOL HEALTH INSTRUCTION

Middle school is a transition from the self-contained classroom in the sixth grade to departmentalized instruction in the high school. It represents a change in the relationship between students and teacher. When the middle grades curriculum is modified by large core areas, the transition for the students is easier, and teachers have a better chance to establish a close relationship with students. Health instruction, as all other instruction at this stage in school, must recognize the factors that motivate students and account for their interests and conduct (Fig. 14-1).

Students between 12 and 15 years of age include children who are in the homophilic, or gang, period, a few who have not yet reached that stage, and perhaps one fifth who can be classed as adolescents. To complicate the picture, a 12-year-old girl is physiologically and socially almost 2 years ahead of a boy.

During the homophilic period, girls are arm-in-arm with girls and boys tend to gang up with boys. Group loyalty is exceedingly important. The teacher should capitalize on the strong desire for approval by their associates and the tendency toward united action by directing

FIG. 14-1. Accepting the individuality of each student helps to give him or her a greater sense of self-worth and interest in school.

health instruction into channels of group approval and action. Group interest can mean group accomplishment and community interest.

Health instruction goals for middle grades

Health practices previously established will continue to be fortified in the middle grades, and new practices, particularly those associated with group health responsibility, will be established. Knowledge to promote understanding of health measures and procedures will be provided in the middle grades. However, greatest attention should be given to the development of attitudes that are essential to provide the necessary intensity to health practices and to ensure the fullest use of health knowledge.

Many health attitudes, in terms of ideal personal and community attainments, will prove to be the most lasting and valuable in terms of the individual's lifelong health measure. Among these are attitudes that are directed toward the following:

1. Resolution to attain a high level of health
2. Pride in a high quality of well-being
3. Application of reasoning to health problems
4. Conviction that only established health principles should be used
5. Acceptance of responsibility for the health of others
6. Ideals of citizen responsibility
7. Cooperation with community health efforts
8. Insistence on high community health standards
9. Pride in community assets

The knowledge of health that the students in the middle grades should acquire is expressed in the areas of primary interest at this level.

SENIOR HIGH SCHOOL HEALTH INSTRUCTION

Health schools of today encompass at least three broad purposes that seek to provide the student with (1) the skills and knowledge needed to continue further study at the higher education level, (2) basic preparation needed for a vocation, and (3) preparation for accepting the responsibilities of adulthood. Health education at the senior high level is most often considered to be one of the essential requirements in this preparation for adulthood.

To be effective, health instruction must be adapted to the distinctive characteristics of the high school age. At times the individual displays the consistency of maturity, and at other times the inconsistency of immaturity. Youth is a period of transition from the dependence of childhood to the independence of adulthood. Self-assertion, determination, and independence reveal the desire of all young people for emancipation from adult domination and for recognition as competent, self-reliant persons in their own right. They want to know *how, why,* and *what.* High school students are imaginative, enthusiastic, sensitive, and idealistic. They seek status within their group and try to merit the respect of their instructors. They need to develop a mature standard of values that will provide a basis for positive motivation. Gaining self-esteem that grows out of successful and satisfying participation is essential to their ultimate well-being.

At the high school level, teachers are working with students who have virtually attained

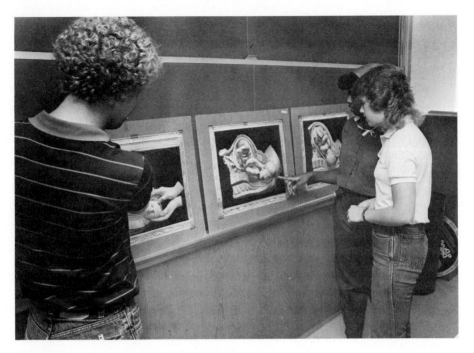

FIG. 14-2. Adolescent girls studying models depicting the anatomy and physiology of the reproductive process during pregnancy and normal delivery.

their maximal level of native intelligence. They will gain a great deal more knowledge from experience and from instructors who can challenge these young people by providing stimulating opportunities for learning. Their experiences can be most meaningful when students have a role in planning and implementing the instructional program. In education, as in self-growth, the individual must participate actively in the process, whether the learning involves memorization, analysis, or creativity. Effective learning must develop as growth from within. The teacher guides this growth by providing motivation through wholesome experiences. Although students will learn something about health without a teacher, a well-designed health instruction program increases both the quantity and quality of student learning (Fig. 14-2).

ORGANIZING FOR HEALTH INSTRUCTION

Health instruction is a recognized area in the curriculum of the middle school, and there are very few that do not offer formal classroom instruction in health. The scheduling of health instruction follows a variety of patterns. Unfortunately in some middle schools health instruction has not been given enough attention and care in planning to ensure its effectiveness. In such schools there is an urgent need to apprise the responsible administrators of the importance of health and what an effective health instruction program can do for students.

Few subject areas offer the student as much in a functional way as does health. Several factors determine the schedule and emphasis assigned to health instruction. The traditional background of the school, state requirements, community demands, the general pattern of the curriculum, the understanding of the administrators, and the competence of the health teachers all affect the nature of health instruction programs.

Correlation of health and other subject fields

In the self-contained classroom of the elementary grades it is both easy and natural for the teacher to recognize and use these health and subject area correlations for more effective teaching. Because correlated instruction is also important at the secondary school level, health instruction should be done through other subject fields. The following discussion applies to middle schools and senior high schools.

Integrated and incidental health learning

The daily experiences of middle school students are rich in health implications. Opportunities for integrated health instructions are plentiful, but usually only the health instructor capitalizes on them. However, if the organized health class does its work effectively, the students will be alerted to the health significance of everyday occurrences. If students are stimulated and challenged by a competent health instructor, a considerable amount of integrated health learning will go on.

In-service preparation of all the school staff in the possibilities and value of integrated health instruction is an ideal that rarely becomes reality. Yet the health coordinator or the health teacher may enlist the cooperation of other staff members, particularly those who have some background in health education or health-related preparation.

Incidental health instruction arises from student-teacher conferences, questions from students in the classroom, injuries to students, news reports, and tests and as an outgrowth of some topic outside the health field. Incidental instruction should not be superficial teaching. Any topic under consideration should be developed sufficiently so that the students understand and appreciate it.

Various activities in the regular program of the school provide health learning opportunities. Assemblies, lunchroom service, projects of the student council, announcements on the bulletin board, safety drives, and health examinations all contribute to the understanding, appreciation, and practice of health.

DETERMINING THE CONTENT OF HEALTH INSTRUCTION

Initiating a course of study through a survey of student health interests illustrates an important principle in curriculum planning: relevance of the instruction. This principle recognizes that (1) learning is more efficient when the subject is of interest to the student, and (2) information is more likely to be applied when it is of interest to the student. However, if the health education curriculum is to include the health content of greatest value to the student, it must draw on at least two additional sources of information. The foundation of the modern school health education curriculum should rest on (1) the health needs and interests of the student, (2) the health needs of the larger society, and (3) the body of health knowledge or the discipline of the health sciences. Examples of health topics identified from each of these sources include the following:

I. Health topics identified by a study of the individual student
   A. Growth and developmental characteristics
      1. Middle school level
         a. Sexual development causes student to be very aware of body changes
      2. Senior high school level
         a. Interest in opposite sex provides incentive for developing responsible adult roles in preparation for marriage
         b. There is growing interest in adult consumer role and many existing misconceptions about medications
II. Health needs of society
   A. Morbidity and mortality data reveal need to prevent such problems as deaths caused by cardiovascular diseases and accidents
   B. Need exists for early detection and treatment of cancer
   C. Smoking causes disease effects caused by smoking
   D. Misuse of drugs cause disease and suffering
III. Data from health knowledge or the health sciences
   A. Human experiences and scientific research have created a body of information that has been organized into broad categories such as nutrition, environmental health, mental health, communicable and chronic diseases, family health, and dental health

Two important publications illustrate the full scope of the content topics that may be treated in a comprehensive health education curriculum. The two examples are the 10 content areas recommended by the School Health Education Task Force of the Education commission of the States (1981) and the Teenage Health Teaching Modules program components (Education Development Center, Inc., 1982). The latter program was developed for the Center for Health Promotion and Education, formerly the Bureau of Health Education, which is located at the Centers for Disease Control in Atlanta.

Content areas recommended by School Health Education Task Force*

The 10 content areas recommended by the task force as minimal elements of a comprehensive school health education program are given below. Following the title of each is a brief list of topics that might be included in teaching this content area. It should be noted that this section is meant to provide *examples* and thus is not all inclusive.

   1. *Personal health:* physical fitness and lifetime physical activities, cardiovascular health, sleep, rest, relaxation, recreation, growth and development, nutrition, oral health, vision and hearing, prevention and control of disease, safety, body systems and their functions, aging, coping with death and dying
   2. *Mental and emotional health:* Positive self-concept, personality, emotional stability, responsibility, motivation, independence, mental disorders, coping with stress, mental health services
   3. *Prevention and control of disease:* contribution of early scientists, causes of disease, pre-

---

*Modified from *Guidelines for improving school health education K-12,* Columbus, 1980, Ohio Department of Education.

ventive measures, chronic disease, degenerative disease, communicable disease, immunization, personal health practices, community efforts

4. *Nutrition:* food choices, elements in food that contribute to good nutrition, factors influencing choices, individual nutritional requirements, food groups and nutrients, food sources, weight control, effects of nutrition on growth and activity, nutritional challenges, food preparations and protection, consumer protection

5. *Substance use and abuse:* personal goals; individual responsibility; substances beneficial to humans; classification of substances and their effects on the body; implications of use of substances; how habits are formed and influence health, use and misuse of tobacco, alcohol, and other drugs; treatment and rehabilitation programs; respect for self and others

6. *Accident prevention and safety:* attitudes toward safety, causes of accidents, home and school safety, traffic (automobile, bicycle, school bus) safety, fire prevention, survival education, environmental hazards, accident prevention—potential hazards, first-aid and emergency health care, safety personnel, resources, and agencies, individual safety precautions, recreational safety, occupational safety, safety rules, laws, regulations, legislation

7. *Community health:* individual responsibility, healthful school, home, community environment, community health resources and facilities, official and nonofficial health agencies, health service careers, pollution control (clean air and water), occupational environments, safety hazards and natural disasters, community involvement—a shared responsibility (health planning)

8. *Consumer health:* individual responsibility, propaganda in advertising, social and economic factors, laws for consumer protection (food labeling), protection agencies, health agencies, and organizations, health insurance, selection of medical services, quackery, reliable sources of health information, evaluating health products and services, use of trained medical personnel

9. *Environmental health:* environmental pollution, effect of environment on health (radiation, pollution), environmental protection agencies, population density, world health

10. *Family life education:* family composition and roles, life cycles (human growth and development), the reproductive process, heredity, marriage, selecting a compatible life partner, family relationships, parenting

Teenage Health Teaching Modules*

The Teenage Health Teaching Modules (THTMs) program consists of 16 teaching modules. Each module is a complete teaching kit for a unit on a designated topic and includes a teacher's guide with pages designed to be duplicated for student handouts. Many modules also include student materials, such as information sheets, posters, educational games, and, in some cases, student booklets. Each module provides 4 to 15 hours of instruction. Many are suitable for grades 7 though 12; some are recommended for either middle school or senior high school.

---

*From Teenage Health Teaching Modules Project, Education Development Center, 55 Chapel St., Newton, MA 02160. Used with permission.

Taken as a whole, the set of modules can constitute an introductory survey course on health. Used independently, modules can be selected to supplement materials already in use. There is no prescribed sequence or required number of modules, so that teachers can, if they choose, introduce one module 1 year and others later on. Activities are designed to be implemented by teachers from a variety of subject areas, such as health, home economics, social studies, science, language arts, and physical education.

Table 14-1 has guided THTM development and illustrates the ways in which the program reconciles the concern for a comprehensive approach, with the need for attention to commonly acknowledged health topics.

Adolescence is a period of rapid and varied physical, cognitive, and psychosocial development. Psychologists have identified many developmental tasks that individuals in our culture confront as they move from adolescent to adulthood. In an effort to combine the principles of developmental theory with those behaviors that are believed to be health promoting, the THTM curriculum has developed the concept of *health* tasks. Health tasks are those physical,

TABLE 14-1. Teenage health teaching modules

Health tasks* of adolescence and program introduction	Personal health	Mental and emotional health	Prevention and control of disease	Nutrition	Substance use and abuse	Accident prevention and safety	Community health	Consumer health	Environmental health	Family life education
Health Is Basic: An Introduction to THTM	X	X	X	X	X	X	X	X	X	X
Understanding Growth and Development	X	X	X	X	X					X
Being Fit	X	X		X						
Eating Well	X	X	X	X				X		
Communicating in Families	X	X								X
Promoting Health in Families	X	X	X		X					X
Having Friends	X	X			X					
Living with Feelings	X	X			X	X				X
Handling Stress	X	X	X		X	X				
Protecting Oneself and Others	X	X			X	X				
Preventing Injuries	X	X				X				
Improving Health and Safety in the Workplace	X	X	X			X	X			
Locating Health Resources	X	X	X	X	X	X	X	X	X	X
Using New Health Research	X	X	X	X	X	X		X		
Acting to Create a Healthy Environment	X	X	X				X		X	
Planning a Health Future	X	X	X	X	X	X	X	X	X	X

From Teenage Health Teaching Modules Project, Education Development Center, 55 Chapel St., Newton, MA 02160. Used with permission.

*Understanding sexuality is a key health task of adolescence. The project plans to develop a module *Sex Education: Deciding What's Right for Your Community,* which would inlcude an annotated bibliography of available materials and guidance for educators and parents to help them decide which approaches and materials on sexuality are appropriate for their community.

mental, emotional, and social tasks adolescents need to resolve to develop to their full health potential. The project has identified 16 critical health tasks and developed modules that focus on each one. The health tasks, which are also the titles of the modules, are listed down the left side of Table 14-1.

In addition to addressing the very special concerns of adolescence, the modules also involve students in an exploration of the traditional health content areas generally recommended for comprehensive school health education programs. The health content areas recommended in the Education Commission of the States publication, *Recommendations for School Health Education: a Handbook for State Policy Makers,* appear along the top of Table 14-1. The X's indicate which content areas are covered in each module. Although each module focuses on a specific adolescent health task and includes explanations of priority health content areas, all modules are carefully constructed to develop skills in five basic areas: (1) self-assessment, (2) communication, (3) decision making, (4) healthy self-management, and (5) health advocacy.

Wrestler charges coach with reckless treatment of injury

EMERGING ISSUE As coordinator of a school health and safety program, you have been summoned by the court to testify as an expert witness relating to a case in which a wrestling coach is being charged with negligent actions, causing further injury to one of his high school wrestlers. The specifics of the case relate to a wrestling workout in which the student suffered a leg injury. The coach undertook an evaluation of the injury and, according to the testimony, pulled on the leg and manipulated the knee. The coach then had the student continue his workout by wrestling a champion collegiate wrestler. The high school wrestler suffered further injury to the knee, resulting in his having to undergo surgery to repair cartilage and ligament damage. In connection with your review of this case, you are asked to respond to the following statements.

Please indicate whether you generally agree or disagree by placing a plus (+) or a minus (−) sign before each statement.

_____ 1. Participation in school athletics involves an assumption of risk. Therefore I have some reservations about charging a coach with negligence.

_____ 2. Coaches are expected to provide first aid for both minor and serious injuries. Therefore I believe that coaches should be granted immunity from acts of ordinary negligence.

_____ 3. School districts have a duty to exercise the same degree of care toward their students as a prudent parent would under comparable circumstances.

_____ 4. I believe that there is contributory fault on the part of the athlete that tends to compromise the charge of negligence.

_____ 5. Conferring *in loco parentis* status on teachers carries with it immunity from liability for negligence.

_____ 6. Public schools as a unit of government have immunity protection against liability for negligence. However, such protection may not extend to its employees.

_____ 7. In my opinion, this coach's action constituted a reckless disregard for the safety of the athlete under his supervision.

_____ If limited to a single choice, I would choose this number.

ADOLESCENT HEALTH AND THE NATION'S OBJECTIVES

Secretary of Health and Human Services Louis W. Sullivan released *Healthy People 2000* on September 6, 1990. The report is the product of an unprecedented cooperative effort among government, voluntary and professional organizations, business, and individuals. It has launched a national initiative to improve the health of all Americans significantly in 10 years through a coordinated and comprehensive push toward prevention. Forming the cornerstone of this effort is a set of national health promotion and disease prevention objectives for the year 2000. Development of the national objectives was coordinated by the U.S. Public Health Service.

Healthy People 2000 sets three broad public health goals for the 1990s:
- Increase the span of healthy life for Americans
- Reduce health disparities among Americans
- Achieve access to preventive services for all Americans

To help meet these broad goals, the 300 specific objectives were arranged into 22 priority areas. Various agencies of the federal government will take the lead responsibility for action toward achieving the objectives. Schools offer the most systematic and efficient means available to enable children and youth to avoid health risks and to improve their health. They provide an avenue for reaching the more than 46 million students each year in addition to the over five million faculty and staff.

Nine objectives from the 22 priority areas that are directly related to the schools' health education and physical education programs have been selected for discussion.

PHYSICAL ACTIVITY AND FITNESS
The problem

Findings from recent surveys have raised concerns about the amount and quality of physical activity and physical education for children and youth. Data from studies conducted in 1974, 1975, and 1984 show that little change has occurred. Less than one half of the children in primary grades (1 to 4) receive a daily program of physical education. The problem is twofold: (1) children in lower grades receive less than a daily program, and (2) a lower proportion of students in the upper grades receive physical education. These results also indicate the need to give more emphasis on lifetime activities to ensure a physically active and fit adult population.

The goals

Increase to at least 50% the proportion of children and adolescents in first through twelfth grades who participate in daily school physical education

Increase to at least 50% the proportion of school physical education class time that students spend being physically active, preferably engaged in lifetime physical activities

The objectives

1. Increase students' knowledge of the role of physical fitness and exercise in maintaining and promoting health
2. Increase students' knowledge of the importance of regular participation in physical activity
3. Increase students' knowledge and acceptance of the *type* and *duration* of exercise that promote cardiovascular fitness
4. Increase students' knowledge of the benefits of cardiovascular fitness in relation to mental health (Fig. 14-3)

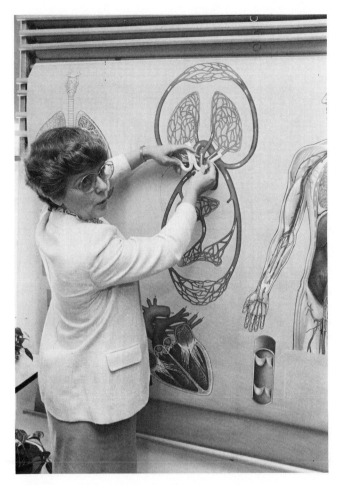

FIG. 14-3. High school health instruction must give greater emphasis to the study of the cardio-vascular system and the prevention of heart and blood vessel disease.

5. Increase students' knowledge of the role exercise plays in a weight control program
6. Increase students' knowledge of the different types of exercise needed to develop general physical fitness, including cardiovascular fitness, flexibility, strength, and coordination

NUTRITION EDUCATION
The problem

Physical activity and dietary patterns are often interrelated factors in the leading causes of death in adulthood. They are related to coronary heart disease, stroke, noninsulin-dependent diabetes mellitus, and arteriosclerosis. For those persons who neither smoke nor drink, eating patterns may have a greater influence on their future health than any other personal choice. In a survey of student food choices, 65% of the respondents say that they buy candy when shopping for snacks. In another survey of eighth and tenth grade students, 48% of the girls and 32% of the boys had not eaten breakfast on 5 or more days during the preceding week.

The goal

Increase to at least 75% the proportion of the nation's schools that provide nutrition education from preschool through 12th grade, preferably as part of quality school health education

The objectives (Box 14-1)

1. Increase students' knowledge of an optimal diet and its relationship to healthy growth and development, to physical activity, to successful reproduction and lactation, and to the maintenance of health
2. Increase students' knowledge of weight control through an appropriately balanced diet and physical activity
3. Increase students' knowledge and acceptance of the U.S. dietary goals and their relationship to disease prevention and health promotion
4. Increase students' knowledge of sodium, calories, fat, and refined sugar as factors in cardiovascular disease
5. Increase students' knowledge and acceptance of the importance of providing appropriate nutrition for infants and young children

TOBACCO EDUCATION
The problem

The use of tobacco is the most important preventable cause of death in the United States, accounting for one of every six deaths, or some 390,000 deaths annually. Cigarette smoking is a major causal factor in coronary heart disease and other blood vessel diseases. It is the most important cause of chronic, obstructive lung disease.

Cigarette smoking during pregnancy is a risk factor for low birth weight, prematurity, miscarriage, sudden infant death syndrome, and other maternal and infant health problems (*Healthy People 2000*, 1990).

The goal

Establish tobacco-free environments and include tobacco use prevention in the curricula of all elementary, middle, and secondary schools, preferably as a part of quality school health education

---

BOX
14-1   **Dietary guidelines for the United States**

The U.S. Department of Agriculture and the U.S. Department of Health and Human Services have issued a dietary guideline for Americans.

1. Eat a variety of foods.
2. Maintain healthy weight.
3. Choose a diet low in fat, saturated fat, and cholesterol.
4. Choose a diet with plenty of vegetables, fruit, and grain products.
5. Use sugars in moderation.
6. Use salt and sodium in moderation.
7. If you drink alcoholic beverages, do so in moderation.

The objectives

1. Increase students' knowledge of cigarette smoking as one of the major risk factors for heart disease
2. Increase students' knowledge and acceptance of cigarette smoking as a major cause of lung cancer and as a contributing factor in other forms of cancer, including laryngeal, esophageal, and bladder cancers
3. Increase students' knowledge and acceptance of cigarette smoking as a major cause of chronic obstructive lung disease, including bronchitis and emphysema
4. Increase students' knowledge and acceptance of the special risks of cigarette smoking for pregnant women

ALCOHOL AND OTHER DRUGS
The problem

Alcohol is a factor in approximately half of all homicides, suicides, and motor vehicle fatalities. The abuse of alcohol and other drugs is related to a number of other social and health problems that directly affect schools, such as early, unwanted pregnancy, delinquency, and school failures. The economic costs related to alcohol abuse are estimated to be approximately $70 billion. Because students take their first drink at an early age, preventive programs must be started at the elementary school level.

The goals

Provide to primary and secondary school children in all private and public schools educational programs on alcohol and other drugs, preferably as part of quality school health education

Reduce the use of alcohol by school children ages 12 to 17 to a level of less than 13%

The objectives

1. Increase students' knowledge and appreciation of the risks associated with alcohol abuse
2. Increase students' knowledge about drugs and their effects
3. Increase students' knowledge and appreciation of the risks associated with regular cigarette smoking, and the use of marijuana and other drugs
4. Increase students' knowledge of the social problems that result from alcohol and drug misuse such as family disruption and crime
5. Increase students' knowledge of the health consequences of drug misuse such as addiction, disability, and automobile accidents (Figs. 14-4 to 14-6)

FAMILY PLANNING
The problem

Family planning as defined in the report *Healthy People 2000* is a "process of establishing the preferred number and spacing of children in one's family and selecting a means by which these preferences are achieved." This approach assumes that a family exists and that planning in this respect is important.

In 1985 there were an estimated 416,170 abortions among U.S. females under age 20, and 16,970 were to females under the age of 15. In 1984 only 6% of the teenagers who obtained abortions were married (U.S. Congress Data from Alan Guttmacher Institute, 1991.)

There is an increasing number of out-of-wedlock births among high school adolescents (Fig. 14-7). The reasons why more pregnant adolescents are remaining unmarried are not clear. It may be that adolescent fathers are unable to support a family. It also may reflect changing societal attitudes toward marriage.

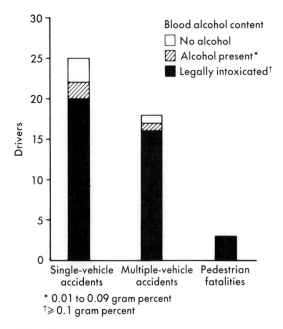

FIG. 14-4. Blood alcohol content of drivers involved in fatal motor vehicle accidents in Fulton County, Ga, 1982.

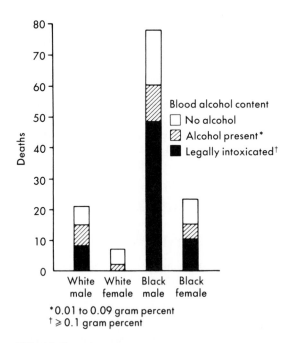

FIG. 14-5. Alcohol use among homicide victims by race and sex in Fulton County, Ga, 1982.

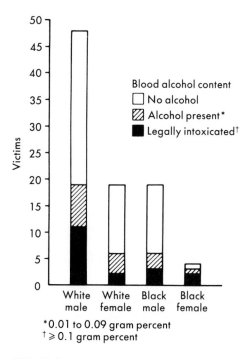

FIG. 14-6. Alcohol use among suicide victims by race and sex in Fulton County, Ga, 1982.

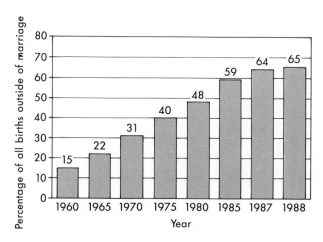

FIG. 14-7. Trends in out-of-wedlock childbearing among U.S. females under age 20, 1960 to 1988.

With respect to health education, school-based sex education has increased student knowledge about issues of sexuality, but apparently has not had an effect on the rates of adolescent sexual intercourse or pregnancy (McGinnis and DeGraw, 1991).

The goals

Increase to at least 85% the proportion of people ages 10 through 18 who have discussed human sexuality, including values surrounding sexuality, with their parents and/or have received information through another parentally endorsed source, such as youth, school, or religious programs

Reduce teenage pregnancies to no more than 50 per 1000 girls ages 17 and under

The objectives

1. Increase students' knowledge and acceptance of the risks of premarital sexual relations and the social, economic, and personal costs of adolescent pregnancy and parenthood
2. Increase students' knowledge and acceptance of the proper uses of fertility control and the appropriate alternatives
3. Increase students' knowledge and acceptance of community family services, including education, counseling, and medical services
4. Increase students' ability to explain the various contraceptive methods, natural family planning, and their relative effectiveness and safety
5. Increase students' knowledge and acceptance of the importance of prenatal visits and prenatal care to the health of the unborn child and to the mother
6. Increase students' knowledge of the ways of protecting and promoting health during adolescent pregnancy and parenthood
7. Increase students' knowledge of adolescent reproductive behavior, pregnancy, and parenthood that will protect and promote the health of the adolescent mother and the child (Fig. 14-8)
8. Increase students' knowledge of the importance of choosing foods wisely, the dangers of cigarette smoking, and the uses of alcoholic beverages and other drugs during pregnancy and lactation
9. Increase students' knowledge and acceptance of their roles as parents in participating in primary health care for their children, including well-child care, growth and development assessment, immunization programs, screening, and diagnosis and treatment of special conditions

VIOLENCE AND ABUSIVE BEHAVIOR
The problem

Violence against children and adolescents at the hands of mothers and their "live-in" companions who may be drug- or alcohol-addicted tends to evoke violent responses from teenagers reared in such an environment. This tragic cycle begins when children grow up witnessing violence and aggressive behavior and they come to accept the use of brute force as an acceptable part of family and social life. Hechinger (1992) points out that youngsters in such a violent environment are at greatest risk of accepting violence as a part of normal life.

Every month nearly 300,000 high school students are physically attacked. A 1987 survey reported that some 338,000 students carry guns to school (Table 14-2). However, on a more promising note, research has demonstrated that children are very resilient. With proper guidance and understanding, children can be taught how to develop gratifying alternatives to violence. The work of Dr. Prothrow-Stith of Harvard is beginning to show that schools can provide a strategic setting for the prevention of violence and abusive behavior (Prothrow-Stith and Weissman, 1991).

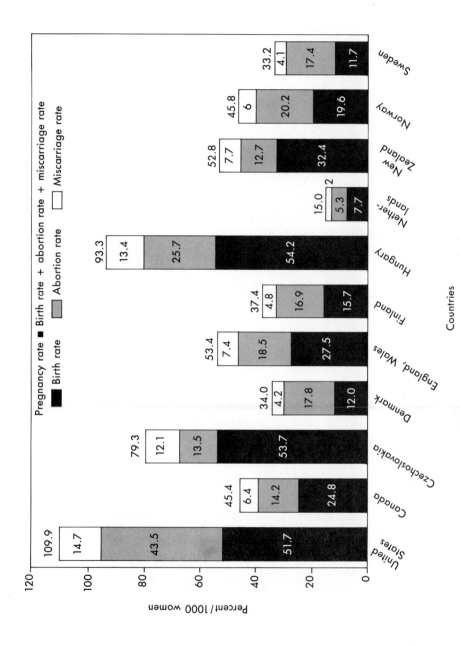

FIG. 14-8. Birth rates, abortion rates, miscarriage rates, and pregnancy rates among females ages 15 to 19 in 11 counties, 1983.

TABLE 14-2. Use of a weapon by institutionalized offenders under age 18 who were sentenced for a violent offense, 1987*

	All violent offenses	Offenders sentenced for:				Other violent offenses
		Homicide†	Sexual assault‡	Robbery	Assault	
Used a weapon...........	40.9%	77.8%	5.3%	44.0%	43.9%	28.1%
Gun	19.7	56.9	1.5	23.7	15.4	13.0
Knife	10.1	17.8	2.6	11.2	9.9	9.5
Other§	11.1	3.1	1.2	9.1	18.6	5.6
Did not use a weapon.	59.2%	22.3%	94.7%	56.0%	56.1%	71.9%
Number of offenders ..	8194	563	955	3204	2985	488

Data from US Department of Justice, Office of Justice Programs, Bureau of Justice Statistics, unpublished data from the *Survey of youth in custody,* 1987, prepared by Beck, AJ, Kline, SA, and Greenfeld, LA, Washington, DC, 1990.
*Survey respondents were residents of long-term, State-operated juvenile facilities. Detail may not total 100% because of rounding.
†Homicide includes murder and all forms of manslaughter.
‡Sexual assault includes rape and other sexual assaults.
§This category includes weapons such as axes, ice picks, scissors, clubs, baseball bats, ropes, vehicles, and objects used for strangulation or suffocation.

The goal

Increase to at least 50% the proportion of elementary and secondary schools that teach nonviolent conflict resolution skills, preferably as a part of quality school health education

The objectives

1. Increase students' knowledge of the circumstances that lead to conflict and violence
2. Increase students' knowledge of the dangers that may result from fighting
3. Increase students' knowledge of how to resolve conflicts nonviolently
4. Increase students' interpersonal and small group skills
5. Increase students' understanding of how to show respect for others

UNINTENTIONAL INJURIES
The problem

Accidental injuries are responsible for more deaths to American adolescents than any other health problem. Approximately half of all deaths and approximately 70% of injury deaths among adolescents ages 10 to 19 were caused by accidental or unintentional injuries. Data from the National Health Interview Survey indicate that injuries were responsible for 8.5% of school-loss days among adolescents. Also, adolescent males had the highest ratio of school-loss days associated with injuries. The leading causes of unintentional injury deaths among U.S. adolescents were vehicles, drowning, firearms, fires, and falls. Sports injuries requiring medical attention accounted for the greatest number of injuries among adolescents ages 13 to 19 years.

The goal

Provide academic instruction on injury prevention and control preferably as part of a quality school health education in at least 50% of the public school systems grades K through 12

The objectives
1. Increase students' knowledge of the various causes of accidents
2. Increase students' acceptance of the use of protective helmets when riding bicycles and motorcycles
3. Increase students' knowledge of the importance of wearing appropriate protective equipment in sports participation
4. Increase students' knowledge and appreciation of the problems arising from adolescent drinking as a factor in automobile accidents
5. Increase students' knowledge and acceptance of using seat belts and child safety restraints in preventing injuries relating to motor vehicle accidents

HIV EDUCATION
The problem

AIDS information and education programs have raised the level of people's awareness and their knowledge about HIV and AIDS. However, there remains misinformation at all levels of society. AIDS is the sixth leading cause of death for U.S. adolescents and young adults. Although the percentage of cases among teenagers remains low, medical authorities believe that many of the young adults ages 20 to 29 years contracted their infections as teenagers. Also of concern is the fact that the number of AIDS cases in the 13- to 19-year age group increased by 51% during the period between 1988 and 1989.

The goal

Increase to at least 95% the proportion of schools that have age-appropriate HIV education curricula for students from the fourth through the twelfth grades, preferably as part of a quality school health education

The objectives

1. For students who have not engaged in sexual intercourse and who have not used illicit drugs, to continue to:
   a. Abstain from sexual intercourse until they are ready to establish a monogamous relationship in marriage
   b. Refrain from using or injecting illicit drugs
2. For youths who have engaged in sexual intercourse or who have injected illicit drugs, schools should encourage these students to:
   a. Stop engaging in sexual intercourse until they are ready to establish a monogamous relationship in marriage
   b. Stop using or injecting illicit drugs
3. For youth unwilling to adopt behavior that would virtually eliminate the risk of being infected, schools in consultation with parents should encourage these students to:
   a. Avoid sexual intercourse with anyone known to be infected or suspected of being at risk of HIV infection
   b. Use a latex condom with spermicide if they engage in intercourse
   c. Seek HIV counseling and testing if HIV infection is suspected

SEXUALLY TRANSMITTED DISEASES
The problem

Included among the sexually transmitted diseases (STDs) are gonorrhea, nonspecific vaginitis, chlamydia, syphilis, human papillomavirus, herpes, chancroid, and pelvic inflammatory disease. Awareness of the risk of sexual behavior and STDs is particularly crucial for adolescents. Through courses in family life and human sexuality education students can develop the knowledge and skills to reduce the risk of contracting an STD (McGinnis and DeGraw, 1991).

Because of the variations in state reporting practices and the reticence of private physicians to make such reports, except for syphilis and gonorrhea, it is impossible to determine the national incidence and prevalence rates of STD. However, in the case of gonorrhea, the incidence rate for adolescents ages 15 to 19 is 1145 cases per 100,000 or an approximate total of 204,023 in 1989. The rates for primary and secondary syphilis have increased substantially since 1977, with an approximate total of 220,000 cases for 15-to 19-year olds. Estimates have been placed as high as 10 million cases for all STDs. Information from the National Adolescent Student Survey revealed that students seemed to know more about HIV transmission and prevention than they do about STDs.

The most effective way to prevent the transmission of HIV and other STD agents is to abstain from sexual intercourse. However, for those who do engage in sexual intercourse, the use of latex condoms has been effective in lowering but not eliminating the risk of STD and HIV infection. (U.S. Congress, 1991)

The goal

Include instruction in STD transmission prevention in the curricula of all middle and secondary schools, preferably as part of quality school health education

The objectives

1. Increase students' knowledge of STDs, including knowledge of how these diseases are contracted and passed to others
2. Increase students' knowledge and acceptance of the importance of early medical diagnosis and treatment of these diseases
3. Increase students' knowledge of the serious complications of these diseases such as infant death, birth defects, and mental retardation

DEALING WITH CONTROVERSIAL SUBJECTS

A realistic assessment of the nature of education indicates that controversy will always surround the educational process. This is a direct result of the role education fulfills in our society. Viewed one way, the role of education is to prepare young people to function effectively within society. Accordingly, education provides young people with the skills that are important for responsible citizenship and effective participation in family and community affairs. Viewed another way, the role of education is to prepare young people to deal with changes in society and to stimulate thinking, creativity, and interpretive skills that may lead to changes within the society. This tension between the role of education as a stabilizing force and the role of education as a vehicle for change often results in controversy.

Controversy presents a useful challenge to school personnel to interpret clearly to the public what they are doing and the value of such action. A community controversy about school-related issues presents a challenge to school personnel to do what they should be most effective at doing: interpreting information in such a way that others can understand and use that information.

Nature of controversy

Controversy occurs for many reasons. At least three different types of controversy can be identified.

Scientific controversy. Through mass communication, the public receives a great deal of conflicting information concerning health-related issues. As new knowledge develops and scientists refine existing knowledge, quite often points of contention occur. One group of scientists will discover the health implications of a particular medicine, food, or personal habit, and another group of scientists will find contradicting information. This is the nature of science: to find the truth through repeated searching and questioning. Scientists anticipate disagreement, but the public does not. Nutrition, for example, is full of topics for which the scientific findings are not yet clear. For the teacher this type of controversy presents a challenge to help students understand the scientific method and the reasons that there are so often contradictions in science. However, until there is clear scientific evidence on a particular point, it would be unwise for a teacher to take sides.

Scientific and religious controversy. Scientific controversy differs greatly from the controversy that pits the findings of science against religious beliefs. For example, there is scientific evidence that fluoride added to public drinking water reduces tooth decay among young people and accordingly enhances health, reduces health care costs, and improves nutrition. However, some communities hold religiously based beliefs that chemicals, such as fluorides, which can be poisonous in large quantities, should not be added to the water. A community's referendums to fluoridate water supplies can often be defeated by these groups. This type of controversy, between religion and science, can be especially costly to a community. In the case of water fluoridation, the first cost is in depriving young people of an effective dental decay prophylaxis, and the second is in the dissension and distrust caused within the community.

Philosophical controversies. Scientific controversy results from different interpretations of scientific findings; controversies involving science and religion contrast the findings of science and the beliefs of religion. Personal philosophies may be based neither on science nor on established religion. Philosophical controversies may surround issues of teaching methods, hiring practices, discipline, and educational philosophy. Today the notion of values clarification as a teaching technique is likely to provoke objection from some and support from others, arousing controversy. The report of the National Commission on Excellence in Education (1983) on the quality of education in the United States, entitled *A Nation at Risk: the Imperative for Educational Reform,* reflects the greatly differing philosophies on how schools should be managed. One example of such a controversial area is seen in the differing values placed on extracurricular activities. Some persons believe that these activities encroach unnecessarily into school time for instruction, whereas others believe that the informal learning resulting from these activities far outweighs the value of the time lost to formal instruction.

Knowledge as a basis of controversy

In our educational system, knowledge is basic. Without knowledge decisions cannot be made, problems cannot be solved, and relationships cannot be established. First and foremost, schools teach facts and information and the methods to derive factual information, the basis of knowledge. The scientific method is the generally accepted method of deriving information or facts and has as its aim the discovery of "truth." A collection of factual information constitutes knowledge.

Knowledge and facts, however, do not represent wisdom. Wisdom is how knowledge is applied and comes with experience and the development of values.

Despite these well-accepted principles of education, the argument is widespread that knowledge about some topics, such as sex, is dangerous. Why should knowledge about sex encourage promiscuous sexual behavior when knowledge about anarchy is not equally feared for encouraging students to become anarchists? In fact, the earlier a person engages in sexual relationships, the less he or she is likely to know anything about sex. Gordon (1981) points out that informed students are most likely to postpone sexual relations until they are emotionally ready, or, when and if these students are sexually active, they act appropriately to avoid pregnancy or sexually transmitted diseases.

To suggest that access to knowledge should be denied because it would foster inappropriate use of that knowledge contradicts the basis of our educational system and the principles of democracy (Fig. 14-9).

Controversy and values

Most often the basis of controversy in a school centers on the issue of values. Questions about what should be taught and who should teach it are an extension of the concern about whose values will be presented to the student along with the factual content material. No teaching is value free regardless of how much teachers may attempt neutrality in their presentations.

FIG. 14-9. Giving a formal report in the health education class provides opportunities for the students to improve their communication skills while gaining self-confidence and greater maturity.

Because most teaching is value laden, there is a concern among parents, school board members, and administrators that the values that are taught, directly and indirectly, have a basis in fact and fall within the range of values of the larger society. A history teacher does not teach the various political systems of communism, anarchy, democracy, and fascism and then suggest that they all have equal merit and that students should select the one they will follow. By word, attitude, and practice the teacher will clearly show a preference for a political system. Similarly the nutrition teacher does not teach about foods without telling students which are the better selections.

In sex education it is clear that it is better for teenagers not to become pregnant for both physiological and psychological reasons. Any teacher who teaches about contraception and does not also present some basic guidelines about the values of avoiding pregnancy is in a sense practicing educational malpractice. However, when a teacher describes contraceptives as a means of avoiding pregnancy, that teacher may still be at odds with some groups in the community who do not accept contraception because it violates religious dictates. Others may believe that giving knowledge about contraception implies tacit approval of premarital sexual intercourse.

Moral and moralistic perspectives

Education takes place in a moral rather than a moralistic context. A moral perspective encourages the acceptance of the aspirations of society but maintains the right of individual liberty. A moralistic context imposes a personal perspective in a persistent and dogmatic way. Gordon (1981) points out that it would be appropriately moral to tell a student that sex before marriage is against the principal teachings of organized religion. It would be moralistic and inappropriate to say that if students participate in sex before marriage they risk damnation. Such a statement, although inappropriate in the public school, may be appropriate in some parochial schools.

The distinction between moral and moralistic perspectives is important when dealing with issues of controversy. The teacher who does not clearly make this distinction is likely to irritate unnecessarily some students or parents. Implicit here is the ability to separate personal values and interpretations from those that represent the views of the larger society. However, it is possible that any specific community may not endorse the views of the larger society, and on some issues there is not a clear position of the larger society. Teachers therefore should be aware of the moral and moralistic perspectives of controversial topics.

When teachers work in areas of controversy, they must be well prepared and knowledgeable about all aspects of the subject. Of course, this is true in all areas of teaching, but it is especially critical in areas that are likely to come under public scrutiny. Fortunately most teachers who are willing to teach in areas of controversy realize this point.

An evaluation of student knowledge gains in selected health education topics taught in a sample of Nebraska schools showed that few schools taught about sex, but in those that did, student knowledge gains, compared with those of students who had not had similar instruction, were significantly higher. Further analysis suggested that teachers willing to teach about this topic prepared themselves especially well. The quality of their teaching and their sensitivity to issues of possible controversy increased, and in so doing they reduced the likelihood of possible community reaction (Newman et al., 1978).

Respecting the rights of all parties

Kirschenbaum (1982) points out that probably as many as half of the school districts in the United States have no clearly stated procedure for dealing with controversy. Kirschenbaum suggests that the following points should serve as guidelines for planning ways to deal with the resolution of controversial situations:

1. Clarify relationships between the school and the community with respect to curriculum and instruction
2. Avoid unnecessary conflict
3. Handle legitimate complaints and controversies in a way that respects democratic principles and professional practice

Relations between the school and community are best clarified with a specific statement on the community's role in the governance of the schools. Obviously this relationship begins with the school board as the community policy-making organization for the schools, but many more forms of relationships can be established by the school board. Advisory panels, expert panels, textbook selection committees, and grievance review panels represent examples of roles for community involvement and relationships between the school and community.

Clearly stated policies that stipulate the responsibilities of these groups will improve their effectiveness and avoid possible confusion.

Conflict can be avoided by administrators who are sensitive to the needs of individuals and who quickly identify and deal with potential conflict situations. Conflict may also be avoided by having ample opportunity for community input and dialog in the planning of new school programs or proposed changes in existing programs. For example, a revision in the school's physical education goals from one of recreation activities to aerobic fitness activities could benefit from public hearings concerning the advantages and disadvantages of the existing programs compared with those of the proposed programs. In this way all sides of an issue can be heard before a final decision is made concerning the proposed change. Even if the change is objected to by some, they will have been given a chance to express their views. Of course, this does not preclude any chance of later conflict, but it reduces the likelihood of such and brings the important issues to the public's attention.

If conflict develops that cannot be dealt with informally, clearly established means to resolve it should exist and be known to those involved. These means of conflict resolution should guarantee the rights of due process and include clear appeal options. A complaint about a curriculum item or teaching method may be dealt with as an administrative matter by the principal or whoever is in charge of curriculum matters. Failure to resolve the issue informally may lead to the issue being referred to a faculty panel. If the issue is still not resolved, a right of appeal may exist to the superintendent, who may appoint a joint school-community review group. Failure at this level may lead to an appeal to the school board. Variations on this hierarchy of conflict resolution steps could be many, but every school board should have a clear and specific set of policies.

On the basis of his work with the National Coalition for Democracy in Education, Kirschenbaum (1982) suggests that the rights and privileges of parents, school members, professional teachers on the school staff, and students all be considered judiciously in dealing with matters of controversy and disagreement.

Parents and community members. Parents are a single group of taxpayers who share, along with other taxpayers, the burden of paying for the schools. Because parents have children participating in the education process, their voices are more clearly heard than other taxpayers and community members in general. However, all citizens share the tax burden of supporting the schools, and so all have the right to participate in the school's governance.

Community members have the right to elect members to the school board and thereby directly participate in the establishment of community education policy. Community members can attend meetings of the school board, express opinions, visit and observe the school in operation, and serve on advisory groups within the school.

Parents have the right to be informed about their children's educational progress, to know of the content of their child's educational experience, and to request that special needs for their children be met. If certain parts of the curriculum are in conflict with the parents' values, they can request that their children be excused from these units. They do not have the right, however, to prevent other children from participating in these units.

School board. School boards serve as the community's representatives to establish goals, set policies, and hire competent professional staff, who in turn will carry out the day-by-day operations of the school and implement the school board's policies. If controversial issues cannot be resolved by the professional staff, the school board will become involved as the final arbitrator. The board's rights and responsibilities include establishing and imposing educational policy, but the board cannot infringe on or impose its will in matters that are not distinctly educational.

Professional staff. The school's professional staff works within the bounds of the policies established by the school board. They are expected to maintain communication with the school's community. The professional staff are expected and have the rights and responsibilities to establish curriculum, determine teaching methods, and revise, replace, and maintain the teaching resources necessary for optimal learning by their students.

Students. Students have the right to expect well-trained and competent teachers, adequate educational resources to facilitate learning, and a broad-based curriculum with a variety of subject matter area. At the same time, students have the right to develop their own opinions, to voice their opinions in appropriate ways and settings, and to choose among a variety of educational opportunities provided by the school. Students also have a right to privacy and due process.

Handling controversy

Controversy is not necessarily bad. Simply put, controversy is a discussion of contrary opinions. Out of controversy may come new agreements, positive ideas, and new energies to solve old problems. Out of controversies may also come dissension, disagreement, and disunity. Each year, hundreds of school districts face controversy and channel the contradictory energies in a positive manner, whereas other districts fail to resolve contrary positions, and accordingly programs, students, teachers, parents, and the communities suffer.

The basic points in dealing with controversy are (1) understanding the nature of the controversy, and (2) having a procedure for handling controversial topics. This procedure must have its foundation in a clear recognition of the legitimate interests and rights of the parties involved. Similarly, these established procedures should be known to all who are interested and involved in the quality of education and the conduct of their community's schools.

INNOVATIVE HEALTH INSTRUCTION: SOME EXAMPLES

Three examples of recent innovative approaches to health instruction are presented. The materials were selected not only because they represent certain innovations but also because they concern topics that have been identified as important to the nation's health objectives and to the health needs of adolescents as well. Also, because of the controversial nature of sexually transmitted disease, it was believed to be of use to both teachers and school officials to learn something of the scope and approach to teaching about these diseases as defined in the California project.

The materials selected represent two state projects, "Decisions about Alcohol and Other Drugs," sponsored by the Nebraska Division on Alcoholism and Drug Abuse, and "Teaching about Sexually Transmitted Diseases," a project of the California State Department of Education. The third example is a health instruction unit for senior high school entitled "Preventing Violence: Non-Conflict Resolution." The material for this latter unit has drawn heavily from Prothrow-Stith and Weissman's book, *Deadly Consequences* (1991).

The materials were selected to illustrate differing aspects of health teaching in today's schools. The Nebraska project offers some important guidelines for teaching secondary school students about alcohol using a decision-making approach. Included is the introduction to the guide, which calls attention to the alcohol problem in American society and the importance of an educational approach to deal with the serious problem of teenage drinking and driving. The guide offers a unique approach to this problem. Traditionally alcohol education has adopted a fear approach that points to the consequences of violating the law or the tragedies resulting from the inexperienced driver and drinker. Increasingly, behavioral scientists are stressing the importance of teaching decision-making skills. Their approach goes beyond the giving of facts about alcohol and helps the student to become aware of the emotional, psychological, and social forces that are shaping the teenager's behavior.

Helping teenagers to become more aware of these influences is a first step in the decision-making process. Helping them to know when more information is needed, to examine carefully the options, to evaluate the consequences of their choices, finally to commit themselves to the decision—living with the decision—is an essential step toward their becoming truly healthy individuals.

The material on sexually transmitted diseases represents an area of the health education curriculum about which very little has been written. In addition to defining the subject, the information for the teacher should be of value in teaching this topic.

Decisions about alcohol and other drugs*

WHY TEACH ABOUT ALCOHOL AND OTHER DRUGS?

Alcohol and other drugs are an almost inescapable part of life in the United States today. Over 80,000,000 Americans drink socially; the vast majority of Americans have taken or will take over-the-counter or prescription medicines at some time; and a rapidly growing percentage of Americans, particularly young people, have used controlled substances for nonmedical purposes.

---

*The material in this section is from *Decisions about alcohol and other drugs: a curriculum for Nebraska schools*, Lincoln, 1982, The Nebraska Prevention Center for Alcohol and Drug Abuse.

Because drugs are powerful substances, with significant and often unpredictable effects on the mind and body, their use is often accompanied by problems. Alcohol, in particular, causes major problems for many people. It has been estimated that more adults are directly or indirectly affected by alcohol-related problems than by any other single health problem.* Other drugs, too, pose serious risks to health and safety. The nature and extent of drug problems vary greatly from community to community, but almost everywhere we see:

- Traffic accidents and fatalities associated with drinking drivers
- Interaction effects resulting from using drugs in combination (particularly mixing alcohol and other drugs)
- Negative effects resulting from drug experimentation, particularly by young people
- Problems caused by alcoholism or other drug dependency, affecting not only the drug-dependent person, but those close to him/her as well

Although parents and teachers recognize that these problems touch both young people and adults, they may not be aware of the full extent of alcohol/other drug use among teens, or of the very real decisions that even elementary and junior high students must make.

Given the problems arising from alcohol/drug use in the society as a whole and the pressure on young people to drink and use drugs, it is important that young people be adequately prepared. They must be ready to handle the experiences they are likely to encounter as teenagers and to anticipate the problems they may encounter as adults.

A measure of the importance of alcohol/drug education to young people is the eagerness with which they seek out information about these substances. Young people are hungry for information about the effects of drugs; they want to discover what others think about drug use and what the actual consequences of a choice to use alcohol or other drugs will be. A school-based alcohol and other drug education program can meet this need for information with *facts* rather than *myths*. But such a program should do more than simply inform. Information alone will not prevent problems. A successful drug/alcohol program must do more. It must help young people to form positive attitudes about themselves and about their ability to make their own decisions, whatever the pressures may be. It must foster a sense of personal responsibility for the consequences of decisions and encourage the development of the ability to cope successfully with life problems. It must, in short, help build the kind of inner strength and sense of self that can make informed, conscious decision-making a reality.

CURRICULUM GOALS AND OBJECTIVES

In line with the assumptions above, the major goal of this curriculum is to help young people make informed, conscious decisions about their personal use of alcohol and other drugs, and hence ultimately to help reduce the incidence of problems associated with the use of these substances. More specifically, students will be able to:

- Identify and practice decision-making skills
- Recognize drugs that they are likely to encounter or use
- Understand the effects of such drugs alone and in combination, and understand the possible consequences of misuse or abuse
- Understand and respect the body's natural functioning and the effects of alcohol and other drugs on that functioning
- Understand and weigh the influence of family, media, and the law on drug/alcohol and other drugs on that functioning
- Recognize the importance of standing up to peer pressure when it conflicts with personal principles and goals

---

*Cited in Finn P, Lawson J: A teacher manual for use with Jackson Junior High, 1982.

- Weigh the consequences of a decision to drink and drive, and make informed decisions based on that knowledge
- Identify and practice alternatives to the use of alcohol or other drugs that satisfy human needs in positive ways
- Develop techniques for handling stressful social situations involving drugs or alcohol
- Recognize when alcohol/drug behavior creates problems for others; and determine appropriate interventions
- Recognize and, if necessary, seek out resources available to help persons with alcohol/drug problems and their families
- Make decisions governing personal alcohol/drug behavior in line with personal principles and goals

This curriculum was developed in a systematic fashion based on the goals listed above. In addition to these broad goals, specific student-oriented learning objectives were developed to aid the formation of each activity. A review of the objectives within this curriculum will be helpful in the development of a specific alcohol/other drug education unit.

CURRICULUM ORGANIZATION

The activities and content information that compose this curriculum are organized into seven major sections or clusters. Each cluster concentrates on a different facet of the overall decision-making process. The first cluster, "Introduction to Decision-making," helps students discover why decisions are important and what elements are involved in making informed, conscious decisions. A five-step decision-making process is introduced, and students have the opportunity to practice working through the process to arrive at a decision. The five steps of the decision-making process are listed below and are presented for use in graphic form throughout the curriculum.

1. Defining the problem
2. Looking at influences
3. Identifying alternatives
4. Looking at risks and results
5. Deciding, acting, and evaluating

The process is discussed in more detail in the introduction to Cluster I. Subsequent clusters expand students' comprehension of the various steps in decision making and provide ongoing practice in making decisions in difficult situations. At the same time, students' understanding of the nature and effects of chemical substances is also enhanced.

As previously mentioned, each section of this curriculum is referred to as a cluster. Each cluster consists of a *Cluster Summary, Activity Summaries,* and, if needed, supplementary *Teacher and Student Information.* The Cluster Summary is found at the beginning of each cluster and is an overall review of the content covered within the cluster. The summary states the concepts of the cluster and reviews what student objectives, activities, and resources are used within the cluster. In observing the Cluster Summary, it should be noted that the objectives, activities, and resources are read from left to right. An objective may have one or more activities that relate to it, or there may be more than one objective that relates to only one activity.

The activities within each cluster are described in the Activity Summary. The Activity Summary is an actual outline of the "steps to learning" that have been identified for each activity. Within the summaries can also be found a synopsis of the activity followed by the student objective(s) that are addressed in the activity. A listing of the resources needed for the activity are found in the left margin of the summary. These resources include handouts for the students, visual aids for the teacher, films, student/teacher information, and an evaluation component.

The handouts intended for use within the activities are duplication masters and are included directly in the activity. The visuals listed are transparency masters, also found in the activity, that may be used by the teacher. Films mentioned within this curriculum are available on request from the sources identified within the Activity Summary. Additional student information is provided and may be reproduced at the teacher's discretion. Supplementary teacher information is included in a few activities and will provide the teacher with an immediate resource. It is suggested that the teacher review each activity in advance of the class period in order to have the appropriate materials produced.

An "Evaluation Component" is included in each cluster to help the teacher evaluate student learning performance. The component consists of a set of test items that are matched with the objectives for each cluster. The objectives that are not accompanied by actual test questions may be assessed as students complete an activity or handout. Teachers will have to observe students working or collect and assess responses on the handouts to assess the objectives. If a teacher would like to construct a pretest to assess students' entry levels, the test items could be combined into one examination. After analyzing the results, the teacher could then select the clusters or specific activities where students have the greatest needs. In a similar fashion, test items from two or more clusters could be combined into a posttest administered at the end of the drug/alcohol unit. Student responses to such a test would provide the teacher with an accurate assessment of the objectives that students have mastered.

An addendum entitled "Drugs and Pregnancy" is included following Cluster VII. This section was prepared to supply educational material dealing with the effects of drug use during pregnancy. The addendum is organized along the same lines as the previous clusters.

A Resource Section is the final unit in this curriculum. This section provides the teacher with immediate information and acts as a reference for much of the content material discussed within the activities. The Resource Section comprises the following components:

- Teaching strategies
- Suggested films
- Sources for drug and alcohol instructional material
- Helping children with alcoholism in the family
- Directory of Nebraska Alcoholism and Drug Abuse Services
- Nebraska alcohol and drug laws
- Glossary
- Bibliography of materials used in developing this curriculum

THE DECISION-MAKING PROCESS

The following example illustrates how the decision-making process can be applied to decision-making dilemmas that teenagers must face.

Situation: Jane is at a party. She drove there with Jim and Jerry in Jim's car. It is getting late. Jim has been drinking heavily all night. His speech is slurred, and he weaves as he walks.

Now Jim wants to leave. "Come on, Jerry and Jane, we're going." Jerry suggests that Jim let him drive. "No way! I'm fine! Come on—*now!*"

Step 1: Defining the problem. Jane definitely sees a problem. On the one hand she needs to get home—she promised her parents she'd be back by 12:30. On the other hand, it doesn't look like

Jim's in much shape to drive. Deciding whether to drink and drive is Jim's problem, but since he's clearly bent on driving, the problem becomes hers as well. She must decide whether to go with him, or if not, what to do. She must also decide whether or not to attempt to influence Jim's decision.

Step 2: Looking at influences. Jane's parents want her home. She likes Jim a lot when he's not drinking and doesn't want to alienate him. Both of these are strong influences that Jane must weigh.

Step 3: Identifying alternatives. Jane has several alternatives:

Go with Jim
Call her parents to come get her
Stay overnight
Call a cab
Find another ride

In terms of influencing Jim's decision, she can:

Do nothing
Steal the car keys
Try to get Jim so drunk he passes out
Mobilize group pressure to influence Jim

In identifying the alternatives she realizes she needs more facts. Is there someone else she can ride with? She asks, and discovers that Barbara is going her way and would be willing to drop her off.

Step 4: Looking at risks and results. To go with Jim means a risk of a serious accident. Jane would call her parents, but then they'd know that drinking had been going on, and they would probably be angry. Staying overnight might also create parental worry. She could call a cab, but that would take most of her spending money for the month. Probably her best bet would be to accept the ride with Barbara.

But what about her feelings about Jim? Jane would prefer not to see him hurt. She could steal the car keys so he couldn't drive, but that would surely anger Jim. She could try to get him so drunk, he'd pass out, but it might not work and besides, she really needs to get home soon. Mobilizing group pressure might not work, and might anger Jim as well, but it could influence him to let Jerry drive.

Step 5: Deciding, acting, and evaluating. Jane decides that the risk of alienating Jim is more than outweighed by the danger of drunk driving. She will not ride with Jim. Her concern for Jim outweighs the risk of angering him by getting the group to pressure him, so she figures she'll try that. Perhaps he'll then let Jerry drive. If not, going with Barbara seems the best bet. Jane talks to several people, including Bob, a person Jim respects highly. Bob and several others reason with Jim. Gradually, Jim is won over. He agrees to let Jerry drive home. After Jane is home, she thinks about what transpired. She's safe, Jim's safe, she's home only a little after 12:30. All in all, it seems as if she made a good decision.

Teaching about sexually transmitted diseases*
INTRODUCTION

The following pages contain suggestions for structuring classroom activities for a 5-day education unit on sexually transmitted diseases (STDs). Since students in middle school and senior high school are at so many different levels of understanding and skill development, a wide variety of learning activities are offered here from which the teacher may choose. Some of these may be more appropriate to the middle school students, others to senior high school students. The activities were designed, at any rate, to provide both the teacher and the students the kind of flexibility that will maximize learning opportunities and minimize the need for previous sophisticated skills or knowledge of the topic.

---

*From Teaching about sexually transmitted diseases: a curriculum guide and resources for grades 7-12, Sacramento, 1980, California State Department of Education.

The unit was designed to be implemented over a period of 5 days in periods approximately 45 minutes long. Individual teachers may wish to depart from this suggested pattern, however, and should feel free to use any parts of the unit that they find helpful. Other teachers may choose to follow the unit exactly as it is outlined. If so, all they need to do is choose the activities they intend to implement and prepare the materials described for those activities. In many cases student worksheets are provided to facilitate completion of the activity. These worksheets are referred to by number and are designed to be copied or displayed via overhead projector.

Although the teacher is encouraged to use the recommended activities and materials in any way he or she wishes, these materials are based on a particular instructional approach that the teacher should clearly understand before beginning the unit.

Too often the primary focus of STD education has been on facts through the heavy use of films, outside health experts, and health pamphlets. This approach assumes that information about STD alone will influence behavior. In reality, a combination of affective and cognitive learning is better suited to the kinds of long-term behavioral changes that STD education attempts to bring about. Therefore the recommended activities for STD education in this unit include opportunities for communication, discussion, consideration of alternative procedures and points of view, and exercising of decision-making skills.

The goal is to encourage an awareness among adolescents about the nature and extent of STDs, ways of preventing them, and the need to seek medical diagnosis or assistance whenever their presence is suspected.

AN OVERVIEW OF SEXUALLY TRANSMITTED DISEASES

Concept 1 STDs may have immediate and long-range effects on individuals and society
Concept 2 Ten specific STDs are a serious health problem because of their incidence or their effects
Concept 3 STDs can be treated and prevented
Concept 4 Individuals have a personal and social responsibility to assist in the prevention and control of STDs

A NOTE ON TERMINOLOGY

Until relatively recently the term "sexually transmitted disease" referred to five specific diseases only. The two most commonly known are gonorrhea and syphilis. The others are chancroid, lymphogranuloma venereum, and granuloma inguinale. Aside from the mode of transmission, sexual relations, these five diseases are completely separate and distinct.

In recent years a number of other diseases that are spread primarily through sexual contact have been added to the list. These include nongonoccocal urethritis, herpes simplex virus 2, and trichomoniasis. However, the discovery and spread of human immunodeficiency virus (HIV), the cause of acquired immune deficiency syndrome (AIDS), have expanded the original definition of sexually transmitted disease. AIDS can be transmitted by contaminated blood, through contact with tainted blood transfusions, from contaminated hypodermic syringes, and through sexual contact. Unfortunately, there is no treatment for AIDS.

Teachers who offer instruction about STDs should be acquainted with all the various terms. They should emphasize throughout the education unit that "sexually transmitted disease" refers to a wide variety of different and distinct STDs.

TO THE TEACHER

Although STDs are widely discussed in the media, they are still cloaked in an aura of secrecy. STDs are essentially a health problem, however, not a moral problem. Consigning these diseases to the realm of guilt and shame makes them diseases that people are less likely to discuss openly and therefore less likely to take action on.

The main role of the teacher in an STD education unit is to create a classroom atmosphere in which these diseases can be talked about openly and comfortably. Therefore the teacher must feel comfortable with these kinds of discussions before initiating them with students. Students may ask direct and specific questions about the use of condoms, sexual intercourse, homosexuality, and similar topics. Moreover, the teacher must feel comfortable not just with the topic, but with informal student discussions in general.

Although the open classroom atmosphere is basic to effective instruction, teachers should not overlook several other principles that can help to make the STD education unit meaningful.

Involve all students. Even when the teacher has succeeded in creating a comfortable atmosphere for discussion, students may be reluctant to express themselves on what they consider to be a potentially embarrassing topic. Some students may even suspect that they are infected with an STD and therefore may be unwilling to betray their anxiety. Although the teacher should not force students to participate in discussions, every effort should be made to elicit input from all the students in the class. This can be accomplished through classroom activities that use both writing and discussion and through occasional small-group activities.

Don't do all the talking. When presentation of facts is required, lectures may be the most efficient technique. If the teacher does too much of the talking, however, he or she will risk creating one-way communication. Use outside experts when possible.

Listen to the students. Even if a teacher avoids doing all the talking, he or she may still not be listening to the students. Listening, in this context, means being responsive to the students' concerns and questions without judging them—in short, structuring the class so that students feel free to ask questions and volunteer their thoughts and opinions.

Vary the pace and style. Mixing different kinds of activities within a single class period will help to sustain the students' attention. The use of different techniques and activities will provide variety and texture to the class.

Avoid the use of slang. Some students have probably already acquired "street knowledge" about STDs. The kinds of attitudes and misinformation commonly associated with street knowledge are counter to the purpose of an effective unit. Therefore from the beginning the teacher should avoid slang and encourage the correct use of terms. (On the other hand, a stilted classroom atmosphere emphasizing *only* the use of proper terminology should also be avoided. Students should be able to feel comfortable discussing this subject.)

SECOND DAY: COMMUNICABLE DISEASES
Rationale

The purpose of this lesson is to begin exploring the content of the unit. Since many students may already be familiar with the communicable disease cycle, the teacher may decide simply to review this information and proceed to the content designed for the following lesson.

Objectives

The teacher will determine whether or not the students are familiar with the communicable disease cycle. If not, the teacher will present this information so that it is clearly understood.

The students will:
- (Objective 1A) Describe the infectious disease cycle
- (Objective 1B) Identify common reportable communicable diseases
- (Objective 1C) Explain why STDs are a serious health problem

Activity 5: Handshake (10 minutes)

Explain that this is an activity designed to offer a concrete illustration of how a communicable disease spreads through a population. Assign a number to everyone in the class. Then tell all the students in the class to shake hands with two other students. After the handshaking, pick two numbers out of a hat and explain that the students who have these numbers are designated as having a communicable disease. Then, in a class discussion, figure out who in the class may have "contracted" the disease through the handshake. The percentages may be made more realistic by figuring the odds of contracting a disease like gonorrhea—20% to 50% for men, and over 50% for women.

Activity 6: The infectious disease cycle (20 minutes)

Draw the diagram of the infectious disease cycle on the chalkboard, and explain the cycle to the students. Ask for student volunteers to assist in the explanation. Duplicate and hand out copies of the infectious disease cycles for measles, syphilis, and gonorrhea (or display them on an overhead projector) and, after making sure that the students understand this material, ask the class to discuss the similarities and differences of the three diseases. Emphasize during this discussion that, while measles creates its own immunity, syphilis and gonorrhea can be contracted through reinfection over and over again. Also emphasize that most other STDs follow cycles that are similar to those of syphilis and gonorrhea.

Teaching about preventing violence through nonconflict resolution

OVERVIEW AND IMPORTANCE OF THE PROBLEM

The Surgeon General's report *Healthy People 2000* calls on the schools to play a key role in the prevention of violence and abusive behavior. Many of today's school children are at risk of becoming victims or are themselves becoming perpetrators of interpersonal violence. Intrafamilial violence is more prevalent than is generally recognized. The relationship between violence and school problems is being explored from many points of view.

From the perspective of a school administrator, Quinn (1991) calls attention to the increasing number of at-risk students in the American public school system. Several factors are contributing to this upward trend, including the large numbers of immigrants from countries that are among the poorest, the increasing number of children born into poverty, the increase in latchkey children, the epidemic of teenage pregnancies, and the number of children suffering developmental disorders.

Of major concern to schools and society in general are the 500,000 students who drop out each year before graduation. This number is part of the 7 million youngsters who engage in high-risk behaviors (Turning Points, 1989). Although much of the research on the at-risk student problems has concentrated on the family, low economic status, and personal problems of students, several investigators have begun to shift the focus of their research on schools as bearing significant responsibility for pupil failures.

For example, Wehlage and Rutter's *Dropout Prevention Theory* (1991) holds that schools must tailor education programs more specifically to the needs of students whose needs often vary widely. Instead, however, schools have been demanding that students adapt to school policies and practices. As a result, the student who fails to attach or bond to the school, who fails to establish social or emotional ties to teachers and peers, often gives up and says, "I don't care."

Howard, in Prothrow-Stith and Weissman (1991), is even more harsh in his criticism of schools and teachers. He contends that there is an unwritten assumption by American educators that only a relative minority of students are bright enough to learn complex material. Students are "pigeon-holed." Consequently, when students fail, educators fall back on their preconceived idea that the child is lacking in ability. This leads to negative expectation and negative reinforcement, according to Howard. The result is "spirit murder." Thus many African-American students, especially boys, begin to "shut down" academically. By contrast, Israel and Japan operate on the assumption that every child can learn sophisticated material.

An article that appeared in the *Milwaukee Journal* in October 1991 perhaps best describes the plight of the African-American student. Statistics from a large metropolitan school system illustrate the gravity of the situation.

". . . of the city's 5,716 African-American males in high school, only 135 (2.3%) earned a B average or higher last year. Overall, African-American males had a grade point average of D-plus . . . While

African-American children account for 55 percent of the system's population, they were handed 94% of suspensions from 1978-1985.''

Some believe that such a situation is a prelude to violence among young Afro-Americans. Much of the information for this unit on ''Violence: Nonconflict Resolution'' has been drawn from Prothrow-Stith and Weissman.

Goals
1. To reduce the incidence of violent behavior and the circumstances leading to homicides
2. To develop student understanding and skills that will enable them to live peacefully with one another
3. To enhance student self-esteem through positive, interpersonal relationships with peers
4. To develop student interpersonal and small group skills, enabling them to manage conflicts constructively

PREVENTING VIOLENCE THROUGH NONCONFLICT RESOLUTION
Student objectives
I. *Understand* the risks of violence
II. *Explain* the circumstances that may lead to violence and injury

Content outline
A. Lessons on violence and homicide
1. Many people are unaware of the fact that the circumstances of most assaults and homicides involve people who are acquainted or are family members, who after drinking become involved in a disagreement and also happen to have a gun.
2. American adolescents are at much higher risk of being victims of gun-inflicted injury or death than are adolescents from industrial countries such as Japan, Germany, Australia and Canada.
3. Young, black males face the most serious threat of harm to life or limb. They are seven times more likely than white youths to die as a result of homicide. Rates for American Indians and Hispanic youth are about three to four times higher than whites. Asians are approximately the same as whites.
4. A 1989 poll reported that three of five Americans own guns.
5. Assault injuries are the consequence of interpersonal violence. A recent survey has shown that, over the 7-year period 1979 to 1986, approximately 2.2 people suffered nonfatal injuries.
6. According to O'Kane, criminologist, without effective gun control, violence will escalate. In response to growing danger in the streets, more people are arming themselves. As a result, teenagers are arming themselves for defensive purposes, afraid that someone will attack them. They carry a gun; someone gets into an argument; the next thing that happens is a dead body.

Student objectives
III. *Understand* how to control anger without hurting themselves or others
IV. *Distinguish* between healthy and unhealthy ways of handling anger

Content outline
A. Lessons on anger
1. Mental health professionals teach that anger is a normal emotion felt by people that may lead them to violent acts when their desires are not satisfied. Anger, as such, is neither good nor bad. It is the way that anger is handled, the way the individual feels that is good or bad. Often an angry person will retaliate by using aggression to physically or verbally hurt someone. A person whose aggression is out of control may hit or strike out in a sim-

ilar circumstance. Aggression explodes when the internal defences to control the anger are not strong enough. The question has been raised as to why there is so much anger among young, black males. Among theories offered as explanations of this phenomenon is "black self-hatred." According to this view, racism has taught poor, black males to hate themselves, causing them to assault and murder others whom they resemble (Prothrow-Stith and Weissman, 1991).

2. Ramey's theory of "free-floating anger" (1980) is explained as a generalized anger accompanied by feelings of frustration and helplessness, resulting in a sense that "the decks are stacked against me." According to Ramey, this is a double whammy of class and race that places young, black males outside the economic and social mainstream of American society. They are left with the belief that they will never find a place in this system. Because of this sense of being disenfranchised, they are perpetually irritable. A free-floating anger means nonspecific feelings that are easily ignited at the slightest provocation or excuse. The young black strikes out, releasing his pent-up rage on the nearest target—usually another black.

3. As Drs. Prothrow-Stith and Weissman point out, there are many reasons why a young minority person might feel anger, such as:
   a. Being poor in America, a nation that admires wealth.
   b. Being the victim of racism.
   c. Attending schools where a student's intelligence levels are preconceived.
   d. Facing a jobless future.
   e. Living in a violent environment where aggressive acts are commonplace.

Student objectives

V. *Understand* the circumstances that lead to fighting

VI. *Explain* the negative or "bad" things that result from fighting

Content outline

A. Lesson: Preventing circumstances that lead to fighting.
   1. These lessons can begin with the transition from the lesson on anger and how students deal with anger. According to Prothrow-Stith and Weissman, "fighting" is always on the list. The approach suggested is a cost-benefit analysis of fighting. Students are asked to create two lists on what is good and bad about fighting. The results of this exercise typically reveal that the "bad things" list about fighting is much longer than the "good things" list. This activity helps students begin to understand that there is much more to lose than to gain from fighting.
   2. Many male students have never before considered *not* fighting. This leads students to begin questioning their own values, which also leads them to begin questioning the teacher. Examples of such questions are as follows:
      a. Does this mean that you would never fight?
   3. In the case of female teachers, boys attribute such an attitude to the sex of the teacher. This may lead to follow-up questions such as:
      a. Would you expect your husband or brother to fight if someone called you a bad name?
      b. What if someone called your mother a bad name?
   4. Such questions are challenging to the teacher. How one responds to questions such as this will be important in helping students achieve the goal of resolving such conflicts nonviolently.
   5. Ferguson offers an important insight. Young men have a difficult time respecting one another. They want to receive respect, but many have not had the proper training to respect one another. According to Prothrow-Stith and Weissman, "Many young black men seem to feel that showing respect for someone is a form of toadying."

Another question often asked is, "What would you do if someone just came up and hit you for no reason at all?" Prothrow-Stith and Weissman's response is, "I don't know what I would do." This observation reveals that young black males, in particular, have a particular concern and heightened sensitivity about their vulnerability.

These authors point to a complicating factor: that early adolescent egocentrism or narcissism (a normal stage of sexual development) puts teenagers at a special risk for violence. Such feelings impair judgment, preventing them (especially young men) from accurately assessing a situation and fleeing from danger. Even if they perceive risk, their overdeveloped narcissistic pride may cause them to fight. In the past, when adolescents fought with their fists, the results were typically bruises, bloody noses, and broken bones. In communities today, however, when the young are armed with guns, fighting can have far more deadly consequences.

Student objectives

VII. *Demonstrate* ways of avoiding a fight (asserting oneself nonviolently)
VIII. *Modify* a mock fight so that it has a nonviolent ending
IX. *Be able to accept* a cooperative role with classmates when working toward a group project or decision
X. *Be able to mediate* the disagreement of others without choosing sides in the dispute

Content outline

A. Guidelines for the skits (mock fights)
  1. They must describe real-life situations.
  2. Students are not allowed to create roles about strangers and criminal violence.
  3. Profanity is not allowed.
  4. Skits continue right up to the moment when the imaginary punch is thrown. The teacher shouts "Cut," and the role play is over.

Teaching-learning activities

A. *Structured controversy*
  1. This class activity is designed to develop interpersonal and small-group skills to manage conflicts. Divide the class into groups of four and then divide each group into two pairs. Select a controversial topic, such as, "Should there be a national gun control law?" or "Should the age of qualification for a driver's license be raised to 18 years?"
  2. Assign pro and con positions to the pairs of students. Supporting reference material should be provided for the student's use. Additional reference materials may be placed in the school library.
  3. Students are to be given the following instructions:
    a. Plan with your partner to develop an effective argument. Use additional material if needed.
    b. Argue forcefully and persuasively, presenting as many facts as possible.
  4. After presenting the arguments, have students reverse their positions and present the opposing argument.
  5. Finally, have the students drop their advocacy positions and reach a consensus decision.
B. *Strategies to prevent a fight*
  1. Responding to a mock insult:
    a. "Why would you want to say that?"
    b. "Why would you want to tell me that I am (ugly, dumb, fat) and hurt my feelings?
  2. Encourage students to think of other nonviolent responses. Other examples:
    a. "This isn't worth fighting about."
    b. "If you have a problem with me, I'll talk, but I don't want to fight."
    c. "I have nothing against you, and I don't want to fight."

C. *Mediation*
1. Organize the class into cooperative learning groups (about five students each). Give each group an assignment to develop a mock conflict. Challenge the students to prepare a situation in which each side has a justifiable complaint.
2. Assign at least two students to prepare each side of the dispute.
3. After each side of the dispute has been prepared, conduct a *hearing* in which each side of the dispute is presented.
4. One student from each of the five conflict groups is assigned to a new group to serve as the mediator.
5. The role-playing mediator must help each of the disputants reach a negotiated settlement of their dispute. The mediator is not allowed to render a decision.

TEACHER PREPARATION IN HEALTH EDUCATION

The field of health education has developed rapidly over the recent past. Together with the increasing number of states that have begun to implement comprehensive school health education programs there has also been an increased demand for the health education specialist. According to recent reports from the Education Commission of the States, an increasing number of states have begun employing health education specialists. This development has also been paralleled by a rapid rise in the number of colleges and universities offering professional preparation in health education. Recent publications such as the Surgeon General's *Healthy People 2000* and the Carnegie Commission reports have given strong support for health education.

Impressive as this progress has been, the developments set in motion by the 1978 Role Delineation Conference and the National Task Force on Preparation and Practice have been even more significant. This has led to the creation of the National Commission for Health Education Credentialing, the formal mechanism for recognition and certification of the health education professional. The work of the task force has helped to define the role of the practicing health educator. Moreover, members of the profession have accepted the definitions, responsibilities, and competencies that are considered basic to the functions of all health educators (Appendix D-1). With the rise of school health education, many state departments of education have adopted certification standards for the health education teacher. The requirements for the Standard High School Certificate established in Illinois are provided as an example (see Appendix D-2). According to these requirements, certification as a high school health education teacher requires at least 32 semester hours of preparation in health education (area of specialization). Those teachers who already hold a teacher certificate in another specialty may qualify to teach health as a second field by satisfactorily completing at least the 20–semester hour–minimum program (see Appendix D). Since the state certification standard is defined as the minimum, colleges and universities offering a major in the field usually establish requirements that go beyond those of the state standard.

SUMMARY

The chapter begins with a discussion of the purpose of secondary education and the controversies that have existed over the years. One group speaks for a "back-to-basics" approach emphasizing the traditional subject-matter curriculum—math, science, English, and art—to prepare students for entrance to college. The other view in this debate holds that the curriculum should serve the needs of the adolescent. The departmental structure of secondary schools clearly reflects a subject matter orientation. Subject areas represent the departments, the formal course offerings, and the teachers themselves, who are prepared as subject matter specialists.

This period of the child's schooling experience between elementary and senior high school is one of transition from the self-contained classroom–integrated learning experience of the elementary school with a single teacher to multiple classrooms, teachers, and special subject departmental organizations of the secondary school. Such a transition can be stressful to the student. As a consequence, today's health education curriculum is placing less emphasis on learning the facts about health and more emphasis on helping students develop new academic and social skills that will help students adjust to the challenges of secondary education.

Curriculum patterns for offering health instruction are reviewed, including the separate health course and the teaching of health in correlation with science. A common curriculum pattern of offering health instruction at the senior high school is the one- or two-semester course scheduling health education and physical education into four 9-week alternating time blocks. A new curriculum for secondary school health education, Teenage Health Teaching Modules, is introduced, together with a scope and sequence chart illustrating its modular teaching plan.

The report *Healthy People 2000: National Health Promotion* and *Disease Prevention Objectives* are examined for their curricular implications relating to adolescent health. Health topics emphasized include physical activity and fitness, nutrition, tobacco, alcohol and drugs, family planning, violent and abusive behavior, unintentional injuries, STDs, and HIV education.

The chapter concludes with selected curriculum examples and a discussion on the teaching of controversial subjects.

G**ET INVOLVED!** Experience has shown that students enrolled in university health education classes often find that their vocational career interests ultimately lead them to choose a health-related field. In an era in which there is a growing public awareness of the importance of preventing disease and promoting health, health education becomes an attractive vocational option. Health education and its relation to the broad field of health promotion may be analogous to the general practitioner in the field of medicine. In this sense, health education becomes a part of all health-related professions. The health education student may prefer to be more of a specialist than a generalist. For example, many health educators become specialists in nutrition education, human sexuality, prevention, or providing rehabilitative education from some disorder or disease entity; or they become substance abuse counselors.

One such specialization is the field of educational therapy, a part of a prescribed medical treatment program for patients who are physically disabled, emotionally disturbed, senile, or acutely or chronically ill. Because of their disability, such patients may be withdrawn, depressed, or detached from normal life and reality. As the name implies, educational therapy is a form of teaching—not as much in the sense of giving knowledge as of stimulating the patient's interest, confidence, and self-esteem to overcome abnormal moods and emotional stress. As a member of the rehabilitation team, the educational therapist evaluates the patient's learning ability, interests, needs, and future goals. The therapist then devises a treatment and/or an educational plan that is fitted to the patient's total rehabilitation program. Course content and teaching methods are adapted to the patient's particular handicap.

Educational therapists may work in Veteran's Administration facilities, hospitals, private and state schools, prisons, job corps, and adult learning centers.

For more information about this field, write to:
The American Association for Rehabilitation Therapy
P.O. Box 6412
Gulfport, MS 39501

STUDY QUESTIONS

1. What is meant by the term *broad-fields approach* when it is applied to organizing the secondary school curriculum?
2. What advantages does a modular scheduling plan offer for health instruction?
3. What is recommended for health instruction at the secondary level, in terms of credit, amount of time, class schedule, and so on?
4. What criteria might the health educator use in determining the content to be included in a high school health course?
5. Given the nation's health priorities, what three major health problems might the health educator include in the high school health course?
6. What are some of the major health and social consequences of teenage alcohol abuse?
7. What different kind of controversy is the health educator likely to encounter in his or her teaching?
8. What guidelines might the teachers and school officials use in handling controversies?
9. What abilities or competencies should the practicing health educator be able to demonstrate? .
10. How do the attitudinal characteristics of the adolescent male make the teaching of conflict resolution difficult?

REFERENCES

Adeyanju M, et al: A three-year study of obesity and its relationship to high blood pressure in adolescents, *J Sch Health* 57(3):109, 1987.

Avruch K, Black P, Scimecca J, editors, *Conflict resolution: cross-cultural perspectives,* New York, 1992, Greenwood Press.

Better health for our children: a national strategy. The report of the Select Panel for the Promotion of Child Health to the United States Congress and the Secretary of Health and Human Services, vol III, a statistical profile. DHHS-PHS Office of the Assistant Secretary for Health and the Surgeon General, Washington, DC, 1981, US Government Printing Office.

Blum R: Contemporary threats to adolescent health in the United States, *JAMA* 257:3390, 1987.

Cissell WB: Teaching about international health in United States public schools, *Health Educ* 18(1):10-11, 1987.

Davidson N, Worsham T, editors: *Enhancing thinking through cooperative learning,* New York, 1992, Teachers College, Columbia University.

Decisions about alcohol and other drugs: a curriculum for Nebraska schools, 1982, The Nebraska Prevention Center for Alcohol and Drug Use.

DiPesi L: Focus on the positive: the campaign for child survival, *Health Educ* 18(2):13-15, 1987.

Education Commission of the States: Recommendations for school health education: a handbook for state policy makers, Denver, 1981, Education Programs Division.

Education Development Center: *Teenage health teaching modules,* Newton, Mass, 1982, the Center.

Ferguson R: The case for community-based programs that inform and mentor black male youth, an urban institute research paper distributed by the Urban Institute, Washington, DC, 1988.

Framework for health instruction in California public schools, Sacramento, Calif, 1978, Office of State Printing.

Gill DG: Illinois State Board of Education, State Superintendent of Education, State Teacher Certification Board, 100 N. First St., Springfield, IL 62777.

Gordon S: The case for a moral sex education in schools, *J Sch Health* 51:214, 1981.

Gordon S, Scales P, Everly K: *The sexual adolescent: communicating with teenagers about sex,* ed 2, North Scituate, Mass, 1979, Duxbury Press.

Greydanus D: Risk-taking behaviors in adolescence (editorial), *JAMA* 258(15):2110, 1987.

Hechinger F: *Fateful choices: healthy youth for the 21st century,* New York, 1992, Hill and Wang.

Horrocks JE: *The psychology of adolescence,* ed 4, Boston, 1976, Houghton Mifflin.

Howard J: Efficacy institute, seminar, comments reported by Weissmann, M. In Prothrow-Stith D, Weissman M: *Deadly consequences,* New York, 1991, Harper Collins.

Hughes LW, Ubben GC: The secondary principal's handbook: a guide to executive action, Newton, Mass, 1980, Allyn & Bacon.

Johnston LD, O'Malley PM, Bachman JG: Use of licit and illicit drugs by American high school students, 1975-1984, DHHS Pub. no. (ADM) 85-1394, Washington, DC, 1985, US Government Printing Office.

Kirschenbaum H: Handling school-community controversies over health education curriculum, *Health Educ* 13:7, 1982.

McClendon EJ, Tayeb RM: *Studying the school health program: a review of the findings,* Kent, Ohio, 1982, American School Health Association.

McGinnis J, DeGraw C: Healthy schools 2000: creating partnerships for the decade, *J Sch Health* 61(7):298-328, 1991.

Miller L, Downer A: AIDS: what you and your friends need to know, a lesson plan for adolescents, *J Sch Health* 58(4):137, 1988.

National Commission on Excellence in Education: A nation at risk: the imperative for educational reform. A report to the nation and the Secretary of Education, US Department of Education, April 1983.

National Education Association: The cardinal principles revisited, *Today's Educ* 65:59, 1976.

Newman I, et al: Adolescent health knowledge revisited, *Neb Med J* 63:406, 1978.

O'Rourke T, Smith B, Nolte A: Health attitudes, beliefs of students grades 7-12, *J Sch Health* 54:210, 1984.

Page R, et al: Interpersonal violence: a priority issue for health education, *J Health Educ* 23(5):286-291, 1992.

Petosa R, Hyner G, Melby C: Appropriate use of health risk appraisals with school-age children, *J Sch Health* 56:52, 1986.

Prothrow-Stith D: *Violence prevention curriculum for adolescents,* Newton, Mass, 1987, Education Development Center, p 106.

Prothrow-Stith D, Weissmann M: *Deadly consequences,* New York, 1991, Harper Collins.

Quinn T: The influence of school policies and practices on drop out rates, NASSP Bulletin, Nov. 1991, pp 73-83.

Ramey L: Homicide among black males, national conference on violence sponsored by the Alcohol Drug Abuse and Mental Health Administration proceedings, *Public Health Rep* 95(6):549-561, 1990.

Scott HD, Cabral RM: Predicting hazardous lifestyles among adolescents based on health-risk assessment data, *Am J Health Prevention* 2(4):23, 1988.

Slaby A: Prevention, early identification, and management of adolescent suicidal behavior, *RI Med J* 69:463, 1986.

Teaching about sexually transmitted diseases: a curriculum guide and resources for grades 7-12, Sacramento, 1980, California State Department of Education.

Turning Points: Preparing American youth for the 21st century: Report of the task force on education of young adolescents, New York, 1989, Carnegie Corp.

US Congress, Office of Technology Assessment: Adolescent Health, vol II: Background and effectiveness of selected prevention and treatment services, OTA-H-466, Washington, DC, 1991, US Government Printing Office.

US Department of Health and Human Services: PHS health education focal points, Atlanta, 1983a, Center for Health Promotion and Education, Division of Health Education, Centers for Disease Control.

US Department of Health and Human Services: Guidelines for effective school health education to prevent the spread of AIDS, *MMWR* 37(suppl s-2):1-14, 1988.

US Department of Health and Human Services, Public Health Service, Office of the Assistant Secretary of Health, Healthy people 2000: national health promotion and disease prevention objectives, DHHS, Pub. no. PHS 91-50213, Washington, DC: US GPO, 1991.

US Department of Health and Human Services, HIV/AIDS prevention, special report, Centers for Disease Control, Public Health Service, Atlanta, Ga, 1991.

Van Til W: *Secondary education: school and community,* Boston, 1978, Houghton Mifflin.

Wehlage G, Rutter RA: Dropping out: how much do schools contribute to the problem? *Teachers College Rec* 3:374-392, 1986.

Yarber WL: *AIDS: what young adults should know, instructor's guide,* Reston, Va, 1987, American Alliance for Health, Physical Education, Recreation and Dance.

Part FIVE

Healthful School Living

Policies and practices in health teaching

OVERVIEW

The focus of this chapter is on the role of school policies and their importance to the conduct of an effective health education program. Policies, in the context of schools, represent the agreements and official position of school authorities regarding a particular issue or issues. As such, policies serve as the basis for communication and understanding. Once a carefully planned policy is adopted, school officials can proceed with a clear sense of direction to establishing goals and the guidelines for teaching and program implementation.

Such controversial topics as drugs, alcohol, tobacco, and sex education have often been the source of tension and conflict concerning the school's responsibility. The problem of adolescent risk-taking behaviors, including drinking, drug abuse, teenage pregnancies, and sexually transmitted diseases, has brought about a new awareness of and concern regarding the school's role in preventive education. Past difficulties with school programs point to limitations in the policy statements. Such weaknesses indicate that the policies do not sufficiently represent the community's views. School officials have been urged to include recommendations from all relevant school and community groups in the policy-making process.

Several of the controversial issues are examined in detail, together with a consideration of their policy implications. Goals and recommendations for the instructional program are offered. The development of effective school policies requires a detailed and comprehensive review of all aspects of the issues. This, together with appropriate participation of school and community groups, provides the basis for effective programming. School policies that evolve from this process and are supported by educational research provide the basis for successful school programs.

OBJECTIVES   After reading this chapter, the student should be able to:

1. Explain the purposes that policies serve in the planning and conduct of programs
2. Identify several steps that are involved in the policy development process
3. Explain the effects of environmental tobacco smoke and the implications for school smoking policy
4. Explain why determining the purposes of alcohol education is more difficult than determining the purposes of smoking education

5. Explain why past efforts in drug education and sex education have been unsuccessful
6. Explain the trends in drug use among adolescents
7. Identify at least three issues that should be considered in developing a school drug education program
8. Explain how the AIDS problem has affected the school sex education program
9. Explain several guidelines for developing a school AIDS education program
10. Identify several findings from research on teaching that are important to health education

---

Policies are general statements often forming the guiding principles relative to an adopted position. Policies determine the course of action to be taken by an organization, group, or an individual. In government, policies bear the same relationship to regulations as rules to law, except that, unlike regulations, policies do not have the force of law.

The process of formulating policy typically involves five steps: (1) identifying the problem or issue, (2) creating an awareness among relevant groups, (3) achieving a consensus position on the problem, (4) issuing a statement of the desired goal, and (5) developing a plan of action that is both prudent and consistent with the goal.

"The influence of volunteer health organizations on national health policies is both unique and necessary." The altruistic nature of organizations such as the American Heart Association, the American Lung Association, and the National Cancer Society adds not only to the importance of their statements and recommendations, but also to their influence on American society.

The policy-making responsibilities for schools rest with the local school board. School policy reflects not only state education laws and regulations, but also state legislation pertaining to the health and safety of students and school personnel. In addition, the board seeks information from the community including parents, teachers, and business and professional leaders. On health issues, the local health department, medical and dental societies, as well as voluntary health agencies may each be called upon for information and technical advice.

The focus of this chapter is on school policies in regard to the controversial health issues, including drug education, sex education, and the policy implications for AIDS education. A brief review of public education history indicates that these issues have been a source of continuing tension between the school and the community. In some instances school policies have failed to provide the scope and the direction needed for effective school health education.

School boards have frequently failed to establish a sufficiently broad base of community support to enable the school to implement its programs. If the school board has not established strong community support for its policies, small-program pressure groups can easily exploit the situation. Such confusion and disruption adversely affect the school's instructional program, which, in fact, may be supported by the community at large.

Good policy-making procedure is directly related to quality education. The Midwest Center for Drug-Free Schools and Communities (1988) has taken the initiative to develop a guidebook to assist schools in establishing sound school-community drug education policies. The staff of this center has recommended that an advisory council of representatives from the community, the school, and law enforcement agencies be created as a first step in developing a drug policy. This council, in addition to helping formulate policy, would also serve as an ongoing reviewer. Specific responsibilities of the council would include defining and redefining the drug problem, updating materials, distributing information, and advising on policy implementation issues.

SMOKING POLICY

All the elements for an effective school policy on smoking are in place. In the years since the Surgeon General issued the landmark report *Smoking and Health* (1964) linking smoking and lung cancer, literally thousands of additional studies have been conducted reaffirming the finding that indeed smoking is a cause of disease. The voluntary health agencies, together with the federal government, have conducted massive informational and educational campaigns to alert the public to this health hazard. In recent efforts aimed at achieving a consensus approach to the smoking problem, the National School Board Association, the American Cancer Society, and the American Heart Association have joined forces on a project calling for a "Tobacco-Free Young America by the Year 2000."

Findings and conclusions drawn from the 1986 Surgeon General's Report on the Health Consequences of Involuntary Smoking have major implications for school smoking policies. The findings summarized in this report reveal that anyone who breathes environmental tobacco smoke is exposed to an increased risk of disease. The principal conclusions from the report are as follows:

1. Involuntary smoking is a cause of disease, including lung cancer in healthy non-smokers.
2. Children of parents who smoke when compared to children of nonsmoking parents have more respiratory infections and lower lung function at maturity.
3. Although separating smokers from nonsmokers may reduce exposure, it does not eliminate the nonsmokers' exposure to environmental tobacco smoke and the increased risk of disease.
4. Laboratory research has now demonstrated that sidestream smoke, the aerosol from the burning tobacco between puffs, is much more toxic than is the exhaled mainstream tobacco smoke (USPHS, 1986).

Although the National School Board Association and the national voluntary health associations have called for a tobacco-free environment by the year 2000, can the educational community afford to wait this long to take steps that will protect the health of today's school children? Providing a special smoking room for school staff, teachers, and administrators is hardly doing the addicted smoker a favor. Being forced to smoke in an even smaller indoor space places the already-at-risk smoker and other inhabitants of the space at an even greater health risk because of the highly concentrated environmental tobacco smoke and its increased levels of toxicity. Separating the smokers from the nonsmokers indoors is not enough; the nonsmoker's right to breathe clean air should not be compromised. A policy that provides indoor restricted smoking areas is no longer defensible, at a time when schools are required to teach about the harmful effects of smoking and when an increasing number of schools are enacting expanded health and wellness programs for students and staff. An increasing number of states are passing legislation banning smoking in public places and work sites, and airlines are prohibiting smoking on planes. Now is the time for educators to assume leadership in the drive for a tobacco-free environment.

Results from a study of school smoking policies conducted for the National School Board Association (Rist, 1986) show that 87% of the responding schools have adopted policies regulating cigarette smoking. Many schools have adopted more restrictive policies since 1980. An important finding from this survey shows that once the school has adopted policies prohibiting smoking, students have been quite cooperative in supporting the policy. However, these results show a serious omission in schools' antismoking policies, since only 2% of the school systems prohibit smoking by school employees. The survey also shows that some 81% of the school systems provide designated smoking areas in school buildings for teachers and administrators. This points to a glaring inconsistency between the policies established for students and those established for adults at the school site. Although the motives of the National School Board Association and the national voluntary health agencies are laudable, their call for action is too delayed and insufficient, given the results from recent research on the toxic effects of environmental tobacco smoke.

Such a policy need not pit youth against adults. As Sagor (1987) has warned, school officials must proceed with caution, lest their position be misunderstood. "The school community's war on drugs has the potential for pitting the two generations against each other."

ALCOHOL AND DRUG POLICY

Research on adolescent involvement with tobacco and alcohol reveals a common pattern of use. Those teenagers who smoke or use alcohol are more likely to smoke marijuana and use other illicit drugs. Concentrating efforts on the development of a nonsmoking policy and the implementation of an effective ban on tobacco use at school has been shown to be an effective first step toward achieving a comprehensive drug policy (Fig. 15-1). For example, one year after implementation of a "no-tobacco-use" policy in the Marietta, Ga, schools (Phillips, 1984), the following positive results were noted:

1. There was a healthier, cleaner environment for all students.
2. There were fewer drug-related problems; there was no evidence of marijuana use at the school.
3. Fewer students were tardy to classes.
4. There were no reported incidents of students being under the influence of drugs.
5. Students performed better academically.

In general, the school drug education policy should address the issues of alcohol, tobacco, and marijuana use. Such a policy, carefully developed and implemented, would make unmistakably clear the school's role in establishing a drug-free environment. More important, it

FIG. 15-1.   Special session of school board members discussing school drug policy with police officer.

would create by precept and by example the essential environmental support and reinforcement so vital to the success of the school drug education program.

Policy statements issued by school officials, as in the following examples, range from one of strict punishment to a caring and advocacy role for the school.

> The schools especially must be unyielding. Students who drink alcohol, smoke marijuana, or use other drugs must understand that the consequences of their behavior are unalterable: expulsion from school and disqualification from all extracurricular activities (Strong, 1983).

The second position is much more compassionate in tone.

> In our zeal to create policies and sanctions that will curb drug abuse, we must not lose sight of the fact that mentally healthy people become that way as a result of a series of caring, one-to-one relationships with parents, teachers, counselors, and others (Sagor, 1987).

Obviously there are problems that must be recognized. A significant number of teenagers will start using psychoactive substances. As a rule, such experimentation is viewed as a natural curiosity, well within the range of normal behavior for the growing and developing young person. Often, after a brief period of experimentation with the drug, the person will refrain from further use. However, there is the risk that such experimentation will lead to the serious problem of habituation and chemical dependency. What may have begun out of a normal curiosity may unfortunately become an acquired habit that is extremely difficult to break. There is a consensus among the public at large that school officials must be unequivocal in their position regarding the use of alcohol, marijuana, and other drugs. Schools must teach abstinence, concentrate on the prevention of drug abuse, make young people accountable for their behavior whenever it deviates from this behavior norm, and administer swift and firm discipline.

THE ALCOHOL PROBLEM AND ALCOHOL EDUCATION

Luce and Schweitzer (1984) calculated that approximately 25% of the total economic cost of illness to the nation is attributable to smoking and alcohol abuse. In addition, there are other costs of alcohol that are estimated to be as high as $6 billion, including property damage from accidents, fires, criminal justice costs, highway safety, and the social welfare system. Not only does alcohol impose a heavy burden of illness on adults, but alcohol use places teenagers and young adults at great risk. Motor vehicle crashes are the leading cause of death for the age group 15 to 24 years. Young persons are 2½ times as likely to be involved in alcohol-related crashes. Data from a recent longitudinal study of a midwestern high school student's drinking pattern reveals that an increasing majority of teenagers are using alcohol during the high school years. Use of alcohol rises from 76% in the ninth grade to 95% at the twelfth grade level. In addition to this increasing prevalence of alcohol use during the high school period, an increasing number of students are drinking to excess. Social drinking in American society is part of the ritual of growing into adulthood (Adeyanju et al., 1987). Tables 15-1 and 15-2 show the average prevalences for alcohol use, smoking, and other drugs for all students in grades 7 through 12.

Investigators attempting to develop strategies dealing with the drinking problem cannot ignore the cultural and social milieu that tolerates drinking and its consequences. The problems of drinking arise from many factors: economic, social, and cultural. These, plus cultural values and society norms, interact in this situation. No single intervention policy can solve society's problem with alcohol.

TABLE 15-1. Annual percentage drug use for youth 12 to 17 years of age

Drug	1972	1974	1976	1977	1979	1982	1985
Marijuana and hashish	—	18.5	18.4	22.3	24.1	20.6	20.0
Hallucinogens	3.6	4.3	2.8	3.1	4.7	3.6	2.8
Cocaine	1.5	2.7	2.3	2.6	4.2	4.1	4.4
Heroin	†	†	†	0.6	†	†	†
Nonmedical use of:							
Stimulants	—	3.0	2.2	3.7	2.9	5.6	4.4
Sedatives	—	2.0	1.2	2.0	2.2	3.7	3.1
Tranquilizers	—	2.0	1.8	2.9	2.7	3.3	3.7
Analgesics	—	—	—	—	2.2	3.7	4.4
Alcohol	—	51.5	49.3	47.5	53.6	47.3	52.0
Cigarettes	—	—	—	—	13.3*	24.8	26.0

National Household Survey on Drug Abuse, Rockville, Md, 1985, National Institute on Drug Abuse, Division of Epidemiology and Statistical Analysis.
—, Not available.
*For 1979, includes only persons who ever smoked at least five packs.
†Less than 0.5%.

TABLE 15-2. Onset of drug use by age

Age	Cigarette (%)	Alcohol (%)	Marijuana (%)
12–13	10	13	4
14–15	22	28	15
16–17	35	25	29
18–21	51	71	31

From Abelson HJ, Fishburn PM, Cisin LH: *National survey of drug abuse,* Rockville, Md, 1982, National Institute on Drug Abuse.

Instead of a single strategy designed for a single high-risk group, Stoudemire, Wallack, and Hedemark (1987) have argued that many initiatives will have to be undertaken through a coordinated plan for this society to move toward achieving a national goal—"the healthiest possible use of alcohol." Although social drinking is a well-established American custom, the achievement of a consensus position on the use of beverage alcohol has proved to be very difficult. Aside from the religious objections to beverage alcohol, critics of the goal "responsible use of alcohol" argue that the human interaction to alcohol is so varied and unique that it is not possible to know who is likely to cross the line from a socially responsible drinker to a problem drinker.

Despite these difficulties, the nation has no workable alternative but to continue the effort to achieve this goal of responsible use. If such an ideal is to be achieved, it will require a coordinated school-community alcohol education program that is based on the following societal norms:

1. Accepting a moderate consumption in *low-risk* situations
2. Actively discouraging moderate consumption in *high-risk* situations
3. Actively discouraging heavy consumption in any situation
4. Accepting abstinence
5. Establishing a high priority on safety and health protection in motor vehicle transportation

Policy initiatives for school also call for comprehensive educational approaches, with careful attention given to the mobilization and coordination of all community resources, including family, churches, voluntary associations, societies, professional organizations, and the local media.

GUIDELINES FOR THE SCHOOL

1. Alcohol education in the schools should begin not later than 12 years of age.
2. The curriculum should include information on the potential risks of alcohol and its misuse.
3. The myths and realities of drinking should include the effect of alcohol on the body, reasons for drinking and not drinking, and the social acceptance of drinking.
4. In addition to cognitive development, the program for preteens and early adolescents must focus on developing decision making, critical thinking, and social skills to help the student cope and resist pressure to use alcohol and drugs.

ANABOLIC STEROID POLICY

Anabolic-androgenic steroids are chemical relatives of male sex hormones. "Anabolic" means that they help build up the muscles and other tissues of the body. "Androgenic" refers to their ability to develop male sex characteristics in the body.

These steroids are used as therapeutic agents to treat stunted growth, and for a limited number of medical disorders. However, they are widely used as performance enhancing drugs by athletes and weight lifters. Their use is intended to increase human muscle mass, strength, or weight or to improve human physical appearance or performance in any form of exercise, sport, or game.

The harmful physical side effects have been well documented. Male teens and athletes may experience accelerated male pattern baldness, acne, decreased sperm production, atrophy of the testes and enlargement of the breast tissue. Female teens and athletes taking anabolic-androgenic steroids may experience virilizing side-effects such as deepening of the voice, baldness, increased facial and body hair growth, and hypertrophy of the clitoris. Other side effects include nausea, vomiting, diarrhea, abnormal liver function, healing problems, and a lowering of the HDL cholesterol level, which can increase the chances of developing coronary artery disease. Psychological alterations include more hostile, aggressive, and assertive behavior.

The State of Illinois Steroid Control Act makes the possession and delivery of steroidal drugs for nonmedical purposes a criminal offense. The bill authorizes the Department of Alcoholism and Substance Abuse to develop an education program to alert the public, particularly student athletes and coaches, of the dangers of abusing anabolic steroids. The legislation amends the Illinois School Code to require all school districts to provide instruction in grades 7 through 12 on the prevention of abuse of anabolic steroids. The Department of Alcoholism and Substance Abuse is working with the Illinois State Board of Education in the development of instructional materials and teacher training.

TEACHING APPROACHES TO DRUG EDUCATION

As Botvin (1983) has observed, the traditional approach to teaching students about smoking, alcohol, and drugs has tended to focus on the factual data and the harmful effects of substances. This approach is based on the assumption that an increase of the students' knowledge will lead to wise choices and ultimately to the rejection of drug use.

This emphasis on the facts of hazardous substance use is a reminder of the past national drug education program of the 1970s and the war on drugs during President Nixon's administration. In its effort to solve this drug problem, the federal government set as a national goal providing every classroom teacher and school administrator with the facts about the nation's drug crisis. A timetable of 1 year was set to accomplish this goal. This plan was based on the assumption that, once the administrators and teachers were informed they in turn could inform the students, and in short order the drug crisis should be solved. However, it became apparent very early that this factual information program was falling short of its goal to reduce drug experimentation and drug abuse. In fact, some of the early studies conducted during this period revealed that not only were the programs not succeeding, but in some instances students who scored the highest on their knowledge of drugs were also the students who were most likely to be experimenting with drugs (Halpin and Thomas, 1977). Generally, an information-based approach to alcohol and drug abuse prevention has not been successful in changing attitudes and behavior.

Because of the concern that drug education was not effective, a national commission on marijuana and drug abuse was appointed in 1973 to evaluate the programs. After an extensive review, the commission concluded that it could not find a drug education program anywhere in the country that it could recommend. The commission went on to state in its report:

> that policy makers should also seriously consider declaring a moratorium on all drug education programs in the schools, at least until programs already in operation have been evaluated. . . . (National Commission on Marihuana and Drug Abuse, 1973, p. 357.)

The Midwest Regional Center for Drug-Free Schools and Communities (1988) offers the following as guides for the development of effective drug education policies:

1. As a first step in the development of policies there should be a careful analysis of existing state and local laws, along with an interpretation of these statutes, especially as they relate to school law. This may require consultation from the state department of education, law enforcement agencies, and the judicial system concerning questions that pertain to such topics as the individual rights of students, parents' consent, and the specific interpretation of "in loco parentis."
2. The school policy-making body should not be confined to the school board and the school district administrator, but rather it should include all persons who, because of interest, knowledge, or job responsibility, can make a contribution. For example, in addition to school administrators, teachers, counselors, and coaches should be represented. Others who should be included are representatives of the court system, city officials, medical and health personnel, representatives of the business community, parents, students, and youth-serving agencies.

Once the policy making body is organized, it should consider several issues such as:

1. The adoption of an appropriate and standardized procedure for reporting substance abuse and suspected illegal substance use activity.
2. A consideration of the appropriate roles of school personnel such as the role of administrators, teachers, and counselors in the implementation of drug policy.
3. Establishment of appropriate due process safeguards to protect the rights of both students and school personnel.
4. Establishment of consistent and reasonable policies relating to suspension and expulsion from school.
5. Establishment of policies concerning substance abuse that reflect a consistent standard of behavior to be applied in evaluating the actions of students and staff.

SEX EDUCATION POLICY

The first step in establishing a policy for sex education, as in all policy development, requires a careful definition and analysis of the subject. When the issue has been sufficiently delineated to secure a general understanding and agreed-upon goals, a plan of action can be undertaken.

Policies are the general guideline statements of principle that provide a frame of reference for school-community agreements. The specific rules or regulations derived from the general principles give direction to the standards of conduct derived from the policy statement. The

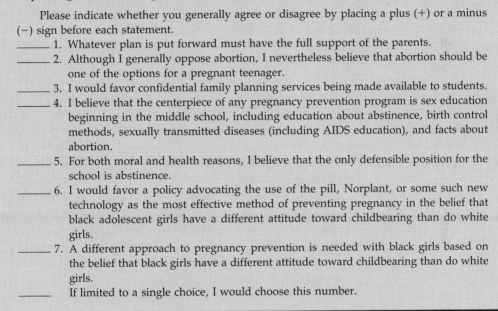

Teen pregnancy—a national dilemma

EMERGING ISSUE   On returning from a national conference on teen pregnancy and the role of the school, administrators in your school system appointed an ad hoc committee to develop a set of policy statements to guide the district's planning. Specifically the charge to the committee is to prepare a set of guidelines that would provide for a broad-based, school-community action program.

In this regard the federal government's National Research Council has just issued a call to all schools and communities—"to give the highest priority to the problem of unwanted pregnancies among the school-age population for both humane and economic reasons."

This statement has added to the sense of urgency and importance of the committee's task. As a health education professional and member of the school health council, you, with other council members, have been asked by the committee to share your thinking on this issue by responding to the following statements.

Please indicate whether you generally agree or disagree by placing a plus (+) or a minus (−) sign before each statement.

_____ 1. Whatever plan is put forward must have the full support of the parents.

_____ 2. Although I generally oppose abortion, I nevertheless believe that abortion should be one of the options for a pregnant teenager.

_____ 3. I would favor confidential family planning services being made available to students.

_____ 4. I believe that the centerpiece of any pregnancy prevention program is sex education beginning in the middle school, including education about abstinence, birth control methods, sexually transmitted diseases (including AIDS education), and facts about abortion.

_____ 5. For both moral and health reasons, I believe that the only defensible position for the school is abstinence.

_____ 6. I would favor a policy advocating the use of the pill, Norplant, or some such new technology as the most effective method of preventing pregnancy in the belief that black adolescent girls have a different attitude toward childbearing than do white girls.

_____ 7. A different approach to pregnancy prevention is needed with black girls based on the belief that black girls have a different attitude toward childbearing than do white girls.

_____   If limited to a single choice, I would choose this number.

over 1 million teenage pregnancies that occur each year serve as a reminder of the need for a more effective program of sex education.

Factors affecting the adolescent pregnancy rates include divorce, the increased number of single-parent families, working mothers, a mobile society, which has underminded the traditional role of the family, and changing cultural values. These forces, together with the influence of the mass media and the lack of supervision and parental involvement for many children, have contributed to the problems of alcohol abuse, drug use, and teenage pregnancy. Authorities point out that the first sex experience typically occurs when both adolescents are intoxicated.

The difficulties encountered in establishing an effective sex education program are somewhat similar to those encountered in establishing an effective program in drug education. In both instances past programs have tended to rely too much on narrowly based information programs without a recognition of important social forces contributing to drug use and sex behavior. Sex, alcohol, and drugs are associated for a variety of reasons. The adolescent boy may use psychoactive substances such as beer or marijuana to overcome his shyness and anxiety in social situations, especially those that include the opposite sex (MacDonald, 1987). The loss of inhibition and control under the influence of alcohol can easily lead the adolescent boy and his partner into sexual intercourse and the possibility of an unwanted or unexpected teenage pregnancy.

MacDonald (1987), a leading public health authority, has spoken out forcefully on the urgent need to upgrade the quality of the sex education program in schools. Gordon (1981) has also identified the ambivalence that characterizes the efforts of American society to deal with sexuality in the educational setting. Despite the fact that surveys indicate that the great majority of parents support sex education in the public schools, studies show that very few comprehensive, high-quality sex education programs exist in American schools.

As a public health official concerned about the teenage pregnancy problem, MacDonald has proposed two models or approaches to more effective sex education: (1) an abstinence ("just say later") model, and (2) a broad-based school-community approach similar to that recommended for school-community drug education. Whatever approach is undertaken, it is essential that schools be quite clear about the objectives and goals for the sex education program. School officials have characteristically been hesitant to express a strong value preference for fear of being misunderstood and of offending certain persons or groups in the community. However, it has become increasingly evident that a neutral approach has not been effective for either sex education or drug education.

There is little doubt as to the information parents and the public want in the sex education course. A strong, clear message—"abstinence for now"—is the cultural imperative standard of behavior. Unfortunately, neither parents nor school officials have made the goal of sex education clear to students. Parents, in particular, have reflected an uncertainty and an ambivalence in communicating with their children about the desired standard of behavior.

Table 15-3 provides important data for analyzing the sex education needs of teenage girls 15 to 19 years of age. The rates of sexual activity given for 1971 and 1982 and the changes that have taken place over this period reveal at least three distinct groups whose needs should be

TABLE 15-3. Rates of sexual activity of girls 15 to 19 years of age

Status	1971 (%)	1982 (%)
Active	27	43
Inactive	72	58
Swing group	16	

For 1971 Zeinick M, Kantner JF: Sexual and contraceptive experiences of young unmarried women in the U.S., 1976 and 1971, *Fam Plann Perspect* 9:55, 1977; *for 1982,* Pratt WF, et al: Understanding U.S. fertility: findings from the NSFG cycle III, *Popul Bull* 39:Table 2, Dec. 1984.
NOTE: The disparity in the percentage differences is attributable to rounding of errors.

recognized when one is planning the sex education program: (1) those girls who remain *sexually inactive,* (2) those who are *sexually active,* and (3) the 16%, labeled the *swing group,* who represent the difference between the 27% active in 1971 and the 43% active in 1982 and are in the process of becoming sexually active. An examination of these data by year shows that the shift to a large extent occurs among the older teens in this age group, an indication that these girls have delayed their decision about sexual activity until 18 and 19 years of age.

If a certain proportion of girls are delaying their decision to become sexually active until 18 or 19 years, sex education in high school provides an important opportunity to reinforce these students' decisions to remain sexually abstinent for now and to protect themselves and others against the threat of AIDS.

Obviously, school officials cannot ignore the needs of the sexually active students. However, this situation places both the parents and school officials in the ambivalent position of teaching abstinence on one hand while at the same time teaching about "safe sex" to the sexually active student. The school sex education program must stress the important responsibility these students have for protecting their own health and the health of their partners.

In view of the urgencies of the public health need, school officials must take the initiative to secure public understanding and the broad-based community support essential to the implementation of an effective sex education program. Emphasizing the "abstinence for now" approach is important because it provides the positive reinforcement for the majority of teenagers who have remained sexually abstinent. This message is particularly important to the 16% of adolescent girls who are most likely to become sexually active. It is these students who are most likely to be responsive to a strong educational message, to peer groups, and to other forms of influence. Teaching students the benefits of delaying their sexual activity should stress the very considerable health risks that pregnancy poses for the teenage girl, including the threat of contracting AIDS. In addition, there are the major social risks, such as interrupting educational plans to take on the heavy economic, social, and personal burdens of pregnancy, marriage, childbirth, and parenting. Teenagers, especially boys, must be helped to realize that sexual activity is not the teenage social norm. The reality is that the majority of teenagers are abstinent. In fact, the rates of sexual activity have leveled for white adolescent girls and have begun to decline for black adolescent girls. For the boys, the objectives are to develop an attitude of respect and caring for one's sexual partner and to appreciate the need to delay the relationship until both persons are prepared to accept the responsibilities that such a relationship entails.

What other topics should be stressed in the sex education curriculum? The concerns over AIDS and the resulting state and national legislation have had a major impact on school sex education. Traditionally, the local school has been given the option of whether to offer sex education and, if taught, what topics to include. However, with the advent of AIDS legislation, Illinois and many other states now mandate the teaching of sex education. The law in Illinois requires that the specific topic AIDS shall be taught, beginning in grade 6.

IMPORTANCE OF COMMUNITY SUPPORT FOR SEX EDUCATION

One of the reasons for the lack of success in sex education during the 1960s and 1970s was the tendency to focus too much on the student to the exclusion of the parent. Also there was the tendency to assume that the schools could provide sex education more or less on their own.

Moreover, parents were often neither comfortable nor sufficiently competent to educate their own children about sex or to teach them how to make good decisions.

This experience has also revealed that certain errors were made in teaching approaches. The well-intended effort to teach children how to make responsible choices and decisions failed to realize that young, immature students may not be able to make decisions in their own best interests. Development of such a highly complex skill requires the support and guidance of parents, teachers, clergy, and others to help the child evaluate the competing options, to anticipate consequences, and to appreciate the full meaning of the consequences that may result from these choices.

AIDS AND PREVENTIVE EDUCATION

Major national policy-making groups, after detailed and exhaustive studies of the *acquired immunodeficiency syndrome* (AIDS), have all issued statements emphasizing the importance of education in the prevention and control of this disease. The Centers for Disease Control, the National Academy of Sciences, the Surgeon General of the United States, and the U.S. Department of Education have recognized that until an effective vaccine and treatment for AIDS has been developed, education is the only effective means by which people can protect themselves.

In addition to these national governmental bodies, leading national professional organizations in the fields of education, public health, and medicine have also endorsed the Guidelines for Effective School Health Education to halt the spread of AIDS. These guidelines were developed through the leadership of the National Centers for Disease Control of the United States Public Health Service (USHHS, 1988).

The manner by which the disease AIDS is spread in children is quite different from the way it is transmitted among adults. In adults, AIDS is spread primarily by sexual intercourse. Surveys show that approximately two thirds of adult AIDS patients are homosexual or bisexual men who have a history of using intravenous drugs. Among children, nearly 80% of AIDS cases are contracted perinatally from infected mothers who are usually linked to intravenous drug usage. Transfusions with infected blood products is a much more significant cause of AIDS in children than in adults. Excluding hemophiliacs, only 2% of adults have contracted AIDS from transfusions, in contrast to 13% of children. Most children who have contracted AIDS from transfusions were infected during their first year of life.

Nearly 90% of pediatric AIDS cases are under 5 years of age and about 50% are diagnosed in the first year of life (Dalton and Burris, 1987).

POLICY FOR AIDS EDUCATION

The AIDS epidemic is of such magnitude that it threatens to overshadow all other experiences with disease in modern history. The fact that there is no likelihood of developing an effective vaccine or therapy for treating the disease in the near future makes preventive education the only option available to society. As a consequence, schools are faced with an unprecedented health education challenge.

This situation requires that all schools should have an advisory body to help develop the policies and plans needed to implement an effective AIDS education program. In addition to the preventive education effort, the advisory council must help the schools and the community keep abreast of current information and developments at the national and state level. Schools should be able to establish orderly procedures that are both appropriate and scientifically sound for the handling of children infected with AIDS. A host of other issues must be considered such as the problem of confidentiality, screening, the legal authority for protecting the infected child, and the rights and responsibilities of all parties concerned.

In addition to policy statements developed by governmental, professional, and commercial agencies, a wide range of curriculum materials on AIDS education is now available. Two such curriculum examples are (1) *AIDS Education: Curriculum and Health Policy,* prepared by Yarber (1987) at Indiana University for the Phi Delta Kappa Educational Foundation and (2) *Guidelines for Effective School Health Education,* developed by the Centers for Disease Control of the USPHS. The Centers for Disease Control suggest these general guidelines as criteria for evaluating an AIDS education program:

1. Are parents, students, health professionals, and appropriate community representatives involved in developing, field-testing, implementing, and assessing the program?
2. Is the program implemented as an integral part of a comprehensive K-12 school health education program?
3. Does the program fairly represent the values and mores of the community?
4. Is the program clearly communicated to both staff and community?
5. Is adequate training provided for those responsible for instruction about AIDS, including school administrators, teachers, nurses, and counselors?
6. Is the program taught by regular classroom teachers at the elementary level, and by teachers who are trained and qualified at the secondary level?
7. Is the program designed to help teenage students recognize the need to avoid specific behaviors that increase the risk of contracting AIDS?
8. Does the program describe and stress the benefits of abstinence for young people and mutually monogamous relationships for adults?
9. Is the program designed to help students acquire essential knowledge and skills to protect themselves from the risk of contracting AIDS if they are sexually active?
10. Is the program designed to help students acquire essential knowledge and skills to protect themselves from becoming drug abusers or to protect themselves from the risk of contracting AIDS if they are drug abusers?
11. Is the program sensitive to young people's stages of psychosocial development, with careful attention to ethno-cultural differences among students?
12. Are sufficient program development time, classroom time, and instructional materials provided for education about AIDS?
13. Is someone assigned to monitor the most recent data to keep the program up to date with current developments?
14. Is there adequate financial support to ensure continuation of the program?
15. Is there a process established for conducting this evaluation?

TEACHING STRATEGIES FOR PROMOTING HEALTH BEHAVIORS

The traditional approach using informational dissemination and fear-arousal messages characteristic of many early drug education programs has not been effective in preventing drug use. Important as student knowledge and attitudes are in the health of the student, researchers have now concluded that the behaviors of smoking, drinking, and other drug uses are symptomatic of larger and more fundamental needs of students. Targeting a specific health behavior and a specific so-called high-risk group of students may not be the most productive approach. As Jessor and Jessor (1984) have established, adolescence is a high-risk time for all youth, many of whom are experimenting with health-compromising behaviors such as alcohol and drugs.

Although there are youths with special needs and who are at special risk, Bernard (1988) has recommended that the school instructional program be placed within a larger context, using a comprehensive approach involving youth, families, schools, and community organizations. The causes of substance abuse are multiple, including personality, environmental, and behavioral factors.

Research concluded during the past decade has provided the basis for new teaching strategies emphasizing personal and social skills, which are proving to be effective in developing students' intellectual and social competencies and at the same time helping them to resist the pressure to become involved with drugs and other risk-taking behaviors.

The personality characteristic of student low self-esteem has taken on increasing significance in the designing of teaching strategies for preventing health-compromising behaviors. Studies have shown that virtually all maladaptive defense behavior patterns in childhood, adolescence, and adulthood are a product of the pain associated with low self-esteem (Mack and Ablon, 1983). This lack of self-esteem has been hypothesized as an important element in many of today's social problems, including child abuse, sexual abuse, domestic violence, delinquency, crime, teenage pregnancy, alcohol and drug abuse, and school failure. A direct concern of the school is students who lack problem-solving skills. An important corollary to these findings is the research showing that children, adolescents, and adults who lack problem-solving skills also share the personality chacteristic of low self-esteem.

This research has brought about a new interest and emphasis on teaching skills for problem solving, decision making, and participation in social situations. Preventive education rests on the assumption that improving the students' problem-solving skills will have a positive effect on several important health behavior outcomes. For example, developing the students' social skills usually leads to improvement in their communication skills and a corresponding reduction of their anxiety in social situations. With these new skills students are able to face challenges with a sense of relaxed confidence that greatly enhances the chances for academic and social success. Achievement in these areas raises students' self-esteem and perception of self-efficacy, enabling them to participate more effectively in problem-solving activities, which continue the cycle of positive outcomes. Problem solving and decision making involve critical thinking; the same skills that are applied to solving interpersonal problems can be applied to solving classroom intellectual problems (Bernard, 1986 and 1988). Longitudinal research demonstrates the value of teaching social problem-solving skills. Observations from these studies show that persons with good problem-solving skills lead productive lives. Children who lack such skills have demonstrated problem behaviors (Box 15-1).

ESTABLISHING AN EFFECTIVE TEACHING-LEARNING ENVIRONMENT

Once the general design of the curriculum has been adopted, it then becomes the responsibility of the teacher and the local school officials to translate the curriculum into workable learning experiences for the students. Until the curriculum is experienced by the student, it is nothing

BOX
15-1   **Drug education curriculum—personal and social skills**

1. Cognitive skills
   a. Myths and realities of drugs
   b. Smoking
   c. Alcohol
   d. Marijuana and other drugs
2. Cognitive skills for personal control
   a. Self-image, self-improvement
   b. Goal setting
   c. Interpersonal influences
   d. Media influences
   e. Cognitive coping skills
3. Problem solving and decision making
   a. Steps in problem solving
   b. Analyzing solutions and consequences
4. Communication skills
   a. Verbal and nonverbal
   b. Avoiding misunderstanding
   c. Asking questions
   d. Communicating with parents
5. Social skills—interpersonal
   a. Overcoming shyness
   b. Conversational skills
   c. Conversing with opposite sex
   d. Social activities
6. Social skills—assertiveness
   a. Resisting peer pressure
   b. Reasons for being assertive
   c. Verbal assertiveness
   d. Nonverbal assertiveness
   e. Resisting peer pressure to drug use

Adapted from Botvin GJ: *Life skills training: teachers manual,* New York, 1983, Smithfield Press.

more than a plan. The process of implementation—moving from a teaching plan into active learning—requires special care in selecting teaching strategies, the content and learning experiences, and the study materials and in assessing the effects of instruction on students.

Although there will always be some intangibles that make for effective teaching (i.e, personality factors and the "art of teaching"), nevertheless, there is also a growing body of research literature that is establishing the scientific basis of education. Given this research base, which generalizations can now be made that will help to ensure an effective learning environment for the student?

Research on learning

Walberg, Schiller, and Haertel (1983) have conducted an exhaustive review of the instructional research covering the period from 1969 to 1979. The following points summarize the key findings from the critical reviews of these authors.

1. *Instructional time* is positively correlated with learning achievement. In general, the more time devoted to instruction, the more students learn. Planning instruction for primary and intermediate-level students must give priority consideration to helping students develop their fundamental skills in reading, writing, and mathematics and to the development of their skills for acquiring information. In this regard, health instruction that is carefully designed in terms of student reading and vocabulary levels has been shown to contribute significantly to the achievement of these fundamentals (Redican, Olsen, and Stone, 1979).

2. *Students learn more when taught in small classes.* For example, elementary school students who are taught in class sizes of 20 or fewer will achieve as much as a 2-year advantage over children taught in larger classes (e.g., 40 students) during the course of their elementary school experience (K-6).

3. *Individualization,* sometimes referred to as a personalized system of instruction, is superior to all other forms of group instruction for cognitive learning. This form of instruction may be characterized as follows:
   a. Reliance on written words
   b. Specific instructional objective
   c. Small units of instruction
   d. Self-pacing of the student through instruction (students proceed through the material at their own rate)
   e. Mastery or near-perfect performance required before the student is allowed to proceed to the next unit
   f. Frequent assessment of the student by repeated testing with maximal credit for success and no penalty for failure

   In this form of instruction, the amount of time for learning is flexible. Although the focus of instruction is on the individual student, providing alternative forms of instruction with opportunities for the student to participate in cooperative group learning with peers has also been found to improve learning.

4. *Direct instruction* has been shown to be particularly effective for student cognitive learning. The term *direct* refers to the fact that the teacher is in control of the teaching-learning situation, including selecting learning activities, sequencing lessons, choosing instructional materials, and monitoring student performance. Students are questioned frequently, and feedback is immediate, emphasizing development of correct responses.

5. *Discussion* as a teaching method is more effective with the older, more mature student. Studies have shown that discussion is almost as effective for student achievement as the traditional lecture method and more effective in helping students to retain information.

6. *Student-centered discussion* (compared with teacher-centered discussion) tends to produce superior results in the effective domain or in attitude changes. The same is true for student-led discussions, which are more effective than teacher-led discussions in achieving desired attitude changes.

7. *Teacher characteristics* are important. These include:
   a. Being able to maintain class control—with gestures, eye contact, proximity control, and use of humor to release tension
   b. Being able to restructure lessons that are not effective
   c. Providing clarity and firmness in communicating expectations regarding students' performance and behavior (Ornstein and Levine, 1981)
8. *Teacher skill in classroom management* has also been shown to be an important factor in student learning. Students' negative perceptions of the classroom tend to have a negative effect on their learning. For example, students may sense friction among classmates, the pressure of small-group cliques, apathy toward the lesson, or that the lesson is disorganized. On the other hand, if students have positive perceptions of the classroom environment, the effect on learning is also positive. For example, students may see the classroom as one of cohesion, in which lessons are difficult but challenging, in which democratic procedures are followed, and in which the physical setting and the materials used are necessary to learning.

Although the results from research on classroom management are less clear, there is the general conclusion that planning and preparation on the part of the teacher are the most effective ways to provide a suitable environment for individual and group learning (Ornstein and Levine, 1981).

Research on school health education

After conducting a comprehensive review of the research literature on school health education, Bartlett (1981) has offered the following perceptive assessment of school health education:

> Evaluative studies of school health education curricula generally reveal that these programs are very successful in increasing knowledge, somewhat successful in improving attitudes, and infrequently successful in facilitating life-style changes.

As previously noted, Botvin (1983) has begun to document the positive effects of the life-skills training program (cognitive and social skills) on the knowledge and attitudes of students with respect to cigarette smoking, drinking, and drug use. This research for the first time demonstrates consistent, positive, behavioral changes in addition to the traditional effects on knowledge and attitudes.

Moreover, teaching for health-behavior change, in addition to involving the student, must go beyond the traditional didactic or information-giving form of teaching. Instead, it is necessary to involve the student much more deeply in the self-management and self-concept development approach to behavior modification. Teaching for behavior change will also require the schools to reach out and involve parents and community agencies if the goal of improved health behavior is to be achieved.

Examples of specific health problem areas that have been found to have high potential for success in developing positive health behavior include the following: (1) the problem of dental care, especially when students perceive the severity of the problem and their susceptibility to dental disease; (2) the problem of unwanted teenage pregnancies, when there is a close working relationship with community agencies coupled with parental support; and (3) smoking prevention education, when there is the opportunity to involve older students in cross-age teach-

FIG. 15-2. Senior high school students interacting in cross-age teaching with middle school students.

ing and peer counseling or tutoring (Fig. 15-2). Also, nutrition education has contributed to improved diet patterns by use of self-management behavior modification techniques with the social support of the family.

Regardless of whether schools will be able to secure the necessary material and human resources to undertake special health education programs aimed at specific health behavior changes, the responsibility to provide basic health information to the public still exists. This health information will form the basis of the public's health knowledge, enabling the individual to exercise his or her full responsibilities of citizenship to make informed decisions affecting personal health, the health of one's family, and the health of the community.

SUMMARY

This chapter discusses the importance of policies to provide a mechanism that establishes a basis for communication and understanding, as well as guidelines for program action. Policy discussion in this chapter is limited to schools and more specifically to several of the controversial issues in school health education: alcohol, marijuana, tobacco, and sex education, including AIDS education. Several steps in the policy development process are reviewed.

School boards are charged with the responsibility for making school policy. An important step in this process is securing strong community support. Historically, schools have had difficulties with the teaching of controversial topics. Because of their sensitive nature, it is very important that the objectives, the teaching methods, and the curriculum materials be approved by the school administration, the school board, and the parents. School boards must involve all the community groups to ensure that all views are properly represented in the policy development. Controversial issues relating to school health education are examined to help school officials clarify the goals and most appropriate teaching methods. The threat posed by the disease AIDS means that schools no longer have a choice as to whether to teach such a controversial issue. All schools are now required to teach sex education and AIDS education as a matter of national interest and public health.

Research has strongly supported the teaching of personal cognitive skills (e.g., problem solving, decision making, and critical thinking) and social skills to help students resist the pressure to engage in risk-taking behaviors. Each of these teaching strategies has been found effective in dealing with the controversial issues.

The chapter concludes with a review of the research on the effective teaching-learning environment. Conclusions are drawn from an exhaustive review of the research literature covering a 10-year period.

GET INVOLVED!

Speech pathology is considered one of the helping professions. An individual trained in this field works with people of all ages with speech problems. For example, infants and children may be delayed in their acquisition of speech and language. Some patients may have a communicative disorder as a result of a cleft palate or some other orofacial abnormality or a neurologic dysfunction such as cerebral palsy, autism, or mental retardation. Speech pathologists work with children who have problems with articulation or vocal or fluency problems such as stuttering. The speech pathologist also works with adults whose communication problems result from head injuries or a stroke, which may cause a condition such as aphasia (inability to speak). Persons trained in this field may also work with persons who stutter or have a foreign dialect.

Undergraduate students are given opportunities to observe and to participate in the delivery of clinical services to those who have communicative handicaps. These students are eligible to become members of the national Student Speech-Language-Hearing Association, which gives them some privileges of the professional association such as receiving the professional journal and the opportunity to attend national meetings at a reduced rate.

Students who have had prior preparation in a health-related field can make the transition to speech pathology with some extra course work as a graduate student. Typically it is important to note that many students enter their training to become speech pathologists as graduate students. Students who have had prior preparation in a health-related field can make this transition by taking some extra course work while studying for the master's degree.

For more information, contact a University Department of Speech and Hearing Science or write to:

The National Student Speech-Language-Hearing Association
10801 Rockville Pike
Rockville, MD 20852

STUDY QUESTIONS

1. Why are policies important to the teaching of controversial topics in health education?

2. What is your position on a school policy that would ban all smoking from school facilities?

3. Explain why you would or would not support a policy that expels students from school for a smoking violation.
4. From the standpoint of prevention, what is an ideal time for introducing drug education into the curriculum?
5. What is the rationale for using a social-skills approach in drug education?
6. What is meant by the statement "responsible use" in alcohol education, and what might that imply from the standpoint of societal alcohol consumption?
7. Identify three points you believe should receive special emphasis in a teenage sex education program.
8. What are the principal conclusions to be drawn from the research on school health education?

REFERENCES

Adeyanju M, et al: The relationship among attitudes, behaviors and biomedical measures of adolescents "at risk" for cardiovascular disease, *J Sch Health* 57(8):326, 1987.

American Heart Association: The influence of voluntary health organizations on national health policies, *Curr Perspect Hypertension* 4:5, 1982.

Barlett EE: The contribution of school health education to community health promotion: what can we reasonably expect? *Am J Pub Health* 71(12):1384, 1981.

Bennett WJ: What works: schools without drugs, United States Department of Education, 1986, Washington, DC.

Bernard B: The issue of self-esteem, *Prevention Forum* 6(3):4, 1986.

Bernard B: Peer programs: the lodestone to prevention, *Prevention Forum* 8(2):6, 1988.

Botvin GJ: *Life skills training, a self-improvement approach to substance abuse prevention*, New York, 1983, Smithfield Press.

Brion-Meisels S, et al: Decisions about drug use, Adolescent Decisions Curriculum, Adolescent Issues Project, United States Office of Education, Special Education Project Grant G008001910, 1982, Boston Judge Baker Guidance Center.

Center for Population Options: *AIDS and adolescents, resources for educators*, Washington, D.C., 1987, the Center.

Crandall DP: Planning issues that bear on the success of school improvement efforts, *Educ Admin Q* 22(3):21, 1986.

Dalton HL, Burris S, editors: *AIDS and the law*, New Haven, 1987, Yale University Press.

Dielman TE, et al: Elementary school-based prevention of adolescent alcohol misuse, *M/Pediatrician* 14:70, 1987.

Dielman TE, et al: Susceptibility to peer pressure, self-esteem, and health locus of control as correlates of adolescent substance abuse, *Health Educ Q* 14(2):207, 1987.

Ellickson PL: *Designing an effective prevention program: principles underlying the Rand Smoking and Drug Prevention Experiment*, Santa Monica, Calif, 1984, Rand Corp.

Ellickson PL: *Project Alert: a smoking and drug prevention experiment, first year progress report*, Santa Monica, Calif, 1984, Rand Corp.

Ellickson PL, Abby R: *A Rand note: toward more effective drug prevention programs*, Santa Monica, Calif, 1987, Rand Corp.

Gordon S: The case for a moral sex education in schools, *J School Health* 51:214, 1981.

Hansen WB, et al: Evaluation of a tobacco and alcohol abuse prevention curriculum for adolescents, *Health Educ Q* 15(1):93, 1988.

Halpin G, Thomas W: Drug education solution or problem? *Psychol Rep* 40:372, 1977.

Health is basic: an introduction to the THTM program for teachers and students, Newton, Mass, 1983, Education Development Center.

Illinois Department of Alcoholism and Substance Abuse, News Release, 1991.

Jessor R, Jessor SL: *Problem behavior and psychosocial development: a longitudinal study of youth*, New York, 1977, Academic Press.

Kirby D, et al: *Emerging approach to improving adolescent health and addressing teenage pregnancy*, Washington, DC, 1985, Center for Population Options.

Lovick SR, Wesson W: *School-based clinics: update*, Houston, 1986, Center for Population Options.

Luce and Schweitzer in USDHSS, Fifth Spinal Report to the U.S. Congress on Alcohol and Health, Washington, DC, 1984, DHHS Publ. no. (ADM) 84-1291.

MacDonald DI: An approach to the problem of teenage pregnancy, *Public Health Rep* 102(4):377, 1987.

Mack J, Ablon S, editors: *The development and sustaining of self-esteem in childhood*, New York, 1983, International University Press.

Midwest Regional Center For Drug-Free Schools and Communities, Chicago, 1988, Brass Foundation.

National Commission on Marihuana and Drug Abuse, Washington D.C., 1973, USDHEW.

Ornstein AC, Levine DU: Teacher behavior research: overview and outlook, *Phi Delta Kappan* 62(8):592-596, 1981.

Phillips JA, Jr: Abolishing tobacco use in secondary schools: a school-based management problem, NASSP Bull, Jan. 1984, National Association of Secondary School Principals, pp. 121-123.

Ray O: *Drugs, society, and human behavior*, St. Louis, 1978, Mosby-n-Year Book.

Redican KJ, Olsen LK, Stone DB: Health education: a positive force in increasing the reading skills of low socioeconomic elementary students, *Urban Rev* 2(4):215, 1979.

Rist MC: Antismoking policies are good for your school system's health, *Am Sch Boards J* 173:25-28, 1986.

Sagor R: Seeking peace in the war on drugs, NASSP Bull, 1987 National Association of Secondary School Principals, pp. 85-87.

Stoudemire A, Wallack L, Hedemark R: Alcohol dependence and abuse. In Amler RW, Dull AB, editors: *Closing the gap: the burden of unnecessary illness*, New York, 1987, Oxford University Press.

Strong G: It's time to get tough on alcohol and drug abuse in schools, *Am Sch Boards J* 170(2):23-24, 1983.

US Department of Health and Human Services: Guidelines for effective school health education to prevent the spread of AIDS, *MMWR* 37:S-2, 1988.

Vincent ML, et al.: Reducing adolescent pregnancy through school and community-based education, *JAMA* 257:24, June 1987.

Walberg HD, Schiller D, Haertel GD: The quiet revolution in educational research. In Moore GW: *Developing and evaluating educational research*, Boston, 1983, Little, Brown.

Yarber WL: *AIDS education: curriculum and health policy*, Bloomington, Ind, 1987, Phi Delta Kappa Educational Foundation.

Healthful school environment

OVERVIEW

The principles of epidemiology indicate that the understanding of a health problem depends on three things: the host, or the person who has the illness; the causative agent, which brought on the illness; and the environment, which brings the causative agent and the host together.

Traditionally school health practice focuses most resources on the host. Through education the school hopes to reduce the risk of illness caused by inappropriate behavior. Through health services the school strives to ensure optimal health, including the early detection of illness and initiation of subsequent treatment. The school environment cannot be overlooked, although it is the least conspicuous element of school health practice.

OBJECTIVES   After reading this chapter, the student should be able to:

1. Describe the health risk posed by the school environment
2. Identify areas of concern in monitoring a healthy school environment
3. Describe basic requirements and suggest how teachers can establish a healthy social environment in the school
4. Discuss basic standards for school food services
5. Specify special environmental concerns in special use areas such as gymnasiums, locker rooms, playground space, swimming pools, and shower rooms
6. Recognize the roles and responsibilities of all school personnel for monitoring the school environment
7. Know of specific hazards associated with particular courses and how to contain these hazards
8. Describe ways the teacher can establish and monitor a healthy psychosocial environment in the school

For the student, school and home are the two environments where he or she spends the most time. The school environment is important to learning in that physically it must not create undue risk of accident or disease and socially it should encourage and support the teaching and learning process. The environment is one of the three elements of public health concern: the agent, the host, and the environment. A good environment contributes to the outcomes of health education and service programs, greatly improving the outcome of society's investment in the educational process.

Architectural, sanitary, aesthetic and social aspects of the school environment must be considered, although the health implications of school architecture may be overemphasized. A well-designed school has greater potential for healthful function than a less well-designed building, but a wholesome environment can certainly be provided in a school of rather poor architectural design (Fig. 16-1).

Sanitation depends on adequate facilities, properly used through sound housekeeping (or school-keeping) practices. All people using the school should actively participate in school keeping. It is unjust to permit students to believe that the building is kept clean and orderly by someone hired solely for the task. Each student and staff person should participate in the chore of keeping "our" school clean, orderly, and attractive. Of course, the school environment cannot be separated from the community environment.

Frequently overlooked in discussions of the school environment is consideration of the ways the environment can promote health. The social and psychological dimensions of the environment are as important as the temperature of the air or the light in a classroom and are discussed in this chapter.

FIG. 16-1. The school environment includes much more than architecture, but the pleasing appearance of a school is important to students and community members alike.

RESPONSIBILITY FOR A HEALTHFUL SCHOOL ENVIRONMENT

Board of education

Sovereignty, or ultimate authority, rests with the people, who delegate its exercise to the board of education. However, the board does not act on its own initiative in plant construction but judges the merits of recommendations made by the professional administrator. A representative community committee is often formed to review the plans and make suggestions. This ensures adequate study of the plan and community understanding of the proposal. When representative community leaders approve the plans, the board of education can proceed in the knowledge that the community understands and supports the project.

If the plan goes forward, an architect is engaged by the board to draw preliminary plans and to make preliminary estimates. The board then takes the necessary steps for financing—usually a bond issue for approval by the electors in a regular or special school district election. If the voters approve, final plans are drawn, bids are called for and opened, and a construction contract is awarded. Because of better school architects, better engineers, illuminating specialists, ventilation experts, and a host of other specialists, school buildings today are a vast improvement over those of a generation ago.

A community's voting to support a bond issue for the improvement of school facilities is a test of a different dimension of the school's environment; it is a measure of the support of the community in which the school resides. If the patrons have reservations about the proposed changes in the school's physical plant, they will not support the raising of the needed dollars through the issuing of bonds. This is clearly a sign that the environment of the school, i.e., its community, is not supportive of the proposed changes. Such bond-issue failures suggest that schools have not adequately communicated their needs for environmental improvement to their communities or have not listened to their communities' concerns about education, or a combination of both. Whichever is the case, when a community is not supportive of the improvement of the school environment, both the community and the school lose. Education has failed in its objective—understanding has not been achieved.

Community standards for fire safety, food handling procedures, building codes, and water supply affect the school environment directly. Working in concert with inspectors and administrators or community regulators can help to create a healthy school environment.

Administrators

Full-time school administrators constantly appraise the school district's needs. Classroom enrollments, age-group populations, migrations, consolidations, real estate developments, industrial changes, and other factors that affect present and future school needs are used as bases for constructing new school buildings or remodeling old ones. Knowledge of the present plant—its shortcomings and possibilities—is necessary to the administrator. The economics of building anew or rebuilding are important.

Once administrators agree on plant expansion, they develop a tentative estimate and general plan. The superintendent submits these recommendations to the board for consideration.

Maintaining the school plant is the responsibility of the superintendent and the administrators, especially the principals. General policies apply to the whole system, and each principal administers the policy to the best advantage for the building for which he or she is responsible. In addition to the physical environment, administrators are also responsible for psychological and social aspects of the environment. The development of personnel policies and discipline codes, the public image of the school, and relationships with parents represent important aspects of the school's responsibility to maintain an environment that encourages learning. Both physical and psychosocial aspects of the school environment are discussed in this chapter.

Teachers

Once the structure is completed and furnished, the teacher's task is to make the building serve the needs of healthful school living and effective education.

A teacher's classroom becomes his or her domain and reflects his or her interests and personality. In this way each classroom assumes a different character, and the school becomes a place of great diversity and considerable interest. The school environment itself should be included as an object of study. Class activities such as safety surveys, testing for light and noise intensity, learning to check water in swimming pools, and learning about sanitation standards in cafeterias are examples of ways teachers can maximize the use of the school as a learning environment.

Some teachers have special responsibilities related to their teaching environment. For example, teachers of home economics, shop, science and physical education all work in classrooms that have special environmental hazards. The use of special equipment and the special activities in each of these areas creates an additional set of expectations and requirements for these teachers to maintain healthful teaching environments. These environmental hazards also represent special teaching opportunities, discussed in more detail later in this chapter.

Students

As much as possible, students should assume the primary responsibility for the order and cleanliness of their school. On a cooperative basis classes can supply additional furnishings for the building. Pictures, vases, bowls, flowerpots, stands, lecterns, and a host of other furnishings are often purchased with funds from class activities. School organizations also contribute to building maintenance and obtain additional equipment.

Special projects such as "Don't Be a Litterbug Week," pickup projects, locker cleanups, rake-up campaigns, and other activities add to the involvement of the students, especially in elementary grades, in maintaining a healthful school environment.

Student pride in the school is not difficult to develop, but it does require some planning and promotion. Loyalties to the school and what it stands for create a desirable atmosphere for wholesome living. With stimulation and guidance, students usually develop appreciation. This can be solidified by having the students assume responsibility for preserving and extending the attractiveness of their common home. Monitors may be designated for specific tasks, but all children should feel they have a responsibility. Monitor selection procedures should be designed to award every youngster a regular assignment.

Custodians

The once nonskilled janitor has been replaced by the qualified custodian. Beside the mechanical skill needed for the assignment, the custodian should know sanitation, control of communicable diseases, and safety. Most states provide in-service preparation to ensure the schools of well-qualified custodians.

Custodians see the school from a different perspective than the rest of the staff. Through their supervisory structure they should have an opportunity to share their views with the student personnel staff—counselors, nurse, principal, and food service director. Custodians may also have useful insights that should be considered when health curricula are being revised.

Today custodians should receive special training in the collection and disposition of body fluids. This new task, necessitated by the HIV/AIDS epidemic, brings custodians into much more frequent contact with teachers. Teachers therefore have to recognize a custodian's special skills and responsibilities and respond to any special directions custodians might provide, both to students and teachers.

In addition to maintenance of the physical plant, custodians have a special opportunity to observe and note aspects of the school's environment that may create risk and danger. Maintenance needs that are often first observed by a custodian should be reported through a formal and responsive communication channel.

Often overlooked is the fact that custodians have unique opportunities to observe students. Custodians often observe behaviors that place individual students at risk or are clearly against the school's rules. Custodians should be given inservice training concerning their responsibilities to report matters of student behavior to appropriate school officials. They deserve rapid responses to their reports and should be told of the outcomes from any event they report. In this sense, the custodian has a responsibility for the physical environment and also the behavioral and social environment of the school, as do all school staff.

Custodian-staff cooperation is a two-way street. Insofar as is possible the custodian's schedule should avoid interfering with the school routine. Time after school and on Saturday is used for cleaning and minor maintenance. Nevertheless, the custodian should not be seen as separate or apart from the process of education.

Lunchroom personnel

Sanitation is more important in the lunchroom than anywhere else in the school. A situation in which sanitation prevents the spread of disease also provides an opportunity for students to observe and learn about proper food-handling conditions and procedures. Lunchroom experiences integrate health practices and instruction.

The facilities and practices in school lunchrooms are those prescribed by public health departments for sanitation regulation in public food establishments. Observance of these regulations is doubly important in the school.

Lunchroom personnel should feel a special obligation to the students, which can be demonstrated by pride in lunchroom work. Personal health habits should be exemplary. If the lunchroom workers suffer from a communicable disease, they should isolate themselves voluntarily. The worker who strives for perfection in sanitary measures is a valuable member of the health instruction team.

Environmental issues related to food service facilities and personnel are clear. Often overlooked, however, are two equally important and interrelated environmental issues: adequate time should be available to use washrooms for washing hands before eating, and there should be enough time to eat to instill a sense of community in the lunchroom.

Large numbers of students and teachers washing their hands before eating places a significant strain on the school's physical plant and resources. Are the bathrooms convenient to the lunchroom and of adequate size to accommodate large numbers of students in a small amount of time? Can students use other washrooms on their way to the lunchroom? Are the washrooms well equipped with hot water, liquid soap, and disposable towels? Are students responsible in their use of soap and towels? Are custodians available to replenish supplies of soap and towels and tidy up and dispose of trash as needed?

Unfortunately, hand washing, one of the most inexpensive and effective means of controlling the spread of communicable diseases, has become a forgotten practice for many students and teachers. Compounding this unfortunate circumstance are school administrators and teachers who no longer expect students to wash their hands before eating and do not provide sufficient time or resources to encourage this practice. When this is the case, the environment, socially and physically, does not support sound health behavior.

LOCATION AND PLAN OF SCHOOL BUILDING

Certain factors in the location and plan of a school building are of direct health significance. To these factors the elementary classroom teacher and the secondary school health instructor should direct their attention. It is not suggested that other things about the building are unimportant, but for present purposes health factors alone will be considered.

Site

School sites should be considered from the standpoint of accessibility, safety, quietness, air cleanliness, adequate drainage, and recreation space. Distance is not so important today as formerly because of improved transportation. Railroad areas, main highways, and through streets are physical hazards to be avoided. City ordinances and state laws usually specify what distance from the school alcoholic beverage dealerships must be located. For clear air and a quiet neighborhood, residential and rural areas are preferable to industrial or other congested areas.

Standards of physical comfort

For the usual school situation, standards for physical comfort have been determined by scientific investigation and practical experience. These standards are expressed in terms of temperature, humidity, and movement of air: i.e. adequate lighting, noise control and an area free of vermin and biological or chemical hazards.

Temperature in the schoolroom should be held between 66° and 70° F (19° to 21° C). In the winter the lower half of this temperature range will feel comfortable as will a room temperature of 70° F (21° C) in the hotter seasons.

Humidity, or air moisture, should be between 30% and 70% of the maximal amount of moisture the air will hold. A humidity of 50% and a temperature of 70° F (21° C) are ideal. Several instruments, such as hygrometers and psychrometers, precisely determine humidity. Without an air-conditioning unit it is difficult to affect the humidity of a classroom.

Air movement carries away body heat and moisture. To be effective, a current of air should be perceptible. The least perceptible current is called the threshold velocity. Under ordinary room conditions air movement should at least be of threshold velocity. A current perceptible at one moment may not be felt a few minutes later. As room temperature declines, the perceptible velocity rises. Since temperature and air movement vary, window ventilation is highly effective because it permits these variations to operate in producing comfortable sensations of the skin. Modern mechanical ventilating systems now do an adequate job but are more expensive to maintain than window-gravity methods of ventilation, which depended on a draft caused by open or partially open windows.

Heating and ventilation

In heating and ventilating schoolrooms, emphasis must be on physical comfort. Body heat and moisture must be removed. When the elimination of heat and moisture is retarded, students experience drowsiness, lassitude, depression, headache, and loss of vigor.

Heat for each room should be controlled individually by a thermostat. Mechanical ventilating systems are usually designed to provide 15 cubic feet (3.8 cu m) of air per occupant per minute. Ventilation in one room does not depend on ventilation in another room. Zoned ventilation is necessary in large school buildings. The gymnasium, auditorium, shop, and cafeteria usually have independent ventilating units. Cloakrooms have separate ventilation. Toilet rooms have ventilating ducts and fans independent of the rest of the system. Chemistry laboratories are provided with fume hoods of acid-resisting construction. Technical standards for special ventilation needs are usually available through engineering and public health organizations.

ILLUMINATION

Proper lighting contributes to the effectiveness of students' work and helps prevent fatigue. Efficiency and comfort of vision are the major considerations of illumination (Fig. 16-2).

A distinction should be made between the terms **light, illumination,** and **brightness.** Light is the source, illumination is the effect, and brightness is the amount of light returned from a surface.

Intensity of visible light is measured in footcandles. A **footcandle** is the amount of light received at a point 1 foot removed from a source of standard candle power.

A **footlambert** is the brightness of any surface produced from the illumination in footcandles and the surface's reflection factor. Thus, if the light units on a task are recorded as 50 footcandles and the reflection factor of the task is 70%, the units reflected to the eye would be 35 footlamberts. The equation is FC/RF = FL. Footlamberts must be considered when the environment is conditioned for visual efficiency and comfort.

Three factors in lighting are important—sufficient light, proper distribution of light, and absence of glare. The amount of needed light depends on a person's activity. Less light is required for a corridor than for a reading area. Distinctness of vision (visual acuity) attains its maximal effectiveness at about 5 footcandles. Speed of vision attains its maximal effectiveness at about 20 footcandles. On a sunny day outdoor illumination may be up to 10,000 footcandles. In a schoolroom the illumination near a window may be above 200 footcandles (Table 16-1).

FIG. 16-2.   Good illumination is essential for learning.

TABLE 16-1.   Recommended lighting levels in schools

Location	Recommended footcandles on task
Classrooms—on desks and chalkboards	70
Study halls, lecture rooms, art rooms, offices, libraries, shops, laboratories	70
Drafting rooms, typing rooms, sewing rooms	100
Auditoriums (not for study), cafeterias, washrooms	50
Open corridors, storerooms	20

Proper distribution of light demands that all areas of the visual field have the same approximate intensity. Recognition of brightness difference has led to the use of lighter-colored chalkboards, woodwork, floors, furniture, and equipment in schoolrooms. **Brightness difference** expresses the brightness of the task as compared with brightness of the surrounding area.

Brightness balance is essential to visual efficiency and comfort. This can be attained when low brightness differences between the task and the surrounding area are maintained. Absolute brightness balance in the classroom is not possible; however, the footlambert brightness of the best-lighted area in the room should not be more than 10 times the footlambert brightness of the poorest-lighted area where tasks are being performed.

Glare is light that causes discomfort, annoyance, or distress to the eyes. It is annoying to face a window or an uncovered light bulb. Reflected light from a tabletop produces glare. Contrast in light disturbs vision. All these conditions produce glare and are much too common in schoolrooms.

Natural light

Natural light should be used to the fullest and most effective extent possible in order to achieve a certain psychological effect and good visual conditions. Ideally, window space should be one fifth of the floor area in rooms not more than 24 feet (7.2 m) wide. Unilateral lighting or lighting from one side is recommended. The left side is preferred, but the right side is acceptable.

NOISE

Noise is unwanted sound. Noise distracts students and teachers from the business of learning and also causes undue fatigue (Fig. 16-3). Noise can be reduced at its source or in its transmission by special modification of the environment. Carpeting and acoustic tiles are two obvious ways to reduce noise transmission.

The original decision of school placement should consider possible noise problems. Traffic and industrial noise can be reduced by the judicious placement of buildings and careful planting of trees.

Students and teachers should not be subjected to average noise levels over an 8-hour period that exceed 85 decibels on scale A. Sound can be measured on many frequencies. Scale A measures sound in the frequency range most closely resembling human speech. Recognizing that noise levels above 65 decibels interfere with speech communication gives meaning to decibel measures.

For students who may be in an especially noisy area such as a shop, swimming pool, or gymnasium, high noise levels for short periods of time are acceptable, but for the teacher who stays in these areas for long periods noise presents a significant health hazard. Such areas should be carefully surveyed to make maximal use of noise-reducing materials, and teaching schedules should be arranged to allow adequate time away from excessive noise. An alternative, but not a particularly satisfactory one except when certain equipment is used in shop classes, is the use of ear plugs. Teachers working in noisy areas should conduct regular noise surveys of these areas, seek ways to reduce noise at its source, and regularly have their hearing checked.

The school environment may meet all noise level recommendations, but modern electronics have made it possible for students to create their own dangerous noise environment. Through devices such as Walkman, sound from personal earphones easily exceeds recommended safe limits. Schools can protect and educate about health and health promotion by judiciously controlling the use of compact cassette players in school and by teaching about the dangers of noise.

FIG. 16-3.   Noise is unwanted sound. Simple reminders to reduce noise level are an effective part of any noise control program.

VERMIN CONTROL

Flies, rats, mice, cockroaches, and other vermin should be controlled by securing doors and windows, eliminating breeding places, and depriving them of food and water sources. These pests are most common in kitchens and lunchrooms. Flies, rats, and mice are easier to control than cockroaches. Because these insects inhabit warm, dark areas and survive on limited amounts of food and water, even scrupulous cleanliness usually cannot eliminate them once an infestation is established. Insecticide sprays should only be used by licensed exterminators and should be used with great care in food preparation areas. Special care should be taken if insecticides and pesticides are stored in school buildings. Containers should be clearly labeled and stored completely separate from any food-related materials.

FIG. 16-4.   Hazardous location for a fountain. To avoid possible injuries to students, a fountain should be set into the wall so that no part of the fountain protrudes and those using the fountain are not likely to be accidentally bumped while drinking.

WATER SUPPLY

School authorities are responsible for providing a safe and adequate water supply for school use. When a municipal water supply is used, primary responsibility for its source and purity rests with the municipality and the public health department. Yet the school district is responsible for proper installation and maintenance of water facilities in the school. In addition to being free from contamination, water should be palatable and sufficiently abundant for normal school needs.

Fountains

Fountains are the most sanitary school drinking facility. One fountain per 75 pupils is an acceptable standard. Recesses in corridor walls provide a safety factor by reducing the likelihood of dental injury from being bumped while drinking (Fig. 16-4).

GENERAL TOILET ROOMS

One washbasin or lavatory for each 40 pupils is recommended. Wash fountains can be substituted for washbasins. Height of the washbasins varies with the age of the students the school serves.

Liquid soap and dispensers are essential. *Paper towels* should be available. *Wastepaper receptacles* large enough to hold waste towels for a half day are necessary for an orderly toilet room.

Toilets and urinals

The number of fixtures will vary for different age levels. Any suggested standard may be unsatisfactory for a specific situation. The basic recommendations are:

Elementary school	Junior and senior high school
1 toilet to 30 girls	1 toilet to 45 girls
1 toilet to 60 boys	1 toilet to 90 boys
1 urinal to 30 boys	1 urinal to 30 boys

ACCESSIBILITY

Schools today serve students with a much wider range of abilities than they served when they were first constructed. Changing educational philosophies and federal regulations encourage schools to serve students of all abilities. For students with different abilities to benefit from the school, many things have had to be changed and upgraded—classroom access, seating patterns, food service facilities, laboratory and classroom equipment, toilets, and recreational facilities. Ramps and elevators have been installed, and school buses modified. Students may have aides to assist them throughout the day, and this requires additional equipment and facilities. Time schedules and classroom organization may be modified.

The cost and short-term inconvenience of modifying the school's physical plant to enable full access is the most visible part of these environmental changes. Other changes are perhaps more important. Helping staff and students understand the reasons for accommodating students of all abilities contributes to an accepting environment. Learning about how to relate to persons with different abilities becomes a critical part of the teaching program. Learning mutual respect for various combinations of abilities is an important outcome of being an educated person.

Access, in other words, like many aspects of the school environment, is most obviously a physical concern; but, more important, it is a social, psychological, and educational concern. Physical dimensions of the school can be relatively easily modified. As a result, students can gain physical access. In some cases it may be harder to make the needed changes in psychosocial environment to create full acceptance of all students. The difficulty some schools have had accepting students who tested HIV-positive illustrates the extreme of the challenge of creating a truly educational environment.

A commitment to equal access to all should drive the schools' policies to create such an environment. State and federal regulations will specify the exact dimensions of the changes that need to occur. School and community attitudes toward making the necessary changes in the physical plant to comply with federal and state regulations will illustrate to students how accepting the school personnel are of the underlying reasons for the changes in the physical environment.

FOOD SERVICE

A food service unit is properly located on the ground floor, conveniently accessible from the outside. It should be planned to facilitate the most direct route from corridor to serving line,

School tobacco policy

EMERGING ISSUE As a middle school counselor from a medium-sized school district, you have been asked to chair a Parent-Teacher Student Association (PTSA) Committee on School Tobacco Policy. Recent action by the district school board has eliminated the designated smoking area for high school students. Dr. Baker, a local physician and also a member of the committee, has been quite outspoken, arguing that the school board should be much more pro-active. He contends that a comprehensive school tobacco policy should be established.

During the first few meetings of the committee, several topics have been introduced for discussion and possible recommendation to the board for policy consideration, including student discipline for possession of tobacco, the role of students and parents in establishing a tobacco-free school, and smoking cessation program services for students, tobacco instruction in the curriculum, and policies on smoking by staff and at school-sponsored events.

As the chair of this committee, please indicate your thinking on this issue by responding to the following statements by marking a plus (+) or a minus (−) sign before each of those statements with which you agree or disagree.

_____ 1. I believe our committee should push for stricter discipline of students and that the possession of tobacco should be treated with the same degree of seriousness as possession of alcohol.

_____ 2. Insofar as students are concerned, the school should be tobacco-free, but I would hesitate to recommend doing away with the teachers' smoking lounge.

_____ 3. I would favor a system of student suspension leading ultimately to expulsion for possession of tobacco.

_____ 4. I believe that the school district should either offer or arrange for a smoking cessation program for students caught smoking or who were found in possession of tobacco.

_____ 5. To strengthen the school's enforcement program, I would favor enlisting both parents and students in the effort to achieve tobacco-free schools.

_____ 6. I believe anti-smoking education should be emphasized in grades 4 through 8.

_____ 7. Believing that addicted student smokers should not be disciplined, I would instead require them to enroll in a smoking cessation program.

_____ 8. I believe that tobacco-free school policies should include both students and staff.

_____ If limited to a single choice, this is the number of the statement I would select.

DiFranza JR: School tobacco policy: a medical perspective, *J Sch Health* 59(9):398-400, 1989.

water cooler, tables, soiled-dish counter, and finally corridor again. Some schools use the dining room for a classroom, for a study hall, and for student activities.

Food service facilities will include:

- *Storage rooms* that should be cool (50° to 60° F [10° to 16° C]), well lighted, adequately ventilated, and vermin free.
- *Refrigeration units* spacious enough to allow ample room for all foods requiring refrigeration. Temperatures must be below 50° F (10° C). Dairy products should be separated from meats or other foods from which they may absorb odors.

- *Manual dish-washing facilities* that include an adequate supply of hot water, a wash sink with detergent and warm water (100° F [38° C]), a rinse sink, and a sanitizing sink containing decontaminant or water above 170° F (77° C).
- *Dish-washing machines* that are checked regularly to ensure unblocked nozzles and adequate water pressure. Temperature of wash water should be between 140° and 160° F (60° and 71° C), and rinse water should be at least 170° F (77° C). Detergent dispensers should regularly be checked. Dishes removed from the machine should be hot enough to dry without toweling in 45 seconds.

PLAY AREAS

The school environment where most accidents and injuries occur is the outside play area. Frequently teachers and administrators overlook this area as an important element of the school health environment. Unprotected posts, gravel-covered playing surfaces, poor drainage allowing ice or mud to accumulate, slippery concrete surfaces, hedges and trees that scratch, uneven surfaces, and poorly constructed or supervised play equipment constitute significant environmental hazards. The environment should be suited to those who use it. Secondary school students can tolerate a greater variety of circumstances in their recreation space than kindergarten students can. Common sense, simple rules, and caution reduce play area hazards to a minimum.

It is important to remember that accidents are a principal cause of death and disability among children and adolescents. School-related accidents don't usually result in death, but they can result in injury that leads to a loss of school days. Estimates of school days lost each year as a result of injuries range upward from 14 million for those ages 6 to 16.

GYMNASIUM AND ACTIVITY ROOM

The gymnasium in junior and senior high schools and the activity room in elementary schools should be clean, well lighted, adequately ventilated, and free from hazards. A hardwood floor with a nonslip finish cleaned daily keeps dust at a minimum. Windows are often more of a detriment than an asset in a gymnasium. Glass bricks are a useful alternative when masonry is used in construction. Artificial lighting as the sole form of illumination is entirely satisfactory. Forced ventilation is necessary when large crowds occupy the gymnasium. Regular inspections of conditions and practices promote safety in the gymnasium.

LOCKER ROOMS

A well-lighted locker room is usually attractive and sanitary. Located adjacent to the gymnasium, the locker room should provide at least 12 square feet (3.3 sq m) of floor space per student, based on the class with the largest number of students. Floors and walls constructed of nonporous material promote sanitation. Floors should have excellent drainage and be cleaned daily. Adequate heat and mechanical ventilation complete the requirements for excellent sanitation.

FIG. 16-5.   Adequate and careful use of light limits fungi and bacterial growth.

SHOWER ROOMS

Nonslip tile flooring is necessary in the shower room. At least 10 square feet (2.7 sq m) of floor space should be allowed for each shower head. The recognized standard is one shower head for every four students, based on the class with the largest enrollment. Shower heads should be at chin height (Fig. 16-5). Whether individual or gang showers are used, water-mixing chambers with wheel-control valves are recommended. The control of water temperature is quicker and easier with this type of equipment. Drying rooms between shower and locker rooms are important.

SWIMMING POOL

Sanitation of the swimming pool is the physical education staff's responsibility. Two factors maintain a sanitary swimming pool—construction and regulation. A properly constructed pool provides for water filtration, chlorination, recirculation, and straining. A chlorine content of 0.2 to 0.5 parts per million inactivates all pathogenic organisms in the water. Daily samples are taken to determine bacteriologic and chlorine contents.

Essential to swimming pool regulation is a qualified person to supervise pool use. Standard regulations to govern pool use are personal cleanliness, freedom from communicable disease, and proper conduct and personal habits. It is essential that everyone who uses the pool take a cleansing shower, wear a clean suit, and use clean towels. Water temperatures between 72° and 78° F (22° and 26° C) and room temperatures between 75° and 82° F (24° and 28° C) should be maintained.

FIRE PREVENTION

Eliminating all risk of fire is impossible, but fire risk can be reduced to a minimum. Construction techniques now make maximal use of fire-resistant building materials, but a great deal of education material (i.e., books and paper) is flammable. Important considerations for fire safety include a building design for easy escape, posted directions for emergency exits, and careful preparation of students and teachers to leave the building quickly and systematically in case of fire.

Areas such as home economics rooms, shops, and laboratories present high fire risk and are usually equipped with special fire-fighting equipment. Students and teachers should be familiar with the use of this equipment and be able to operate it in an emergency. However, the first responsibility of all is evacuation. Containing the fire is a secondary concern better left to fire department personnel.

SPECIAL ENVIRONMENTAL CONCERNS RELATED TO INSTRUCTION

This section discusses environmental hazards that relate directly to instruction. As instructional resources become more sophisticated and instructional patterns strive to approximate reality, it is only natural that risks from these new instructional patterns may increase. Instructions related to biology and chemistry are used to illustrate this concern, but other instructional areas also involve some degree of risk. Also, risks are not limited to physical consequences. New teaching techniques related to developing refusal skills, for example, are not without psychological risk. These are discussed in the section on the psychosocial environment.

Biological hazards

Any biological agent capable of reproducing may be detrimental to other forms of life. When a biological agent is detrimental to other forms of life, a hazard exists. Bacteria, viruses, molds, rickettsiae, parasites, venomous vertebrates, and invertebrate animals and plants that may be toxic all represent potential biological hazards. The hazard may be present whether the agent is alive or dead. The implications of biological hazards in the school environment are many.

Animals in the classroom require the teacher to be knowledgeable about their care, feeding, and husbandry. If animals are used in experiments of any type, standards of humane treatment must be recognized. Disposal of animals' bedding, waste, and carcasses require forethought and may require compliance with local and state laws.

The science lab of today is more likely to be the site of the study of microorganisms and other biological hazards than it was when it was designed and built. Accordingly, special care and caution may be required. The National Institute of Occupational Safety and Health has established standard procedures for working with biological agents in classes.

Although it is not the job of the health teacher to impose safety standards in other classes, the health teacher should be aware of potential hazards and of the health-related learnings that can occur in these classes. The health teacher should be aware of strategies students can use to protect their health, even in other classes. For example, knowledge on the use of liquid disinfectants that can be used effectively with biological wastes is important in any environment. Knowledge that easily available substances like liquid chlorine bleach can be diluted to effectively destroy biological agents on dishes and laboratory glassware and for cleaning up some biohazard spills is useful in many situations.

Indoor air pollution, or "sick building syndrome" as it is sometimes called, represents another example of a biological hazard. Sick building syndrome, which causes residents of certain buildings to become ill, can generally be tracked to a biological, chemical, or other environmental hazard. Inadequate ventilation sometimes contaminated by improperly applied pesticides, boiler additives, improperly diluted cleaning agents, tobacco smoke, or combustion gases from cafeterias and laboratories are the principal causes. Building contamination also occurs from microorganisms such as bacteria, fungi, protozoa, or other microbial products resulting in such health conditions as hypersensitivity, pneumonitis, allergic rhinitis, conjunctivitis, upper respiratory infections, or allergic asthma.

Chemical hazards

The danger of exposure to chemical hazards has been recognized for centuries, long before the dangers of biological hazards were recognized. Chemicals enter the body through inhalation, ingestion, inoculation, and absorption through the skin or mucous membranes. The reaction of the human depends on the toxicity of the chemical, the concentration of the exposure, the length of the exposure, and the individual's susceptibility.

Specific health concerns in schools begin with contamination of the building air. Asbestos fibers, for example, have become a significant concern for educators. In 1985, it was estimated that asbestos-containing material could be found in about 31,000 schools. Asbestos is used in acoustical ceilings, pipe wrappings, floor tiles, and art materials. As long as these products remain in good condition there is little risk. However, with time, asbestos-bearing products break down, and asbestos fibers are released. Today there are rigorous standards for the materials being introduced to schools and also rigorous standards for procedures to remove asbestos from existing school buildings. The cost to school districts is significant.

An interesting point related to teaching about asbestos is to place the expenditures and efforts to reduce asbestos hazards in some context. It is usually possible to find out how many dollars are being spent in a state for asbestos removal from schools. It is also possible to find out how many asbestos-related deaths occurred in the state in the previous ten years. This type of information can then be compared with the amount of dollars spent to reduce other airborne health hazards. For example, the dollars spent in a state to reduce cigarette consumption provides an interesting counterpoint. This is not to suggest that asbestos is not a critical health problem or that efforts to remove it are misplaced, but simply to illustrate how some obvious health hazards are overlooked when health policies or priorities are established.

Directly related to the teaching function of schools is the presence of hazardous chemicals for science labs, art classes, and maintenance of the physical plant. The Occupational Safety and Health Administration has proposed standards regulating classroom laboratories. The Environmental Protection Agency also has standards related to chemicals and their disposal.

To reduce the hazards associated with chemicals, four actions are effective. First, the design and construction of school laboratory and storage rooms must be adequate to meet modern standards. Labs and storage areas in older schools were often not designed to accommodate the hazards that are recognized today. Remodeling is an effective preventive strategy. Second, safety equipment should be available and in functioning order, and all students should know how to use it. Third, schools should provide adequate protective apparel for students and staff who work with chemicals and biological hazards. Fourth, teachers must teach about and insist that established safety practices and procedures are carried out.

PSYCHOSOCIAL DIMENSIONS OF THE SCHOOL ENVIRONMENT

Much can be done within the limits of the physical dimensions of the school to make it safe. Regardless of the nature of the physical space, the potential for learning within that space will ultimately depend on the way people interact with each other. True, the interactions can be affected by the nature of the space and the health and safety considerations of that space, but, given a reasonable physical plant, it is the person-to-person interactions within the school that will most affect learning. The contact between people in schools is generally the responsibility of teachers and the students themselves. Classroom management, in other words, will largely prescribe the nature of the psychosocial environment. Although the community, the administration, the parents, and the principal all influence what happens in the school, it is the classroom teacher, along with the students, who determine what is learned, how it is learned, and how well it is learned.

On entering a school, one can often "sense" the atmosphere of the place. That sense begins with the physical environment, its upkeep and appearance; but the real sense of the school comes from the "spirit" of the way people relate to each other: tense, happy, efficient, caring. This "sense" is difficult to measure, but nevertheless it is real. In most cases the school administration, the principal and their assistants, set this tone. It filters into the classroom but can differ greatly from one classroom to another.

The classroom as a learning environment

The classroom environment begins with the physical space, but it is the use of that space that is critical, and it is the individual teacher who dictates how that space is used.

Classroom management differs greatly from teacher to teacher and should not be confused with classroom discipline. The assertive discipline of an earlier era established a beginning point for learning by establishing order, but it did not ensure learning. Effective classroom management is a recurring element of a healthy psychosocial environment, but it is not a sufficient condition for learning.

In reality there are two basic tasks faced by the classroom teacher: (1) establishing order and (2) ensuring learning. Establishing order is a management task that requires rules, procedures, and consequences. Enabling learning involves creating an environment in which the maximum amount of time is spent on activities with learning as their objective. These activities are appropriate to learning and encourage satisfaction, achievement, and reward compared to activities that are inappropriate to learning and become the focus of discipline and punishment. Once control is established, the development of the learning environment is the next step.

Once a learning environment is established, the next step is to develop a clear system of expectations and a subsequent system of accountability. As a consequence of these steps the students should clearly recognize their responsibilities to achieve the learning objectives. They should also recognize the system of accountability and, consequently, receive recognition

FIG. 16-6. As part of the psychosocial environment, teachers can provide desirable social experiences to create a wholesome environment.

when learning is occurring. The structure of the classroom, the student-teacher interaction, and the behavior of the teacher to a large degree determine the successes of the students. Special teacher training and skills of the teacher that ensure such success set teachers apart as members of a respected profession (Fig. 16-6).

An effective learning environment means that activities run smoothly, that resources are available and in place before the class, and that the teacher is a good organizer and manager. The beginning of any course, the first few lessons, and the first few days are critical to the development and maintenance of an environment that enables learning. It is best if little time is lost in organizational matters at the beginning of the course. Certainly rules, procedures, and consequences must be outlined, but the learning objectives are just as important. In a new class becoming involved in activities aimed at specific learning objectives and in interacting with other students in the class sets the tone for all subsequent classes throughout the semester. These initial activities should leave little opportunity for students to be idle or to talk about other topics. They should involve a review of information already known and lead to high levels of success. Such a process allows students be become acquainted and to "catch the spirit" of the class as a learning place, and at the same time to receive rewards for completing initial steps with a good level of success.

Although rules, procedures, and consequences are important to classroom management and may be introduced on the first day, they will no doubt be described in more detail in later classes. More important to the health of the class is a sense of the personal relevance of the class content, of the specificity and focus of the learning activities, and of achievement for completing learning activities. Research on classroom effectiveness suggests that time on task and the minimum amount of time lost in transitional activities are two important elements for a successful class and a healthy classroom. The first few days or weeks of a class establish responsibilities for the teacher and the student. Learning is a joint responsibility. When students and teachers accept this point, there is opportunity for later independent learning.

Small things are important: good organization so time is not spent on administrative and management activities at the expense of learning activities; direct eye contact with the entire class and a friendly smile; a high level of involvement with the class; reinforcing appropriate behavior and discouraging inappropriate behaviors. Being sensitive to who is behind a disturbance or a question, allowing targeted responses, attending to more than one activity at a time and providing feedback and encouragement as often as possible are the skills of a professional teacher.

In a classroom, appropriate behavior is not the absence of inappropriate behavior. However, the teacher is primarily interested in increasing appropriate behavior and only secondarily in reducing inappropriate behavior.

It is beyond the scope of this chapter or this book to describe all the methods available to the teacher to encourage appropriate behavior. It is useful, however, to review a few of the important points to reinforce the concept of a healthy psychosocial school environment.

The simplest and most effective strategy is simply to emphasize the positive. The teacher's task is to "catch students being good" and to acknowledge that behavior. Inappropriate behavior in the short term can be ignored. Nonverbal reactions may range from a simple "look" to moving closer to the source of the disruptive behavior. A simple request to cease the behavior may suffice, but it should be timed so it is heard and comprehended by the offending students and targeted at the right person. Separate discussions with persistently disruptive students may lead to some type of behavioral contracting or to removal from the class. The clarity of the rules and regulations of the class and how they were presented determine how well these strategies work.

The important point is that rules and regulations are designed to encourage learning and appropriate behaviors. They should be presented in the spirit of positive learning. Rules should identify the general expectations of the class and whenever possible be written in positive terms. At the same time they need to specify what behaviors are not acceptable. The number of rules should be kept to a minimum. Rules should be stated in positive terms if at all possible, avoiding "don't" and "no." Rules should be posted and distributed and, when appropriate, students should be involved in the final form that the rules take. The rules should be taught. If "treating others with respect" is a rule, it will be useful to show, teach, and allow practice of the meaning of treating others with respect.

The consequences of breaking rules should also be clearly stated and understood. Consequences may include: a gradation of responses beginning with the first offense and possible warnings and increasing with subsequent offences until ultimately the principal, or parents may be involved and dismissal from class may be a consequence. Procedures for rule enforcement should be clearly described.

Expectations and accountability are important elements of the psychosocial environment of the school. Students are more likely to meet expectations when the expectations are appropriate, challenging, and clearly understood. Teachers who have high expectations and consistently adhere to those expectations focus everybody's efforts on the learning objectives. When expectations are clear and learning cues guide progress toward these expectations, progress can usually be seen by both students and the teacher.

Although all education should be relevant to learning, the health teacher has a clear opportunity to make the learning they direct specially relevant to each individual student. To a degree each student represents or brings to class his or her own laboratory: a site where health-related actions affect their own personal health. Students should begin to see how their health-related behaviors affect how much they enjoy life, how they affect other people, how much sickness they will experience, and ultimately how long they might live. Helping students discover direct relevance from the subject matter is an opportunity not to be overlooked. Therefore expectations should relate to personal outcomes and should challenge thought and suggest behavior. Neither low nor high expectations encourage learning; and high, unrealistic expectations cause frustration. Again, the skill of the teacher sets the tone of the classroom.

Special applications for the health teacher

Because health teachers deal with topics that are sometimes controversial and because they focus on the development of health-enhancing skills, there may be some special challenges in maintaining a healthy classroom.

Managing the discussion of topics that touch on different moral and ethical positions illustrates one of the special challenges for health teachers: the discussion of abortion, for example. Although this is not a text on teaching methods, the handling of such potentially controversial topics will influence the psychosocial environment.

First, before any discussion of a controversial topic begins, the teacher should be well aware of the school's policy on discussing and teaching about specific controversial topics and the degree of support the teacher has from the administration. Obviously there are limits to the discussion of any topic, and the classroom teacher should be aware of the limits established by the school administration.

The second point is the challenge to set the ground rules for discussion. Part of any discussion is ensuring that sufficient time is available to allow all points of view to be discussed. Discussion should be focused on specific topics and should clearly be directed by specific educational objectives.

Third, at closure, teachers should be able to summarize the discussion clearly and concisely and relate the findings back to the educational objectives of the class.

Another special challenge that is important to the health teacher is the teaching of social skills that involve role play and simulations. Because students are being led through new behaviors and others are observing their performance, there is a special challenge to maintaining a healthy psychosocial environment.

Role play and simulation are excellent teaching strategies but not without some risk. Some community members may not approve of schools' teaching specific behaviors; thus it is important to keep parents informed and involved in understanding the school's programs.

Selecting participants for role play situations can be a positive or a negative experience for all involved. Role play situations should be demonstrated by teachers and volunteer students. Role play situations that involve students working in small groups of two or three students help avoid situations of a few students in front of the class. Once students are used to the notion of participating in simulated situations and have had practice in dealing with problem situations, they will more readily become involved in role play interactions in front of the class.

As a simple rule of thumb, role play situations should involve as many students as possible as quickly as possible. Small groups working simultaneously enable this. Role play situations should provide ample opportunity for rewarding the participants. An important part of any role play is for those who are not playing roles to be able to experience vicariously the roles they are watching. Accordingly, role plays best meet their educational objectives if they are well done. Opportunity to practice roles helps improve quality. A day to think about a role play situation helps. Clear guidelines and objectives for each person in a role play situation help keep the situation focused. Role play simulations should not be embarrassing for any participant but they should encourage experimentation with new behaviors.

SUMMARY

Changing the environment is the fundamental principle of primary prevention. We change the environment to reduce the likelihood that disease conditions can occur. For schools, there is a responsibility to provide an environment not only that is safe from undue hazards, but also one that facilitates learning. Such an environment includes both the physical characteristics that encourage good teacher-student interaction and the psychosocial characteristics that create an atmosphere of calm and confidence that enhances learning.

The environment is the responsibility of all who work and learn in a school, reflecting the values of the total community. The ideal environment enables all to work together to maintain optimal opportunities for students to learn and teachers to teach.

GET INVOLVED!

Dietitians or nutritionists are professionals trained in the application of principles of nutrition to food selection and meal preparation. They counsel individuals and groups in diet preparation and supervise food service institutions such as hospitals and schools. They promote sound eating habits through education.

In addition to assessing nutritional needs and developing diet plans for individual patients, dietitians or nutritionists may perform adminstrative and managerial functions.

With the exception of smoking and drinking, food choices and eating patterns may exert the most important influence on the indivdual's health.

To qualify as a registered dietetian, the American Dietetics Association recommends a 4-year undergraduate program, an accredited dietetic experience and an extended clinical experience in a dietetic internship. After completing the bachelor's or master's degree, graduates must then complete a 6-month approved work experience.

Dietitians who prefer to teach may take additional work in education and become practicing health educators in their specialty of nutrition education.

For more information about the field of dietetics, write to:
The American Dietetic Association
216 W. Jackson Blvd.
Chicago, IL 60606-6995

STUDY QUESTIONS

1. Identify the areas of a school most likely to create a risk to health.
2. Who has the responsibility for monitoring a healthy school environment? What are the actual responsibilities of the people you have just listed?
3. What are the important environmental considerations in planning the location of a school?
4. List the variables important to a healthy environment inside the school.
5. In what ways are brightness, balance, and glare important to students' learning?
6. What would dictate practical standards for noise in the school building?
7. How can the psychological environment of a school be improved?
8. Why are public health officials concerned about the possible spread of infection via the school lunchroom?
9. What is the primary function of school ventilation?
10. Why do some school authorities prefer all artificial lighting in schools?
11. What would you rate as the most important requirements in school sanitation?
12. What can each teacher do to promote more healthful school living?
13. What are the most critical factors in establishing a healthy psychosocial environment?
14. How can teaching styles and classroom management affect the health of a student?
15. In what ways does a teacher create the psychosocial environment of the classroom?

REFERENCES

Arlin M: Teacher transitions can disrupt time flow in classrooms, *Am Educ Res J* 16:42, 56, 1979.

Basic concepts of environmental health, Pub No. 80-1254, Washington, DC, 1980, National Institutes of Environmental Health Sciences, Public Health Service/ National Institutes of Health, US Department of Health, Education and Welfare.

Brophy J: How teachers influence what is taught and learned in classrooms, *Elementary Sch J* 83:1-13, 1982.

Canter L, Canter M: *Assertive discipline: a take charge approach for today's educators,* Seal Beach, Calif, 1976, Canter Associates.

Doyle W: Classroom management and organization. In Wittrock M, editor: *Handbook of research on teaching,* ed 3,.MDNM/ New York, 1986, MacMillan.

Emmer E, et al: *Classroom management for secondary teachers,* Englewood Cliffs, NJ, 1984, Prentice-Hall.

Evertson C, et al: (1984). *Classroom management for elementary school teachers,* Englewood Cliffs, NJ, 1984, Prentice-Hall.

Gottfredson GD: An empirical test of school-based environmental and individual interventions to reduce the risk of delinquent behavior, *Criminology* 24:705-731, 1986.

Hawkins JD, et al: Childhood predictors of adolescent substance abuse: toward and empirically grounded theory, *J Child Contemporary Society* 18:1-65, 1986.

Johnson D, et al:: Effects of cooperative, competitive, and individualistic goal structures on achievement: a meta analysis *Psychol Bull 89:47-62, 1981.*

Jones VF, Jones LS: *Classroom management: motivating and managing students,* ed 3, Boston, 1990, Allyn and Bacon.

McGinnis E, Goldstein A: *Skillstreaming the elementary school child,* Champaign, Ill, 1984, Research Press.

Olds RS, Eddy JM: Negative health messages in schools, *J Sch Health* 56:334, 1986.

Pukey WW, Novak JM: *Inviting school success,* ed 2, Belmont, Calif, 1986, Eadsworth Publishing.

Purdom WP: *Environmental health,* New York, 1979, Academic Press.

Rowe DE: Healthful school living: environmental health in the school, *J Sch Health* 57:426, 1987.

Sadker MP, Sadker DM: *Sex equity handbook for schools,* New York, 1982, Longman.

Schultz EW, Glass RM, Kamholtz JD: School climate: psychological health and well-being in school, *J Sch Health* 57:432, 1987.

Wagner RH: *Environment and man,* New York, 1978, W.W. Norton.

Wiatrowski MD, Gottfredson G, Roberts M: Understanding school behavior disruption, *Environment Behav* 15:53, 1983.

Willgoose CE: *Environmental health: commitment for survival,* Philadelphia, 1979, Saunders.

Wolfgang C, Glickman C: *Solving discipline problems,* Boston, 1986, Allyn & Bacon.

Zeisell J: *Stopping school property damage,* Arlington, Va, 1976, American Association of School Administrators.

Part SIX

Appraisals in School Health Practice

CHAPTER
17
Evaluation

OVERVIEW

Evaluation data provide the basis for decision making. Frequently people are unaware that they are conducting evaluation activities. A simple action such as crossing the street requires an evaluation of existing conditions compared to the recollections of what happened the last time similar conditions occurred. If evaluation is considered an ongoing process, an integral part of living, it becomes less ominous than when viewed as an action to tell whether a program was good or bad.

In school health practice, evaluation continues on many levels. Each day the teacher, nurse, principal, and aide evaluate aspects of their programs. As a result of these ongoing evaluations they also change and improve programs. Ongoing evaluation of this type is referred to as process, or formative, evaluation. The second principal type of evaluation is product, or summative, evaluation and is carried out after a program is completed. Both types are equally important.

When an evaluation is planned, knowing clearly why it is conducted and who will use the results are equally critical to the planning process. Formal evaluations should be conducted for a specific cause, which focuses the evaluation efforts. Informal evaluations are ongoing. Anyone involved in educational programs will, consciously or unconsciously, evaluate the program constantly. At the same time minor program changes result from these informal evaluations. Most of what is discussed in this chapter refers to the more formal and structured evaluation activities carried out to meet a specific purpose.

Evaluation activities begin when project objectives are established. Today, more than ever before, evaluation activities are seen as important considerations in program planning. Well-conducted evaluations provide the single greatest opportunity to improve school health practice.

OBJECTIVES   After reading this chapter, the student should be able to:

1. Define evaluation
2. Differentiate between formative and summative evaluations
3. Outline basic procedures in any evaluation activity
4. Describe a variety of evaluation devices and techniques
5. Define and differentiate between the concepts of objectivity and reliability
6. Suggest ways that the health status of children can be evaluated and how these evaluations are significant in the planning of health services and health education
7. List the important program elements to be examined in a review of health practice administrative policies and practices
8. Describe important criteria in evaluating the school environment
9. Describe, develop, and use a variety of measurement techniques to assess the outcomes of health education programs

How much has the school health program improved students' health status? How effective is the school health program? Does it measure up to recognized standards? Is health instruction effective? Does the school meet healthful living standards? All these are inevitable and logical questions for those concerned with the school health program. To what extent school health activities meet the general and specific objectives of the health program is of concern to students, parents, the community, school administration, and, particularly, health teachers and school health service personnel.

Ideally, evaluation includes both objective measurements and the subjective judgments of experts. In school health, evaluation determines the effectiveness of the program by measuring the degree to which the school's health objectives are achieved. It encompasses the purely subjective, transient judgments as well as highly objective, scientific measurement of factors affecting health. Thus evaluation is inherent not only in the teacher's observation of a students' attitude but also in the dental examination.

PURPOSE OF EVALUATION

The purpose of evaluation is not to prove or disprove but to improve. Program improvement is the single most important purpose of evaluation. Proper improvement occurs when programs have clarity and specificity in their objectives, when they are carried out with rigor and integrity, and when they closely measure their specified outcome. Evaluation carried out as a program is being developed and tested is called **formative evaluation**. Evaluation activities to measure how well a program conformed to its original plan, sometimes called program integrity, are called **process evaluation,** and activities to see how well a program actually met its objectives are called **outcome** or **summative evaluation**.

Evaluation audience

The actual conduct of any evaluation follows some generally accepted steps. However, the most important decision is determining why the evaluation is being conducted. Who wants the evaluation? Who will use the results of the evaluation? Why is the evaluation being carried out? If the school board wants an evaluation of a health education program, members will be interested in such things as the evaluation of teachers, the curriculum materials used, parents' satisfaction with the program, and student interest in elective health courses. Teachers, on the other hand, are likely to be interested in students' knowledge gains and behavior changes.

Specifying the reason for an evaluation aids in the implementation of its recommendations. If the evaluation is requested because of public complaints about a program, it will differ significantly from one conducted as a part of a self-study in preparation for an accreditation review.

Reasons for planning and carrying out evaluation activities include but are not limited to the following:

1. To determine the present status of the school health program
2. To assess progress toward achievement of program objectives
3. To provide information about program strengths and weaknesses
4. To provide data to justify additional support and funds for the program
5. To provide information about program activities such as health services and health instruction to modify the program and improve it

Important purposes of pupil health evaluations are as follows:

1. To enable teachers and school officials to adapt school programs to meet the health and educational needs of children
2. To determine pupil health status, as well as individual health knowledge status
3. To inform parents of their children's health status
4. To provide information to enable students to adjust their study programs to progress more rapidly
5. To provide data on students' learning achievement that can serve as a basis for grading students

EVALUATION PROCEDURES

The ideal school health program involves a number of elements. These were described in Chapter 1 and include health services, school health environment, the integration of school and community health promotion efforts, physical education, food services, health promotion programs for teachers and staff, guidance and counseling, and health instruction.

Because each of the elements in the school health program should be evaluated, and recognizing the variety of conditions and situations under which evaluation must be done, it is not possible to set out a step-by-step procedure that will serve all purposes. Yet certain principles apply, some of which are as follows:

1. The general program goals must be clearly stated.
2. Specific objectives that relate to individual parts of the program must be stated precisely in order to serve as measurable outcomes.
3. All products, records, and instruments of an evaluation should be preserved, since they can be of value in assessment of the effects of the program on participants.
4. Methods and instruments used to collect program information must meet the standards of objectivity, reliability, and validity.
5. Information about the program should be collected early enough to be useful in revising or modifying the program.
6. In health education evaluation, efforts should be made to determine whether students apply what they learned or exhibit skills they learned from the health instruction program.
7. Evaluation of the total school health program may require that information be collected from many different sources, including the school, the home, the neighborhood, and the larger community.
8. The value of any school health program will depend on the collection of valid data followed by expert judgment to arrive at program recommendations.
9. The results of the evaluation must be presented in a usable and easily readable form for application to future situations.

EVALUATION INSTRUMENTS

There are few things that can be proved without qualification. The best that can be done is to present evidence one way or another. This should be kept in mind in selecting and using any

School-based prevention program

EMERGING ISSUE Your school district superintendent has arranged for a weekend retreat to which you, as district health education representative, and approximately 20 other people from the district and community have been invited. Among those who will be attending are teachers, counselors, administrators, supervisors, and representatives of parents and social agencies. The apparent inability of the school to cope effectively with problems such as teen pregnancies, substance abuse, school dropouts, racial tensions, and the rising threat of AIDS to the adolescent population has set the stage for this conference. The charge contained in the letter of invitation is to "consider a new role for schools" on the basis of the following assumptions:

1. Serious problems affecting today's school-age population result from a failure of the socialization process (e.g., many adolescents have failed to internalize the values held by the larger society).
2. Contemporary school intervention programs have generally been ineffective.

The conference has been organized into four working groups: (1) classroom management, (2) instructional practices, (3) curricula, and (4) school organization and climate.

As preparation for the conference, you are asked to respond to the following statements by placing a plus (+) or a minus (−) sign before each of the statements with which you generally agree or disagree.

_____ 1. Although I agree that schools must put more emphasis on the teaching of values, I'm concerned about the possible effects of multicultural education on the mainstream values of a democratic society.

_____ 2. Although I believe such a conference is needed, I would like more assurances about administrative commitment and support of recommendations coming out of the conference.

_____ 3. Although I am concerned about these health and social problems, I have serious reservations about the ability of the schools to impact such problems.

_____ 4. Given the difficulty we have had in establishing a comprehensive health education program, I am not optimistic about the prospects of the conference for success.

_____ 5. Given the categorical approach of the government to funding such programs as drug education and AIDS prevention, I believe that the government is not likely to support a broad-based approach such as this.

_____ 6. I believe that it is imperative that schools become more inclusive by involving parents, by working more closely with health and social agencies, and by using multicultural education for the teaching of social values.

_____ If limited to a single choice, I would choose this number.

evaluation instrument, which is merely a device for obtaining evidence. A human being must interpret and weigh the evidence. Some instruments provide fairly precise data, whereas others yield only general tendencies or relative differences. Many evaluation devices that have recognized mechanical faults and qualitative shortcomings may, nevertheless, serve worthwhile purposes in certain situations. A critical analysis should be made of every measure used, but the instrument should also be appraised in terms of the service it performs and the purpose for which it is used.

This section will present a wide range of instruments and techniques useful in program evaluation. It is important to keep in mind that the school health program includes many components. Some of the techniques described will be especially useful in evaluating one component of the school health program but of little value in evaluating others. No single instrument or technique is equally effective in evaluating all areas of school health practice.

Observation

Observation, the most frequently used instrument in school appraisal, can be both meaningful and valuable in health evaluation. To be most effective, observation must be critical and precise. By using carefully prepared observation protocols and maintaining clear standards of objectivity a teacher can develop a highly accurate level of discrimination. Teachers who notice deviations in the behavior or performance of a student should confirm or note subsequent changes at the end of each week. Repeated variations suggest a student may need special assistance. Some teachers like to review their class lists at the end of every week or two to record special observations on any children so they will be more sensitive to observed changes over time.

Interviews and conferences

Interviews and conferences reveal information that other techniques cannot elicit. Conferences with students, parents, and friends who know a child are highly productive in providing health-related information. Interviews with students can be conducted in small groups but need to focus on specific topics.

Self-appraisal

Student analysis of their own health provides information and stimulates interest. A checklist is a useful tool to guide self-appraisals. Original comments will add to the data gathered.

Questionnaires

A series of specific questions can be used to obtain information on health practices and problems. A variety of standard health questionnaires are available.

Checklist

Checklists are composed of objective items that usually consist of yes-or-no answers or descriptive lists. They are frequently used for studies of such things as sanitary conditions or health practices.

Surveys

Surveys relate to people, including sociological facts and psychological data, such as knowledge, attitudes, and practices, as well as health status.

Records

Family and personal health records can be rewarding sources of data. School health records should be sufficiently complete to be a dependable source of information.

Reports

Accounts, descriptions, or statements, either incidental or developed for a special purpose, have value, especially when correlated with other data.

Achievement tests

The most commonly used form of measurement in the school is the written or oral test. Both are adaptable to health instruction and are particularly effective in revealing the nature and extent of student learning.

Simulations

To assess how students may behave, the conditions of an actual situation are simulated. Sometimes simulations are called situation tests. Role playing can be used to simulate real health-related situations.

Self-critique (teachers)

All the foregoing strategies apply to students or the school environment. Although teachers are evaluated annually by the principal or department head, they may wish to initiate their own personal evaluation/improvement activities. As part of their professional development, and perhaps independent of the school administrators, teachers may identify areas in their own performance that can be improved. By a process of personal analysis teachers may create specific objectives for their own performance and create a personal plan to improve. Writing out such a plan, setting specific objectives, and creating strategies to improve and developing a timeline makes evaluating one's self development process more meaningful.

The careful completion of self critiques of this type provides useful information to share with supervisors at the annual review. Involving another teacher may also provide ideas and insight on how to improve.

From each of these techniques two types of information can be obtained. One type of information is the numeric data that come from counting, such as test scores, screening results, or the number of times a behavior was observed. This type of information, amenable to statistical analysis, has long been an important part of evaluation. From statistical data, the establishment of norms provides a standard for comparison. Numerical scores are precise, objective, and definite. Averages, variations, and consistencies can be determined with a high degree of accuracy. Health knowledge tests are particularly amenable to statistical treatment. Raw scores can be made more meaningful if specific sections of the test and the types of errors are analyzed. Statistical methods, when applicable in the measurement of health outcomes such as knowledge and attitudes, should be given preference. However, care should be taken in the interpretation of statistical results, as well as other data. A high correlation does not establish a cause-and-effect relationship.

The second type of information is less objective and less amenable to statistical analysis but no less valuable. These are data from observations and interpretations, often described as clinical appraisals or clinical evaluations. Clinical evaluations, less precise and standardized than statistical evaluations, are the only means available for appraising some activities in health. The determination of a student's health status does not lend itself readily to statistical treatment. The findings of the physician and dentist, the observations of the nurse and teacher, the personal history of the child, and the report of the parents may be adequate for clinical evaluation of the student's health. Although lacking statistical precision, the purpose of health evaluation may be well served. Up to now, no completely satisfactory standardized test of health attitudes has been developed. Nevertheless, teachers can devise techniques for attitude appraisal by systematically observing children in situations that reflect their choices and attitudes toward health. Norms cannot be determined and perhaps are unnecessary. Many health activities and objectives involve too many intangible values to be gauged with objective test instruments. Clinical appraisals are used to obtain a general evaluation of various health factors.

DATA FOR PLANNING AND EVALUATION

Today there are more data available for planning school health programs than ever before. The amount of data on adolescent health, other than morbidity and mortality, has been increasing steadily since 1989 when a consortium of school health organizations published data from students in grades 8 and 10 as part of the National Adolescent Student Health Survey.

The Centers for Disease Control (CDC) has provided funding for states to gather data on adolescent risk behaviors under the headings of Youth Risk Behavior Surveys. In addition, the CDC has gathered similar data for a national sample of students in grades 9 to 12. A number of states have carried out telephone surveys of the health risk behaviors of adults, providing a view of adult health risk behavior. These state and national data provide a benchmark for local education planners in setting direction and developing program objectives.

ESTABLISHMENT OF EVALUATION CRITERIA

The processes of evaluation, including procedures and instruments, should meet the criteria of objectivity, reliability, validity, and the practical considerations of use.

Objectivity

Objectivity implies the elimination of personal bias and self-interest. It is the opposite of subjectivity, where personal interest colors the decision or choice. Certain laboratory tests used in health examinations may be totally objective. An electrocardiograph gives an objective measure of the frequency and rhythm of the heartbeat and the action of the heart. The recording of blood pressure is considered objective, though human judgment is involved. However, whenever human judgment is involved, the evaluation cannot properly be totally objective.

No test a teacher uses to measure learning is totally objective. Although the test may be written in an objective form, such as a multiple-choice test, the selection of the item and judgment as to its quality constitute a subjective process. The practical approach in evaluation is to reduce subjectivity to a minimum. Understanding validity is a way to increase the objectivity of any testing procedure.

Validity

Validity is the extent to which a test measures what it is designed to measure. In testing terms, validity can be assessed in four ways: content validity, concurrent validity, predictive validity, and construct validity.

Content validity indicates how well a test or evaluation instrument actually samples the unit being measured. In some cases this is obvious. If a teacher wants to test students' knowledge of the bones in the arm and leg, he or she can ask them to list all the bones in the arm and leg. If, however, the educational task is more complex (e.g., learning all the major bones in the body), it would be impractical to ask students to list them all. However, questions asking students to name a sample of the entire list of bones would be adequate to estimate their knowledge.

Concurrent validity indicates how well a test score relates to an accepted performance criterion. Knowing the names of all the major bones in the body, for example, probably has little relationship to knowing how to lift heavy weights without risking injury. However, knowledge about levers, muscle origins and insertions, and kinesiology relates to knowing how to lift heavy weights.

Concurrent validity is a control issue in evaluation of health education programs. The question is how well knowledge, attitude, and practice measures on a test actually relate to behavior. High concurrent validity indicates that there is a good correlation between test scores and actual health practice.

Predictive validity is concerned with present test scores and future measures of performance. If students who score well on a written test of skills to resist social and peer pressure to smoke are actually less likely to become cigarette smokers, this test has good predictive validity for future smoking behavior.

Construct validity, the last of the four types of validity, is the least specific and is based on logical inferences drawn from various evidence to indicate that the test actually measures what it was designed to. If one hypothesizes that knowledge about advantages of a particular behavior relates to the likelihood that the behavior will be carried out, a degree of construct validity exists.

Validity is not a simple generalized concept but should be viewed four different ways as an indicator of an evaluation tool or a technique's usefulness.

Reliability

Reliability is the consistency of measurement and can be assessed three ways: internal consistency, equivalence, and stability.

Reliability is usually expressed as a correlation coefficient. Measures of **internal consistency** show the consistency of performance of two parts of a single test. The coefficient is computed by comparison of one part of the test with another part ("split half") using a Spearman-Brown formula or by an item analysis using the Kuder-Richardson formula.

A **coefficient of equivalence** measures the relationship between two forms of the same test administered at close to the same time.

The relationship of two measures taken at two different times using the same test represents a **coefficient of stability.**

High reliability coefficients indicate that what is being measured has a degree of constancy and is therefore probably a stable construct, not affected by transient pressures but can be affected over time by focused programs.

EVALUATION OF CHANGE IN THE HEALTH STATUS OF STUDENTS

Because the school health program emphasizes building up and maintaining the highest possible health level in every student a reliable means for measuring health status change would be extremely valuable. No single scale or measure has been devised, but combining several tests and methods can produce a workable profile of a student's health status.

A recent thorough health examination obviously gives the best indication of the child's health. Comparison with previous examinations is relatively simple for children who have had defects corrected during the interim. However, for many youngsters no such corrections are necessary, and evaluating any change in health status commands the skills and expert judgment of the physician.

In the absence of a health examination the teacher's own assessment of a child's health level will be of value. Although highly subjective, the appraisal considers attitude, pleasure in activity, vigor, endurance, ability to relax, absence of defects, and adequate social adjustment. The appraisal can be supplemented by data from the child's school health record, such as dental corrections, vision tests and corrections, hearing tests, weight and height changes, and records of illnesses. The physical growth charts in Chapter 4 can be used to chart the child's developmental status.

Supplementing the teacher's appraisal with the judgment of other teachers who have had ample opportunity to observe the child and obtaining the parents' assessment will reduce the subjective factor.

More objective measures can also be used to assess health status (e.g., the number of days absent for illness, the number of visits to the school nurse, and the need for medication). Certain measures of fitness and strength taken in physical education classes and grades received for regular class work also add perspective to health status. Taken together several of these measures would give a useful evaluation of changes in health.

EVALUATION OF ADMINISTRATIVE PRACTICES AND POLICIES

School health work is advanced or retarded in terms of administrative policies and practices related to it. An insight into the success or failure of the health program may be gained by a survey of administrative practices and policies that relate to the health program. The usual survey is made by means of a checklist of widely accepted school health responsibilities of the administrator. Such a list should include the following:

1. Recognize health as a basic objective of education and reflect this priority in the school's written administrative practices and policies

2. Secure and budget adequate funds for health programs
3. Regularly keep parents informed of the health program
4. Establish an appropriate cooperative relationship with community health agencies
5. Maintain communication with community organizations
6. Employ qualified school health service personnel
7. Become informed about health problems of the school-age group
8. Arrange the school day in accord with sound health practice
9. Establish an effective system for keeping health records
10. Establish a policy on school health examinations
11. Provide for health observations by the teachers
12. Establish a systematic referral program
13. Promote measures to ensure services for every child in need of such services
14. Institute program policies aimed at control of injuries and communicable diseases
15. Procure necessary materials, time, facilities, and equipment for health instruction
16. Appoint only qualified teachers for health instruction
17. Provide a healthful and safe physical environment
18. Ensure adequate food services
19. Provide facilities, personnel, and an established plan to meet emergencies
20. Provide health services for professional personnel
21. Provide in-service health education for teachers
22. Provide adequate faculty sick leave
23. Enable communication between school counselors and the school teachers and the school nurse
24. Provide health promotion activities for teachers and staff

This checklist does not include all the health responsibilities of the administrator but specifies essential minimal practices to serve as a practical, realistic measure of the administration's contribution to the school health program. The school health program checklist properly illustrates how all the essential elements of a school health program can be checked for evaluation purposes.

EVALUATION OF THE SCHOOL HEALTH PROGRAM

Appraisal of the overall school health program is necessary to measure the completeness of the program, its function, and its effectiveness. A valid program evaluation points up its strengths and weaknesses. Despite the recognized need for such an evaluation instrument, very few such appraisal forms are available. In consequence, most program assessments are either general surveys or evaluations of specific phases of the program, notably the health instruction phase.

Available standard forms differ in purpose, scope, and composition. They can be used to advantage, particularly if supplemented by other evaluative devices to serve specific situations and needs.

An example of a comprehensive instrument is included in Appendix B. This self-appraisal checklist was developed by the Nebraska Department of Education with financial support from the Centers for Disease Control. This evaluative checklist is based on the

Kolbe-Allensworth model of a comprehensive health education teacher training program (CHETT).

EVALUATION OF HEALTH SERVICES

Circumstances may make it desirable to evaluate health services independently of other phases of the health program. Such an evaluation includes the nature and frequency of health examinations; dental examinations; screening of vision, hearing, weight, and height; and the teacher's appraisal of the child's health. The follow-up program and correction of defects must be included. Prevention and control of diseases, emergency care, and first-aid provisions are also appraised.

Teachers and administrators can make effective use of two types of resources in evaluating school health services: (1) the evaluative checklist type of instrument in Appendix B, and (2) the published formal statements of standards from authoritative bodies such as the American Academy of Pediatrics. The academy's book *School Health: a Guide for Physicians* presents a useful set of standards and supplementary information.

EVALUATION OF THE SCHOOL ENVIRONMENT

Any assessment of the school environment must extend beyond the mere static physical environment. It should encompass the activities and practices in the school that affect health promotion, disease prevention, safety, social adjustment, and esthetic appreciation. Evaluation should include factors affecting physical and mental health.

No phase of the school health program is as easy to appraise as the physical environment. Sanitary facilities are tangible, can be counted or tabulated, and involve relatively little analysis or subjective judgment. Even the safety elements of the school environment are easy to identify and tabulate. Perhaps for these reasons sanitary surveys of schools have long been routine in school practice. Certainly these surveys should continue, but they should be expanded into an evaluation of total healthful school living. Appendixes B and C provide useful checklists for this purpose.

In evaluating the school environment the evaluator should view the school as a dynamic community of students and school personnel. The various forces and factors that affect the student's well-being are included and evaluated in terms of their influence on the student's total health. In addition to appraising school life in action, this process can serve as a stimulating instructional instrument. Students can participate in the evaluation of the total school health environment.

EVALUATION AND HEALTH INSTRUCTION

Two aspects of evaluation can be applied to health instruction. One aspect is evaluation of the health instruction program based on the quality and appropriateness of instructional activities. The second aspect can be based on the learning achieved by students.

What should be included in a health instruction program? What objectives should be recognized? What time allotment is made? What facilities, equipment, and materials are available? What methods are being used? To what extent do integration and correlation take place? What preparation should teachers have in health education? These are questions that must be answered in an evaluation of the school health instruction program.

Because schools vary greatly in their perception of health instruction aims, developing a universally applicable scale is difficult. Any form broad enough to encompass all purposes and situations would be so all-inclusive as to be impractical. The problem is to determine essentials of health instruction and to construct a scale to evaluate such a program. Each school can rate itself in terms of these basics and then supplement the rating with an evaluation of the special features of its own program. An evaluation of a specific health course can be done with a checklist or inventory that includes the important criteria of classroom practice applied to health education.

Inventory of the health course

1. Objectives of health instruction
   a. Are there both general and specific objectives?
   b. Are the objectives stated in terms of student behaviors?
   c. Do the statements of objectives specify the type of behavior and the content or subject matter to be learned?
   d. Are the objectives related to the health needs and interests of both students and society?
   e. Are objectives stated in terms of attitudes, skills, and practices, as well as knowledge?
2. Course organization and content
   a. Is there use of conceptual statements or generalizations to facilitate organization and understanding of health content?
   b. Is there a logical order of health content?
   c. Is there a logical sequence of topics to be covered?
   d. Is the content or subject matter scientifically accurate?
   e. Are health topics correlated or integrated with other school subjects?
3. Learning activities and materials of instruction
   a. Do class activities relate to student interests?
   b. Are a variety of methods used in teaching?
   c. Are there a variety of materials and instructional aids used in teaching?
   d. Are provisions made for individual differences and for individualized instruction?
   e. Are materials current and scientifically accurate?
   f. Are students given frequent positive responses for achieving the program's educational objectives?
4. Evaluation of instruction
   a. Is the classroom atmosphere conducive to learning?
   b. Do students appear alert and interested in the health instruction?
   c. Are students given ample opportunity for class participation?
   d. Are student objectives, content, learning activities, and materials effectively related?
   e. Is student progress effectively measured in terms of course objectives?
   f. Is the course of curriculum regularly evaluated and revised?

Developing instruments to evaluate health instruction effectiveness requires an understanding of the subject, a grasp of outcomes toward which health instruction is directed, competency in test construction, and a willingness to put forth creative effort. Whether a teacher needs a simple survey of health practices or a complex objective test to measure students' understanding and appreciation of health values, demands on time, patience, ingenuity, and energy are involved.

Test construction and testing are competencies that every classroom teacher should strive to master. Standard tests have their place and value, but constant reliance on such tests indicates a limited classroom testing program. Standard tests cannot replace teacher-made tests. A rich, meaningful evaluation program means that tests and testing are integrated with the objectives, procedures, activities, experiences, techniques, concomitant learning, skills, and values developed in the class. Testing can be mastered by study and practice. A teacher need not attain the competence of a specialist to do an acceptable job of testing. In addition to its contribution to the instructional program, testing competency personally and professionally gratifies the teacher.

Tests are used for diagnostic purposes, to determine progress and to measure final achievement. In all cases, tests should reveal the nature and extent of learning. They can be tailored to fit each situation and can be both enjoyable and stimulating. Tests should be considered a means to facilitate learning. Students should be encouraged to view tests as an opportunity to demonstrate knowledge and skill. Students' fear of tests can be overcome by using tests frequently as another method of teaching. Instead of using test results only for the purpose of grading, tests can be used as a means of review and of stimulating learning. By developing high quality tests and using them properly, teachers help students develop positive attitudes toward testing. In all testing, teachers should make an effort to put students in a proper frame of mind before the test.

The steps in test construction should follow a fairly well-developed set of procedures such as the following:

1. Prepare a list of major objectives
2. Develop a content outline of topics to be covered
3. Develop a comprehensive list of specific objectives
4. Classify the objectives into categories such as the following:
   a. Cognitive or knowledge facts, terminology, application, analysis, interpretation, synthesis, and evaluation
   b. Effective interests, attitudes, appreciations, and values
   c. Psychomotor skills, practices, and technical performances
5. Devise test situations to reveal what students have learned in relation to the specific objectives
6. Prepare test items appropriate to the different types (domains) of objectives and different levels of learning
7. Try out the test to determine the following:
   a. The degree of difficulty of items
   b. The discrimination index of items
   c. General utility of the test
8. Revise the test to overcome weaknesses revealed in pretesting.

Health behavior inventories should do more than measure the pupils' knowledge of health practices. Such inventories have value for answering the pertinent question of whether knowledge is being applied.

Since health practices are stressed at all grades, adequate evaluation of the health instruction program should examine the extent to which health practices are affected. The Youth Risk Behavior Survey developed by the CDC illustrates an attempt to assess the extent of a range of behaviors that are related to major causes of death and disability.

However, some important health practices are considered either personal or in some cases illegal. It is reasonable to expect a student readily to report food choices in a food diary but not so readily to report sexual practices or alcohol, marijuana, or tobacco use. Therefore health practice inventories are limited by the validity and reliability of the data obtained and will vary greatly from one area of health behavior to another.

For research and special evaluation efforts there are sophisticated ways to obtain reasonably accurate information on health behavior. Such procedures often require persons other than the teacher to gather the data, with assurances of anonymity and the fact that school personnel will see the data only in aggregated form. Sometimes these inventories include the gathering of physiological measures to ensure more accurate self-reporting of behaviors. For example, gathering saliva samples for chemical analysis to detect chemical indicators of nicotine in the body usually increases the number of students who indicate on a health behavior inventory that they smoke cigarettes.

Health attitude tests

A great deal of attention has been paid to attitude as an evaluation measure in health education. Despite this attention there is much yet to be learned about attitudes and their measurement. The relationships between knowledge, attitudes, and behaviors are unclear. Although it is logical to assume that these relationships exist, it has not been shown, for example, that change in knowledge will result in a change in attitude or that a change in attitude necessarily predicts a change in behavior. Attitudes can exist in the absence of supporting knowledge, and behaviors can exist in the absence of attitudes and knowledge as to why the behavior is carried out.

Frequently attitudes are simply considered a response on a scale to a statement of fact:

	Strongly agree	Mildly agree	Neither agree nor disagree	Mildly disagree	Strongly disagree
Smoking is a dirty habit.	_____	_____	_____	_____	_____
Jogging is boring.	_____	_____	_____	_____	_____

Carefully conceived, this type of measuring technique provides some useful data, but often it is difficult to tell whether attitude or knowledge is being measured.

The construct of attitudes can be used in many ways. Teachers and others readily admit that youngsters who smoke cigarettes have a different general attitude from those who do not. Everyone acknowledges that attitudes are associated with behaviors, but the precise meaning of attitude escapes consensual definition. The psychological and educational literature over the years has included a large number of definitions of attitude. In general, an attitude is often seen as an emotionally toned idea.

Fishbein (1973) has described an attitude in a way useful to health educators and has suggested some effective ways of measurement. He has defined an attitude as a "learned predisposition to respond in a consistently favorable or unfavorable manner with respect to a given object." Although Fishbein's work with behavior acknowledges the influence of social norms, his means of measuring an attitude has clarified the value of attitude measurement in health education.

Fishbein suggests that an attitude can be derived from an assessment of *beliefs* about a behavior and an *evaluation* of the *consequences* of these beliefs. Beliefs are an assessment of the subjective probability that performing a behavior may lead to a particular consequence. For example, the belief that smoking cigarettes can be habit forming may be assessed by some to be very likely whereas others may judge it to be very unlikely. The second component of attitudes, according to Fishbein, is the evaluation of the consequences of this particular behavior. In this example the second component of attitude measure is an assessment of whether respondents consider the forming of habits to be good or bad. An attitude then is a representation of the beliefs concerning the consequences of a particular behavior and an evaluation of the consequences.

A series of scales could be developed to measure both beliefs about cigarette smoking and beliefs about the consequences of smoking, as follows.

BELIEF ABOUT THE BEHAVIOR

1. Smoking cigarettes in the company of others is upsetting to them.
   Likely _____:_____:_____:_____:_____:_____:_____ Unlikely
2. Smoking cigarettes is an unnecessary expense.
   Likely _____:_____:_____:_____:_____:_____:_____ Unlikely

EVALUATION OF THE CONSEQUENCES

1. Upsetting others is
   Good _____:_____:_____:_____:_____:_____:_____ Bad
2. Unnecessary expenses are
   Good _____:_____:_____:_____:_____:_____:_____ Bad

This is not the only way to measure attitude, but it is an especially interesting one because it measures two important components. These components of attitude can be summarized as follows:

Attitude = Beliefs $\times$ Evaluations

Using the types of scales illustrated above and scoring each response $+3$ to -3 provides a standardized way to compare attitude scores. Each belief score is multiplied by its corresponding evaluation score, and the resulting scores are summed to provide an attitude score.

It is clear that this technique for measuring attitude has clear advantages over the single-dimension scales frequently used for attitude evaluation.

Health knowledge and understanding tests constitute the health teacher's principal evaluation instruments. Knowledge as a recognized objective of health is amenable to fairly precise measurement, and many test forms can serve this purpose. Understanding is equally important as an objective and, though more difficult to measure than knowledge, can be evaluated by means of tests built on recognized principles of test construction.

Certain forms and criteria are recognized in test item construction. They are helpful in aiding the health teacher to develop classroom tests that both challenge the students and truly evaluate aspects of health education.

Essay tests

The essay examination has considerable merit. It can reveal the students' general grasp of a subject and their ability to organize and express understanding. These are skills or attitudes that the whole school program seeks to develop. The essay test is especially valuable for diagnostic purposes. An essay question should call for a sequence of ideas, for the development of logical thinking, or for support for an idea.

Some suggestions for the construction, use, and scoring of essay tests can be channeled into the health teacher's needs. Questions might be structured as follows:

1. Elicit reactions to a situation, not merely a description of it.
2. Base items on how, why, or the significance of a particular piece of information rather than merely restating facts.
3. Call for definite, precise points and ask that the most important points in the answers be underlined.
4. Work out several model answers for use in grading and set up certain pertinent points.
5. Read the first question on all papers, then the second on all papers, and on through the last to give uniformity to grading; subjectivity can be reduced when you take the average score of several qualified graders, but several graders are not likely to be available in the usual school situation.
6. Use either the positive approach in scoring by adding points for each contributing statement or the negative approach of starting the reading by giving the question an arbitrary value (e.g., 20) and then deducting from the maximal score as the answer is deficient in meeting the model or standard answer.
7. Read selected answers in class to help students evaluate their own performance and understand what a high-quality answer is.

True-false tests

To many people an objective test means only one thing: true-false test. Most widely used, most abused, and most maligned, the true-false test can be a useful testing technique. It is easy to construct, useful in testing for misconceptions, especially suitable for situations involving just two alternatives (such as infectious or noninfectious), and easy to score; and it provides for wide sampling.

Testing, as well as teaching, should discourage rote learning without understanding. For this reason, subtracting the number of wrong answers from the number of right ones (R − W = S) to obtain the score discourages both rote memorizing and guessing. For a single test, correction for guessing (R − W = S) quite likely will produce a distribution of letter grades different from that when no penalty is received for an incorrect answer.

R equals number of right answers
W equals number of wrong answers, not counting omissions
S equals score corrected for guessing

The most acceptable scoring procedure for objective tests is to give the same credit for each correct answer and to provide a correction for questions omitted. Correcting for omissions is in effect a correction-for-chance, as shown by the following example. On a 100-item true-false test, student A had 60 correct answers and 40 incorrect answers. Thus he received a score of 20. Student B, on the same test, also had 60 correct answers but he had only 20 incorrect answers with 20 items omitted. Therefore student B received a higher score of 40 (60 − 20 = 40). However, over a period of time (e.g., a semester) that involves several tests, the final distribution of letter grades will be much the same under either plan.

A good test uses new terms and phrases, cast in a new mold, and avoids common word associations and textbook statements. A good test favors the student whose preparation has been thorough and who understands the material. It penalizes and confuses the student whose preparation has been superficial and who tries to get by through cleverness and outguessing the tester. A few suggestions may be helpful.

1. Use true and false statements approximately in equal proportions.
2. Make the important factor in the statement apparent to the student.
3. Use straightforward statements, not confusing or trick statements.
4. State exactly what is meant and avoid ambiguity.
5. Use quantitative rather than qualitative terms.
6. Do not depend on recalling a precise figure or word to determine whether the statement is true or false.
7. Exercise caution in the use of the following:
   a. Absolute words, such as *only, never, always,* and *all* are usually found in false statements.
   b. Qualifying words such as *usually, frequently,* and *almost* are more often used in true statements.
   c. The longer the statement, the more likely it is to be true.

A modified true-false test has items in which one or more key words are underlined. If the statement is correct, it is marked true. If the statement is incorrect, the underlined term is crossed out and a correct term substituted in the blank space.

Other variations of the true-false test include the alternate response test, which permits only two possible responses such as yes-no, correct-incorrect, and same-opposite. Still other forms of this test include the use of S and U for satisfactory and unsatisfactory or the use of A, D, and U to designate agree, disagree, and undecided.

The following sample true-false items illustrate the enumerated suggestions. Some common errors in item construction have been purposely included. Can you identify these? The last item shows an example of the modified true-false question with an underlined term.

Items 1 to 5 are true-false questions. If the statement is true, circle the T; if false, circle the F.

T F 1. There is no single index of the quality of a child's health.
T F 2. Large persons always have good health.
T F 3. A mentally healthy person never gets angry.
T F 4. A balanced diet is one having the same number of calories each meal of the day.
T F 5. Alcohol is always a *stimulant* to the human body.

Material that lends itself to modified true-false items can usually be converted to simple true-false or short-answer items.

Multiple-choice tests

Superficially all multiple-choice questions appear to be similar, but a wide variety of items are included. In general, multiple-choice items should contain at least four responses, and five responses are preferred if all the options appear plausible.

If tests are machine scored, numbers may be used for responses in place of letters.

The first type is a direct question followed by five possible responses, one of which is correct or the best answer. For example:

_____ 6. The statement "In solving one problem we often create a new problem" is best illustrated by which of the following?
    A. The discovery of penicillin put the producers of tincture of iodine out of business.
    B. Controlling infectious diseases has made new immunization methods necessary.
    C. Prolonging the length of life has resulted in new economic and social needs.
    D. The decline of infectious disease has created the problem of an oversupply of physicians.
    E. The discovery of the electron microscope has added new diseases to be conquered.

In the second type of multiple-choice test, the items are stated as incomplete sentences; there are five proposed completions, one of which is the best:

_____ 7. The expression "Nature grants biological function without social favor" means:
    A. Reproduction is solely a function of socially well-adjusted people.
    B. Only responsible people should have children.
    C. Some people, capable of being fathers and mothers, are incapable of being proper parents.
    D. The ability to reproduce is independent of economic or educational level.
    E. Sterility does not occur among the more socially fortunate.

In the third type of multiple-choice test, one key with five responses for a series of statements is used:

Key for items 8 to 12
A. Favorable for prevention of respiratory infection
B. Unfavorable for prevention of respiratory infection
C. Not related to prevention of respiratory infection
D. Favorable for prevention of respiratory infection only when a person is under 10 years of age
    _____ 8. Vigorous exercise
    _____ 9. Avoiding crowds
    _____ 10. Avoiding night air
    _____ 11. Fatigue
    _____ 12. Taking a laxative

Another design of multiple-choice test may stimulate analytical thinking:

Key for items 13 to 17
A. Statement is correct; reason is correct.
B. Statement is correct; reason is incorrect.

C. Statement is incorrect; reason is correct.

D. Statement is incorrect; reason is incorrect.

13. All overweight people should exercise vigorously because exercise increases metabolism.

14. Drinking fluids before or during a meal will stop digestion because water will dilute stomach acid.

15. Regularity is favorable to good digestion because it permits a cycle or rhythm in the function of the digestive system.

16. Dentifrices should be used in brushing teeth because dentifrices are antiseptics.

17. Fluoride prevents decay for adults because it destroys bacteria.

Another variation in multiple-choice tests is a chart on which designations are used as the key and the items refer to the designations on the chart.

In the construction, use, and scoring of multiple-choice items, certain safeguards are suggested:

1. There should be only one correct or best answer.

2. The position of the correct response should be changed from item to item. There is a tendency to make the second response the correct one most frequently.

3. Skill in constructing alternative answers (foils) is the key to good multiple-choice test construction.

4. Foils should be attractive and vary in degree of plausibility.

5. One item may ask the student to select the exception to the other four items.

6. Direct statements are preferable to incomplete sentences.

7. If incomplete sentences are used, the responses should come at the end of the sentence.

8. All responses to incomplete sentences should be grammatical completions.

9. Responses should be as homogeneous as possible.

10. When multiple-choice items are placed in a block, the student is aided and scoring is more simple.

11. Avoid words in the response that repeat words in the sentence, except when inserted as foils to counter attempts to outguess the test.

12. Correct responses should not be conspicuous by being long or short.

13. Avoid the use of direct phrases from the text.

14. If the five response items are well constructed, deducting ¼ point for each error ($R - \frac{1}{4}W = S$) will spread the scores and reduce guessing.

15. The multiple-choice test lends itself to the effective measurement of understanding.

Matching tests

Matching tests are a modification of the multiple-choice test. Two columns are used; one is either incomplete statements or a list of questions, and the other is a list of responses. Another form of matching test consists of parallel columns.

From the key at the right, select the best response to each statement in the column to the left. Place the letter of that response in front of the number of the statement.

_____ 18. Health of the gum	A. Vitamin A
_____ 19. Important for thyroxin production	B. Vitamin B

_____ 20. Elevates a schoolchild's intelligence
_____ 21. Necessary mineral for red corpuscles
_____ 22. Helps prevent infection
_____ 23. Bone growth and development
_____ 24. Growth and repair of tissues
_____ 25. Citrus fruits

C. Vitamin C
D. Vitamin D
E. Fat
F. Iodine
G. Iron
H. Protein
I. None of the above

Statements in items 26 to 29 are to be compared quantitatively.
   Key for items 26 to 29:
   A. The quantity of M is greater than the quantity of N.
   B. The quantity of M is less than the quantity of N.
   C. The quantity of M is the same as the quantity of N.

Statement M	Statement N
_____ 26. Number of chomosomes in a sperm	Number of chromosomes in a mature ovum
_____ 27. Number of ova in newborn girl	Number of sperm in newborn boy
_____ 28. Rate of maturation in the male	Rate of maturation in the female
_____ 29. Action of progesterone before ovulation	Action of esterone before ovulation

Matching tests are quickly constructed and require little space. For broad subject areas they are satisfactory but are not readily adaptable to limited ones. Matching tests are excellent for testing knowledge and association but have limited value for testing analysis and interpretation.
   In the construction, use, and scoring of matching tests, certain suggestions are helpful:
   1. Using the same number of terms in each column should be avoided.
   2. Statements should be in the left column and responses in the right column.
   3. The same response may be used more than once.
   4. Each statement should have at least two plausible answers that serve as foils in addition to the correct response.
   5. A single block should contain only homogeneous material from a single area.
   6. Sentence structure and the form of the responses should be consistent.
   7. The students should understand the mechanics of the test.
Deduction for errors presents a problem. If a deduction is to be made, the number of possible choices must be considered. An arbitrary formula of $(R - \frac{1}{4}W = S)$ serves in most instances, since usually no more than four foils would likely apply to the statement.

Completion tests

Incomplete statements are given, and the student either selects the correct responses from a list or writes in the appropriate terms. It is used almost excessively because it is easy to construct. Convenient for small areas of subject matter, it can be objective if terminology is not a major consideration. Completion tests are used frequently to test student recall of sheer factual material. Care should be taken in sentence structure to prevent confusion.

For items 30 to 41 in each blank space place the letter of the term that best completes the statement.

Key for items 30 to 41

A. Age
B. Building
C. Carbohydrate
D. Energy
E. Fat
F. Height
G. Organic
H. Protein
 I. Regulation
 J. Sex
K. Upkeep
L. Weight

A food is any substance that provides cells with (30)_____ , materials for (31)_____ and (32)_____ , or that provides for the (33)_____ of functions. Only (34)_____ foods are digested, and these are of three classes, (35)_____ ; the sugars and starches, (36)_____ , which contains nitrogen; and (37)_____ . Placed in alphabetic order four factors are important in determining a person's basal metabolic rate: (38)_____ , (39)_____ , (40)_____ , and (41)_____ .

There is merit in using more responses than blanks. This type of test can be challenging and even takes on some of the aspects of a puzzle. Deduction for errors is difficult to determine.

A simple type of completion test is one in which a short key applies throughout:

Key for items 42 to 46

A. Increase (increased)
B. Decrease (decreased)
C. No change (not changed)

Regular exercise may (42)_____ one's resistance to disease and (43)_____ one's immunity to infection. Regular exercise will (44)_____ one's predisposition to a particular disease. Regular exercise will (45) the output of the thyroid. According to present studies, an athlete's life expectancy will (46) as a result of athletics.

Short-answer tests

In short-answer tests the student completes the statement by writing a short answer in the space provided. Credit should be given for reasonably correct responses. Textbook sentences should not be used, and care should be taken to avoid revealing the correct response. Sentence structure is highly important. The shorter the answer required, the less the grader's subjective judgment enters into the scoring. A few examples of short-answer items, shown in the following, illustrate this type of test.

Items 47 to 52 are short-answer questions.

In your words complete the following sentences with a brief statement:

47. A food is any substance that _____.
48. The most nearly perfect food is _____.

49. The best way for a person to lose weight is _____ .
50. Infection is _____ .
51. As a cause of death in the United States, communicable diseases are _____ .
52. Three of the five leading causes of death in the United States are _____ .

Although limitations inherent in the short-answer tests are obvious, they can be used to some advantage. They can be constructed quickly, which is especially helpful when a limited area of material is to be tested.

As part of the government efforts to encourage better planned and better evaluated health education programs designed to improve the health of young people, a series of books of possible test questions has been published by IOX, a California based evaluation group. These manuals provide a range of questions useful for evaluation purposes in the areas of drug abuse, stress, smoking, diabetes, alcohol abuse, nutrition, and physical fitness.

GRADING

No matter how you grade, some students will be unhappy. Grades are designed to communicate educational status rather than to guarantee happiness; thus it is important that grading schemes reflect educational status. Some schools have replaced grades with anecdotal records. Some use anecdotal records to supplement grades. However, the demand for a single indicator of grade equivalency means that grades will be with us for a long time.

Teacher-generated grades require the establishment of a standard against which to compare student performance. Standards for comparison are either absolute or relevant.

Absolute values

The absolute system of grading uses a preestablished standard for course or examination expectations. Subjectivity occurs in determining what the standard is. Three examples of absolute grading systems follow.

Percentage grading

Percentage grading implies that 100% represents all possible learning and 0% represents no learning at all. Some arbitrary standard usually is established to represent the passing grade (e.g., 70%). A 70% implies that 70% of the materials was learned or mastered. Percentage scores can be converted to letter grades by the establishment of a range, i.e., *A* equals 93% to 100%; *B* equals 85% to 92%.

The teacher's goal is to prepare a test that truly reflects course content and to write test items that allow the assessment of acceptable learning to fall in a relatively small range of scores such as 70% to 100%.

Adjusted percentage scores

In recognition of the difficulty in test making, the "adjusted" approach usually allows the highest score achieved to be adjusted to equal 100%. If the highest grade is 85, then 85 is defined to equal 100%, and all the other scores are adjusted accordingly. In this way student performance anchors the scale. Comparison of scores between different groups of students becomes impossible, however, because members of each group are compared only with each other.

Competency-based grades

The level of acceptable competency is determined in advance, and students are judged as passing or not passing a certain "benchmark" of competency. With this approach, students are given multiple chances to pass or master a defined area of competency.

Relative values

Grading on a curve. This system implies that grade distribution reflects a normal curve and establishes quotas for each grade. For example, this system may dictate that only the highest 8% can get an *A*, even if many students cluster close to this cut-off point. This approach presupposes that even at the end of the course students will still be distributed across a normal curve, which implies that a significant number of students did not learn much.

Distribution gap grading. Distribution gap grading involves ranking all grades achieved in the class and recording their frequency. Natural clusters are then assigned a letter grade. The highest grades may cluster anywhere on the scale, and they represent a common grade, i.e., the highest grade. The next cluster of grades represents the next highest grade, and so on. If grades do not cluster clearly, the teacher is still faced with the subjective task of deciding the point at which one grade ends and another begins.

TABLE 17-1.   Comparison of absolute and relative grading system

Relative grading system (comparison with other students)	Absolute grading system (comparison with an established standard)
Advantages	
1. Individuals with exceptional ability will be recognized.	1. Course expectations must be communicated clearly to students.
2. This is the common and accepted system in many schools, and so results can be interpreted easily.	2. Most or all students can obtain high grades if they work well.
	3. Course grades represent the degree of achievement of course objectives.
	4. Students do not influence their grades if they help each other in preparing for exams and tests.
Disadvantages	
1. No matter how good or bad the reference group is, some students will always get high grades and some will always get low grades. Accordingly these grades are difficult to interpret without additional information.	1. It is difficult to establish ahead of time what the course standards will be for each grade.
2. Grades are influenced as much by the quality of students in the class as by real differences in performance.	2. Reasonable student achievement levels need to be identified and measured by teacher-made tests.
3. Grades tend to fluctuate from one class to another depending on the quality of students.	

Adapted from Fisbie DA, et al: Assigning course grades, Office of Instructional Resourses, University of Illinois at Champaign-Urbana, 1979.

Table 17-1 contains a summary of the advantages and disadvantages of these two approaches.

Grading tends to create a difficult situation for students and teachers. However, grades are inevitable, and in one form or another are experienced throughout life. The important point for teachers is to ensure that students know exactly what they are expected to learn, how their achievement will be measured, the consequences of not meeting certain standards, and where they can go for help and special assistance.

Summary

Individual instructors find certain types of tests preferable to others. Doubtless the instructor's particular skill is reflected in the preference. Practical considerations of a busy teacher frequently determine the type of test developed. Ideally, test results should be analyzed statistically, but the health teacher has neither the time nor the inclination for such an analysis. For that reason the occasional use of a standard health knowledge test may be advisable. Several standard health knowledge tests are available.

To ask for perfection in a health test is to ask for the impossible. These tests depend on words, and although words are our best tools for conveying ideas, they are also the biggest obstacle to understanding. Different connotations and shades of meaning are an ever-present difficulty. Health tests need not be perfect to be valuable. A precise measure to the most minute increment is unnecessary in the practical affairs of life.

A health test is not the end of health education; it is a record of the past and a barometer for the future. Evaluation is a continuous and never-ending process, an integral part of learning.

The objective of evaluation is not to approve or disapprove but to improve. Evaluation outcomes should always be expressed in ways that are comprehensible and encourage improvement. Evaluation should always be presented as a positive and constructive process.

GET INVOLVED!   Individuals preparing to enter a health or health-related field may have an interest in or a need to become involved with the field of safety and accident prevention. The fact that unintentional injuries are the leading cause of death for all children is reason enough for educators to want to help reduce this threat to life and health.

With motor vehicle crashes being the principal cause of injury and death, the field of driver and safety education presents both a challenge and an opportunity for a young person entering the field of health education of a related field today.

There are more than 40 different national organizations related to the field of safety. These range from very specific interests such as aviation safety to more general concerns such as industrial safety, human factors research, and safety management. There are two organizations an educator may elect to join: the Safety Society and the American Driver and Traffic Safety Association. Typically, qualification for teaching driver education is like acquiring a teaching minor or a secondary field.

Most safety organizations are affiliated with the National Safety Council, one of the largest organizations in the United States. The National Safety Council membership is composed of both individual professionals and organizations. The purpose of the Council is "to arouse and maintain the interest in safety and accident prevention." In addition to annual meetings, the Council publishes journals covering research, safety standards, and policy issues relating to family safety, traffic safety, school safety, farm safety, and industrial safety.

For specific information concerning driver education qualifications, write to a local school superintendent's office or to your State Department of Education.

For information concerning career opportunities in the field of safety and accident prevention, write to:

The Safety Society
American Alliance for HPERD
1900 Association Dr.
Reston, VA 22091

American Driver and Traffic Safety Education Association
239 Florida Ave.
Salisbury, MD 21801

STUDY QUESTIONS

1. In the final analysis, what is the true measure of the effectiveness of a school health program?
2. Distinguish between subjective and objective evaluation.
3. What are the advantages of using a standardized test instrument in evaluation in the school health program?
4. How can an inventory be useful in evaluating a school health program?
5. Why are objectives of a program necessary as a guide in developing evaluation instruments?
6. When subjective judgments are necessary, how can subjectivity be reduced?
7. To what extent is testing a specialty?
8. A youngster's health status may decline so little each day that it will be imperceptible to the teacher. How then can teachers identify the youngster whose health is declining?
9. Distinguish between the different types of validity and the different types of reliability of a test.
10. How valid are health attitude tests with which you are familiar?
11. "Essay tests are not outmoded and can be highly valuable for certain evaluation purposes." Explain.
12. Make an appraisal of true-false tests.
13. What is an attitude, and how can it be measured?
14. What is the relationship between attitudes, knowledge, and practice?
15. In multiple-choice tests why is the construction of foils the critical skill demanded?
16. Interpret the statement, "A student who does well on one type of test usually does well on any other type of test."
17. What are the basic requirements of a good multiple-choice question?
18. What is the purpose of evaluation in school health practice?

REFERENCES

Anderson LW: *Assessing affective characteristics in the school,* Boston, 1981, Allyn & Bacon.

Centers for Disease Control: Results from the National Adolescent Student Health Survey, *MMWR* 38:147-150, 1989.

Centers for Disease Control: Behavioral risk factor surveillance, 1988, *MMWR* 39(suppl SS-2):1-22, 1990.

Diederich PB: *Short-cut statistics for teacher-made tests: 1983-1984 test and measurement kit,* Princeton, NJ, Educational Testing Service.

Fishbein M: The prediction of behaviors from attitudinal variables. In Mortensen CD, Sereno KK, editors: *Advances in communication research,* New York, 1973, Harper & Row.

Fitz-Gibbon CT, Morris LL: *How to analyze data,* Newbury Park, Calif, 1987, Sage.

Fitz-Gibbon CT, Morris LL: *How to design a program evaluation,* ed 2, Newbury Park, Calif, 1987, Sage.

Gay LR: *Educational evaluation and measurement,* Columbus, Ohio, 1980, Charles E. Merrill Publishing.

Hawkins JD, Nederhood B: Handbook for evaluating drug and alcohol prevention programs: staff/team evaluation of prevention programs (STEPP), Rockville, Md, DHHS, PHS, ADAMHA, Office of Substance Abuse Prevention, DHHS Publication No. (ADM) 87-1512, 1987.

Herman JL, Morris LL, Fitz-Gibbon CT: *Evaluator's handbook,* Newbury Park, Calif, 1987, Sage.

Hills JR: *Measurement and evaluation in the classroom,* Columbus, Ohio, 1981, Charles E. Merrill.

Kolbe LJ: Indicators for planning and monitoring school health problems. In Kar S, editor: *Health promotion indicators and actions,* New York, 1989, Springer.

Kolbe LJ: An epidemiological surveillance system to monitor the prevalence of youth behaviors that most affect health, *Health Educ* 21(6):44, 1990.

Lidz CS: *Improving assessment of school children,* San Francisco, 1981, Jossey-Bass.

Making the classroom test: a guide for teachers, 1983-1984 test and measurement kit, Princeton, NJ, Educational Testing Service.

McKenzie TL: Observational measure of children's physical activity, *J Sch Health* 61(5):224, 1991.

Morris LL, Fitz-Gibbon CT: How to deal with goals and objectives, In Morris LL, editor: *Program evaluation kit,* Newbury Park, Calif, 1978, Sage.

Nader PR, editor: *Options for school health,* Germantown, Md, 1978, Aspen Systems Corp.

Proctor SE: Evaluation of nursing practice in schools, *J Sch Health* 56:272, 1986.

Rowe DE: Healthful school living: environmental health in the school, *J Sch Health* 57(10):426, 1987.

Shick J: Those tantalizing textbook tests, *Health Educ* 18(6):42, Dec 1987/Jan 1988.

Shick J: Tantalizing textbook tests, part II: true-false, matching, completion and essay, *Health Educ* 20(2):18, 1989.

Siegel LP, Krieble TA: Evaluation of school-based, high school health services, *J Sch Health* 57(8):323, 1987.

Swezey RW: *Individual performance assessment: an approach to criterion referenced test development,* Reston, Va, 1981, Reston.

Trotter CE: *Guide for evaluation of school facilities,* Knoxville, 1977, School Planning Laboratory, University of Tennessee.

APPENDIX

A

General criteria for evaluating instructional materials

The following criteria are to help you evaluate instructional materials. Indicate your judgment by circling the appropriate number. Each item must be rated. A separate evaluating sheet is necessary for each set of materials considered for recommendation.

NOTE: Comments that would add to this evaluation would be appreciated. Please use last page.

Evaluated by _____ Date _____

Committee _____ School _____

Data for evaluated materials

Author _____
Title _____
Publisher _____ or _____ producer _____
Copyright date _____ Type of materials _____
Grade level of material being evaluated _____
Is this material part of a series? Yes ☐ Series grade level _____
No ☐

Title of series _____
Cost per item _____

SUMMARY OF EVALUATION

	High				Low	M*	NA†
I. Text format	5	4	3	2	1	0	0
II. Audiovisual format and considerations	5	4	3	2	1	0	0
III. Organization and overall content	5	4	3	2	1	0	0
IV. Bias content	5	4	3	2	1	0	0
V. Teacher's guide for texts or audiovisual materials	5	4	3	2	1	0	0
VI. Additional support materials	5	4	3	2	1	0	0

*Missing: material should have had item but does not.
†Not applicable.

TEXT FORMAT

	High				Low	M	NA
1. General appearance	5	4	3	2	1	0	0
2. Size and color practical for classroom use	5	4	3	2	1	0	0
3. Binding: durability and flexibility	5	4	3	2	1	0	0
4. Quality of paper	5	4	3	2	1	0	0
5. Readability to type	5	4	3	2	1	0	0
6. Appeal of page layouts	5	4	3	2	1	0	0
7. Usefulness of chapter headings	5	4	3	2	1	0	0
8. Appropriateness of illustrations	5	4	3	2	1	0	0
9. Usefulness of references, index, bibliography, appendix	5	4	3	2	1	0	0
10. Consistency of format	5	4	3	2	1	0	0

AUDIOVISUAL FORMAT AND CONSIDERATIONS

	High				Low	M	NA
1. Sound quality	5	4	3	2	1	0	0
2. Picture quality	5	4	3	2	1	0	0
3. Emotional impact	5	4	3	2	1	0	0
4. Other qualities: vitality, style, imagination	5	4	3	2	1	0	0
5. Authoritative and well-researched, free of propaganda	5	4	3	2	1	0	0
6. Length suitable to audience and content	5	4	3	2	1	0	0
7. Durability	5	4	3	2	1	0	0
8. Usefulness in more than one subject area: write areas here _____							

_____

_____

ORGANIZATION AND OVERALL CONTENT

Use the specific criteria developed for the subject area if available. Otherwise, use the following guidelines.

Guidelines for organization and overall content	High				Low	M	NA
1. Currency of content	5	4	3	2	1	0	0
2. Consistency of organization	5	4	3	2	1	0	0
3. Clarity and conciseness of the explanation	5	4	3	2	1	0	0
4. Unit organization: follows logical sequence	5	4	3	2	1	0	0
5. Usefulness of illustrations in enhancing the content	5	4	3	2	1	0	0
6. Consistency of point of view with basic principles of subject area	5	4	3	2	1	0	0
7. Usefulness in furthering the systematic and sequential program of the course of study	5	4	3	2	1	0	0
8. Interest appeal: provisions for student differences and backgrounds	5	4	3	2	1	0	0
9. Usefulness in stimulating critical thinking (i.e., problem solving situations, etc.)	5	4	3	2	1	0	0

	High ─────── Low					M	NA
10. Usefulness in stimulating students toward self-evaluation and formulation of their own goals	5	4	3	2	1	0	0
11. Usefulness in facilitating lesson planning by the way the material is organized	5	4	3	2	1	0	0
12. Adaptability of content to varied instructional methods	5	4	3	2	1	0	0
13. Adaptability of content to varying abilities of individual students (i.e., vocabulary and reading levels)	5	4	3	2	1	0	0
Above average							
Average	5	4	3	2	1	0	0
Below average	5	4	3	2	1	0	0
14. Adequacy of learning activities							
Quality	5	4	3	2	1	0	0
Quantity	5	4	3	2	1	0	0
15. Provision for review and maintenance of previously acquired skills	5	4	3	2	1	0	0
16. Provision for measuring student achievement	5	4	3	2	1	0	0

BIAS CONTENT

	High ─────── Low					M	NA
1. Presents more than one viewpoint of controversial issues	5	4	3	2	1	0	0
2. Presents accurate facts when generalizations are made	5	4	3	2	1	0	0
3. Includes all socioeconomic levels and settings and all ethnic groups	5	4	3	2	1	0	0
4. Gives balanced treatment of the past and present	5	4	3	2	1	0	0
5. Promotes the diverse character of our nation by:	5	5	3	2	1	0	0
a. Presenting the positive nature of cultural differences							
b. Using languages and models that treat all human beings with respect, dignity, and seriousness							
c. Including characters that help students identify positively with their heritage and culture							
d. Portraying families realistically (one-parent, two-parent, several generations)							
e. Portraying the handicapped realistically							
6. Includes minorities and women by:	5	4	3	2	1	0	0
a. Presenting their roles positively but realistically							
b. Having their contributions, inventions, or discoveries appear alongside men							
c. Depicting them in a variety of occupations and at all levels in a profession							

    d. Having their work included in materials
    e. Presenting information from their
       perspective
    f. Having appropriate illustrations

TEACHER'S GUIDE FOR TEXTS OR AUDIOVISUAL MATERIALS

	High				Low	M	NA
1. Easy to use	5	4	3	2	1	0	0
2. Answers provided	5	4	3	2	1	0	0
3. Background information	5	4	3	2	1	0	0
4. Teaching strategies	5	4	3	2	1	0	0
5. Ideas for motivation, follow-up, extension	5	4	3	2	1	0	0
6. Guidelines for evaluation	5	4	3	2	1	0	0
7. Inclusion of script	5	4	3	2	1	0	0
8. Bibliography	5	4	3	2	1	0	0

ADDITIONAL SUPPORT MATERIALS THAT ACCOMPANY TEXT

Please list the materials (e.g., workbooks, tests) ___
and use separate form for each one listed _____
_____

USE THIS SPACE FOR COMMENTS:

School health program evaluation

The Nebraska Department of Education, with financial support from the Centers for Disease Control, developed a comprehensive health education teacher training program (CHETT) for the teachers of Nebraska. The basis for this training program is the Kolbe-Allensworth model of comprehensive school health programs described in Chapter 1. The CHETT program trains teams of school personnel (administrators, counselors, teachers, nurses, and parents) in a thorough understanding of all aspects of a school health program. As part of that training and follow-up activities, the CHETT team assesses the quality of the health program of their school. The following checklist was designed specifically for that purpose and is based on the Kolbe-Allensworth model. Note that the questions are designed specifically to identify measures that are common across all types and sizes of schools and are representative of the issues included in each of the categories of a school health program. Also, note that on the last page a method is presented to quantify the results of this assessment so that scores are established to represent the quality of the school's program. Therefore subsequent measures can be used to assess progress in its improvement.

HOW HEALTHY IS YOUR SCHOOL?*
Background

This survey is designed to help school personnel develop a profile of their school as a source of health promotion for students and teachers.

Answer all the questions, and then follow the instructions to summarize the results. The summary statement on p. 497 will identify the areas in which your school is making a difference in health promotion activities and the areas in which your school's contribution could be improved.

One survey should be completed for each administrative unit within your school system. An administrative unit means a school facility (building) with a principal or head teacher. If a junior and a senior high school or an elementary school and a junior high school share a building but have different administrations (principals), separate surveys should be completed.

This survey is based on a model of a comprehensive school health program developed by Diane Allensworth and Lloyd Kolbe.† This model suggests that there are several components

---

*School health program evaluation; revised April 2, 1992

†Allensworth D, Kolbe L: The comprehensive school health program: exploring an expanded concept, *Health* 57:409, 1987.

to a good school health program, including health services, health instruction, healthy environment, school and community health promotion activities, physical education, food services, counseling, school-site health promotion, and administrative support. Coordinated activities in each of these areas represent the school's best chance to support and enhance the health of students and teachers.

Instructions

Answer all questions. A judgment will be called for in many cases because the questions are answered with a Yes or No. "To a degree" answers are not possible. Therefore you will need to decide whether or not your school indeed does what the question asks.

Follow the instructions at the end of each section to create a percentage score. Enter the percentage score for each section on the appropriate scales on p. 497.

THE SCHOOL HEALTH ENVIRONMENT

The school environment should be safe and conducive to learning. The school environment should enable and reward health-enhancing behaviors. The school environment should encourage acting out health-enhancing behaviors and principles learned in the classroom.

1. Do all classrooms and other teaching areas present a satisfactory physical environment for learning (adequate light, air circulation, no excessive noise)? YES NO

2. Is all classroom equipment, including chairs and tables, in good repair and functional? YES NO

3. Would you say the school presents a positive emotional climate conducive to learning and personal growth for all students? YES NO

4. Are all facilities used by students completely accessible to the handicapped? YES NO

5. a. Are all buildings smoke-free? (If "yes," go to question 6. If "no," go to question b.) YES NO
   b. If all buildings are not smoke-free, do designated smoking areas fully separate nonsmokers from passive smoke? YES NO

6. Are all student washrooms provided with an adequate supply of soap and disposable towels? YES NO

7. Is there an established policy for periodic safety inspections of all buildings? YES NO

8. Are safety inservices conducted for all faculty and staff at least once a semester? YES NO

9. Are plans for building evacuation for fire, tornadoes, and other disasters clearly posted indicating procedures to follow? YES NO

10. Are the warning devices and fire extinguishers functional with up-to-date inspections? YES NO

11. Are evacuation drills held at least twice a semester? YES NO

12. Do all school personnel know the location of emergency alarms? YES NO

13. Is a first aid/infection control kit available in every classroom? (A first aid/infection control kit should contain gloves and materials for handling bodily fluids.) YES NO

14. Are persons trained in first aid/infection control procedures known by all school personnel and available whenever school activities are in progress? YES NO

15. Is the environment inside the school kept clean and well maintained? YES NO

16. Are the school grounds maintained year round to ensure safety? YES NO

17. Is playground equipment inspected and repaired on a routine basis? YES NO

18. Is a specific individual charged with the responsibility of monitoring the school environment (buildings and grounds) for all matters related to the health of students and school personnel? YES NO

Interpretation

How many yes answers were marked in this section? → _____

Use the table below to convert the number of yes answers to a percentage score
and enter percentage score here: → _____

Enter the percentage score under School Health Environment on p. 497.

No. yes	Percentage score	No. yes	Percentage score	No. yes	Percentage score
1	5.0	7	39.0	13	72.0
2	11.0	8	44.0	14	78.0
3	16.0	9	50.0	15	83.0
4	22.0	10	56.0	16	89.0
5	28.0	11	61.0	17	95.0
6	33.0	12	67.0	18	100.0

SCHOOL HEALTH SERVICES

School health services include those things a school does for its students to assist in the early detection of health problems that may interfere with learning. School health services also include actions the school takes to assist students with special health needs to gain the full benefit of the school's educational programs.

19. Does your school provide regular screening programs, by qualified nurses or other trained personnel? YES NO

If yes, do the screenings include:

20. Hearing YES NO

21. Vision YES NO

22. Scoliosis YES NO

23. Blood pressure YES NO

24. Dental YES NO

25. Is screening equipment maintained in good condition? YES NO

26. Does an educational session for students explaining the purpose of screening and the screening test precede the screening activity? YES NO

27. Is there an established mechanism for counseling and/or referral for students and parents following screening? YES NO

28. Is there an established liaison with community agencies to assist in obtaining needed services for students? YES NO

29. Is there an established procedure for following up with students/parents who have not acted on the screening recommendations within 30 days? YES NO

30. Is there an established procedure for teachers to identify students experiencing difficulty in school and refer them to a specially trained team of teacher counselors for recommended remedial action (such as SCIP or similar program)? YES NO

31. Is at least one person in each building certified in CPR? YES NO

32. Is at least one person in each building certified in first aid? YES NO

33. Is there an adequately equipped nurse's office or sick room that provides a private, quiet place for sick or injured students? YES NO

34. Does the school maintain current immunization records on all students? YES NO

35. Does the school have clear procedures for forwarding students' health records to the new schools when the student moves or transfers? YES NO

36. Does the school maintain a current file on the special medical needs of all students (allergies, special emergency needs)? YES NO

37. Does the school have a communicable disease policy, which includes infectious disease control procedures, that is known by all staff? YES NO

38. Does the school have an HIV/AIDS policy that is known by all teachers?   YES / NO

39. Are the infectious disease control procedures known by all staff?   YES / NO

40. Does the administration take steps to ensure that the infectious disease control procedures are adhered to at all times?   YES / NO

41. Does the school conduct annual inservice programs to ensure all staff know the school's policies on communicable diseases/HIV/AIDS and alcohol and other drugs?   YES / NO

42. Does the school provide special services to all students who have special health related needs such as physical, mental or emotional handicaps?   YES / NO

Interpretation

How many yes answers were marked in this section? →   _____

Use the table below to convert the number of yes answers to a percentage score and enter percentage score here: →   _____

Enter the percentage score under School Health Services on p. 497.

No. yes	Percentage score	No. yes	Percentage score	No. yes	Percentage score
1	4.0	9	38.0	17	71.0
2	8.0	10	42.0	18	75.0
3	13.0	11	46.0	19	79.0
4	17.0	12	50.0	20	83.0
5	21.0	13	54.0	21	88.0
6	25.0	14	58.0	22	92.0
7	29.0	15	63.0	23	96.0
8	33.0	16	67.0	24	100.0

ADMINISTRATIVE SUPPORT

This section asks questions to assess the extent and the degree of administrative support for the school's health program. Administrative support comes from the school board and from the school administration (prinicpal). Administrative support is visible in clear management of the school's comprehensive health promotion activities.

43. Does the school have an advisory committee, including a variety of school and community representatives, charged with encouraging and supporting the school's health promotion efforts?   YES / NO

44. Does the school have a staff person designated the health coordinator or health program manager with release time to ensure the success of all aspects of the school's health program?   YES / NO

45. Is there a separate budget for special health promotion activities for students and/or staff?   YES / NO

46. Does the school have a set of health goals for students?   YES / NO

47. Does the school have a set of health goals for staff?   YES / NO

48. Are community and parent representatives involved in assisting the school with its health program?   YES / NO

49. Does the administration evaluate the full range of the school's health related activities at least once every 2 years?   YES / NO

50. Are district funds allotted for all aspects of the school's health program?   YES / NO

51. Is the school board briefed annually about the status of student health and the student health issues faced by teachers?   YES / NO

52. Are the school board's health-related policies combined in a separate document and made available to teachers and staff?   YES / NO

Interpretation

How many yes answers were marked in this section? →   _____

Use the table below to convert the number of yes answers to a percentage score
and enter percentage score here: →   _____

Enter the percentage score under Administrative Support on p. 497.

No. yes	Percentage score	No. yes	Percentage score	No. yes	Percentage score
1	10.0	5	50.0	8	80.0
2	20.0	6	60.0	9	90.0
3	30.0	7	70.0	10	100.0
4	40.0				

SCHOOL PHYSICAL EDUCATION

Physical edcuation classes provide an opportunity for school personnel to add to a student's education through the physical senses: by movement, kinesthetics, strength, flexibility, and endurance. Physical education classes are an important element of a school's health program.

53. Is physical education required of all students in all grades in your school?   YES NO

54. Do physical education classes include information and formal discussions to illustrate the value of class activities to personal health?   YES NO

55. Do physical education classes include homework focused on the benefits of physical education?   YES NO

56. Do physical education classes earn students a grade of the same type as any other academic subject?   YES NO

57. Do all teachers exhibit personal fitness and exemplify the objectives of the physical education program?   YES NO

58. Does the school have a policy prohibiting the substitution of other courses or activities for physical education classes?   YES NO

59. Are all teachers of physical education classes certified to teach physical education?   YES NO

60. Do all physical education classes require at least 30 minutes of vigorous exercise three times per week during both semesters of each year?   YES NO

61. Do physical education classes teach skills beyond those associated with the school's athletic program?   YES NO

62. Are individualized and/or adaptive physical education programs provided to assist those who are not able to perform in regular physical education classes?   YES NO

63. Do all physical education courses focus on developing students' flexibility, strength, and endurance?   YES NO

64. Are at least 50% of physical education class activities noncompetitive?   YES NO

65. Does the school have an adequate facility for conducting physical education classes throughout the school year?   YES NO

66. Is there coordination between the curriculum in physical education and the curricula in health, science and home economics classes?   YES NO

67. Do all school personnel see physical education as critical and co-equal to other elements of a student's educational program?   YES NO

68. Would you say the emphasis in your school's physical education program is toward health-related physical fitness and away from athletic ability?   YES NO

69. Do physical education students complete exams at the end of each semester as do students enrolled in other courses?   YES NO

70. Does the school library contain adequate materials and information to supplement the learning in physical education classes?   YES NO

Interpretation

How many yes answers were marked in this section? →   _____

Use the table below to convert the number of yes answers to a percentage score
and enter percentage score here: →   _____

Enter the percentage score under School Physical Education on p. 497.

No. yes	Percentage score	No. yes	Percentage score	No. yes	Percentage score
1	5.0	7	39.0	13	72.0
2	11.0	8	44.0	14	78.0
3	16.0	9	50.0	15	83.0
4	22.0	10	56.0	16	89.0
5	28.0	11	61.0	17	95.0
6	33.0	12	67.0	18	100.0

SCHOOL HEALTH INSTRUCTION

Instruction is a primary element for enhancing the health of young people. The scope and sequence of a school's health instruction program and how health instruction relates to other instructional programs affects a student's knowledge and shapes his or her attitudes and behaviors. Even if your school does not have a separate health class at each grade, these questions should still be answered.

71. Does your school have a written statement of the goals and objectives of its health instruction program?   YES   NO

72. Are those teaching health-related issues endorsed to teach health?   YES   NO

73. In health classes do students earn the same type and amount of credit toward graduation as in any other academic subject?   YES   NO

74. Is health instruction required of all students at all grade levels?   YES   NO

75. Do all instructors of health-related issues know what their students were taught in preceding years so each grade level complements and expands the student's knowledge base?   YES   NO

76. Is there an effective mechanism that ensures clear integration between what is taught in health classes and the other subjects in the curriculum?   YES   NO

77. Do health classes include homework in type and amount comparable to other subjects?   YES   NO

78. Does the content of the health curriculum at each grade level clearly relate to the needs of the students?   YES   NO

79. Does the school have a policy of evaluating its health curriculum at least once every 5 years?   YES   NO

80. Does the school library contain adequate materials and information to supplement the learning in the health classes?   YES   NO

81. Is the scope and sequence of the health curriculum known to other teachers of each grade level?   YES   NO

82. The following questions refer to the integration of instruction on health-related topics across the curriculum. Use the following codes to indicate which other courses integrate health topics. There may be more than one course integrating health at any grade level. Answer only for those grades served by your school.

    P   for Physical Education course
    H   for Home Economics course
    S   for Social Studies course
    Sc   for Science course
    M   for Mathematics course
    E   for English course
    X   for other classes such as family life, psychology, etc.

83. At which grade levels are the following subjects taught? Indicate with a check mark. Answer only for those grades served by your school.

84. Rate the primary objectives of each grade level of the health instruction program in your school according to the following outcomes. In each grade range, for each of the three domains, rate the focus of your school's health education program as it is now conducted.

	K–3	4–6	Middle/ junior high	Senior high
Personal and physical health				
Mental and emotional health				
Prevention and control of disease				
Nutrition				
Substance use and abuse				
Accident prevention and safety				
Community and environmental health				
Consumer health				
Family life education				
Death and dying				
Causes of mental retardation				

Interpretation

How many yes answers were marked for questions 71 to 82 in this section? → _____

Use the table below to convert the number of yes answers to a percentage score and enter percentage score here: → _____

Enter the percentage score under School Health Instruction on p. 497.

No. yes	Percentage score	No. yes	Percentage score	No. yes	Percentage score
1	5.0	9	41.0	16	73.0
2	9.0	10	45.0	17	77.0
3	14.0	11	50.0	18	82.0
4	18.0	12	55.0	19	86.0
5	23.0	13	59.0	20	91.0
6	27.0	14	64.0	21	95.0
7	32.0	15	68.0	22	100.0
8	36.0				

Interpretation of question 82 for scoring purposes:

For the grades served by your school, count the number of topics integrated into at least two subject areas. The total score possible for this question is 11.

	K	1	2	3	4	5	6	7	8	9	10	11	12
Personal and physical health													
Mental and emotional health													
Prevention and control of disease													
Nutrition													
Substance use and abuse													
Accident prevention and safety													
Community and environmental health													
Consumer health													
Family life education													
Death and dying													

Mark as follows: 1 for principal focus
2 for some focus
3 for minor or no focus

	K–3	4–6	Middle/ junior high	Senior high
Increasing health knowledge				
Changing health beliefs/attitudes				
Influencing health behavior				

Interpretation of questions 83 and 84:

Questions 82 and 83 are not included in the scores used to create the school profile on p. 497. These two questions are designed to give an overall profile of the health instruction program at your school.

THE SCHOOLSITE HEALTH PROMOTION PROGRAM FOR FACULTY AND STAFF

Schoolsite health promotion programs provide an important academic and financial benefit for school personnel and serve to illustrate to students and the community the school's commitment to active health promotion.

85. Does the school's sick leave policy encourage the early identification and treatment of illness? YES NO

86. Does a school/medical society/ community committee exist to explore or oversee the school's health promotion activities? YES NO

87. Does the school have policies that YES
encourage health and health promotion activities for faculty and staff (i.e., smoke-free buildings/space, access to lockers and exercise facilities, food service alternatives)? NO

88. Are health screenings routinely available to all school personnel? YES NO

89. Can school personnel obtain a personal fitness appraisal with school sponsorship? YES NO

90. Is nutritional analysis and counseling available from school personnel or with school sponsorship? YES NO

91. Does the school conduct educational programs addressing health promotion options for school personnel? YES NO

92. Does the school have an employee assistance program (EAP) that encourages early access to treatment services?

    YES
    NO

93. Does the school conduct an annual inservice for all personnel on health promotion and the relationship between health and learning?

    YES
    NO

Interpretation

How many yes answers were marked in this section?→ _____

Use the table below to convert the number of yes answers to a percentage score and enter percentage score here:→ _____

Enter the percentage score under Schoolsite Health Promotion for Faculty and Staff on p. 497.

No. yes	Percentage score	No. yes	Percentage score	No. yes	Percentage score
1	11.0	4	44.0	7	78.0
2	22.0	5	56.0	8	89.0
3	33.0	6	67.0	9	100.0

COORDINATION OF THE SCHOOL HEALTH PROGRAM WITH THE SCHOOL'S COMMUNITY

The school is a vital part of any community. Its operation is influenced by the community and it in turn influences the community. Cooperative ventures, open communications and mutual trust are important for a school to be effective in its educational mission.

94. Does the school have a parent advisory group that provides an organized way for parents to share health-related concerns with school administrators?

    YES
    NO

95. Does the school have a health service advisory group/committee that includes members from the local medical community, business community, and other significant community representation?

    YES
    NO

96. If there is a local health department, is there ongoing contact between the school and the local health department?

    YES
    NO

97. Are the results of ongoing health education, health promotion, and screening programs reported regularly to the community?

    YES
    NO

98. Is there an effective network of health-related contacts that ensure that the students with special health needs can access needed services?

    YES
    NO

99. Does the school have a school-based or school-linked clinic?

    YES
    NO

100. Does the school participate in local community health promotion activities such as health fairs?

    YES
    NO

101. Does the school actively encourage student participation in community projects and programs designed to promote healthy life-styles?

    YES
    NO

102. Are community members who are health professionals involved in the school's health instruction program?

    YES
    NO

Interpretation

How many yes answers were marked in this section? → _____

Use the table below to convert the number of yes answers to a percentage score and enter percentage score here: → _____

Enter the percentage score under Coordination of School Health Program with Community on p. 497.

Continued

No. yes	Percentage score	No. yes	Percentage score	No. yes	Percentage score
1	11.0	4	44.0	7	78.0
2	22.0	5	56.0	8	89.0
3	33.0	6	67.0	9	100.0

GUIDANCE AND COUNSELING

School counselors are an important part of any school's staff. The degree to which they are sensitive to the health needs of students and actively involved in the school health promotion program will directly influence the quality of the school's health promotion efforts.

103. Does your school have a student personal services team consisting of at least a counselor, nurse, teacher, and an administrator that meets regularly to consider options for students having difficulty in school?   YES NO

104. Does your school have a student assistance team or program?   YES NO

105. Do the students (as reported by the counseling staff and nurse) experience flow of information about health-related problems from the student personal services team to teachers working on the revision and content of the health-related curricula?   YES NO

106. Are counselors, teachers of health issues, and school nurses involved each year in educational programs for parents?   YES NO

107. Are counselors, teachers of health issues, and school nurses involved in educational programs for parents of entering students at K-1, middle/junior high school, or senior high school?

108. Is information on the health problems of students reported regularly to parents through a school or principal's newsletter?   YES NO

109. Are support groups available for students with special needs?   YES NO

110. Is there an established liaison with community agencies to assist in obtaining needed services for students?   YES NO

111. Does the school have established plans and procedures to handle "crises" such as a student or staff death, suicide, violence, or HIV/AIDS infection?   YES NO

112. Do school personnel have communication with the religious leaders of the community?   YES NO

113. Are the school counselors appropriately credentialed/certified?   YES NO

114. Can any student see a school counselor within 2 days of his or her request?   YES NO

115. Are there adequate facilities for counselors to meet privately with students and hold conferences with parents?   YES NO

116. Are counselors involved in teaching sections of the health curriculum?   YES NO

Interpretation

How many yes answers were marked in this section? → _____

Use the table below to convert the number of yes answers to a percentage score and enter percentage score here: → _____

Enter the percentage score under Guidance and Counseling on p. 497.

No. yes	Percentage score	No. yes	Percentage score	No. yes	Percentage score
1	7.0	6	43.0	11	79.0
2	14.0	7	50.0	12	86.0
3	21.0	8	57.0	13	43.0
4	29.0	9	64.0	14	100.0
5	36.0	10	71.0		

FOOD SERVICES

The provision of food services is an integral part of the school's service activities. The food service program provides an important opportunity for complementing the school's overall health promotion activities.

117. Do all meals served at the school meet USDA/DHHS guidelines? YES NO
118. Are food service staff careful to serve food low in salt, fat, and calories? YES NO
119. Is the school's program to supplement the costs of meals for students from low-income families handled confidentially and professionally? YES NO
120. Has the school board developed a set of goals and objectives related to student nutrition and school food servers? YES NO
121. Are food service staff credentialed by the American Food Service Association (AFSA), or are they actively encouraged to obtain certification? YES NO
122. Are food service personnel involved in planning the school's nutrition education curricula? YES NO

123. Does the school food service program have educational objectives indicated by such things as informational food labeling, food selection advice, and appropriate posters and educational materials in the food service area? YES NO
124. Does a policy exist that determines the nutrional content and availability of snack of foods in vending machines? YES NO
125. Are students actively encouraged to wash their hands before eating? YES NO
126. Do food service staff conduct an annual evaluation of the food service program, involving students, faculty, and staff? YES NO
127. Is information on the food service program and nutritional advice a regular feature in the school's communication with parents through such means as pamphlets and newsletters? YES NO
128. Is the school board briefed annually on the school's food service program? YES NO

Interpretation

How many yes answers were marked in this section? → _____
Use the table below to convert the number of yes answers to a percentage score and enter percentage score here: → _____
Enter the percentage score under Food Services on p. 497.

No. yes	Percentage score	No. yes	Percentage score	No. yes	Percentage score
1	8.0	5	42.0	9	75.0
2	17.0	6	50.0	10	83.0
3	25.0	7	58.0	11	92.0
4	33.0	8	67.0	12	100.0

INTERPRETATION

To help interpret the results of this survey, mark a point corresponding to the percentage score for each section of the survey under the appropriate heading. Connect the points with a line to create a graph. This is your school profile.

Prioritize the areas of needed attention by considering the magnitude of deviations from 100% and the feasibility and likelihood of action to move the school toward 100% in the next year.

%	School health environment	School health services	Administrative support	School physical education	School health instruction	Schoolsite health promotion for faculty and staff	Coordination of school health program with community	Food services	Guidance and counseling
100-									
95-									
90-									
85-									
80-									
75-									
70-									
65-									
60-									
55-									
50-									
45-									
40-									
35-									
30-									
25-									
20-									
15-									
10-									
5-									
0-									

Survey of conditions and practices affecting safety in the school environment

REPORTING OF ACCIDENTS

1. Are accident report cards or forms available?
2. Is a complete written report on file for every accident that results in an injury?
3. Is a special study made of the causes of each accident?
4. Is an adequate, constructive follow-up study made after accident analysis to prevent recurrence of the accident?
5. Is a regular inspection (weekly) made of the building and grounds?
6. Are adequate first aid equipment and personnel available at all times?

FIRE PROTECTION

1. Are vacant rooms, basements, and attics free from flammable material?
2. Is there proper insulation between heating equipment and flammable material?
3. Are there two or more exits from every floor with doors swinging outward?
4. Are there adequate fire escapes on buildings of two or more stories?
5. Are fire extinguishers of an approved type provided for every 2000 square feet of floor space?
6. Are fire extinguishers tested regularly?
7. Do the older pupils know how to use the fire extinguishers?
8. Are fire alarms centrally located?
9. Are fire drills so proficient that the building can be emptied in an orderly manner in less than 3 minutes?
10. Are student organization and lines of exit well established (see Fig. 9-3)?

GYMNASIUM, POOL, AND LOCKER ROOMS

1. Is equipment in good condition?
2. Are all exposed projections covered?
3. Is the floor treated to prevent its being slippery?
4. Are doors of a safe construction?
5. Are fountains in a safe location?
6. Are definite rules for the use of the gymnasium and pool posted and practiced?
7. Are students properly dressed for gymnasium activities?
8. Is horseplay prohibited?
9. Is unsupervised use of the gymnasium and pool prohibited?
10. Are pool users classified according to skill?

HALLS AND STAIRS

1. Are all obstructions removed?
2. Are the floors and stairs treated to prevent them from being slippery?
3. Are worn or broken stairs replaced?
4. Are railings provided so that every person using the stairs can hold a railing?
5. Is undue congestion of hall traffic prevented by changing routes, practices, and schedules?
6. Are horseplay and running in the halls prohibited?

SHOPS, LABORATORIES, AND HOME ECONOMICS ROOMS

1. Is all equipment in good condition and regularly inspected?
2. Are all possible safety devices and attachments available and in working order?
3. Are good housekeeping practices followed?
4. Are lighting and space adequate?
5. Are machines stopped for oiling and adjustment?
6. Are safety rules posted and practiced?
7. Are students properly instructed in the use of equipment?
8. Are horseplay and running prohibited?
9. Is the unsupervised use of the shop, laboratory, or home economics rooms prohibited?
10. Is protective clothing and eyewear worn?
11. Are first aid supplies immediately available?

CLASSROOMS AND AUDITORIUMS

1. Are all obstructions removed?
2. Are exposed projections covered?
3. Are sharp objects placed in protected places?
4. Are radiators and electric fixtures properly protected?
5. Are dropped objects picked up immediately?
6. Is an orderly routine followed, with running and pushing prohibited?

PLAYGROUND

1. Is the playground space allocated in terms of safety?
2. Is apparatus in safe condition and checked regularly?
3. Are children taught the proper use of each piece of apparatus?
4. Is supervision always provided when the playground is used?
5. Do new students in kindergarten and first grade receive special instruction and supervision?
6. Are horseplay and stunting prohibited?
7. Are caution and courtesy stressed at all times?
8. Do the children assume cooperative responsibility for playground safety?
9. Is the playing surface in good condition and nonslippery?

ATHLETICS

1. Is the playing area constructed in terms of safety?
2. Are all hazardous obstructions removed?
3. Is approved equipment used?
4. Has every participant received medical approval?
5. Is competent supervision always provided?
6. Are the participants properly trained and sufficiently skilled?
7. Is parental approval required for participation in vigorous athletic events?
8. Is parental approval required if students are to be transported for athletic contests?
9. Are adequate first aid and medical services available?

GOING TO AND FROM SCHOOL

1. Are studies made of hazards children may encounter going to or from school?
2. Are specific routes outlined for students?
3. Are the routes direct, requiring a minimal use of roadways and busy intersections?
4. Are stop and go signals, stop signs, school signs, police supervision, and one-way streets used to the greatest advantage?
5. Are ice, glass, and other hazardous obstructions removed from walks?
6. Do children stay on the walks and in crosswalk lanes; and do they obey rules, signs, and traffic directors?
7. If school traffic patrols are organized, are the patrols under proper adult supervision?
8. Is maximum use made of traffic enforcement officers and facilities?
9. Are bus riders given instruction on entering and leaving the bus, as well as on conduct in the bus?
10. Are bicycle riders given special instruction and supervision?
11. Are student motor vehicle drivers given special instruction and supervision?
12. Are the parents enlisted in the safety program to and from home?

Responsibilities and competencies for entry-level health educators

RESPONSIBILITY I: ASSESSING INDIVIDUAL AND COMMUNITY NEEDS FOR HEALTH EDUCATION
Competency A

Obtain health-related data about social and cultural environments, growth and development factors, needs, and interests.

Sub-competencies

1. Select valid sources of information about health needs and interests.
2. Use computerized sources of health-related information.
3. Use or develop appropriate data-gathering instruments.
4. Apply survey techniques to acquire health data.

Competency B

Distinguish between behaviors that foster, and those that hinder, well-being.

Sub-competencies

1. Investigate physical, social, emotional, and intellectual factors influencing health behaviors.
2. Identify behaviors that tend to promote or compromise health.
3. Recognize the role of learning and affective experience in shaping patterns of health behavior.

Competency C

Infer needs for health education on the basis of obtained data.

Sub-competencies

1. Analyze needs assessment data.
2. Determine priority areas of need for health education.

RESPONSIBILITY II: PLANNING EFFECTIVE HEALTH EDUCATION PROGRAMS
Competency A

Recruit community organizations, resource people, and potential participants for support and assistance in program planning.

Sub-competencies

1. Communicate need for the program to those who will be involved.
2. Obtain commitments from personnel and decision makers who will be involved in the program.
3. Seek ideas and opinions of those who will affect, or be affected by, the program.
4. Incorporate feasible ideas and recommendations into the planning process.

Competency B

Develop a logical scope and sequence plan for a health education program.

Sub-competencies

1. Determine the range of health information requisite to a given program of instruction.
2. Organize the subject areas comprising the scope of a program in logical sequence.

From National Task Force on the Preparation and Practice of Health Educators: A framework for the development of competency based curricula for entry-level health educators, New York, 1985, National Task Force on the Preparation and Practice of Health Educators. Reprinted New York, 1990, National Commission for Health Education Credentialing, Inc.

Competency C

Formulate appropriate and measurable program objectives.

Sub-competencies

1. Infer education objectives facilitative of achievement of specified competencies.
2. Develop a frame-work of broadly stated, operational objectives relevant to a proposed health education program.

Competency D

Design educational programs consistent with specified program objectives.

Sub-competencies

1. Match proposed learning activities with those implicit in the stated objectives.
2. Formulate a wide variety of alternative educational methods.
3. Select strategies best suited to implementation of educational objectives in a given setting.
4. Plan a sequence of learning opportunities building upon, and reinforcing mastery of, preceding objectives.

RESPONSIBILITY III: IMPLEMENTING HEALTH EDUCATION PROGRAMS
Competency A

Exhibit competence in carrying out planned educational programs.

Sub-competencies

1. Use a wide range of educational methods and techniques.
2. Apply individual or group process methods as appropriate to given learning situations.
3. Use instructional equipment and other instructional media effectively.
4. Select methods that best facilitate practice of program objectives.

Competency B

Infer enabling objectives as needed to implement instructional programs in specified settings.

Sub-competencies

1. Pretest learners to ascertain present abilities and knowledge relative to proposed program objectives.
2. Develop subordinate measurable objectives as needed for instruction.

Competency C

Select methods and media best suited to implement program plans for specific learners.

Sub-competencies

1. Analyze learner characteristics, legal aspects, feasibility, and other considerations influencing choices among methods.
2. Evaluate the efficacy of alternative methods and techniques capable of facilitating program objectives.
3. Determine the availability of information, personnel, time, and equipment needed to implement the program for a given audience.

Competency D

Monitor educational programs, adjusting objectives and activities as necessary.

Sub-competencies

1. Compare actual program activities with the stated objectives.
2. Assess the relevance of existing program objectives to current needs.
3. Revise program activities and objectives as necessitated by changes in learner needs.
4. Appraise applicability of resources and materials relative to given educational objectives.

RESPONSIBILITY IV: EVALUATING EFFECTIVENESS OF HEALTH EDUCATION PROGRAMS
Competency A

Develop plans to assess achivement of program objectives.

Sub-competencies

1. Determine standards of performance to be applied as criteria of effectiveness.
2. Establish a realistic scope of evaluation efforts.
3. Develop an inventory of existing valid and reliable tests and survey instruments.
4. Select appropriate methods for evaluating program effectiveness.

Competency B

Carry out evaluation plans.

Sub-competencies

1. Facilitate administration of the tests and activities specified in the plan.
2. Use data-collecting methods appropriate to the objectives.
3. Analyze resulting evaluation data.

Competency C

Interpret results of program evaluation.

Sub-competencies

1. Apply criteria of effectiveness to obtained results of a program.
2. Translate evaluation results into terms easily understood by others.
3. Report effectiveness of educational programs in achieving proposed objectives.

Competency D

Infer implications from findings for future program planning.

Sub-competencies

1. Explore possible explanations for important evaluation findings.
2. Recommend strategies for implementing results of evaluation.

RESPONSIBILITY V: COORDINATING PROVISION OF HEALTH EDUCATION SERVICES
Competency A

Develop a plan for coordinating health education services.

Sub-competencies

1. Determine the extent of available health education services.
2. Match health education services to proposed program activities.
3. Identify gaps and overlaps in the provision of collaborative health services.

Competency B

Facilitate cooperation between and among levels of program personnel.

Sub-competencies

1. Promote cooperation and feedback among personnel related to the program.
2. Apply various methods of conflict reduction as needed.
3. Analyze the role of health educator as liaison between program staff and outside groups and organizations.

Competency C

Formulate practical modes of collaboration among health agencies and organizations.

Sub-competencies

1. Stimulate development of cooperation among personnel responsible for community health education program.

2. Suggest approaches for integrating health education within existing health programs.
3. Develop plans for promoting collaborative efforts among health agencies and organizations with mutual interests.

Competency D

Organize in-service training programs for teachers, volunteers, and other interested personnel.

Sub-competencies

1. Plan an operational, competency-oriented training program.
2. Use instructional resources that meet a variety of in-service training needs.
3. Demonstrate a wide range of strategies for conducting in-service training programs.

RESPONSIBILITY VI: ACTING AS A RESOURCE PERSON IN HEALTH EDUCATION
Competency A

Utilize computerized health information retrieval system effectively.

Sub-competencies

1. Match an information need with the appropriate retrieval system.
2. Access principal on-line and other database health information resources.

Competency B

Establish effective consultative relationships with those requesting assistance in solving health related problems.

Sub-competencies

1. Analyze parameters of effective consultative relationships.
2. Describe special skills and abilities needed by health educators for consultation activities.
3. Formulate a plan for providing consultation to other health professionals.
4. Explain the process of marketing health education consultative services.

Competency C

Interpret and respond to requests for health information.

Sub-competencies

1. Analyze general processes for identifying the information needed to satisfy a request.
2. Use a wide range of approaches in referring requesters to valid sources of health information.

Competency D

Select effective educational resource materials for dissemination.

Sub-competencies

1. Assemble educational material of value to the health of individuals and community groups.
2. Evaluate the worth and applicability of resource materials for given audiences.
3. Apply various processes in the acquisition of resource materials.
4. Compare different methods for distributing educational materials.

RESPONSIBILITY VII: COMMUNICATING HEALTH AND HEALTH EDUCATION NEEDS, CONCERNS, AND RESOURCES

Competency A

Interpret concepts, purposes, and theories of health education.

Sub-competencies

1. Evaluate the state of the art of health education.
2. Analyze the foundations of the discipline of health education.
3. Describe major responsibilities of the health educator in the practice of health education.

Competency B

Predict the impact of societal value systems on health education programs.

Sub-competencies

1. Investigate social forces causing opposing viewpoints regarding health education needs and concerns.
2. Use a wide range of strategies for dealing with controversial health issues.

Competency C

Select a variety of communication methods and techniques in providing health information.

Sub-competencies

1. Use a wide range of techniques for communicating health and health education information.
2. Demonstrate proficiency in communicating health information and health education needs.

Competency D

Foster communication between health care providers and consumers.

Sub-competencies

1. Interpret the significance and implications of health care providers' messages to consumers.
2. Act as liaison between consumer groups and individuals and health care provider organizations.

D-2

Standard high school certificate for State of Illinois

The Standard High School certificate is valid for 4 years for teaching in grades 6 through 12 of the common schools. This certificate may be issued to graduates with a bachelor's degree from a recognized college who present certified evidence of having earned credits as follows:

	Semester hours
A. General education	42
1. Language arts	8
2. Science and/or mathematics	6
3. Social science (including a course in American history and/or government)	6
4. Humanities	6
5. Health and physical education	3
6. Additional work in any above fields and/or psychology (except educational psychology) to total	42
B. Professional education	16
1. Educational psychology (including human growth and development)	2
2. Methods and techniques of teaching at the secondary level or in a teaching field	2
3. History and/or philosophy of education	2
4. Practice-student teaching clinical experiences equivalent to 100 clock hours*	

	Semester hours
5. Student teaching (grades 6–12)	5
6. Electives in professional education may be taken from the above fields and/or guidance, tests and measurements, methods of teaching reading, and instructional materials to total	16

If the grade level of your student teaching was not on the high school level, it will be necessary for you to submit a letter of verification of successful teaching experience from the appropriate school district official in which you were employed. This letter should state all employment dates, the schools in which you were employed, your assignment, and the type of teaching certificate held. Verification of Chicago, Ill., teaching experience should be obtained from the Director of Personnel of the Chicago Board of Education. These official letters must be submitted to the office of the Regional Superintendent of Schools of the Illinois county in which application is being made.

	Semester hours
C. One major area of specialization	32
or	
three minor areas of specialization (24 each)	72
D. General electives to make a total of	120

---

*Applicants with successful teaching experience at the 6 to 12 level need not complete prestudent teaching clinical experiences.

Applicants presenting the required credit in student teaching and evidence of successful teaching experience need not complete another student teaching experience.

If your area of specialization is the same as one of the general education categories, the same course may be used for both requirements.

State Board of Education Document No. 1 (Oct. 1977)

HEALTH EDUCATION

20 semester hours in the field

REQUIRED HEALTH EDUCATION COMPONENT

One course from each of the following areas to total 10–14 semester hours:

1. Advanced concepts of health
2. Programs in school health
3. Programs in community health
4. Curriculum development and evaluation in health education

ADDITIONAL HEALTH EDUCATION COMPONENTS

One course from at least three of the following areas to total 6 to 10 semester hours:

1. The growing and developing organism
2. Ecological relationships
3. Disease control
4. Human sexuality and family life
5. Food practices and eating patterns
6. Consumer health sources and resources
7. Safety
8. Mood-modifying substances
9. Personal health practices
10. Mental/emotional health

Illustration credits

CHAPTER 1

Fig. 1-2. From US Congress, Office of Technology Assessment: Adolescent health. Volume 1: Summary and policy options, OTA H-466, Washington, DC, 1991, US Government Printing Office, p. 8.

Fig. 1-3. From US Congress, Office of Technology Assessment: Adolescent health. Volume 1: Summary and policy options, OTA H-466, Washington, DC, 1991, US Government Printing Office, p. 10.

Fig. 1-4. From US Congress, Office of Technology Assessment, Adolescent health. Volume 1: Summary and policy options, OTA H-466, Washington, DC, 1991, US Government Printing Office.

Fig. 1-5. Copyright by David Riecks.

Fig. 1-6. From Nader PR: The concept of "comprehensiveness" in the design and implementation of school health programs, *J Sch Health* 60(4):133-138, 1990.

Fig. 1-7. Copyright, Parke, Davis and Company, and reproduced by special permission of Parke, Davis & Company.

CHAPTER 2

Fig. 2-1. Adapted from Centers for Disease Control. Courtesy Laura Kann.

Fig. 2-4. From US Congress, Office of Technology Assessment: Adolescent health. Volume 1: Summary and policy options, OTA H-466, Washington, DC, 1991, US Government Printing Office, p 9.

CHAPTER 4

Fig. 4-3. Courtesy Bill Weigand.

Fig. 4-4. Redrawn from *Good housekeeping: family health and medical guide*, New York, 1980, Hearst Books.

Fig. 4-5. From Tanner JM, Whitehouse RH, Takaishi M: Standards from birth to maturity for height, weight, height velocity, and weight velocity, *Arch Dis Child* 41:455-471, 1966.

Fig. 4-6. Courtesy Bill Weigand.

Fig. 4-7. From Tanner JM. In Forfar JO, Arneil GC, editors: *Textbook of paediatrics*, Edinburgh, 1962, Churchill Livingstone.

Fig. 4-8. From Tanner JM. In Forfar JO, Arneil, GC, editors: *Textbook of paediatrics*, Edinburgh, 1962, Churchill Livingstone.

Fig. 4-9. From Valadian I: Proceedings of the National Nutrition Conference, US Department of Agriculture, Nov. 1971.

Fig. 4-10. Courtesy William H. Creswell III.

Fig. 4-12. From Larson RL: Physical activity and the growth and development of bones and joint structures. In Rarick G, editor: *Physical activity: human growth and development*, New York, 1973, Academic Press.

Fig. 4-13. From Cheek DB: Body composition, hormones, nutrition, and adolescent growth. In Grumbach MM, Grave GD, Mayer FE, editors: *Control of the onset of puberty*, New York, 1974, John Wiley & Sons. Copyright 1974, reprinted by permission of John Wiley & Sons.

Fig. 4-14. From Cheek DB: Body composition, hormones, nutrition, and adolescent growth. In Grumbach MM, Grave GD, Mayer FE, editors: *Control of the onset of puberty*, New York, 1974, John Wiley & Sons. Copyright 1974, reprinted by permission of John Wiley & Sons.

Fig. 4-15. From Cheek DB: Body composition, hormones, nutrition, and adolescent growth. In Grumbach MM, Grave GD, Mayer FE, editors: *Control of the onset of puberty*, New York, 1974, John Wiley & Sons. Copyright 1974, reprinted by permission of John Wiley & Sons.

Fig. 4-16. From The Champaign-Urbana News Gazette June 1, 1992.

Fig. 4-17. Copyright by David Riecks.

Fig. 4-18. Modified from the National Center for Health Statistics: Monthly vital statistics report, vol 25, no 3, suppl [HRA] 76-1120, 1976. Courtesy Ross Laboratories, Columbus, Ohio.

Fig. 4-19. Modified from the National Center for Health Statistics: Monthly vital statistics report, vol 25, no 3, suppl [HRA] 76-1120, 1976. Courtesy Ross Laboratories, Columbus, Ohio.

CHAPTER 5

Fig. 5-1. Copyright 1983 by Jim Whitmer.

Fig. 5-3. Copyright by David Riecks.

CHAPTER 6

Fig. 6-1. Copyright by David Riecks.

Fig. 6-2. Copyright by David Riecks.

CHAPTER 7

Fig. 7-1. Copyright by Jim Whitmer.

Fig. 7-6. Copyright by David Riecks.

Fig. 7-10. Copyright by David Riecks.

CHAPTER 8

Fig. 8-2. From Centers for Disease Control, Atlanta, Ga.
Fig. 8-3. From Centers for Disease Control, Atlanta, Ga.
Fig. 8-4. From Centers for Disease Control, Atlanta, Ga.
Fig. 8-5. Copyright by David Riecks.
Fig. 8-6. Redrawn from US Department of Health and Human Services: Healthy people 2000:national health promotion and disease prevention objectives (Full Report, With Commentary), Washington, DC, 1991, US Government Printing Office, DHHS Publication No. (PHS) 91-50212, p. 513.

CHAPTER 9

Fig. 9-3. From US Congress, Office of Technology Assessment: Vol 2, Adolescent health, Washington, DC, 1991, US Government Printing Office.
Fig. 9-4. From National Safety Council.
Fig. 9-5. From National Safety Council.

CHAPTER 10

Fig. 10-1. Top, Copyright by David Riecks. *Bottom left* and *right,* Copyright by Jim Whitmer.

CHAPTER 11

Fig. 11-1. From Blum HL: *Planning for health: development and application of social change theory,* New York, 1974, Human Sciences Press.
Fig. 11-4. Courtesy Champaign Public Schools, Champaign, Ill.
Fig. 11-5. Copyright by David Riecks.
Fig. 11-7. From Becker MH, editor: *The health belief model and personal health behavior,* Thorofare NJ, 1974, Charles B Slack.
Fig. 11-9. From Ajzen I, Fishbein M: *Understanding attitudes and predicting social behavior,* Englewood Cliffs, 1990, Prentice-Hall. Reprinted with permission.

CHAPTER 12

Fig. 12-2. From Posner GJ, Rudnitsky AN: *Course design: a guide to curriculum development for teachers,* ed 2, New York, 1982, Longman. Reprinted with permission.
Fig. 12-4. Modified from School Health Education Study, Inc: Health education: a conceptual approach to curriculum design, Washington, DC, 1967, St. Paul, Minn,

1968, 3M Education Press, p 20. Artwork courtesy William H. Creswell III.
Fig. 12-5. Grade six National Center for Health Education, New York.
Fig. 12-11 From Pratt D: *Curriculum: design and development,* New York, 1980, Harcourt Brace Jovanovich. Reprinted with permission of the publisher.
Fig. 12-12. Adapted from Teen-age health teaching modules, field-tested edition, 1983, and from Muth K and Alermann D, 1992.

CHAPTER 13

Fig. 13-1. Copyright by David Riecks.
Fig. 13-3. Copyright by David Riecks.
Fig. 13-4. Copyright by David Riecks.

CHAPTER 14

Fig. 14-2. Courtesy Mary E. Allen.
Fig. 14-3. Courtesy Mary E. Allen.
Fig. 14-4. From US Department of Health and Human Services: *MMWR* 32:47, 1983.
Fig. 14-5. From US Department of Health and Human Services: *MMWR* 32:47, 1983.
Fig. 14-6. From US Department of Health and Human Services: *MMWR* 32:47, 1983.
Fig. 14-7. Redrawn from Office of Technology Assessment, 1991, based on US Congress, House of Representatives, Select Committee on Children, Youth, and Families, *US children and their families: current conditions and recent trends, 1989* (Washington, DC: US Government Printing Office, 1989); US Department of Health and Human Services, Public Health Service, Centers for Disease Control, National Center for Health Statistics, Division of Vital Statistics, "Advance Report of Final Natality Statistics, 1988," *Monthly Vital Statistics Report* 39 (no 4, suppl), DHHS Pub. No. (PHS) 90-1120, Aug 15, 1990.
Fig. 14-8. Redrawn from Alan Guttmacher Institute: *Teenage pregnancy in the United States: the scope of the problem and state responses,* New York, 1989.
Fig. 14-9. Courtesy Mary E. Allen.

CHAPTER 16

Fig. 16-1. Copyright by David Riecks.
Fig. 16-2. Copyright by Jim Whitmer.
Fig. 16-3. Courtesy Mary E. Allen.

Index